Love and Death in Goethe: "One and Double"

Studies in German Literature, Linguistics, and Culture

Edited by James Hardin
(*South Carolina*) ·

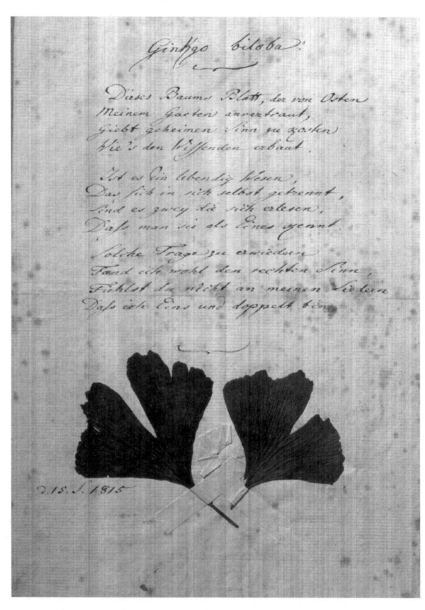

Goethe's poem "Ginkgo biloba," in Goethe's handwriting and with crossed ginkgo leaves pasted at the bottom by him. Courtesy of the Anton and Katharina Kippenberg Foundation, Düsselldorf.

Love and Death in Goethe

"One and Double"

Ellis Dye

CAMDEN HOUSE

First published 2004
by Camden House

Camden House is an imprint of Boydell & Brewer Inc.
668 Mt. Hope Avenue, Rochester, NY 14620, USA
www.camden-house.com
and of Boydell & Brewer Limited
PO Box 9, Woodbridge, Suffolk IP12 3DF, UK
www.boydell.co.uk

ISBN: 1–57113–300–3

Library of Congress Cataloging-in-Publication Data

Dye, Ellis, 1936–
    Love and death in Goethe: one and double / Ellis Dye.
        p. cm. — (Studies in German literature, linguistics, and culture)
    Includes bibliographical references and index.
    ISBN 1–57113–300–3 (hardcover : alk. paper)
    1. Goethe, Johann Wolfgang von, 1749–1832 — Criticism and in-
terpretation. 2. Love in literature. 3. Death in literature. I. Title.
II. Series: Studies in German literature, linguistics, and culture (Un-
numbered)

PT2177.D94 2004
832'.6—dc22

                                                            2004014264

A catalogue record for this title is available from the British Library.

This publication is printed on acid-free paper.
Printed in the United States of America.

For Carol

Contents

Acknowledgments

I WISH TO THANK THE EDITORS of the following journals for permission to republish here, extensively revised, material that earlier appeared in their pages: "Goethe's Line 'In der Finsternis Beschattung,'" *Germanic Notes and Reviews* 18 (1987): 20–21; "Werther's Lotte: Views of the Other in Goethe's First Novel," *Journal of English and Germanic Philology* 87 (1988): 492–506; "Goethe's 'Die Braut von Korinth': Anti-Christian Polemic or Hymn of Love and Death?" *Goethe Yearbook* 4 (1988): 83–98; "Goethe's 'Der Fischer,' or the Non-rescue," *The Germanic Review* 64 (1989): 51–57; "'Selige Sehnsucht' and Goethean Enlightenment," *PMLA* 104 (1989): 190–200; "Wilhelm Meister and Hamlet: Identity and Difference," *Goethe Yearbook* 6 (1992): 67–85; "Goethe's *Die Wahlverwandtschaften:* Romantic Metafiction," *Goethe Yearbook* 8 (1996): 66–92; "On Inchoatives & Cessatives, and on Glowing and On-glowing in Goethe," *Germanic Notes and Reviews* 34:1 (Spring 2003): 10–12; and "Substitution, Self-blame, and Self-deception in Goethe's Stella: Ein Schauspiel für Liebende," *Goethe Yearbook* 12 (2004).

I am pleased to express my thanks to Macalester College for unhesitating support, and to James Hardin, General Editor of Camden House, both for encouraging me to submit the manuscript and for his wise counsel as well as to James Walker for his expert management of its preparation and publication. My thanks also to the conscientious and perceptive copyeditor, Sue Innes, who does not hesitate to challenge an author on matters of substance and interpretation and who overlooks nothing, and to editorial assistant Jane Best for her superb handling of this book's production and her willingness to go the second mile. Thanks also to John Haiman for ideas originating in a 1997–98 seminar "Repetition, Quotation, Imitation" and for many stimulating conversations; as well as to Jane K. Brown, Jocelyne Kolb, Kiarina Kordela, Deirdre Vincent, Linda Schulte-Sasse, and Bonnie Watkins for criticism, for valuable insights, and for assistance and inspiration at crucial times. Gitta Hammarberg read the entire manuscript and provided many helpful suggestions. Our departmental office manager, Lana Larsen, has been supportive and helpful, as have librarians at Macalester and at the University of Minnesota Wilson Library. My thanks to my daughters, Ellen, Marianne, Martha, and Sarah for not unduly doubting whether I would ever finish this book. My hope that they would be proud of it has motivated me more than they know.

I am grateful to my Rutgers University teacher, Professor Israel S. Stamm, for true friendship while he lived and for lasting guidance in matters intellectual, ethical, and aesthetic. My parents, Mar and Neva Dye, believed in me and gave me the respect for the truth that is my highest value and my most cherished possession.

My thanks, finally, to my wife Carol, who perceptively critiqued more than one version of my manuscript and without whose patient good sense, understanding, constant support, and unreserved devotion neither scholarship nor some more important things would have been accomplished. I dedicate this book to her.

E. D.

January 2004

Abbreviations

DjG   Fischer-Lamberg, Hanna, ed. *Der junge Goethe*. 6 vols. Berlin: Walter de Gruyter, 1963–74.

DVjs   *Deutsche Vierteljahrsschrift für Literaturwissenschaft und Geistesgeschichte.*

E   Goethe's letters to Eckermann (in FA 2,12).

FA   Goethe. *Sämtliche Werke. Briefe, Tagebücher und Gespräche.* Edited by Hendrik Birus, Dieter Borchmeyer, Karl Eibl, Wilhelm Voßkamp, et al. 40 vols. Frankfurt am Main: Deutscher Klassiker Verlag, 1985–2003. *Frankfurter Ausgabe.* Numbers indicate section, volume, and page.

GA   Goethe. *Gedenkausgabe der Werke, Briefe und Gespräche.* Edited by Ernst Beutler. 24 vols. Zurich: Artemis, 1948–1954.

HA   Goethe. *Werke.* Edited by Erich Trunz. 14 vols. Hamburg: Christian Wegner, 1948–60; Munich: Beck, 1981. *Hamburger Ausgabe.*

JEGP   *Journal of English and Germanic Philology*

KA   Friedrich Schlegel, *Kritische Friedrich-Schlegel-Ausgabe.* Edited by Ernst Behler et al. 35 vols. Munich, Paderborn, Vienna: Ferdinand Schöningh, 1958–2002.

MA   Goethe. *Sämtliche Werke nach Epochen seines Schaffens.* Edited by Karl Richter with Herbert G. Göpfert, Norbert Miller, and Gerhard Sauder. 21 vols. in 31. Munich: Carl Hanser, 1985–1998. *Münchener Ausgabe.*

PEGS   *Publications of the English Goethe Society*

SA   Freud, Sigmund. *Studienausgabe.* Edited by Alexander Mitscherlich, Angela Richards, and James Strachey. 11 vols. Frankfurt am Main: S. Fischer, 1969–75.

WA   Goethe. *Werke: Weimarer Ausgabe.* Edited by Gustav von Loeper, Erich Schmidt, et al., im Auftrage der Großherzogin Sophie von Sachsen. Four parts, 133 vols. in 143. Weimar: Hermann Böhlau, 1887–1919.

Werke Nietzsche, Friedrich. *Werke in drei Bänden.* Edited by Karl
Schlechta. Munich: Carl Hanser, 1966

References to *Die Leiden des jungen Werthers* are cited using the date of the
letter and the page number in FA 1,8, "Fassung B." The Editor's report to
the reader is cited by page alone.

Introduction

IN JOHANN WOLFGANG GOETHE'S *Prometheus,* an early dramatic fragment (1773), Pandora rushes into the arms of her father, Prometheus, and breathlessly reports that she has witnessed what must have been sexual intercourse between her friend Mira and Mira's lover Arabar in an open meadow. Pandora is overwhelmed by what she has seen — Mira's initiation into womanhood — and by the nameless, vicarious passion ignited in herself. "Er küßte sie tausendmal," she reports. "Und hing an ihrem Munde, / Um seinen Geist ihr einzuhauchen." Alarmed by Pandora's outcry, Arabar had fled and left Mira to exhaust her still live desire in Pandora's embrace, who remains aflame with excitement. "Was ist das alles," the girl asks her father, "was sie erschüttert / Und mich?" Prometheus answers with one of the oldest of conceits, "Da ist ein Augenblick, der alles erfüllt. / Alles, was wir gesehnt, geträumt, gehofft. / Gefürchtet meine Beste, — Das ist der Tod!" (FA 1,1:222, lines 334–36, 355–56, 389–91). In an undulating crescendo reminiscent of the *Liebestod* music of *Tristan und Isolde,* an extended protasis rises to an explosive, orgiastic "dann" in the apodosis: "Dann stirbt der Mensch" (line 404). Life is extinguished at the moment of greatest intensity. "O Vater, laß uns sterben!" cries Pandora (405). Thus does Goethe draw on the tradition of love and death, for the first time with this degree of explicitness.[1]

This book examines Goethe's use of the theme of love and death — the *Liebestod* — and the issues of selfhood and individuation that inform it. Focus is on Goethe, one of history's most virtuosic and most subversive users of traditional thematic material, both because he made frequent, heretofore unexamined use of this Romantic theme and because his intellectual and artistic preeminence *as part of European Romanticism* is insufficiently recognized.

The linking of love and death, Eros and Thanatos, has been a commonplace in literature, music, and art from the abduction of Persephone, as told

---

[1] Love and death are linked early in Goethe's writing, e.g. "Miteinander ins Bett oder ins Himmelreich" in the 1773 farce *Ein Fastnachtsspiel vom Pater Brey* (line 94). "An Christel," also 1773, ends with: "Und endigt sich nicht meine Qual / Sterb ich an ihrer Brust." Unless otherwise stated, references are to the *Frankfurter Ausgabe* of Goethe's works: *Sämtliche Werke. Briefe, Tagebücher und Gespräche,* 40 vols, ed. Dieter Borchmeyer et al. (Frankfurt am Main: Deutscher Klassiker Verlag, 1985–2003).

in the Homeric *Hymn to Demeter,* to the coincidence of love and death in *Aida, Tristan und Isolde,* and *The Mill on the Floss,* or even on the evening news. In Dante's *The Divine Comedy* Virgil names a number of great historical and mythical figures whose love resulted in death — Cleopatra, Helen, Achilles, Paris, Tristan, "and more than a thousand shades whom love had parted from our life" ("Inferno," Canto V, lines 63–69). Freud's psychoanalytic theory is formulated in terms of the Eros-*Todestrieb* opposition and shows his indebtedness to German Romanticism, in which the *Liebestod* is a primary topos.

The association of love with death is often little more than a clever conceit or rhetorical flourish. Hamlet comments bitterly on his mother's marriage to Claudius within a month of the king's death, "The funeral bak'd-meats / Did coldly furnish forth the marriage tables" (1.2.180–81[2]). In Schiller's *Maria Stuart,* Queen Elizabeth's secretary hopes the queen will consent to marry her French suitor, Duke Francis of Anjou, and sign the order of execution for her rival Mary Stuart, "*Sie* geht / Ins Brautgemach, die Stuart geht zum Tode" (2.1). Here love is the opposite of death, although they coincide in time, whereas the delights of love would have caused Rousseau's death, or so he imagines: "Ah, if ever in all my life I had once tasted the delights of love to the full, I do not think that my frail existence could have endured them; I should have died on the spot."[3] When Wilhelm Tell must wait for a wedding party to pass through the "hohle Gasse" by Küßnacht before he can assassinate the tyrant Gessler, the connection, apparently, is not obvious enough, so Schiller makes it explicit. "Hier wird gefreit und anderswo begraben," says Stüssi, a passer-by. "Und oft kommt gar das eine zu dem andern," replies Tell (4.3). "O nuziali tede, abborrite," sings Guiletta in Bellini's *I Capuleti e I Montecchi,* "così, così fatali" (1.2).[4] Bellini's *Norma* also ends with the death of Norma and Pollione on the funeral pyre. In Blake's "O Rose, thou art sick" and Goethe's "Erlkönig," suitor and predator are one. In Claudius's "Der Tod und das Mädchen" (like "Erlkönig," the Claudius poem is most familiar in Schubert's musical setting), in paintings across the centuries from Hans Baldung[5] to Egon

---

[2] The Shakespeare edition referred to throughout this work is *The Complete Works of Shakespeare,* ed. George Lyman Kittredge (Boston: Ginn and Co., 1936).

[3] Jean-Jacques Rousseau, *The Confessions,* trans. J. M. Cohen (Harmondsworth, Middlesex, England: Penguin, 1954), 210.

[4] "O nuptial torches, abhorred, / so fatal" (Vincenzo Bellini, *I Capuleti e I Montecchi,* libretto by Felice Romani, trans. Gwyn Morris, EMI Classics, 1975). Unless otherwise stated, any translations from the German are by the author.

[5] Hans Baldung, aka. Hans Baldung Grien, 1484/85–1545. In Baldung's *The Three Ages and Death* (Vienna) a girl contemplating herself in a mirror is approached by

Schiele, in much German baroque poetry, and in the 1934 movie "Death Takes a Holiday," reproduced in 1998 as "Meet Joe Black," the "supple Suitor" (Emily Dickinson) is Death himself. Jakob Balde (1604–68) imagines longing for death as the passionate desire of a virgin who calls Death her bridegroom: "Trauter Tod, du Freund und Wonne, düsterschönes Leichenlicht, Schattenmann, du meine Sonne, Küsse doch mein Angesicht. . . . Komm doch, komm mich zu umfangen."[6] "It was Death himself who stood behind me," recalls the heroine in Atwood's *Alias Grace* — "with his arms wrapped around me as tight as iron bands, and his lipless mouth kissing my neck as if in love. But as well as the horror, I also felt a strange longing."[7]

"The grave's a fine and private place," protests Andrew Marvell, "but none, I think, do there embrace."[8] In Mozart's *The Magic Flute* Monostatos offers Pamina a choice: "Liebe oder Tod!" (2.10), while Goethe's Claudine of Villa Bella must love Crugantino or *he* will die by his own hand (FA 1,4:612). Love and death may be locked in mortal combat, love always strong enough to "kill" death (Donne: "Death, thou shalt die"), or at least durable enough to survive it, remaining unforgotten beyond the river Lethe, as in Propertius, Quevedo, or Hölderlin. "Es ist die Glut, das Feuer, die 'Flamme' (*llama*), wie [Quevedo] hier sagt, seiner Liebe, die unzerstörbar bleibt, die keinem Gesetz gehorcht, die selbst das kalte Wasser des Todes und des Vergessens 'durchschwimmt.'"[9]

Love and death constitute a *coincidentia oppositorum*, an identity within a stated opposition, as when in Thomas Mann's *Der Zauberberg* Hans Castorp compares himself with his terminally ill cousin, "Il est moribond, et moi, je suis amoureux, eh bien!"[10] Or when, in a double synecdoche, Pamina

death from behind. Reproduced by Sabine Melchior-Bonnet in *The Mirror A History*, trans. Katharine H. Jewett (New York and London: Routledge, 2001), 211.

[6] Trans. Georg Philipp Harsdörffer (1607–58). From Walther Rehm, *Der Todesgedanke in der deutschen Dichtung vom Mittelalter bis zur Romantik*, 2nd ed. (1928; repr. Tübingen: Niemeyer, 1967), 217.

[7] Margaret Eleanor Atwood, *Alias Grace* (New York: Nan A. Talese, 1996), 280.

[8] Andrew Marvell, "To His Coy Mistress," *The Complete English Poems*, ed. Elizabeth Story Donno (New York: St. Martin's Press, 1972), 51. Cf. Rosalind: "The poor world is almost six thousand years old, and in all this time there was not any man died in his own person, videlicet, in a love cause. . . . Men have died from time to time, and worms have eaten them, but not for love" (Shakespeare, *As You Like It*, 4.1).

[9] Walter Naumann, "'Staub entbrannt in Liebe': Das Thema von Tod und Liebe bei Properz, Quevedo und Goethe," *Arcadia* 3 (1968): 165.

[10] Thomas Mann, *Gesammelte Werke in zwölf Bänden* (Oldenburg: S. Fischer, 1960), 3:472 ("Walpurgisnacht").

"Im Kriege kommen Eros und Todestrieb zu ihrem eigentlichen Ziel, der lust- und grauenvollen Auflösung des Individuums in Matsch und Schlamm. [*Der*

says to her dagger, "Du also bist mein Bräutigam?" (2.27). To the Baron in Pushkin's *The Miserly Knight,* the insertion of the key into the lock of his chest is like thrusting a knife into a victim and yields a corresponding erotic release. Dickens takes the reader's familiarity with the coincidence of love and death for granted, knowing he will be understood when Ralph Nickleby says, "One would think . . . that there was a funeral going on here, and not a wedding" (712).[11] John Irving does the same in *The World According to Garp* when, in the collision of Garp's car with the parked vehicle in which his wife and her graduate student are engaged in oral sex, Garp's son is killed and Mrs. Garp bites off her lover's penis. In Vonnegut's *Hocus Pocus* the protagonist calculates that the number of women he has made love to is exactly the same as the number of men he killed in Vietnam. Rilke's *Weise von Liebe und Tod des Cornets Christoph Rilke* proclaims its theme in the title. And the prominence of the *Liebestod* in opera has yielded Peter Conrad's title *A Song of Love and Death: The Meaning of Opera.*[12] The theme is parodied in the Langston Hughes libretto for Kurt Weill's *Street Scene* when Sam says: "Now love and death have linked their arms together / and gone away into another bourn; . . . They have gone and left us here to mourn." The last line of Giordano's *Andrea Chénier,* in which Madeleine and Andrea go to the guillotine together, is "Viva la morte insiem!" which echoes Verlaine's "Mourons ensemble, voulez-vous?" ("Les Indolents"). Returning to his beloved young wife before the fatal jealousy sets in, Otello sings to Desdemona: "Venga la morte! Mi colga nell' estasi / Di quest' amplesso / Il momento supremo!" (Were I to die now! No delight up in paradise is so divine as this supreme moment, 1.3). After he has killed her he says: "When I entered here I kissed you ere I killed you. Now I'm dying, and night enshrouds my senses . . . to kiss you . . . once more to kiss you . . . once more to kiss you" [Otello dies] (4.4).[13] "In a score of sentimental novels (and in the tales of that supereminent necrophile Poe) the grave proves the only marriage bed; and the dust of those who cannot on earth embrace without guilt mingles innocently there."[14] Jean Paul Friedrich Richter presents a male-male *Liebestod* in *Siebenkäs.* When the page and her king die in battle,

---

Zauberberg] ist eine gewaltige Entgrenzungsphantasie" (Hermann Kurzke, *Thomas Mann: Das Leben als Kunstwerk* [Munich: C. H. Beck, 1999], 329).

[11] In Ovid's stories of Tereus and Procne and of Orpheus and Eurydice the wedding turns into a funeral.

[12] Peter Conrad, *A Song of Love and Death: The Meaning of Opera* (New York: Poseidon, 1987).

[13] Giuseppe Verdi, *Otello,* libretto by Arrigo Boito, trans. Walter Ducloux (New York: Schirmer, 1962). Trans. slightly modified.

[14] Leslie Fiedler, *Love and Death in the American Novel,* rev. ed. (1960; repr., New York: Stein and Day, 1966), 57.

in Conrad Ferdinand Meyer's "Gustav Adolphs Page," it is discovered that the page is a woman. At their funeral they are "bedded" together before the altar in the church.

Love and death pervades pop psychology[15] and is everywhere in film, for example in Woody Allen's wacky *Love and Death* (1975) and Marguerite Duras's *La maladie de la mort* (1982). In *High Noon* Gary Cooper, must "face the man who hates me . . . on this, our wedding day." In *Duel in the Sun*, branded "lust in the dust" when it was released (1946), Gregory Peck and Jennifer Jones shoot and wound each other from a distance at Squaw's Head Rock before her slow, tortured crawl up the rock toward him and their last rendezvous. In *Guilty as Sin* (1991), the adversaries in a deadly erotic game pull each other over the balustrade and fall four stories, but, landing on the back of his head, the villain cushions his intended victim's fall. The positions are reversed when the author of *French Lessons,* Alice Kaplan, tells of making love on Alice Bergstrand's gravestone, "cool marble below; warm thick Ted above." In *The Skull beneath the Skin,* P. D. James recalls that "eighteenth-century whores had copulated with their clients on the flat tops of tombs in London's East End graveyards." *Newsweek* magazine takes its readers' familiarity with the love-death topos for granted when reporting that in *The Widow of St. Pierre,* "a proud French officer . . . and his idealistic wife . . . take in a prisoner condemned to death in Patrice Lacont's gripping, romantic nineteenth-century epic about — what else? — love and death."[16] The *Liebestod* even occurs in a title about digital culture: Katie Hafner's *The Well: A Story of Love, Death, & Real Life in the Seminal Online Community.*[17] Journalism loves such headlines as "Teen-Age Films: Love, Death and the Prom,"[18] and finds space for a report about a wedding couple with a macabre sense of humor, the man wearing a skull-emblazoned T-shirt, black tux, and plastic skull scepter, the woman death-head earrings, a black dress, and black veil. To their disappointment, this bride and groom were prevented from sealing their troth in the graveyard. People who owned lots in the cemetery found the couple's plans "degrading."[19] On 10 May 1994, American Public Television broadcast a program entitled "Romeo and Juliet in Sarajevo" (ad-

---

[15] Witnesses of a shooting on a New York street, a husband and wife take to their bed. "Shaken, the two went home; after a large glass of cognac each, . . . they made love quickly and urgently and only then fell asleep, exhausted" (Lesley Hazleton, *The Right to Feel Bad: Coming to Terms with Normal Depression* [Garden City, New York: Doubleday, 1984], 157–58).

[16] Newsweek, 12 March 2001, 74

[17] Katie Hafner, *The Well: A Story of Love, Death, & Real Life in the Seminal Online Community* (New York: Carroll & Graf, 2001).

[18] *New York Times,* Sunday, August 16, 1987.

[19] *Saint Paul* (Minnesota) *Pioneer Press Dispatch,* Sunday, November 1, 1987.

vertised before the showing as "Love and Death in Sarajevo") about the
death by sniper fire of a Serbian boy and a Muslim girl in the no-man's land
between Serb and Muslim territory. The boy died instantly, but the girl was
able to crawl a few feet and embrace her dead lover. Their bodies lay in the
heat for two days before they could be retrieved. They died on a bridge.
There is a self-conscious example of the link between love and death in
Diana O'Hehir's *I Wish This War Were Over*. Here the heroine agrees to
have sex with her mother's boyfriend after he has run over a Labrador re-
triever and finished off the animal with a wrench. "I pushed my forehead
into the dashboard. 'We'll go back. And get into bed.' For some reason I felt
that if we actually did act it out, this seduction scene we had been pretending at, that would give the dog's death some meaning." Initiated readers
may hear an echo here of an early event in Thomas Mann's *Der Erwählte*,
where Wiligis cuts the throat of the good dog Hanegiff for fear that his
howling will awaken the household and prevent the consummation of his
love for his twin sister Sibylla.

Linking love and death is a vital, on-going tradition. R. K. R. Thornton
gives thirty-six poems under the heading "Love and Death" in his anthology
Poetry of the Nineties. The theme has yielded numerous dissertations and
scholarly books. It would exceed the bounds of an introductory chapter just
to list titles bearing the words "love and death."[20] A recent Internet search
with the key words "love and death" produced 67,600 entries. If yet another
book on this subject is presented here, it is because none so far has adequately explored the epistemological or emblematic significance of the
Liebestod; because there is no monograph on the theme of love and death in
Goethe; because his appropriation of this theme links him to his younger
contemporaries and underscores his pioneering role in the Romantic movement; and because the primacy of the theme in German literature has been
overlooked by historians of culture.

What is a *Liebestod*, and when is a *Liebestod* not a *Liebestod*? For a love-
death to count as a *Liebestod* —what Bijvoet calls a "double love-death"[21] —

[20] A few additional examples: Romain Rolland, *Le jeu de l'amour et de la mort* (1925);
Roger Stilling, *Love and Death in Renaissance Tragedy* (1976); Theodore D.
Papanghelis, *Propertius: A Hellenistic Poet on Love and Death;* Michel Fougères, *La
Liebestod dans le roman français, anglais et allemand au XVIIIe siècle*, 9 (1974); *Love
and Death in a Barn, or The Sad Sorrowful Life of Beautiful Kate Harrington in
Philadelphia; Love and Death in a Hot Country; Love and Death on Long Island; Love
and Death in the Fictional Works of Madame de Lafayette (1971);* Ulrich Irion, *Eros
und Thanatos in der Moderne* (1992); Michael Sevastakis, *Songs of Love and Death:
The Classical American Horror Film of the 1930s* (1993); Lawrence Kramer, *After the
Lovedeath: Sexual Violence and the Making of Culture* (1997).

[21] Maya C. Bijvoet, *Liebestod: The Function and Meaning of the Double Love-Death*
(New York and London: Garland, 1988).

two lovers must die at the same time and in each other's arms, as do (*more or less* at the same time and *more or less* in each other's arms) Tristan and Isolde, Romeo and Juliet, Aida and Rhadames, and Vrenchen and Sali in Keller's "Romeo und Julia auf dem Dorf" (also in Delius's opera "A Village Romeo and Juliet"). Love and death must coincide and, ideally, be seen as identical, as in the example from Goethe's *Prometheus* with which we began. Actually, lovers seldom die together, any more than Jacob and Esau were born simultaneously. Rather, as Hans Castorp, protagonist in *Der Zauberberg*, realistically ponders about the end of *Aida*, "zwei lebendig Begrabene würden, die Lungen voll Grubengas, hier miteinander, oder, noch schlimmer, einer nach dem anderen, an Hungerkrämpfen verenden, und dann würde an ihren Körpern die Verwesung ihr unaussprechliches Werk tun, bis zwei Gerippe unterm Gewölbe lagerten, deren jedem es völlig gleichgültig und unempfindlich sein würde, ob es allein oder zu zweien lagerte" ("Fülle des Wohllauts," *Gesammelte Werke*, 3:896). In John Updike's *Brazil,* Isabel "lay down beside [the dead Tristão] and kissed his eyes, his lips" (260) but, unlike her medieval prototype, she does not die. Stefan Zweig and his wife took poison together in Brazil in 1942.

Lovers can simultaneously undergo "la petite mort," a common term for orgasm which explains the superstition, referred to in Donne's "The Canonization," that each orgasm subtracts a day from one's life." The *Liebestod* is a formula and a fiction — an ideal that, like all ideals, is always only approximated, never fully realized. Literary linkings of love and death constitute a class best defined not as the sum total of particular events satisfying an essential criterion of inclusion such as the literal simultaneous death of two tightly embracing lovers (which would be a class with no members), but as all of those instances that refer to this paradoxical concept, address it, and approximate it to a recognizable degree. Category theorists speak of "membership gradience" — the idea that some categories have "a center of a rather vague extensity" but no clear boundaries, allowing for degrees of membership.[22] Goethe's "Der Fischer" and "Erlkönig" depict borderline love-deaths, since in these poems only one of the interlocutors dies, raped by a supernatural lover with a lethal touch, while the "undead" bride of Corinth demands that her Christian mother arrange for the immolation of herself and her lover.

[22] Stephen C. Pepper, *World Hypotheses: A Study in Evidence* (Berkeley: U of California P, 1957), 164. George Lakoff, *Women, Fire, and Dangerous Things: What Categories Reveal about the Mind* (Chicago and London: U of Chicago P, 1987), 12.

Among the purposes of this study is to fill a gap left in the historical discussion of love and death left by Denis de Rougemont,[23] Edgar Wind, and other writers. De Rougemont disposes of German Romanticism in two pages, and Wind justifies his neglect of the love-death topos in post-Romantic German literature with the lame excuse that this theme, having "passed through the 'denser mists of German romanticism,'"[24] is thereby made irrelevant. Our concern here is with works in which love and death relate to each other, and with the paradoxical thematic link between love and death in the writings of Goethe in particular — with *his* use of the *Liebestod* as a topos. To the extent that it confines itself to illustrations from Goethe, while cross-referencing others, this book's organization is loosely chronological. It examines works in which the theme of love and death or some isomorph of this theme is central, but it provides more than a catalogue of occurrences of its theme, exploring the significance of the love-death topos for Goethe's symbolic practice, his epistemology, and his place in literary history. It aims to show what Goethe's use of a literary commonplace reveals about Romanticism, about the construction of meaning, and about an aspect of Goethe's distinctive orientation and genius. His awareness of the conventionality of language, thought, and creativity reflects both the thinking of the age in which he lived and his own personal doubts and beliefs, but it also shows that conventions may be used in creative and surprising ways,[25] especially by an author conscious of their conventionality. We will notice themes and structures that were popular in the literature and culture from which Goethe emerged, which he helped shape, and which have lost none of their vitality today. Even apparent arbitrariness may betray a convention at work. Instances of love and death that lack any discernible dialectic between the two, however, are beyond our scope. Love triangles that result in somebody's death but do not signify a union of lovers in death will not long detain us. An exception is Goethe's *Stella,* which only in the second and less convincing version ends with the death of the protagonists, the first version culminating in a state of happy three-in-one polyamory.

As noted, the *Liebestod* is an example of the paradox of unity in duality, one and double, often referred to as a *coincidentia oppositorum* and launched

[23] Denis de Rougemont, *Love in the Western World,* trans. Montgomery Belgion (1940; rev. ed. New York: Pantheon, 1956; Random House, 1983; English translation of preface and postscript by Princeton UP, 1983).

[24] Edgar Wind, *Pagan Mysteries in the Renaissance* (1958; rev. ed., New York: Norton, 1968), 166–67 n. 57.

[25] Every repetition is "nicht nur re-produktiv (d.h. eine starre Konvention wiederholend [*sic*]), sondern auf systematisch unkontrollierbare Weise schöpferisch" (Manfred Frank, *Die Unhintergehbarkeit von Individualität* [Frankfurt am Main: Suhrkamp, 1986], 125).

upon its course through intellectual history by the German humanist, scientist, statesman, and philosopher Cardinal Nicholas Cusanus (1401–64)[26] — or perhaps nearly two thousand years before that by Heraclitus, who said, "From the strain of binding opposites comes harmony."[27] Tristan and Isolde are such opposites, as are love and death in the *Liebestod* they enact. The *coincidentia oppositorum* works its magic in Hegel, Marx, and every other dialectical philosophy and is the fulcrum around which Romantic rhetoric and thought revolve. This term covers many pairs of strange bedfellows — any bridging of opposition in which the sense of opposition hovers in unstable tension with a unifying counterforce. The sublation of contraries in a higher synthesis (of man and wife in marriage, of creature and Creator in Jesus Christ, or of sulfur and mercury in the panacea that is actually a deadly poison[28]), is structurally homologous with the coincidental affirmation and denial of opposite meanings in the form of equivocation known as Romantic irony or in oxymorons such as the *delectatio morosa* or Cusanus's doctrine of *docta ignorantia*. Of these, Goethe, like Donne and Congreve, is conspicuously, almost self-indulgently, fond. His recourse to such formulations as "offenbares Geheimnis,"[29] when straightforward, linear logic falls short, links him with Cusanus and with Hegel, among other partisans of paradox. Because he saw no way of stripping truth down to its naked essence, his revelations contain an element of mystery. "Da sich gar manches unserer Erfahrungen nicht rund aussprechen und direkt mitteilen läßt," he wrote to a fellow writer, Carl Jacob Ludwig Iken, "so habe ich seit langem das Mittel gewählt, durch einander gegenüber gestellte und sich gleichsam ineinander abspiegelnde Gebilde den geheimeren Sinn dem Aufmerkenden zu

[26] See Dorothea Waley Singer, *Giordano Bruno: His Life and Thought* (New York: Henry Schuman, 1950). Singer explains that both Bruno and Nicolaus Cusanus hold to this doctrine. "They both cite Pseudo-Dionysius (fifth century) who held that God transcends all contraries. His work was commented on by Johannes Eriugena (d. 877); by St. Thomas (1225–74); by Albertus Magnus (1193–1280); by Meister Eckhart (d. circ. 1327) and by Marsillio Ficino (1433–99). All these writers except Eckhart are cited by Bruno" (80–81).

[27] Heraclitus, *Fragments: The Collected Wisdom of Heraclitus*, trans. Brooks Haxton (New York: Viking Penguin, 2001), 31.

[28] With this combination Faust's father sought to cure people of the plague (lines 1042–49). Michelsen believes "Quecksilberoxyd [= mercuric oxide] and Salzsäure [= hydrochloric acid] were the "widrige" compounds (Peter Michelsen, *Im Banne Fausts: Zwölf Faust-Studien* [Würzburg: Königshausen & Neumann, 2000], 62).

[29] Goethe saw F. W. Gotter's *Das öffentliche Geheimnis*, which he calls "das Offenbaare Geheimniss," in September 1781 (Johann Wolfgang von Goethe, GA, 616); "Heilig öffentlich Geheimnis" occurs in the poem "Epirrhema," and a *West-östlicher Divan* poem is entitled "Offenbar Geheimnis."

not clear whether G. is

offenbaren" (27 September 1827).[30] Goethe shows that language, like the painted panes of Faust's study, is a "trübes" — that is, an obfuscatory medium, which generates the truth by refracting it. The line to Nietzsche and to Heidegger is a direct one. "Die Gesetzgebung der Sprache gibt auch die ersten Gesetze der Wahrheit," wrote Nietzsche (*Werke*, 311). "A language is only symbolic, only figurative, and never expresses its objects immediately," says Goethe. Thus one can only bring together a variety of "formulas as a way of approaching them" — by analogy (FA 1,23,1:244). We reach for truth and grasp soap bubbles. Goethe doubts that the thing in itself can be accessed through language, which is always insufficient in its anthropocentricity, conventionality, and ephemerality and always as much a barrier as a gate, arresting in its very concreteness. "We live among derivative phenomena," he was forced to conclude, "and have no knowledge of how to reach the *Urfrage*" (FA 1,13:76). The love-death theme, noteworthy in its own right, is a metaphor for paradoxical approaches to the primal question.

Attention to the theme of love and death illuminates Goethe's poetry and many of his longer works, including *Faust,* and provides support for the growing recognition that Goethe, by his self-conscious and sophisticated use of language and its tropes, coincides with his younger contemporaries — the Romantics, whom he sometimes sharply criticized and with whom he is supposed to have been at odds. The *Liebestod* is the Romantics' favorite topos, and Goethe is foremost among them in the frequency and brilliance of his use of it. In his reliance on the *coincidentia oppositorum,* of which the *Liebestod* is a parade example, he is united not only with the Schlegels, Schelling, and Novalis — and, later, with Nietzsche, who is "soaked in Goethe"[31] — but with Herder, Hamann, Jacob Boehme, Cusanus, and, farther back, Heraclitus.

"We need to have a better understanding of why certain tropes and topoi become fashionable expressions of social and political reality at critical historical junctions."[32] To be sure, such constitutive facts of life as our exis-

---

[30] Friedrich Schlegel remarked, "Hat man nun einmal die Liebhaberei fürs Absolute und kann nicht davon lassen: so bleibt einem kein Ausweg, als sich selbst immer zu widersprechen und entgegengesetzte Extreme zu verbinden" (Friedrich Schlegel, *Kritische Friedrich-Schlegel-Ausgabe,* ed. Ernst Behler et al., 35 vols. [Munich: Ferdinand Schöningh, 1958–2002], sec. 1, vol. 2, *Charakteristiken und Kritiken 1,* ed. Hans Eichner [1967], 164); Blütenstaub, no. 26.

[31] Barker Fairley, "Nietzsche and Goethe," *Bulletin of the John Rylands Library,* Manchester, 18 (1934): 302. Cf. Faust's "Die Erde hat mich wieder" with Nietzsche's "Ich beschwöre euch, meine Brüder, *bleibt der Erde treu* und glaubt denen nicht, welche euch von überirdischen Hoffnungen reden!" (*Also Sprach Zarathustra,* in *Werke* 2:280).

[32] Azade Seyhan, *Representation and its Discontents: The Critical Legacy of German Romanticism* (Berkeley: U of California P, 1992), 163.

tence in time and, less definitely, our gender determine the very possibility of historical junctions and decide not only our being but how we conceptualize being. The polarity of articulation and submergence,[33] for which Goethe coined the verb *sich verselbsten,* and its opposite, *sich entselbstigen,* has its own historical dynamic. An individual's physical separation from his or her mother at birth may be unaffected by history, but life generates agonies and desires that demand conceptualization in whatever materials history happens to provide, for example, the threat provided by the Dionysian substratum of Greek culture to the *principium individuationis,* which Nietzsche assigns to Apollo (*Werke,* 1:23–24, 27). Yet individuality remains. It hurt his mother to behold Jesus on the cross, but not in the same way, and probably not as much, as it hurt Jesus himself. The German Romantics exhibit serious pain at the individual's isolation. They are uncomfortable with the opposition between subject and object and long for unity. That the love-death topos mirrors their effort to highlight and bridge the chasm and allies them with Goethe will, I hope, become plain.

An articulated worldview is one thing; habits of mind and conventions taken for granted are something else again, and are at least as revealing. All readers and students of literature profit from paying attention to women or men whose reception and rearticulation of their cultural inheritance has a distinctive stamp and a lasting effect. Goethe was such a man — an exemplary recycler and a fecund creator of culture. And largely through this one man, who coined the term "Weltliteratur," the cultures of many lands were introduced to a broad German readership. It is an understatement when Walter Kaufmann says, "Nineteenth-century German philosophy consisted to a considerable extent in a series of efforts to assimilate the phenomenon of Goethe."[34] Goethe's influence, in the West overall as well as in Germany, was pervasive — on the French (e.g. Berlioz, Gounod, Massenet, Hugo), on the Americans (Emerson, Longfellow, Fuller, Hawthorne), and on the British (Byron, Carlyle, Sir Walter Scott, George Eliot). Even the once skeptical T. S. Eliot eventually recognized Goethe's greatness and kept a drawing of him on his mantelpiece. The twentieth century neglected him, however — in the Anglo-Saxon countries as the result of the two wars in which Germany was the adversary, and in Germany as a reaction to his having been made an

---

[33] These terms are borrowed from Benjamin Bennett, *Goethe's Theory of Poetry: Faust and the Regeneration of Language* (Ithaca, NY: Cornell UP, 1986), passim.

[34] Walter Kaufmann, *From Shakespeare to Existentialism* (Garden City, New York: Doubleday, Anchor, 1960), 58–59. "The unparalleled impact of Goethe's personality, life, and works on nineteenth century German thought can hardly be exaggerated" (Kaufmann, *Nietzsche: Philosopher, Psychologist, Antichrist,* 4th ed. [Princeton: Princeton UP, 1974], 378 n. 10).

icon of German culture by nineteenth-century *Bildungsbürgertum*. All of us have been impoverished.

In the course of this study I explore a variety of matters that are associated with the theme of love and death — lovesickness, venereal disease (syphilis, AIDS), predatory women as targets of love and agents of death, the equation of womb and tomb (*Romeo and Juliet* 2.3.9–10), the *vagina dentata*, woman as object, Frau Welt, the Charybdis, the Lorelei, Undine, the possible asymmetry between male and female attitudes toward the *Liebestod* — as well as others less obviously linked to it but no less germane, such as Goethe's awareness of the split that semiologists identify in the sign (and his understanding of this split as analogous to the split between self and other), linguistic alienation and iconicity, paradox, virtuosity, and Romantic irony.

Readers will see the similarity between Romeo and Juliet's dying "together" and the confluence of two drops of water on the petal of a rose as they combine and disappear into the blossom's calyx in Hebbel's poem "Ich und Du." Octavian puts it this way to the Marschallin in act 1 of "Der Rosenkavalier": "Was heißt das 'du'? Was 'du und ich'? . . . Das sind Wörter, bloße Wörter, nicht? . . . Wie jetzt meine Hand zu deiner Hand kommt, / Das Zudirwollen, das Dichumklammern, / das bin ich, das will zu dir, / aber das Ich *vergeht* in dem Du." Readers may notice that the narrator's hope at the end of *Die Wahlverwandtschaften* for a joint resurrection of Eduard and Ottilie, buried side by side in the chapel, bears a resemblance to the immolation sought by the Bride of Corinth for herself and her Athenian lover. Whether the narration of this tale is straightforward or ironic, whether the narrator is competent to interpret the events related, and whether the bride's rejection of Christianity represents Goethe's own views are also interesting and valid questions. But the conceptual structures — *Denkbilder* or *Sinnfiguren* — informing works of the imagination, or, as Goethe put it, the author's "Vorstellungsart" or way of thinking about things (FA 1,25:31), say more about his or her literary-historical location than does the adoption of a position, either pro or con, at a lower level of abstraction.

Goethe, who has been accused of ignoring crucial differences when he makes "no abrupt distinction between 'Idee' and 'Erfahrung' . . . between logical or conceptual antitheses on the one hand ('Plus-Minus,' 'Ideales und Reales') and empirical opposites on the other hand ('Gelb-Blau,' 'zwei Körperhälften,' etc.)" . . . and of treating "all such pairs as if they were of the same order,"[35] found conventional conceptual systems and established hierarchies suspect. His unsystematic openness to a variety of configurations and arrangements of ideas is evident in his fiction as well. In *Die Leiden des jun-*

---

[35] H. B. Nisbet, *Goethe and the Scientific Tradition* (London: Institute of Germanic Studies, 1972), 45.

gen Werthers, Lotte's Albert faults Werther's analogies and thinks his rea-
soning borders on empty prattle.[36] There is similarity and difference in every
analogy; no metaphor "runs on four legs" (Coleridge). One thing may substitute for another to a greater or lesser degree and in one way or another.
But many factors affect our belief that similarity or difference is more important in a given case or that one *tertium comparationes* is more important
than another.[37] Which similarities are definitive and which differences incidental depends on the frame of reference — usually a preestablished and
dogmatic set of ideas. "Kant . . . illustrates at some length the distinction between an actual and an analogical resemblance. In an analogy, the sensory
properties of the *analogon* are not the same as those of the original, but they
function according to a similar formal principle."[38] In claiming that there are
no facts, only interpretations, Nietzsche reflects Goethe's influence.[39] We can
agree, without supposing that no reading is better than any other or that
understanding is only a matter of taste and does not require serious thought.

Goethe views humans as having only mediate, that is, only *symbolic* access to such ultimates as God, truth, or immortality. It was he who first defined humans as symbol-using animals, and his works abound in symbols of
symbolism — symbols of our dependence on symbols as mediators of truth.
Since poetry is itself a "medium," he features a symbol of mediation in the
dedicatory poem to his collected works — the veil, which conceals but also
reveals. Elsewhere a serpent converts its arched body into a bridge from one
side of a river to the other, a noblewoman's head is transposed onto the
body of a bajadere or prostitute, which enables her to mediate between pariahs and the great god Brahma, and a child asleep on the carpet links the
kneeling Wilhelm Meister and Natalie, the "Beautiful Amazon."[40] A fresco of
Iris, the goddess of the rainbow, adorns the ceiling of the front stairwell in

---

[36] Albert finds Werther's ranking of suicide among other great deeds "paradox! sehr
paradox!" (12 August 1771).

[37] Asked which word didn't belong to the set "add, subtract, multiply, increase," the
scientist Dean Kamen chose "add" because all of the others had eight letters
(*Newsweek,* June 10, 2002, 54).

[38] Paul de Man, "The Epistemology of Metaphor," *Critical Inquiry* 5, 1 (1978): 13–
30, repr. in *Aesthetic Ideology,* ed. Andrzej Warminski (Minneapolis, MN: U of
Minneapolis P, 1996), 46.

[39] "Gegen den Positivismus [which supposes that] 'es gibt nur *Tatsachen,*' würde ich
sagen: nein, gerade Tatsachen gibt es nicht, nur *Interpretationen*" (Nietzsche, *Werke*
3:903).

[40] A tableau mirrored in the story "Sankt Joseph der Zweite" from the *Wanderjahre.*
The widowed Marie is delivered of a baby boy who is held by Frau Elisabeth into the
space "gerade zwischen mich und die Mutter." The boy, like the lily stem,
symbolizes "ein reines Verhältnis," mediation (FA 1,10:38–39). There can be no
unmediated relationship between opposites.

Goethe's house am Frauenplan in Weimar — a different kind of bridge from that on which the young lovers in Sarajevo died. The stairway enables two-way traffic between above and below, and suggests the reversibility of our own exit from unity into selfhood and back again. Next to the door separating this entryway from the main part of the house and in front of a statue of the *Magna mater* stand the twins Sleep and Death, proclaiming what Hannelore Schlaffer has called "den unseligen Zusammenhang von Sinnlichkeit und Tod."[41]

A topical approach to any writer's *oeuvre* entails at least two risks: (a) thematic purity can become a criterion of value and cause neglect of important intellectual, ethical, or aesthetic qualities — a charge often made against the study of the history of ideas; (b) the prevalence of a theme may seem to heighten its significance and obscure the limits of its application in particular cases. I try to avoid these mistakes through a judicious selection of examples and through inquisitive reading as well as through reflection on the larger cultural context and the function of conventions. I wonder what the *Liebestod* tells us about Goethe, about the works in which this theme occurs, about the discourse of which it is a staple, and about the culture it reflects. His use of a traditional theme also provides an occasion to reflect on the originality and the quality of the works in which love and death play a part, and to ponder originality as a literary value. I do not refrain from making non-thematic, for example linguistic and aesthetic, observations about the works considered. Poems, in particular, are addressed as artifacts, not as mere nodes of intersection in an intertextual system. In them I look for cohesiveness, integrity of design, and special meanings and effects. On the other hand, no work of art is an atomistic organic whole, separate from its cultural history and context.

My subtitle "One and Double" is from a *West-östlicher Divan* poem: "Gingo Biloba" and evokes the unity in duality informing the love-death tradition. Of Tristan and Isolde Gottfried writes, "si wurden ein und einvalt, / die zwei und zwîvalt waren ê."[42] Other possible titles might have been "Strange Bedfellows" or, from *Faust*, "Geeinte Zwienatur" (line 11962). The *Faust* line, which might be rendered into English as "Twin Natures Combined" or into non-English as "united twinature" (cf. "twilight" with German "Zwielicht") comes as close as any short formula to expressing the unity and "polarity" of love and death as a coincidence of opposites. The

---

[41] *Stuttgarter Zeitung,* July 3, 1993, 49. Christa Lichtenstern discusses this in "Jupiter — Dionysos — Eros/Thanatos: Goethes symbolische Bildprogramme im Haus am Frauenplan" in the *Goethe-Jahrbuch,* 112 (1995): 343–60.

[42] "They became one and single, / Those who had once been two and double" (Gottfried von Strassburg, *Tristan und Isolde,* in Auswahl herausgegeben von Friedrich Maurer [Berlin: Walter de Gruyter, 1986], lines 11716–17).

ginkgo leaf with its divided, heart-shaped periphery and its undifferentiated internal unity, symbolizes, like Goethe's title *West-östlicher Divan,* the unity of West and East, Goethe's brotherhood with the Persian poet Hafiz: "Lust und Pein / Sey uns den Zwillingen gemein!" ("Unbegrenzt"), and his unity in love with Marianne von Willemer, who authored several of the poems herself. Love and death — those "twin enchantments of the romantic imagination"[43] — like body and soul, or creator and creature in the person of Jesus Christ, or like Tristan and Isolde united in a *Liebestod,* are themselves twins, and show that "twinness" implies opposition as well as unity. Some twins, such as Wiligis and Sibylla, are sexual opposites, yet narcissistically in love with themselves in each other, but all twins are opposed when they face one another or when they both want the same toy or lover. Love and death, too, are at once opposites and an identity. As the author of "Gingo Biloba" mischieviously inquires, "Fühlst du nicht an meinen Liedern, daß ich eins und doppelt bin?"

---

[43] Erich Heller, *Thomas Mann: The Ironic German* (Cleveland, OH: World Publishing Co., 1961), 61.

1: Issues: Some Implications of the Link between Love and Death

"LIEBEN UND UNTERGEHN: das reimt sich seit Ewigkeiten," says Nietzsche. "Wille zur Liebe: das ist, willig auch sein zum Tode."[1] "L'amour, la mort, sont sans doute les événements majeurs qui affectent la condition humaine."[2] The antipodes "l'amour et la mort," near homonyms in French, are linked in titles like that of Gautier's "La Morte Amoureuse," for which Goethe's "Die Braut von Korinth" was probably a source.[3] Philipp Otto Runge's desire for fusion with Pauline Bassenge was a "Sehnsucht und . . . Wille" which are "nur das Innere und Äußere, . . . das ist das *Ich* und das *Du*, das kann nicht verbunden werden als durch den Tod; ich meine, daß sie völlig eins sind, wie sie im Paradies gewesen."[4] In *Die Wahlverwandtschaften* Eduard and Ottilie overcome their separateness and individuality: "Dann waren es nicht zwei Menschen, es war nur Ein Mensch im bewußtlosen, vollkommnen Behagen mit sich selbst zufrieden und mit der Welt" (FA 1,8:516).

Love creates life, death destroys it. To love is to live — to experience an extreme of vitality at the farthest remove from the oblivion which is death.[5] On the other hand, to love is to surrender one's selfhood to another. Lovers live *and die* on love. Only when in love is the individual truly him- or herself, yet when in love he or she is no longer a self at all, but part of a higher unity. "Dieß ist das Geheimniß der Liebe," writes Schelling, "daß sie solche verbindet, deren jedes für sich seyn könnte und doch nicht ist, und nicht

---

[1] Friedrich Nietzsche, *Also Sprach Zarathustra,* in *Werke* 2:379.

[2] Georges Gargam, *L'Amour et la Mort* (Paris: Editions du Seuil, 1959), 7.

[3] Virginia M. Allen, *The Femme Fatale: Erotic Icon* (Troy, NY: Whitston, 1983), 63.

[4] Letter of April 1803, in Philipp Otto Runge, *Briefe und Schriften,* ed. Peter Betthausen (Munich: C. H. Beck, 1982), 140.

[5] "Die Höhe des Daseins als Subjektivität ist die Liebe; die Liebe, entgegengesetzt dem Tode, als Entfaltung aller menschlichen Kräfte, und zwar eine Entfaltung, die alle Grenzen zu übersteigen beansprucht, unendlich sein will, qualitativ und quantitativ, intensiv und extensiv" (Alfred Focke, *Liebe und Tod: Versuch einer Deutung und Auseinandersetzung mit Rainer Maria Rilke* [1885; rpt. Vienna: Herder, 1948], 37).

seyn kann ohne das andere."[6] For to love is to die as an individual and escape from the prison of selfhood. "Plato calls Love a bitter thing," writes Ficino. "And not wrongly, because anyone who loves, dies."[7] The Romantic physicist Johann Wilhelm Ritter calls love and death "synonyms," since "in beyden wird die Individualität aufgehoben, und der Tod ist die Pforte des Lebens."[8] "Was stürbe wohl [dem Tode], als was uns stört, was die Einigen täuschend entzweit?"[9]

Individuation

The *Liebestod* is part of a broad paradigm — "Entindividuation," the desire to escape from the loneliness of selfhood into union with an opposite — with another person, with God, or with the world.[10] It reflects a concern with the self and with what it means to be an individual, an issue implicit in the injunction "Know thyself!"[11] and in every treatment of the love-death theme since antiquity. The desire to possess, blend with, incorporate, or be absorbed in an other or a world of others informs the myth of Venus and Adonis and the stories of Hero and Leander, Orpheus and Eurydice, Admetus and Alcestis, Protesilaus and Laodamia, Pyramus and Thisbe, and Tristan and Isolde, all of which Goethe knew at a young age. In the hymns "Prometheus" and "Ganymed," he articulates the polarity "sich verselbsten" and "sich entselbstigen" — the contradictory urge in every human breast both to assert and to "unself" itself through self-submergence or self-transcendence in the ecstasy of love (FA 1,14:385).

As Eagleton notes, an individual is a "very different animal" from a particular, for individuation raises the question of the individual's relation to the

---

[6] Friedrich Wilhelm Joseph von Schelling, *Sämmtliche Werke,* ed. K. F. A. Schellin (Stuttgart: Cotta, 1860), 1, 7:408.

[7] Marsilio Ficino, *Commentary on Plato's 'Symposium' on Love,* trans. Sears Reynolds Jayne (Dallas, TX: Spring Publications, 1985), 55.

[8] Johann Wilhelm Ritter, *Fragmente* (1810; facsimile reprint Heidelberg: Lambert Schneider, 1969), 205.

[9] Thomas Mann, *Tristan,* in *Gesammelte Werke in zwölf Bänden,* 8:246.

[10] Freud says the object is "das variabelste am Triebe, nicht ursprünglich mit ihm verknüpft, sondern ihm nur infolge seiner Eignung zur Ermöglichung der Befriedung zugeordnet" (Freud, "Trieb und Triebschicksale [1915c], in *SA* 3:86).

[11] Charles Taylor, *Sources of the Self: The Making of the Modern Identity* (Cambridge, MA: Harvard UP, 1989), 113. Schmitz writes: "Der Mensch [ist] für Goethe mit seiner Individualität keineswegs identisch . . ., sondern diese [tritt] seinem innersten Wesen und Wollen als ein auferlegtes beschränkendes Sollen entgegen" (Hermann Schmitz, *Goethes Altersdenken im problemgeschichtlichen Zusammenhang* [Bonn: H. Bouvier, 1959], 419).

universal.[12] Manfred Frank, quoting Goethe's word "Individuum est ineffabile,"[13] says it is the particular, not the individual, that relates to the universal.[14] The features and actions of an *individual* cannot be inferred from the category to which it belongs. "Individualität" is "ein Einzelnes . . ., das nicht kontinuierlich aus einem Allgemeinen abzuleiten ist."[15] "Ein Element, das aus einem Ganzen durch Eingrenzung ausgesondert werden kann (oder wie ein Fall unter eine Regel fällt), heißt ein Besonderes."[16] To be sure, individuals affect, and are affected by, the systems of relations in which they reside or with which they collide, but they cannot be inferred or derived from these systems. While particulars are specimens of their class or genus, individuals generate and express novelty. It would be a dull world that had only classes and particulars, but no individuals.

Goethe is more interested in the existential predicament of the lone individual than in the logical or ontological status of the individual as a category. "Jeder ist selbst nur ein Individuum und kann sich auch eigentlich nur fürs Individuelle interessieren. Das Allgemeine findet sich von selbst, dringt sich auf, erhält sich, vermehrt sich. Wir benutzen's, aber wir lieben es nicht" (FA 1,13:211). He showed his admiration for the rugged individualist "Kraftkerl" in his early *Sturm und Drang* dramas and displayed his own personal individuality in original verse forms and in the mildly outrageous conduct of his early Weimar years. *Götz von Berlichingen* asserts the rights of the free individual, which it is the function of government, in the person of the Kaiser, to serve,[17] while *Stella* carries individualism to the extreme of implying that one lover is never replaceable by another, and love for one person not in conflict with a simultaneous love for another.[18]

[12] Terry Eagleton, *The Idea of Culture* (Oxford: Blackwell, 2000), 55.

[13] Goethe to Johann Caspar Lavater, 20 September 1780, quoted in Frank, *Die Unhintergehbarkeit,* 112. Dirk Kemper advertises a forthcoming book on '*individuum est ineffabile: Goethe und die Individualitäts-problematik der Moderne,* in "Goethes Individualitätsbegriff als Receptionshindernis im Nationalsozialismus," *Goethe-Jahrbuch* 116 (1999): 135 n. 8.

[14] Manfred Frank, *Was ist Neostrukturalismus?* (Frankfurt am Main: Suhrkamp, 1984), 459. A particular is an instantiation of "ein Allgemeines" — a general. The features of an individual, however, are not inferable from its class.

[15] Frank, *Die Unhintergehbarkeit,* 67.

[16] Frank, *Die Unhintergehbarkeit,* 111. "Individuell ist . . . was von jedem Universalitätsanspruch ausgenommen und aus einem Allgemeinen auch nicht bruchlos deduziert werden kann. Ein aus einem Allgemeinen Ableitbares nenne ich ein Besonderes, nicht ein Individuelles" (25).

[17] Kemper, "Goethes Individualitätsbegriff," 129–43.

[18] "Goethe persuades us that, in breaking the bounds of society and morality, his heroes discover a deeper meaning in life, a fullness and richness unknown to those governed by external codes. This highest intensity of being is at the extreme of

A sense of incompleteness and the yearning for fulfillment in love and death may be familiar to most of us.[19] Everyone has experienced at some level of consciousness a longing for release from individuality and alienation and for a return from our terrestrial peregrination or voyage as a Wandering Jew, a Kundry or a Flying Dutchman, never at home, yet always propelled onward by the hope that there *is* a home somewhere and a complement to our imperfection. We seek a resting place and someone to lie down with, a union in which we are no longer guests or restless wanderers, but "Liebende" and in "Ruh." Yet we fear this rest too, which is the peace of death, "die unbedingte Ruh,"[20] thus our ambivalence toward sex. "Identity and absorption emerge as the threat of sex itself,"[21] for the threat of sex is the threat of death, and has given rise to such bizarre myths as that of the *vagina dentata,* the vagina with teeth.

The *Divan* poem "Selige Sehnsucht" depicts the flight of a moth into the flame of a candle in search of a more sublime mating than the sexual union in terrestrial darkness to which it owes its existence. One may lose oneself temporarily, as in love, or permanently, as in death. The *Liebestod,* the *coincidentia oppositorum* employed by Romanticism to encode the return from individuation or "Spezifikation"[22] into a primal unity, is all about erasing boundaries. "Consume my body with spiritual fire," said Novalis, "that I may mix more intimately and airily with thee; let the wedding night last forever" (*Hymns to the Night,* 1st hymn). Novalis equates the benefits of wine, benzaldehyde, and opium with the intoxicating allure of a maiden's womb

individualism. At the other end is its dissolution, its self-loss in feeling, in nature, in God" (Roy Pascal, *The German Sturm und Drang* [New York: Philosophical Library, 1953], 145).

[19] Freud considers whether the drives are "regressive" and aim at "Wiederherstellung eines früheren Zustandes." "Jenseits des Lustprinzips," *SA* 3:266–67. Eagleton says that we are driven by "a desire to scramble back to a place where we cannot be harmed, the inorganic existence which precedes all conscious life, which keeps us struggling forward: our restless attachments (Eros) are in thrall to the death drive (Thanatos)" (Eagleton, *Literary Theory: An Introduction,* 2nd ed. [Minneapolis, MN: U of Minnesota P, 1996], 161). Cf. Georges Bataille, *Death and Sensuality: A Study of Eroticism and the Taboo* (New York: Walker, 1962), 15.

[20] "Die Braut von Korinth," line 193; *Faust,* lines 340–41.

[21] Susan Stewart, *Crimes of Writing: Problems in the Containment of Representation* (New York: Oxford UP, 1991), 244.

[22] "Über Metamorphose und deren Sinn; Systole und Diastole des Weltgeistes, aus jener geht die Spezifikation hervor, aus dieser das Fortgehn ins Unendliche" (*Tagebuch* 17. Mai 1808, in FA 2,6:306). The term comes from Samuel Richter, pen name: Sincerus Renatus. See Rolf Christian Zimmermann, *Das Weltbild des jungen Goethe: Studien zur hermetischen Tradition des deutschen 18. Jahrhunderts,* vol. 1 (Munich: Wilhelm Fink, 1969), 191.

and bosom in a darkness devoid of "leuchtende Kugeln," a night into which the bodies of lovers evaporate.

Openings to the self and the injection or infusion of natural fluids such as semen and blood — "ein ganz besondrer Saft" — or drugs, poisons, potions, and all kinds of substances with the power to penetrate the membranes and orifices of the self play a prominent role in the history of the love-death theme, which depends on someone's desire to cross the line between oneself and one's lover. For the self is neither indivisible nor impermeable; it allows a flow of fragrances, fluids, and fictions in and out of seemingly hard, impenetrable bodies, vessels, and ideologies of many kinds. "[Er] hing an ihrem Munde, / Um seinen Geist ihr einzuhauchen," says Pandora. Metaphors of flowing, confluence, influence, often linked with potions (*Tristan und Isolde, Faust*), poisons (*Romeo and Juliet*), and ointments are essential to the love-death tradition. What part of Donna Anna's essence is in the narrator's private box and what is still down on the stage from where her fragrance wafts up to him, in Hoffmann's tale about Mozart's *Don Giovanni*? How much of Don Juan has flowed into Donna Anna if she has succumbed to him, as the narrator believes? What measure of Christ's spirit lives in Christian believers, and how much of them inhabits the body of the Church? To what extent are we always already in the world, and to what extent does the world always reside and preside in us? Adelheid von Walldorf "sucks" her lovers into death with poison. Faust hopes the contents of his "einzige Phiole" will launch him on a flight through the ether (line 704).

How do individuals come into being in the first place? Given Goethe's debts to Plato and Plotinus, we might expect the "idea" or the universal to be his basic reality, individuals emanating from it through a process of mirroring or separation,[23] and in one of his early *Ephemerides* (February 1770) Goethe did declare his belief in the "systema emanativum" (FA 2,1:192). Whether a given life trajectory flows out of a "parent" with which it was never identical or emanates from an original unity has been the subject of centuries of debate. In the emanation model only the emergent individual, not the parent, suffers from nostalgia for completeness, the gods being blessedly devoid of passions, "schicksallos, wie der schlafende Säugling" (Hölderlin, "Hyperions Schicksalslied"), since they are already perfect. They dine "an goldenen Tischen," oblivious to the sufferings of "Erdgebornen" (Iphigenie's "Gesang der Parzen"). It is no skin off their nose if their creatures suffer torment or privation. Emanation impoverishes only the emergent individual, not the gods, even if the idea that the self could ever be separate and alone can only be an illusion. But insofar as subjectivity is defined by longing, only the creature, not the Creator, is possessed of subjectivity. The

---

[23] To separate = prepare itself; "Alle Endlichkeit beruht auf Negation/Einschränkung" (Frank, *Die Unhintergehbarkeit*, 109).

other side of the coin is that parents are dependent on their offspring. "Denn weil / die Seligsten nichts fühlen von selbst, / muß wohl . . . in der Götter Namen / teilnehmend fühlen ein andrer. Den brauchen sie" (Hölderlin, "Der Rhein"). "Am Ende hängen wir doch ab / Von Kreaturen, die wir machten," is how the sage Mephistopheles puts it (*Faust*, lines 7003–4).[24] Goethe's focus, however, is not on the agonies of a prior, transcendent ego, but on the lonely, indivisible self that enters being and time through a separation at a particular instant in time from the primal unity, and whose earthly sojourn is propelled by its desire to return — to home, to the mother, or into the open arms of God, as Werther hopes and as the hymn "Mahomet's Gesang" depicts.[25]

The *Liebestod* is preeminently concerned with the boundary between inside and outside[26] — outside either in the sense of "away from home," like the Prodigal Son, or alienated from the world in which one resides, as in much modernist writing. Though unpredictable, individuals, like particulars, do always refer back to their source or to their prototype, like variations on a theme, or to the community that defines their expatriation. En route they experience unforeseen encounters, dialogue and conflict, as in the second of Goethe's "Orphic Primal Words." The self is enriched and transformed by contact with the non-self. "Nicht einsam bleibst du, bildest dich gesellig" ("TYXH, *Das Zufällige*"). The lamp awaits the flame that will ignite it. There is an existentialist tinge to Goethe's (neo)platonism that resists the submergence of the individual in a crowd and denies the relevance of any general rule. This complicated his reception by the Nazis.[27] Twentieth-century existentialism derives from Romanticism, and its stress on human independence is a manifestation of an inherited common culture. We are not alone in our loneliness.

Goethe does not imagine individuation either as the division of a prior unity such as the manwoman split by Zeus in Aristophanes' tale in Plato's

[24] To Eckermann's reflections on these lines Goethe replied, "Ein Vater, der sechs Söhne hat, ist verloren, er mag sich stellen wie er will" (FA 2,12:365–66).

[25] Goethe anticipates both of two contrary psychoanalytical theses — that the aim of a drive is (a) the "Herstellung einer Identität des Subjekts mit dem Objekt," and (b) the "Aufrechthaltung der psychischen Individualität des Subjekts" (Peter Zagermann, *Eros und Thanatos*. [Darmstadt: Wissenschaftliche Buchgesellschaft, 1988], 3).

[26] Jacques Derrida, *Dissemination,* trans. Barbara Johnson (Chicago: U of Chicago P, 1981), 103; Charles Taylor, *Sources of the Self,* 111, 113; Maggie Kilgour, *From Communion to Cannibalism: An Anatomy of Metaphors of Incorporation* (Princeton: Princeton UP, 1990), 4 and passim.

[27] See Kemper, *Goethes Individualitätsbegriff,* 129–43. According to Rudolph, Werther rejects Albert's appeal to a general *Menschenverstand* as an unjustified restriction of human individuality (Enno Rudolph, "Individualität," *Goethe-Handbuch* 4/1 [Stuttgart: Metzler, 1998]: 530).

Symposium, the broomstick split by the apprentice sorcerer's ax, or as a separating out of an original multiplicity in which the individual self resides as a discrete potentiality even *prior to* its emergence as a phenomenon. In the last case, the individual would not *come into* being but always already be. Goethe draws an analogy to the conflict between the orthodox doctrine of the trinity, implying the consubstantiality of Father, Son, and Holy Ghost, and the Arian view of God's indivisibility, the Son and the Holy Spirit being offspring of the Father, not particles first embedded in, then dispersed out of, His essence.[28] Casting himself as the Arian of the science of optics struggling against the Athanasian orthodoxy of the followers of Newton,[29] he contrasts Newton's division of light into seven discrete colors with his own view that pure white light is indivisible. Life's "ringing play of colors" results from the interaction of light and dark, positive forces both, just as individual selves are shaped and hardened by fortuitous accidents and obstacles met along the way. In the sonnet "Mächtiges Überraschen," the landslide "Oreas" blocks the path of the onrushing mountain stream, splashes it back into itself and creates "ein neues Leben." Error and superstition, too, interact with truth to yield the peculiar understandings and beliefs that mark a human individual.[30] Whether as an *ex nihilo* creation, a reflection, a spark or a splinter, the individual proceeds according to its own essential law: "So mußt du sein, dir kannst du nicht entfliehen, / So sagten schon Sibyllen, so Propheten; / Und keine Zeit und keine Macht zerstückelt / Geprägte Form, die lebend sich entwickelt' ("Urworte. Orphisch, ΔAIMΩN, *Dämon*").

Emanation is a proceeding forth from a point of origin, but sometimes Goethe speaks of symmetrical division. "Erscheinung und Entzweien sind synonym," he says. Appearing as a phenomenon is synonymous with "sich *trennen, sondern, verteilen*" (GA 17:395, 700).[31] Originating in a primeval

---

[28] Goethe understands Newton as saying, "die Farbe [sei] dem Licht nicht nur eingeboren, sondern die Farben in ihren spezifischen Zuständen seien in dem Licht als ursprüngliche Lichter enthalten, welche nur durch die Refraktion und andre äußere Bedingungen manifestiert, aus dem Lichte hervorgebracht und in ihrer Uranfänglichkeit und Unveränderlichkeit nunmehr dargestellt würden" (FA 1,23,1:805).

[29] Albrecht Schöne, *Goethes Farbentheologie* (Munich: C. H. Beck, 1987), 68–75.

[30] "Das Subjekt, in der Erscheinung, [ist] immer nur Individuum . . ., und [bedarf] daher eines gewissen Anteils von Wahrheit und Irrtum . . ., um seine Eigentümlichkeit zu erhalten" (Letter to Arthur Schopenhauer, 16 November 1815, in GA 21:114). Cf. Haller's "Vom Ursprung des Übels," in which error is seen as a consequence of limitation: "Zudem, was endlich ist, kann nicht unfehlbar sein, / Das Übel schlich sich auch in uns durch Irrtum ein."

[31] "Was in die Erscheinung tritt, muß sich trennen, um nur zu erscheinen" (GA 16:864). Weinhandl argues that unity is also prior in Goethe (Ferdinand Weinhandl, *Die Metaphysik Goethes* [Berlin: Junker & Dünnhaupt, 1932; reprint, Darmstadt:

division, individuals mourn their loss and rejoice in finding each other: "Allah braucht nicht mehr zu schaffen, / Wir erschaffen seine Welt" ("Wiederfinden").

Strife, not love, is the usual relationship of individuals to one another, according to the Görlitz mystic, Jacob Boehme. In Goethe too: "Was nebeneinander existiert, scheint nur zum Streit berufen zu sein" (To Charlotte v. Stein, 19 November 1807). The aim of Eros, by contrast, is to burn individuality away. "Individual beings were but so many defects and eclipsings of the one and only Being; and as such none was susceptible of being really loved."[32] In Romantic literature the ground into which one longs to be reabsorbed is as formless as the night, as in Young's *Night Thoughts* and Novalis's *Hymns to the Night* — implicit also in Juliet's dismissal of the "garish sun" (3.2). Darkness, declared the mother of light by Mephistopheles, finds herself in mortal combat with her ungrateful offspring, through whose agency bodies have a transitory being (*Faust*, lines 1349–58). She is independent of the things on which light shines in order to show itself. When they pass away light itself will disappear. "Alles was entsteht, / Ist wert, daß es zu Grunde geht" (lines 1339–40), but that which never originated will never cease to be.[33] Behind the concept of "Mother Night," which is semiotically linked with water (Freud's "oceanic")[34] and with God, is the dichotomy of unity versus separation, the One and the Many.

The paradox that personal identity arises out of *a loss* of identity with the source is at the core of the Romantic world view and the premise on which all of its struggles are based. Indeed, belief in the individual as a unique essence defined by self-consciousness is the founding error of all modernism, an "error" insofar as it is blind to the complex ways in which the self is embedded in a world and is a manifestation of its world. The desire to lose a sharply delineated selfhood in an enveloping liquid All informs Romantic yearning and explains the prominence of the *Liebestod* in its artistic expres-

Wissenschaftliche Buchgesellschaft, 1965], 75–76): "Also auch für das Getrennte, das ursprünglich Entzweite ist Verbindung von Goethe immer schon vorausgesetzt" (75).

[32] Denis de Rougemont, *Love in the Western World*, trans. Montgomery Belgion (New York: Fawcett, 1940; rev. ed. New York: Pantheon, 1956).

[33] Cf. Franz to Adelheid in the first version of *Götz von Berlichingen:* "O das geht über alle Höllenstrafen die glückseligkeit des Himmels nur einen kleinen Augenblick zu genießen. Tausend Jahre sind nur eine halbe Nacht. Wie haß ich den Tag. Lägen wir in einer uranfänglichen Nacht, eh das Licht gebohren ward. Oh. Ich würde an deinem Busen der ewigen Götter einer sein, die in brütender Liebeswärme in sich selbst wohnten, und in einem Punkte die Keime von tausend Welten gebaren, und die Glut der Seligkeiten von tausend Welten auf einen Punckt fühlten" (FA 1,4:237–38).

[34] On the "oceanic," see Freud, *Das Unbehagen in der Kultur*, in *SA* 9:197–98.

sion.[35] Human love is a temporary, proleptic fulfillment of the longing for ultimate self-surrender: "Und immer sehnt sich fort das Herz, / Ich weiss nicht recht ob himmelwärts, / Fort aber will es hin und hin, / Und mögte vor sich selber fliehn. / Und fliegt es an der Liebsten Brust / Da ruht's im Himmel unbewusst" ("Was wird mir jede Stunde so bang?"). The individual's longing for love is ultimately satisfied not in sexual orgasm — "la petite mort" — but in the lovers' death together, just as the merging of individuals into an identity entails their submergence in eternal love: "Ungehemmt mit heißem Triebe / Läßt sich da kein Ende finden, / Bis im Anschaun ewiger Liebe / Wir verschweben, wir verschwinden" ("Höheres und Höchstes").

As Eibl notes, Faust "fühlt sich 'beschränkt,' 'umstellt,' er empfindet Herzbeklemmung, Hemmung seiner Lebensregung, fühlt sich 'verengt,' 'gedrängt,'"[36] not by the world around him but by the walls of his own self. As Goethe wrote to Charlotte von Stein, "Wundersam ist doch ieder Mensch in seiner Individualität gefangen" (30 June 1780). In a variation on the ancient metaphor of the soul imprisoned in the body, Werther imagines selfhood as a "Kerker" whose walls the self longs to scale and surmount. He tells of a noble race of horses who bite open an artery when the pressure becomes too great. The sibylline Makarie in *Wilhelm Meisters Wanderjahre* sees into "die innere Natur eines jeden durch die ihn umgebende individuelle Maske" (FA 1,10:379). Beyond the shell of a person's body and personality there is an ideal boundary of the self — an "ideele geistige Gränze"[37] — that we long in vain to transgress.

"Goethe's fusion of love and death reminds one of the romantic notion of the *Liebestod* but is really very different," says Hatfield. "In Wagner or Novalis, the 'love-death' expresses a longing for Schopenhauerian nothingness or for ecstasy gained by the Dionysiac loss of individuality. For this, the sexual act as such is the appropriate symbol. For Goethe, the ecstasy has the aim of metamorphosis to a higher form: the embrace leads to the conception of a new being; dying, to new life."[38] Hatfield has a point. In *Prometheus* the

---

[35] The essence of philosophy, according to Friedrich Schlegel, is "Sehnsucht nach d[em] Unendlichen." KA 2,18:418; *Philosophische Fragmente: Zweyte Epoche,* no. [1168].

"Je weiter die Selbstwerdung fortschreitet, desto größer wird die Sehnsucht nach Entäußerung," notes Peter Huber. "Die Fluktuation zwischen beiden Polen führt zur Entgrenzung im Liebestod" (FA 1,4:857).

[36] Karl Eibl, *Das monumentale Ich: Wege zu Goethes "Faust"* (Frankfurt am Main & Leipzig: Insel, 2000), 89.

[37] Note to "Kunst und Altertum am Rhein und Main" (1816), FA 1,20:87; Schmitz, *Goethes Altersdenken,* 268.

[38] Henry Hatfield, *Goethe: A Critical Introduction* (Norfolk, CT: New Directions, 1963), 118.

intercourse witnessed by Pandora foreshadows a resurrection or a rebirth (lines 411–12). In "Selige Sehnsucht" death is followed by a rebirth at the level of accidence that masks a continuity of essence.[39] Goethe envisions an oscillation *between* self-assertion and resubmergence, as instances of the law of polarity he saw at work everywhere — in the expansion and contraction of matter, the exhaling and inhaling of the breath, the systole and diastole of the heartbeat, and the interaction of the sexes.[40] Each separation along life's road is a reenactment of the original individuating event, and each coming together anticipates the final reunion. The alternation of self-articulation and resubmergence was affirmed by the alchemists, whose writings Goethe studied in the months between Leipzig and Strassburg and whose "great work" is conceptualized as an ascending series of dyings and becomings. Uncomfortable with finality, Goethe sometimes depicts a reunion as only a bridge to subsequent separations and reunions, forays outward and returns at a higher level, in an ascending spiral. At other times the paradigm seems static, his characters propelled by the desire to escape temporality in search of an enduring, timeless spatiality. In conflict with itself, the self seeks both self-preservation and surrender to unity. This is at the root of Romantic irony and analogous to the simultaneous desire for identity (= presence) and for meaning (= representation = non-identity).

The *Liebestod,* a *Coincidentia Oppositorum*

The unity of love and death is manifest in the paradox of the *Liebestod*. Love is ecstasy — "Lebensgenuß," "[des Lebens] Nonplusultra," hence the opposite of death,[41] while, on the other hand, love and death both reverse individuation and restore unity. Love unites opposed selves temporarily; death does so absolutely.[42] Both love and death return the self to its origin and des-

---

[39] The young Schelling too affirms an indestructible self when he says: "Schwerlich hätte je ein Schwärmer sich an dem Gedanken, in dem Abgrund der Gottheit verschlungen zu seyn, vergnügen können, hätte er nicht immer an die Stelle der Gottheit wieder sein eigenes Ich gesetzt. Schwerlich hätte je ein Mystiker sich als vernichtet denken können, hätte er nicht als Substrat der Vernichtung immer wieder sein eigenes Selbst gedacht" (*Sämmtliche Werke* 1,1:319).

[40] See Rolf Christian Zimmermann, "Goethes Polaritätsdenken im geistigen Kontext des 18. Jahrhunderts," *Jahrbuch der Deutschen Schillergesellschaft* 18 (1975): 304–47.

[41] Rudolph Drux, "'Wie reimt sich Lieb und Tod zusammen?': Gestalten und Wandlungen einer Motivkombination in der barocken Lyrik," *Der Deutschunterricht: Beiträge zu seiner Praxis und wissenschaftlichen Grundlegung* 37.5 (1985): 25.

[42] "The union, which is the effect of love . . . is real union, which the lover seeks with the object of his love. . . . *Aristophanes stated that lovers would wish to be united both into one, but since this would result in either one or both being destroyed,* they seek a suitable and becoming union; — to live together, speak together, and be united to-

tiny. Like an open secret, like the *pharmakon* that is both poison or potion and a panacea,[43] or like Jesus Christ, who is both creator and creature, large enough to encompass the universe and small enough to dwell in Mary's womb, they are antitheses but also an identity, a *coincidentia oppositorum*.[44]

gether in other like things" (Thomas Aquinas, *Summa Theologica*, 3 vols., trans. Fathers of the English Dominican Province [New York: Benzinger Brothers, 1947–48], 1:710).

[43] "As Starkey wrote: 'this Water is by Philosophers called their Venom, and indeed it is a very strong poison. . . . But as concerning the Medicine that is made by it, it is certain that of all Medicines in the World it is the highest, for it is the true Arbor Vitae'" (Ronald D. Gray, *Goethe the Alchemist* [Cambridge, UK: Cambridge UP, 1952], 227). Mephistopheles says of theology: "Es liegt in ihr so viel verborgenes Gift, / Und von der Arzenei ist's kaum zu unterscheiden" (lines 1986–87). This is a topos. "Es ist Arznei, nicht Gift, was ich dir reiche," says Lessing's Nathan in attacking his daughter Recha's pious superstition that an angel has rescued her from the fire (1,2). The philter drunk by Tristan and Isolde both restores them and destroys them as individuals. "The Greek word from which *pharmaco-* and all its variants derive is *pharmakon*, which can mean 'drug, medicine, or poison'" (Mark C. Taylor, *Erring: A Postmodern A/Theology* [Chicago: U of Chicago P, 1984], 117). "Jedem Gift ist nicht nur sein Gegengift gewachsen, sondern die ewige Tendenz der waltenden lebendigen Kraft geht dahin, aus dem schädlichsten Gift die kräftigste Arznei zu bereiten" (Johann Gottfried Herder, *Sämtliche Werke*, ed. Bernhard Suphan [Berlin: Weidmann, 1881], 17:27). "Je giftiger ein Ding ist, je schärfer probiert es ein Ding" (Jakob Böhme, *Magnum mysterium*, 1623, as quoted by Wilhelm Dobbek, "Die coincidentia oppositorum als Prinzip der Weltdeutung bei J. G. Herder wie in seiner Zeit," in *Herder Studien*, ed. Walter Wiora with Hans Dietrich Irmscher [Würzburg: Holzner, 10 (1960)]: 27). "Was mich nicht umbringt, macht mich stärker" (Nietzsche, *Götzen-Dämmerung, oder wie man mit dem Hammer philosophiert*, in *Werke* 2:943). Cf. Mynheer Peeperkorn (Thomas Mann, *Der Zauberberg*, "Mynheer Peeperkorn, des weiteren," *Gesammelte Werke* 3:801).

[44] Franz Koch identifies Goethe's conception of the symbol as a *coincidentia oppositorum*. *Goethes Gedankenform* (Berlin: Walter de Gruyter, 1967), 254. See Ernst Cassirer, *The Individual and the Cosmos in Renaissance Philosophy*, trans. Mario Domandi (New York: Barnes & Noble, 1963), 7–45, 123–91, and Edgar Wind, *Pagan Mysteries in the Renaissance* (New Haven: Yale UP, 1958; rev. and enlarged edition, New York: Norton [The Norton Library], 1968), 105–12, 191–238. M. H. Abrams discusses the connections between Romanticism and neoplatonism in *Natural Supernaturalism: Tradition and Revolt in Romantic Literature* (New York: W. W. Norton, 1971), 141–54. McFarland surveys the reception of Bruno, Cusanus, Paracelsus, and Böhme by the Romantics, pointing out that Coleridge's early reading of these authors preceded that of their German descendants; see Thomas McFarland, *Romanticism and the Forms of Ruin: Wordsworth, Coleridge and the Modalities of Fragmentation* (Princeton, NJ: Princeton UP, 1981), 289–341. See also Alice D. Snyder, *The Critical Principle of the Reconciliation of Opposites as Employed by Coleridge* (Ann Arbor, MI: Ann Arbor Press, 1918), 289 n. 42. For Böhme and the

Like Tristan and Isolde, or like a straight line and a circle with an infinite radius, or like freedom and fatality,[45] love and death are two and yet one — one in uniting the opposed forces within a single human soul or two human opposites into a new identity, as in Paul Fleming: "Ich irrte hin und her und suchte mich in mir, / Und wuste dieses nicht, daß ich ganz war in dir."[46] In Johann Christian Günther's poem "Als er der Phyllis einen Ring mit einem Totenkopf überreichte," we sense the poet's pleasure in linking "Eis und Flammen," "Lieb und Tod." "Denn beide sind von gleicher Stärke / Und tun ihre Wunderwerke / Mit allen die auf Erden gehn." From the man's point of view — it may compute differently for women — both lovers, losing themselves in each other, gain something more valuable. "Der Liebende will im Grunde gar nicht zu sich zurückkehren, weil er nur durch die Geliebte Leben erhält oder, in negativer Paradoxie, seiner selbst nicht innewürde, wenn er sich nicht liebend entäußerte."[47] Wagner's Tristan and Isolde long for the unity in which they are "nicht mehr Tristan, . . . nicht mehr Isolde" (2.2). Catherine in *Wuthering Heights* declares, "I *am* Heathcliff — he's always, always in my mind — not as a pleasure, any more than I am always a pleasure to myself — but, as my own being — so, don't talk of our separation again — it is impracticable." "I am thee and thou art me and all of one is the other," says Maria to Robert Jordan in *For Whom the Bell Tolls*. "Erst als Liebende(r) ist ein Mensch ganz er selbst, aber zugleich nur der Teil einer Einheit in der Zweiheit."[48] "Der Eros . . . strebt nach Vereinigung, Aufhebung der Raumgrenzen zwischen Ich und geliebtem Objekt," says Freud.[49] "Auf der Höhe der Verliebtheit droht die Grenze zwischen Ich und Objekt zu verschwimmen. Allen Zeugnissen der Sinne entgegen behauptet der Verliebte, daß Ich und Du eines seien, und ist bereit, sich, als ob es so wäre, zu benehmen."[50]

German Romantics, see Paola Mayer, *Jena Romanticism and Its Appropriation of Jakob Böhme* (Montreal & Kingston: McGill-Queen's UP, 1999).

[45] See Cassirer, "Giovanni Pico Della Mirandola," *Journal of the History of Ideas* (1942): 323. Baudelaire: "Non seulement il y aura, dans le cas de progrès, identité entre la liberté et la fatalité, mais cette identité a toujours existé." From Maria Moog-Grünewald, "Die Frau als Bild des Schicksals: Zur Ikonologie der Femme Fatale," *Arcadia* 18:3 (1983), 245 n. 13.

[46] Paul Fleming, *Deutsche Gedichte,* ed. J. M. Lappenberg, 2 vols. (Stuttgart: Litterarischer Verein, 1865; repr. Darmstadt: Wissenschaftliche Buchgesellschaft, 1965).

[47] Rudolf Drux, "Lieb und Tod," 28.

[48] Rüdiger Schnell, *Suche nach Wahrheit: Gottfrieds "Tristan und Isold" als erkenntniskritischer Roman* (Tübingen: Max Niemeyer, 1992), 220.

[49] "Hemmung, Symptom und Angst," *SA* 6:265.

[50] *Das Unbehagen in der Kultur, SA* 9:199.

How does the *coincidentia oppositorum* work? Wilhelm Dobbek defines thinking dialectically as the contemplation of opposed phenomena in their mutual interdependence. The unity of contraries is never simply a compromise, but a tense and productive interaction of genuine antitheses (17–18).[51] This takes the rhetorical, pragmatic dimension of Goethe's writing into account and explains his fascination with the *coincidentia oppositorum* as a provocative and dynamic alternative to unambiguous representation. It also exposes "unitarian" interpretations of *Faust* as reductionist attempts to simplify a great, unparaphrasable work. According to Dobbek, the *Goethezeit* combines the idea of immanence (against transcendence) with a dynamic conception of unification in time (against a timeless unity in space). Goethe's conception of individuation as a punctual splitting off adds force to this idea. It is hard to identify Goethe with either tendency, as though he himself were a timeless, unchanging identity and his thought an established, undeveloping and undialectical pledge to dynamic development from his youth in Frankfurt until his old age. Rather, each concept serves a local, limited poetic need and is not binding in a *weltanschaulich* sense. Yet he does rely on a fairly stable set of categories, while keeping an ironic distance from them and absorbing infusions from many sources.

Dialectical thinking remains productive today, especially in non-Anglo-Saxon philosophical discourse. Paul Ricoeur assigns a strong meaning to "as" as not only the "as" of comparison (oneself as *similar to* another) but that of a consequence (oneself as a result of *being* another)."[52] The structure of unity in opposition ("Geeinte Zwienatur") informs every dialectic, as well as such rhetorical figures as the oxymoron, the paradox, and the equivocation known as Romantic irony (which asserts and denies at the same time). The *femme fatale's* strength — her irresistible sexual power — is also her weakness. She is powerless to control its effects. In Grass's *Katz und Maus* Joachim Mahlke's too-large penis and Adam's apple cause an inferiority complex that he tries to offset with the ornaments he hangs from his neck, eventually the iron cross. The too much is, without an *aufhebend* counterweight, too obviously too little.

---

[51] Wilhelm Dobbek, *Coincidentia oppositorum*, 17–18.

[52] Paul Ricoeur, *Soi-même comme un autre*, trans. by Kathleen Blamey as *Oneself as Another* (Chicago: U of Chicago P, 1992), 3 — emphasis added. Frank reads Schelling as saying, "Ein reines Satz-Subjekt bleibt so lange bedeutungslos, wie das Prädikat nicht präzisiert, *als was* denn das in Subjektposition Gesetzte näherhin existiert" (e.g. A as B in the identity A = B). "A als reines Wesen, als transitives Subjekt alles Etwas-Seins, wäre an und für sich nichts. Um nicht nur an ihm selbst, sondern als dies oder das zu existieren, muß es sich entäußern. Und jede Entäußerung impliziert Veränderung" (Frank, *Selbstbewußtsein und Selbsterkenntnis* [Stuttgart: Reclam, 1991], 134–35).

Boyle suggests that a Leibnizian anxiety about the autonomy of the self may account for the German preoccupation with the polarity of individuation and reassimilation.[53] "The monad was a proto-self," says Charles Taylor.[54] In the Renaissance, according to Bakhtin, the human body came to be seen as "a strictly completed, finished product . . . isolated, alone, fenced off from all other bodies. . . . The ever unfinished nature of the body was hidden, kept secret; conception, pregnancy, childbirth, death throes, were almost never shown. The age represented was as far removed from the mother's womb as from the grave."[55] Belief in a punctual self generates both the desire for self-preservation and the abiding *Angst* of separation; thus the iconic prominence of Mary and Venus in any representation of the plight of modern man. As stereotypical but antithetical representations of woman, Mary and Venus are objects of a man's longing for, and fear of, submergence in the womb that is also a tomb.

The desire for unity in love and death, then, follows from the fact of individuation, just as unity may derive from differentiation in logic.[56] Theologically this would imply the contingency of God himself. If, on the other hand, unity is prior and multiplicity secondary,[57] this may attest to the lateness and modernity of Romanticism. For Goethe, in any case, "the human tragedy" is "the tragedy of life apart from a primal center of significance and hence limited to eternal derivations."[58] The desire for a blending devoid of all differentiation coupled with the sense that this is impossible characterizes the thought of the younger Romantics, for whom the *Liebestod* symbolizes victory over division of every kind, including that between signifier and signified in the sign, which both eclipses its referent and, in *re-presenting* it, brings it once again into view. Every union, therefore, is a *coincidentia op-*

[53] Nicholas Boyle, *Goethe: The Poet and the Age*, 1 (Oxford: Clarendon P, 1991), 13–16, 161.

[54] Charles Taylor, *Sources of the Self*, 375.

[55] Mikhail Bakhtin, *Rabelais and His World*, trans. Hélène Iswolsky (Cambridge, MA: MIT Press, 1968), 29.

[56] "There is no principle of unity where there is no principle of differentiation" (Peter F. Strawson, *Individuals: An Essay in Descriptive Metaphysics* [London: Methuen, 1959; paperback reprint 1990], 103).
Goethe allows for either originary unity or originary division. "Einheit und Mannigfaltigkeit [sind] . . . unaufhebbar aufeinander angewiesen . . ., und . . . wir [haben] es nun bald mit einer Einheit, die der Entzweiung fähig ist, ebensowohl aber auch bald mit einer ursprünglichen Entzweiung [zu tun], die einer Vereinigung fähig ist" (Weinhandl, *Metaphysik*, 152).

[57] See R. Howard Bloch, *Medieval Misogyny and the Invention of Western Romantic Love* (Chicago: U of Chicago P, 1991), 25–26.

[58] Clark S. Muenzer, *Figures of Identity: Goethe's Novels and the Enigmatic Self* (University Park: Penn State UP, 1984), 161 n. 37.

positorum, a fusing of opposites still preserved in their fusion. Complete, unambiguous presence is as unattainable as it is desirable, which may explain the Romantics' recourse to irony and paradox, and their fondness for oxymorons. Goethe's younger contemporaries share his passion for a unity that is more than the bridging of difference: "zwey Seelen sollen sich in einen Leib, zwey Leiber in eine Seele schicken" (FA 1,20:495) and thereby produce a third, in a union that is greater than the sum of its parts. It is hard to see why the prospect of an open-ended universe did not deny Nietzsche, who is otherwise so dependent on Goethe, his belief in the eternal recurrence of the same. Implicit in the idea of organicism, it is a crucial, indispensable insight — one not congenial to mechanistic world views.

Other Explanations of the Link between Love and Death

The pervasive link between love and death in the history of literature, religion, and philosophy has been explained in a variety of ways. As opposed forces, love and death are a near match for each other, love being strong enough to cancel out death. *The Song of Solomon* says "love is as strong as death." "Many waters cannot quench love neither can floods drown it" (8:6–7).[59] Wilde's Salomé says love is stronger: "le mystère de l'amour est plus grand que le mystère de la mort."[60] Elaine E. Boney sees equal intensity as the common element in the fires of love and death,[61] while H. W. Munzer and Patrick Brady believe that love and death are paradoxically linked by their opposite effects, love tending toward activity, death toward stasis.[62] Death destroys the organism while love provides for the continuation of the species or "Gattung" (a word linked to the word for coupling or mating, as Munzer points out). This distinction originates with Schopenhauer, and is commented on by Freud: "Für [Schopenhauer . . . ist] ja der Tod 'das eigentliche Resultat' und insofern der Zweck des Lebens . . ., der Sexualtrieb aber die Verkörperung des Willens zum Leben" (*SA* 3:259). Love obstructs death's disintegrating power. It both extends the lovers' lives through the creation of offspring and rejuvenates the love partners themselves (*SA*

---

[59] *The Bible,* Revised Standard Version (Oxford UP, 821). On *Die Legende von Paul und Paula,* the *Neue Züricher Zeitung* says, "Ihre Liebe war so stark wie der Tod."

[60] Oscar Wilde, *Salomé,* in *The Collected Works,* ed. Robert Ross, vol. 2 (London: Routledge, 1993), 80.

[61] Elaine E. Boney, "Love's Door to Death in Rilke's Cornet and Other Works," *Modern Austrian Literature* 10 (1977): 23.

[62] H. W. Munzer, "Das Liebesproblem und Todesproblem bei Johann Christian Günther." Diss. U of Pennsylvania, 1951. Patrick Brady, "Manifestations of Eros and Thanatos in *L'étranger,*" *Twentieth Century Literature* 20 (1974): 183–88.

3:264). Freud distinguishes between "Ich-triebe = Todestriebe" and "Sexualtriebe = Lebenstriebe" (*SA* 3:261), later recast as "Lebens- [Eros] und Todestriebe" (262), the aim of the *Todestriebe* being to put an end to "Vitaldifferenzen" (264) and restore an original state of things" (266). According to Norman O. Brown, "Eros is the instinct that makes for union, or unification, and Thanatos, the death instinct, is the instinct that makes for separation, or division."[63]

Any discussion of Eros and Thanatos that casts them only as opposites and ignores their coincidence misses the implicit paradox. Love and death *both* coincide *and* oppose each other; *sie heben einander auf.* Love fosters *both* the extinction and the preservation of the self, while the prospect of death may intensify someone's desire for love. But what love and the death principle ultimately aspire to is neither survival nor self-perpetuation but rest and permanence, a timeless moment to which one might say, "Verweile doch! du bist so schön!" *Both* love and death seek stasis and *both* express a wish for escape from time and temporal struggle into a lasting bliss. A moment of ecstasy so strong that he would want time to stop would be the death of Faust, which is not only a risk he is willing to take but a consummation he would gratefully embrace: "Dann will ich gern zu Grunde gehn.The oddest attempt so far to explain the link between love and death is that of Denis de Rougemont in *Love in the Western World.* De Rougemont provides a historical-psychological, and, at points, psychoanalytical explanation of the love-death topos, while searching for its "existential *meaning*."[64] The reason for the passion of Tristan and Iseult, according to de Rougemont, is that their love is dangerous, illicit, forbidden. We want what we are denied (an explanation entertained by Lotte for Werther's passion, which he dismisses as unworthy of her [20 December 1772, FA 1,8:221]). Since erotic passion is incompatible with marriage and a Frau Isolde unthinkable, according to Rougemont, the novel of adultery is the quintessential narrative of passion. The twists and turns of the story's plot are due to the principals' psychological need for barriers, which the lovers themselves are sometimes obliged to erect. This is why Tristan places his sword between himself and Iseult in the forest, why he leaves Mark's court after Iseult's acquittal of the charge of adultery (although her innocence, hence his own, has been proven by the God's Judgment), and why he marries Iseult of the White Hand although his love for Iseult the Fair keeps this marriage from being consummated. "The most serious obstruction is . . . the one preferred above all. It is the one most suited to intensifying passion."[65] A milquetoast

[63] Norman O. Brown, *Love's Body* (New York: Random House, 1966), 80.

[64] Preface, Denis de Rougemont, *Love in the Western World.*

[65] De Rougemont, 44. Subsequent references to this work are cited in the text using the page number.

husband like King Mark is easily outwitted, but his presence obviates the lovers' need to invent an obstacle of their own. Since society won't tolerate an overt desire for death, however, the absolute obstacle to love, the *Todestrieb* is expressed as a lesser passion — love. "The existence of a repressed wish is invariably manifested, though in such a way as to disguise the true nature of this wish" (47).

De Rougemont perceives no identity, analogy, or homology between love and death, and views the relationship between them mechanistically. Love is linked with death because it may eventuate in death. A passion may be fatal. Passion is a diminished and socially tolerable surrogate for death, since both passion and death are suffered rather than committed. To be sure, passion (German *Leidenschaft*) is suffering (*Leiden*), but de Rougemont mistakes the terms of the traditional equations: individuation = life, and love = death, and puts in their place the equation passion = death. The sword between Tristan and Iseult is "a self-imposed chastity . . . a symbolical suicide . . . 'Passion' triumphs over desire. Death triumphs over life" (45). But death and dying are not the same thing. There is no such thing as death, only dying. Dying is part of life and living *is* dying. Both birth and dying are suffered. We are thrown into life and yanked out of it again by agencies greater than ourselves. Desire is a part of life, not a lesser death. Nor is death a more intense passion, but release from passion. A. H. Harrison gets it right: "For [Swinburne's] Rosamond, death becomes the only possible respite from the suffering intrinsic to passion . . .: 'I wish we were dead together to-day, / Lost sight of, hidden away out of sight, / Clasped and clothed in the woven clay, / Out of the world's way, out of the light.'"[66] We suffer many things while alive, but death is not something we experience at all. We live until we are dead.

Goethe can be counted on to use traditions logically. To him, an anxious, self-protective chastity would be equivalent to egoism. In resisting absorption in another we may hold death temporarily at bay. It is when we submit to love that we are lost. Only a daredevil who prizes love *above life* may fall in love: "Wer sich der Liebe vertraut hält er sein Leben zu Rat?" ("Amyntas"). But love *is* life, as well as its opposite, so anyone's being, prior to the experience of love, is a kind of pre-life or a "Beharren im (Noch-) Nichtsein" — a being not yet pregnant, or a pregnant non-being: "Alles muß in Nichts zerfallen, / Wenn es im Sein beharren will" ("Eins und alles").

Love will not tolerate separation and individual identity. In the paintings of Munch, Klimt, and Behrens, observes Horst Fritz, a kiss encodes "die Verschmelzung der beiden menschlichen Gestalten zu einer neuen

---

[66] A. H. Harrison, "Eros and Thanatos in Swinburne's Poetry: An Introduction," *Journal of Pre-Raphaelite Studies* 2.1 (November 1981): 26.

Ganzheit."[67] "Orgasm is often experienced and described as a death-like state, as a loss of boundary, of identity, of contingency; there is a merging with the loved object, or a merging of both self and other into some larger unit" — thus the term "la petite mort."[68] The womb, like the earth, is *both* a tomb *and* an incubator of new life — a burial plot and a soil in which to sow one's seed.[69] The grave is at once the womb that we re-enter and the tomb in which we decompose — the place where sexuality and difference of every sort are abolished. To die is to complete the cycle of life and return to the source — ultimately to return to God. Ethical love is a renunciation of oneself for the sake of another, as in the psychology of Eric Fromm. Bataille includes the poetic with love and death as "an expression of the desire of being for triumph over the contingency of individualism and for continuity, which is, finally, assimilable both to death and to the poetic."[70]

Anti-Individualistic, Anti-Humanistic Bias

The love-death topos contains an anti-individualistic, therefore an anti-humanistic bias. The quest for love and death devalues the human and the individual, for love and death mix the separate and discrete and usher in unity, disorder, and oblivion. This anti-individualistic (also anti-intellectual tendency — for intellectual order requires the clear discrimination of ideas[71]) in favor of the communal, the transcendent, and the confused accounts for Naphta's delight in pointing out to Hans Castorp that the higher degrees of freemasonry, which the humanist Settembrini so fervently admires, were once accused of obscurantism and "waren . . . in der Hauptsache große Alchimisten." "Ein Symbol alchimistischer Transmutation," explains Naphta, "war vor allem die Gruft. . . . Sie ist der Inbegriff aller Hermetik,

---

[67] Horst Fritz, "Die Dämonisierung des Erotischen in der Literatur des Fin de Siècle," in *Fin de siècle: Zu Literatur und Kunst der Jahrhundertwende,* ed. Roger Bauer et al (Frankfurt am Main: Klostermann, 1977): 452.

[68] Rosemary Gordon, "The Death Instinct and its Relation to the Self," *The Journal of Analytic Psychology,* no. 2 (1961): 131–32.

[69] "Zu den Grundanschauungen der antiken Mysterien aber gehört eben die Identität von Hochzeit und Tod" (Karl Kerényi, "Das ägäische Fest: Die Meergötterszene in Goethes 'Faust II,'" [1949], repr. in *Aufsätze zu Goethes "Faust II,"* ed. Werner Keller [Darmstadt: Wissenschaftliche Buchgesellschaft, 1992], 172).

[70] R. Howard Bloch, *Medieval Misogyny,* 175–76.

[71] Chasseguet-Smirgel identifies denomination as the means of "Trennung" and unraveling of chaos: "Die gesamte Schöpfung ist somit eine Teilung des Chaos, von der die Namengebung ein Sonderfall ist. Solange ein Ding keinen Namen hat, bleibt es aufgelöst im großen Ganzen. Mit der Namengebung gelangt es zur Existenz" (Janine Chasseguet-Smirgel, "Vorwort" to Peter Zagermann, *Eros und Thanatos* [Darmstadt: Wissenschaftliche Buchgesellschaft, 1988], xviii).

nichts anderes als das Gefäß, die wohlverwahrte Kristallretorte, worin der Stoff seiner letzten Wandlung und Läuterung entgegengezwängt wird."[72]

Treatments of love and death rely on metaphors of mixing and mingling — the mixing of dust in the grave, the incorporation of blood and flesh in stories of vampires and cannibals, the symbolic loss of form implied by drownings (water is chaos, the dissolution of form, thus the prominence of sirens, mermaids, the Charybdis, and the various Loreleis, Melusines and Undines as agents of absorption and dissolution), in the erasure of individual outlines in darkness, and in the mixing of ashes on the funeral pyre.[73]

Mass movements are imbued with the love- and death-drive. Intoxicated with love's heady liquor, death-hungry partisans bow to the influence of charismatic preachers and succumb to the psychosis of the crowd (of which Baudelaire says "C'est un *moi* insatiable de *non-moi*"[74]). The new theater erected by the director in Dürrenmatt's story "Der Theaterdirektor"— an amorphous, nondescript leader whose grip on the city leads through an orgy of death to the imposition of a new totalitarian order — is "eine ungeheuerliche Mischung aller Stile und Formen."[75] In partaking of the Eucharist, the believer is absorbed into the body of Christ. Novalis develops the full mystical-erotic possibilities of this set of ideas in one of his *Geistliche Lieder,* the "Hymne," where conjugal union and religious communion are metaphorically connected and a time is foreseen when "alles Leib, [ist] / Ein Leib, / In himmlischem Blute / Schwimmt das selige Paar."[76] Embracing the collective, the Kridwiss circle in Mann's *Doktor Faustus* exhibits an orgiastic contempt for the individual.[77] Leverkühn makes extensive use of the glissando, which erases the boundaries between discrete tones and notes.

[72] Thomas Mann, *Der Zauberberg, Gesammelte Werke,* 3:705–6.

[73] In a flash of illumination, Charles Smithson "suddenly . . . comprehended . . . why he felt this terrible need to see [Sarah] again; it was to possess her, to melt into her, to burn, to burn to ashes on that body and in those eyes" (John Fowles, *The French Lieutenant's Woman* [New York: Signet, 1969], 272).

[74] Charles Baudelaire, *L'Art Romantique, Oeuvres Complètes de Charles Baudelaire,* ed. F.-F. Gautier, vol. 4 (Paris: Éditions de la Nouvelle Revue Française, 1923), 219.

Janine Chasseguet-Smirgel, quoting Heine and Walter Darré, sees the Nazi "Blut und Boden" myth as a manifestation of the drive toward union with the mother imago. "Diese Vereinigung mit der Mutter ist eine Hochzeit, die tausend Jahre dauern soll" (Chasseguet-Smirgel, "Vorwort," xvii).

[75] Friedrich Dürrenmatt, "Der Theaterdirektor," *Die Stadt* (Zürich: "Die Arche," 1952), 66.

[76] Novalis, *Schriften: Die Werke Friedrich von Hardenbergs,* ed. Paul Kluckhohn and Richard Samuel, 3rd ed. (Stuttgart: W. Kohlhammer, 1977), 1:167.

[77] "Es wurde sehr stark empfunden und objektiv festgestellt: der ungeheure Wertverlust, den durch das Kriegsgeschehen das Individuum als solches erlitten hatte, die Achtlosigkeit, mit der heutzutage das Leben über den einzelnen hinwegschritt,

Ocularcentric Romanticism

The love-death topos, though ancient, is peculiarly at home in Romanticism, which is essentially informed with a conception of knowledge as seeing and with the subject-object dichotomy. Goethe says of his friendship with Schiller: "[Wir] besigelten . . ., durch den größten, vielleicht nie ganz zu schlichtenden Wettkampf zwischen Objekt und Subjekt, einen Bund, der ununterbrochen gedauert, und für uns und andere manches Gute gewirkt hat" (FA 1,24:437). As Wellek notes, "the concern for the reconciliation of subject and object, man and nature, consciousness and unconsciousness," the ambition for "the reconciliation of art and nature, language and reality," the "endeavor to overcome the split between subject and object, the self and the world, the conscious and the unconscious" is what constitutes Romanticism.[78] Although a limited historical phenomenon, not a timeless mode of feeling, and although it varies according to nationality and other synchronic differences, all of modernism, broadly defined, splits the world into self and other. This split is what produces romantic striving and accounts for the prominence of the *Liebestod* as the preeminent symbol of reunion in Romanticism. "The very notions of subject and object in their modern sense come to be within [a new localization in which the subject is . . . over against the object]. The modern sense is one in which subject and object are separable entities," whereas in antiquity — as is evident in both Plato and Aristotle, despite their differences — "people accepted without resistance their insertion in a universe of meaningful order."[79] It is the subject's alienation that generates the tension between subject and object and the desire to overcome the chasm between them. No chasm, no need to build bridges. Every age since Descartes has found its own way of articulating estrangement, twentieth-century modernism focusing on the individual's alienation from bourgeois society. The existential fact of individuation underlies all such permutations. Thus the *Liebestod* has enjoyed a dramatic flowering in modern culture. Freud and his most important mediator to the world of literature, Lacan, seek to balance the recognition of subjects as separate cen-

---

und die sich denn auch als allgemeine Gleichgültigkeit gegen sein Leiden und Untergehen im Gemüte der Menschen niederschlug" (Thomas Mann, *Doktor Faustus, Gesammelte Werke* 6:484).

　　Frank notes that in the pre-history of fascist worldviews, "der Wunsch nach Abdankung des souveränen und autonomen Subjekts . . . eine unvergeßliche Rolle gespielt hat und noch spielt" (*Die Unhintergehbarkeit*, 10).

[78] René Wellek, "Romanticism Re-examined," in *Concepts of Criticism,* ed. Stephen G. Nichols, Jr. (New Haven: Yale UP, 1963), 218, 220. Also: "The Concept of Romanticism in Literary History" (1949); repr. in *Concepts of Criticism,* 162.

[79] Charles Taylor, *Sources of the Self,* 188, 192.

ters of initiative with an acknowledgment of each subject's contamination by history and society.

Love-Death Topos a Male Construct?

The love-death topos may be a peculiarly male construct, in Klaus Theweleit's term "eine Männerphantasie."[80] Pioneer feminists such as Nancy Chodorow have studied "separation and individuation from a gendered perspective."[81] In Chodorow's view, "mothers are more likely to allow their sons to separate [than their daughters], both because they see them as other and because the culture demands that, to establish a male identity, the boy must not only identify with father but disidentify with mother," while "girls develop more fluid boundaries than boys, and their sense of self is rooted in relationship."[82] Chodorow's psychoanalytic and sociological models respect differences in historical and cultural articulations of the problem of individuation. Because most children are "mothered" by women and socialized by female care-givers, not just because girls are anatomically similar to their mothers, girls enjoy a sense of community that mitigates the pain of indi-

---

[80] Klaus Theweleit, *Männerphantasien* (Frankfurt am Main: Verlag Roter Stern, 1977). Translated as *Male Fantasies* by Stephan Conway with Erica Carter and Chris Turner, with a foreword by Barbara Ehrenreich (Minneapolis, MN: U of Minnesota P, 1987).

> Freud observed that every female genital is the "place where we have once been," is the home we as men long to go home to, is the mother. Thus the reconstitution of the androgyne during intercourse, the union which re-establishes the unity, is a brief return to the primal state of completeness from which, as created and shaped matter, as self-aware, distinct individuals, we are otherwise in permanent exile.
>
> It is really strange, this *pars pro toto;* and strange how very deeply we dip when we dip into woman.
>
> As an adolescent I learned that just to place my nose into the warm and intimate shelter of my hand made me feel warm and sheltered all over, . . . It was a foretaste of that other sheltering insertion which is equally partial in extent and even more total in effect, bringing with it a sense of peace and completeness comparable to immersion in a warm, long-forgotten ocean; a state of being before thought and before pain, an oceanic feeling less nostalgic than that which overcomes us in nature, but equally related to the mother: the visit home, the only way we 'can go home again' before that final homecoming of death. (Wolfgang Lederer, *The Fear of Women* [New York: Grune & Stratton, 1968], 230)

[81] Lynne Layton, "Current Issues in Theories of the Self," paper given at MLA, December 1991, p. 10; Nancy Chodorow, *The Reproduction of Mothering: Psychoanalysis and the Sociology of Gender* (Berkeley: U of California P, 1978).

[82] Lynne Layton, "Current Issues in Theories of the Self."

viduation. Every boy, by contrast, must face his difference, and suffers a consequent discontinuity and generalized loneliness as well as the fear that he can never again know the sense of oneness and fusion that he knew as an infant. "Men can never recreate this state of total union," writes Cynthia Wolff. "Adult women can — when they are pregnant. Most pregnant women identify intensely with their unborn children, and through that identification in some measure reexperience a state of complete and harmonious union."[83]

These ideas suggest that because of their different feelings toward selfhood, men may have a stronger need for erotic love and a stronger *Todessehnsucht* than women, a stronger urge to return to the womb as tomb and to escape from the prison of the self. Several female readers of this chapter have protested, however, that love carries no connotation of blending or loss of selfhood for them. A separate female culture has survived male cultural dominance, they say. Vulnerable to rape and pregnancy, women want to fortify boundaries, not break them down. This may actually confirm Chodorow's thesis and lend paradoxical support to the idea that men are individualistic and women communal, that men have the martial talents and women the social ones, men showing a proclivity for self-destruction and a willingness to risk the destruction of the world, while women's sense of belonging prevents any rush toward the abyss and permits sympathy, and trust, and encourages both self-affirmation and affirmation of life. "Die Männer," says Charlotte in *Die Wahlverwandtschaften*, "denken mehr auf das Einzelne . . ., die Weiber hingegen mehr auf das was im Leben zusammenhängt, . . . weil ihr Schicksal, das Schicksal ihrer Familien an diesen Zusammenhang geknüpft ist, und auch gerade dieses Zusammenhängende von ihnen gefordert wird" (FA 1,8:274–75).

The Oedipus complex is in the first instance a yearning for union on the part of the child, which may account for adversarial relationships among boys and men, the boy competing with his father for the affection of his mother. To the lonely male, woman is the goal and the instrument of his deliverance.[84] Melanie Unseld sees "Widersprüchlichkeit" as the quality that

---

[83] Cynthia G. Wolff, "Thanatos and Eros: Kate Chopin's 'The Awakening,'" *American Quarterly* 25 (1973): 469.

[84] "Jean Baker Miller, Nancy Chodorow, and Carol Gilligan suggest that men define themselves through individuation and separation from others, while women have more flexible ego boundaries and define and experience themselves in terms of their affiliations and relationships with others. Men value autonomy, and they think of their interactions with others principally in terms of procedures for arbitrating conflicts between individual rights. Women, on the other hand, value relationships, and they are most concerned in their dealings with others to negotiate between opposing needs so that the relationship can be maintained" (Patrocinio P. Schweikert, "Toward a Feminist Theory of Reading," in *Gender and Reading: Essays on Readers,*

causes men to identify women with death.[85] But this identification more probably occurs because men view women, like death, as a means of escape and self-abandon, seeking and fearing them in a *delectatio morosa*. Knowing sisterhood from the beginning, and becoming mothers while still in their childhood, women *are* (and thus do not *seek*) the matrix to which it is every man's desire to return. Already embedded in a network that provides an anonymous security, women embrace independence. Men, on the other hand, who are essentially needy, long to return to the womb — all the while anxious to preserve their individuality. Nothing illustrates ambivalence as vividly as does men's attitude toward women. Yet even this ambivalence is not unambiguously male. Ellen Greenberger found in a "Thematic Apperception Test" that "romantic fantasies were found to occur significantly more often in women confronting death than in control patients." Episodes of rape, abduction, seduction, and infidelity "typically involved a man whose identity was very nebulous. In considering the meaning of these episodes, and the identity of the male, it was suggested that perhaps Death itself was the mysterious lover."[86] We are back with Baldung and Schiele.

In sexual intercourse it is the man who is incorporated and the woman who incorporates.[87] To be sure, literature is replete with love- and death-hungry *females,* such as Goethe's bride of Corinth, Brentano's "Lore Lay," Flaubert's Emma Bovary, Tolstoy's Anna Karenina, and Ibsen's Hedda Gabler, the last of whom expresses her desire for "release" before shooting herself at the play's end. Yet not only are these all works by male authors, but the dominant culture has projected onto women a desire for conjunction equivalent to that characteristic of men, which amounts to the absence of the female voice from literature. Although the *Liebestod* theme occurs in women writers and female mystics from as far back as Sappho and Hildegard von Bingen and is pervasive in the work of Margaret Fuller, George Eliot, Iris

---

Texts, and Contexts, ed. Elizabeth A. Flynn and Patrocinio P. Schweikert [Baltimore: Johns Hopkins UP, 1986], 54–55).

[85] Melanie Unseld, *"Man Töte Dieses Weib!" Weiblichkeit und Tod in der Musik der Jahrhundertwende* (Stuttgart & Weimar: Metzler, 2001), 92.

[86] Ellen Greenberger, "'Flirting' with Death: Fantasies of a Critically Ill Woman," *Journal of Projective Techniques and Personality Assessment,* 30, 2 (1966): 197, 199 n. 4.

[87] "On the level of social metaphor, to love was . . . an act of incorporation. You preyed, or were preyed upon. Love and depredation went hand in hand. That is why Freud . . . had come to the conclusion that love and death were pretty much one and the same thing, especially if you happened to be the one being incorporated rather than the one doing the incorporating" (Bram Dijkstra, *Evil Sisters: The Threat of Female Sexuality in Twentieth-Century Culture* [New York: Henry Holt, 1996], 80).

Murdoch, Kate Chopin,[88] and P. D. James, this may be less an expression of native female experience than a manifestation of women's subjugation. Is "woman" not only what men want from sex but what men have made women believe — a co-option of their professional sisters into their own worldview and a projection of the male mind set onto the daughters of their imagination? The series of *femmes fatales* beginning with George Lillo's Millwood (in *The London Merchant*, 1731) and extending through Lessing's Marwood (in *Miß Sara Sampson*, 1755), Goethe's Adelheid von Walldorf (1773), Schiller's Lady Milford (in *Kabale und Liebe*, 1784), Hauptmann's Anna Mahr (in *Einsame Menschen*, 1891), to Ibsen's Hedda Gabler, Mann's Claudia Chauchat and beyond, are creations not only of male authors but of the male characters in the fictions they inhabit — Marwood says so explicitly, as Rolf-Peter Jantz has pointed out.[89] Even Medea, with whom Marwood compares herself, is the creature of Jason. The "viciousness" of these women is explicitly (in the case of Lady Milwood) or implicitly (in the case of Marwood) blamed on their male counterparts, which makes the *femmes fatales* themselves mere accessories to a bad faith dialogue in which men both engender vice and seek to divest themselves of responsibility for it. After vicarious alienation through the medium of the male consciousness, can women ever regain their natural, unalienated attachment to their mother? Would women's desires be different in an uncontaminated female culture? We will never know.

If the love-death theme is implicitly sexist, it must also be time-bound, ephemeral, a passing fancy, its hoary antiquity notwithstanding. We may someday see fascination with love and death as a mark of a particular broad era, of which Romanticism is the last full flowering and of which an implicit belief in the atomized self, accompanied by defensiveness and dread, is a defining characteristic. The various "postmodernisms" are united in their acceptance of larger systems of order from which it is supposed to be impossible to disengage the individual. If so, we may be in the dawn of a new era. Perhaps, however, the root desire informing the love-death topos is the desire to escape the ravages of time, as is indicated by the time metaphors in Faust's wager. Being *is* time, and time is constitutive of being, while both love and death imply stasis, an endless, but eternally unavailable spatial presence. There is no indivisible now — no present whose parts do

---

[88] In Chopin's *The Awakening*, Edna's "yearning for suffusion and indefinable ecstasy" is as strong as the desire attributed to any female character by any male author. "The fundamental significance to Edna of an awakening," says Wolff, "is an awakening to separation, to individual existence, to the hopelessness of ever satisfying the dream of total fusion" (Wolff, "Thanatos and Eros," 468–70).

[89] Rolf-Peter Jantz, "'Sie ist die Schande ihres Geschlechts.' Die femme fatale bei Lessing," *Jahrbuch der Deutschen Schiller-Gesellschaft* 23 (1979): 210–12.

not belong to the future or the past, so there is no abiding, indivisible past or future either. Faust demands a moment so lovely that he will want it to stay. He wants permanence, and wants it the more because time is so fleeting — because "at my back I always hear / Time's wing'd chariot hurrying near," as Marvell puts it in "To His Coy Mistress." Thus Mephistopheles arranges the meeting with Margarete and the taste of an ecstasy available only in death.

Is "the womb-tomb-urn complex," then, "intellectually insulting in its simplicity"[90] or is it simply fundamental? No search for meaning can be complete that does not explain why we use such conventions. Are they, like language in general, as Chomsky believes, a manifestation of human nature without practical utility, or do they represent a form of agreement that contributes to the survival of the social unit? The recognition that human intercourse is informed with topoi subverts the pre-Romantic over-estimation of originality as a primary source of literary value. The topos of love and death continues to be repeated. Why do we love it so much? We will not know what it means to love and die until we know what it means to be, perhaps not even then. Culture is contamination.

---

[90] Stephanie in A. S. Byatt's *The Virgin in the Garden* (London: Chatto and Windus, 1978; New York: Vintage, 1992), 251.

2: Incorporating Tradition

Originality and Intertextuality

GOETHE READILY acknowledged his indebtedness to tradition. "Goethe ist kein Prophet," writes Friedrich Sengle, "sondern ein gewaltiger Erbe der Tradition."[1] In "Bedeutende Fördernis durch ein einziges geistreiches Wort," Goethe says he took into the repository of his memory the themes for several of his most famous ballads and let them incubate there for forty or fifty years, until they ripened toward a new representation. "Ich will hievon nur die *Braut von Korinth,* den *Gott und die Bajadere,* den *Grafen und die Zwerge,* den *Sänger und die Kinder,* und zuletzt noch den baldigst mitzuteilenden *Paria* nennen" (FA 1,24:596). Elsewhere he employs weaving metaphors to denote the interactions of life and the intertextuality of literature, their pertinence being apparent in the very idea of "text" and its derivatives. The Earth Spirit describes his incessant activity as weaving: "So schaff' ich am sausenden Webstuhl der Zeit, / Und wirke der Gottheit lebendiges Kleid" (*Faust I,* lines 508–9). It is impossible to keep the strands of tradition out of one's weaving, but loose ends may be tied up and given a place in a new tapestry. The inverse of Goethe's metaphor, which exalts the writer as the agent of incorporation and re-presentation, is the assignment of agency to tradition itself, which incorporates the writer and gives him or her back to the world in a series of new incarnations. To understand the ways in which traditions engage or are engaged by a poet and weave or are woven together to yield what Stephen C. Pepper, the philosopher of contextualism, calls "emergent qualitative novelty" is an ambitious goal.[2] Even if we restrict ourselves to what may seem to be atomistic thematic traditions, we are likely to favor those that bear a name (such as the love-death tradition) and leave underlying concepts or less clearly outlined ones unremarked. Every insight entails blindness, every perception some repression. Threads in a fabric both retain their identity and serve a

---

[1] Friedrich Sengle, "Die didaktischen und kulturkritischen Elemente im 'West-östlichen Divan,'" in *Neues zu Goethe: Essays und Vorträge* (Stuttgart: Metzler, 1989), 189.

[2] Stephen C. Pepper, *World Hypotheses: A Study in Evidence* (Berkeley: U of California P, 1957), 257.

larger pattern, one that may repeat, or contrast with, a past or hidden referent. Among the strands woven together in Goethe's "Die Braut von
Korinth" are elements of early Christian history, Enlightenment militancy
toward positive religion, the topos of woman as an agent of engulfment,
revenants, vampires and the meaning of the Eucharist, and religious eighteenth-century millenarianism, *Jenseitigkeit*.[3]

Prominent in Goethe's inheritance is the "Hermetic" tradition of alchemy, in which everything in the world is sexually marked. In Faust's
description of his father's striving to produce the magnum opus in the
scene "Vor dem Tor," the Lion Red, a wooer bold, is wed "in tepid bath" to
the Lily. These contraries are then tortured from one bridal chamber into
another until the young queen (the pharmakon, the panacea, the philosophers' stone) appears in the glass (lines 1034–47). Androgynous in most
pictorial representations, the philosophers' stone is an exemplary *coincidentia
oppositorum*. Except for Goethe's familiarity with pietist tradition, gained
through conversations with Susanna von Klettenberg and his visits to
pietist conventicles during his convalescence from the illness that had be-
fallen him as a student in Leipzig, *Die Leiden des jungen Werthers* might
never have taken the form that it did. Goethe was guided by, and he sometimes rejected, traditional literary genres that became trendy in the 1770s,
largely as a result of his own experiments with the ballad form and what he
regarded as "Shakespearean" drama. The "Kraftmensch" Crugantino in
Claudine von Villa Bella sings a ballad to the assembled company at the castle and gives voice to the popularity of the old folk genres with their perceived naturalness and simplicity: "Alle Balladen, Romanzen, Bänkelgesänge
werden jetzt eifrig aufgesucht, aus allen Sprachen übersetzt" (FA 1,4:614).
Crugantino's ballad — "Es war ein Buhle frech genung" — is an *original*
ballad by Goethe, but indebted, of course, to the traditions of which
Crugantino speaks.

The volume *Goethe und die Tradition* outlines Goethe's indebtedness to
many traditions,[4] including Western humanism, which favors the mythology
and the texts of Greece and, to a lesser extent, Rome and of which Goethe's
writings from his earliest efforts through *Faust: Der Tragödie zweiter Teil* are
a part. Goethe saw in the collision of Hellenism and Christianity in the first
century and the resulting blending of Hellenism into Christianity a rich
quarry for poetry.[5] Because he knew his place and function in the larger system of intertextuality, Goethe lets Faust question whether such alien infu-

---

[3] E.g. in Lavater's *Aussichten in die Ewigkeit*, in Werther's hope to be united with
Lotte beyond the grave, and in Luise Miller's renunciation of her claim to her lover
Ferdinand until after her life in a world marred by class differences.

[4] Hans Reiss, ed., *Goethe und die Tradition* (Frankfurt am Main: Athenäum, 1972).

[5] Conversation with Kanzler von Müller, 6 June 1824 (GA 23:348–49).

sions *can* be cast out: "Das ist im Grund der Herren eigener Geist, / in dem die Zeiten sich bespiegeln" (lines 577–79). He believed neither in any kind of ahistorical autonomy nor in a primitive ideal of national cultural purity. "Bedenkt man, daß so wenig Nationen überhaupt, besonders keine neuere, Anspruch an absolute Originalität machen kann; so braucht sich der Deutsche nicht zu schämen, der seiner Lage nach in den Fall kam seine Bildung von außen zu erhalten, und besonders was Poesie betrifft, Gehalt und Form von Fremden genommen hat" ("Über das lyrische Volksbuch 1808," FA 1,19:400).

Goethe's use of more "alien" traditions such as the poetic traditions of Persia and Islam in the *West-östlicher Divan,* or of China in the *Chinesisch-deutsche Jahreszeiten* and in *Elpenor* shows his commitment to "Welt-literatur," his own coinage.[6] The synthesis he achieves in "mating" with the Persian poet Hafiz is marked as a linking of opposites in the title "West-östlicher Divan," an isomorph of the coincidence of contraries named in the title of *Dichtung und Wahrheit.* Contrasting Goethe's sometimes contradictory reception of the Orient with that of the Romantics, Kontje analyzes his orientalism, sees evidence in it of his "ironic awareness of the Western desire for Oriental origins" and interprets it as a defense of the pastiche of his own eclectic *Altersstil.* "Throughout the *Divan* we catch glimpses of self-deprecating humor, the sense that the elderly poet has been there before and that the present moment is a repetition of events that recede into the distant past."[7]

Coming out of the *Sturm und Drang,* which prized originality — the term "Originalgenie" was put into circulation by Edward Young's "Conjectures on Original Composition" (1759) — Goethe later often emphasized how little of what he or indeed anyone had done was truly "original" and how overrated "originality" is. "Man spricht immer von Originalität," he said to Eckermann, "allein was will das sagen! Sowie wir geboren werden, fängt die Welt an, auf uns zu wirken, und das geht so fort bis ans Ende. Und überall! was können wir denn unser Eigenes nennen, als die Energie, die Kraft, das Wollen! — Wenn ich sagen könnte, was ich alles großen Vorgängern und Mitlebenden schuldig geworden bin, so bliebe nicht viel übrig" (E, 158). Goethe knows that he is in good company in mining

[6] Asked by Eckermann whether a Chinese novel that Goethe had been reading was one of their best, Goethe answered: "Keineswegs. Die Chinesen haben deren zu Tausenden und hatten ihrer schon, als unsere Vorfahren noch in den Wäldern lebten" (Goethe's letter of 31 January 1827 to Eckermann, FA 2,12:224).

[7] "It is not so much a question . . . of Goethe's generous understanding of the East, but more of his ironic awareness of the Western desire for Oriental origins," writes Kontje, "that casts a kinder light on his multicultural masquerades." Todd Kontje, "Goethe's Multicultural Masquerades" (paper presented at MLA 2000, Washington, DC, December 2000), 8–9.

sources. "Wenn ich bedenke, wie *Schiller* die Überlieferung studierte, was er sich für Mühe mit der Schweiz gab als er seinen *Tell* schrieb," he said, "und wie *Shakespeare* die Chroniken benutzte und ganze Stellen daraus wörtlich in seine Stücke aufgenommen hat, so könnte man einem jetzigen jungen Dichter auch wohl dergleichen zumuten. In meinem *Clavigo* habe ich aus den Memoiren des Beaumarchais ganze Stellen" (E, 348–49).[8] Laura Martin points out that the story "Die pilgernde Törin," a translation from the French, acquires new meaning in the context of the *Wanderjahre*.[9] Albert Leitzmann provides helpful information on the sources of Goethe's and Schiller's ballads.[10]

Clavigo, written in one May week in answer to a challenge from Goethe's "pretend wife" Susanne Magdalene Münch and the first work that Goethe published under his own name, is based on an inset in part four of Pierre Augustin Caron de Beaumarchais's *Mémoires: Fragment de mon voyage d'Espagne*. Goethe's *Clavigo* has been part of the theatrical repertoire since its first performances, including one in Augsburg in the autumn of 1774. Returning from Vienna to Paris in 1774 as a secret agent of the French royal house, Beaumarchais himself stopped at Augsburg. Seeing his own name on the playbill, he went to the local performance of *Clavigo* and witnessed the protagonist's assassination by the fictional Beaumarchais's hand as well as the "stage death" of his own sister. Although he did not understand German, Beaumarchais was not pleased by Goethe's additions to the events recounted in his memoir: "l'Allemand avait gâté l'anecdote de mon mémoire en la surchargeant d'un combat et d'un enterrement, additions qui montraient plus de vide de tête que de talent."[11]

In *Clavigo* Goethe displays not only his dramatic talent and his knowledge of literary convention but also his command of the grammar and idiom of *Empfindsamkeit*. The play is also confessional, according to *Dichtung und Wahrheit*. The titular hero is weak and ambitious and, at the urging of his friend Carlos, breaks not one but two promises of marriage to Marie Beaumarchais (just as Goethe felt that he had broken an implied promise to

[8] "Düntzer vermutet, daß Goethe eine Ballade aus Percy, 'Lucy and Collin' meint, die von Herder unter dem Titel 'Röschen und Kolin' übersetzt wurde" (HA 10:603).

[9] Laura Martin, "Who's the Fool Now? A Study of Goethe's Novella 'Die pilgernde Törin' from His Novel *Wilhelm Meisters Wanderjahre*," *The German Quarterly*, 66.4 (1993): 431–50.

[10] Albert Leitzmann, *Die Quellen von Schillers und Goethes Balladen* (Bonn: A. Marcus & E. Weber, 1911).

[11] Anton Bettelheim, *Beaumarchais: Eine Biographie* (Frankfurt, Rütten & Loening, 1886), 335. See Georges Lemaitre, *Beaumarchais* (New York: Alfred A. Knopf, 1949), 150; see also FA 1,4:928.

Friederike Brion). Yet he is not without remorse. When Marie dies of a broken heart, Clavigo is himself heartbroken, and, happening onto her funeral procession on a Madrid street, delivers himself over to a just retribution at the hand of her brother, who appears on the scene just as Clavigo throws back the lid of the coffin with the words: "Marie! Nimm mich mit dir! Nimm mich mit dir!" With Beaumarchais' dagger buried in his chest, Clavigo says, "Ich danke dir, Bruder! Du vermählst uns," before planting a "bridegroom's kiss" on Marie's "kalte Totenhand" and sprinkling her "Brautschmuck" with roses of blood — instead of the flowers with which her brother had hoped to adorn not her coffin but her bridal bed.[12]

Like *Clavigo*, *Stella*, subtitled "Ein Schauspiel für Liebende" (1775), has been successful on the stage, most successful in the first version with the prospect of a sublime polyamorous love of the three principal characters. At the urging of Schiller, who had earlier sworn that his love for both of the von Lengefeld sisters did not reduce his affection for either one,[13] Goethe wrote a second, tragic version for Weimar theatergoers who would have been scandalized by the *ménage à trois* proposed by Cezilie in the original version.[14] Goethe had justified suicide in *Die Leiden des jungen Werthers,* and in *Stella* he recommended a marital arrangement that was seen as not just kinky or impractical but as potentially disruptive of the ethical and social order.

Goethe's writing in these early plays was nevertheless conventional. The language of the heart that is given such eloquent expression, the envisioned utopia in which true love transcends the topoi of property and economics and, later, the tragic ending of the second *Stella* are all incorporations, if also transmutations, of ready-to-hand cultural material.[15] Even *Götz von Berlichingen* is a testimony to the young Goethe's indebtedness to traditions of many kinds.

[12] FA 1,4:491–92. See the reprint of a D. Berger copper engraving ("nach Chodowiecki") in FA 1,4:816.

[13] Schiller wrote to Charlotte and her sister Caroline von Beulwitz: "Wie könnte ich mich zwischen euch beiden meines Daseins freun, wenn meine Gefühle für euch beide nicht die süße Sicherheit hätten, daß ich dem anderen nicht entziehe, was ich dem einen bin" (15 Nov 1789). It was the jealous Charlotte von Kalb who coined the term "Doppelliebe" for Schiller's relationship to the two sisters. (Friedrich Burschell, *Friedrich Schiller: Mit Selbstzeugnissen und Bildokumenten* [Hamburg: Rowohlt, 1958], 90).

[14] A third — the fourth, if we count the revision made by Goethe for *Schriften,* 1787–90 (see FA 1,4:978) — is from the pen of someone else. See David G. John, "Ein neuer Schluß für Goethes *Stella,*" *Goethe Jahrbuch* 111 (1994): 91–101.

[15] "[Ich] war längst überzeugt," says Goethe, "es gebe nichts Neues unter der Sonne, und man könne gar wohl in den Überlieferungen schon angedeutet finden, was wir selbst gewahr werden und denken, oder wohl gar hervor bringen. Wir sind nur Originale weil wir nichts wissen" (FA 1,24:425).

"Heidenröslein"

Goethe's first attempt at "folk poetry," also his first *Kunstballade* and first significant treatment of the theme of love and death, is the famous and simple "Heidenröslein" (1771). The background of "Heidenröslein" is known, although there is uncertainty about the specifics. Borrowing the refrain and some phrasings from a longer poem by Paul von der Aelst, published in 1602 in a song book of which Herder owned a copy, he composed "Heidenröslein."[16]

Herder then incorporated it "from memory," with no mention of the author, into "Auszug aus einem Briefwechsel über Ossian und die Lieder alter Völker," one of the essays in *Von deutscher Art und Kunst* (1773), as an authentic, anonymous "folk song." The ballad documents Goethe's and Herder's reception of premodern poetry and their desire to infuse some of its vitality into an anemic contemporary literary corpus. Like "Erlkönig," with which it has structural and morphological as well as thematic similarities, "Heidenröslein" has been made more famous by Schubert's setting than it might otherwise have become. One cannot actually speak of love and *death* in this poem, only of love and aggression, love and violation. In a version by Herder with the title "Die Blüthe," however, sent to his fiancée Caroline Flachsland to be copied into her "Silbernes Buch," the heath rose is made into a fruit blossom that is broken off and dies: "Das Blüthchen starb so schnell darnach" (*DjG* 2:298). Goethe's and Herder's versions are both tragic.

We can better appreciate Goethe's fondness for ballads (which appears again in the compositions of 1797 for Schiller's *Musenalmanach*) if we contrast them with the fashionably gallant poetry popular in the courts and even with the "anacreontic" poetry of bourgeois poets from the generation just older than Goethe or with the young Goethe's own virtuosic exploitation of contemporary poetic fashion in the poems of "An Annette" and the pastoral play "Die Laune des Verliebten." "Heidenröslein" hides its sophistication and is dressed as something simple, plain, and strong. But this too was a passing phase. As Crugantino's remark shows, Goethe saw enthusiasm for the primitive as a fad, and by 1775 had distanced himself from it.

With his coinage "Volkslied" Herder meant simply a popular song in any national literature. "Heidenröslein," like its model and other, older poems — none of them the work of any collective but simply poems or songs of anonymous authorship — is the story of a young woman's struggle

---

[16] Paul van der Aelst, *Blumm und Außbund Allerhandt Außerleser Weltlicher / Züchtiger Lieder und Rheymen . . . so wol auß Frantzösischen / als Hoch- und Nider Teutschen Gesang- und Liederbüchlein zusammen gezogen / und in Truck verfertigt* (Deventer 1602). Gerhard Sauder, "Heidenröslein," *Goethe-Handbuch* 1 (Stuttgart: Metzler, 1996): 128.

against a force stronger than herself. It is an allegory of our common vulnerability to violence at the hands of things that are bigger than we are and that, as Schiller pointed out in his essay "Über das Erhabene," in threatening our freedom also threaten our humanity, to which individual free agency is essential. Schiller's question, and, implicitly, that of Goethe's poem, is: How can we preserve our humanity in the face of irresistible violence? How can we preserve our freedom, given the existential fact of human contingency and the fact that all of us are always at the mercy of forces greater than those under our control?

"Das Heidenröslein" is more dramatic and elliptical than most ballads, which, like Gottfried August Bürger's "Lenore," often spell out an explicit moral: "Mit Gott im Himmel hadere nicht." (To be sure, these words can be read as ironic and may have been so intended by Bürger himself.) Herder's "Die Blüthe" is heavy-handedly didactic: if you break the blossom, there will be no fruit (*DjG* 2:298). Don't kill the goose that lays the golden egg. Goethe's poem is spare. A youth sees the Rose (described as "jung" and "morgenschön" — the latter compound typical of the diction in Goethe's early work),[17] and, aroused, proceeds to take her for his own, despite her threat to prick him with her thorns: "Knabe sprach: Ich breche dich, / Röslein auf der Heiden! / Röslein sprach: Ich steche dich, / Daß du ewig denkst an mich." The Heath Rose's thorns, like her "Weh und Ach," provide no protection. "Mußt' es eben leiden." The repetition of the refrain after each of the three strophes softens, or perhaps intensifies,[18] the brutal message that nothing much changes between the sexes, or, by extension, between suffering humanity and the gods, who kill us for their sport. This poem anticipates "Erlkönig" and, at a greater remove, such "philosophical" poems as "Gesang der Geister über den Wassern," "Das Göttliche," and the Harfner's song "Wer nie sein Brot mit Tränen aß" in *Wilhelm Meisters Lehrjahre* — also, since we are all patients, or, optimistically, receivers of divine gifts: "Alles gaben Götter, die unendlichen." All of these poems, like *Die Leiden des jungen Werthers,* have human suffering as their theme, highlighting our station as recipients of the bolts, thrusts and — sometimes, fortuitously — gifts that come from a world in which we are vulnerable, ephemeral phenomena — *Eintagsfliegen.* It is the lot of humans to "leiden," to be passive reactors to God or the gods as personifications of pure activity. Human contingency is a basic Goethean theme, the poems in which it occurs foreshadowing Hölderlin's "Hyperions Schicksalslied" with its visual display of human falling. "Das ist der Lauf der Welt," as Mephistopheles says

---

[17] Cf. "Fremdlingsreisetritt" in "Der Wandrer," "siegdurchglühter" in "Wandrers Sturmlied" and "Knabenmorgenblütenträume" in "Prometheus."

[18] Responding to my word "softens," Jocelyne Kolb writes, "For me it does rather the contrary."

to Frau Marthe Schwerdtlein in response to her observation that Faust is attracted to Margarete (line 3204), as though libido must always result in the victory of the stronger — however Pyrrhic this victory, for the victim may scratch and scar the attacker, inflicting regret or venereal disease, for this too may be a message in "Heidenröslein." Carl August, Goethe's friend and patron, was a sufferer, and Goethe's fear of syphilis is well documented.

Like Weislingen in *Götz von Berlichingen*, Clavigo, Fernando in *Stella*, and, finally, Faust, "Heidenröslein" may be intended to be confessional, the youth another of Goethe's self-portraits.[19] If so, it *anticipates* his betrayal of Friederike Brion, whereas the other "confessional" figures reflect a regretful hindsight. The poem was written in the summer of 1771, before Goethe left Strassburg, hence before he wrote to Frederike terminating their relationship but prior to his celebration of William Shakespeare's name day, 14 October. He recalls his remorse in *Dichtung und Wahrheit:* "Ich fühlte nun erst [i.e. after receiving her disappointed reply] den Verlust den sie erlitt, und sah keine Möglichkeit ihn zu ersetzen, ja nur ihn zu lindern. . . . Ich konnte mir mein eignes Unglück nicht verzeihen" (FA 1,14:566). But he sought absolution in poetry and invoked a tradition of "poetische Beichte" and "selbstquälerische Büßung" (568) by sympathetically depicting the two Maries in *Clavigo* and *Götz von Berlichingen* and exposing the sorry figures cut by their respective lovers to deserved spectatorial criticism.

Goethe left Strassburg and Frederike in August — perhaps without making it clear that his departure was an irrevocable good-bye. His subsequent self-reproach may not have been as heartfelt as he and some of his biographers pretend. He records melancholy feelings on visits to Sesenheim in anticipation of the time, "da ich so viel Liebes und Gutes, vielleicht auf immer, verlieren sollte" (FA 1,14:505). If he did feel guilt after the fact, it may have been aggravated by his knowledge that his high-handedness was premeditated and by some shame over the frivolous liberties he took in approaching the Brions. His heart may have been lightened, on the other hand, by a self-exculpatory satisfaction in the surprising depth and sincerity of his remorse. In the version of Goethe's poem published by Herder it is the youth rather than Heidenröslein who is the subject of "leiden," and it seems clear that his soon forgotten suffering is caused by the rose's thorns: "Das Röslein wehrte sich und stach, / Aber er vergaß darnach / Beim Genuß das Leiden!" (FA 1,1:125). In the *Ausgabe letzter Hand,* the poem appears ambiguous: "Half *ihm* doch kein Weh und Ach, / Mußt es eben leiden." Since Goethe must

---

[19] Boyle thinks so: "A personal confession here insinuates itself into the shared language and collective literary repertoire of a 'people'" (Nicholas Boyle, *Goethe: The Poet and the Age,* vol. 1: *The Poetry of Desire (1749–1790),* vol. 2: *Revolution and Renunciation (1790–1803)* [Oxford: Clarendon Press, 1991, 2000], here 1:113).

have sanctioned this final version,[20] a reader might wonder whether "ihm" refers here to "dem wilden Knaben" ("ihm" = him) or, as is usually, and no doubt correctly, assumed, to the neuter diminutive "dem Röslein" ("ihm" = her). In the first collection of his poems published by Goethe and usually regarded as authoritative,[21] there is no ambiguity: "Half *ihr* doch kein Weh und Ach." Both the *Münchener Ausgabe* and the *Frankfurter Ausgabe* adopt this wording (MA 1,1:163–64; FA 1,1:278), Eibl explaining: "Erst in der Ausgabe letzter Hand dann biedermeierliche Glättung durch grammatisches Geschlecht 'ihm,' vermutlich durch den Setzer" (FA 1,1:830). But Goethe did bear scars from his affair with Friederike. Friedenthal hears his lament to her father about the pesky Rhine mosquitoes as a metaphor for his own pangs of conscience. No angel with a flaming sword had driven Adam and Eve from the garden, said Goethe to the good Reverend Brion. The mosquitoes from the Tigris and the Euphrates were deterrent enough.[22]

On his first visit at the Pfarrhaus in Sesenheim Goethe presented himself in two separate disguises, first as a poor theology student and then in the clothes of the son of the innkeeper in the nearby village of Drusenheim (FA 1,14:468). Although the second disguise was hastily improvised in the wake of his embarrassment about the first, and deceived nobody or at least only momentarily, he was interested in the way in which these "masks" affected his reception. Comparably, in representing herself "as" someone that she is not, Beethoven's Leonore enacts the apophatic "as" implicit in every substitution (Leonore *as* Fidelio) — even in the incarnation of the god in "Der Gott und die Bajadere" and every representation of Zeus as something that he is not or, rather, perhaps *is* ("Ganymed"). Every disguise is a "Betrug" — a displacement as much as a deception. Rilke's poem "Leda" says of Zeus, "Schon aber trug ihn sein Betrug zur Tat." A deception has carrying power. One is reshaped and moved forward by a disguise.

In his mind Goethe dresses the entire Sesenheim episode in characters, categories, tropes, and topoi borrowed from *The Vicar of Wakefield,* not only in retrospect but while experiencing it. He conversed at the time with his friend Weyland about how uncannily the family at Sesenheim resembled that of Goldsmith's vicar, and in *Dichtung und Wahrheit* even substitutes the name Olivie for Friederike's younger sister, after first identifying her by her real name Sophie. The conclusion seems inescapable that the young author, not yet twenty-two years old, saw the entire Sesenheim affair in the light of a literary tradition and as grist for his own mill.

---

[20] See Eibl, FA 1,1:734.

[21] Göschen (1789).

[22] FA 1,14:508; Richard Friedenthal, *Goethe: Sein Leben und Seine Zeit* (Munich: R. Piper, 1963), 108.

"Heidenröslein" has occasioned surprisingly little commentary, considering how famous it has become in Schubert's sprightly G-major setting for high voice and piano. A more mournful melody, familiar in German-speaking lands, does it better justice, for it is not an amusing tale that is told here.[23] It is even more remarkable that, sensitized to the pervasive misogyny in the literary tradition, we even now hardly raise an eyebrow at what is unmistakably a rape scene — as though "Heidenröslein" were a benign little skit of bucolic playfulness. I would not call the poem pornographic. It has dramatic power, a deftness and economy of portraiture, a lullaby-like musicality and authenticity not found in pornography. But stripped of the patina of respectability afforded it by its canonization and reduced to the event depicted, it is far removed from the "Kinderton" that Herder claimed to hear in it and from Schubert's bouncy melody (FA 1,1:125). To read it adequately is to shudder at its invitation to enjoy a voyeuristic pleasure in the destruction of a girl by a red-blooded, therefore violent young man. As in the rape of the boy in "Erlkönig" and the violent execution of Adelheid von Walldorf after the executioner has first propositioned her, "Heidenröslein" seeks beauty in violence. Trite but true, all art is violence, whether a sculptor carves a Galatea out of a stone, an artist imposes order on a "natural" landscape, or a writer presses human suffering into the conventions of poetry or song.

But as Goethe says, "der Mensch will leben" (FA 1,1:520). In 1771 he was a vigorous, enterprising young man and an ambitious talent conscious of his powers, trying out new forms of life and poetry, and willing to exploit not only his own experience in his art. His attitude toward Friederike was possibly of the sort of which Wackenroder's Berlinger accuses the decadent artist. Coming upon suffering families — "Väter, Mütter und Kinder" — "das verweichlichte Künstlergemüt" views them as an interesting compositional group and attempting, although ashamed of himself, "aus dem elenden Jammer irgend etwas Schönes und kunstartigen Stoff herauszuzwingen,"[24] or, in the words of John Fowles, "Now what could I do with you?"[25]

A later poet, Eduard Brauer, who was convinced that "Heidenröslein" was about Friederike, made a pilgrimage to her grave. His ode to her, fifty-four years after her death, ends with the strophe: "Nun hast du

[23] At least 154 melodies have been written for Goethe's text (Sauder, "Heidenröslein," 1:128).

[24] Stuart Atkins, *The Age of Goethe: An Anthology of German Literature 1749–1832* (Boston: Houghton Mifflin, 1969), 423.

[25] As the suddenly dramatized narrator of *The French Lieutenant's Woman* thinks to himself as he and Charles Smithson sit opposite each other in a train compartment (John Fowles, *The French Lieutenant's Woman* [New York: Signet, 1969], 317).

längst geendet, / Hörst nicht des Pilgers Reim, / Der frommen Gruß dir spendet, / Rose von Sesenheim."[26]

"König in Thule"

The ballad "König in Thule" is sung by Gretchen to calm her uneasiness about having attracted Faust's attention on her way home from church. In its dramatic context it is tragically ironic since its theme is loyalty in love, and Gretchen will soon be loved and forsaken by Faust. Pregnant, disgraced, and driven to distraction by the persecution of the townspeople, she will drown her child and be imprisoned and executed for the crime of being female and having fallen for a frivolous, self-indulgent man. Gretchen's singing bespeaks both happiness and graveyard whistling — "die Ahnung von Glück ebenso wie das bange Vorgefühl der Katastrophe."[27] It is likely that this ballad, one of Goethe's favorites, was composed independently of *Faust*. According to Beutler, it represents an evolution from "Hoch auf dem alten Thurne steht," which Goethe read to friends on a boat trip from Ems down the Lahn in the summer of 1774.[28] As Beutler points out, its insertion into *Faust* may reflect a Shakespearean influence. "Desdemona singt in der dritten Szene des vierten Aktes des 'Othello' vor dem Schlafengehen ein schwermütiges Volkslied [i.e. before being killed by the jealous Othello]. So singt auch Gretchen, indem sie ihre Flechten um's Haupt ordnet" (FA 1,1:338). Bohm hears an echo of Ariosto's *Orlando Furioso*.[29]

"Es war ein König in Thule" tells of a wizened old king in the mythical land of "Thule,"[30] who, unlike Belshazzar, whose last banquet comes to mind, commits no hubris in his night of feasting and drinking in his castle by the sea, but, instead, divides up his kingdom and all of his moveable goods among his heirs — everything but a goblet presented to him on her deathbed by his beloved that has become a symbol of their untransferable

---

[26] Raymond Matzen, *Goethe: Friederike und Sesenheim* (Kehl: Morstadt, 1989), 156.

[27] Werner Ross, "Johann Wolfgang Goethe: Es war ein König in Thule," in *Wege zum Gedicht* 2: Balladen, ed. Rupert Hirschenauer and Albrecht Weber (Munich & Zürich: Schnell und Steiner, 1963), 147.

[28] Ernst Beutler, "'Der König in Thule' und die Dichtungen von der Lorelay," in *Essays um Goethe*, 1947 (repr. Frankfurt am Main: Insel, 1995), 336. For date of composition and publication dates — 1782, 1790, 1800, 1815, and in the Ausgabe letzter Hand, see also Per Øhrgaard, "Der König in Thule," *Goethe-Handbuch* 1 (1996): 134.

[29] Arnd Bohm, "The Tell-Tale Chalice: 'Es war ein König in Thule' and *Orlando Furioso*," *Monatshefte für deutschsprachige Literatur und Kultur* 92,1 (2000): 20–34.

[30] "In der antiken Geographie (bei Virgil, Georg. I 30) als 'Ultima Thule' die nördlichste Insel der Welt und Name eines Reiches" (MA 1,1:885).

love. Wellbery argues that the cup is "a metonymy for the beloved. Its significance for the king stems from the fact that it comes from her, and, like a memento, it will accompany the king after his separation from her, recalling her to him, evoking her presence in absence."[31] Any souvenir is at least theoretically transferable, and could commemorate the same person to a second lover, or a third, although not in the same way. The meaning of a memento is decisively affected by the peculiar, if not unique knowledge and experience of its recipient. Goethe's *Stella* radically proposes an exclusivity in love that does not preclude loving more than one other person, serially or at the same time. Each lover's experience is, more or less, extraordinary. This does not mean that love itself is transferable, only that multiple loves are possible and, indeed, common in human experience, each of them irreplaceable. What I cannot pass on to my heirs, as Wellbery notes, is "my own singular identity" (239), including my love: "*I am my love, my desire*" (243, his italics) — neither *my* identity nor the identity of the person or persons that I love — the king's "Buhle," in the case at hand.

The king is not just an old "Zecher"; he is first and foremost a king. There are many drinkers, but only a few of them are kings. It is the king who "trank letzte Lebensglut." Attention has been given to the ritual character of ceremonial drinking as well as to the emotion that wells up in the king when the meaning of his drinking comes to mind. Note that it is not precisely the cup as such that brings the emotion-laden meanings to mind, or else he wouldn't have to drink from it to activate them. The drinking itself is significant. "Die Augen gingen ihm über / So oft er trank daraus." The ritual re-enacts a mingling of substances, as must have occurred when the king's "Buhle" was still alive. As Wellbery notes, Werther wants to "drink" Lotte.[32]

The word "Glut," as in the line "Trank letzte Lebensglut," and its verbal counterpart "glühen," Goethe's favorite words for intense human passion, occur early and often in his writings. In the second version of the early anacreontic poem "Hochzeitlied an meinen Freund," Goethe substitutes "glühst" for "blickst" in the first version: — "Wie glühst du nach dem schönen Munde, / Der bald verstummt und nichts versagt." It is not yet the transitive "Glüh entgegen" of "Wandrers Sturmlied," the "anglühst" of "Ganymed" — "Wie im Morgenrot / Du rings mich anglühst / Frühling Geliebter!" or the "durchglühst" of "Pilgers Morgenlied": "Allgegenwärt'ge

---

[31] David E. Wellbery, *The Specular Moment: Goethe's Early Lyric and the Beginnings of Romanticism* (Stanford, CA: Stanford UP, 1996), 234. Cf. Hofmannsthal, "Die Beiden," where the girl bearing the cup "is [herself] the cup she carries, filled to the brim and ready to be drunk" (Robert M. Browning, *German Poetry: A Critical Anthology* [New York: Appleton-Century-Crofts, 1962], 313).

[32] Wellbery, "Morphisms of the Phantasmatic Body: Goethe's 'The Sorrows of Young Werther,'" in *Body & Text in the Eighteenth Century,* ed. Veronica Kelly and Dorothea von Mücke (Stanford, CA: Stanford UP, 1994), 192.

Liebe! / Durchglühst mich," but it is fervent enough.[33] In the tower scene of *Götz von Berlichingen* the cessative "verglühst" expresses not merely the dying out of speech (Götz's alarming silence) but of life itself. Elisabeth says to Götz: "Du verglühst in dir selbst." The "Lebensglut" of the old king, like that of Götz, is about to die out. He takes a last drink in memory of the beloved gone on before and dies. But first he casts the goblet over the cliff,[34] watches it fall, fill up with water, and sink into the sea. The king's eyes sink too. He never drinks another drop.

Note the parallelism between "Trank nie einen Tropfen mehr" and the last line of "Der Fischer": "Und ward nicht mehr gesehen." If, as Ross points out, the king throwing his goblet is like the Doge von Venice throwing his ring into the sea, "um die Vermählung der Seestadt mit dem Meer zu erneuern,"[35] then the goblet is a metonymy for the king, rather than for his lover, and it is the sea which becomes a metonymy for his "Buhle," the equation of woman with water being among the most pervasive of all topoi. He drinks her, but she drinks him too.

Achim von Arnim and Clemens Brentano relocated in their imagination the king's last supper from its mythological seaside setting to a castle above the vineyards sloping into the Rhine. Standing on one of these hills in 1801 the twenty-three-year-old Brentano saw *himself* as a "König in Thule." "Nicht ins Meer sinkt der Becher, er stürzt in den Rhein."[36]

Goethe's early ballads were composed in the afterglow of Percy's *Reliques of Ancient English Poetry* (1765) and reflect the warmth for *das Volkstümliche* that enlivened the last quarter of eighteenth-century intellectual life. One is struck by the apparent affinity between theme and genre, an impression reinforced by the ballads of 1797. Why love and death find a home in the ballad, in particular, is a question we won't answer here, but it is clear that conventions of genre, like other conventions, have a bearing on an author's choice of theme. Eibl objects, for instance, about "Heidenröslein" that "man . . . nicht an dem Befund vorbeikommen [wird], daß hier die Geschichte einer Vergewaltigung geboten wird, die eher in den Bereich der Ballade gehört," that is, rather than in that of the *Lied* (FA 1,1:830).

---

[33] Cf. "Und ihr Kuß war Himmelsbrot, / Glühend wie der Wein" ("Der neue Amadis"). Werther writes to Lotte: "Keine Ewigkeit soll das glühende Leben auslöschen, das ich gestern auf deinen Lippen genoß, das ich in mir fühle!" (FA 1,8:251).

[34] Ross reminds the reader of the "Minnetrunk," the old Germanic custom where "bei besonderen Festen das mit Met gefüllte Horn" was emptied "zu Ehren eines Toten" ("Johann Wolfgang Goethe," 151).

[35] Ross, "Johann Wolfgang Goethe," 151.

[36] Ernst Beutler, "'Der König in Thule,'" 351, 359.

"Das Veilchen" and
"Es war eine Ratt' im Kellernest"

"Ein Veilchen auf der Wiese stand," Erwin's song from the Singspiel *Erwin und Elmire* (1775), depicts the happy death of a lover despite his beloved's indifference, while "Es war eine Ratt' im Kellernest" ridicules a death due to a penetrating, impregnating poison that acts like love. In "Das Veilchen," a copy of which Lotte Jacobi sent to her brother Georg on 25 January 1774, a young violet is inadvertently trampled to death by its beloved, but dies happily because its death comes through her — "durch sie, durch sie" — and at her feet. That, Elmire believes, is Erwin's fate. The song is always on her mind, and when she finishes singing it, it is, "als hätt' ich einen Gifttrank eingesogen"! (FA 1,4:512). The refrain of another song ends, "O Liebe! Gib mir den Tod" (509). We should perhaps not extract too much emotion from either song. Goethe is after a poignantly melancholy touch. The reference to "Gifttrank" is arresting, however, for a year after writing "Der König in Thule" Goethe wrote the wicked parody of the "Liebestod," sung by one of the perennial students, Brander, in the "Auerbachs Keller" scene of *Faust* — "Es war eine Ratt' im Kellernest," about a rat poisoned by the cook. Racing about the house, its entrails burning "als hätt sie Lieb im Leibe," the rat succumbs at the foot of the sadistic cook who scattered the poison, just as the violet dies at the foot of his beloved. This coarse lyric, which mocks the plight of the lovesick knight held at a cruel distance by his liege lady, grotesquely mirrors — according to his own testimony in a letter to Auguste Stolberg, 14–19 September 1775 — Goethe's own state in 1775. "Mir wars in all dem wie einer Ratte die Gift gefressen hat, sie läuft in alle Löcher, schlurpft alle Feuchtigkeit, verschlingt alles Essbare das ihr in Weeg kommt und ihr innerstes glüht von unauslöschlich verderblichem Feuer" (*DjG* 5:258–59). It also mirrors the frenzy of the knowledge-hungry Faust, racing through the curricula of the university, then resorting to experiments in magic, and finally attempting to escape the confines of self-hood. Its "*pointe*," as Atkins notes, is "the equation of physical suffering with love, for three reasons — that of frustration in the first stanza, that of satiety in the second, and in the last that of a similarity between death spasm and sexual orgasm."[37] It also portends the death of Margarete as a result of "love in her body." The rat's inability to quench its passion is like Faust's inability to sate the hunger that drives him on, its burning stomach a grotesque parody of Faust's "deeply-moved breast," as unsatisfied by nearness as by the promise of a distant fulfillment.[38] There is an echo of the rat's

---

[37] Stuart Atkins, *Goethe's Faust: A Literary Analysis* (Cambridge, MA: Harvard UP, 1958), 59.

[38] Atkins, *Goethes Faust*, 306–7.

unquenchable passion in Hölderlin's picture of the bereaved Meno driven like a wounded deer in search of some balm for its injury: "Aber nimmer erquickt sein grünes Lager das Herz ihm / wieder, und schlummerlos treibt es der Stachel umher . . . ihm bereitet umsonst die Erd' ihr stärkendes Heilkraut, / und sein schäumendes Blut stillen die Lüftchen umsonst" ("Elegie," later "Menons Klage um Diotima"). Since "insatiability" defines Faust (line 1863), absolute rest (line 341) will be the death of him — inevitable in any case, but not immediately. Faust, however, survives and dedicates himself to a life of tumult and pain — healed of his "Wissensdrang" (line 1768), but desire only for academic, non-experiential knowledge. He now wants to experience what his fellowmen experience. In the frantic deeds and frenetic events of Faust's life, as in the rat's aimless racing about, we see Being's erring toward entropy, drawn on by the promise of rest or relief. It is to postpone this consummation until Faust's life is complete that the provocateur Mephistopheles is allowed to tempt him, "so lang' er auf der Erde lebt" (line 315). Temptation will whet his passion until it is quenched in the "ewiger Augenblick" of the love-death.

Part of the wicked joke in Brander's song is that rat poison, like the potion that rejuvenates Faust in the Witch's kitchen, is an aphrodisiac: "Du siehst, mit diesem Trank im Leibe / Bald Helenen in jedem Weibe" (lines 2603–4). After drinking the potion Faust sees a paragon of female beauty, and this prompts him to seek fulfillment with a woman, which he does on the streets of Gretchen's provincial town, a quest parodied in the poem's "vulgar pun of 'allen Pfützen.'"[39] The cook's sadistic glee will obviate any suspicion of sentimentality about love in *Faust:* "Da lachte die Vergifterin noch: / Ha! sie pfeift auf dem letzten Loch, / Als hätte sie Lieb' im Leibe." That even this grotesque parody is subject to musical softening, however, is demonstrated by Berlioz's popular setting in *La Damnation de Faust.*

"Ganymed"

Zimmermann notes the parallel between Mira's experience of self-surrender in *Prometheus* and Ganymede's in the eponymous hymn. Pandora, who has become a kind of Ganymede, feels everything she witnessed and felt in Mira's experience, but at the appropriate level, the religious level. This lan-

---

[39] Arnd Bohm, "Typology and History in the 'Rattenlied' (*Faust I*)," *Goethe Yearbook* 10 (2001): 69. Cf. the scatological: "Und was bleibt denn an dem Leben, / Wenn es alles ging zu Funken, / Wenn die Ehre mit dem Streben / Alles ist in Quark versunken. // Und doch kann dich nichts vernichten, / Wenn, Vergänglichem zum Trotze, / Willst dein Sehnen ewig richten / Erst zur Flasche, dann zur . . . [Fotze]" (FA 1,2:850).

guage had to be learned.[40] Zimmermann speculates that Goethe's "Gany-med" was originally composed as a dramatic monologue, the intro-ductory scene of the third act of the *Prometheus* fragment. Fifty years later Goethe thought he had intended the antithetical hymn "Prometheus" to appear in this position, but he was confusing the two.[41] Starting with Goethe's collection of 1778 (see FA 1,1:735), "Ganymed" has been printed *after* the hymn "Prometheus" in collections of Goethe's works, and inter-preters have connected the two as representing opposite poles of the "sich verselbsten"–"sich entselbstigen" polarity, despite uncertainties about the dating of the two poems, "Ganymed" possibly being the earlier of the two.[42] If so, the inversion by Goethe in printed editions of his poems may contain a deliberate allusion to the "exitus-reditus" narrative: first individuation, then reassimilation, an inner logic overriding the chronology of composition.

"Ganymed" has been interpreted in many ways. It is part of the paean tradition, for example: "Das Gedicht selbst hebt mit der begeisterten Invokation des Frühlings an und wird so in die Tradition des Päans, des am Frühlingsanfang zu Ehren Apolls gesungenen Hymnus, gerückt."[43] Whether its addressee is the god or the season in the several manifestations recounted in the poem, it is first and foremost a love poem ("Frühling, Geliebter!), and, given the personification, a homoerotic love poem. In its heterosexual counterpart, depicted twice in *Faust II*, Zeus takes on the form of a swan to couple with Leda and sire Helen of Troy, but "Ganymed" is about the god's abduction of a receptive shepherd boy and is echoed in "Mahomets Gesang" in the father's awaiting those who yearn for him — "seine Sehnenden." In "Ganymed," "Die Wolken neigen sich der sehnenden Liebe." Reciprocity, not yet coalescence, rules throughout the poem. It is still a matter of one in-dividual embracing another, as we do not need to count the pronouns to feel: "Du, Dein, dich, deine Blumen, mein Herz, Mir, mir, Du kühlst" — culminating in the line "Umfangend umfangen," of which Goethe must have been proud. Note that he does not say "umfassend umfaßt," perhaps not only because this would be less euphonious but because it connotes only a blissful holding fast, not an anxious/delightful grasping for the new lover, lest he escape. Cf. "Du faßtest mich auf's beste, / Und hieltest mich so feste, / Ich sank in deinen Schoß" ("Blinde Kuh"). The word "fassen" occurs ear-

---

[40] Rolf Christian Zimmermann, *Das Weltbild des jungen Goethe: Studien zur hermetischen Tradition des deutschen 18. Jahrhunderts,* 2 vols. (vol. 1. Munich: Wilhelm Fink, 1969; vol. 2: Munich: Wilhelm Fink, 1979), 2:159.

[41] Zimmermann, *Weltbild,* 2:161.

[42] Eibl guesses "1773/74/75?" for "Prometheus" and "1772/73/74/75?" for "Ganymed (FA 1,1:735). Gloël arrives at the date of 1772 for "Ganymed" (from Eibl, FA 1,1:929).

[43] Rudolf Drux, "Ganymed," *Goethe-Handbuch* 1 (1996): 116.

lier and is preliminary to "umfangen": "Daß ich dich fassen möcht' / In diesen Arm." The phrase "Umfangend umfangen" suggests a having caught and been caught — captured, not just caught, a pursuer embraced by the quarry at the moment of capture. By contrast, the "hypothetical" suicide with whom Werther sympathizes "streckt endlich ihre Arme aus, all ihre Wünsche zu umfassen," but "ihr Geliebter verläßt sie."

There is alternation between warmth and coolness in the poem. Love manifest as a morning breeze cools Ganymede's burning thirst, but as morning redness it glows upon his coolness and warms him. A shepherd awakening in the cool morning air exults in the warmth of morning redness. Love, however, is not drawn passively from a chaste coolness.[44] As in "der Liebesnächte Kühlung" of "Selige Sehnsucht" or, in the coolness of the fisherman in "Der Fischer" ("Kühl bis ans Herz hinan"), Ganymede's coolness *anticipates* and invites love's glow. A coolness poised in anticipation of warmth. In the history of art Ganymede is an icon of *the desire* for love. And love awakens in answer to this desire, just as the nix's appearance in "Der Fischer" is in answer to something in the fisherman himself. The warm glow of Ganymede's morning is the glow of *new* love. There is a kinship between his rejoicing in the warmth of spring and Werther's letter of 10 May 1771, which precedes his acquaintance with Lotte, as well as between Ganymede's ascension and Werther's and Faust's desire to levitate, they too being lifted up by the awakening of spring.

Expectancy, rather than fulfillment, is implied by the time of day in "Ganymed" — "*Morgen*glanze" — and by the fact that Ganymede is an adolescent, having not even yet arrived at young manhood. There is growing warmth: "Mit tausendfacher Liebeswonne / Sich an mein Herz drängt / Deiner ewigen Wärme / Heilig Gefühl." The warmth of love answers the coolness of anticipation. In the erstwhile coolness of these poems there is

---

[44] One thinks of Blackall's memorable commentary on the plural "Kühlungen" in Klopstock's "Die Sommernacht": "Wenn der Schimmer von dem Monde nun herab / In die Wälder sich ergießt, und Gerüche / Mit den Düften von der Linde / In den Kühlungen wehn." "The sense would seem, at first sight, to be 'cool places,'" says Blackall, "and as a formation one might compare English 'clearings.' The effect is quite charming. And the abstractness seems to enhance the effect. There is a coolness everywhere which is, in fact, various sorts of coolness, produced by different contributory factors in different sets of circumstances. Coolnesses. The word has an embracing power. It is something more than 'cool *places*'; coolnesses. There are coolnesses everywhere, all pervaded by scents and perfumes. Each different in itself, but each cool. And all of them transfigured by the calm light of the summer moon and brought to coolness by it; so that the forest is an amalgam of coolnesses. The plural and the abstractness are essential to the peculiar nature of the poetic idea" (Eric A. Blackall, *The Emergence of German as a Literary Language 1700–1775* [Cambridge, UK: Cambridge UP, 1959], 339).

something akin to the virginity of Elena Luksch-Makowsky's portrait of ado-
lescence (1903).[45] As Ritter-Santini puts it, "es ist die Verführung einer
jugendlichen, noch schlummernden Kraft, die mit der Wärme der Natur in
einer neuen Jahreszeit, dem Frühling erwacht."[46] The love that ensues is not
the white heat of passion, but a love that warms and enlightens, casting a
warm glow on the person in love and on the world around. The world of
love is a sunny world in whose warmth the shivering lover basks. Recall the
sudden warm glow of Quinquin and Sophie in the presence of each other at
the beginning of act 2 of *Der Rosenkavalier*. Also the chastely erotic love of
Quinquin and the Marschallin at the opera's beginning, soon to give way to
the Marschallin's melancholy reflections on time. A person in love basks in
the incredible lightness of being. Love transforms and transports the world.
"Was war's das alles, Fernando ohne dich?" says Stella. What does she care
about fortune and property, how vital even was the uncle who loved her like
a father and whom she forsook for Fernando's sake? (FA 1,4:564). Love is a
passion for shared experience: "Meine Liebe, wie ganz anders war's damals,
da dein Vater noch mit mir reiste," says Cezilie to her daughter Luzie, "da
wir die schönste Zeit unsers Lebens in freier Welt genossen; die ersten Jahre
unserer Ehe! Damals hatte alles den Reiz der Neuheit für mich. Und in
seinem Arm vor so tausend Gegenständen vorüberzueilen; da jede
Kleinigkeit mir interessant ward, durch seinen Geist, durch seine Liebe!"
(FA 1,4:535). Love warms the world. "Er ist wieder da!" says Stella. "Und
in einem Wink steht rings um mich die Schöpfung lebevoll — ich bin ganz
Leben — und neues wärmeres glühendes Leben will ich von seinen Lippen
trinken (561–62).[47] Goethe's purpose is not to contrast true and false love or
higher and lower forms of love, but rather to display what extraordinary
affection for another, or for more than just one other, can confer on a
person privileged to experience love. For someone in love the earth glows —
glows transitively, lifting up and transforming the person touched by its
glow. The warmth of new love is why the neologism "anglühst" in "Wie im
Morgenglanze / Du rings mich anglühst, / Frühling, Geliebter!" is the
strongest word in the poem. The god's glow comes as a surprise and sparks
an ejaculation of happy astonishment. If only Goethe's word were available
in English — to "onglow" or, weaker, "glow at" someone! That's what a
lover can do.

[45] Upper Belvedere, Vienna.

[46] Lea Ritter-Santini, *Ganymed: Ein Mythos des Aufstiegs in der deutschen Moderne*,
trans. Birgit Schneider (Munich: Carl Hanser, 2002), 37.

[47] Recall Wellbery's point that Werther wants to "drink" Lotte ("Morphisms," 192).
According to Brown, "The act of drinking" is also the play *Faust's* "central image of
achieving unity with the Absolute" (Jane K. Brown, *Goethe's Faust: The German
Tragedy* [Ithaca: Cornell UP, 1986], 100).

"Ganymed" is so vaguely ecstatic a depiction of an individual's elevation by love as to make some readers question the poem's connection with the concrete Greek myth and to make them question the title. It is true, very little in the poem is addressed to a specific, personal lover, rather more to springtime in all of its manifestations, including the bubbling in the blood that a vernal love provokes. Is it about falling in love with someone at all or just about love in general and about the lover's readiness for love? Yet "Ganymed" *is* addressed to a lover, however vague and extensive this lover's outlines. Personification there is, but broadly and inclusively. Indeed the grand comprehensiveness of the season with its warm, transitive glow, its translucent beauty, the lovely morning breeze, the nightingale's song, and even the cool grass prickling the lover's breast — in particular, the reference to the "Nebeltal," from which the call to the poem's persona comes — may remind of Corregio's painting of Io, in which Zeus is a nearly featureless mist — here it is *Wolken,* not *Nebel,* both elements lacking clear boundaries. Goethe eventually purchased a "Karton" by Asmus Jakob Carstens, "Ganymed, vom Adler getragen" (1793), in which, as Ritter-Santini puts it, "die großen Flügel des Vogels scheinen bereits zum Körper des Jünglings zu gehören" (55). In the Corregio Zeus is identifiable as a person mainly by the one diaphanous arm reaching to embrace the willing Io. Like Io in the painting, Ganymede feels "the primal allure of life itself,"[48] and, also like Io, Goethe's Ganymede responds: "Ich komm! Ich komme! / Wohin! Ach Wohin!" The destination matters, and the still uncertain boy does not know "wohin." The answer that comes is: "Trust me!" Love calls for surrender, and surrender entails trust, as when Don Carlo hands over his sword (in Verdi; in Schiller, it is his letters) to Rodrigo/Posa — or, a thought that is hard to suppress, especially if one has the "Erlkönig" in mind, it entails acquiescence or resignation to the overture of a superior power. In "Ganymed," however, there is no fear or even reluctance. All is reciprocity — "Umfangend umfangen!" — a divergence from the classical story, as Boyle has pointed out, since there "Jupiter's love for Ganymede, which caused him to pluck the boy up into heaven to be his cup-bearer, was certainly not dependent on Ganymede's love for the god."[49] In Goethe's "Ganymed," too, the overture comes from beyond: "Wie . . . Du rings mich anglühst, / Frühling, Geliebter!" But the boy is receptive. One thinks of Leda as "die Aufgetane" in Rilke's poem about a parallel event. It is the god who approaches, but she is open to his approach. No one who has glowed at another person or felt him- or herself "glowed on" by someone else will ever forget these lines or fail to exult in the encounter and mutual coming to-

---

[48] Ingrid Rowland, "The Genius of Parma," *The New York Review of Books* XLV, no. 10, June 11, 1998, 4.

[49] Boyle, *Goethe: The Poet and the Age,* 1;160.

gether. Hence the clouds hover downward, drawn earthward by love's long-ing, "to me, to me!" And, after a moment's hesitation, Ganymede reaches out to what is coming, and is carried, upwards, "an deinem Busen / Alliebender Vater," embracing while being embraced.

As Sauder observes, "Der trotzigen Abgrenzung von den Göttern in *Prometheus* entspricht hier eine Phantasie der Vereinigung, Verschmelzung. In der Zeile 'Umfangend umfangen' wird die Bewegung von oben und das 'Hinauf' des sehnenden Ichs durch die Verknüpfung von Passiv und Aktiv in außerordentlicher Verkürzung zum Zentrum des Gedichts. Was sich im *Maifest* bereits ankündigte, das Verschwimmen der Grenzen von 'Natur' und 'Liebe,' von Subjekt und Objekt, Innen- und Außenwelt, wird hier bis zur Selbstvergötterung gesteigert. Denn wer 'umfängt' und wer 'umfangen wird,' der 'allfreundliche Vater' oder das Ich, ist nicht zu unterscheiden. Die Erfahrung der Natur entspricht der erfahrenen Liebe" (MA 1,1:873–74). Sauder's verb "entspricht" fits, since it illustrates Goethe's characteristic use of paradigms in which particular topoi — isotopes, as it were — may be in-terchangeable. Boyle argues that Ganymede's identity remains intact. "Even at the climax of the poem it is as true to say that he absorbs the other into himself, as that he is absorbed into the other."[50] But does not such absorp-tion, by whichever party in whichever other, erase the boundaries of the self? "Selbst dann bin ich die Welt," sing Wagner's Tristan and Isolde in act 2. Not quite. Not yet in this poem. If I am the world, then "I" have no boundaries and *am* no longer. If, on the other hand, the boy Ganymede is an autonomous self, an embrace, but not yet complete fusion, is what tran-spires. To the extent that this is the case, "Ganymed" is a classic instance of the love-death, which never does and never could quite depict a full "Verschwimmen der Grenzen," to borrow Sauder's word, although this is always the goal and in Goethe's poem, as in many pictorial depictions, a goal articulated by the representation of Zeus as mist or clouds. As Ritter-Santini points out, Faust, at the beginning of *Faust II*, act 4, will be borne aloft by the clouds into which Helena's garments have been transformed, not in the talons of an eagle, comfortingly, but by a diaphanous manifestation of the maternal, "das Ewig-Weibliche."[51] Faust as Ganymede! For like Ganymede, Faust is transported not by his own agency, but by someone else, just as at the beginning of his adventures he is carried away on Mephisto's magic cloak. There is an implicit foreshadowing here of his elevation by the angels at the play's end. Love's transports, like all passion and all tradition, origi-nate outside the self.

According to Sauder, "Ganymed" is "Reflex früher Erfahrung von Trennung, enttäuschter Wünsche nach Einheit. Das Phantasiebild einer

[50] Ibid., 1;161.

[51] Ritter-Santini, *Ganymed,* 83.

(narzißtischen) Vereinigung wird von der trennungsgesättigten Alltagswelt provoziert" (MA 1,1:874). Separate identities are marked, so division remains. The desire for reunification is its consequence, as the participle "*sehnende* Liebe" makes clear. We long for what we lack. But "Enttäuschung" in a vision of such promise? There is no trace of disappointment in the poem, just anticipation and a mutual embrace that is as close as individuals ever come to forgetting themselves.

3: Frau Welt. Venereal Disease. *Femmes Fatales.*

WOMAN, IN THE *LIEBESTOD* TRADITION, is both a love object and an agent of death. Charlotte, for example, is both a madonna and *femme fatale* to Werther, a paragon of lust-defying purity but as seductive as the magnetic mountain in Werther's grandmother's tale, a mountain that pulls the hardware out of passing ships and sends them to a watery grave (16. and 26. Julius 1771). The narratives that evolved around Friederike Brion, too, rely on stereotypes of woman as virgin and woman as whore.[1] The Princess von Este in *Torquato Tasso* appears first as Tasso's muse, and then, in *his* inconstant eyes, as a siren and Armida, when he embraces her and is rejected (FA 1,5:830–31, lines 3333, 3349). Stella's cascading locks of hair might become chains for Fernando like Armida's for Rinaldo. No suggestion that she is a Medusa, although Medusa is part of the tradition, one Goethe breezily alludes to in the *Divan* poem "Locken, haltet mich gefangen."

The *femme fatale, Machtweib,*[2] peril to male innocence, devouring female, *instrumentum diaboli,* and host of venereal disease, is to the masculine consciousness the bringer of death. As love object, she *promises* release from individuation; as a *femme fatale,* she *threatens* it, inspiring both rapture and terror.[3] She is attractive for the liberation she promises, offering both ecstasy and fulfillment. As either mother or menace, woman is an object to the male

---

[1] Helga Stipa Madland, "Poetic Transformations and Nineteenth-Century Scholarship: The 'Friederikenliteratur,'" *Goethe Yearbook* 8 (1996): 38.

[2] Ursula Friess, in *Buhlerin und Zauberin: Eine Untersuchung zur deutschen Literatur des achtzehnten Jahrhunderts* (Munich: Wilhelm Fink, 1970), traces the genealogy of the "Machtweib" in eighteenth-century German literature, starting with Lessing's Marwood and covering the Countess Orsina, Lady Milford, Julia Imperiali, Klinger's female characters, Lenz's Donna Diana, the "Markgräfin Mathilde," and Adelheid's literary descendants. She finds that "im Roman der hohen Literatur, von Wieland bis zur beginnenden Romantik" there occurs an "'Entdämonisierung' der 'Buhlerin' und 'Zauberin' . . . Die 'gefährliche' Verführerin aber lebt im Trivialroman weiter" (144). In Friess's classification, Marwood is the archetypal *Buhlerin* and Adelheid the archetypal *Zauberin* (166, 190).

[3] Revlon markets a perfume "Ciara Femme Fatale," so-called "Because the female of the species is more dangerous than the male" — from Kipling's poem "The Female of the Species."

consciousness.[4] Linking love and death in her person, she inspires such titles as *Fatal Attraction* and *Liaisons Dangereuses* and such mixed feelings as the *delectatio morosa.* She is at once "abstoßend und zugleich begehrenswert, . . . niedrig und göttlich, . . . Heilige und Hure," and constitutes a *coincidentia oppositorum* all by herself — at once the "Devil's gateway" and the "Bride of Christ."[5] She is a contradiction — "ambiguity, paradox, enigma."[6]

From Eve on, woman has been portrayed as more receptive to the Devil than man. This misogynous cliché is repeated in the *Faust* scene "Walpurgisnacht," where the *Hexenmeister* say: "Wir schleichen wie die Schneck' im Haus, / Die Weiber alle sind voraus. / Denn, geht es zu des Bösen Haus, / Das Weib hat tausend Schritt voraus" (lines 3978–82). Women are quicker than men to sin, according to the *Malleus Maleficarum* by the Dominicans Heinrich Kramer and Jacob Sprenger (1487); in Schöne's words: "Das männliche Geschlecht, in dessen Gestalt Christus Mensch wurde, [sei] dem Zugriff des Bösen weit weniger ausgesetzt . . . als die ihrer Natur nach von unersättlicher sexueller Gier getriebenen Weiber" (FA 1,7,2:350). Goethe expressed the same sentiment to Riemer: "Wenn ein Weib einmal vom rechten Wege ab ist, dann geht es auch blind und rücksichtslos auf dem bösen fort; und der Mann ist nichts dagegen, wenn er auf bösen Wegen wandelt. Denn er hat immer noch eine Art von Gewissen. Bei ihr aber wirkt dann die bloße Natur" (8 [18?] August 1807).[7] By definition, woman as succubus copulates with demons, "gaining knowledge . . . by physical means."[8] The question of knowledge is at the core of *Faust,* as of the book of Genesis. "Knowing" and "carnal knowledge" are familiar euphemisms for sexual intercourse.[9] According to Nietzsche, however, Adam

[4] Perhaps not only to the *male* consciousness. "[Die Mutter] (resp. ihre Imago) ist . . . der psychische Summenbegriff des Objekts an sich, das Objekt der Objekte" (Peter Zagermann, *Eros und Thanatos* [Darmstadt: Wissenschaftliche Buchgesellschaft, 1988], 6).

[5] Maria Moog-Grünewald, "Die Frau als Bild des Schicksals: Zur Ikonologie der Femme Fatale," *Arcadia* 18,3 (1983): 239–57, here, 254.

[6] R. Howard Bloch, *Medieval Misogyny and the Invention of Western Romantic Love* (Chicago: U of Chicago P, 1991), 90, 91.

[7] GA 22:471. Cf. *Goethes Gespräche,* auf Grund der Ausgabe und des Nachlasses von Flodoard Freiherrn von Biedermann, ed. Wolfgang Herwig, vol. 2 (Zürich and Stuttgart: Artemis, 1969), 251, no. 2527, 8 (18?) August 1807. There is uncertainty about the date.

[8] Walter Stephens, *Demon Lovers: Witchcraft, Sex, and the Crisis of Belief* (U of Chicago P, 2002), 36.

[9] This generates the humor in a joke about Vice President Dan Quayle some years ago: "What did Marilyn Quayle say to Dan the morning after their wedding night?" Answer: "I *knew* Jack Kennedy, and you're no Jack Kennedy." In a vice-presidential debate between Senator Lloyd Bentsen and Quayle (Omaha, Nebraska, 5 October

and Eve are punished not because sex is a sin but because knowledge is a sin: "Der Mensch war [Gottes] *größter* Fehlgriff geworden, er hatte sich einen Rivalen geschaffen, die Wissenschaft macht *gottgleich,* — es ist mit Priestern und Göttern zu Ende, wenn der Mensch wissenschaftlich wird! — *Moral:* die Wissenschaft ist das Verbotene an sich — sie allein ist verboten. Die Wissenschaft ist die *erste* Sünde, der Keim aller Sünde, die *Erb*sünde. Dies *allein ist Moral.* — 'Du sollst *nicht* erkennen'" (*Werke* 2:1213).

Frau Welt

The medieval personification of the *femme fatale* is the allegorical figure "Frau Welt." A playful vignette of Frau Welt — one would like to say, a *rococo* vignette, if the morbid antitheses personified in Dame World were not more characteristic of the baroque — occurs in Goethe's *West-östlicher Divan,* where the Schenke, who once *knew* "Welt," boasts of having made his escape in the nick of time. He lost both faith and hope to "jene garstige Vettel / die buhlerische," but, luckily, managed to rescue caritas. Now in love with Suleika, he has also recovered faith — faith in her love. With her on his lap and a cup of saki in hand, who needs hope? (FA 1,3,1:109, 413–14).[10] Goethe here treats a grotesque figure with his characteristic lightness, a gift from the anacreontic culture in which he made his first poetic forays.

The history of literature and art is replete with *femmes fatales,* including the sirens and harpies of antiquity: Calypso, Venus, Helen of Troy, Armida, Eve, Delilah, Jezebel, Judith, Salome, the Medusa, and numerous sphinxes, nymphs, and Amazons, and "Frau Welt." One of the four women sculpted into the façade of the Strassburg cathedral provides a seemingly mild example, displaying nothing more malignant than the toads climbing up her legs. Her image also adorns the south portal of the Cathedral of Worms. She is "a fine lady, well-dressed, graceful and smiling, and adored by a little knight who rapturously hugs her knees" but her naked back is being "eaten by maggots and crawling with toads."[11] Toads were supposed to be poisonous,

1988), Bentsen charged Quayle with pretending to be a second JFK and spoke the words attributed in the joke to Mrs. Quayle.

[10] Note the triad "Glaube, Hoffnung, Liebe" from Corinthians 1:13. In the masquerade scene of *Faust II,* Hoffnung and Furcht, "zwei der größten Menschenfeinde" because deterrents to purposeful action in the present, are led in chains by "Klugheit" (lines 5403–44).

[11] Wolfgang Lederer, *The Fear of Women* (New York: Grune & Stratton, 1968), 37. Cf. Faust kneeling at Helena's feet, lines 9270–72. Sander L. Gilman reproduces a photograph of the "Frau Welt" from the portal of the St. Sebaldus Church in Nuremberg in his book *Disease and Representation: Images of Illness from Madness to AIDS* (Ithaca: Cornell UP, 1988), 255. Illustrations can also be found in Wolfgang Stammler, *Frau Welt: Eine mittelalterliche Allegorie.* (Freiburg/Schweiz: Uni-

like snakes, and, also like snakes, allied with the devil. Hexed onto his body, they could cause an enemy to languish and die.[12] If the turn-coat Weislingen looked into the mirror he would see "Kröten und Schlangen," says Götz von Berlichingen (FA 1,4:146).

In Simrock's reconstruction of the *Faust* story,[13] Helena turns into an abominable snake in Faust's arms, exuding pestilential breath.[14] "In *Purgatorio* 19 Dante turns Lady Philosophy into the Siren associated with Ulysses, and reenacts his hermeneutics from the *Convivio* as the stripping of a beautiful woman, which reveals that the naked truth is rotten to the core."[15] *Nuda veritas* is always female, complete with pubic hair in Klimt's painting. Like the Lorelei, she holds a mirror.

Although the *Frau Welt* tradition is redolent of misogyny, the gender of the Latin word for "world" is masculine — *mundus* — and Stammler shows that the masculine personification of the world, as the Prince of the World, is older than its female counterpart.[16] From the twelfth century on, especially in German, where the gender of *Welt* is feminine, the world is represented as a woman[17] — a seductress promising happiness, wealth and fulfillment, but delivering disloyalty, disease and decay, as in Walther von der Vogelweide's "Elegie": "Diu Werlt ist uzen schoene, wiz, grüen unde rot / und innan swarzer varwe, vinster sam der tot."[18]

Frau Welt is often identified with Venus or with Voluptas, another allegorical figure, for example in a fifteenth-century dialogue, where Voluptas, rather than Venus, tries to bind the love-hero Tannhäuser to her service.[19] In Wagner's *Tannhäuser,* as in that of Heine (Wagner's source), it is again Venus. Heine's pope says to Tannhäuser: "Der Teufel, den man Venus nennt, / Er ist der Schlimmste von allen; / Erretten kann ich dich

versitätsverlag Freiburg, 1959). See also Thiel, *Das Frau Welt-Motiv in der Literatur des Mittelalters* (diss., Saarbrücken, 1956).

[12] Stammler, Frau Welt, 32–33.

[13] Karl Simrock, ed., *Faust: Das Volksbuch und das Puppenspiel,* 3rd ed. (Basel: Benno Schwabe, 1903).

[14] Karl Eibl, *Das monumentale Ich: Wege zu Goethes "Faust"* (Frankfurt am Main & Leipzig, 2000), 229–30.

[15] Maggie Kilgour, *From Communion to Cannibalism: An Anatomy of Metaphors of Incorporation* (Princeton, NJ: Princeton UP, 1990), 70.

[16] Among Stammler's pictorial examples, including the one from the cathedral in Worms, there are several of the masculine Fürst der Welt, who often holds an apple, incongruously, as does his female counterpart (Bild X & XI). Stammler, *Frau Welt.*

[17] Stammler, *Frau Welt,* 35.

[18] "Externally the world is beautiful, white, green and red / but colored black inside, dark as death" (quoted in Stammler, *Frau Welt,* 44).

[19] Stammler, *Frau Welt,* 66.

nimmermehr / Aus seinen schönen Krallen" (lines 137–40). Venus is the conventional foil to the Virgin Mary, implicitly in Goethe's "Der Wandrer," as well, although the madonna of this idyll is only obliquely opposed to the pagan goddess in the ruins of whose temple she innocently resides.

In Rabelais and an uncounted array of other authors, woman is metonymically the abyss, a hole that no man can fill,[20] in others she is the boundless, engulfing sea. Portraying her as a harpy is a favorite way of demonizing a woman and one exploited in the journalistic annihilation of Marie Antoinette prior to her execution in the flesh in 1793.[21] Danton's wife Julie is a grave in *Dantons Tod,* Büchner's tragedy of the French Revolution: "Die Leute sagen, im Grab sei Ruhe, und Grab und Ruhe seien eins. Wenn das ist, lieg ich in deinem Schoß schon unter der Erde. Du süßes Grab, deine Lippen sind Totenglocken, deine Stimme ist mein Grabgeläute, deine Brust mein Grabhügel und dein Herz mein Sarg" (1.1). Frau Peachum's song of sexual subjugation in Brecht and Weill's *Dreigroschenoper* is more succinct and earthier: "Und er beginnt nun zu verstehn / Daß ihm des Weibes Loch das Grabloch war."

Grimmelshausen's "Landstörtzerin Courasche" (1670 A.D.) is at once a Frau Welt and a simple, strong, maternal woman struggling to survive the Thirty-Years War.[22] She has been seen as the counterfigure to the sinful saint, Maria Aegyptiaca,[23] who appears at the end of *Faust* (lines 12053–60) and is, *mutatis mutandis,* an ancestress of Adelheid von Walldorf. In Johann Beer's *Der Simplicianische Welt-Kucker,* the allegorical figure Miseria uses the Frau Welt-like deterioration of another woman, Helena, as a warning against whoredom: "Zuvor ein Wunder der Welt / itzt ein Abscheu aller Menschen. Zuvor von den allerstärckesten Helden geküsset / itzt von den Würmern gefressen. Zuvor mit dem herrlichsten Geruch bereichert / itzt ein stinckendes Toden — Aß."[24] Frau Holle, the Danish Ellefruen (elfins) and the Swedish Skogssnufva all have hollow, rotting backs, and Robert Burns exposes the futility of cosmetic cover-ups in his poem about a church lady

---

[20] Kilgour, *From Communion to Cannibalism,* 90

[21] See Pierre Saint-Armand, "Terrorizing Marie Antoinette," trans. Jennifer Curtis Gage, *Critical Inquiry* 20,3 (spring 1994): 379–401; here, 395, figure 4.

[22] Gerhart Hoffmeister, "Dirnen-Barock: "Evil Women" in 17th-Century German Prose and its Roots in Reality," in *Studies in German and Scandinavian Literature after 1500: A Festschrift for George C. Schoolfield,* ed. James A. Parente Jr. and Richard Erich Schade (Columbia, SC: Camden House, 1993), 72.

[23] Richard Schade, "Thesen zur literarischen Darstellung der Frau am Beispiel der Courasche," in *Literatur und Volk im 17. Jahrhundert,* part 1, ed. W. Brückner et al (Wiesbaden: Harrasowitz, 1985), 232. See Hoffmeister, *Dirnenbarock,* 72.

[24] Beer, *Der Simplicianische Welt-Kucker,* 174–75; cited in Hoffmeister, *Dirnenbarock,* 73.

with a louse on her bonnet. In Coleridge's "Christabel," the vampire Geraldine is a "Frau Welt." "Her silken robe, and inner vest, / Dropt to her feet, and full in view, / Behold! her bosom and half her side — / A sight to dream of, not to tell! / O shield her! shield sweet Christabel!" (248–54). "The expurgated line (between 252 and 253) depicts Geraldine as a horrible creature, whose bosom and side 'are lean and old and foul of hue.'"[25]

The lamia, who appear as lust-filled vampires in *Faust,* are humanized in Keats's eponymous poem. The central figure of his "Belle Dame Sans Merci" has more literary descendants, including Claudia Chauchat in *Der Zauberberg* — slovenly of manner and tubercular inside.[26] She is ambiguous, an "Angst- und Wunschbild zugleich."[27] In Baudelaire's "Les métamorphoses du vampire," when the poet goes to kiss "La femme [dependant] de sa bouche de fraise, / En se tordant ainsi qu'un serpent sur la braise," she becomes "une outre aux flancs gluants, toute pleine de pus!" Opening his eyes he finds "Tremblaient confusément des débris de squelette.[28] "In Max Beerbohm's *Zuleika Dobson,* the *femme fatale* drives hundreds of men to drown themselves simultaneously. For the Duke, her primary victim, love and death . . . were exquisitely one."[29]

In *Evil Sisters* Dijkstra demonstrates the pervasiveness of the idea of woman as vampire not only in the arts and pop culture but in twentieth-

---

[25] From Arthur H. Nethercot, *The Road to Tryermaine* (Chicago: U of Chicago P, 1939), 121, who in turn refers to *"Christabel" by Samuel Taylor Coleridge: Illustrated by a Facsimile of the Manuscript and by Textual and Other Notes by Ernest Hartley Coleridge* (London, 1907), 75 n. Geraldine is "a doomed creature herself, who at times seems controlled by ominous forces" (Lieselotte E. Kurth-Voigt, "La Belle Dame sans Merci: The Revenant as Femme Fatale in Romantic Poetry," in *European Romanticism: Literary Cross-Currents, Modes, and Models,* ed. Gerhart Hoffmeister [Detroit: Wayne State UP, 1990], 255–56).

[26] Settembrini calls Frau Chauchat a Lilith and a pomegranate — food for the dead (*Der Zauberberg, Gesammelte Werke,* 456, 493). She represents those dark, nameless forces that a man must know if he would grow and develop, according to the novel's doctrine of *placet expiriri.* "Vernünftwidrigerweise" Hans Castorp goes ahead and tastes of the pomegranate.

[27] Rolf-Peter Jantz, "'Sie ist die Schande ihres Geschlechts.' Die femme fatale bei Lessing," *Jahrbuch der Deutschen Schiller-Gesellschaft* 23 (1979): 207–21: here, 214.

[28] Baudelaire, *L'Art Romantique: Oeuvres complètes de Charles Baudelaire,* ed. F.-F. Gautier, 14 vols. (Paris: Éditions de la Nouvelle Revue Française 35 & 37, 1918), 1,1:161–62. Horst Fritz writes: "Ein literarischer Extremfall ist [Ladislaw] Przybyszewski, in dessen Erzählung 'De Profundis' die begehrte Frau schließlich zum blutsaugenden Vampir sich windelt" ("Die Dämonisierung des Erotischen in der Literatur des Fin de Siècle," in *Fin de siècle: Zu Literatur und Kunst der Jahrhundertwende,* ed. Roger Bauer et al. [Frankfurt am Main: Klostermann, 1977], 442–64; here, 451).

[29] Steven Jaksa, term paper, spring 2000, p. 7.

century "science." Theda Bara was the quintessential sexual predator on the silver screen. The thrill her performances gave their male audience depended on their vicarious fulfillment of the ambivalent desire of men both to submit to and to kill the vampire. Lene in Hauptmanns "Bahnwärter Thiel" and the prostitutes who betray Mac the Knife show woman's power as well as every-man's "sexuelle Hörigkeit." Jenny Diski writes mockingly of "men's fear of helplessness, suffocation and submergence, in the inescapably female and deliquescent form of uterus, breast and vagina. . . . Women drip with danger for men, who, as we know, first can't live without us and then can't live with us. . . . [Women] as like as not are plotting against you with their sexuality and secretions while trying to abort your sons on whom the patriliny depends. . . . Men suffer. No, they do. It's awful. We hear . . . Lear railing against 'the sulphurous pit,' Milton moaning about 'this fair defect of Nature,' Swift sniffing about 'all her stink' and Yeats complaining that 'Love has pitched his mansion in the place of excrement.'"[30] The fear of the pollution caused by women occurs in the Marquesas islands and among the Mayas, the Island Caribs, the orthodox Jews of the Shtetl, and the Japanese.[31] "Pornography constructs what a woman is in terms of its view of what men want sexually. . . . It institutionalizes the sexuality of male supremacy, fusing the eroticization of dominance and submission with the social construction of male and female."[32]

The most notorious myth of all on dangerous women is that of the *vagina dentata*. In his chapter "A Snapping of Teeth," Lederer says "the myth of the *vagina dentata*" led, in various cultures, to the appointment of specialist heros whose risk-fraught occupation was to defoliate and to "entzahnen" the vaginas of brides, making them "safe" for their husbands. "We cannot help but envy them their courage," he wise-cracks (44). The myth of the *vagina dentata* overdetermines the idea of incorporation, combining the concept of engulfment by the enveloping womb with the idea of oral devouring. The vagina becomes a mouth, and the mouth a tunnel to the source. In Dürer's woodcuts the maws of hell are the mouth of a mine, and in Romantic imagery the mine is the vagina of the earth, an abyss that swallows and devours. In *Being and Nothingness* Sartre analyzes "the viscous, the thick, sticky substance that would entrap [a man's] liberty like the soft threat

[30] Jenni Diski "Oh, Andrea Dworkin," *London Review of Books* 23, 7 (6 September 2001): 11–12.

[31] Lederer, *Fear of Women*, 35–40.

[32] Catharine A. MacKinnon, "Pornography, Civil Rights and Speech," *Pornography: Women, Violence and Civil Liberties,* ed. Catherine Itzin (Oxford UP, 1992), 461, 463.

of the body of a woman."[33] Inside a woman's vagina there may be other dangers than glue or sharp teeth — serpents, for instance, which link the *vagina dentata* with the myth of the Medusa, who is alluded to in "Locken, haltet mich gefangen" and mentioned by Mephistopheles in "Walpurgisnacht" (line 4194). "Poe's obsession with teeth has been interpreted psychoanalytically as a product of his fear of being destroyed by women (the motif of the *vagina dentata*) or as a surrogate for his obsessional attachment to the womb."[34]

Monte Gulzow and Carol Mitchell have recognized male fear of the *vagina dentata* in the belief of American soldiers in Viet Nam that Asian prostitutes placed razor blades or broken glass in their vaginas: "Like — man — like I heard that them whores would put razor blades in their pussies and the G.I. would be fucking like crazy [hips moving in a rotation] and like they couldn't feel nothing man, and they pull it out, ya know, and it would be shredded. SP4 Army Active, Age 21."[35] SP4 is not far out of the mainstream, as the other interviews by Gulzow and Mitchell show. A soldier may pine for *la petite mort,* but he fears mutilation.[36]

The danger of making love to a prostitute and the greater, but often ignored, threat to a woman by a promiscuous man is the threat of venereal disease, in particular of AIDS, which is now a "pandemic." Portrayals of syphilis have borrowed heavily from the *Frau Welt* tradition. Thus the vignette on the title page of August Barthelemy's translation of Fracastorius's Latin poem *Syphilisa* (1840) shows Dame Syphilis as a pretty young thing in a crinoline, a garland in her hair and long black tresses dangling down. Her pretty face is a mask, behind which lurks the death head.[37]

Syphilis emerged as a subject of concern, first in medical then in belletristic literature, in the late fifteenth and early sixteenth century. A 1495 edict of the Emperor Maximilian (1459–1519) "describes a 'new' disease that was ravaging his empire, the *pösen plattern,* probably the first reference

[33] William Barret, *Irrational Man: A Study in Existential Philosophy* (Westport, CT: Greenwood Press, 1977), 258.

[34] Theodore Ziolkowski, "The Telltale Teeth: Psychodontia to Sociodontia." *PMLA* 91 (1976), repr. in *Varieties of Literary Thematics* (Princeton, NJ: Princeton UP, 1983), 15.

[35] Monte Gulzow and Carol Mitchell, "'Vagina Dentata' and 'Incurable Venereal Disease': Legends from the Viet Nam War," *Western Folklore* 39 (1980): 307.

[36] In a notorious case, Lorena Bobbitt cut off her husband's penis and tossed it from a car at an intersection in Manassas, Virginia, where it was rescued by the local fire department. The headline in the *Saint Paul Pioneer Press* read "Public and privates: Trials turn spotlight on wife's conjugal cut" (Monday, November 8, 1993, p. 2A).

[37] Reproduced in Sander L. Gilman, "Black Bodies, White Bodies: Toward an Iconography of Female Sexuality in Late Nineteenth-Century Art, Medicine, and Literature," *Critical Inquiry* 12,1 (1985): 236, fig. 17.

to syphilis in a printed document." "Less than a year after Maximilian's edict, Konrad Schellig, physician to Philip, Elector Palatinate, and a spectator at the Diet . . ., argued that syphilis had existed for many years."[38] "On 1 August 1496, the first visual representation of the syphilitic appeared, a broadside by Theodoricus Ulsenius, with an illustration by Albrecht Dürer."[39] Ulrich von Hutten, who eventually died of syphilis, wrote his *De Guaiaci Medicina et morbo Gallico* (1519) on the failures of the medical establishment and the benefits of treating syphilis with a powder made from guaiac wood.[40] Benvenuto Cellini (1500–71), whose autobiography Goethe translated, suffered from syphilis, as did Schubert, Nietzsche and, possibly, Heine. Syphilis figures prominently in Shakespeare, as Bentley shows. In German baroque literature, syphilis, known as "die welsche Krankheit" or "Franzosenkrankheit" is a common theme. Johann Balthasar Schupp's *Corinna: Die erbare und scheinheilige Hure* (1660) dies of syphilis but at peace with the church, after repenting and receiving forgiveness for her sins.[41] In the Venusberg incident in Grimmelshausen's *Der abenteuerliche Simplicissimus,* Simplex, here known as Beau Alman, believes that he has contracted "die lieben Franzosen" or "mal de Nable," so called because it was supposed to have first appeared in the army of Charles VIII of France, before Naples, in 1494.[42] Four years before Goethe's birth, William Hogarth's *Marriage à la Mode* portrays "both the money-hungry aristocrat and the title-hungry alderman's daughter . . . as syphilitics."[43] In Mann's *Doktor Faustus,* Adrian Leverkühn deliberately contracts syphilis, as the almost omniscient Devil knows: "Du, mein Lieber, hast wohl gewußt, was dir fehlte, und bist recht in der Art geblieben, als du deine Reise tatest und dir, salva venia, die lieben Franzosen holtest" (305). In Brecht's *Mutter Courage,* Yvette is infected.

Bohm believes that syphilis is the plague referred to in the *Faust* scene "Vor dem Tor" ("Rattenlied," 72–73), and Baus argues that Goethe was

[38] Greg W. Bentley, *Shakespeare and the New Disease: The Dramatic Function of Syphilis in Troilus and Cressida, Measure for Measure, and Timon of Athens* (New York: Peter Lang, 1989). 8.

[39] Gilman, *Disease and Representation,* 248–49.

[40] Jon Arrizabalaga, John Henderson, and Roger French, *The Great Pox: The French Disease in Renaissance Europe* (New Haven, CT: Yale UP, 1997), 99–103.

[41] Gerhart Hoffmeister, "Dirnen-Barock," 69. Beer's *Der Simplicianische Welt-Kucker* also has a Venusberg into which the protagonist is lured by a "welsche Gräfin."

[42] Hans Jakob Christoph von Grimmelshausen, *Der abenteuerliche Simplicissimus,* ed. Alfred Kelletat (1956; repr. Darmstadt: Wissenschaftliche Buchgesellschaft, 1967), 320, 322.

[43] Gilman, *Disease and Representation,* 1988, 255–56.

himself a syphilitic.[44] K. R. Eissler shows that Goethe was at least syphilophobic.[45] "At no other place did Goethe express his horror of venereal disease as strongly as in the *Roman Elegies*" (1053 n. 74). Both Roman Elegy no. 16 (as originally numbered): "Zwei gefährliche Schlangen," which Goethe chose not to publish, and no. 20: "Eines ist mir verdrießlich," which his offended readers saw as a sacrilegious claim that the only reason for loyalty in love was to provide security against venereal disease, stand "under the sign of anxiety."[46]

In one of his "Venetian Epigrams," "Goethe tells that two prostitutes in a tavern recognized him as a stranger by his imperviousness to their overtures: "O so wißt ihr warum blaß der Venetier schleicht" (FA 1,1:471). Eissler hears "a warning" in the posthumous epigram # 39 about G. A. Camper, who lectured in Rome on his father's anatomical theories until he contracted syphilis as a just retribution for linguistic mistakes (Eissler, 1350). The Weimar Duke, Carl August, was a sufferer. "Sagen Sie mir gelegentlich ein Wort wie Sie sich befinden," Goethe wrote to him on 6 April 1789. "Ich fürchte das leidige Übel hat Sie noch nicht verlassen. Ich werde ihm ehestens in Hexametern und Pentametern aufs schmählichste begegnen, das hilft aber nicht zur Kur" (FA 1,1:1118). It seems unfair that bad grammar could cause disease but good poetry could not cure it.

Woman is a more interesting and more threatening phenomenon for another reason than that she might dominate, devour, smother in slime, or infect with a fatal disease. She is a challenge, whether as a sorceress, like Armida in Tasso's *Gerusalemme Liberata,* a Charybdis to be entered only by the most fearless diver, as in Schiller's "Der Taucher," or a shrew in need of taming. Not only elusive and dangerous, but unformed and malleable, she brings out a man's creativity, like the stone that Pygmalion transforms into Galatea. Wagner's Kundry is a redeemable penitent, like the penitent woman at the end of *Faust.* As a predator needs a prey, a real man *needs* something to domesticate and reform, perhaps even redeem, knowing that he is ultimately in need of redemption by her.

Adelheid von Walldorf

George Lillo, Lessing's predecessor in the genre of bourgeois tragedy, Lessing himself, and, later, Schiller all mitigate the corruption of the Ladies Millwood, Marwood, and Milford in these authors' respective plays by show-

[44] Lothar Baus, *Johann Wolfgang Goethe — Ein "genialer" Syphilitiker: Das Ende einer langen Kontroverse* (Homburg/Saar: Asclepios, 2001).

[45] K. R. Eissler, *Goethe: A Psychoanalytic Study 1775–1786,* 2 vols. (Detroit: Wayne State UP, 1963), 1024, 1347.

[46] Eissler, *A Psychoanalytic Study,* 1268–69.

ing that they have all been victims of men. Less the Enlightener but a more probing psychologist, Goethe does not demystify the erotic power of Adelheid von Walldorf in *Götz von Berlichingen*. To him, personality is the most fascinating of mysteries and related to what he later dubbed "das Dämonische" — charisma combined with a sense of irresistible destiny.[47] Of such "dämonisch" persons he says, "Eine ungeheure Kraft geht von ihnen aus, und sie üben eine unglaubliche Gewalt über alle Geschöpfe, ja sogar über die Elemente. . . . Alle vereinten sittlichen Kräfte vermögen nichts gegen sie; . . . die Masse wird von ihnen angezogen" (FA 1,14:841–42). It was the young Goethe's interest in strong personalities that led him to the autobiography of Gottfried von Berlichingen and to Faust, Prometheus, and Mohammed. Like Brentano's Lore Lay, Adelheid von Walldorf is mysterious even to herself, as is Helena in *Faust:* "Welch streng Geschick / Verfolgt mich, überall der Männer Busen / So zu betören, daß sie weder sich / Noch sonst ein Würdiges verschonten" (9247–50). In Adelheid's encounter with the gypsies the stage directions are: "ADEL. *will los, Zig.<euner> faßt sie mit beiden Armen, und will sie küssen. Adel.<heid> schreit:* Ai!" (FA 1,4:221). Blessed or cursed with what Goethe calls *attrativa,* Adelheid wantonly kills lovers and is driven irrepressibly toward an irresistible fulfillment, like the river in "Mahomet's Gesang" — or like the prophet whose uninterruptible course is symbolized by the river. In *Werther* Goethe ridicules the efforts of philistines to reinforce a river's banks and control its course (26 May 1771). As the river threatens the buildings and gardens of an ordered municipality, a strong woman threatens male power and hegemony. This was the fate of Marie Antoinette, who passed through Strassburg on her way to the French throne while Goethe was a student there in 1770 and upon whose short, unhappy life he casts a nostalgic glance in *Dichtung und Wahrheit.*

    Götz von Berlichingen mit der eisernen Hand: Ein Schauspiel is studied for its historical-political significance. The play "eröffnete . . . die Geschichtsdichtung der neueren Weltliteratur," writes Wittkowski.[48] It established Goethe's fame in the German-speaking lands and spawned a host of

---

[47] "In [Adelheid] sieht man eigentlich erst [den Typus der 'dämonischen Frau'] und hat dann in der Erkenntnis der Zusammenhänge diese Bezeichung auch auf die Marwood übertragen" (Friess, *Buhlerin und Zauberin,* 84). Hermann Schmitz, in his book *Goethes Altersdenken im problemgeschichtlichen Zusammenhang* (Bonn: H. Bouvier, 1959), distinguishes between "das Dämonische" and "Dämon" or Daimon = "die notwendige . . . Individualität der Person" (217, cf. 278). To Goethe, that which is *dämonisch* manifests itself in contradictions and cannot be subsumed under a concept, less still, a word and must be represented "mit Ironie" (FA 1,23,1:14).

[48] Wolfgang Wittkowski, "Homo homini lupus. Homo homini Deus: 'Götz von Berlichingen mit der eisernen Hand,'" in *Andeuten und Verschleiern in Dichtungen von Plautus bis Hemingway und von der Goethezeit bis Sarah Kirsch* (Frankfurt am Main: Peter Lang, 1993), 31–56; here, 32.

imitations. As an interpretation of history, it merits historiographical study, both as a product of the *Sturm und Drang* and as an early instance of the kind of conflict that informs Friedrich Hebbel's tragedies — the great man resisting and destroyed by the *Zeitgeist*. Remarkably, in view of her prominence, especially in the first, unpublished version — the *Geschichte Gottfriedens von Berlichingen mit der eisernen Hand dramatisiert* (1771) — Adelheid is neglected in the handbooks but she is recognized as an agent of love and death by Friess.[49] Adelheid embodies the promise and the threat of woman — that she will draw men out of their lonely selves into an enveloping, liquid female All. She is the "natural" female — ambitious, manipulative, ruthless and beautiful — a Venus at the provincial court of Bamberg, eventually condemned by a secret court and killed by its appointed executioner. Her stereotypical foil is Götz's sister, not coincidentally named Maria. "Maria ist liebreich und schön," says the page Franz, "und einem Gefangenen und Kranken kann ich nicht übel nehmen der sich in sie verliebt. In ihren Augen ist Trost, gesellschaftliche Melancholie. — Aber um dich Adelheid ist Leben, Feuer, Mut — Ich würde! — Ich bin ein Narr — dazu machte mich Ein Blick von ihr" (FA 1,4:311).

We have listed Adelheid's typological ancestors. Among her *descendants* are Büchner's Marie (although an adulteress, she is essentially a victim), and Franz von Stuck's various allegories of "sin," Wilde's and Strauss's Salomé (1893 and 1905), Wedekind's (and Pabst's and Berg's) Lulu,[50] Lola Lola (in *Der blaue Engel*), Lola in *Damn Yankees* — also Lorelei Lee, the Marilyn Monroe character in *Gentlemen Prefer Blondes*,[51] and Claudia Chauchat. In the first version of *Götz*, Adelheid is separated from her entourage by gypsy

---

[49] "Man muß im Hinblick auf Adelheids 'Größe' und auf das Leiden Weislingens wie Franzens, die sie nach der Fassung A 'zum Todte gesaugt' (Friess, *Buhlerin und Zauberin*, 281) hat, von 'Liebe und Tod' sprechen. Auch Weislingens 'elendes Fieber' (ibid., 270), das sie ihm durch 'Gift,' nicht mehr durch echten Zauber bereitet, ist das Leiden des in der Liebe Gefangenen, jener Liebe, die z. B. auch mit dem Namen Venus verbunden ist" (ibid., 192).

[50] Wedekind's *Die Büchse der Pandora* (1904), G. W. Pabst's movie of the same name (1928), Alban Berg's opera *Lulu* (1937). "Lulu stirbt gleichsam einen negativen Liebestod — bezeichnend gegen Ende ihr Interesse für Wagners 'Tristan' — da jede positive Form der Erfüllung Gefahr liefe, affirmativ jenem falschen Glücksbegriff anheimzufallen, hinter dem nur die brutale Zweckrationalität der Gesellschaft lauert" (Fritz, "Die Dämonisierung des Erotischen," 462).

[51] Tunner contemplates the etymology of "lurelei," "lur," "luren," "lauern," etc. and notes that "lur" may connote "a secret melancholy, originating in a long and vain wait for release, whether in love or death" (Erika Tunner, "The Lore Lay — a Fairy Tale from Ancient Times?" in *European Romanticism: Literary Cross-Currents, Modes, and Models*, ed. Gerhart Hoffmeister [Detroit: Wayne State UP, 1990], 269–86; here, 270).

magic and lured into the gypsies' camp, a place beyond the fringe of normal European society but congruous with her as elemental being. She is a forerunner of Mérimée's and Bizet's Carmen, "the outcast woman as the destroyer of male innocence," as well as of the mysterious widow in Kazantzakis's *Zorba the Greek,* who, since no Jesus intervenes on her behalf, gets her head cut off.

As the weaker sex, women are by nature dependent not on force but on cunning, "daher ihre instinktartige Verschlagenheit und ihr unvertilgbarer Hang zum Lügen."[52] While a man must consider his honor, nobility, and dignity, woman will throw virtue to the wind when her survival or, especially, the survival of her offspring, is at stake. Beyond the pale of civilization, women are allowed to fight dirty, and are characterized, for instance in fairytales, by their ruthless Odyssean cunning (it is the wicked stepmother in *Hänsel und Gretel* who insists on abandoning the children in the forest, and Gretel, not Hänsel, who outsmarts the witch), while a man is constrained by a code of honor that renders him defenseless against adversaries willing to hit below the belt. "Weibliche List" is a stronger weapon than a man's physical strength. Woman's wiles, however, reveal her natural vileness and excuse men's brutality toward her. This is part of a misogyny dating from a time before the Christian era. One may see in such systems the cunning of culture, which conspires to make woman contemptible, an object on which violence may and must be exercised. This is the double-bind in which woman finds herself and explains the *Lustmord* as a pattern.[53] The way to restore an ailing world is to excise the cancer at its core.

Ornament and sex toy of those in power, Adelheid uses her sexual allure to further her ambitions. She destroys the renewed bond of friendship between Weislingen and Götz, seduces the page Franz, who poisons Weislingen at her behest (FA 1,4:380). Franz would murder his own father if he stood in the way of his love for her (366). Adelheid is fundamentally weak, however. She cannot control the effect of her powerful sexuality on the quick excitability of men, which is a topical paradox of the *femme fatale* tradition. Even the son of an old gypsy woman in the forest, "beißt die Zähne zusammen . . . faßt sie mit beiden Armen und will sie küssen" (FA 1,4:220–21). The *femme fatale* is herself always a victim — even in her temporary dominance, which always causes her to be victimized anew. Unable to control the effects of her strength, she is both *anziehend* and *abstoßend,* desired and feared — a coincidentia oppositorum.

---

[52] Arthur Schopenhauer, *Parerga and Paralipomena: Werke in zwei Bänden,* ed. Werner Brede (Munich: Carl Hanser, 1977), 2:712.

[53] See Maria M. Tatar, *Lustmord: Sexual Murder in Weimar Germany* (Princeton, NJ: Princeton UP, 1995).

The *Fehmgericht* that condemns Adelheid is a kind of star chamber court that, in Walter Scott's translation, is said to have provided the model for the practices of the Ku Klux Klan. The authorities of this court decide that she must be destroyed, with "Strang und Schwert" for having committed adultery and "*sucked*" her husband and his page into death — "durch geheime verzehrende Mittel" (FA 1,4:243).[54] Her lurid execution after she first repulses the executioner's advances enables any reader or spectator with a taste for the sadistic to revel in her downfall, like the aroused Mortimer in Schiller's *Maria Stuart,* who enjoys a voyeuristic sexual satisfaction as he imagines the axe slicing through Mary's "blinding white neck" (3.6, line 2556). Western culture still confers sexual power on leading women and provides their destroyers with "jouissance" and "orgasmic bliss,"[55] excusing even the rapist, at least in his own eyes, as it once justified the executioner of witches.[56] Adelheid's executioner, an ancestor of Jack the Ripper, fits the type, just as Adelheid is a forerunner of Lulu.

Adelheid's execution is depicted only in the first version of *Götz* and takes place only after the executioner propositions her and is repulsed. Admonishing her to appeal to the heavenly avenger to accept her death as a just penalty for her crimes, he is temporarily distracted by her radiant beauty. Like the hunter sent to dispatch Snow White, he considers deceiving his commissioners and sparing her. Or perhaps he is more like the fanatical Mortimer, who in *Maria Stuart* would rescue the woman Elisabeth calls "eine listige Armida" (line 2374) *for himself.* "In ihren Armen würd ich elender ein Gott sein," says Adelheid's assassin. He actually demands of her "Was ein Mann verlangen kann, von einer schönen Frau! in tiefer Nacht." But her "Maß ist voll." With futile dignity, she tries to defend herself with a dagger, only to suffer the decreed fate after a brief struggle. Bleeding from his wounds, her murderer repents of his "blutig Gelüst," throttling the "Schlange" and repeatedly thrusting his own dagger into her with the rapt,

---

[54] Freud and his followers also employ the sucking metaphor, speaking of "The fusionary suction of the primary object" — "the fusionary mother" — in her capacity as the object of the *Todestrieb.*" She is "interesting, desirable, *dämonisch* as a passageway, as the door to non-being, to the annihilation of the self as of the psychic object" (Zagermann, *Eros und Thanatos,* 109).

[55] Saint-Armand, "Terrorizing Marie-Antoinette," 387.

[56] In Mann's *Doktor Faustus* the loathsome Eberhard Schleppfuß tells the tale of Heinz Klöpfgeißel and his beloved Bärbel. Because on a visit to a whore house and again in the arms of the inn-keeper's wife Heinz is unable to perform, Bärbel is made to confess that while lying in his embrace she applied to his back a salve made of the fat of an unbaptized infant. Both Bärbel and the old witch who provided the specific, whose purpose was to bind Heinz to his wife and to her alone, are burned at the stake as the only means of saving their eternal souls (Thomas Mann, *Gesammelte Werke in zwölf Bänden* 6:143–47).

blasphemous utterance, "Gott, machtest du sie so schön, und konntest du sie nicht gut machen" (246–47). The scene underscores the relationship between misogyny and sadism, which better explains the orgiastic ecstasy experienced by males in destroying a powerful woman than does the thesis of an abstract, generic hatred for the female sex. Male sadism is often linked with female masochism (as in Wedekind's *Frühlings Erwachen,* in which Wendla Bergmann taunts Melchior Gabor until he beats her with the stick she gives him, then with his fists). The "blâme des femmes" topos is operative throughout.[57]

Note the similarity between the execution of Adelheid and the destruction of the Heidenröslein in Goethe's early ballad, who is likewise vanquished by a would-be lover. The crime of both women is that they are irresistible. Like the Lorelei and like Helena in *Faust II,*[58] they are punished for their sexual allure in what Beutler calls "die Tragödie der übermäßigen Schönheit" (366). The attacker's pleasure in pursuing and destroying them, however, is both part of their allure and an excuse for his satisfaction in their destruction. It would be a stretch to cast the "Knabe" of "Heidenröslein" as an ancestor of Jack the Ripper, but Adelheid anticipates his victims in important ways. Vile because of her beauty,[59] she is to blame for her own death. It is significant that Adelheid is a widow. There is no sexual power like that of a woman of experience.

In 1773, Goethe published, at his own expense, a second version of his play under the title *Götz von Berlichingen mit der eisernen Hand: Ein Schauspiel,* Johann Heinrich Merck having loaned him enough money to buy the paper. He himself had fallen under Adelheid's thrall, he later wrote, and allowed her to take over the action to such an extent that its unity was destroyed (FA 1,14:621). Accordingly, he deleted Adelheid's encounter with the gypsies and greatly reduced the love scenes with Franz in acts 4 and 5.

---

[57] Jonathan Beck, "Formalism and Virtuosity: Franco-Burgundian Poetry, Music, and Visual Art, 1470–1520," *Critical Inquiry* 10 (1984): 644–67; here, 649.

[58] Helena's "god-given" beauty so dazzles the watchman Lynkeus that he fails to announce her arrival in Faust's palace. She pardons him with the words, "Das Übel, das ich brachte, darf ich nicht / Bestrafen. Wehe mir! Welch streng Geschick / Verfolgt mich, überall der Männer Busen / So zu betören, daß sie weder sich / Noch sonst ein Würdiges verschonten" (lines 9246–50).

[59] "Marie Antoinette fulfills her destiny as *fascinum* by undergoing what Leo Spitzer called *Entlarvung,* a movement by which a positive quality is converted into a negative quality, a greatness into vileness" (Saint-Amand, "Terrorizing Marie-Antoinette," 391, quoting Claude Reichler, *L'Age libertin* [Paris: Minuit, 1987], who, on p. 134, refers to Spitzer's use of this term).

Helen

Paulet, the Puritan guard of Maria Stuart in Schiller's tragedy, can think of nothing worse to say about his charge than "O Fluch dem Tag, da dieses Landes Küste / Gastfreundlich diese Helena empfing" (1.1: lines 83–84). Helen of Troy, the most beautiful woman ever, has been a scandal for millennia: "Bewundert viel und viel gescholten, Helena" (*Faust,* line 8488). "The truth of Helen must encompass, it seems, not only the bed of love but also the bed of death."[60]

Lessing discusses in *Laokoon* the impotence of literature, the verbal art, in representing Helen's matchless beauty, and proclaims that Homer wisely showed it *indirectly,* by its effects.[61] Goethe agrees: "Da die Schönheit untheilbar ist und uns den Eindruck einer vollkommenen Harmonie verleiht, so läßt sie sich durch eine Folge von Worten nicht darstellen" (*Kunst und Altertum,* 1826; FA 1,22:250–51). The Olympians of ancient Greece, says Nietzsche, display a "phantastischen Überschwang des Lebens" and see, wherever they turn, the "in süßer Sinnlichkeit schwebende' Idealbild ihrer eigenen Existenz," Helen, smiling at them" (*Werke* 1:29). Helen was the tastiest morsel that the *Wanderbühnen* and the puppet theaters had to offer their eager audience. Like her immortal prototype, Aphrodite, Helen is the heathen and paragon of sensuality that Nietzsche holds up as an "üppiges, ja triumphierendes Dasein" in contrast to the "unleiblicher Vergeistigung" worshipped by Christians (*Werke* 1:29). She is the disreputable and available beauty, like Schiller's Mary Stuart, of whom Elizabeth says, "es kostet nichts, die allgemeine Schönheit / zu sein, als die gemeine sein für alle!" (lines 2417–18). Helen is the ancestor of every adulteress and, indeed, any woman with any kind of checkered past, including the penitent women mentioned at the end of *Faust:* first and foremost, Gretchen.

Goethe's Helena, however, is not a *femme fatale* at all. In *Faust,* predatory sexuality is ascribed not to her, the "buhlerisches Teufelsgespenst" of the chapbooks (HA 3:579, but, rather, to the lamiae — "lustfeine Dirnen" (line 7235) who are supposed to have died between betrothal and marriage and who in their sexual frustration try to seduce even Mephistopheles, a fellow more attracted to young boy angels. Goethe's Helena is a persecuted and anxious refugee, pursued by her husband Meneläus, combining in her own narrative and that of Phorkyas the many different histories that myth

[60] Robert Emmet Meagher, *Helen: Myth, Legend, and the Culture of Misogyny* (New York: Continuum, 1995), 29.

[61] On the men of Troy, one of whom proclaims that such beauty is worth years of conflict. Gotthold Ephraim Lessing, *Laokoon,* in *Sämtliche Schriften,* ed. Karl Lachmann, 3rd rev. ed. by Franz Muncker, 23 vols. (vols. 1–11, Stuttgart: Göschen, 1893; vols. 12–22, Leipzig; vol. 23 Berlin, Leipzig: de Gruyter, 1886–1924), 9:129–30.

assigns to her. As the personification of classical beauty and the ideal complement to the occidental, medieval Faust, she *is* what he seeks. Together, she and Faust constitute a *coincidentia oppositorum*, a "Synthese des Edeln mit dem Barbarischen,"[62] "Zum ersten Mal edle Gräzität mit hoher Romantik," in the words of the Bremen scholar Iken, an insight confirmed by Goethe with the words: "Es ist Zeit, daß der leidenschaftliche Zwiespalt zwischen Klassikern und Romantikern sich endlich versöhne" (FA 2, 10:547). Eibl employs Zimmermann's term "Consensus" to describe this reconciliation,[63] which is less a matter of agreement than yet another coincidence of opposites, thus yet another manifestation of Goethe's romanticism.

The Helena act was the first part of *Faust II* to be published, in volume 4 of Goethe's *Werke,* in 1827. The first 8802 lines had been written around the year 1800, a decade after Goethe's "classical" phase. The episode was expanded, and parts of it underwent many revisions. However one may classify the story of Helena's union with Faust — as a play within a play, as an opera, or as a dream — it does not portray a fulfillment in time or the end of time. Quoting the extant eleven versions of verses 9939–40: "Daß Glück und Schönheit dauerhaft sich nicht vereint," Eibl notes that they bring the problem of time back into the foreground.[64] When Euphorion crashes, Helena's garments turn into clouds. They envelop Faust, "heben ihn in die Höhe und ziehen mit ihm vorüber" (9945–54). A female counterpart to the cloud-clad Zeus of "Ganymed," Helena "verschwebt," and this is the last we see of her, while Faust goes on to other adventures — not yet to "neue Sphären reiner Tätigkeit."

---

[62] Schiller·to Goethe, 23 September 1800 (FA 2,5,2:74).

[63] Karl Eibl, "Consensus: Eine Denkfigur des 18. Jahrhunderts als Kompositionsprinzip Goethescher Gedichtsammlungen," in *Insel-Almanach auf das Jahr 1999: Johann Wolfgang Goethe: Zum 250. Geburtstag* (Frankfurt am Main and Leipzig: Insel, 1998), 93–112. See also FA 1,1:815–16.

[64] Eibl, *Das monumentale Ich,* 277–78.

4: *Die Leiden des jungen Werthers*

TWO OF THE WORKS THAT GOETHE WROTE in 1774 end with a *Liebestod*. *Clavigo*, an enduringly popular play, does not actually celebrate the blending of the lovers in a death-transcending union: Its horizon is more social than existential and revolves around Clavigo's difficulty in choosing between love and ambition, between ascendancy in society and government on the one hand and marriage to the *declassé* Marie Beaumarchais on the other. The dilemma is resolved by the thrust of a dagger from Marie's brother, the mortally wounded Clavigo falling on the coffin of the woman he has wronged. He grasps her cold hand, saying "Du bist die Meinige — Und noch diesen Bräutigamskuß. Ach!" (FA 1,4:492).

The protagonist of Goethe's sensational novel *Die Leiden des jungen Werthers* envisions his suicide in terms of a *Liebestod*, and *Werther* is one of the most important works structured around this topos in world literature. The novel also involves matters social, however, and is often interpreted, famously by Georg Lukács,[1] as a reflection of the struggle of a middle class now feeling its oats against the prevailing feudalistic structure: Werther indulges appetites that social developments have awakened but that a repressive class structure cannot yet tolerate. Mainstream critics, however, focus on Werther's frustrated love and his suicide, on his progress from initial self-affirmation to his eventual self-surrender, in a vain hope — so recognized by Werther himself — of being united with Lotte beyond the grave. That he does not seriously believe in the narrative to which he claims to subscribe and according to which he stages his death does not alter the trajectory of his life, but it bears importantly on the question of his character.

The appearance of *Werther* in 1774 made its author an international celebrity, and it remained the work for which he was best known throughout his life, a fact the subsequent notoriety of *Faust* and Goethe's greater pride in the *Farbenlehre* tend to make us forget. *Werther* elicited comment, pro or con, from almost every belletrist of the time. Two French versions and a French dramatization appeared in the first year after its publication. Translated into English in 1779 (seven more English editions came out in the next twenty years), the work was available in most European languages by 1800. We know that Napoleon claimed to have read *Werther* seven times and carried it with him on his Egyptian campaign. On October 2, 1808, he

---

[1] Georg Lukács, *Goethe und seine Zeit* (1936; repr. Bern: Francke, 1947), 17–30.

summoned Goethe to his headquarters in Erfurt for conversation about the novel. Napoleon wanted to meet "the other great genius of the time," as he is supposed to have said. He is also supposed to have said, as Goethe left the audience, "Voila un homme!" Napoleon objected to the "episode" — the eighteenth-century's pejorative term for extraneous events or sub-plots in a narrative — depicting Werther's employment as secretary to the pedantic ambassador; Napoleon thought that this detracted from the novel's main theme of frustration in love and the principle of unity of action.[2]

It was no exaggeration when Goethe said that the effect of its publication was like that of "lauter Brandraketen" (E, 528). The book's notoriety made it a nuisance to its author, who was forced to travel incognito in order to avoid answering, "ob denn auch alles fein wahr sei."[3] This question has been answered, but interest in *Werther* remains high. There is a consensus that the book is revolutionary, whether in its novel use of the epistolary form (all of the letters are by the protagonist), in its infectious sensibility and rhetorical power, in its protest against the class system, or, finally, in its challenge to orthodox theology. Readers are given an intimate account of the suffering of a real young man, not a heroic example, as in accounts of the suicides of Cato, Dido, or Lucretia.[4]

This, however, remains the main issue — whether Werther, the man, has enough stature to be the proper subject of a tragedy or whether he is morally deficient and his story a cautionary tale. Among the responses to *Werther*, psychological interpretations predominate, many of them resonating in one way or another with Werther's own reference in a conversation with Albert to a "Krankheit zum Tode" (12 August 1771; FA 1,8:99).[5] The writings of

---

[2] H. G. Gräf, *Goethe über seine Dichtungen,* 3 parts in 9 vols. (Frankfurt am Main: Ruetten & Loening, 1901), 1,1:580, 660. See Klaus Scherpe, *Werther und Wertherwirkung* (Bad Homburg: Gehlen, 1970), 64.

[3] "Ob denn auch Werther gelebt? ob denn auch alles fein wahr sei? / Welche Stadt sich mit Recht Lottens der Einzigen rühmt? / Ach wie hab ich so oft die törigten Blätter verwünschet, / Die mein jugendlich Leid unter die Menschen gebracht" (*Römische Elegie* no. IV, FA 1,1:398).

[4] Blackall finds that Werther "cuts a sorry figure alongside, say, Hedda Gabler, and as a ritual suicide his cannot compare with that of Sappho, Empedocles, or even Madame Butterfly" (Eric A. Blackall, *Goethe and the Novel* [Ithaca, NY: Cornell UP, 1976], 38).

[5] A history of psychology could be written on reactions to Goethe's novel, from the views of contemporaries to the crude Freudianism of an M. D. Faber, "The Suicide of Young Werther," *Psychoanalytic Review* 60 (1973): 239–76; here, 270. Cf. Ernst Feise, "Goethes Werther als nervöser Charakter," *The Germanic Review* 1 (1926): 185–253; Max Diez, "The Principle of the Dominant Metaphor in Goethe's *Werther*," *PMLA* 51 (1936): 821–41; 985–1006; Robert T. Clark, Jr., "The Psychological Framework of Goethe's *Werther*," *The Journal of English and Germanic Phi-*

Lacan have exerted a great deal of influence on recent interpretations of the novel as on literary criticism generally. Generation after generation of critics have identified Werther as a particular psychological type, depending on prevailing fashions in psychology. Matthias Claudius and Jakob Michael Sailer scorned him as childish, and the physicist Lichtenberg saw him as a "Geck" and a "Quodlibet von Hasenfuß und Weltweisen."[6] Greek and Roman youths would not have committed suicide because of a hopeless love, said Lessing. According to Blanckenburg, however, Werther's passion for Lotte follows naturally from his fervent personality rather than from Lotte's unique attractions — an explanation similar to Granville-Barker's observation that Romeo is in love with love before he ever meets Juliet.[7] Ernst Feise, Max Diez, Robert T. Clark, Stuart Atkins, and Hans Reiss have described Werther as more or less pathological, the last explicitly designating the novel as "a clinical case in the disintegration of a personality,"[8] an assessment that Christian Garve anticipates by two centuries. Blackall diagnoses Werther as "narcissistic."[9] Feise sees him as a "nervöser charakter"[10] and Tellenbach claims he is afflicted with "endogenic melancholia,"[11] the quaintness of which classifications should alert us to the ephemerality of psychological diagnoses generally.[12]

Blackall divides interpretations of *Werther* into "three main groups. On one hand it is claimed that it is Werther's temperament alone that leads him to destruction — he could not have survived in any world. Ilse Graham sees

lology 46 (1947): 273–78; Stuart Pratt Atkins, "J. C. Lavater and Goethe: Problems of Psychology and Theology in *Die Leiden des jungen Werthers*," *PMLA* 63 (1948): 520–76; repr. in Jane K. Brown and Thomas P. Saine, eds., *Essays on Goethe* (Columbia, SC: Camden House, 1995), 23–82. Hans Reiss, "*Die Leiden des jungen Werthers:* A Reconsideration," *MLQ* 20 (1959): 81–96: here, 91; Reiss, *Goethes Romane* (Bern and Munich: Francke, 1963), 14–71.

[6] Contemporary reactions are in *Zeitgenössische Rezensionen und Urteile über Goethes "Götz" und "Werther,"* ed. Hermann Blumenthal (Berlin: Junker und Dünnhaupt, 1935).

[7] Blumenthal, 76. Harley Granville-Barker, *Prefaces to Shakespeare,* 2 vols. (Princeton, NJ: Princeton UP, 1947), 2:339.

[8] Hans Reiss, "A Reconsideration," 91

[9] Blackall, *Goethe and the Novel,* 43.

[10] Ernst Feise, "Goethe's Werther als nervöser Charakter," *The Germanic Review* 1 (1926): 185–253.

[11] Hubertus Tellenbach, "The Suicide of the 'Young Werther' and the Consequences for the Circumstances of Suicide of Endogenic Melancholics," *Israel Annals of Psychiatry and Related Disciplines* 15 (1977): 16–21.

[12] On the ephemerality of medical taxonomy, see Daniel Pool, *What Jane Austen Ate and Charles Dickens Knew: From Fox Hunting to Whist — The Facts of Daily Life in Nineteenth-Century England* (New York: Simon & Schuster, 1993), 246–49.

Werther as entrapped within the prison of his own psyche and therefore as oblivious to the reality beyond himself.[13] At the opposite extreme is the claim that the inflexible forms of society drive him to his death. The third position, Blackall's own, "holds that he comes to grief because of the opposition between his own inner world and outer reality."[14] "Das Entscheidende," says Trunz, "ist nicht die äußere Situation, daß Lotte verheiratet ist, sondern die innere, daß Werther die Liebe zu etwas Absolutem macht" (HA 6:557). Steinhauer claims that "for Werther the outside world is but a reflection of his inner mental state. Things exist only in the meaning which he assigns to them. He is one of the first of those modern men whose attitude is summed up in the words of Schopenhauer: the world is my representation."[15]

The history of sociological or socio-political interpretations is shorter but still occupies a sizeable block of literature. Times and circumstances have changed, if not for the better, then at least in a way that may seem to weaken the urgency of the "to-be-or-not-to-be" question, the high suicide rate notwithstanding. Goethe's novel must, of course, be seen in its historical context but not so radically historicized as to erase the similarity between a suffering young man in 1772 and one today. Scherpe's sociological approach in *Werther und Wertherwirkung,* which elicited a sharp rebuttal by Gerhard Kaiser,[16] takes alternative views into account and now seems moderate. Lukács's 1936 interpretation is fresher than most of those produced since.

It is impossible to separate reader responses to Werther as a character from the fortunes of the book. If Werther's struggle against the limits of individuation and his longing for love and death are due to exceptional personal weakness, not only he but also the book is diminished. Many critics try to elevate the author by lowering his creature, accrediting Goethe with an exposé of a pathetic, sentimental mentality for which they themselves lack sympathy. To be sure, after the storm of protest elicited by his novel Goethe provided some support for this view. In a second edition he introduced both the first and the second book with verses — Book Two with the words ". . . Sieh, dir winkt sein Geist aus seiner Höhle: / Sei ein Mann und folge mir nicht nach." His correspondent and confidante, Auguste Gräfin Stolberg,

---

[13] Ilse Graham, "*Die Leiden des jungen Werther:* A Requiem for Inwardness," *Goethe and Lessing: The Wellsprings of Creation* (London: Paul Elek, 1973), 115–36; here, 119.

[14] See Blackall, *Goethe and the Novel,* chapter 2, "Soliloquy in the Epistolary Mode," n. 11 (281–83). Blackall finds that the narration does yield a view of reality that is independent of Werther's consciousness but that Werther has no access to it (282).

[15] Harry Steinhauer, "Afterword," in *Goethe: The Sufferings of Young Werther,* trans. Harry Steinhauer (New York: Norton, 1970), 110.

[16] Klaus Scherpe, *Werther und Wertherwirkung.* Gerhard Kaiser, "Zum Syndrom modischer Germanistik," *Euphorion* 65 (1971): 194–99.

feared that readers would believe Goethe shared Werther's views.[17] And there are *ex post facto* remarks by Goethe himself that can be made to serve an exculpatory critical purpose — for example, his observation that "Werther praised Homer while he retained his senses, and Ossian when he was going mad."[18]

The most persuasive evidence is on the other side, however, including Goethe's self-identification with Werther by assigning him his own birth date, his regret, in denouncing "die törigten Blätter" that had made "*mein jugendlich Leid*" public (FA 1,1:398), his admission to Lavater, "Und nun hab ich seiner [des lieben Jungen] Geschichte meine Empfindungen geliehen" (26 April 1774), and his accreditation of Werther's gift of "einer tiefen reinen Empfindung und wahrer Penetration."[19] Years later he wrote to Charlotte von Stein, "Ich korrigiere am Werther und finde immer daß der Verfasser übel getan hat sich nicht nach geendigter Schrift zu erschiesen" (25 June 1786), and to Zelter, "Da begreift man denn nun nicht, wie es ein Mensch noch vierzig Jahre in einer Welt hat aushalten können, die ihm in früher Jugend schon so absurd vorkam."[20]

Vincent has shown that the second version of the book was affected by events in Goethe's life.[21] In its time *Werther* was read as a *roman á clef*. Since Goethe had known Carl Wilhelm Jerusalem in Wetzlar and heard of Jerusalem's suicide from Kestner, readers assumed that it was Jerusalem's story that he had told. Werther's failure to come to terms with life disturbed a readership still uncertain about the difference between fiction depicting a "heterocosmic world" and the "reality" in which they lived, while struggling to believe in a harmonious creation. To those who identified with Werther (mostly younger readers), it was very disturbing that this man of feeling and intelligence experienced the world as inhospitable and took early leave, not before admonishing the divine Father to be as forgiving and welcoming to *his* Prodigal Son as is the mortal father of Jesus's parable (the blasphemous implications of the comparison were not lost on Goethe's contemporaries). Younger readers resonated also to Werther's struggle to transcend the walls of selfhood and become united with a beloved he regards as an ideal complement to himself. Let us keep in mind Goethe's remark that "gehindertes

---

[17] Ich fürchte, viele werden glauben, daß Goethe selbst so denkt." To Heinrich Christian Boie, 14 November 1774, in Wilhelm Bode, *Goethe in vertraulichen Briefen seiner Zeitgenossen*, 3 vols. (1917; new ed. Berlin: Aufbau, 1979), 1:85.

[18] Henry Crabb Robinson, *Diary,* ed. Th. Sadler (London 1869), 2 August 1829, 2:432; HA 6:541. Hans Gerhard Gräf, *Goethe über seine Dichtungen*, 2:688.

[19] To Gottlieb Friedrich Ernst Schönborn, 1 June–4 July 1774.

[20] To Zelter, 26 March 1816, after the suicide of Zelter's son.

[21] Deirdre Vincent, *Werther's Goethe and the Game of Literary Creativity* (Toronto: U of Toronto P, 1992).

Glück, gehemmte Tätigkeit, unbefriedigte Wünsche sind nicht Gebrechen einer besonderen Zeit, sondern jedes einzelnen Menschen, und es müßte schlimm sein, wenn nicht jeder einmal in seinem Leben eine Epoche haben sollte, wo ihm der 'Werther' käme, als wäre er bloß für ihn geschrieben" (E, 529). These are not the words of a man diagnosing a peculiar psychological syndrome or regretting a particular cultural development.

Interpretations that distinguish the "objective" state of affairs from Werther's perception of them depend on the ideology of modernism and betray a naive conception of reality as that which stands opposed to the alienated, suffering self. Werther's mistake, it is supposed, consists in his failure to come to grips with an objective "reality," while we in our armchairs, sit on *terra firma,* helpless witnesses to *his* ever more grievous alienation. "We have all been brought up as imagists," writes Robert Scholes. "We assume that a complete self confronts a solid world, perceiving it directly and accurately, always capable of capturing it perfectly in a transparent language."[22] Goethe, like Hegel, had a better understanding of the complex interactions of the inner life and external reality and less confidence in our ability to draw clear boundaries between subject and object. Like the ballad "Erlkönig," written six years later, *Werther* interrogates the nature of reality and the way in which it is constructed. In both the novel and the ballad, the relation of self and other is questioned. Beyond that, Werther's problem involves not so much a failure to discern differences between the world and his private delusions as an unwillingness to accept a world clearly seen and judged wanting. Werther does exhibit a rich inner life and is glad when this is nourished by his experience of nature and the society. When he finds himself in conflict with things as they are, he is frustrated, not because of a fatal astigmatism or because he is a misfit in an otherwise well-designed creation, but as a critic of a world in which Lotte can be married to a man who neither appreciates her special merits nor resonates to the finer vibrations of her soul (29. Julius 1772, 157). Werther sees discontinuities everywhere, such as in the disappointment of the schoolmaster's daughter, whose husband (a *Heimkehrer* like Werther) returns ill and empty-handed from his trip to Switzerland to receive his inheritance, only to be greeted on arrival with news of the death of their youngest son: "Es geht mir nicht allein so. Alle Menschen werden in ihren Hoffnungen getäuscht, in ihren Erwartungen betrogen" (4 August 1772, 159). Another illustration of the paradigm of disappointed expectations is the Bauerbursch, added in the second version, who kills his rival instead of himself: "Du bist nicht zu retten, Unglücklicher! Ich sehe wohl daß *wir* nicht zu retten sind" (207 — my emphasis). Goethe stresses Werther's identification with the lad by having both of them (and the Editor as well)

---

[22] Robert Scholes, "Is There a Fish in this Text?" in *On Signs,* ed. Marshall Blonsky (Baltimore, MD: The Johns Hopkins UP, 1985), 308–20; here, 310.

employ the same vocabulary, "kleine Vertraulichkeiten," to describe the intimacies afforded the two unhappy lovers by their respective mistresses.[23] Werther also identifies with the psychotic Heinrich, who finds no flowers for his beloved on the bare November hills and whose story as an alternative scenario to Werther's own Goethe perhaps overstresses by making a hopeless love for Lotte the cause of his psychosis (1 December 1772, 191).

Unlike previous writers in the epistolary form, Goethe provides no explicit corrective to Werther's point of view. Our independence as readers might be enhanced, but the subtlety of the work diminished, if we were given direct access to Lotte's thoughts and feelings. Albert too might provide helpful information. Both Lotte and Albert must have spoken with the Editor of Werther's papers, but not even he is privileged. When he relates what he could not have known — Werther's thoughts as he goes to meet Lotte on the day the peasant lad is arrested or Lotte's feelings toward Werther and toward her husband on 21 December — he is best understood as employing a kind of "veracious imagination."[24] From the Editor's account and from Werther's letters we can draw some inferences that diverge from Werther's own judgments, but neither Werther himself nor the Editor is omniscient or infallible. Both augment the facts with conjectures, or fantasies, about Lotte and Albert and the other characters as well. Yet because there are two narrators and because the events reported by each lend themselves to a variety of interpretations, the reader is afforded a measure of independence, as is generally agreed. And this was Goethe's intention, at least in the second version. He wrote in a letter to Johann Christian Kestner of 2 May 1783, "Dabey war unter andern meine Intention Alberten so zu stellen,

[23] 16. Julius 1771, FA 1,8:79; 4 September 1772, FA 1,8:163; cf. "eine glückliche Vertraulichkeit," FA 1,8:255.

[24] George Eliot's term, which she defines in "Leaves from a Note-Book" as "the working out in detail of the various steps by which a political or social change was reached, using all extant evidence and supplying deficiencies by careful analogical creation" (*Essays of George Eliot*, ed. Thomas Pinney [New York: Columbia UP, 1963], 446).

Blackall (*Goethe and the Novel*, 47, 49, 55); and Benjamin Bennett ("Goethe's *Werther:* Double Perspective and the Game of Life," *German Quarterly* 53 [1980]: 64–81; here, 64) believe that Werther and the Editor share an identical perspective and that the "fictive editor" is only a "device" used to objectify and relativize Werther's point of view. Thomas P. Saine finds him to be an "'omniscient narrator' who can penetrate first Werther's, then Lotte's state of mind" (Saine, "The Portrayal of Lotte in the Two Versions of Goethe's *Werther*," *JEGP* 80 [1981]: 54–77; here, 72). The Editor, however, is a separate, finite character within the novel who is careful to indicate his sources and the limits of his competence. Footnotes give additional information or explain that to say more would be indiscrete, disloyal, or injurious to someone, giving a patina of authenticity for readers still unsure about the difference between "fiction" and lies.

daß ihn wohl der leidenschaftliche Jüngling, aber doch der Leser nicht verkennt. . . . Ich hoffe Ihr werdet zufrieden seyn." In preserving the autonomy of secondary characters, in refusing to allow them to coalesce as *manifestations* of the one subjectivity that is the primary conduit of information about them, Goethe creates a subtle metaphor for one of the novel's primary themes — Werther's loneliness — and, by extension, the separateness and loneliness of everyone.[25] Goethe's innovation, maintained until the days immediately prior to Werther's death, is to restrict the point of view to that of only one person. And he achieves this unity of perception and intensity of focus while affording glimpses of a reality beyond Werther's mind. The novel portrays not just Werther but Werther in context and conflict. This is what makes it a tragedy and not just a "a psycho-pathological case history"[26] or a satire on whatever neurosis or weakness the critic may abhor.

It is through Werther, then, not directly from Lotte, that we learn of her pleasure in talking and flirting with him, *he* who reports the "kleine Vertraulichkeiten" she grants him — accidental bumpings of feet under the table, her "unschuldig" propensity for placing her hand on his and moving so close to him "im Interesse der Unterredung" that he can feel her heavenly breath on his lips (16. Julius 1771, 79), her kind, or penetrating, or soulful glances (21 November 1772, 183; 22 December, 251), and the distinctions she confers on him at the dance by waltzing with him (at the time, a sign of extraordinary intimacy) and singling him out by giving him a slap on the cheek when he miscounts or hesitates during the parlor game that she devises to distract timid members of the party from the fury of the storm. We have no reason to doubt Werther's report that she did organize such a game, that she did slap him (among others who miscounted), that she was reminded by the storm of Klopstock's "glorious ode" in which just such a storm is depicted, or that she expressed appreciation of Klopstock's success in capturing the essence of such a storm in his poem by uttering the poet's name, revealing a literary enthusiasm she shares with Werther and confirming their joint membership in the esoteric society of Klopstock admirers. We can also give Werther the benefit of the doubt when he says that she employed the affectionate salutation "lieber Werther" (21 November 1772, 183) (whether or not this is packed with as much feeling as Werther supposes), that she assigns him errands as a pretext for seeing him, that she once sent him a bouquet of flowers after being unable to spend time with him in a larger social gathering, or that she makes the bold gesture of enclosing a pink ribbon from her dress in her (and Albert's!) birthday present to him, a fetish that Werther asks to have placed in his coffin. Finally, Lotte pays Wer-

---

[25] Graham, "A Requiem for Inwardness," 119.

[26] Detlev Schumann, "Some Notes on *Werther*," *JEGP* 55 (1956): 533–49; here, 533.

ther the compliment of saying that her mother would have deserved to know him (10 September 1771, 121). And while he may exaggerate the significance of her statements and actions, he clearly has grounds for believing that she is encouraging him and is even in love with him. Small wonder that it drives him crazy when she lets her canary fly from her lips to his, that he awakens disappointed at not finding her in his bed, and that, after reading the line from Ossian, "Morgen wird der Wanderer kommen, kommen der mich sah in meiner Schönheit, ringsum wird sein Auge im Felde mich suchen und wird mich nicht finden" (245), he responds to her rush of tears by taking her into his arms and kissing her trembling, stammering lips. Lotte's situation and her actions are aspects of the objective state of affairs with which Werther wrestles and which, finally, seems to require that he leave the world.

We cannot know with certainty whether Lotte is surprised when Werther draws her to his breast and kisses her on the lips, but she has little choice but to act as though she were. Thrice repeating his name, she draws herself up, and "in ängstlicher Verwirrung, bebend zwischen Liebe und Zorn" (in the Editor's words, who must have been told of the incident by Lotte herself), she withdraws, uttering the fateful words, "Das ist das letzte Mal! Werther! Sie sehn mich nicht wieder" (247). Given the differences between Werther's and the Editor's assessments of her feelings on 21 December and their thoughts about her thoughts as she hands over the pistols (which makes Werther believe she sanctions his plan), we can only guess at Lotte's feelings, but there is plenty of evidence of her independence of mind and action. She is a genuine "other" to Werther, and her otherness, both as a different personality and as the ideal complement to his being, is part of her attractiveness to him.

Blackall refers to Werther's "longing to be free of individual existence, to abandon individuation."[27] The consistency with which the idea of the self as a prison, from the older theme of the body as a prison of the soul,[28] is thematized in the novel tells us much about Lotte's meaning to Werther. As Trunz observes, "Werther empfindet den Tod als Befreiung aus einem Kerker . . ., als Entgrenzung des Ich" (HA 6:548). Werther refers to himself as an "Eingekerkerten" (12 December 1772, 213) and to the world that the thoughtful observer of human nature will construct "aus sich selbst" as a "Kerker." He also speaks of turning back into himself and finding a world there (22 May 1771, 23) and later of having created "Welten um mich" (3 November 1772, 179) — worlds more congenial than the "real" world in which he is forced to reside. His mention of "die Wände, zwischen denen man gefangen sitzt" is an allusion to the self as a monad, which has no win-

---

[27] Blackall, *Goethe and the Novel*, 35.
[28] Cf. *West-östlicher Divan*, FA 1,3,1:106.

dows but which becomes a "Welt" when its walls are decorated with colorful forms and illusory bright vistas (22 May 1771, 23). The pervasive polarity of "Einschränkung" versus "Freiheit" is a variation on the theme of the self as a prison and Werther's vacillation between the antithetical desire to affirm his selfhood and to submerge it in a higher unity.[29] This vacillation is a human universal, says Goethe in *Dichtung und Wahrheit,* and imposes the duty "uns zu erheben und die Absichten der Gottheit dadurch zu erfüllen, daß wir, indem wir von einer Seite uns zu verselbsten genötigt sind, von der andern in regelmäßigen Pulsen uns zu entselbstigen nicht versäumen" (FA 1,14:385). Early in the novel Werther longs to become lost in the beckoning greenness of the forest (21. Junius, 57), later in the flood waters raging through the valley in which Werther has enjoyed moments of intimate conversation with Lotte (12 December 1772, 213). These are examples of what Trunz calls Werther's longing for "Entgrenzung." Zimmermann discusses Goethe's view that every human creature is dependent on the dynamic of expansion and concentration and thinks that Werther's problem is his one-sidedness. Propelled by a ganymedian desire for harmonious union with the whole and the divine, he lacks egoism, the drive for self-preservation, and the sense of self-assured completeness.[30] Géza von Molnár examines the alternation between the honorific and the pejorative connotations of "Einschränkung" and "Freiheit" in *Werther.*[31] Here "the field . . . of corporeal alterity" disappears. . . . "The dancing couple [at the ball] becomes a transfinite body, isolated because unrelated to any alterity, and yet within this isolation total unto itself.[32] This is the context for Werther's desire to possess a Lotte who is at once a beloved other and a means of escape from the confines of the self — an *arché* and *telos* to which being can return and disappear.

The tension between self and world and self and other, and Werther's desire to transcend this boundary is a pervasive theme in *Die Leiden des jungen Werthers.* At an earlier, happier time, he had longed to overcome gravity and fly with the wings of a crane to the shore of the immeasurable ocean, "aus dem schäumenden Becher des Unendlichen jene schwellende Lebenswonne zu trinken" and feel in his own breast a drop of the blessed-

[29] Trunz, HA 6:570–71.

[30] Rolf Christian Zimmermann, *Das Weltbild des jungen Goethe: Studien zur hermetischen Tradition des deutschen 18. Jahrhunderts,* 2 vols. (Munich: Wilhelm Fink, 1969 [vol. 1] and 1979 [vol. 2], 2:176).

[31] Géza von Molnár, "Confinement or Containment: Goethe's *Werther* and the Concept of Limitation," *German Life and Letters* 23 (1970): 226–34.

[32] David E. Wellbery, "Morphisms of the Phantasmatic Body: Goethe's 'The Sorrows of Young Werther,'" in *Body & Text in the Eighteenth Century,* ed. Veronica Kelly and Dorothea von Mücke (Stanford, CA: Stanford UP, 1994), 183–84.

ness of the Being that creates all within and through itself (18 August 1771, 107).[33] Werther takes in his destiny orally, his "hyperbolic orality" undergoing a reversal of valence by the end of Book One, where "the oral cavity becomes a 'yawning,' bottomless grave: an 'abyss' or 'Abgrund.' Second by second the world is eaten up ('verzehrt'), so that all that Werther can see is the infinitely consuming, infinitely chewing monstrosity of the omnivorous world-mouth."[34] Werther exhibits, in Lacanian terms, "a 'cannibalisme fusionnel': the eater eaten, the eager drinker gulped."[35] Or we might say with "The Bride of Corinth" in mind, a 'vampirisme fusionnel.' Ingestion is not, however, the only metaphor designating the blending of self and other or the dialectical interaction of opposed essences or qualities. Infusion is at least as common, as in Faust's willingness "ins Nichts dahinzufließen" if he cannot rise to "neuen Sphären reiner Tätigkeit" (line 705). Either he will achieve self-realization or he will flow back into nothingness. Heidegger says in "Was ist Metaphysik" that science dismisses "das Nichts" as "das, was 'es nicht gibt,'"[36] but the Faustian *Nichts* is clearly a feminine *something*[37] — whether a "marine and salty female wave-water," [put together like Venus Anadyomene] "out of the crud of male semen scattered on the deep at the moment of the emasculation of Father Time by his Oedipal son,"[38] or a more solid receptacle, into which the lonely masculine ego can surrender his agonistic self. Later, Mephistopheles mocks Faust's "überirdisches Vergnügen, . . . In Nacht und Tau auf den Gebirgen liegen, / Und Erd' und Himmel wonniglich umfassen, / Zu einer Gottheit sich aufschwellen lassen, . . . In stolzer Kraft ich weiß nicht was genießen, / Bald liebewonniglich in alles überfließen" (lines 3282–89).[39] Deliquescence into

---

[33] Among the limitations on the individual is gravity. In *Faust,* the mystical impulse is expressed either as a desire flow into nature or nothingness or to overcome gravity in flight (e.g. lines 1074–88). Cf. Werther: "Wie oft hab ich mich mit Fittigen eines Kranichs, der über mich hinflog, zu dem Ufer des ungemessenen Meeres gesehnt" (18 August 1771, 107).

[34] Wellbery, "Morphisms," 181–208, 193–95.

[35] Wellbery, "Morphisms," 193 n. 22.

[36] "Die Wissenschaft gibt [das Nichts], mit einer überlegenen Gleichgültigkeit gegen es, preis als das, was 'es nicht gibt'" (Martin Heidegger, *Gesamtausgabe* 1, 9:106–7 (Frankfurt am Main: Vittorio Klostermann, 1975–2004).

[37] Cf. "Das Nichts von Zuhandenheit gründet im ursprünglichsten 'Etwas,' in der *Welt*" (Heidegger, *Sein und Zeit*, 16th ed. [Tübingen: Niemeyer, 1986], 187).

[38] A. S. Byatt, *Possession: A Romance* (New York: Random House, 1990), 266.

[39] "Fließen" is a favorite Goethean metaphor. In "Nacht" Faust blames himself for the presumption of desiring "schon durch die Adern der Natur zu fließen / Und, schaffend, Götterleben zu genießen" (lines 619–20). In Margarete's bedroom he again reproaches himself: "Mich drang's, so g'rade zu genießen, / Und fühle mich in Liebestraum zerfließen" (2722–23). Mephisto reminds him: "Erst

nothingness, like overflowing into everything, is a kind of ejaculation, and impregnating Lotte would be an even more satisfying mixing of essences for Werther than to "drink her." Yet any fusion implies the destruction of separate selves and is therefore threatening as well as appealing, which accounts for Werther's ambivalence. It is a short step from this metaphorical field to that of the *vagina dentata* discussed in chapter 3.

Casting Lotte as his other, Werther avails himself of the two stereotypes about women that dominate Western literature. She is first a mother — a healthy young madonna — and doubly attractive in this quality to a man longing to return to the womb. The theme of the mother as womb and tomb ("Du Mutter, die mich selbst zum Grab gebar")[40] is pervasive in Goethe. Werther first sees her in the act of cutting bread for "her" children (16. Junius 1771, 41), which stamps her image as "eine wahre Mutter" on his consciousness forever (Albert's word, 10 August 1771, 91). It is as a mother that she wishes Werther to view her when she relates to him the solemn charge given her by her own mother on her death bed to be a mother to her younger siblings. And Werther complies, affecting a kind of Mariolatry in his attraction to her and declaring her shielded from the thrust of profane erotic desire (16. Juli. 1771, 79). But then he looks for her in his bed (21 August 1771, 109; 14 December 1772, 215). Werther identifies with Lotte's children and excuses the child in himself for grasping Tantalus-like for the charming and nubile young woman whom fate dangles before him: "Weiß der große Gott, wie einem das tut, so viel Liebenswürdigkeit vor einem herumkreuzen zu sehen und nicht zugreifen zu dürfen; und Das Zugreifen ist doch der natürlichste Trieb der Menschheit. Greifen die Kinder nicht nach allem, was ihnen in den Sinn fällt? — Und ich?" (30 October 1772, 177). Christ preferred children to adults, who fail to grasp that they are themselves only children.

But Lotte is also a Venus, both "Heilige und Hure." Pop psychology has invented a name — the "prostitute-Madonna complex."[41] However unintentionally, she does have a destructive effect on Werther and, is, to that extent, a *femme fatale* and a paradox. She is not deliberately malevolent; it is her innocence that makes her so seductive and so dangerous. Like Nature,

kam deine Liebeswut übergeflossen, / Wie vom geschmolznen Schnee ein Bächlein übersteigt; / Du hast sie ihr [Gretchen] ins Herz gegossen" (3307–9). Cf. "Wenn im Unendlichen dasselbe / Sich wiederholend ewig fließt" (FA 1,2:680); also: "Was kann der Mensch im Leben mehr gewinnen / Als daß sich Gott-Natur ihm offenbare? / Wie sie das Feste läßt zu Geist verrinnen, / Wie sie das Geisterzeugte fest bewahre" (FA 1,2:685).

[40] "Der ewige Jude," MA 1,1:242. Cf. Gerhard Kaiser: "Mutter Natur ist nicht nur Schoß, sondern zugleich Grab allen Lebens" ("Goethes Naturlyrik," *Goethe-Jahrbuch* 108 [1991]: 65).

[41] Virginia M. Allen, *The Femme Fatale: Erotic Icon* (Troy, NY: Whitston, 1983), 8.

she is both a "Schauplatz des unendlichen Lebens" and the "Abgrund des ewig offenen Grabes," "ein ewig verschlingendes, ewig wiederkäuendes Ungeheuer" (18 August 1771, 107). She is the objective correlative of Werther's ambivalence toward his own selfhood and its inevitable limits.

Die Leiden des jungen Werthers would not have had the impact that it has had if it did not depict Lotte's attractive personal qualities — her spontaneous simplicity and common sense, her prudential wholesomeness and matter-of-fact serenity, her infectious good nature and endearing practicality, her inclusive maternal sympathy for suffering creatures, her unselfish charm, even her flirtatiousness. She is far more to Werther than (if she were not already attached) an ideal potential wife, for whom only theoretically a Fräulein von B., or Frederike, the daughter of the Pastor von St. . ., "die einen die kurze Zeit über wohl unterhalten hätte" might substitute (1. Julius 1771, 63). It is part of her charm that she does not understand her unique importance to him. Why not find someone who is unattached instead of coveting the "Eigenthum eines andern?" she asks, thoughtlessly expressing the conventional belief that we covet most what we are denied, the greener grass on the other side of the fence. She considers fixing Werther up with a friend. To him, however, she is the unique human counterpart, the only suitable complement, to his own needy essence and, since she is unavailable, symbolic of the futility of our highest aspirations. Werther's frustration at being denied her makes him doubt the possibility of human fulfillment as such. Informing his desire for Lotte is a teleological question: is human nature susceptible of perfection, or are we doomed to frustration and incompleteness in a world we never made? His is essentially the question of the meaningfulness of the creation. As the physicist Steven Weinberg put it in his book *The First Three Minutes*, "The more the universe seems comprehensible, the more it also seems pointless."[42] Recall the hilarious account in *Dichtung und Wahrheit* of the boy's conversations with the odd pessimist Wilhelm Friedrich Hüsgen who confidentially "drückte . . . das blinde linke Auge stark zu, blickte mit dem andern scharf hervor und sagte mit einer näselnden Stimme: Auch in *Gott* entdeck' ich Fehler" (FA 1,14:178).[43] Whether or not the six-year-old Goethe was as disturbed by the Lisbon earthquake as he says, the *Kosmos*- and *Gotteskritik* in his early writings is unmistakable.

Lotte, the non-metaphysician, does not worry about such things. Her relationships are not romantic, let alone metaphysical, but social and philanthropic — coquettish at worst. She is at ease as a married woman. Friendship

---

[42] Quoted by Freeman J. Dyson in "Science & Religion: No Ends in Sight," *The New York Review of Books*, vol. 49, no. 5 (March 28, 2002): 4.

[43] Also *Gotteskritik:* "O Gott, bestrafest du die Liebe, Du Wesen voller Lieb und Huld?" ("Elegie auf den Tod des Bruders meines Freundes," FA 1,1:64).

with Werther, whom she esteems and surely even loves, is enough and, or so she wishes to believe, compatible with her love and affection for her husband, like Cathy in *Wuthering Heights,* who loves Edgar as well as Heathcliff. Werther is not far off the mark when he imagines her showing the shrewd eye for their own advantage that he attributes to women in general: "Wenn sie zwei Verehrer in gutem Vernehmen mit einander erhalten können, ist der Vortheil immer ihr so selten es auch angeht" (30. Julius 1771, 85). Werther's love, by contrast, is exclusive and passionate. The letter in which he becomes convinced that Lotte loves him is the one in which he reports how deflating it is to him when she speaks affectionately of her fiancé — he feels like a soldier in disgrace, stripped of his medals and his sword (13. Julius 1771, 77). She does not comprehend "was er an mir find't" (*Faust,* line 3216). Her natural cheerfulness makes her the more appealing to the agonistic Werther as his opposite and complement. Werther loves her resilient acceptance of life — of its limitations, its conventional arrangements, and the cycle of births and deaths.[44] Like Gretchen, in her naive comfort with things as they are, she is a kind of primitive, a noble savage, and admired by the reflective Werther because of her naturalness.

Werther does imagine Lotte wishing to reject the institution of wedlock, which holds for this world only, and to partake of the ecstasy of loving him and him alone in a hierogamy that would make the earth move — or fade away into oblivion (247). But heaven can wait. "Ich gehe voran! gehe zu meinem Vater, zu deinem Vater. Dem will ich's klagen, und er wird mich trösten, bis du kommst, und ich fliege dir entgegen und fasse dich und bleibe bei dir vor dem Angesichte des Unendlichen in ewigen Umarmungen" (22 December 1772, 251).

Werther's is a story of return, a paradigm prefigured and marked as a leitmotif in numerous images and allegories of "Heimkehr," including those of the vagabond seeking submergence in the cool darkness of the forest (21. Junius 1771, 57) and Werther's return to the village of his childhood upon leaving the post with the ambassador. The novel is replete with illustrations of aborted undertakings, withdrawals, and new disappointments. The return to his home town is a nostalgic feast, and Werther relishes each moment from the time he exits the coach at the linden tree outside the town gates until he arrives at the courtyard by the river that had been the scene of his childhood *Fernweh.* "Damals sehnte ich mich in glücklicher Unwissenheit hinaus in die unbekannte Welt, wo ich für mein Herz so viele Nahrung, so

---

[44] On Lotte's chatter with a friend about acquaintances who are ill, Werther comments, "meine Einbildungskraft versetzte mich ans Bett dieser Armen; ich sah sie, mit welchem Widerwillen sie dem Leben den Rücken wandten, wie sie — Wilhelm! und meine Weibchen redeten davon, wie man eben davon redet — daß ein Fremder stirbt" (26 October 1772, 175).

vielen Genuß hoffte, meinen strebenden sehnenden Busen auszufüllen und zu befriedigen. Jetzt komme ich zurück aus der weiten Welt — o mein Freund, mit wie viel fehlgeschlagenen Hoffnungen, mit wie viel zerstörten Planen" (9 May 1772, 151).[45] How different everything is now, the place changed, Werther himself filled with disillusionment. You can't go home again. In taking employment in the *Residenz,* Werther tries to embrace life. He comes up empty-handed and retreats, like a horse, which, after a good start, must be returned to the stall. His mother will be disappointed. Ultimately he retreats from life itself into what he imagines as the waiting arms of God.

Werther is a "Wandrer, ein Waller auf der Erde" (16. Junius 1772, 157), but, like that of the river in "Mahomets Gesang" or of the moth in "Selige Sehnsucht," his journey is never an aimless roaming, but an undivertible quest for resubmergence. In asking to borrow Albert's pistols, he says he is going on a journey. Then he settles his accounts and takes a mournful look at his favorite constellation, not coincidentally "der Wagen" (the big dipper, irrelevantly, in English), before setting out toward "home" and the reunion with the father in whose presence he and Lotte will dwell with arms and souls intertwined throughout eternity, like Tristan and Isolde, who are metonymically intertwined by the briar rose growing out of Tristan's grave and into Isolde's, or like the letters E and O engraved in Eduard's cup in *Die Wahlverwandtschaften.*

Werther, however, is not confident that there will be recompense in the world beyond, or even that a God awaits him with open arms. He experiments with conventional paradigms, only to recognize their vacuousness, without always admitting this to himself. In his last letter to Lotte he pretends to be dying for her sake, and the sake of her marriage to Albert. "Eins von uns dreyen muß hinweg, und das will ich seyn!" (21 December 1772, 225). This has been held against him by critics. Even though Werther triumphs over his desire to murder Albert or — another possibility — Lotte herself, he undeniably inflicts an unhealable scar on their marriage. But he acknowledges his crime with brutal honesty and self-awareness. To Albert he says, "Ich habe den Frieden deines Hauses gestört, ich habe Mißtrauen zwischen euch gebracht. Leb wohl! . . . O daß ihr glücklich wäret durch meinen Tod!" To Lotte he says, "Daß ich des Glückes hätte theilhaftig werden können, für *dich* zu sterben! Lotte, für *dich* mich hinzugeben! Ich wollte muthig, ich wollte freudig sterben, wenn ich dir die Ruhe, die Wonne deines Lebens wiederschaffen könnte. Aber ach! das war nur wenigen Edlen gegeben, ihr Blut für die Ihrigen zu vergießen, und durch ihren Tod ein

[45] "Ein Trieb wäre . . . ein dem belebten Organischen innewohnender Drang zur Wiederherstellung eines früheren Zustandes" (Sigmund Freund, *Jenseits des Lustprinzips, SA* 3:246).

neues, hundertfältiges Leben ihren Freunden anzufachen!" (22 December 1772, 261, 263). Werther's reality testing is good, even in this moment of extremity. He knows that his suicide will not benefit those he leaves behind.

Werther's "Christusleeres Christenthum" (Johann Caspar Lavater's term), which in *Werther* excuses, even justifies, suicide, belongs in the same category as his demand for postmortal compensation for the dissatisfactions of life in this world. Lacking in faith, he is the brother of Faust, the "unbehauster Mensch": "Die Botschaft hör' ich wohl, allein mir fehlt der Glaube" (line 765). Both Werther and Faust suffer from the *principium individuationis,* from the sense of alienation from the source. Both have the same mystical longings, both seek to overcome division and isolation, whether in love or in direct, unmediated knowledge. *Faust,* like *Werther,* is full of metaphors of life and selfhood as a prison, from which escape in death is the ultimate release. The question with which both works struggle is, how can you know that from which you are separated and to which you have no access? For Werther, Jesus Christ is not *the way* back to the Father in the sense that mortals are dependent on Christ's mediation. Werther hopes he may be among the chosen few who have immediate, *unmediated,* access to God (15 November 1772). Just as the young Goethe himself regarded Jesus, Socrates and other notable figures of history and myth only as extraordinary, but not essentially dissimilar, embodiments of the divine in man,[46] so Werther chooses to view the death and resurrection of Jesus not as the unique link between the antipodes of necessary and contingent being, but as a model to emulate in his return to the Father. In arranging for a "last supper" of bread and wine before his suicide, Werther commemorates his own kinship with Jesus in choosing to die and be reborn to eternal life in the bosom of God. Christ was not appointed to atone for everybody. "Sagt nicht selbst der Sohn Gottes, daß die um ihn sein würden, die ihm der Vater gegeben hat? Wenn ich ihm nun nicht gegeben bin? Wenn mich nun der Vater für sich behalten will, wie mir mein Herz sagt?" (15 November 1772, 181).

Verging on hysteria, Werther admonishes God the Father to be as humane as a finite, human father — the father of the Prodigal Son, for instance, who welcomes *his* son and does not turn him away. Note the

---

[46] Jesus was in a series with "Moses! Prophet! Evangelist! Apostel, Spinoza oder Machiavell" (To Johann Caspar Lavater and J. K. Pfenninger, 26 April 1774). "Denn da Gott Mensch geworden ist, damit wir arme sinnliche Kreaturen ihn möchten fassen und begreifen können, so muß man sich vor nichts mehr hüten, als ihn wieder zu Gott zu machen" ("Brief des Pastors zu *** an den Neuen Pastor zu ***!" [DjG 3, 110]). A letter to Lavater of 22 June 1781 contains the reproach that it is unjust and a rape to pluck out "alle köstliche Federn, der tausendfachen Geflügel unter dem Himmel, . . . als wären sie usurpiert . . ., um deinen Paradiesvogel ausschließlich damit zu schmücken."

imperatives: "Vater, den ich nicht kenne! Vater! der sonst meine ganze Seele füllte und nun sein Angesicht von mir gewendet hat! rufe mich zu dir! Schweige nicht länger! dein Schweigen wird diese dürstende Seele nicht aufhalten" (30 November 1772, 191). But even though God remains silent, Werther will not be deterred. God's silence is the salient feature of Werther's religious experience, just as Lotte's inaccessibility is the decisive fact of his experience of love.

Unlike Iphigenie, who "is allowed to leave the island of Tauris only after she has abandoned the island of her former self,"[47] Werther does not succeed in escaping from the island of *his* self. He reaches out, but, like the young woman whose suicide Werther explains to Albert, he is able to grasp nothing and, like her also, he will seek in "einem rings umfangenden Tode" (12 August 1771, 101) compensation for his failure to know the embrace of a mortal woman. He is the man of the empty embrace.[48] Werther's final letter to Lotte attempts to confirm her love for him and to convey his desire to her that they be united in death. This is his vision of eternity. Unfailingly conscious of alternatives to his own way of thinking, he protests to imagined doubters that it is no dream. "Ich träume nicht, ich wähne nicht! — nah am Grabe ward mir's heller. Wir werden sein, wir werden uns wiedersehn!" (251).

Paulin finds in Werther's final letter "a raving, deluded perversion of these hopes [for reunion beyond the grave] and the culture in which they stand."[49] Werther's vision of eternity in his last moments, however, is first and foremost an expression of anxiety, mediated, to be sure, through the culture and fashion of self-expression of the time. His recitation of the sentimental theme, "Wer werden uns wiedersehen," his identification with Jesus Christ (cf. "Mein Gott! Mein Gott! Warum hast du mich verlassen?" 15 November 1772, 181), and his refashioning of Christian theology are desperate efforts to find support in conventional ideas as he advances toward death, the ultimate incomprehensibility. In the face of the abyss he avails himself of cultural topoi — the eternal union of lovers in death, for example — but this does not prove his confidence in them. They seem a weak reed in his

[47] Heinz Politzer, "No Man is an Island: A Note on Image and Thought in Goethe's *Iphigenie*," *The Germanic Review* 37 (1962): 42–54; here, 52.

[48] John Francis Fetzer, "Schatten ohne Frau: Marginalia on a *Werther* Motif," *The Germanic Review* 46 (1971): 87–94. Roger Paulin believes the passage at the end of Book One in which Werther sees Lotte's white dress "nach der Garthenthüre schimmern, ich streckte meine Arme hinaus, und es verschwand" to be the first expression, repeated in other works, of the theme of "the beloved floating away, and disappearing, cloudlike" (Roger Paulin, "'Wir werden uns Wieder Sehn!': On a Theme in Werther," *Publications of the English Goethe Society*, N. S. 50 [1980]: 66). Like Helena, Lotte "verschwebt."

[49] Paulin, "'Wir werden uns Wieder Sehn!': On a Theme in Werther," 75.

moment of fear and trembling. Not Werther alone, but the book itself lodges its protest and declares, "Gott giebt Regen und Sonnenschein nicht unserm ungestümen Bitten" (3 November 1772, 178–79).

5: *Stella: Ein Schauspiel für Liebende*

STELLA HAS BEEN CALLED A "Pendant zu *Werther* . . .; die Figuren der Dreiecksgeschichte sind vertauscht" (MA 1,1:757), for while in *Werther* it was one woman between two men, in *Stella* it is one man between two women. *Werther* ends in the death of the protagonist, *Stella* does so only in a late, second version, no longer subtitled "Ein Schauspiel für Liebende," but simply "Ein Trauerspiel." Both works pose the question of the uniqueness of personalities and raise the possibility of one lover replacing or standing in for another. In *Stella,* substitution is thematized, as part of a demonstration that, just as Werther claims, every lover or beloved is unique and irreplaceable.

In this play about polyamorous love, Madame Sommer, as Cezilie is known until she and Fernando meet and acknowledge each other in act 3, arrives with her daughter Luzie at an inn managed by a robust Postmeisterin in the village where Luzie is to take employment with Stella, a young noblewoman. Cezilie has fallen into near indigence since she was deserted by her husband. Stella too is an abandoned woman, forsaken by the same man who had earlier left Cezilie, but, although still in mourning over the loss of Fernando and the death of their child, she is productively engaged in teaching peasant girls useful skills and then placing them in good houses. Coincidentally, Fernando, the partner *absconditus* of both adult women and Luzie's father by Cezilie, arrives at the same inn. He had left Stella in a vain search for Cezilie and then, to his shame and regret, fought in the foreign service to suppress "die sterbende Freiheit der edlen Corsen" (560). He now intends to return to Stella, whom he had first swept away from the home of her rich uncle and then, five years later, left behind on the estate they had occupied together. He has been gone for three years.

Fernando's reunion with his wife and child in the village in which he had abandoned Stella ignites a fierce conflict in his breast. His first impulse is to forsake Stella anew, and take flight with Cezilie, but Cezilie has now met Stella, admires her and knows that she is far more to Fernando than a mere replacement for herself, and decides to withdraw her prior claim and leave the two of them and their love a clear field (570–71). She proposes that he and she can write letters and remain friends at a distance. When Fernando rejects this solution as the result of self-deception on Cezilie's part and when Cezilie herself sees that it would impose an extra burden on its intended beneficiaries, she recalls the story of the Graf von Gleichen who returned from a Crusade accompanied by the Muslim woman who freed him from her father's prison. The waiting wife's grateful acceptance of the Count's rescuer as her equal in their marital bond promised eternal happiness *à trois*. Fernando, Cezilie and Stella will emulate the legendary example: "Eine Wohnung, Ein Bett, und Ein Grab" (573). "Mein! Mein," says Fernando. "Ich bin dein!" says Stella. "Wir sind dein!" says Cezilie, in the play's last line.

Clever of Goethe to have it be the wife who proposes what may have been his own *Wunschtraum*. It is characteristic of him to try to cover his tracks, as Vincent has shown.[1] As Freud said in accepting the Goethe Prize in 1930, Goethe was "nicht nur als Dichter ein großer Bekenner . . ., sondern auch trotz der Fülle autobiographischer Aufzeichnungen ein sorgsamer Verhüller" (SA 10:296). It was a typical obfuscation when he prefaced the second edition of *Werther* with the verses: "Sieh, dir winkt sein Geist aus seiner Höhle: / Sei ein Mann und folge mir nicht nach," authorizing the tenacious fiction that Werther was not the self-portrait that contemporaries supposed, and that Goethe was, instead, making *Empfindsamkeit* a target of satire. To be sure, while on one level, Werther and Fernando are Goethean self-portraits, just as Weislingen and Clavigo are proclaimed by Goethe to be, no literary character can fully represent or stand in for its creator. Nor can a confession by a fictional surrogate compensate for the absence of a direct personal admission of the real live author's guilt.

In their first conversation Stella actually discusses with Cezilie, Fernando's lawfully wedded wife, the difference between an "Ersatz" and an "Entschädigung," and does so in an almost professorial way. Cezilie says to Stella that "Geschäftigkeit und Wohltätigkeit" may take the place of romantic love in the lives of "unglückliche liebende Herzen."[2] No, there can be no "Ersatz" for a lost love, answers Stella — "Entschädigung wohl, nicht Ersatz — Etwas anstatt des Verlornen, nicht das Verlorne selbst mehr — Verlorne Liebe, wo ist da Ersatz für!" But a female-female friendship might serve as at least an "Entschädigung," for the love of a man. "Wir wollen einander das sein, was [die Männer] uns hätten werden sollen!" (547). Schiller similarly describes male-male friendship as a "Surrogat" for heterosexual love (3:172).

Experimentation with an economy of substitution informs Goethe's work from beginning to end. In the anacreontic poem "Unbeständigkeit," the young Goethe gives the jaded advice that women are interchangeable in a young man's life: "Es küßt sich so süße der Busen der zweiten / Als kaum

---

[1] Dierdre Vincent, "Text as Image and Self-Image: The Contextualization of Goethe's *Dichtung und Wahrheit* (1810–1813), *Goethe Yearbook* 10 (2001): 129.

[2] FA 1,4:547. Unless otherwise indicated, parenthetical references to *Stella* are to this volume and this, the first, version.

sich der Busen der ersten geküßt." Werther sends his servant to Lotte in place of himself when he is unable to go see her, "nur um einen Menschen um mich zu haben, der ihr heute nahe gekommen wäre." Except that he is embarrassed to do so, he would have liked to hug and kiss the boy on his return and muses about the Bononischen Stein, which shines for a while in the night after having been exposed to light. (18. Juli 1771, 81). When Werther's Lotte lets her canary first "kiss" her and then Werther, it is almost as though he were kissing her lips directly (FA 1,8:167, 2nd version only). Yet she later tries to persuade Werther that she is only a placeholder in his life and that he could fall in love with another woman if he would only put his mind to it, indeed that it is only her preemption by another man that makes her attractive to him (FA 1,8:221).

In *Iphigenie auf Tauris* Iphigenie, the Greek priestess living among the Taureans, is an image and representative of the goddess Diana. The play's plot revolves around the confusion in the minds of the principal characters as to which image and substitute for the goddess must be brought back to Greece to expiate the curse on the house of Atreus. When Orest realizes that it is his sister Iphigenie and not the stone image who is the true "image" ("Ebenbild") of the goddess, a peaceful resolution of the conflict with King Thoas becomes possible.[3] In *Wilhelm Meister's Lehrjahre* a mischievous baroness, aware of the growing fondness between Wilhelm and the pretty young Countess, attires Wilhelm in the Count's housecoat and places him where the Countess will find him in her husband's favorite chair, since, the baroness suspects, he has already *replaced* him in the woman's heart. In the same work Lothario is astonished to encounter on a ride through the country a living image of a long-ago sweetheart Margarete, seemingly unchanged despite the intervening ten years. The girl is actually a niece of the young woman he once loved (and still holds dear). On a return visit he enjoys a reunion with his early love, now surrounded by her several children (FA 1,9:848). At the close of the *Lehrjahre*, Natalie takes the place of Therese, a wife destined for Lothario, and becomes an "Entschädigung" for the errant Wilhelm's loss (FA 1,9:990). Since Natalie is the perfect partner for Wilhelm, Friedrich's preposterous charge that she would step in wherever a bride was wanting and marry out of "Gutherzigkeit . . . als Supplement irgendeiner Existenz" is frivolous, as the dismissive "irgendeine Existenz" makes clear (FA 1,9:946), but Friedrich's compliment to his sister mirrors the work's pervasive reliance on substitution. The husband in the eponymous "Sankt Joseph der Zweite" in the *Wanderjahre* is a stand-in

---

[3] They had misunderstood the words of the god: "'Bringst du die Schwester, die an Tauris' Ufer / Im Heiligtum wider Willen bleibt, / Nach Griechenland, so löset sich der Fluch.'" "Wir legten's von Apollens Schwester aus, / Und er gedachte *dich!*" (lines 2113–17).

for Joseph of Nazareth, just as Marie is adored by Wilhelm as an image of the original Mary.

In *Die Wahlverwandtschaften* Ottilie replaces Charlotte and becomes a compensation to Eduard for his loveless marriage, although, like Natalie to Wilhelm, she is far more to him than just a compensation. As Charlotte's second husband, Eduard is himself already a surrogate, soon replaced in Charlotte's heart by the captain, to whom he has already surrendered his given name, the palindrome Otto. After Ottilie's death Eduard discovers that the glass engraved with the entwined letters E and O is a substitute for the one tossed into the air by the young mason and caught by an onlooker at the laying of the cornerstone on Charlotte's birthday. No one knows whether the letters E and O stand for Eduard's alias and his true name or for Eduard and Ottilie. The division of the compound A and B and the new combinations of B and D and A and C according to the novel's titular metaphor, along with the assignment of only one name to the main characters (Otto twice, Ottilie, Char*lotte*, young Otto who drowns), suggests that everyone is replaceable and shows the paradigmatic structure of Goethe's account of erotic relations.

The "Paris" of Goethe's story "Der neue Paris" is as much a substitute for the Homeric seducer of Helen as is his "neue Melusine" for the mermaid masquerading as a human in myth and ancient fiction.[4] In "Der Mann von funfzig Jahren," Flavio, a comical sight in his father's ill-fitting clothes, takes the place of the Major in Hilarie's heart. The antiphonal poems that Flavio then reads to Hilarie were inspired by his own prior object of admiration, his merry widow, but Hilarie is a happy substitute and as moved by the passion expressed in the poems as if they had been originally addressed to her. In the system of distributional equivalences underlying these substitutions, everything can represent almost everything else, in one way or another. Jane Brown has noted imitations in Goethe's life of events and characters in Rousseau's *Confessions* and proposed that Charlotte von Stein was Goethe's Madame de Warens while Christiane Vulpius was Goethe's Therese.[5] Vincent interprets the rewriting of the *Die Leiden des jungen Werthers* as a coded record of Goethe's relations with Charlotte von Stein and an updated, esoteric version of the relationship depicted in the novel.[6]

---

[4] Cf. "Der neue Amor," "Der neue Amadis," Rousseau's *La nouvelle Héloïse,* trans. Judith H. McDowell (University Park: Pennsylvania State UP, 1968), and "La nouvelle Justine, ou les malheurs de la vertu" by Donatien Alphonse François Marquis de Sade.

[5] Paper given at the German Studies Association Conference in October, 2001.

[6] Deirdre Vincent, *Werther's Goethe and the Game of Literary Creativity* (Toronto: U of Toronto P, 1992).

Even Goethe's use of non-rhyming substitutes for an expected rhyme illustrates his virtuosic play with surrogates, as when "Morgenröte" is "rhymed" with "Hatem" in the poem "Locken! haltet mich gefangen!" (FA 1,3,1:87). Mommsen notes subtler uses of implied rhyme, such as the implicit reference to the Bible as the "Buch der Bücher" in place of the spoken "Tuch der Tücher" in the *Divan* poem "Beiname," the "Tuch" in question being the veil of Saint Veronika, on which was imprinted the image of the Lord and which was worshipped as an icon — thus a substitute — for the Lord himself.[7] Throughout the *West-östlicher Divan* Hatem is a stand-in for Goethe, just as the Western poet casts himself as a twin of his Persian brother and forerunner Hafiz. It is part of the ideology implicit in this work that lovers are carbon copies of each other, and Goethe draws this conclusion explicitly in his notes to the *Divan*. "Und der Wandrer wird kommen / Der Liebende! Betritt er / Diese Stelle, ihm zuckts / Durch alle Glieder. / 'Hier! vor mir liebte der Liebende. . . . Er liebte! Ich liebe wie er, / Ich ahnd' ihn!'" (FA 1,3,1:603).

The substitutes in *Stella* provide an especially good example. We learn early on that Stella's benevolent uncle became an *Ersatz* for her deceased father, and we have noticed how the two women consider whether their friendship might be an acceptable substitute for the love of a man. There are abundant other examples. The *Postmeisterin*, who has lost her first husband and feels over-extended running her inn without a man at her side, would take a second husband, if only as an ally who would make the servants look alive. Stella is herself an *Ersatz*, for Cezilie, and Fernando would banish the "teur[en] Schatten meines unglücklichen Weibes" in the arms of the angel to whom, having failed to find Cezilie, he now plans to return (FA 1,4:540). In the first moments of his reunion with Stella he risks an allusion to Tasso's *Gerusalemme Liberata* and relates her to the *femme fatale* of Tasso's poem. Her cascading locks of hair might become chains for him as do Armida's for Rinaldo and Suleika's locks are bidden to do in "Locken! haltet mich gefangen." About to leave home late in the play, Stella plans to take Fernando's portrait along — a poor substitute for the man himself, as is Eduard's portrait for the only man in Ottilie's life in *Die Wahlverwandtschaften*,

---

[7] Katharina Mommsen, "Spiel mit dem Klang: Zur Reimkunst im 'West-östlichen Divan,'" in "*Sei mir Dichter, willkommen!*" ed. Klaus Garber and Teruaki Takahashi, Europäische Kulturstudien 4 (Cologne, Weimar, Vienna: Böhlau Verlag, 1995), 29–46; here, 33–34. Bahr writes, "Das Schweißtuch der Veronika ist ein Bild, das Realpräsenz Christi *bedeutet,* aber nicht *ist.* So stehen die 'entferntesten Dinge' in Verbindung, aber sie sind nicht identisch" (Ehrhard Bahr, *Die Ironie im Spätwerk Goethes: Studien zum "West-östlichen Divan," zu den "Wanderjahren" und zu "Faust II"* [Berlin: Erich Schmidt Verlag, 1972], 61).

In *Götz von Berlichingen* Olearius refers to the corpus juris by the emperor Justinianus as "ein Buch aller Bücher" (FA 1,4:148).

but a comforting presence nevertheless.[8] Cezilie congratulates the fatherless Luzie on having "noch nichts verloren, das nicht zu ersetzen gewesen wäre" (FA 1,4:535). Pikulik observes that in *Stella* romantic love is a terrestrial equivalent of eternal salvation.[9] At the play's end Cezilie proposes an "Ehe zu dritt" in place of the conventional "Ehe zu zweit."

Just as a portrait may stand for a person, living persons may represent pictures, as in the Christmas tableaux vivants in *Die Wahlverwandtschaften*. In one of these, Ottilie, a "scheinbare Mutter," represents the Virgin Mary and is adored in this capacity by the architect who designed the crèche tableau (FA 1,8:438–39).[10] It is useful to have Goethe's play with equivalences in mind while observing Charlotte, who objects to the applicability of the concept of elective affinities to humans, try to salvage the concept of individuality: "Diese Gleichnisreden sind artig und unterhaltend," she says, "und wer spielt nicht gern mit Ähnlichkeiten! Aber der Mensch ist doch um so manche Stufe über jene Elemente erhöht" (FA 1,8:305). Charlotte argues that individuals are incapable of replacing, or being replaced by, one another. She insists on exclusivity in romantic relationships and thinks this ideal follows from the uniqueness of the individual personality.[11] In romantic love, no substitution is allowed or even possible.

Stella prefigures *Die Wahlverwandtschaften* in many ways.[12] In supplanting conventional with unconventional social arrangements, including the substitution of a polyamorous *ménage à trois* for monogamous marriage,

---

[8] "Die Unterhaltung mit einem geliebten Bilde, selbst wenn es unähnlich ist, hat was Reizendes," she writes in her diary. "Man fühlt auf eine angenehme Weise, daß man zu zweien ist und doch nicht auseinander kann" (FA 1,8:403). See Günter H. Hess, "*Stella* und *Die Wahlverwandtschaften*," *Seminar* 6 (1970): 218 and David G. John, "Ein neuer Schluß für Goethes *Stella*," *Goethe Jahrbuch* 111 (1994): 91–101; here, 100.

[9] Lothar Pikulik, "Stella: Ein Schauspiel für Liebende," in *Goethes Dramen: Neue Interpretationen*, ed. Walter Hinderer (Stuttgart: Reclam, 1980), 89–103; here, 98.

[10] The beloved in "Künstlers Morgenlied" is envisioned as a "Madonna . . . ein Erstlingskind, / Ein heilig's, an der Brust." Lotte is first encountered and admired by Werther in the role of mother to her siblings. Faust admires Gretchen as a substitute mother to her baby sister as well. Reverence for maternity inspires the young Goethe's invocation to the "Genius unsers Vaterlands" to let a German youth such as himself go forth and find a maiden, "the *second* mother of her family," who will give truth and living beauty to his songs (*DjG* 2:274). It is as a madonna that the woman of the idyll "Der Wandrer" is first perceived and saluted: "Gott segne dich, junge Frau, / Und den säugenden Knaben / An deiner Brust!" (FA 1,1:208, 342).

[11] On exclusivity as an element in the code of romantic love, see Niklas Luhmann, *Liebe als Passion: Zur Codierung von Intimität* (Frankfurt am Main: Suhrkamp, 1982), 163–82.

[12] Hess, "*Stella* und *Die Wahlverwandtschaften*," 215–24.

however, *Stella* is a characteristic manifestation of *Sturm und Drang* rebelliousness. It is also typical of the *Sturm und Drang* in honoring individual uniqueness.[13] Far from denying the individuality of lovers, it suggests that a special, untransferable love for one person does not preclude a simultaneous, equally untransferable love for someone else.[14] As noted, Manfred Frank, who is fond of Goethe's phrase "individuum est ineffabile,"[15] argues that individuals are capable of surprising, introducing novelty and altering the relational system they inhabit or with which they intersect.[16] This is consistent with Goethe's usage, early and late, and contradicts the principle that everything is replaceable. Meeting and loving someone new effects an expansion or at least an alteration of the universe, which is not a zero-sum game in which each novelty must supplant its predecessor and each signification replace an anterior signification, but one in which the new token or edition may constitute a genuine gain and is therefore not a token at all. Cezilie and Stella may seem to alternate with each other as Fernando's lovers in what has been called "serial monogamy," but as individuals and fully rounded characters, each woman occupies a different place in his heart and, for that matter, in each other's store of love objects. The replacement of one lover with another is compatible with a Romantic belief in unique personalities, inasmuch as the second is only functionally or chronologically a replacement for the first. In emotional terms they do not replace each other at all, each loving and being loved in a unique way. Neither can eclipse the other, and the exclusion of either Stella or Cezilie from Fernando's life or of him from theirs would be an unsatisfactory solution to their dilemma. The women in *Stella* explicitly justify his fickleness, implicitly acknowledging the possibility of loving more than one person, consecutively or at the same time. In the second, tragic version (1816, performed on stage in 1806) Fernando says to Stella: "Wenn ich dich ansehe, . . . verlischt jedes andre Bild in meiner Seele!" (FA 1,6:542), but the original *Stella* proclaims that exclusivity in one's human relationships and the institution of monogamy do not imply each other. As Cezilie says, "Jede soll ihn haben, ohne der andern was zu rauben" (FA

---

[13] "In his greatest works Goethe persuades us that, in breaking the bounds of society and morality, his heroes discover a deeper meaning in life, a fullness and richness unknown to those who observe external codes. This highest intensity of being is the extreme of individualism, but at the same time its dissolution, its self-loss in feeling, in nature, in God" [Pascal, *The German Sturm und Drang* (New York: Philosophical Library, 1953], 145).

[14] Thanks to Bonnie Watkins for pointing this out to me.

[15] To Johann Kaspar Lavater, 20 September 1780; quoted in Manfred Frank, *Die Unhintergehbarkeit von Individualität* (Frankfurt am Main: Suhrkamp, 1986), 112.

[16] Frank, *Die Unhintergehbarkeit*, 67

1,4:573). In the second version these same words are sadly illusory. Stella has already taken poison.

As has been widely speculated, the young Goethe may have been caught between love for Lili Schönemann, to whom he was engaged, and his spiritual kinship with Auguste Stolberg. Remarkably, he presented Lili with a copy of *Stella* containing a hand-written dedicatory poem (FA 1,1:176; 1,4:977), but, as Huber speculates, he may never have achieved the closeness with her that he achieved in his correspondence with Auguste Stolberg (FA 1,4:990). Although Goethe never met Auguste in person, she may have established a paradigm in his mind for intimate soulful communication to be occupied by a series of subsequent ideal lovers, each a substitute for her predecessor.[17]

Goethe was intrigued by the possibility of alternatives to, or refinements on, the ideal of exclusivity. Werther's Lotte would like to keep both Werther and Albert for herself, if she could, and seeks a match for Werther in one of her friends, whether as a stand-in for herself or only as a convenient way of keeping him nearby (FA 1,8:229), not unlike the Herzog in Schiller's *Kabale und Liebe,* who promotes a marriage between Ferdinand and Lady Milford as a means of having his cake and eating it. The rebellious Ferdinand would rather die. He is Luise's and Luise's alone. The tragedy in Schiller's play hinges on the fact that Luise has dual loyalties — to Ferdinand *and* to her father. Like the heroine of *Sophie's Choice,* she is required by a malevolent authority to choose, and looks forward to an afterlife in which overlapping loves will be allowed.

The issues addressed in *Stella* were in the air in the 1770s,[18] but *Stella* intensified the debate about sexual relations and inspired several parodies, two by Kotzebue alone, who saw that Goethe's play encoded the claim, ridiculous in Kotzebue's view, that love for more than one person may be natural and honorable. Goethe, however, expected incomprehension from those who were not themselves in love, thus the subtitle: "Ein Schauspiel für Liebende." A unique problem, occasioned by the intersection of the lives of unique individuals, requires a unique solution, whether sanctioned by conventional wisdom or not. If Goethe was torn between Lili and Auguste, this would have strengthened his sympathy for Fritz Jacobi, who was in love both with his wife Betty von Clermont and his childhood sweetheart

[17] Nicholas Boyle, *Goethe: The Poet and the Age,* vol. 1: *The Poetry of Desire (1749–1790);* vol. 2: *Revolution and Renunciation (1790–1803)* (Oxford: Clarendon Press, 1991, 2000), 1:216, 261.

[18] The Fürstin Gallitzin in Münster, who paid Goethe a visit in September 1785, believed that one person could "love many and each one fully" and viewed the institution of monogamous marriage as a "social arrangement" for the purpose of procreation. (Paul Kluckhohn, *Die Auffassung der Liebe in der Literatur des 18. Jahrhunderts und in der deutschen Romantik* [1922; repr. Tübingen: Max Niemeyer, 1966], 232).

Johanna Fahlmer. Johanna was Jacobi's aunt and eventually (1778) replaced Goethe's deceased sister Cornelia by marrying Schlosser, Cornelia's widower, five months after her death. Gottfried August Bürgers "Doppelehe" was a scandal. Kluckhohn lists other literary precedents and sequels.[19] And providing what at first glance might seem to be an eponymous title for Goethe's *Stella* is Jonathan Swift's love for the two women he called Stella (Esther Johnson) and Vanessa (Esther Vanhomrigh). Goethe probably also knew of Lavater's advice to two young women against entering into a triangular relationship with the man they both loved (details in FA 1,4:984 and MA 1,2:712).

These examples from Goethe's own life or the lives of others cover only the issue of multiple objects of affection and the question whether one may replace another. A related question is to what extent literary characters may represent their creators. Is Fernando an effigy of Goethe himself, not only in his capacity to love more than one woman at the same time but in his failure to remain loyal to one to whom he promised or, at least, seemed to promise exclusive devotion? In *Dichtung und Wahrheit*, Goethe claims that the fickle and blameworthy characters Weislingen and Clavigo amount to a poetic confession — a confession of his guilt in loving and leaving Friederike Brion. They are objective correlatives of his own transgression — self-portraits, or so he says. Fernando, Faust, and, possibly, the Knab' of "Heidenröslein" can be added to the rogues' gallery. Goethe speaks of his self-torment after breaking with Friederike, of a "selbstquälerische Büßung" and of "reuige Betrachtungen" (FA 14,1:568).

Weislingen and Clavigo, among other fictional targets of blame, are stand-ins for Goethe himself. But even his self-portrait in *Dichtung und Wahrheit* is such a target.[20] The principle at work is like that of voodoo, with the important difference that killing or convicting the effigy actually saves and absolves the original. In killing off Weislingen, Clavigo, and Werther and in exposing Faust, Fernando, and his own youthful self, as it were, to the most searing blame, Goethe enacts a displacement that may be shrewdly self-exculpatory. This would not be unheard of. Rousseau, for example, taxes Montaigne with "false ingenuousness," writing of "his pretense of confessing his faults while taking good care only to admit to likeable ones."[21] Heine in turn accuses Rousseau of preferring to confess his shame for sending his

---

[19] Kluckhohn, *Auffassung der Liebe* (211–12; 233–39).

[20] Fritz Jacobi saw a resemblance, not to Clavigo but to Carlos, a character "worin Göthe so ganz leibt und lebt" (to Johanna Schlosser, 10 Nov 1779, quoted in Wilhelm Bode, *Goethe in vertraulichen Briefen seiner Zeitgenossen*, 3 vols, [1917, new ed. Berlin: Aufbau, 1979], 1:247).

[21] Jean-Jacques Rousseau, *The Confessions*, trans. J. M. Cohen (Harmondsworth, UK: Penguin, 1954), 479.

children to a foundlings' home to the more disgraceful admission that he was incapable of paternity and that Therese's children were sired by other men.[22] An author may create counterfeit selves with the purpose of drawing fire away from his or her "true" self, like holding up a hat on a stick. In his early plays and in *Dichtung und Wahrheit* Goethe may be employing the rhetorical figure "confessio" or "paromologia," confessing the venial sin of abandoning Friederike in hopes of being excused for the worse one of entering into an intimate relationship with her without ever intending a serious commitment, indeed of using her as a *Versuchsobjekt* on which to practice his own powers of personality and poetic expression.

"Ich fühlte nun erst [i.e. after receiving Friederike's disappointed reply] den Verlust den sie erlitt, und sah keine Möglichkeit ihn zu ersetzen, ja nur ihn zu lindern," writes Goethe later (FA 1,14:566). What rings false is the adverb "erst," since he and Friederike's sister Sophie, who was "voraussehender oder offener" than Friederike, seem to have spoken about his "vermutlichen Abschied" (FA 1,14:543). But did he not anticipate Friederike's disappointment? And what does he mean when he then says: "Ich konnte mir mein eignes Unglück nicht verzeihen" (FA 1,14:566), which echoes Fernando's words to himself in *Stella:* "o, wenn's in dir liegt, so zu fühlen, und so zu handeln, warum hast du nicht auch Kraft, dir das geschehene zu verzeihen?" (FA 1,4:555–56). Was Goethe, like Fernando, pretending to blame himself for not being as callous and remorseless as a manly man should be? Fernando is not only a self-portrait of his fickle creator; he is an effusive confessor in his own right, calling himself a "Bösewicht, und feige" and confessing to Stella that he has "das Herz nicht dir den Dolch in die Brust zu stoßen, und will dich heimlich vergiften, ermorden!" (FA 1,4:565). There is an echo here of Faust's self-reproach in "Wald und Höhle": "Ihren Frieden mußt' ich untergraben!" (*Faust I*, line 3360 — *Urfaust*, line 1426).[23] It is no idle threat when the Heidenröslein says to the boy who is about to rape her, "ich steche dich, / Daß du ewig denkst an mich." As noted, Friedenthal interprets Goethe's joke to Friederike's father about the Rhine mosquitoes as a metaphor for Goethe's conscience pangs. But conscience pangs for what, precisely? For planning to forsake a young

---

[22] Heinrich Heine, *Geständnisse, Sämtliche Schriften,* 6 vols. (Munich: Carl Hanser Verlag, 1968–75), 6,1:448.

[23] The *Urfaust* was of slightly earlier composition than *Stella*, which was composed between February and April 1775 (MA 1,2:712). "Als Boie am 15. Okt. 1774 in sein Tagebuch eintrug, der Faust sei 'fast fertig' (Gräf II 2, 15), konnte dieser Eindruck der Vollständigkeit wohl nur entstehen, wenn die Szenenfolge von 'Strase' bis 'Kerker' vorlag" (*DjG* 5:477).

"*Faust* war schon vorgeruckt, *Götz von Berlichingen* baute sich nach und nach in meinem Geiste zusammen" (FA 1,14:552–53).

woman who has "given herself" to him, or for having used her from the beginning as a means to an egotistical end?

Elizabeth Powers proposes that in telling his story "Die neue Melusine" to the company at Sesenheim, after Friederike's father, the vicar, had gone to take his afternoon nap, Goethe was issuing a veiled warning to her, an announcement that "that he will . . . behave in the mold of the evil Squire Thornhill, Burchell's attractive but disreputable nephew."[24] "Die neue Melusine" does seem to encode Goethe's doubts about marriage, for eyes not too blinded by love to see. It seems likely that Goethe regarded his time with Friederike as a dalliance and a pastoral interlude from the outset, and, as he himself claims, that he experienced the events at Sesenheim in terms of the characters, categories and topoi of *The Vicar of Wakefield* while he was experiencing them and not only in recalling them forty years later. If so, his "falling in love" with her was a staged affair, an reenactment of an existing text. His wicked comment to Charlotte von Stein that he needed to experience what he was going to depict — that he needed to fall in love with a princess in order to continue his *Tasso* (Charlotte herself not having been princess enough) and to sell his soul to the devil in order to write *Faust* (10 January 1788) — may sanction the thought that in trying on surrogate identities while in Sesenheim he was in search of vicarious social and sexual experience that would enrich him as a writer and that what he sought while there was not so much sex as knowledge — insofar as these can be differentiated. His arrival there in one and then another costume before revealing "himself" reinforces this impression. It is hard to think, in any case, that Goethe ever had any intention of settling permanently into the idyll of Sesenheim or that, in another case, he coveted Kestner's domestic responsibilities, however pleasant the fantasies about replacing him in the arms of Charlotte Buff after sundown. Safely back in Frankfurt he writes: "Es kostete mich wenig, und doch begreif ich nicht wies möglich war" (10 April 1773). Like the narrator of "Die neue Melusine," he knew when to make his escape, and could then lament Friederike's loss at leisure, when compensation was no longer possible. As Schiller's Musikus Miller says to his daughter Luise, who would drown herself in the river and pray for forgiveness as she sank to the bottom: "Du willst den Diebstahl bereuen, sobald du das Gestohlene in Sicherheit weißt" (5.1).

Already *Die Leiden des jungen Werthers* was confessional: "Und nun hab ich [Werthers] Geschichte meine Empfindungen geliehen." And not only his "Empfindungen," but many concrete details, such as his own birthday. He should perhaps not have been as vexed as he later was about the impertinent

---

[24] Elizabeth Powers, "The Artist's Escape from the Idyll: The Relation of Werther to Sesenheim," *Goethe Yearbook* 9 (1999): 65.

inquiries as to whether everything really happened as portrayed in the novel. In his letters to Johann Christian Kestner he avoids sounding as though his passion for Kestner's Charlotte was all-consuming or that he was truly jealous. "Lotte hat nicht von mir geträumt. Das nehm ich sehr übel, und will dass sie diese Nacht von mir träumen soll, diese Nacht, und solls Ihnen noch dazu nicht sagen" (25 September 1772). "Wir redeten wies drüben aussäh über den Wolcken, das weis ich zwar nicht, das weis ich aber, dass unser Herr Gott ein sehr kaltblütiger Mann seyn muss der euch die Lotte lässt. Wenn ich sterbe und habe droben was zu sagen ich hohl sie euch warrlich. Drum betet fein für mein Leben und Gesundheit, waden und Bauch pp und sterb ich, so versöhnt meine Seele mit Trähnen, Opfer, und dergleichen sonst Kästner siehts schief aus" (10 April 1773). A letter to his friend Salzmann in October 1773 does not sound remorseful either — more like a Lovelace who "scored" and pretends to a blasé indifference. He asks Salzmann to forward a copy of *Götz* to "Msll. [Brion]" in hopes "the poor girl may find consolation in the fact that Weislingen gets poisoned." The bravado in these letters may mask Goethe's genuine sense of loss, in the case of Lotte, and, in the case of Friederike, his real guilt — guilt both for his cavalier treatment of her and for his lack of a more heartfelt regret. He must have known that confession is not enough — that in merely excoriating unfaithful lovers in print he was not paying a fair price for having been one, and that, in indicting his fictional stand-ins, he was both compounding his sin and increasing his suffering, in full knowledge of the hope, unworthy in his own eyes, that self-flagellation might preempt condemnation by others. But is anyone deceived: Salzmann and Kestner, we, his readers, or even Goethe himself?

The Frankfurt edition of *Dichtung und Wahrheit* speaks of confession as "das poetologische Prinzip" of Goethe's autobiography (FA 1,14:1147), but what are the purpose and the effects of confession? Is it *really* therapeutic and good for the soul in expelling guilt from one's innermost self, as Goethe claimed,[25] or does it, rather, reinscribe and deepen the guilt, like the ill-fated machine in Kafka's "The Penal Colony"? How can we tell when confession is sincere and when it is simply self-serving, an attempt to reduce the negative balance in the bottom line by claiming one's remorse as a credit? The autobiographies of the Pietists asked the great auditor "über den Wolcken" to accredit the sinner's sincerity against the guilt confessed and seem to have sought understanding from human readers as well. Or, since the very idea of a genre implies repetition, is the use of the confessional genre an attempt to minimize one's crimes by appealing to precedents, in the belief that unoriginal sin is less grievous? Mephisto's purpose in observing that Gretchen is not

---

[25] "Ich fühlte mich, wie nach einer Generalbeichte, wieder froh und frei, und zu einem neuen Leben berechtigt" (FA 1,14:639).

the first woman to pay the price of love — "Sie ist die erste nicht!" but only the latest and nearest token, is to deaden Faust's conscience and help him see that he is not the first hit-and-run lover: "*Ich* bin der erste nicht." In a worse rationalization still, Adelheid's executioner in *Götz von Berlichingen* consoles himself with the words "Du bist nicht der erste" (FA 1,4:246–47).

Cezilie excuses Fernando on the ground that men deceive themselves in deceiving their women: "Wir glauben den Männern! In den Augenblicken der Leidenschaft betrügen sie sich selbst — warum sollten wir nicht betrogen werden?" (FA 1,4:547). But who deceives whom when one deceives oneself? Who has been abandoned by whom if Fernando is "verlassen von mir selbst"? (FA 1.4:561). All such formulations as "self-esteem," "self-projection," "self-representation," "self-criticism," "self-blame," and "self-deception" derive from a reflexive model of "self-consciousness" in which a knowing subject is presumed to be able to observe itself as object and, as an author, free to represent or misrepresent a more or less accurately discerned self. "My purpose is to display to my kind a portrait in every way true to nature," writes Rousseau, "and the man I shall portray will be myself." Frank critiques this model of self-consciousness, and, by extension, the notion that it is in the power of any writer to portray him- or herself. He sees the beginning of German philosophical idealism in Fichte's rejection of "der optischen Metapher der Intro-spektion und der Selbst-wahrnehung."[26] If Frank is right, the idea of self-representation, or, for that matter, *self*-deception, is a trap set for us by language, since the self portrayed or deceived cannot coincide with the self doing the portraying or the deceiving. Every self-portrait, whether critical or honorific, is a caricature, a counterfeit self in place of the original, as Heine notes.[27] The eye I see when I look at myself in the mirror is not the eye doing the looking. Even the most truthful art must be partly a fiction: Dichtung *und* Wahrheit.

Temporarily relieved of his troubles after returning to Stella, Fernando says, "Fernando, kennst du dich noch selbst?" (FA 1,4:553), a self-doubt anticipated in Faust's remark in Gretchen's room: "Armsel'ger Faust! ich kenne dich nicht mehr." A "*Be*kenntnis" presupposes "Selbst*erkenntnis*," but, in fact, says Goethe, "Selbsterkenntnis," is not to be had, at least not through introspection. In "Bedeutende Fördernis durch ein einziges geistreiches Wort" he expresses a tongue-in-cheek suspicion that the ancient admonition, "Erkenne dich selbst" was a trick of secret, conspiratorial priests whose aim was to confuse humankind by leading us "zu einer innern falschen Beschaulichkeit." "Der Mensch kennt nur sich selbst, insofern er die Welt kennt, die er nur in sich und sich nur in ihr gewahr wird" (FA

[26] Franck, *Die Unhintergehbarkeit,* 34.
[27] Ibid, 447.

1,24:595–96).[28] The Harfenspieler in *Wilhelm Meisters Lehrjahre* is preoccupied with himself to the point of being delusional. The "schöne Seele" of book 6 is also guilty of "zu viel Beschäftigung mit sich selbst" (FA 1,9:897).[29] Wilhelm Meister accuses the other actors of being "mit sich selbst unbekannt" (FA 1,9:810)[30] and thinks the ghost who left the veil urging him to flee (697) might better have advised him to turn inward into himself (801). But Wilhelm does not merit the name of actor, in Jarno's opinion, because he can only play "himself" (931). We might quibble that since the "hohles leeres Ich" (812–13) on which the Harfenspieler is focused is inevitably a *Nicht-Ich*, he is technically in compliance with Goethe's dictum that one can gain self-knowledge only via a detour through the world of objects, for which the *Nicht-Ich* ought to be as good a placeholder as anything else. But the point seems to be that a narcissistic self-centeredness is harmful precisely because it involves self-deception. Wilhelm, the *schöne Seele,* and the Harfenspieler are all mistaken in thinking that the self with which they are obsessed is their own real self instead of the effigy and surrogate that it must be.[31] The opposite and right course is implied in Friedrich's famous summation near the end of the novel: "Du kommst mir vor wie Saul, der Sohn Kis, der ausging seines Vaters Eselinnen zu suchen, und ein Königreich fand" (992). We find happiness where we least expect it. And we think where we are not.[32] True confession is impossible.

As a particular kind of misrepresentation, self-deception is a theme in *Stella* and in the young Goethe generally. "Fühlen Sie nicht, daß Sie sich betrügen, sich mit Willen zu Grunde richten?" says Lotte to Werther (FA 1,8:220). Not only does Fernando repeatedly deceive himself, but the nurse who attended to Stella's sick child also succumbed to wishful thinking, believing that her ministrations had succeeded and that the child had been revived. "Ach, und sie hatte sich betrogen!" says Stella. "Tot lag es da, und ich neben ihm in wütender, grasser Verzweiflung" (FA 1,4:548). It is almost as

---

[28] Elsewhere Goethe affirms the possibility of self-knowledge: "Wir handeln eigentlich nur gut, insofern wir mit uns selbst bekannt sind; Dunkelheit über uns selbst läßt uns nicht leicht zu, das Gute recht zu thun, und so ist es denn eben so viel, als wenn das Gute nicht gut wäre" (to Knebel on 8 April 1812: FA 2,7:44).

[29] It is one of Lotte Buff's merits that such as she are "nicht allzu sehr mit sich selbst beschäftigt: sie haben Zeit die Außenwelt zu betrachten, und Gelassenheit genug sich nach ihr zu richten, sich ihr gleich zu stellen" (FA 1,14:590).

[30] Stella too, in the second version, is described as "das schöne, mit sich selbst und der Welt unbekannte Kind" (FA 1,6:543).

[31] Rousseau says of his enemies: "They could draw another man and give him my name, but they could only deceive those who wished to be deceived" (*Confessions,* 590).

[32] Lacan, Jacques. *Ecrits: A Selection,* trans. Alan Sheridan (New York: Norton, 1977), 166.

though Stella had been conditioned by the nurse's mistake to expect deceit everywhere. Thus she responds to Luzie's astonished claim, on seeing Fernando's portrait, that this is the very man with whom she has just eaten lunch with the words: "Du betrügst dich! Du betrügst mich!" Wilhelm, the servant, is ordered to go over and check. "Seh Er," says Luzie, "ob ich mich betrüge" (549). When Cezilie, planning her exit, suggests in act 5 that she and Fernando correspond and remain friends, he says "Wer nicht fühlte, . . . daß du dich selbst betrügst, indem du die marterndste Gefühle, mit einem blendenden eingebildeten Troste schweigen machst. Nein, Cezilie! Mein Weib, nein!" (571). Cezilie's reply is: "Wer betrügt sich? Wer betäubt seine Qualen, durch einen kalten, ungefühlten, ungedachten, vergänglichen Trost? Ja ihr Männer kennt euch" (572), which rather seems to mean: "Ihr Männer kennt euch *nicht*!" We might ask, though, in view of Goethe's own doubts about the possibility of self-knowledge and also with an eye to his later revision of this play: Does the solution proposed by Cezilie: "Eine Wohnung, Ein Bett, und Ein Grab" represent a case of self-deception on Goethe's part, a desire to make himself think he believes what he cannot and a need to propose a solution in which he does not firmly believe and which he later rejected, or does this solution stand as an affirmation of one's right and ability to love more than one person at a time? That the tragedy of the second version is already implicitly present in the first has been claimed by more than one critic.[33] Which ending is the more plausible one?

"Alles, was . . . von mir bekannt geworden, sind nur Bruchstücke einer großen Konfession," said Goethe (FA 1,14:310). Even a fiction is, at the very least, a disclosure of the author's consciousness and frame of mind: "Dichterische Äußerungen sind unwillkürliche Bekenntnisse, in welchen unser Innres sich aufschließt und zugleich unsre Verhältnisse nach außen sich ergeben."[34] The act of confession may be more revealing than what is confessed. And deceptions, even self-deceptions, may unveil deeper truths.

---

[33] E.g. Huber (FA 1,4:992), Pikulik ("Stella," 101), and Beutler (GA 4:1088). Sauder sees the happy ending of the original as an acceptable "denkbaren Schluß einer Fiktion," although "utopisch und ironisch" (MA 1,2:711), and Castle long ago declared "die Handlung [to be] durchaus auf kein tragisches Ende angelegt" (Eduard Castle "*Stella*: Ein Schauspiel für Liebende," 1924, reprint in *Jahrbuch des Wiener Goethe-Vereins* 73 [1969]: 134). "Ein tragischer Ausgang hätte von Anfang an andere Veranstaltungen erfordert," observes Staiger (*Goethe*, 3 vols. [Zürich und Freiburg: Atlantis, 1956–59, 1:186, while Boyle believes that "there is in the play the material of tragedy," but that the play lacks the "sense of the rootedness of its dilemmas, either in the historical data of the national life (as in *Götz* and *Werther*), or in the unasked-for destiny of the literary genius (as in *Clavigo* and *Claudine von Villa Bella*), which gives to the fate of Goethe's other heroes a specific and bitter necessity" (*Goethe: The Poet and the Age*, 1:217).

[34] To King Ludwig I. of Bavaria, 14.4.1829; FA 2,11:108.

Vincent says that "the chief joy [Goethe] derived from writing lay precisely in the concealment of his confessional input."[35] He projects onto Stella his own fondness for games of hide and seek. "Wahrlich man ist doch ein großes Kind," she says, "und ist einem so wohl dabei. — Eben wie die Kinder sich hinter ihr Schürzgen verstecken und rufen Pipp! daß man sie suchen soll!" (FA 1,4:546). This writer's father-in-law used to play a game with his children called: "Here I am, there I go." He would point to where he had ostensibly just gone and the kids would at least start off in the wrong direction. It worked every time. And so it is with the poet's word. "Here I am" Goethe says — or, at least, "there I went." But the feint is as transparent as a mosquito's wing and the pain as temporary as its sting. The truth is the pair of mischievous eyes shining through the ribs of a fan, as in the poem "Wink" from the *West-östlicher Divan.*

Mattenklott speaks of Goethe's technique as an "Erzeugen der Wahrheit durch die imaginative Montage der Gegensätze in ein und dasselbe Bild" and recalls what Walter Benjamin reading Baudelaire later called "dialektische Bilder."[36] Bahr says: "Es ist die Struktur der Goetheschen Ironie: zwei gegensätzliche Begriffe sind zueinander in die Schwebe gebracht und verweisen auf einen dritten."[37] "Nicht Gewißheit und Sicherheit [werden] gegeben, sondern nur ein Wink, sich über die polaren Gegensätze zu erheben."[38] But what must be acknowledged is Goethe's awareness of the conventionality of knowledge and his clear understanding that every representation is informed with antecedents as well as shaped by its conceptual context. Far from flaunting his superior aloofness, his ironic fictions bespeak our common becloudedness and our common reliance on models. Language, which functions only by analogy ("gleichnisweise," FA 1,23,1:244) is a "trübes" medium, like the prism, the atmosphere, or a veil — "der Dichtung Schleier aus der Hand der Wahrheit." Because the would-be conveyors of truth — language or the forms of the imagination — are, indeed, *Eintagsfliegen,* here today and gone tomorrow, truth must be represented "mit Bewußtsein," "Freiheit," and "Selbstkenntnis" or, in other words, "*mit Ironie*" (FA 1,23,1:14). Respect for truth requires that we display our means of representing it, including the clutter in the writer's own consciousness. "Bei jedem aufmerksamen Blick in die Welt [theoretisieren] wir" (FA 1,23,1:14). When Nietzsche said, "gerade Tatsachen gibt es nicht, nur Interpretationen" (*Werke,* 3:903), he was echoing Goethe, who exposes

---

[35] Vincent, "Text as Image," 129.

[36] An "Erzeugen der Wahrheit durch die imaginative Montage der Gegensätze in ein und dasselbe Bild" (Gert Mattenklott, "Faust II," in *Goethe-Handbuch* 2 [Stuttgart: Metzler, 1997]: 391–477; here, 400).

[37] Bahr, *Die Ironie im Spätwerk Goethes,* 106 and passim.

[38] Ibid., 107

the fallacy in every claim of transparent representation, for instance, in the realistic novel or confessional autobiography.

Is the "Ehe zu Dritt" proposed in the first version of *Stella,* then, perhaps just one possible scenario among others, a contingency plan, and one which, because it is only a fantasy, could be replaced by another, just as the story of the Bauerbursch who attempts to rape his mistress and murders his rival or that of Heinrich who becomes psychotic represent alternative scenarios to Werther's suicide in the second version of *Werther?* Did Goethe the more readily acquiesce to Schiller's urging that he provide a more conventional, tragic ending for his "Schauspiel für Liebende" because the framework on which his fictions are mounted is the paradigm?[39]

David John has discovered a third ending to *Stella,* which sends Stella to a nunnery. John shows that this outcome, by an anonymous author, is motivated by the religious ideas present in the drama and by the character portrayal and the diction employed earlier in the play. In experimenting with alternative endings, Goethe anticipates John Fowles in *The French Lieutenant's Woman* and Max Frisch in *Biographie* two centuries later. There has been a lot of argument about which of the endings of *Stella* is truly organic, but I would suggest that the prominence of the theme of substitution within the play provides a tentative and relative sanction for them all.

The tragic ending of *Stella,* second version — now no longer "ein Schauspiel für Liebende" but "Ein Trauerspiel" — is the opposite of a *Liebestod,* but in departing from this paradigm it gives a nod to it nevertheless. "Alles um Liebe, war die Losung meines Lebens. Alles um Liebe," says Stella, "und so nun auch den Tod" (FA 6,1:564). "Großer Gott!" says Cezilie. "Und so stehe ich, im fürchterlichsten Augenblick, zwischen Zweien, die ich nicht trennen und nicht vereinigen kann. *Es fällt in der Ferne ein Schuß.*" Thus does this version yield to the conventional idea that love must be exclusive, after all, that each person may unite with only one single opposite and that, on the other hand — for this is the double bind — the very fact of individuation prevents a perfect union. The dying Stella dispatches both Cezilie and Luzie to the dying Ferdinand and says "*sinkend:* Und ich sterbe allein," which suggests that, if die one must, it is better to die in the arms of one's beloved than all alone. No worse fate than for lovers to die alone, unless it be for them to have to *live* apart. Like a disappointed rhyme, a convention may be most visible when it is transgressed, a paradigm most meaningful when it is announced and then left unfilled.

---

[39] Goethe viewed monogamy itself as a matter of convention: "[es] kam zur Sprache, daß nach unsern Sitten, die ganz eigentlich auf Monogamie gegründet sind, das Verhältnis eines Mannes zu zwei Frauen, besonders wie es hier zur Erscheinung kommt, nicht zu vermitteln sei und sich daher vollkommen zur Tragödie qualifiziere" (FA 1,19:684).

6: Intrusions of the Supernatural

WITH THE FELICITOUS OXYMORON "*Natural Supernaturalism*" Meyer H. Abrams captures a coincidence of opposites constitutive of Romanticism.[1] Not only do nature and the natural have pride of place on Romanticism's scale of values, but its fascination with the supernatural is itself natural. As Goethe enjoyed pointing out, every manifestation of *culture* is natural. Dress, manners, habits of mind and behavior, traditions, rituals, language and its rules, and the generic and thematic conventions of literature, religion, and philosophy are all natural.

The love-death theme is especially at home — it is not a "guest" — in Goethe's ballads. These ballads transgress many boundaries of theme, style, genre, and levels of abstraction as well as the threshold between "high and low culture." In "Bedeutende Fördernis durch ein einziges geistreiches Wort," Goethe names several ballads that illustrate how he incorporated traditional material into his consciousness and let it ripen there toward a purer form and a more definite re-presentation: "die *Braut von Korinth, den Gott und die Bajadere,* den *Grafen und die Zwerge,* den *Sänger und die Kinder,* und . . . *Paria*" (FA 1,24:596). He borrowed the ending of *Clavigo* from an English ballad and "ganze Stellen" from Beaumarchais. The image of absorbing, incubating and re-presenting an inherited theme, such as the theme of the Prodigal Son in *Werther,* is a good illustration of the "inside-outside" dichotomy, which Derrida regards as the basis of all other binary oppositions.[2] A boundary is crossed when a wayfarer enters the terrain of the mother and child in "Der Wandrer." In Roman Elegy VII (the numbering

---

[1] Meyer H. Abrams, *Natural Supernaturalism: Tradition and Revolt in Romantic Literature* (New York: W. W. Norton, 1971).

[2] Derrida, *Dissemination,* trans. Barbara Johnson (Chicago: U of Chicago P, 1981), 103. "Nichts ist drinnen, nichts ist draußen; / Denn was innen, das ist außen" (Goethe, "Epirrhema"). Contemplating Gretchen at her window, Michelsen remarks: "Der Mensch an der Grenze seiner Behausung . . . erfährt die Spannung zwischen Innen und Außen als Sehnsucht, als Nicht-Erfülltsein seiner gegenwärtigen Existenz im begrenzten Bereich seiner Lebenswelt. Bei Gretchen hat sich dieser Zustand zur Ex-Zentrik radikalisiert, zu einer Ausgerichtetheit ihres ganzen Wesens aus sich heraus, nach einem außerhalb ihrer liegenden Bezugspunkt" (Peter Michelson, *Im Banne Fausts: Zwölf Faust-Studien* [Würzburg: Königshausen & Neumann, 2000], 85). "Denn das ist der Natur Gehalt," writes Goethe in one of his *Zahme Xenien,* "daß außen gilt was innen galt" (FA 1,2:677).

varies in different editions) another wanderer apologizes for entering the house of Zeus: "Empfänget / Dein ambrosisches Haus, Jupiter Vater, den Gast?" (FA 1,1:410–11), but a boundary is also crossed in literary translation, as in Herder's translation of the Scottish ballad "Edward," with which Goethe's "Erlkönig" shares the theme of conflict between a parent and a child or in his translation of the Danish "Ellerkonge's Tochter," which inspired "Erlkönig."

A book's chapter, too, has traversable borders and tentacles reaching beyond its boundaries, since similarities and differences reside at different levels and any individual can belong to several classes or categories at the same time. The nix of "Der Fischer" is as much a *femme fatale* as the bride of Corinth, and both might have been dealt with in chapter 4 or, as ballads with traditional themes, in chapter 3.[3] Since "Der Fischer," "Erlkönig," and "Die neue Melusine" all depict an intrusion of the supernatural into the human realm, I consider them here rather than there. But is the Erlkönig first and foremost an "homme fatal," an alien intruder, or, rather, a sexual predator, alien or not? Is he an external threat or an internal one? Does the poem depict a case of the predation on children by adults or is it best grouped with other Enlightenment attacks on superstition? Is the tiny princess in "Die neue Melusine" a *femme fatale,* an alien, or, like the nix in "Der Fischer," an icon of the traditional metonymic and sexist association of woman with water, water with drowning, and drowning with the submergence of selfhood and identity in an encompassing, chaotic all? Should "supernatural" predators like the Erlkönig or the revenant in "Die Braut von Korinth" be separated from "natural" ones like the youth in "Heidenröslein" and from elemental ones like the "Erdgeist" in *Faust* and the nix in "Der Fischer"? What are the important differences between the Erlkönig and Zeus in "Ganymed," or Zeus and Shiva (Mahadöh) in "Der Gott und die Bajadere"? Whether Mephistopheles is *the* devil or just *a* devil or only an urbane cavalier sharing the quality of "humoristische Anmut" with the mythical or supernatural figures in the most playful ballads is a question requiring attention to the matter of rhetorical distance and the very large issue of literature and belief.[4]

[3] Quoting the last lines of Goethe's "Der Fischer," Jung writes: "Die Nixe ist eine noch instinktivere Vorstufe eines zauberischen weiblichen Wesens, welches wir als Anima bezeichnen. Es können auch Sirenen, Melusinen, Waldfrauen, Huldinnen und Erlkönigstöchter, Lamien und Sukkuben sein, welche Jünglinge betören und ihnen das Leben aussaugen" (C. G. Jung, "Über die Archetypen des kollektiven Unbewußten," 1934, in *Gesammelte Werke,* 20 vols. [Stuttgart: Rascher, 1958–1994; reprint, Olten und Freiburg im Breisgau: Walter-Verlag, 1966–1994], 9,1:34).

[4] In fairy tales this "scherzhaft-ernste" quality (Hans Rudolph Vaget, "'Mäßig boshaft': Fausts Gefährte: Goethes Mephistopheles im Lichte der Aufklärung," *Goethe-Jahrbuch* 118 [2001]: 234–46; here, 246) comes "aus der Verbindung des

What is inside a national culture and what outside? Is Goethe's adaptation of Herder's (mis)translation of the "Ellerkonge's Tochter" a more integral part of German literature, because of the closer linguistic and cultural relationship between things Danish and German, than his appropriation of themes from the Persian poet Hafiz in the *West-östlicher Divan*? Is the domestic divinity Mahadöh in "Der Gott und die Bajadere" "a stranger god" (Nietzsche's term), and does Goethe's story of his intrusion represent yet another infusion of foreign culture into Goethe's work — one repeated in the borrowings in the *West-östlicher Divan* from Persia and in *Elpenor* and *Chinesische-deutsche Jahreszeiten* from China? Is the receiver of alien cultural material better viewed as a victim or as a parasite? There are both benign and malignant donors as well as both benign and malignant extractors of blood, semen, blessings and culture. Who is the giver and who the receiver in the symbiosis of the ivy and the elm?

A. Above and Below, The Wet and the Dry: "Die neue Melusine," "Der Fischer," Women and Water

The legendary Melusine, an example of the "Erlösungsbedürftigkeit der elementarischen Frau,"[5] is mentioned in several texts by Goethe.[6] Although he told his story "Die neue Melusine" to the company at the Brion household in Sesenheim while visiting from Strassburg, he did not write it down for another thirty-seven years (FA 1,14:485; see also HA 9:785). Except for its title, which like "Der neue Paris" and "Der neue Amadis" acknowledges

Unmöglichen mit dem Gemeinen, des Unerhörten mit dem Gewöhnlichen" and Goethe says he sought to produce this effect in "Die neue Melusine" (*The Foreign Quarterly Review*, 38, no. 1 [July 1827]: 129–31; FA 1,22:711).

[5] Melanie Unseld, *"Man Töte Dieses Weib!" Weiblichkeit und Tod in der Musik der Jahrhundertwende* (Stuttgart and Weimar: Metzler, 2001), 53.

[6] As a boy Goethe picked up a copy of the ancient story of Melusine among other "sales" books "für ein paar Kreutzer" (FA 1,10:1206). Melusine is mentioned in *Werther* (May 12, 1771), in the *Unterhaltungen deutscher Ausgewanderten* (FA 1,9:1036), and in *Dichtung und Wahrheit* (FA 1,14:505). Goethe wrote to Charlotte von Stein: "Ich strich um mein verlassen Häusgen, wie Melusine um das ihre wohin sie nicht zurückkehren sollte, und dachte an die Vergangenheit von der ich nichts verstehe, und an die Zukunft von der ich nichts weis" (17 November 1782).
    The Danish "Erlkönigs Tochter" and Goethe's "Erlkönig," "are alike in that they are based on the belief, common in northern mythology, in elves, who, as cloud or storm spirits, were feared because of their habit of stealing children and young men in order to increase their race" (James Boyd, *Notes to Goethe's Poems*, 2 vols. [Oxford: Basil Blackwell, 1944], 1:173). In "Die neue Melusine" the tiny princess tries to keep the narrator in her realm in order to preserve, if not increase, her race, although, of course, there is nothing malevolent about her.

older stories to which he is indebted, and Goethe's reference to its heroine in a letter to Schiller, as ein "undenisches Pygmäenweibchen" (7 August 1797), Goethe's story contains few reminders of its aquamarine genealogy — internally only the fact that *his* Melusine belongs to the "Geschlecht der Nixen und Gnomen" (FA 1,10:642) and the narrator's revealing refusal to accept his beloved's admonition about too much wine with the words: "Wasser ist für die Nixen!" — a sly wink from the author to the reader (FA 1,10:645).[7] A traveling barber meets a beautiful woman and falls in love with her. She places a dainty "Kästchen" in his custody and asks him to keep it in a separate room whenever he stops for the night. The barber is rescued from one scrape after another by his beloved, who always seems to appear out of nowhere. One night he sees light shining from the not fully closed box and, peeking through the opening, sees her in miniature form and in a miniature world. Demanding an explanation, he learns that she is a princess in an ancient race of dwarfs which is threatened with extinction and can only be restored through her union with a human. Rather than lose her, the barber agrees to be shrunk down to her size and marry her, but he soon feels regret, regains his previous dimensions, and sells the now useless "Kästchen." The story has been read as reflecting Goethe's fear of marriage, and as a forewarning to Friederike.

Like "Erlkönig," "Die *neue* Melusine" tells of the intrusion of an extranatural being into the human realm. It is the story of her romance with the young man she has chosen as a mate. The Erlkönig, too, takes the boy back to his own supernatural dwelling. "Der Fischer" might seem to invert the scenario, inasmuch as the fisherman's descent into the "deep heaven" where the nix and her brood are at home is "halb" voluntary, but in all of these cases the destination is an exotic elsewhere, and in each case transliminal communication takes place. Woman — she who lacks boundaries — is the agent of such border crossings, the maternal *Wunderschoß* of night (*Faust,* 8665), a vessel of mixing, mingling and transformation. This is why such agents of engulfment as "the Phorcides (7969–8033) or Graeae of the Classical Walpurgisnight," who "live 'Versenkt in Einsamkeit und stillste Nacht,'"[8] are conventionally female. In a paralipomenon to *Faust* Satan instructs: "Euch giebt es zwey Dinge / So herrlich und groß / Das glänzende Gold / Und der weibliche Schoos. / Das eine verschaffet / Das

[7] "Herrn Winfreds Meerfahrt" by Strachwitz has an encounter of "Held und Nixe" (Rupert Hirschenauer, "Johann Wolfgang Goethe: Erlkönig," in *Wege zum Gedicht* 2 (Interpretation von Balladen), ed. Rupert Hirschenauer and Albrecht Weber [Munich: Schnell & Steiner, 1963; repr, 1964], 159–68; here, 160).

[8] Stuart Atkins, *Goethe's Faust: A Literary Analysis* (Cambridge, MA: Harvard UP, 1958), 181.

andre verschlingt."[9] Like Wedekind's Lulu, woman is the "*Erd*geist." One may even wonder if the *Erdgeist* of *Faust I,* as the *anima mundi* or *anima terrae,*[10] is not female and whether "his" words "Geburt und Grab / Ein ewiges Meer" (504–5) is not a self-reference — a possibility masked by the masculine gender of the noun *Geist* but made visible by the semiotic field of the metaphors employed.[11] Jane Brown finds that "the Mothers are . . . an equivalent for the earth spirit adapted to the changed focus and more abstract character of Part II."[12] What Faust seeks in every re-immersion is transformation and regeneration, which is also the goal of Homunculus,[13] Faust's stand-in, in the pageantry of the Classical Walpurgisnacht, as, "von Pulsen der Liebe gerührt" (8468), he plunges into the water and breaks his phial against the conch of Galatee, extinguishing his flame in order to unite with his aqueous opposite and advance toward rebirth in a higher form.

In German literature, the link between women and water on the one hand and the male's desire for and dread of love and death on the other is often personified by the maiden Lorelei, who in numerous and various incarnations beckons seductively to the Romantic male self,[14] as well as by naiads and other water sprites — the "lovesick and cruel female[s] who [are] out to lure a man down into [their] abode."[15] At the head of this tradition is

---

[9] "Paralipomena" to *Faust,* H P50, FA 1,7,1:553 — spoken by Satan.

[10] "The picture of nature as being both womb and grave is . . . common in Renaissance poetry, and familiar from Spenser, Shakespeare, and Milton" (Harold Jantz, *Goethe's Faust as a Renaissance Man* [Princeton, NJ: Princeton UP, 1951], 85). See also 84, 88, 92.

[11] As to gender, cf. the *Fürst der Welt* who becomes *Frau Welt* and, in the masquerade of *Faust II,* Geiz, who, as Avaritia, was once female but is now "männlichen Geschlechts" (5665) and played by Mephistopheles.

[12] Jane Brown, *Goethe's "Faust": The German Tragedy* (Ithaca: Cornell UP, 1986), 163.

[13] "'Inside a woman,' notes Lawrence Lipking, 'is also where men take form' (128)." Quoted in Helen Sword, "Leda and the Modernists," *PMLA* 107 (1992): 305–18; here, 310. Cf. Rilke's "Leda": "und wurde wirklich Schwan in ihrem Schoß."

[14] Lortzing's romantic opera *Undine* is based on the story by Friedrich de la Motte-Fouqué. The Rhein maidens in *Rheingold* and *Götterdämmerung* are mermaids of a sort, and a mermaid occurs in Weber's *Oberon,* based on Wieland's poem. Dvorak's Rusalka desires to become human and marry the Prince. When the Prince abandons Rusalka for the Foreign Princess, both he and Rusalka die, but his repentance ensures the water nymph a human soul.

[15] "Psychoanalysis is accustomed to the symbolism of water as representing birth, and [Marie] Bonaparte interprets . . . 'bottomless lakes,' . . . as relating to those waters in which we have truly once resided, the amniotic fluid. That water, in all these tales, is a feminine element, cannot be doubted: only feminine creatures emerge from it, or lure into it. But furthermore it is the darkness and the mystery, the impenetrable se-

Goethe's "Der Fischer." Heine's is the most famous of the Lorelei poems, but Brentano's "Lore Lay" precedes his, and the figure appears in the work of countless minor poets, as well as in Mörike's "Schiffer- und Nixen-Märchen" and "Die schlimme Greth und der Königssohn," and in Fouqué's *Undine,* whose heroine murders her mortal husband Huldbrand with a kiss when he denies their marriage and tries to marry the daughter of a Duke.[16] The theme is present in the last song of Schubert's setting of Müller's *Die schöne Müllerin* where the brook sings a lullaby to the miller boy who has sought solace in her depth. The river nymphs sing to Faust: "Am besten geschäh' dir / Du legtest dich nieder, Erholtest im Kühlen / Ermüdete Glieder, / Genössest der immer / Dich meidenden Ruh; / Wir säuseln, wir rieseln, / Wir flüstern dir zu" (7263–70). Faust's temptation from the beginning is to immerse himself in a liquid opposite — "in deinem Tau gesund mich baden" (397) — and in his apostrophe to the moonlight in the scene "Nacht." The new day that Faust salutes upon resisting the allure of suicide is a "new shore" (701), a refuge from the boundless liquid in which he had been on the verge of dissolving into nothingness (cf. 719).

Stories of Melusine conventionally involve a woman wronged — as in "Lore Lay" and in Andersen's story of the little mermaid. The Lorelei's predations, moreover, are involuntary; she is victim of an irresistible compulsion, like Goethe's Bride of Corinth, or of her own charms, like Brentano's Lore Lay. The femme fatale . . . "is usually not subject to her conscious will, . . . she is not the subject of power but its *carrier.*"[17] Lore Lay is *not* a revenant and was betrayed by her lover, not sacrificed by her mother, as was Goethe's Bride, but both females destroy their lovers. Lore Lay then atones by diving from her rocky perch into the Rhine, while the vampire of "Bride"

cret, that are feminine and ever alluring to man; they are ever connected with danger and with death — the ultimate return to the Mother" (Wolfgang Lederer, *The Fear of Women* [New York: Grune & Stratton, 1968], 235).

[16] "Could it perhaps be that [the story of the Lorelei] is not a fairy tale at all, but rather the melody of love and death of one of those androgynous beings from the realm of the Undines, Melusines, and sirens, upon whom the romantics could never sate themselves — 'outsiders of the second sex'?" (Erika Tunner, "The Lore Lay — a Fairy Tale from Ancient Times?" in *European Romanticism: Literary Cross-Currents, Modes, and Models,* ed. Gerhart Hoffmeister [Detroit: Wayne State UP, 1990], 269–86; here, 269). This is a reference to Hans Mayer's "Das zweite Geschlecht und seine Aussenseiter," in *Aussenseiter* [Frankfurt am Main: Suhrkamp, 1981], 33). "Maurice Genevoix meditates on the question of the 'German psyche' in his novel *Lorelei* (1978)" (Tunner, "The Lore Lay," 269). In another work, an "undine," who reminds the protagonist of Goethe's Mignon, almost drowns Pechorin, who can't swim (Lermontov, *A Hero of Our Time,* trans. Vladimir Nabokov & Dimitri Nabokov [New York: Doubleday Anchor, 1958], 73–80).

[17] Mary Ann Doane, *Femmes Fatales: Feminism, Film Theory, Psychoanalysis* (New York and London: Routledge, 1991), 2.

asks that she and her "fiancé" be burned on a funeral pyre. Eichendorff's Lo-relei, in "Waldgespräch," would prefer not to harm the knight who happens on her in the forest, but the compulsion to avenge her injury overrides the desire to spare her innocent prey. The tradition is seldom without the impli-cation that the man *desires* to be destroyed, as in the "Song by the Sea" by Laurie Lee, whose composition may have had an onomastic motivation. In this poem the speaker longs for submergence at the hands of the enchant-ress: "Girl of green waters, liquid as lies, / . . . From my attic brain and pris-oned eyes / Draw me and drown me now" (15).[18]

Kurth-Voigt points out that in the verse preface to the third edition of Heine's *Buch der Lieder* (1839), as earlier in Eichendorff and Mérimée, "a statue of a beautiful woman . . . comes alive and enters into a potentially le-thal relationship with a young man."[19] In *Le Rhin* (1840–41) Hugo remarks that "l'oréade de Lurley, jadis courtisée par tant de princes et de comtes my-thologiques, commence à s'enrouer et à s'ennuyer"[20] "For Gérard de Nerval, *Lorely: Souvenirs d'Allemagne* (1852), she becomes once again a symbol of all seduction, whereby he anticipates Jean Lorrain, alias Paul Duval," whose prose poem "Loreley" (1897) is based on Violetta's Lore Lay song in Bren-tano's *Godwi*. Apollinaire published a "Lorely' in the cycle 'Rhénanes' in his volume of poetry *Alcools* (1903).[21] As Tunner notes, the Lorelei is "une chanson du mal aimé."

The Semiotics of Drowning

The story of Melusine links women and water as agents of dissolution and transmutation.[22] The sirens and the Charybdis in the *Odyssey* — the latter a

---

[18] Cf. Shakespeare, *The Comedy of Errors,* 3.2: S. Ant: "O, train me not, sweet mermaid, with thy note, / To drown me in thy sister's flood of tears. / Sing, siren, for thyself, and I will dote. / Spread o'er the silver waves thy golden hairs, / And as a bed I'll take them, and there lie / And in that glorious supposition think / He gains by death that hath such means to die. / Let Love, being light, be drowned if she sink!"

[19] Lieselotte E. Kurth-Voigt, "La Belle Dame sans Merci": The Revenant as Femme Fatale in Romantic Poetry," in Hoffmeister, *European Romanticism,* 247–67; here, 260.

[20] Victor Hugo, *Le Rhin: Lettres a un Ami, Oeuvres complètes, 28* (Paris: La Librairie Ollendorff, 1906), 136.

[21] Examples from Erika Tunner, "The Lore Lay," 283.

[22] "Love and death, eroticism and time, are related to one another in the symbol of the Rhine. The symbolic fusion of woman and water is based on old European tradition, and yet it only takes on its especially uncanny aspect in the nineteenth century" (Tunner, "Lore Lay," 272).

swirling female whirlpool who sucks sailors into the sea — mermaids,[23] nixes, Undines and water nymphs (as in the story of Hylas, companion of Hercules during the argonautic expedition) are interchangeable personifications of the same equation of woman with water. They are "seductive and impenetrable female representative[s] of the dark and magic underwater world from which our life comes and in which we cannot live."[24] To be immersed in them is to forfeit one's characteristic form — to re-enter primeval chaos and cease to appear as an identifiable individual. The alchemistic *Aurea Catena Homeri* and the *Opus Mago-Cabbalisticum* by Welling, both of which young Goethe read, speak of the "chaotisches Urwasser."[25] Ursula, in the movie "The Little Mermaid," "is portrayed . . . with extremely gynephobic imagery: as she sings to Ariel about the construction of femininity, for example, there is one scene in which Ursula launches her body toward the 'camera lens' and engulfs it with the dark void located in the middle of her octopus legs."[26]

What ails Isolde, in Gottfried von Strassburg's triple pun on "l'amour," "la mort," and "la mer"[27] is *"Lameir"* — "'*Lameir* is what distresses me,' answered Love's falcon, Isolde, 'it is *lameir* that so oppresses me, *lameir* it is that pains me so.'"[28] Water, the formless element, is a familiar death symbol. A person's immersion in water, has come to symbolize the destruction of his

[23] A sailor of Henry Hudson's saw one on June 15, 1608; Hudson's ship escaped harm, but to see a mermaid is generally unlucky, and to listen to her song is to risk both body and soul (Gwen Benwell and Arthur Waugh, *Sea Enchantress: The Tale of the Mermaid and Her Kin* [1961, repr. New York: Citadel, 1965], 95). Female figures associated with water constitute a sub-class of the *femme fatale*. "In Nina Auerbach's analysis of the Victorian 'myth of womanhood,' the mermaid submerges herself in order to conceal her power: 'the mermaid exemplified the secrecy and spiritual ambiguity of woman's ascribed powers. Fathomless and changing, she was an awesome threat to her credulous culture'" (Lynda Hart, *Fatal Women: Lesbian Sexuality and the Mark of Aggression* [Princeton NJ: Princeton UP, 1994], 35; note regarding Nina Auerbach, *Woman and the Demon* [Cambridge: Harvard UP, 1982], 7–8).

[24] Dorothy Dinnerstein, *The Mermaid and the Minotaur: Sexual Arrangements and Human Malaise* (New York: Harper Colophon, 1977), 5.

[25] Wachsmuth, Andreas B. "'Sich verselbsten' und 'entselbstigen' — Goethes Altersformel für die rechte Lebensführung," *Goethe (Jahrbuch der Goethe-Gesellschaft)*, 11 (1949): 263–92; here, 268.

[26] Kate Copeland in a term paper, Spring 2000, 12.

[27] Brangäne, on hearing that Tristan and Isolde have drunk the love potion, says, "Ah, Tristan and Isolde, this draught will be your death!" (Gottfried von Strassburg, *Tristan*, trans. A. T. Hatto, [1960; rev. ed. Harmondsworth: Penguin, 1967], 195). The potion has the immediate effect of transforming the erstwhile adversaries into the most passionate of lovers.

[28] Gottfried, *Tristan*, 199.

or her characteristic form and thus death, as in Christian baptism (preliminary to "rebirth" as a new person). Women and Water both represent the termini of life — origin and destiny. Both have the power to release and recollect, like a fisherman casting out a lure and reeling in his catch.[29] The mermaid is a marine *femme fatale* and is typically portrayed as contemplating herself in a mirror. Water is also a "symbol of . . . consciousness — in its capacity to reflect the formal reality of the visible world."[30] As Goethe pointed out, however, even mirrors falsify, through inversion (FA 1,13:306).

To die in water is to reenter the fluid medium from which we all issued forth, to return to the womb and be welcomed back into the enfolding element of the sea. This is why, at the end of *Death in Venice*, Gustav Aschenbach, who sought "refuge from the thronging manifold shapes of his fancy in the bosom of the simple and vast," is beckoned out to sea — the "oceanic," in Freud's term[31] — by Tadzio, a "charming boy" bearing attributes of both Eros and Thanatos (such as the crossed legs). Mann's Little Sir Friedemann finds death in the water at the feet of the brutal Gerda von Rinnlingen, "den Spiegel des Wassers in ihren Augen." In Wagner's *Der fliegende Holländer* Senta and the Dutchman die and arise out of the water together in a classic *Liebestod,* as do Sardanapalus and Myrrha at the end of Byron's drama. Of Klein's drowning, in *Klingsor,* Hesse writes, "Seit dem Moment . . . wo er sich mit ganzem Wollen, mit ganzem Verzicht auf jedes Wollen, mit ganzer Hingabe hatte vom Bootsrand fallen lassen, *in den Schoß der Mutter,* . . . hatte das Sterben keine Bedeutung mehr." Drownings occur at the end of *La nouvelle Héloïse, Die Komödie der Verführung* by Schnitzler, *The Mill on the Floss, Romeo und Julia auf dem Dorf,* and Grass's *Katz und Maus* (when Mahlke, who aims first his prayers and then his tank gun at the Virgin Mary's womb, returns to the belly of the sunken mine-sweeper). At the end of Kate Chopin's *The Awakening,* Edna commits suicide by drowning: "The touch of the sea is sensuous, enfolding the body in its soft close embrace." Condemned by his father, Kafka's Georg Bendemann drowns himself. In *Possession* A. S. Byatt recreates Virginia Wolfe's suicide by sending the lesbian lover of Christabel LaMotte, author of *The Fairy Melusina,* to her death in the river.

---

[29] Cf. Barbara Ehrenreich, foreword to Theweleit, *Male Fantasies,* trans. Stephan Conway, with Erica Carter and Chris Turner (Minneapolis, MN: U of Minnesota P, 1987), 1:xiii, xv. On the connection between woman and water, see Theweleit 249–94. Cf. Eliade, *The Forge and The Crucible,* trans. Stephen Corrin (1962; New York: Harper Torchbook, 1971), 41.

[30] J. E. Cirlot, *A Dictionary of Symbols,* trans. Jack Sage (New York: Philosophical Library, 1962), 201.

[31] On the "oceanic," see Freud, *Das Unbehagen in der Kultur, SA,* 9:197–98.

Drownings in Goethe

The lines "Wenn in öder Winternacht / [Der Fluß] vom Tode schwillt" in "An den Mond," probably written in the same year as "Der Fischer" (1778), are commonly understood as reflecting the death by drowning of Christel von Laßberg on 17 January 1778, an event the more affecting to Goethe because the young suicide had a copy of *Die Leiden des jungen Werthers* in her bag. Werther empathizes with a young woman who, jilted by her lover, sought comfort in "einem rings umfangenden Tode" (12 August 1771). At the end of *Ossian* the principal characters all drown, one after the other. Shortly after reading to Lotte from his translation of Ossian, Werther resists the urge to plunge into the flood, which has inundated sites of his former intimacy with her: "Ach, mit offenen Armen stand ich gegen den Abgrund und atmete hinab! hinab! und verlor mich in der Wonne, meine Qualen, meine Leiden da hinabzustürmen! dahinzubrausen wie die Wellen!" (12 December 1772). Kaempfer notes Werther's equation of Lotte's eyes with the sea, "das alte Synonym fürs Weibliche."[32]

Gretchen drowns her baby in *Faust*. The drownings and near drownings in *Die Wahlverwandtschaften* — the boy who almost drowns on Ottilie's birthday and the girl in the inset novella "Die wunderlichen Nachbarskinder," as well as the drowning of Charlotte's child while in the care of Ottilie — led Wilhelm von Humboldt to regard "das häufige ins Wasser Fallen und die wiederholten Rettungsversuche" as "eine Sonderbarkeit" of the novel.[33] There are drownings and near drownings in *Wilhelm Meister* as well, among them Wilhelm's story in *Die Wanderjahre* about his youthful love for the son of the fisherman, who, with four other boys, drowns while collecting crabs for the pastor's wife (FA 1,10:544–49).[34] A strong swimmer, the fisherman's son could have saved himself, had the others not dragged him down (548). Since the youthful lovers, after swimming together, admire each other's naked bodies and seal their eternal friendship "unter den feurigsten Küssen" (545), this text has been interpreted as proof of Goethe's (latent) homosexuality.[35]

---

[32] Wolfgang Kämpfer, "Das Ich und der Tod in Goethe's *Werther*," in *Goethes "Werther": Kritik und Forschung*, ed. Hans-Peter Hermann (Darmstadt: Wissenschaftliche Buchgesellschaft, 1994), 278.

[33] Letter from Wilhelm von Humboldt to Friedrich Gottlieb Welcker, 23 December 1809 in *Die Wahlverwandtschaften: Eine Dokumentation der Wirkung von Goethes Roman 1808–1832*, ed. Heinz Härtl (Berlin: Akademie-Verlag, 1983), 88.

[34] See H. M. Waidson, "Death by Water: or, the Childhood of Wilhelm Meister," *Modern Language Review* 56 (1961): 44–53.

[35] K. R. Eissler, *Goethe: A Psychoanalytic Study 1775–1786*, 2 vols. (Detroit: Wayne State UP, 1963), 2:1451.

Seekers of death by drowning share a lack, something insufficient about their mortal existence, and a desire for relief and plenitude in the cool, liquid non-self. For the movement from plurality or duality into identity, the idea of drowning is ready to hand — the absorption of the individual into an encompassing liquid female medium. You can drown in a woman, who to a man is comprehensible only as a vast, unsurveyable sea. "Ah! quand les femmes écrivent," wrote Jules Barbey d'Aurevilly in *Les Bas-bleus* (1878), "c'est comme quand elles parlent! Elles ont la faculté inondante; et comme l'eau, elles sont incompréhensibles."[36] An individual's absorption into something larger — whether a sexual opposite, a social group, one's work when in "flow," or a class-creating *Vorstellungsart,* depends on the idea of identity and difference. To have an identity is to be separate, to stand apart as an identifiable or self-identifiable essence, while to identify with something is to traverse the boundary between oneself and something else. Either individuation or identification is an event and involves the idea of time. Only a recollection of twoness can make oneness appear as the result of a movement, and vice versa. Indeed, unity makes sense only in contrast with plurality or, at least, with duality.[37]

B. "Der Fischer"'

In an early Rococo poem of Goethe's ("Rettung," early 1770s), a young man in despair over the fickleness of his flame stands on a river bank with thoughts of suicide. About to plunge into the stream, he hears another pleasant female voice warning him of the water's depth and is saved. He owes his life to the pretty new acquaintance, but won't she be his happiness as well? She winsomely casts down her eyes, kisses follow — and all thought of death is postponed.

It may seem irreverent to compare this trifle with "Der Fischer," a ballad esteemed for its unsettling evocation of the magic power of nature. Yet the protagonist in both cases is a young man with a void in his heart, and at the water's edge each encounters a female figure who becomes instrumental to the man's fulfillment. Both poems show the attraction of drowning for an

[36] From Howard Bloch, *Medieval Misogyny and the Invention of Western Romantic Love* (Chicago: U of Chicago P, 1991), 16.

[37] But "Hölderlin und Novalis . . . werden zeigen, daß, wenn einmal eine Dualität von Momenten in die Dimension des Selbstbewußtseins eingeführt ist, ihre Präreflexivität nicht mehr erklärt werden kann. Niemals könnte eine Zweiheit als Grund von strenger Identität aufgeboten werden. Diese Kritik setzt eine Radikalisierung der Bedeutung des Terms 'Identität' voraus, denn Identität ist in der Tradition durchaus als Relation bestimmt worden" (Manfred Frank, *Selbstbewußtseins-theorien von Fichte bis Sartre,* ed. Manfred Frank [Frankfurt am Main: Suhrkamp, 1991], 450).

aching heart. But whereas the jilted lover in the first poem is saved by his new acquaintance, the fisherman in the second is lured down into the water and never seen again.

Goethe later downplayed the significance of "Der Fischer." "Es ist ja in dieser Ballade bloß das Gefühl des Wassers ausgedrückt, das Anmutige, was uns im Sommer lockt, uns zu baden; weiter liegt nichts darin" (E, 67). Goethe's claim that "Der Fischer" is not suited for pictorial representation is rather an understatement. The fisherman encounters not just water (and water signifies more than merely a means of cooling off and refreshing oneself) but also the alluring female who emerges out of the water, assailing him with a reproach and then cajoling him down into the water with her.

Scholars have seen in Goethe's ballad a rendition into folk poetry of his own susceptibility to the magic of nature and to water as a specific manifestation of "Naturmagie." It is thus a "naturmagische Ballade."[38] Critics have experienced little difficulty in getting from the inanimate world, "die außersittlichen Kräfte der Natur"[39] to the animate and ethically informed one of myth and *Märchen,* from the poet's susceptibility to nature as naked, inhuman and "magic" power (the antithesis to human culture) to the fisherman's surrender to the blandishments of the nix. The usual stratagem is to identify the poet with his creature, Goethe with the fisherman, and then, via a traditional metonymy, to accept the mermaid, or river nix, as a personification of water. Gundolf accredits Goethe with tying "unmittelbar" into the tradition of the folk ballad.[40] Zimmermann draws out some of the ethical and psychological implications that always burden personifications and concludes that in transforming a natural world vulnerable to human exploitation into a fairy tale realm that ensnares the human heart Goethe both reveals and masters his own vulnerability to the magic of nature.[41] Trunz too sees nature as the subject of the poem and stresses the novelty of Goethe's treatment of it. Goethe's susceptibility to the allure of water is on record in a letter to Charlotte von Stein (19 January 1778). The assumptions underlying the best-known interpretations of this ballad are: (a) that the mermaid stands for water; (b) that water stands for nature; (c) that the fisherman stands for Goethe; (d) that Goethe was nakedly and peculiarly open to nature *qua* na-

---

[38] A term coined by Paul Ludwig Kämpchen, *Die numinose Ballade,* Mnemosyne 4 (Bonn: Ludwig Röhrscheid, 1930) as an indicator of the special qualities of a small group of Goethe's early ballads, including this poem, "Erlkönig" and "Gesang der Elfen." The term has become common among critics.

[39] Werner Zimmermann, "Johann Wolfgang Goethe: Der Fischer," in Hirschenauer, *Wege zum Gedicht* 2:154–58; here, 154.

[40] Gundolf, *Goethe* (1930; repr., Darmstadt: Wissenschaftliche Buchgesellschaft, 1963), 507.

[41] Zimmermann, "Der Fischer," 156, 158.

ture (i.e. as opposed to being alert to the symbolic significance of nature); (e) that, unspoiled by prevailing literary fashion, Goethe had a natural receptivity to myth and folk poetry; and (f) that in this poem raw experience is composed and compressed — "verdichtet"[42] — into myth and thus transmuted, alienated, and aesthetically mastered in a brilliant example of "gaiety transfiguring all that dread."[43] But this was not simply an unmediated, personal response to an element *qua* element or a historically unprepared act of natural and naive poetic self-expression. The meeting between man and mermaid incorporates multiple legacies of form and content.

Goethe's "feuchtes Weib" is the immediate ancestor of Brentano's Lore Lay,[44] which makes all subsequent Loreleis her progeny. In almost all of the stories of water nymphs a female figure is in pursuit of a man, even when, as in Hans Christian Andersen's "The Little Mermaid" or Goethe's "Die neue Melusine," a decided sympathy for her predicament is evoked. No longer simply a personification of the allure of a natural element, the mermaid is visible as a female and a predator, at once threatening and seductive, and recognizable as a part of the world of male fantasies about women. As the womb into which man desires to return, woman is the tomb in which sexuality and indeed difference of every sort will be abolished. Like water, she is a focus of man's yearning for reassimilation and his dread of engulfment. To be sure, there are mermen as well as mermaids, as in Matthew Arnold's "The Forsaken Merman," and an early effort by Tennyson,[45] but these are minor novelties, whereas the mermaid (like the witch) reflects the abiding power of the idea of woman as erotic peril, sometimes as revenge for abuse at the hands of a man. Thus Goethe's "feuchtes Weib" lures her prey down to a watery grave, in retaliation for his own predation of marine life and in recognition of his death yearning. Because her actions follow from an injury suffered at the hands of an exploitive, abusive, or unfaithful man, the mermaid has a kinship with the ladies Millwood, Marwood, and Milford. In German literature, lack of purity is honorific. Experienced women are more interesting than virgins, as Lessing pointed out.[46] Examples in Goethe are Adelheid

---

[42] For example, Kayser, *Geschichte der deutschen Ballade,* 117; Gundolf, *Goethe,* 507).

[43] Yeats, "Lapis Lazuli."

[44] Ernst Beutler, "'Der König in Thule' und die Dichtungen von der 'Lorelay'" in *Essays um Goethe* (1947; repr., Frankfurt am Main: Insel, 1995), 333–88; here, 351.

[45] "The Merman," with a companion piece, "The Mermaid" — both 1830.

[46] "Der schlimmere Charakter, welcher mehr Anteil an der Handlung nimmt, als dem vollkommnen seine Seelenruhe und festen Grundsätze zu nehmen erlauben, [wird] ihn alle Zeit ausstechen" (materials to Gotthold Ephraim Lessing, *Laokoon,* in *Lessings sämtliche Schriften,* ed. Karl Lachmann, 3rd expanded ed. by Franz Muncker, 23 vols.; [vols. 1–11, Stuttgart: Göschen; vols. 12–22, Leipzig; vol. 23, Berlin, Leipzig: de Gruyter, 1886–1924], 14:355).

von Walldorf, Gretchen, the penitent women with whom she's associated at the end of *Faust II,* and the bajadere of "Der Gott und die Bajadere."

The fisherman represents a cluster of associations hardly less important than those surrounding the water maiden. First, this is a generic fisherman, a man identified by occupation, his introduction: "Ein Fischer saß daran," being typical of "naturmagische Balladen,"[47] which do not refer to a definite time or deal in persons of specific identity (cf. *"der* Vater mit seinem Kind" — "Erlkönig").[48] Since this poem is about the allure of death, encoded as the allure of water in the personification of a mermaid, the choice of fisherman as protagonist and victim is a natural one. But why not a skipper on the Rhine, a seafarer unbound from the mast, a Hylas in search of water for cooking, or simply a disappointed lover on a river bank, as in "Rettung"? "Fisherman" has connotations of seeker, as we know from the New Testament.[49] The fisherman who uses lures is a deceiver as well, a con artist, as Goethe spells out in a later poem, "Lust und Qual": "Knabe saß ich, Fischerknabe, / Auf dem schwarzen Fels im Meer, / Und, bereitend falsche Gabe, / Sang ich, lauschend ringumher." In Christian Daniel Schubart's poem "Die Forelle," the fisherman is a "thief" who deceives the trout "in cold blood." This naive and ruthless exploitation becomes a political contest and a route to education in Goethe's ballad. The nix's challenge to the fisherman's world of values exposes both its reliance on deception and its thoughtless cruelty, and creates the possibility of freedom — the awareness of alternatives and compensations that sparks a desire for liberation.

The fisherman is not identified by name, but we are given some information about his emotional state, such as that he was "kühl bis ans Herz hinan" and that, upon seeing and hearing the nix, "sein Herz wuchs ihm so sehnsuchtsvoll, / Wie bei der Liebsten Gruß." Of the maiden, by contrast, we have only an exterior view. She is the other here, whether an autonomous reality or the fisherman's own dreamy creation. The man is the work's sentient center.

The poem's narrator is distinguishable from the fisherman and, in his choice of narrative tense, his diction, and his use of other familiar poetic conventions, makes his mediating presence clear. His tale is told in the past tense or, in the case of lines 5–8, the historical present, and thus clearly assigned to the never-never-land of fiction. The term "ein feuchtes Weib," which introduces the maiden as erotic object, expresses astonishment and

---

[47] Kayser, *Geschichte der deutschen Ballade,* 116.

[48] Even when a time is specified (e.g. the age of chivalry, as in F. L. von Stolberg's ballads — see Kayser, *Geschichte der deutschen Ballade,* 106) or characters denominated ("Edward," "Lenore," "Schön Rohtraut," etc.), ballads do not narrate history; rather, they remain mythical and general.

[49] Matthew 4.18–20, rev. standard ed.

delight on the narrator's part quite independent of the fisherman's own response; as comical as it would be to say "Lo, a damp wench!" in English. As Kommerell notes, the narrator does not partake of any *Urschauer vor dem Elementaren*.[50] If Goethe here expresses an elemental shudder of his own, he does so through the medium of a modern playfulness and detachment from the mermaid figure — a kind of "humoristische Anmut" — that is not far removed from the gaiety of the later ballads (e.g. "Der Zauberlehrling," "Hochzeitlied," "Der Totentanz") but that does not fully mask the threat she represents. The parallelisms "Das Wasser rauscht,' das Wasser schwoll," "Sie sang zu ihm, sie sprach zu ihm" (and its inverse in line 29), and "Halb zog sie ihn, halb sank er hin," and the use of alliteration and rhyme all bespeak the narrator's lyric purpose. The line "Und ward nicht mehr gesehn" has a long literary history, as Rölleke has shown, and illustrates the incestuousness of literature.[51] Far from offering untransmuted emotion to the auditor or reader, this narrator is a part of a tradition and uses generic convention to modulate the events depicted.

The water is turbulent, rushing and swelling. A fisherman sitting on the shore appears to seek something — fish, no doubt, but something more, something audible and intelligible or at least interpretable, since he *listens,* although the primary indices to which a fisherman must respond *as a fisherman* are visual and tactile. As Zimmermann notes, the rhyme "lauscht" — "rauscht" suggests that the nix's appearance is in answer to his listening.[52] The ballad's plot is as an example of the quest, "a dominant plot in masculine literature,"[53] in which the water maiden is instrumental to the fisherman's fulfillment. Two earlier, discarded titles of a poem with a related plot were "Selbstopfer" and "Vollendung." Their abandonment in favor of "Selige Sehnsucht" may have been because the later poem's subject is not the *achievement* of ecstasy but the flight toward it. In "Der Fischer" too,

[50] Max Kommerell, *Gedanken über Gedichte* (Frankfurt am Main: Vittorio Klostermann, 1943), 348.

[51] In *Der Ohrenzeuge,* Canetti wrote, "und *wurde* nicht mehr gesehn." From Heinz Rölleke, "Und ward nicht mehr gesehen: zur Geschichte eines Goethe-Zitats," *Germanisch-romanische Monatschrift* 58, N.F. Bd. 27, 4 (1977): 433–45; here, 445 n. 17.

[52] Zimmermann, "Der Fischer," 156.

[53] Josephine Donovan, "Toward a Women's Poetics," *Tulsa Studies in Women's Literature* 3 (1984): 99–110; here, 104. Kathryn Rabuzzi "concludes that 'both history and story, traditionally so full of quests as to be virtually synonymous with them, may not be formally appropriate to express traditional feminine experience'" (Donovan, 105; ref. to Rabuzzi, *The Sacred and the Feminine: Toward a Theology of Housework* [New York: Seabury, 1982], 153). Cf. John S. Irving. "The Quest/Goal Pattern and its Thematic Transformation in Goethes Works Through 1786: An Experiment in Morphological Criticism," Diss., UCLA, 1964.

something ("Wohligsein," "Gesundheit") is lacking which, in finally sinking into the water, the fisherman expects to recover.

The word "kühl," which stands in contrast to the "Todesglut" into which the fisherman would lure the denizens of the deep, transfers the quality of coolness from the water to the fisherman himself, who is expectant, like Ganymed in the cool morning air. Like the word "Kühlung" in "Selige Sehnsucht" and, as a plural, in Klopstock's "Die Sommernacht," it suggests that the fisherman is poised and ready to respond. He listens calmly — "ruhevoll," half mesmerized by the restful bobber riding the waves of a rough sea, when the nix emerges and begins to speak.

She opens with a challenge and reproach, denouncing not only "Menschenwitz" as a system of thought and values but the deviousness of "Menschenlist" and its techniques for luring *her* "scaly brood" from their natural element into the fires of death. The possessive "meine Brut" denotes her partisan maternal interest and frankly advertises her subsequent verbal tempting not as mysterious and spontaneous seduction but as a countermove to a provocation, a parry in defense of her own kind. At one level, hers is a *class* action, and the fisherman's eventual acquiescence implies acknowledgment of the justice of her case and acceptance of the penalty.

The word "Todesglut," which relates to the death eroticism of Goethe's other uses of "Glut," has been a problem for critics and translators.[54] It seems calculated to have a startling effect, for no one talks about the *death* of a fish, anymore than we talk about fishing as an act of murder. It highlights and exposes one exemplary human code — that other forms of life exist for human use and that deception is a legitimate way of appropriating them — and, by implication, putting other aspects of "Menschenwitz" into question. This ballad is not only about the threat and the attraction of women and water but about cultural codes in general (including those of our patriarchal, androcentric culture) and the ways in which these are made visible and relative when challenged by an outsider. It is about *difference* and about meaning as a function of difference.

But, one and double, it is also about *sameness*. The nix's restricted criticism of the fisherman, before proceeding to seduce him *in answer to his listening,* raises questions of authorship and of the limits of personality. What is

[54] Cf. "nur soviel Glut" in "Wandrer's Sturmlied," "Wie du mich anglühst, Frühling, Geliebter ("Ganymed") and "Wie glühst du nach dem schönen Munde" ("Brautnacht"); also, after he has revived Faust's appetite for Gretchen in "Wald und Höhle" (3366–67). As Boyd notes, Mme. de Stael reported that Goethe criticized her rendition of the word into French as 'l'air brûlant' and maintained that he intended to convey the heat of the kitchen. Düntzer took the word as referring to the warm surface water, but Boyd agrees with Loeper (who finds an antecedent in Homer) in preferring "relatively hot and, for the fish deadly air" (Boyd, *Notes to Goethes Poems* 1:149–50).

he listening for ultimately? And is she who responds not, so to speak, "des Herrn eigner Geist"? The fisherman might well wonder with Goethe, "Ist es der Gegenstand oder bist du es, der sich hier ausspricht?" (FA 1,13:500). Is the criticism in fact *self*-criticism, the seduction a manifestation of a predisposition for self-submergence? For not only does the nix appear in response to the man's listening, she appears as he would have her, in conformity with masculine categories of mind. To see a mermaid is to see woman as a danger and a prize — as a threat to a man's self-preservation and as the means of escape from individuation.

The relationship between self and non-self was Goethe's life-long preoccupation and made him campaign ever more aggressively for clear, objective vision and against self-contemplation as a false route to self-knowledge. In view of this, the maiden's reference to her victim's narcissism, the suggestion that the image of himself in the water ought to attract him most of all, encourages a suspicion of the fisherman's ability to discern and valorize only himself in the other — the "Selbstbezogenheit"[55] for which Werther and Wilhelm Meister are notorious.

The possibility of the maiden's only chimerical reality would accord with the illusoriness of the world to which she draws the fisherman's attention. The sun and moon only *seem* to bathe themselves in the water; in fact, they are absent and are so marked by their reflections, a *Schein* in place of a *Sein*. And if the image is more beautiful than its referent, this is because of the reflection's idealizing and therefore falsifying effect. What warranty here that drowning would be pleasant, or that a man submerged in the watery depths could partake of the well-being enjoyed there by fish? Unlike a fisherman's deceptions, however, the maiden's enticements are not realistic but self-deconstructive, as the oxymorons "wellenatmend," "der tiefe Himmel," and "in ew'gen Tau" suggest. The lures she dangles before the fisherman cannot be decisive. Nor can her persuasiveness be attributed to the hypnotic power of her words or to her ethos as a singer — her coquettish intellectual charm[56] — although this undeniably has its effect. Rather, we must look below the surface of her argument to its substance. What she points to, but does not display, is a well-being beyond the prison of individuation, a happiness of which a "trüber Gast" on dry land has only the dimmest intimation, but an intimation nevertheless. She indexes a world through the looking glass and invites the fisherman to behold the truth beyond the illusion, an endless spatial stability beneath the shimmering and changeable surface of

---

[55] Heinz Politzer's term; see "Das Schweigen der Sirenen," *Deutsche Vierteljahrsschrift für Literaturwissenschaft und Geistesgeschichte* 41 (1967): 444–67; here, 457.

[56] H. A. Korff, *Goethe im Bildwandel seiner Lyrik*, 2 vols. (Hanau am Main: Werner Dausien, 1958), 248.

temporality and mortality. There is both play and deadly seriousness here. The mermaid seizes on the weakness of her adversary, sees that he yearns vaguely, indistinctly, and offers the comfort of oblivion and the freedom that is death. Goethe said of the ballad that it has "etwas Mysterioses, ohne mystisch zu sein" (FA 1,21:39), but the mysticism here is undeniable.

The question, "Lockt dich dein eigen Angesicht / Nicht her in ew'gen Tau?" alludes to the folk myth that to see one's own double or "Spiegelbild" is to have a premonition of death,[57] as well as a reference to the mermaid's own narcissism, her traditional pose with a mirror as she combs her hair of green or gold. In suggesting that the fisherman would be enamored of his own countenance, the nix insinuates that he shares her own pleasure in self-contemplation. If I am right, however, in claiming that the nix expects her adversary to recognize difference and absence as well as sameness and presence in reflections — their reversal of image and the opposition of subject and object they inevitably mark — and if she knows him to suffer from the discontinuity, the young man's own mirror image cannot be "der entscheidende Köder" either.[58] Rather, he is moved by the promise of release from the confinement of the self and of union with her in the fluid and formless meta-self of the sea. This is paradoxical, but symbolism — and Goethe's symbolism in particular, which is fundamentally deictic — does not either depend on identity or restrict itself to what was been called "associative analogy" between signifier and signified.[59] It employs a variety of ways of pointing. Thus the transitory is a "Gleichnis" of the eternal (*Faust II*, lines 12104–5), and the spectrum of colors in the rainbow, the "farbiger Abglanz" (line 4727), points to the pure white sunlight of which each color is a corruption. Usually similarity and difference are combined, as when the contingent and mortal "good human being" prefigures "jene geahneten Wesen," the gods ("Das Göttliche"), or when sexual union (the lower) prefigures *unio mystica* (the higher, in "Selige Sehnsucht") or the "erklingend Farbenspiel" of lovers in search of each other, in all its lively multi-sensuous excitement ("Wiederfinden"), leads and points inexorably to the silent night

[57] Brentano's Lore Lay says that her glance is deadly — even to herself. Mörike's "Erinna an Sappho" develops the traditional motif that to see one's double (thus one's "Spiegelbild") is to have a premonition of death. This belief informs the incident in *Wilhelm Meisters Lehrjahre* in which the Count interprets the apparition of himself seated in his favorite chair (actually Wilhelm, disguised by the playful Baroness in the Count's morning gown) as a sign of his imminent death.

[58] Politzer, "Das Schweigen der Sirenen," 451. Politzer finds the fisherman's narcissism reflected in the very verses of the poem, which, for example, converts the sentence: "sie sang zu ihm, sie sprach zu ihm" into its mirror image at the beginning of the last strophe (452).

[59] Earl R. Wasserman, "The English Romantics: The Grounds of Knowledge," *Studies in Romanticism* 4 (1964): 17–34; here, 19.

of "ewige Ruh' in Gott dem Herrn" ("Wenn im Unendlichen dasselbe"). That is why pictures can be symbolic, why "deines Geistes höchster Feuerflug / Hat schon am Gleichnis, hat am Bild genug" ("Prooemion") and why the reflection of the fisherman's external appearance (itself only an icon of a selfhood that can never be fully objectified) can point to something larger than, and inclusive of, his self. The scale of difference approximates that implied in the oxymoron "in ewigen Tau." The waters of the deep are not evanescent like the dew that is gone by noon, but everlasting — as durable as death and as lethal as love.

The simile, "Wie bei der Liebsten Gruß," brings out the erotic character of the fisherman's temptation. That his heart waxes "sehnsuchtsvoll," reveals the maiden's presence to be in reality only a promise of presence, an objective correlative of the void she does not yet fill and *will* fill only when conjoined with the fisherman in a "shared nonbeing."[60] If she is his own self-projection, she represents self-alienation and the fisherman's yearning for a still outstanding self-identity. At the same time, Goethe's incorporation into his ballad of both male fantasies and a challenge to such codes by the embodiment of these fantasies may reflect his own dialectical movement toward resolution and wholeness. Until closure is achieved, there will always be "Sehnsucht." "Balde / [but not yet] Ruhest du auch" ("Wanderer's Night Song II"). Thus the fisherman is ready when the water laps at his feet, prompting him to yield to the maiden's pull and accept her cool embrace. He responds and, half drawn, half sinking of his own accord, is never seen again. "Das Ewig-Weibliche (you saw it coming) zieht ihn hinunter."

In "Rettung," the void in the young man's heart is filled by the fortuitous appearance of a winsome replacement for the disloyal sweetheart. To the fisherman of "Der Fischer," such a rescue would be a non-rescue — his reincarceration in selfhood and incompleteness. And the non-rescue that he embraces is the true rescue — a flight into freedom. Perhaps this is why George Eliot gave the title "The Final Rescue" to the last chapter of *The Mill on the Floss*, the chapter in which Tom and Maggie Tulliver drown together.

C. Enigmas of "Erlkönig": Then and Now

Goethe's ballad "Erlkönig" has been studied almost to death. Yet it lives on, familiarly in Schubert's song with its difficult piano accompaniment echoing the hoof beats of the galloping horse and its taxing vocal range, as the dialogue shifts from the narrator to the father, to the child, and to the Erl King. "Erlkönig" is a product of Goethe's second wave in the genre of *Kunstbal-*

---

[60] I borrow this happy term from Paul Robinson, *Opera and Ideas* (Ithaca, NY: Cornell UP, 1985), 83.

lade, after "Heidenröslein," "König in Thule," "Vor Gericht," and "Der Fischer" and before the ballads of 1797. It was sung by Corona Schröter in the park on the bank of the Ilm in Tiefurt on July 22, 1782 as part of the *Singspiel Die Fischerin,* and, according to Eibl, was intended "als eher schlichtes Liedchen . . ., dessen unheimliche Seite quasi naiv-unbewußt mitgetragen wird" (FA 1,1:1022). Schröter's singing may have intensified the ballad's terrifying content, while Schubert's overstatement diminishes it.

We will listen here for the ontological undertones of "Erlkönig," in hopes that hearing them may help explain the poem's power. For the ballad is concerned with questions of being and non-being, being and identity — what it means to be, and what it means to be someone or to be in a particular way — for example, to be at the mercy of unseen or uncomprehended beings, beings whose being is at once doubtful and all too threateningly present. We have become so used to the verb 'to be' as a copula that we have lost our ear for its ontological meaning. In special, fixed situations — "to be or not to be," "I am the great 'I am'" — this most basic verb has preserved its force, but in unbound situations we require a complement: "John is here." "John is my brother." "John is trustworthy."[61] In German, the ontological meaning of *sein* is still common[62] and was taken for granted in Goethe's discourse and that of his pietist friends. Lotte proclaims to Werther on the eve of his departure from Wahlheim "Wir werden sein!" (10 September 1771), words repeated by Werther in his last letter to Lotte. "Wie kann ich vergehen? wie kannst du vergehen? Wir *sind* ja! (FA 1,8:249). "Die goldne Zeit," says the Princess von Este in *Tasso,* sie war . . . so wenig als sie ist, / Und war sie je, so war sie gewiß / Wie sie uns immer wieder werden kann" (FA 1,5:762). In Kleist's *Prinz Friedrich von Homburg,* Rittmeister von Mörner erroneously reports, "Der Kurfürst ist nicht mehr" (2.5). And the Prince pleads with the Kurfürstin to intervene and prevent his execution or tomorrow he will lie decaying between two narrow boards "und ein Gestein sagt dir von ihm: er war" (3.5). To her mother's musing, "Wer weiß, wie du sein wirst, wenn sich die andern [Mädchen] entwickelt haben," Wendla Bergmann, in Wedekind's *Frühlings Erwachen,* replies presciently, "Wer weiß — vielleicht werde ich nicht mehr sein."

---

[61] "Aristotle distinguished between 'to be A' (for instance, to be thought of) and 'to be' without qualification. He made the same remark about the 'being A' of that which has 'ceased to be'; for instance, from 'Homer is a poet' it does not follow that 'Homer is.' Some such distinction seems necessary, since among the A's that one can be is 'dead' or 'no longer existent.' . . . Elsewhere [Aristotle] suggested that propositions equivalent to 'Socrates is ill' and 'Socrates is well' imply the plain 'Socrates is'; 'neither is true if Socrates does not exist at all'" (*The Encyclopedia of Philosophy,* 3:141, article "Existence").

[62] "Wenn ich bin," says the Devil to Adrian Leverkühn in Thomas Mann's *Doktor Faustus,* "so kann ich nur Einer sein" (*Gesammelte Werke,* 6:300).

Heidegger questioned a conventional science that dismissed "das Nichts" as simply that which *is not*, but, in a complex metonymony, *is* something, for instance, in Faust's realization on Easter morning that in drinking the poison he will risk flowing into nothingness — "ins Nichts dahinzufließen" (line 719). He was also resisting the ocularcentrist conception of being, which is challenged by a character in Thomas Mann's *Der Erwählte:* "Sollten wir als Kristen Unsichtbarkeit gleichsetzen mit Nicht-Sein?" Faith, we remember, is the evidence of things not seen. To the extent that *sein* survives as more than a copula, we may hear a contradiction in the words "In seinen Armen das Kind war tot."

"Erlkönig" was inspired by Herder's translation of a Danish folk ballad, to which he gave the title "Erlkönigs Tochter" as a result of his misunderstanding of the Danish "eller" in "ellerkonge."[63] Thus in Goethe's ballad the Danish "King of the Elves" becomes the "Erlkönig" or, as it were, King of the alder people or the tree spirits. George Henry Lewes gives the plot of the Danish poem in order to show the "difference between a legend and a perfect poem."[64] Whether or not "Erlkönig" is a *perfect* poem, the mysterious monarch whose blandishments and threats attract and terrorize the boy to whom they are addressed is more famous than any other elfin king has a prayer of becoming. Goethe's poem has inspired a host of imitations, including Matthison's "Die Elfenkönigin," Anastasius Grün's "Elfenliebe," Annette von Droste-Hülshoff's "Der Heidemann," and Uhland's "Die Elfen" and "Harald"[65] and even such schoolyard parodies as the one recalled by James Simpson: "Wer reitet so spät auf Mamas Bauch? Es ist der Vater mit seinem Schlauch";[66] or in references to George W. Bush as "der Öl-König." "Erlkönig" has been set to music at least forty-four times (GA 2:729–30), five times during Goethe's lifetime.[67]

---

[63] = king of the elves, as equivalent to Low German "Eller," (High German "Erle" = alder), and of ellerkone (= Elfenweib) as the *daughter* of the alder king. The stage directions of *Die Fischerin* contain the words, "Unter hohen Erlen am Flusse stehen zerstreute Fischerhütte[n]" (Boyd, *Notes to Goethes Poems,* 1:170). "Auch in dem Elfenlied *Um Mitternacht . . .* tanzen die Elfen *auf Wiesen an den Erlen*" (Trunz, HA 1:565).

[64] George Henry Lewes, *The Life and Works of Goethe,* 2nd ed. (1864; repr. New York: F. Ungar, 1965), 490.

[65] Boyd, *Notes to Goethes Poems,* 1:171.

[66] James Simpson, "Freud and the Erl King," *Oxford German Studies* 27 (1998): 30–63; here, 54.

[67] Staiger judges Loewe's setting to be better than Schubert's, "dessen bekanntere Komposition, bei aller Genialität, doch nicht die dunkelsten Gründe des Textes ermißt" (Emil Staiger, *Goethe,* 3 vols. (Zurich and Freiburg: Atlantis, 1956–59), 1:345). See also Hirschenauer, "Erlkönig," 168 n. 4.

"Erlkönig" is often read as part of the reaction of the *Sturm und Drang* to the Enlightenment and as Goethe's personal "Beziehung . . . zu den magischen Elementen der beseelten Natur."[68] Psychoanalytical interpretations abound as well. And the fact that the Erlkönig's passion for the boy is the passion of an adult male for a male child has been disturbing to generations of critics. Boyle describes "Erlkönig" as "the most terrifyingly erotic poem of [Goethe's] life,"[69] which may raise questions about the source of its erotic power. Curiously, Karl Hugo Pruys makes nothing of the fact in *Die Liebkosungen des Tigers: Eine erotische Goethe Biographie* (1997), which claims that Goethe was a closet homosexual.[70]

Herder's method of explaining things cultural by their genesis led to the nineteenth century's preoccupation with biography, among other things. It also blurs and subverts the Enlightenment distinction between superstition and true religion. If religions, like organisms and ecosystems, are the result of their ontogeny, they must all be equally valid as authentic expressions of their originary circumstances. Blindness to the naturalness of culture and the ideologies informing conceptions of nature, coupled with a failure to recognize the equivalence and equivocity of religious beliefs, may produce melancholy ironies, as in the case of Malchen's fear that an ugly beard will grow on her cheek where the impulsive Werther has kissed her. If she hurries and washes her face in the fountain, Lotte assures her, everything will be all right. When later that same evening a visitor protests that Lotte did wrong to encourage superstition in children, Werther recalls that the man had presented a child for baptism just the week before (6. Julius 1771) and reflects that all of us are dependent on illusions of one kind or another.[71] The disapproving Enlightener enjoys a simple faith in the Christian sacraments, while embracing with the other side of his brain Enlightenment views that were lapping away at the foundations of positive religion.

[68] Benedikt Jeßing, *Johann Wolfgang Goethe* (Stuttgart and Weimar: Metzler, 1995), 31.

[69] Nicholas Boyle, *Goethe: The Poet and the Age,* vol. 1: *The Poetry of Desire* (1749–1790); vol. 2: *Revolution and Renunciation* (1790–1803) (Oxford: Clarendon Press, 1991, 2000), 1:339.

[70] Cf. "In der Oluf-Ballade ging es um die Konkurrenz von ehelicher Liebe und nicht-lizenziertem Eros, hier tritt noch die sexuelle Inversion hinzu, der Erlkönig wird durch die schöne Gestalt des Knaben gereizt und ist zu Gewaltanwendung, zu Vergewaltigung bereit, ein Skandalon, das schwer zu entwörtlichen ist (Alexander von Bormann, "Erlkönig," *Goethe-Handbuch* 1 [Stuttgart, Weimar: Metzler, 1996]: 212–17; here, 214).

[71] Goethe later observes, "daß practisch genommen, sich Glaube und Aberglaube nicht unterscheiden lasse, und daß man . . . wohl thue, sich in diesen bedenklichen Regionen nicht zu lange aufzuhalten" ("Der deutsche Gil Blas, Fromme Betrachtung," FA 1,21:63).

The young Goethe honored naive faith while refusing to accredit New Testament miracles or to grant supernatural status to Jesus Christ. Gottfried August Bürger wanted his "Lenore" to be read under low candle light, with a death head as a prop, for the sake of atmosphere, which suggests the artificiality of the situation. Bürger's care for special effects does not suggest that he believed in revenants or that he would have been scared if one had sauntered into the room. Did Emily Brontë believe in them? With what intensity? In what way? Was she, too, fond of special effects, or only a practitioner of literary realism, letting Heathcliff's troubled mind manifest its delusions as symptoms of his affliction? Does belief imply conviction that what the unreligious regard as fictions are not fictional but truly "real"? To honor a set of beliefs is one thing, to have internalized it and be governed by it is another.

"Erlkönig" reflects the conflict between secular reason and religious devotion, between the attack on pietism in such works as *Die Pietisterey im Fischbeinrocke* and the letters of Susanna von Klettenberg. The forces of light and dark, however, were not as clearly juxtaposed as this contrast suggests. Rather, the struggle within each soul, even the souls of the champions of Reason, was one of the propelling forces of the age, as people sought to distinguish fact from fiction, *Vernunft* from folly, charlatanry from true apostleship, as in Molière's *Tartuffe*. Goethe's *Satyros* and *Der Groß-Cophta* dramatize aspects of this struggle. But "Erlkönig" questions not only the depths and kinds of belief, but also the modes of being of visions and ideas.

"We are nowhere asked to believe," says Boyd, that the boy actually sees and hears the Erl King, and feels his terrible grip; this "may all be a figment of his fevered imagination."[72] Boyd finds the "gain in rationality in Goethe's poem" to be "a decided advance" over Herder's tale of diabolical elves and their innocent victim.[73] Yet nothing in "Erlkönig" authorizes talk of the boy's "hallucinations," and so Staiger and Hirschenauer, among others, accredit the child's visions as revealing truths to which cold reason is blind.

The narrator provides little help.[74] The boy *sees* the Erl King and his daughters, *hears* the king's words, and dies. Whether the father believes in his own reassuring comments or prevaricates in order to comfort his boy, and whether he preserves his naturalistic beliefs or gives them up in the

---

[72] Boyd, *Notes to Goethes Poems*, 173.

[73] Ibid., 174.

[74] Schöne's remark on the narrator of Bürger's "Lenore" applies also to the narrator of "Erlkönig." He is "ein Erzähler, . . . der zwar nirgend ausdrücklich vorgeführt oder genannt wird, als sprechende Figur aber deutlich greifbar ist und keineswegs einfach mit dem Dichter gleichgesetzt werden kann" ("Lenore," in *Die deutsche Lyrik: Form und Geschichte*, ed. Benno von Wiese, 2 vols. [Düsseldorf: August Bagel Verlag, 1964], 1:190–210; here, 1:198).

face of his loss, is left unanswered at the poem's end — even if the loss is viewed as a consequence of illness. For how can illness take a child away? Nevertheless, we should not mistake the poem's brevity and the narrator's reticence as signs of a smug agnosticism on the part of the author, who struggled early and late with the mystery of being and non-being.

The theological issue informing the ambiguities of "Erlkönig" is the *disseits-jenseits* dichotomy, a variation on the inside-outside dichotomy mentioned above. Beginning with Elizabeth Rowe's *Friendship in Death: In Twenty Letters from the Dead to the Living* (1728) and continuing with Young's popular *Night Thoughts on Life, Death, and Immortality* (1742–45), fascination with the hereafter and with beloved friends and relatives beyond the veil was all the rage. In Germany, Wieland's *Briefe von Verstorbenen an hinterlassene Freunde* (1753) preceded Lavater's *Aussichten in die Ewigkeit* (1768–78) by fifteen years. But Werther's and Lotte's talk of where and when they will see each other again is an even more prominent illustration. "Wir werden uns wiedersehn," says Werther on he eve of his departure from Wahlheim at the end of the first book. Lotte thinks he means on the morrow, but his plan is to leave Wahlheim forever. When later in Book Two he embraces her against her will, she says, "Das ist das letzte Mal! Werther! Sie sehn mich nicht wieder" (FA 1,8:246–47).[75] Werther eventually finds consolation in the hope that he will hold Lotte in his arms in the hereafter — "vor dem Angesichte des Vaters in ewigen Umarmungen" (250–51). In Goethe this dialectic of here and hereafter is recast into a dichotomy of the world of sense perceptions and a variety of twilight zones that are other and alien but that may intrude into the world of here and now. The still unravished bride of Corinth walks the corridors as one of the undead and eventually claims her prize in a sacrament of love and death. A princess from the kingdom of the dwarfs lures a young man into her realm and tries to wed him there in order to preserve her race,[76] a theme which "Die neue Melusine" (FA 1,10:633–56) has in common with the Danish prototype of "Erlkönig."

[75] "Das Wiedersehn im Jenseits kommt im 18. Jahrhundert . . . ganz allgemein in der Dichtung und Popularphilosophie, z.B. bei Young und Richardson, . . . bei Mendelssohn in seinem 'Phädon,' 1767, und bei Klopstock in seinen Oden, z.B., 'An Fanny.' Werther kennt Klopstocks Oden, und er weiß, daß Lotte in ihnen gelesen hat. — In dem Bericht Kestners über Jerusalem heißt es: 'Mendelssohns Phädon war seine liebste Lektüre.' — Vgl. 117,32ff. u. Anm." (E. C. Mason, "'Wir sehen uns wieder!' Zu einem Leitmotiv des Dichtens und Denkens im 18. Jahrhundert," *Literaturwissenschaftliches Jahrbuch der Görres-Ges.* 5, [1964]: 79–109. Quoted by Trunz in HA 6:579).

[76] The Danish "Erlkönigs Tochter" and Goethe's "Erlkönig" "are alike in that they are based on the belief, common in northern mythology, in elves, who, as cloud or storm spirits, were feared because of their habit of stealing children and young men in order to increase their race" (Boyd, *Notes to Goethe's Poems* 1:173).

Cathy haunts the moor of *Wuthering Heights*. Demons from the nether-world snatch away children. Ancient beliefs about alternative worlds and enthusiasm for "heterocosmic poetry" become strange bedfellows.[77] When the ghost of Hamlet's father returns and demands vengeance, says Lessing, we can see that the world of *Hamlet* is a world in which ghosts are real.[78] To Derrida, Marxism is a ghost haunting the post-Marxist world. The study of its presence would be called "hauntology."[79] In "Das Unheimliche" Freud says it is "zweifelhaft, ob wir es [in Hoffmann's "Der Sandmann"] mit einem ersten Delirium des angstbesessenen Knaben oder mit einem Bericht zu tun haben, der als real in der Darstellungswelt der Erzählung aufzufassen ist."[80] Books like Whitley Strieber's *Confirmation: The Hard Evidence of Aliens Among Us* find a ready market.[81] In the movie *The Sixth Sense* a psychologist succeeds in helping a boy who sees dead people only because the psychologist is himself dead, therefore visible and available to the boy with the sixth sense. To recognize the possibility of alien intrusions is to concede that boundaries whose imperviousness we assume can be traversed and penetrated, and to cast being in a new light, to inquire what it means to be in a new way — as ontology or as *hauntology*. It is to recognize that both the autonomy of the self and the solid, impenetrable reality inhabited by the self are fictions. Only the uninquisitive philistine is safe in his comfortable, well-padded world.

[77] Tom Stoppard recalls Richard Eyre's *Hamlet,* "in which the ghost of Hamlet's father was interpreted as a projection of young Hamlet's neurosis, existing only in Hamlet's mind. He conjured up his own ghost scene, the actor speaking both roles in different voices" ("Pragmatic Theater," *The New York Review of Books,* 46, 14 [23 September '99]: 8).

[78] Lessing, *Hamburgische Dramaturgie,* 11. Stück, *Sämtliche Schriften,* eds. Lachmann and Muncker (Stuttgart: Göschen, 1893), 9:227–30.

[79] "*What is* a ghost?" asks Derrida. "What is the *effectivity* or the *presence* of a specter, that is, of what seems to remain as ineffective, virtual, insubstantial as a simulacrum? . . . Let us call [the opposition between the thing itself and its simulacrum] a *hauntology*" (Jacques Derrida, *Specters of Marx: The State of the Debt, The Work of Mourning, and the New International* [New York and London: Routledge, 1994], 10).

[80] *SA* 4:252. See Simpson, "Freud and the Erl King," 35.

[81] Whitley Strieber, *Confirmation: The Hard Evidence of Aliens among Us* (New York: St. Martin's Press, 1998). This and two other books, David M. Jacobs, *The Threat* (New York: Simon and Schuster, 1998) and Jodi Dean, *Aliens in America: Conspiracy Cultures from Outerspace to Cyberspace* (Ithaca, NY: Cornell UP, 1998) are reviewed by Frederick Crews in *The New York Review of Books,* vol. 45, no. 11 (June 25, 1998): 14–19.

Does the assumption that the child in "Erlkönig" is delirious explain anything at all?[82] How does a neurological condition cause the mind to hallucinate? How, for that matter, does the *healthy* mind produce imaginary creatures, in fantasy or in dreams?[83] But even if we knew the neuroscientific facts, what bearing would they have on the reality of hallucinations? What is the mode of existence of delusions or figments of the imagination, which are never reducible to the underlying biological structures? When Goethe said, "Es ist eine Gotteslästerung zu sagen: daß es einen *optischen Betrug* gebe," he meant that what the crude materialist Benjamin Graf Rumford called an illusion was precisely the reality in need of study and explanation.[84] Why does the mind produce a *particular* narrative, a symbolic structure, or any special arrangement of imaginary phenomena? Neither Freud nor Lacan has brought us any closer to knowing either how visions are produced or what they mean, despite lengthy speculations on the latter point.

In *Disease and Representation,* Gilman registers the role of culture and belief in our understanding and representation of disease and of our interest in marking off and distancing sick persons from ourselves by referring to them as "cases."[85] Our notions of illness change over time, so that the very term "mental illness" is now recognized as a misnomer.[86] Freud believed in

[82] Leverkühn tries to explain away his interlocutor, the Devil, as a product of his own fevered brain: "Nach meiner starken Vermutung seid ihr nicht da. . . . Viel wahrscheinlicher ist, daß eine Krankheit bei mir im Ausbruch ist und ich den Fieberfrost, gegen den ich mich einhülle, in meiner Benommenheit hinausverlege auf eure Person und euch sehe, nur um in euch seine Quelle zu sehen" (302). Thomas Mann, *Gesammelte Werke* 6:302. Cf. "Verrätst dich und nennst mir selber die Stelle in meinem Hirn, den Fieberherd, der dich mir vorgaukelt, und ohne den du nicht wärst" (312).

[83] The question of brain and mind is still mysterious and much discussed by John Searle and his adversaries in neuroscience. See Searle's review of Ray Kurzweil in the *New York Review of Books,* April 8, 1999; also the exchange between the two authors in *NYRB,* May 20, 1999, 74, plus Colin McGinn's review of Searle's *Mind, Language, and Society: Philosophy in the Real World* (New York: Basic Books, 1998) and Paul M. Churchland and Patricia S. Churchland's *On the Contrary: Critical Essays, 1987–1997* (Cambridge: Bradford/MIT Press, 1998) in *NYRB* 46, no. 10 (June 10 1999): 44–48. See also "Don't Bet the Chicken Coop," Jerry Fodor's review of *Thinking About Consciousness* by David Papineau (Oxford UP, 2002). Fodor's review is in *The London Review of Books,* 24 (5 Sept 2002): 21–22. McGinn ends his review with a reference to "matters about which human beings are still deeply ignorant" (48), Fodor his with the words "Nobody has a clue."

[84] Boyle, *Goethe: The Poet and the Age,* 2:268.

[85] Sander L. Gilman, *Disease and Representation: Images of Illness from Madness to AIDS* (Ithaca: Cornell UP, 1988), 4, 14–17.

[86] Pool discusses ague, cholera, consumption, croup, diphtheria, dropsy, dyspepsia, gout, palsy, pleurisy, quinsy, typhoid fever, typhus, and yellow fever in Victorian

schizophrenogenic mothers, but the "mentally ill" suffer not so much from poor parenting as from a malfunction of the brain — with the direst of consequences for the mind, and sometimes for the body.[87] Schizophrenia and bipolar illness do generate delusions and, because all of us are insecure about our ability to distinguish the true from the false, are regarded by the ignorant as something to be ashamed of. We are jealous of our hold on "reality." From the point of view of the father in "Erlkönig," what the child sees and hears is not there. But the narrator does not say that it *is* not there. We know only that the father either cannot see or hear it or that he denies that he can in hopes of calming his child. Consciousness is a first-person phenomenon and never fully explicable by the observations of third persons.

Like "Die Braut von Korinth," "Erlkönig" explores the relationship between a parent and a child, a theme also at the center of the ballad "Edward," which Herder translated. It has not been remarked upon, to my knowledge, that the father in "Erlkönig" is a brother in arms to Laocoon, Ugolino, and every other parent struggling to protect a child from hostile powers. Other examples are Rigoletto, Anna Fierling in *Mutter Courage und ihre Kinder,* the Queen of the Night, and Roberto Benigni in the hit movie *Life is Beautiful* (1998). Goethe's *Die natürliche Tochter,* about the loss of a child,[88] is another example.[89] That this father's defense has to be conducted on the level of percept and concept and not in physical combat makes it anything but a "schlichtes Liedchen."

Commentators on "Erlkönig" pay little attention to the father, except to notice the insufficiency of his commonsense naturalism. They ignore his loss at the poem's end and the threat of loss with which he struggles in the drama played out in the ballad. He is more than a foil to the child. It is *his* identity as a father that is inquired after in the poem's first line, indeed its first word ("*Wer* reitet so spät?). He *is* terrified, knowing that his child is threatened by an assailant against which he is helpless and whom he can neither see nor hear. His seemingly confident "Ich seh es genau" ironically

England. "Psychophenia," "dementia praecox," etc., had, of course, not yet been discovered.

[87] In Elizabethan England syphilis was understood to cause not only madness but also melancholy. Syphilis is understood as having this effect in *Hamlet* (Greg Bentley, "Melancholy, Madness, and Syphilis in *Hamlet,*" *Hamlet Studies* 6 [1984]: 75–80).

[88] Boyle, *Goethe: The Poet and the Age* 2:43.

[89] On the loss of his nine-year-old son in Rome in 1803, Wilhelm von Humboldt wrote to Schiller: "Ich vertraue nicht meinem Glück, nicht dem Schicksal, nicht der Kraft der Dinge mehr . . . Ich habe den Tod nie gefürchtet und nie kindisch am Leben gehangen, aber wenn man ein Wesen todt hat, das man liebte, so ist die Empfindung doch durchaus verschieden. Man glaubt sich einheimisch in zwei Welten" (27 August 1803, in *Briefwechsel zwischen Schiller und Wilhelm von Humboldt,* 3rd expanded ed., ed. Albert Leitzmann [Stuttgart: Cotta, 1900], 302).

documents his blindness to the poem's central phenomenon. "Genau" is precisely *not* how he sees. He only hears his child scream, "Mein Vater, mein Vater, jetzt faßt er mich an." Not only the life of his child, but also his very comprehension of reality, his world, is at stake as well, and it is his horror that is in focus in the final strophe ("Erreicht den Hof mit Mühe und Not; / In seinen Armen . . ."). If the poem does not valorize the father's world view, it does certify and dignify his terror and his grief: "Dem Vater grauset's; er reitet geschwind." We might even wonder whether the father is not the primary target of the Erl King's assault. But whether or not this father's "Grausen" is intended by the assailant, it is an important factor in the narrative.

What does the demon want? If he loves the boy, how can he destroy him? How can the "Knabe" *break off* the rose in "Heidenröslein" if he loves her? To what extent does the fear of violence haunt every child's imagination? An adequate reading of "Erlkönig" will see the rape of the child as a *Lustmord,* like the execution of Adelheid in *Götz von Berlichingen.* It will consider what the violation of children and of women have in common. In any case, "Raub, Entrückung, Entführung beinhalten stets eine Form von äußerer oder innerer Gewalt, wie bei der Verführung, gleich, in welcher Figur sie vollzogen wird."[90] Is "Erlkönig," then, about a different reality or a different view of reality, about a child's terror, a parent's struggle and loss, violent crime, the effects of disease, or the mystery of death? What does the poem say about being? *Is* the boy still, somewhere, at the poem's end, or *is* he no longer? What is the mode of being or non-being of the being he sees and hears? *Who* or *what* is this Erlkönig?

At the poem's end the boy's mortal shell is held still in the arms of his father, as the mortal shell of the boy Miles remains in the governess's arms in "The Turn of the Screw." Neither death is a tragedy, since a tragedy must be comprehensible. "Erlkönig" does not rationalize or soften, except formally, in its matchless, cruel beauty. The message is plain and stark. The child *is dead.* The last line, adopted almost verbatim from "Erlkönigs Tochter," says so: "In seinen Armen das Kind war tot." But "dead" is not among the things that one can be, as we admit when we refer to a person's "remains" or to "the body." How can anyone *be* dead?

D. "Die Braut von Korinth"

Ilse Graham has written sensitively about the deliberations of Goethe and Schiller during "das Balladenjahr" 1797 and about the quagmire represented by the ballad form, "von welcher man weder wußte, was sie an das Licht des

---

[90] Lea Ritter-Santini, *Ganymed: Ein Mythos des Aufstiegs in der deutschen Moderne* (1998), trans. Birgit Schneider (Munich: Carl Hanser, 2002), 114.

Tages fördern, noch ob sie den Sänger loreleihaft in den Sog seines Unterbewußtseins hinablocken würde."[91] The ballad genre, or so Graham suggests, was a *femme fatale.*

"There is a dimension to the meaning of the femme fatale," notes Virginia Allen, "suggesting that even though she might die, she will not be obliterated. She will rise to claim another victim, perhaps as one of the living dead, a vampire."[92] A founding document of the gothic tradition, Goethe's "The Bride of Corinth" predates and probably influenced the many nineteenth-century vampire stories in various national literatures,[93] e.g. Baudelaire's "Les métamorphoses du vampire" or Przybyszewski's "De Profundis" and Bram Stoker's *Dracula.* It has generally been allowed to interpret itself. More precisely, the heroine of the poem, the revenant, has been accepted as the voice of authority on the meaning of her own story. Whichever set of opposites is taken as the underlying polarity, whether Hellenism versus Christianity, nature versus culture, sensualism versus asceticism, humanism versus theism, progressive materialism versus reactionary otherworldliness, or mother versus daughter, most readers have been untroubled by doubt as to which antithesis is affirmed and which condemned.[94] The

---

[91] Ilse Graham, "Die Theologie tanzt: Goethes Balladen 'Die Braut von Korinth' und 'Der Gott und die Bajadere,'" in *Goethe: Schauen und Glauben* (Berlin: Walter de Gruyter, 1988), 253–84; here, 254.

[92] Pater describes Leonardo's *La Gioconda* as "older than the rocks among which she sits; like the vampire she has been dead many times, and learned all the secrets of the grave" (Walter Pater, *The Renaissance: Studies in Art and Poetry,* 2nd ed., revised, [London: Macmillan, 1877], 135; quoted in Virginia M. Allen, *The Femme Fatale: Erotic Icon* [Troy, NY: Whitston, 1983], 3).

Baudelaire's *Metamorphoses of a Vampire* was "one of the half dozen poems for which he was prosecuted, and [which he was] forced to exclude from the second edition of *Les Fleurs du Mal*" (Allen, *The Femme Fatale,* 76).

[93] Revenants are a staple of the love-death tradition. Clara Wieck named the fourth of her compositions in 1836, opus 5: "Ballett des Revenants." Kurth-Voigt provides a catalogue of revenants, e.g. those in Heine's *Atta Troll* (1847), including Goethe ("La Belle Dame Sans Merci," 261)! Helena is also a sort of revenant and says to the protagonist of Heine's *Doktor Faust* (1851), "Ich trinke deine Seele aus, / Die Toten sind unersättlich." In Heine's "Die Beschwörung," "Die arme verstorbene Schönheit kommt, / In weißen Laken gehüllet. / Ihr Blick ist traurig. Aus kalter Brust / Die schmerzlichen Seufzer steigen. / Die Tote setzt sich zu dem Mönch, / Sie schauen sich an und schweigen." Moritz Stiefel returns after his suicide in Wedekind's *Frühlings Erwachen.*

[94] See the following interpretations: James Boyd, *Notes to Goethe's Poems,* 2:82–93; Ernst Feise, "Die Gestaltung von Goethes 'Braut von Korinth,'" *Modern Language Notes* 76 (1961):150–54; Johannes Klein, *Geschichte der deutschen Lyrik von Luther bis zum Ausgang des zweiten Weltkrieges,* 2nd ed. (Wiesbaden: Franz Steiner, 1960), 342–44; Max Kommerell, *Gedanken über Gedichte,* 361–64; H. A. Korff, *Bildwandel,*

judgment against Christianity or allied perversions in favor of the natural or classical, or whatever else is deemed wholesome and correct, has been common if not quite unanimous. And why not, since this is the judgment passed by the bride herself?

Readers of fiction are not obliged, however, to accept the opinions of fictional characters as authoritative for the work in which they exist. I would suggest that, despite an overlay of anti-Christian polemics, the primary emphasis in the poem is on the bridging of distance and difference, on conjunction and integration, and that its contrasting stress on difference and opposition serves as much to heighten the love interest and the mythical import of the plot as to express Goethe's objections to the Christian religion.

Goethe derived his subject from an earlier source and claimed to have preserved it in his imagination for forty or fifty years. Only after renewal and transformation in the crucible of his consciousness did it become purified and ripe for the re-presentation which we know as "Die Braut von Korinth." What possibilities Goethe saw in the inherited subject may be suggested by what it became and what it remained in his own rendition. His narrative tells of a young traveler from Athens who has come to the home of family friends in Corinth. While still children, the Athenian youth and the daughter of the Corinthian family had been betrothed by a handshake of the respective fathers, and the young man hopes that the early plan to link the families through marriage can now be realized. A troubling development since the betrothal, however, is the conversion of the family in Corinth to Christianity, which raises doubts in the youth's mind about how he will be received and whether, or at what price, love and lovers' vows will still be honored.

Only the mother is awake when the youth arrives. She welcomes him, shows him to a well-appointed room, serves him a supper of bread and wine, and bids him good night. Without tasting either food or drink, he stretches out on the bed and dozes off, only to be awakened when a maiden enters the room, which she had thought unoccupied. She is embarrassed to have intruded upon him there and would withdraw, but he begs her to stay and

2:58–70; Walter Müller-Seidel, "Goethe: Die Braut von Korinth," in *Geschichte im Gedicht*, ed. Walter Hink (Frankfurt am Main: Suhrkamp, 1979), 79–86; Emil Staiger, *Goethe* (Zurich: Atlantis, 1956), 2:307–15; Hans-Günther Thalheim, "Goethes Ballade 'Die Braut von Korinth,'" *Goethe* 20 (1958): 28–44; Elizabeth Wright, "Ambiguity and Ambivalence: Structure in Goethe's 'Die Braut von Korinth' and 'Der Gott und die Bajadere,'" *Publications of the English Goethe Society* 51 (1981): 114–32; Ilse Graham, "Die Theologie tanzt,"; Mathias Mayer, "Goethes vampirische Poetik. Zwei Thesen zur *Braut von Corinth*," *Jahrbuch der deutschen Schillergesellschaft* 43 (1999): 148–58. Müller-Seidel's is an exception to the general tendency to make a binary choice in favor of the "natural." Boyd points out that Goethe's ballad is "no mere 'Tendenzstück' advocating this or that faith" (*Notes to Goethes Poems*, 87).

partake with him of the gifts of Bacchus and Ceres which his hostess has provided. The gifts of Amor will be her own contribution and make the evening complete. But things are not this easy. The maiden tells the youth that she is one of many sacrifices to the new religion and that she is now beyond the reach of earthly joys. This only makes him the more ardent, and, realizing that she is in fact the promised bride of his childhood, he redoubles his solicitations. She weakens and presents him with a necklace, while declining the silver chalice that he has brought and accepting only a lock of his brown hair. Again he demands love and, at her repeated refusal, throws himself upon the bed amidst tears of despair. When she points to the coldness of her limbs, he replies that his love would warm a corpse. Finally they come together in love and desire, "Eins ist nur im andern sich bewußt" (line 123).[95] As she devours his words of passion, his ardor warms her congealed blood. "Doch es schlägt kein Herz in ihrer Brust."

At the cock's crow, the mother is still up and busy with household chores. Offended by the unmistakable sounds from the guest room, she bursts in and discovers that her own deceased daughter is the wench in the visitor's bed. The maiden had been sent to a nunnery as a votive offering for her mother's recovery from serious illness and had there perished. The girl now rises up and denounces the new and false faith that denied her the human fulfillment that is a pre-condition of a restful grave. Citing breach of promise, she is driven to seek the lost good and will suck the life blood of her once intended groom. And she must prey on other young men too unless she and her lover can be brought to rest in the flames of a funeral pyre. Rising from the blaze, they will hasten back to the gods of old.

Although Goethe denies it, his source may have been a tale by a certain Pflegon, freedman under the emperor Hadrian, which Goethe read in the Anthropodemus Plutonicus of Praetorius.[96] In this story the lovers' tryst does not take place in Corinth, but in the Syrian city of Tralles, and the theme of religious difference does not occur. Philinion, the pretty daughter of a noble

---

[95] Rüdiger Schnell observes that love between Riwalin and Blanscheflur and between Tristan and Isolde is a function of absolute honesty and clarity (Lauterkeit) between them. "Im Erkennen des anderen kommt der Mensch zur Erkenntnis seiner selbst; durch die Reinheit des anderen hindurch sieht er sich selbst, unabhängig von den Rollen, die er nach außen hin zu spielen hat. Liebe bedeutet also nicht nur Durchsichtigkeit, sondern auch Reflexion, Spiegelung des einen im anderen (lines 11726, 11973)" (Rüdiger Schnell, Suche nach Wahrheit: Gottfrieds "Tristan und Isold" als erkenntniskritischer Roman [Tübingen: Max Niemeyer, 1992], 219–20).

Cf. Goethe: "Man weiss erst daß man ist wenn man sich in andern wiederfindet" (Goethe to Auguste Gräfin von Stolberg, 13 February 1775, DjG 5:9).

[96] Johannes Praetorius, Anthropodemus Plutonicus (Magdeburg, 1666). Cited in Leitzmann, Die Quellen von Schillers und Goethes Balladen (Bonn: A. Marcus & E. Weber, 1922), 34–37.

couple, has died inexplicably, and she comes upon the young visitor, Machates, not by chance but full of amorous purpose, even threatening him with a lawsuit (before which agency is not clear) if he is not complaisant. When the lovers are discovered and the ghost exposed, she reproaches her parents only with a spiteful interruption of her pleasure. Her revenge is to die anew and remain lifeless at their feet. Presents given to her by Machates are found in her grave. To prevent the loud mourning of the parents from causing a riot in the town, a guard is set up around the house and the girl's body is thrown to the wild animals outside the city gates, while offerings and sacrifices are made to the gods. Machates soon dies too, inexplicably. Praetorius interprets these marvels as an example of the devil's characteristic practice of occupying the bodies of the dead in pursuit of his diabolic ends.

Goethe claimed to have got his story *not* from Phlegon but from "wo anders her."[97] His innovations and alterations in the plot are, in any case, numerous — the transformation of the revenant into a vampire, the change of venue, the deletion of personal names (perhaps for the sake of breadth of application), and the more detailed and sympathetic portrayal of the love scene, which is transmuted from damnable lust into chaste love — the ceremonial union of two sympathetic young people (despite all the repugnance of vampirism as an idea, the lovers of Goethe's ballad are reminiscent of Romeo and Juliet, here bridging the gap between rival religions as their star-crossed prototypes linked hostile factions), some substitutions in the gifts exchanged by the lovers that underscore the permanence of their bond,[98] and, above all, the theme of conflicting religions. These are considerable accretions and imperfectly explained with the metaphors of ripening and purification that Goethe employed to describe his subject's maturation in his mind over the years. On the other hand, the theme of love and death is retained, developed, purified in fact (for example, eliminating the salaciousness in the source) and made symbolic — all of which did not stop Herder from viewing this ballad and "Der Gott und die Bajadere" as a self-indulgent display of Goethe's offensive sensuality: "Priapus [spielt] eine

---

[97] Conversation with Kanzler F. von Müller, 6. Juni 1824, GA 23:348.

[98] In Phlegon, after "offtmals wiederholten Küssen und Vermischung" (Leitzmann, *Die Quellen*, 35), the ghost presents her lover with a tucker and a golden ring, rather as a gratuity. For these gifts Goethe substitutes a necklace as a stronger symbol of their bond. The youth offers a chalice to his bride, as in the Phlegon story, but Goethe's Bride rejects it, requesting instead a lock of her lover's hair. "Der Todesgott weiht die dem Tode Bestimmten durch Abschneiden einer Locke der Unterwelt. So versucht die Tote, den Jüngling durch die Locke an sich und an das Totenreich zu binden" ("Staiger in der Manesse-Ausgabe Bd. I, S. 472," in HA 1:664). There is a variation on this motif in Mörike's "Erinna an Sappho." There as here the lock symbolizes a bond between the living and the dead, a bond reinforced in Goethe's poem by the symbol of the chain.

große Rolle, einmal als Gott mit einer Bajadere . . ., das zweite Mal als ein Heidenjüngling mit seiner christlichen Braut, die als Gespenst zu ihm kommt und die er, eine kalte Leiche ohne Herz, zum warmen Leben priapis-iert — das sind Heldenballaden!"[99]

One of Goethe's purposes in so radically recasting and re-presenting his inherited materials was probably to break a lance for greater naturalness in intercourse between the sexes. Although a sexual meeting with necrophilic overtones is a sensational topic, he was not just provoking for the sake of provocation or of contributing something eye-catching that would enhance the circulation of Schiller's *Musenalmanach,* where the ballad was published in 1798. The classicism of Goethe's middle period, to which this ballad be-longs, includes an advocacy of natural sexuality, an affirmation of the erotic fulfillment that is every person's birthright and the happy pursuit of which, in the *Römische Elegien,* is shown as uniting the ancient gods with the Ro-man poets and with the visitor from the North who, newly arrived in the city of love, discovers there his oneness with prototypes in history and myth. In the poem before us, the bride's first words to her Athenian lover indict Christianity as hostile to life. Lives are sacrificed to this "falsch Gelübd'" — "Weder Lamm noch Stier, / Aber Menschenopfer unerhört" (lines 172; 61–63). This coincides with other anti-Christian and pro-Hellenistic statements of the time, such as Schiller's "Die Götter Griechenlands" and Wordsworth's "The World Is Too Much With Us." Goethe's Corinthian bride explicitly contrasts Hellenistic religion with a Christian culture in which natural values are abandoned or suppressed. Her parents' decision to commit their daugh-ter to a convent is a crime against nature, a violation of the girl's natural right to human fulfillment through the consummation of her desire to love and marry. She is the typical revenant — a soul that can find no rest because her business among the living was left unfinished.[100] Indeed, her vampirism represents on one level the perversion of natural desire and is a manifestation of the topos of aborted natural development, according to which such evils as predation and malignant growth result from the obstruction of a natural purposiveness. An oak whose crown is broken off by the storm becomes mis-shapen, ugly, and threatening, extending tentacles that tear at the cloak of a nocturnal wanderer. The same topos underlies many of the portraits of predatory women in literature, including those of Medea, the various sirens, Loreleis, and Venuses of Romanticism, the thirteenth fairy godmother in the fairy tale "Sleeping Beauty," and the series of femmes fatales descending

[99] To Karl Ludwig von Knebel, 5 August 1797, in Herder, *Briefe in einem Band* (Berlin: Aufbau, 1970), 350.

[100] Like Anne Boleyn in the song: "With 'er 'ead tucked underneath 'er arm, she walks the bloody tower." "Die Seele, der im Leben ihr göttlich Recht / nicht ward, sie ruht auch drunten im Orkus nicht" (Hölderlin, "An die Parzen").

from George Lillo's Millwood, whose vileness to the young London merchant, George Barnwell, is a direct consequence of her abuse by unscrupu-
lous men. That the vampire of Goethe's ballad is a ghost and an unwilling
seductress are details which in no wise separate her from other figures in this
tradition; she was cut off in her prime and is now propelled by a drive, unimpeded by the boundary between life and death, to seek what she has been
denied. "Ach, die Erde kühlt die Liebe nicht!" (line 168).

Goethe's indictment of Christianity as inhospitable to natural human
impulses and ultimately as hostile to life is familiar. The feeling that his own
growth had been held up by the proscriptions of institutionalized Christianity may have motivated his enthusiasm for the greater naturalness he observed in the culture of Greece, and his pro-Hellenistic statements as well as
his personal defiance of some of the ruling social and sexual conventions
contributed to his reputation as a sensual pagan, a pervasive image in Germany even today. However, he never supposed that he could escape the influence of Christianity, and he was never without appreciation for its history,
myths, sacraments, and values, as the ballad "Die Braut von Korinth" itself
shows.[101]

There can be little doubt that the importance of Corinth in early Christian history, plus the fact that it contained a temple of Venus, accounts for
Goethe's choice of this venue for his story. The apostle Paul had preached in
Corinth and wrote four epistles to the infant congregation there, the last
three of which are known as Corinthians 1 and 2 in the New Testament.
The first letter is lost; the third is thought to consist of chapters 10–13 of
2nd Corinthians. While Goethe may have intended no more than to give the
proper setting for the religious conflict that he wished to dramatize, two issues, which come up in different ways in Goethe's ballad, are prominent in
the first of Paul's extant letters to the Corinthians — the question of celibacy
and that of the meaning of the Eucharist. Regarding the former, Paul responds to what seems to have been a supposition of accomplished salvation
in the minds of some believers, saying that he has encouraged them to remain celibate not because as Christians they have already overcome the
world and entered the Kingdom of God (in which there is neither male nor
female, neither marrying nor giving in marriage), but because (as he believed) the end of the world is imminent. Paul realistically admits that sexuality is a governing fact of human life and that not everyone has the gift of
celibacy. "If [the unmarried and the widows] cannot exercise self-control,

---

[101] Goethe had only sarcasm for the notion that he had forsaken his inherited culture
and religion. "Ich heidnisch?" he remarked to General Rühle von Lilienstern. "Nun
habe ich doch Gretchen hinrichten und Ottilie verhungern lassen; ist denn das den
Leuten nicht christlich genug? Was wollen sie noch Christlicheres?" (as reported by
K. A. Varnhagen von Ense, 1809, GA 22:579).

they should marry. For it is better to marry than to be aflame with passion."[102] Celibacy is not a principle of faith or a badge of induction into the Kingdom, but rather an expedient dictated by the impending trauma.[103] Nevertheless, Paul's sermons as well as his example would have encouraged the congregation in Corinth to regard celibacy as the ideal state.[104] The mistake of the bride's mother lies not so much in any misunderstanding of Paul's exhortations as in her fanaticism and her disregard for the autonomy of her daughter, who is unconverted to the Pauline ideal and has her own desires and purposes. The mother's crime is exploitation; the daughter was made to enter a monastic life that was not of her own choosing.[105] She has lain unreconciled in the grave and returns to exact her revenge and to achieve the non-celibate fulfillment that she regards as her natural right and just due. Not so dissimilarly, Goethe "attributed his 'physical-moral troubles' of the last years before the Italian journey partly to his unnatural, celibate life style. On his return to Weimar he lost little time in ensuring that he would not make the same mistake again. "As Mars took Rhea Sylvia on her way to draw water at the Tiber, so Goethe took Christiane and made her his mistress."[106]

The second of the issues discussed in Paul's letters to the Corinthians that are echoed in Goethe's ballad is the taking of the bread and the wine. In Goethe's poem this issue is employed not as a vehicle of religious contrast but as a means of sanctifying the "wedding" of Christian bride and Greek groom and of symbolizing their communion. In the Christian context, partaking of bread and wine commemorates Jesus' last meal with his disciples, and its "repetition . . . spontaneously brings to mind Jesus' death," and signifies "a mythic (or 'spiritual') participation in the death [on the part of the partaker]."[107] Through the Eucharist the Christian believer identifies with Christ in death, anticipating at the same time his or her own death and resurrection through Christ's agency. Participation in the Lord's Supper, like baptism, also "effects incorporation into the Body of Christ."[108] In commun-

---

[102] 1. Cor. 7.8; rev. standard ed.

[103] Calvin J. Roetzel, *The Letters of Paul: Conversations in Context,* 2nd ed. (Atlanta: John Knox Press, 1982), 2, 59.

[104] Graham's essay "Die Theologie tanzt," which interprets the significance of Paul's letters for Goethe's ballad differently than I do, came to my attention only after my essay was first published, in 1988.

[105] Cf. Müller-Seidel, "Die Braut von Korinth," 84–85.

[106] Humphry Trevelyan, *Goethe and the Greeks* (Cambridge, UK: Cambridge UP, 1941), 181.

[107] Roetzel, *The Letters of Paul,* 85.

[108] Ernst Käsemann, "The Pauline Doctrine of the Lord's Supper," in *Essays on New Testament Themes* (London: SCM Press, 1964), 111.

ion the believer is united with Christ and with other partakers of the sacrament. They come to together in a community. Novalis develops the full mystical-erotic possibilities of this set of ideas in one of his *Geistliche Lieder*, the "Hymne," where conjugal union and religious communion are metaphorically connected and the time is foreseen when "alles Leib, [ist] ein Leib, / In himmlischem Blute / Schwimmt das selige Paar."[109]

Although the emphasis varies, the conjoining and death-foreshadowing meanings are present wherever Goethe mentions the Lord's Supper (e.g. FA 1,14:316–17). Young Werther, for example, in whose "Christusleere" theology Jesus is no longer "the Way," but rather only a role model whose death and resurrection he may voluntarily emulate, orders bread and wine as his last supper. Here solidarity with Jesus Christ is limited to what Werther regards as imitation. Faust, by contrast, brings a chalice of poison to his lips early on Easter morning and is then reminded by Easter ceremonies in a neighboring church of the necessity of Christ's mediation in effecting the translation of men from mortality to immortality and is deterred at the last moment from hubristically attempting self-translation. Contingency is here the operative idea.[110]

In "Die Braut von Korinth," the bread and wine are initially provided not as a sacrament but only as a supper. This acquires sacral significance when it is employed by the lovers as a wedding feast, and its peculiarly Christian meanings are enlivened when it is seen to be part of a *Liebestod*. The proverb, "Ohne Wein und Brot leid't Venus Not," which, as Boyd notes (89), is derived from Terenz's "Sine Serere et Baccho friget,"[111] is pertinent but, by itself, an insufficient explanation of the supper's centrality.[112] Wine and bread may enhance love (and the bride's wish to hasten to the gods of old — line 196 — means, above all, to hasten under the aegis of Venus), but

---

[109] Novalis, *Schriften: Die Werke Friedrich von Hardenbergs,* ed. Paul Kluckhohn and Richard Samuel, 3rd ed., 4 vols. in 7 (Stuttgart: W. Kohlhammer, 1977–99), 1:167.

[110] Robert Ellis Dye, "The Easter Cantata and the Idea of Mediation in Goethe's Faust," *PMLA* 92 (1977): 963–76; here, 963, 966–68.

[111] James Boyd, *Notes to Goethe's Poems,* 2 vols. (Oxford: Basil Blackwell, 1944 & 1949), 2:89.

[112] "One example [of the association of erotic love and food in Byron's *Don Juan*] is the significant . . . association in Canto 2 of Venus with vermicelli: 'While Venus fills the heart (without heart really / Love, though good always, is not quite so good) / Ceres presents a plate of vermicelli, — / (For love must be sustained like flesh and blood), — / While Bacchus pours out wine or hands a jelly: / Eggs, oysters too, are amatory food (Byron, *Don Juan,* 2.170)" (Jocelyne Kolb, *The Ambiguity of Taste: Freedom and Food in European Romanticism* [Ann Abor: The U of Michigan P, 1995], 59). See also Byron, *Don Juan,* 16.86 as cited in Kolb, *The Ambiguity of Taste,* 60.

the special case here is a love unto death. The supper signifies the lovers' communion in love and in death.

It is in the fate of the non-Christian of the poem, the bridegroom, that the meaning of the Eucharist as anticipatory to death is unambiguously realized. The bride herself, who is a baptized Christian, is already dead and therefore refuses the bread as food for the living, while accepting the wine.[113] Her Athenian lover reciprocates in the drinking of the wine (and presumably takes bread as well) and then dies when his blood is sucked out by the vampire; her actions become dense with significance when we consider that she drinks blood first symbolically and then literally, uniting his substance with hers. The Christian symbol is divided, as it were, into signifier and signified; the effect may be to revive a metaphor for the reader.[114] However unwillingly, the maiden had become a celibate Christian in life and had presumably drunk often of the blood of Christ, who was her spiritual bridegroom. She had entered into his body and he into hers. Upon returning as a ghost, she again partakes of the wine before gulping the blood and causing the death of her mortal bridegroom.[115] Her participation in this sacrament anticipates and makes possible her eventual communion in death with the bridegroom whom she "weds" and with the gods to whom she wants to return. The sexual union with a lover represents, and is instrumental to, union with the divine, an idea found in some first-century mystery religions and one informing the *Liebestod* topos throughout its long history.

In depicting this variously meaningful "Brautnacht" and last supper, Goethe is engaged less in marking religious boundaries than in celebrating a mythical conjunction across multiple barriers. The ballad turns less on religious difference than on the pivotal encounter between male and female, the quick and the dead, Christian and Greek (a more complete coming together than the rapprochement of Taurian and Greek in Iphigenie auf Tauris). As Müller-Seidel has pointed out, there is no objection to a marriage with the

---

[113] Staiger, *Goethe* 2:309.

[114] Byron associates cannibalism and transubstantiation in *Don Juan* (ii. 44). The surgeon drinks Pedrillo's blood, whereas Juan "refuses to 'dine on his pastor and his master' (ii. 78)" (Kolb, *The Ambiguity of Taste,* 145). Note the cannibalism in Dante [Ugolino], "which provides the literary 'legitimization' for Byron's subject" (ii. 83). Heine plays on the Eucharist as cannibalism: "Trotzen kann ich deinen Geistern, / Deinen dunklen Höllenpossen, / Denn in mir ist Jesus Christus, / Habe seinen Leib genossen. // Christus ist mein Leibgericht" (ibid., 129–30). The Eucharist figures in the poems "Vitzliputzli" and "Disputation," which conclude the first and final books in the *Romanzero* cycle (ibid., 174).

[115] Goethe likes images of incorporation. In the poem "An den Geist des Johannes Sekundus," for instance, he says his beloved "Mehr möchte haben von mir, und möchte mich Ganzen / Ganz erküssen, und fressen, und was sie könnte."

second daughter.[116] Goethe goes out of his way to dignify the participants and to identify them as types and representatives before subordinating accidental human differences to transcendent existential concerns. The youth seems the very epitome of Athenian masculinity, and the vampire has none of the ghastly characteristics usually associated with her kind; though resentful, she is a paragon of Christian modesty and virtue. Dressed in a white veil and gown with a band of Christian black and gold around her forehead, she walks "sittsam still" into his room (line 31)[117] with no purpose of either seducing or harming him. Her act of vampirism, the unavoidability of which only gradually enters her consciousness,[118] is kept discreetly offstage and is best understood as a further metaphor of their union, her absorption of his substance into herself. Of course, in the context of her sharp rejection of Christianity, the thought may occur to us that Christians are here being branded as vampires all, predators upon healthier cultures — feeding on a borrowed vitality as, in the sacrament, they feed on the blood of their god and as that god himself became bloated at the cost of his Hellenistic rivals. "Einen zu bereichern, unter allen, / Mußte diese Götterwelt vergehn," was how Schiller put it in "Die Götter Griechenlands" — words that closely parallel lines 57–60 of Goethe's ballad. So hostile an interpretation of the meaning of the Christian-vampire-bride would agree with the bride's own judgment of Christianity and is a factor in the poem's ambiguities. The dominant impression conveyed, however, is not that Goethe is using the figure of a vampire to castigate Christianity, but that he is exploiting the rituals of Christianity to extract mythic significance from a case of vampirism. On another level he is expressing the parasitic nature of all acts of communion and intercourse, whether of cultures or of individuals, including his own dependency on inherited models and traditions.

In a context unrelated to our topic, Miller has reflected on the words "parasite" and "host." "'Parasite,'" he observes, "is one of those words which calls [sic] up its apparent opposite. . . . There is no parasite without its host."[119] The same is true of the word "guest," a prominent word here and elsewhere in Goethe's writings. In the ballad, there is interaction between guests and hosts on a number of levels. The Athenian youth is a guest of the host family in Corinth — "[the mother] empfängt den Gast mit bestem Willen" and shows him to a room. No sooner has he lain down on the bed, however, than "ein seltner Gast" comes in at the door that he has left unlocked. There is a nesting and a reciprocity of the use of the word "Gast"

[116] Müller-Seidel, Walter, "Die Braut von Korinth," 82.
[117] Cf. Elizabeth Wright, "Ambiguity and Ambivalence," 117–18.
[118] Boyd, *Notes to Goethes Poems,* 2:92.
[119] J. Hillis Miller, "The Critic as Host," in *Deconstruction and Criticism,* ed. Harold Bloom (New York: Seabury P, 1979), 217–54; here, 218–19.

here. The maiden is the young man's guest, while he is the guest of her family and thus of herself as well. They belong to each other as reciprocal guests to hosts, and in intercourse with each other they lose their self-awareness, or rather the self-awareness of each is preserved only through the medium of her/his consciousness of the other (line 123).[120] With each other they are at home. On the other hand, the maiden is as alien and as much a guest in her mother's house and religion as is the young pagan, her lover. Neither one belongs in this sectarian and thus inhospitable domicile, but when joined together in love and fire they will hurry after the gods who were driven from the premises (lines 57–58). In another sense, the youth is host to his bride in her role of parasite. In the course of their love feast he presumably partakes of the host of the Eucharist (an etymologically unrelated word but one bearing pertinent connotations here) and is then preyed upon by his vampire bride, who, like the black-widow spider, destroys the mate whose blood makes her meal. Thus is he consumed and united with her, metaphorically returned to the womb, before their joint transmutation and reunion with their gods. And, indeed, the point of another use of the word "Gast" by Goethe — "ein trüber Gast" in the poem "Selige Sehnsucht" from the West-östlicher Divan — is that until we are consumed in the flames of a higher mating, we remain untransformed and doomed to a lonely and obfuscated existence as eternal guests on the dark earth. To die and become is essential to becoming at home, so that only by killing her lover and herself can she unite with him and overcome their mutual strangeness and detachment — annihilate him and herself as guests and eternal outsiders, yet always propelled onward by the hope that there is a home somewhere — a resting place and someone to lie down with, in union with whom we are no longer guests or restless wanderers, but "Liebende" and in "Ruh" (line 193).

Readers with some awareness of the range of meaning of the *Liebestod* theme will not facilely take the bride's Hellenism and her rejection of the Christian religion as a final und unambiguous representation of the meaning of "Die Braut von Korinth." The humanistic and individualistic values implicit in her nostalgia for the anthropomorphic gods of sunny Greece are only part of the story, the greater part being her reluctant but ineluctable surrender to her own erotic longing and her quest for peace and dissolution with her lover in the flames. Her preference for Hellenistic polytheism over a monotheistic Christianity reflects the intellectualism and partisanship that is an undeniable part of her nature, a tendency to differentiate and take sides,

---

[120] Cf. Hegel: "In der Liebe hat ein Individuum das Bewußtsein seiner in dem Bewußtsein des andern, ist sich entäußert, und in dieser gegenseitigen Entäußerung hat es sich (ebenso das andre wie sich selbst als mit dem andern eins) gewonnen" (*Vorlesungen über die Philosophie der Geschichte*, in *Werke in zwanzig Bänden*, ed. Eva Moldenhauer and Karl Markus Michel, vol. 12 [Frankfurt am Main: Suhrkamp, 1970], 60).

but the wedding and welding of nun and pagan that she and her lover enact can be read against the grain of her religious polemicising as a metaphor for the historical mixing and blending that in fact took place, revealing Christianity not as adversary, but as lover and consumer of the Hellenism that it embraced and destroyed. Müller-Seidel has questioned on other grounds whether it was Goethe's purpose in this poem to play off the richness of Greek antiquity against the impoverishment effected by the rise of Christianity and regards the issue of religious difference as at most a secondary concern of the poem.[121] He points to beliefs and practices that unite the two families of the ballad and offset their differences, such as their common and mistaken supposition that it is the parents' prerogative to use their children as they wish (an abuse of parental power to those schooled in Kantian ethics and thus to the mature Goethe and Schiller). But we can take note of anachronistic ethical ideas in the ballad while taking its historical setting seriously and acknowledging the general cultural compatibility of Corinth and Athens in the first century, the emergence of religious novelty in Corinth notwithstanding. In any case, the poetic effect of the radical metaphors of vampirism and erotic union in death is to overshadow such distinctions as that between Hellenism and Christianity, and ultimately to minimize the significance and value of separate identity altogether, in favor of the mixing and blending that is Romanticism's answer to the existential loneliness of separate human selves. There is no need to discount the bride's resentment and her anti-Christian rhetoric in order to see that the poem's double *Liebestod* — first the death of the youth in erotic union with the revenant, then the (anticipated) immolation of both of them — is the poem's central event and the key to its meaning. Despite the bride's explicit Hellenism, her classicism, as it were, what we have above all in this ballad is a celebration of the vanquishing of distance and difference in love and death and thus a fundamentally Romantic poem. And although the bride brands Christianity as pernicious and praises Hellenism as wholesome, the work in which she resides decries not only religious sectarianism, the bride's as well as her mother's, but all kinds of differentiation and binary choices and celebrates unity, self-surrender, and transcendence.

For death is not the end of the story. The bride's projected scenario employs the familiar concept of rebirth, which makes dying and becoming sequential in an eternal cycle or spiral. The lovers' rest will be followed by their return, as a couple, to the gods of their childhood. This, at least, is her request. As all Goethe students know, transmutation, metamorphosis, death and resurrection are but different, interchangeable metaphors for what is fundamentally the same process — the destruction of one form of being and its recreation as something higher. The process may take place in an al-

---

[121] Müller-Seidel, "Die Braut von Korinth," 82.

chemical retort, a cocoon, or a sepulcher and usually involves the combining of opposites, as in the mating of the Lion red and the Lily "im lauen Bad" to produce the young Queen who personifies both a medication and a deadly poison (*Faust,* 1042–47) or the wedding of fire and water in the persons of Homunculus and Galatee in the pageant on the Aegean Sea, whereupon Homunculus hopes to "entstehn" (line 8246). The mating of opposites (such as acids and alkalis — to give one final example — which, according to the Hauptmann of *Die Wahlverwandtschaften,* show "eine entschiedene Vereinigungslust" [FA 1,8:303]) are "hierogamous" unions that make the earth shake or, as in Werther, make the world fade into oblivion (FA 1,8:246–47), and the disparateness of the partners is a prerequisite.[122] "Obgleich einander entgegengesetzt und vielleicht eben deswegen, weil sie einander entgegengesetzt sind," remarks the Hauptmann, the antipodal mates "suchen und fassen, . . . modifizieren [sich] und [bilden] zusammen einen neuen Körper" (FA 1,8:303). But Goethe is nothing if not virtuosic in his manipulation of symbols. And knowing this, we may delight in recognizing the wedding and then the projected immolation and rebirth of our ballad's contrasting lovers, on the one hand, and Goethe's account of the generation of the poem itself, on the other, as the combination and transmutation of inherited and borrowed subject matter in the crucible of the poet's consciousness as containing the same root metaphor. The ballad's content as well as the story of its gestation exhibits the cycle (or, rather, the spiral) of sequential *Liebestode* and resurrections — unions, deaths, and becomings, "Gestaltungen" and "Umgestaltungen" — which informs Goethe's concept of dynamic existence and bears his unmistakable signature.

But equally characteristic of Goethe is the *Friedfertigkeit* and the partiality for "geeinte Zwienatur," for unity over division and love over war that is implied by the convergence and the mergings of opposed forces and entities in this poem — of male and female, of the quick and the dead, of Athenian youth and Corinthian bride of Christ (and, at a greater referential distance, of Hellenism and Christianity or the blending of Hellenism into Christianity: the poet believed that the contrasts between these offered a rich quarry for poetry).[123] We might even see in the vampire's drinking of the soul of her lover a symbol of Goethe himself as a modern imbibing the spirit of a more whole and harmonious past age and the marriage of Christian bride and pagan youth as an affirmation of the interaction and interdependence, the communion, of all individuals and all cultures that connect and interfuse. In honoring the naturalness and vitality of Greece, Goethe incorporated some of that naturalness and vitality into himself. But the process is reciprocal;

---

[122] Evelyn J. Hinz, "Hierogamy versus Wedlock: Types of Marriage Plots and Their Relationship to Genres of Prose Fiction," *PMLA* 91:5 (1976): 900–913; here, 907.

[123] Conversation with Kanzler F. von Müller, 6. Juni 1824, GA 23:348–49.

Greece likewise underwent a transfusion from him, absorbed some of his spirit — as the past always does when appropriated by the present. Ulrich von Wilamowitz-Moellendorff employed the Homeric image of ghosts revived by the blood of the living to make the point: "We know that ghosts cannot speak until they have drunk blood; and the spirits which we evoke demand the blood of our hearts. We give it to them gladly; but if they then abide our question, something from us has entered into them." It is "something alien, that must be cast out in the name of truth!"[124] Because he knew his place and function in the larger system of intertextuality, Goethe has Faust question whether such alien infusions *can* be cast out (lines 577–79). Conversely, he neither expected nor desired independence from the past nor believed in the possibility of achieving any kind of ahistorical autonomy. He was grateful for the legacy and fond of images of contingency, parasitism, and symbiosis as metaphors for the interdependence of all creatures. Thus ants sucking the "filtrirten Safft" from the bodies of aphids are seen as analogous to the exploitation of the peasants by the nobility (to Knebel, 17 April 1782) and in the poem "Amyntas," an apple tree pleads that the ivy that drains off its life juices be spared. As Demetz notes, "the ivy, like a vampire, 'lives on' the tree and . . . drains away his life and infects his sap with carnal passion, if not with foul disease."[125] "Amyntas" ends with the question, "Wer sich der Liebe vertraut, hält er sein Leben zu Rat?" Ultimately, the yearning for love and death is not wholesome, and Goethe's "Die Braut von Korinth" is not a paean to life, at least not to the fiction that we live as autonomous subjects, unaffected by history and environment. There is a definite stress on synthesis, on con-fusion, communion, and community in the poem. Love, communion, dissolution, and rest from wandering are the goals of Goethe's vampire-bride, who nevertheless seeks a sunny happiness beyond death, amidst the glorious gods of Greece. Without love, she seems to say, we are dismal guests indeed, but with it we rest in the bosom of Venus until morning awakens.[126]

---

[124] Hugh Lloyd-Jones, *Blood for the Ghosts: Classical Influences in the Nineteenth and Twentieth Centuries* (Baltimore: Johns Hopkins UP, 1982), 5.

[125] Peter Demetz, "The Elm and the Vine: Notes Toward the History of a Marriage Topos," *PMLA* 73 (1958): 521–32; here, 529. See also Mandy Green, "'The Vine and her Elm': Milton's Eve and the Transformation of an Ovidian Motif," *The Modern Language Review* 91, part 2 (April 1996): 301–16.

[126] "In the novel of adultery by a strange inversion form can become greedy for formlessness, and there are recurrent signs of a regressive guest for the unstructured or prestructured state. Chaos is a state in which there are no marriages and hence no identification of offspring, and hence an inability to establish names" (Tony Tanner, *Adultery in the Novel: Contract and Transgression* [Baltimore: Johns Hopkins UP, 1979], 61–62).

E. "Der Gott und die Bajadere"

Goethe's early ballads, under the influence of Percy's *Reliques of Ancient English Poetry* and imbued with the young Goethe's enthusiasm for "folk poetry," have a power and immediacy he never again achieves in the ballad form and never seriously tries to achieve. His later ballads, especially those composed for Schiller's *Musenalmanach* 1798, reflect a still live, but transmuted enthusiasm for the ballad form. They are not wanting in feeling. With Christiane Vulpius in mind, Max Kommerell calls "Der Gott und die Bajadere" Goethe's "most personal poem."[127] But the feeling is well-clothed. Beyond that, the later ballads are exercises in virtuosity or, in Graham's term, "eine Gratwanderung"[128] of form and feeling in which a virtuosic, alienating form keeps raw feeling under control and mediated through an aesthetic prism. Only a year later Goethe translated the "Kerker" scene of *Faust* into verses, "da dann die Idee wie durch einen Flor durchscheint, die unmittelbare Wirkung des ungeheuern Stoffes aber gedämpft wird'" (to Schiller, 5 May 1798).

"Der Gott und die Bajadere" has the same theme as Mozart's *Die Entführung aus dem Serail* (which Goethe directed forty-nine times in Weimar),[129] Beethoven's *Fidelio* and, with a bewildering series of complications, Kleist's *Amphitryon:* loyalty in love. *Die Entführung* also shares the ballad's orientalism, attributing superior uprightness to a non-European, and Leonore in *Fidelio* displays the same unconditional love as is shown by the bajadere. These are all cases of *the woman's* loyalty in love. Not that the man's is in question, but the sexist cliché of the loyal woman is implicit in these creations by male authors. Perhaps it is the inverse of Goethe's pretense of cynical wisdom in the early poem "Unbeständigkeit," where a youth's fickleness is legitimated, as though the poem's persona were a Viennese man of the world. Both this early poem and "Der Gott und die Bajadere" appear more sexist than, for instance, Schnitzler's cynically nostalgic *Reigen,* which even-handedly portrays the fickleness of *both* sexes.

[127] Max Kommerell, "Goethes indische Balladen," in *Goethe-Kalender auf das Jahr 1937,* ed. Frankfurter Goethe-Museum (Leipzig: Dieterich 1937): 158–85; here, 164.

[128] Ilse Graham, "Die Theologie tanzt," 253.

[129] "The five most performed plays in Weimar were by Mozart or Schiller during Goethe's direction of the theater" (Jane K. Brown, "The Theatrical Practice of Weimar Classicism," forthcoming in The Camden House History of German Literature volume 7: *The Literature of Weimar Classicism,* ed. Simon J. Richter, 2005). Mozart, with only seven titles, was given 304 performances overall, after Kotzebue's 641 with 96 titles, Iffland's 371 with 32 titles, and Schillers' 313 with 15 titles (figure 1). As Brown points out, Mozart was "much the longest runner" on the Weimar stage," his average run being 43 performances (8, figure 3).

The theme of loyalty in love is prefigured in "Es war ein König in Thule" and by Klärchen in *Egmont,* who resembles Beethoven's Leonore and, like Leonore, has political as well as personal purposes. In Klärchen Goethe had "glorified a feminine capacity for love and passionate devotion that refused to count the cost. The changes made to *Erwin* and *Claudine* reflect the same altered notion of the feminine ideal also, for a new female character was introduced into both plays, a woman for whom love is all and whose attitude acts as a foil to the behavior of the existing central female figures, Elmire and Claudine."[130]

Can the polyamory of *Stella* be reconciled with the fidelity of Klärchen, or that of the old king in Thule, the vampire bride of "Die Braut von Korinth," and the Indian bajadere? Recall the example of the Graf von Gleichen brought up by Cezilie in *Stella*. Life may sometimes generate loyalty to more than one person, none of them supplanting each other or inevitably in conflict. Monogamy and loyalty in love, Goethe seems to say, are not synonymous. Such an extreme of loyalty as self-immolation upon the death of a spouse, however, was expected only of women, and not of women generally, but only of a lawfully wedded wife. The "non-wife" of the ballad has no obligation, as the priests point out. Yet, as in both *Fidelio* and "Der Gott und die Bajadere," the loyalty of the woman in question is neither culturally determined nor required by the prevailing legal code, but individual. Likewise, in gaining the favor and trust of the governor of the prison and throwing herself in front of her husband at the moment of his intended execution, Lenore transcends the duty and creativity of any wife.

A smug acceptance of suttee (sati) in the spirit of "andere Länder, andere Sitten" would be opprobrious today and was so already in Goethe's day. "Für die Zeit Goethes [war die Witwenverbrennung] ein aktueller Musterfall für mögliche Verirrungen des Menschlichen" (Eibl, FA 1,1:1239). Goethe himself says that aspects of "indische Dichtungen" come from the conflict between "der abstrusesten Philosophie" and "der monstrosesten Religion" ("Indische und chinesische Dichtung," HA 12:301), including, or so Schaub reads him as meaning, the Hindu ceremony of suttee.[131] Goethe's appropriation of the theme of suttee may render him vulnerable to anachronistic and uncomprehending condemnation by naive readers. It is a manifestation of our somewhat arbitrary selectiveness among available

[130] Deirdre Vincent, *Werther's Goethe and the Game of Literary Creativity* (Toronto: U of Toronto P, 1992), 101.

[131] Ute Liebmann Schaub, "'Gehorsam' und 'Sklavendienste': Komplementarität der Geschlechtrollen in Goethes Ballade 'Der Gott und die Bajadere,'" *Monatshefte* 76.1 (1984): 31–44; here, 32. Norbert Mecklenburg shares Hermann Hesse's view that Goethe was unsympathetic toward Indian mythology ("Poetisches Spiel mit kultureller Alterität: Goethes 'indische Legende' *Der Gott und die Bajadere*," *Literatur in Wissenschaft und Unterricht* 33 [2000]: 107–16; here, 111).

causes and issues that the theme of vampirism today flourishes in popular literature but that a writer must think twice about telling a tale that would seem to condone the burning of widows or let his or her narrator seem to smile on an unconsecrated "wife" who voluntarily throws herself into the fire in which her deceased husband is being cremated. Vampirism is sufficiently farfetched and exotic that we gain a harmless amusement from a fundamentally monstrous theme, while suttee and all that it implies is still too close and too real, like female genital mutilation. The idea that Goethe was condoning suttee is preposterous, but there appears to be a lingering suspicion among readers today that he failed to feel the required indignation at such a barbarous practice and that he personally identified with the god. As Adorno sarcastically put it, with an allusion to Lessing's patriarch, "Der Bürger braucht die Bajadere, nicht bloß um des Vergnügens willen, das er jener zugleich mißgönnt, sondern um sich recht als Gott zu fühlen. . . . Die Nacht hat ihre Lust, aber die Hure wird doch verbrannt."[132] Eibl thinks that interpretative difficulties arise "daraus, daß man dem Gedicht sogleich ein affirmatives Verhältnis zu den fremdkulturellen Voraussetzungen unterstellt" (FA 1,1:1239), but to subscribe to this reservation would be like reading *Werther* as an exercise in cultural criticism. One seldom goes wrong in presupposing Goethe's sympathy for his characters. The reader's task is always to discern the tone and the nuances of communication between her/him and an author. In fabulous tales such as Thomas Mann's "The Transposed Heads" or "The Holy Sinner," where the protagonist shrinks to the size of a hedgehog and lives on earth milk, we have no problem. No child worries when George explodes from eating too many cookies. The "Disneyfication" of Grimms' (or, for that matter, even Hans Christian Andersen's) fairy tales for American children, on the other hand, suggests that their violence, sexism, prejudice, and brutality *is* still a problem. Although the Grimms' stories are more or less fictional (and Andersen's entirely fictional), they are too realistic and sad, for all their artifice and conventionality. As a real historical institution, suttee was "worse" and poses a bigger interpretative challenge. The whole question of rhetorical "distancing" needs further study.

Pervasive in Goethe's works is the idea of metamorphosis, often cast in religious terms as transformation or transfiguration or alchemical ones as transmutation. It is this *Denkfigur* that underlies every initiation or initiatory rite. As Schaub observes, the bajadere undergoes, under the leadership of the god, first an initiation[133] and then, through the "Stirb und werde" of the fu-

---

[132] Theodor W. Adorno, *Minima Moralia: Reflexionen aus dem beschädigten Leben,* in *Gesammelte Schriften,* 22 vols. (1951; repr. Frankfurt am Main: Suhrkamp, 1971–80), 4:196.

[133] "Der rigorose Prüfungsvorgang, dem die Bajadere unterworfen wird und dem sie sich auch willig-willenlos unterwirft, ist von Goethe als ein mystisches Initiations-

neral pyre, a transmutation (there is a leader and an initiate or ephebe in every initiation).[134] The god's descent to test his creatures and the theme that he finds the socially despised to be the most worthy is widespread. The gods test Brecht's "guter Mensch von Sezuan" too, and in his sonnet "Über Goethes Gedicht 'Der Gott und die Bajadere,'" Brecht offers his own take on "Der Gott und die Bajadere." "Beneidet / Von allen hob er sie am Schluß zu sich empor!"[135]

Although "Die Braut von Korinth" may betray Goethe as the old pagan and adversary of the crucifix that he sometimes makes himself out as being, "Der Gott und die Bajadere," does not make him into a Hindu. His use of the idea of incarnation, which is common to both Christianity and Hinduism and which Kommerell finds congenial to his mind-set as an older man,[136] does not commit him to either religion. Goethe salutes unreserved love.

As both Eibl and Wild point out,[137] there is no evidence of the remorse that the ballad's "moral" intones in the third-to-last line: "Es freut sich die Gottheit der *reuigen* Sünder" (my emphasis). The God, whom Staiger and Kommerell take to be a Goethean self-portrait, condescends to save the bajadere. Says Knopf, "Das wäre der Kitsch-Traum oder auch der Topos vom großmütigen Retter gefallener Mädchen, die nach ihrer Reue von allen Sünden gereinigt werden."[138] However, the bajadere shows no remorse and has no need of any, in particular from a Hindu point of view.[139] She is sanctified because of her unconditional love, her love unto death, not because she repents. Like "Die Braut von Corinth," composed only a few days earlier, "Der Gott und die Bajadere" celebrates the blessedness of love and the natu-

geschehen gestaltet, wie es vor allem im orientalischen religiösen Denken begegnet" (Schaub, "'Gehorsam' und 'Sklavendienste,'" 38).

[134] Goethe, like Hölderlin, chooses death on the funeral pyre — the "Flammentod" — as the preferred symbol of self-sacrifice. "Denn was das Feuer lebendig erfaßt, / Bleibt nicht mehr Urform und Erdenlast. / Verflüchtigt wird es und unsichtbar, / Eilt hinauf, wo erst sein Anfang war" (FA 1,2:380).

[135] Jan Knopf, "Kritiker und Konstrukteur der erlesenen Kunstgebilde: Zur Goethe-Rezeption im Werk Bertolt Brechts am Beispiel von 'Der Gott und die Bajadere,'" in *Spuren, Signaturen, Spiegelungen: Zur Goethe-Rezeption in Europa,* ed. Bernhard Beutler and Anke Bosse (Cologne: Böhlau, 2000), 367–79. Reprinted in MA 4,1:1218–19.

[136] Kommerell, *Gedanken,* 368.

[137] FA 1,1:1240; MA 4,1:1223. Eibl says, "Deutungsvorschlag: Der formal 'korrekte,' inhaltlich inadäquate Schluß soll eine ironische Aufhebung des exoterischen Verständnisses berwirken, den Stoff in seiner Besonderheit 'vernichten' und dadurch auf ein esoterisches Text-Verständnis hinleiten."

[138] Knopf, "Kritiker und Konstrukteur," 375–76.

[139] See E. M. Butler, "Pandits and Pariahs," in *German Studies Presented to L. A. Willoughby* (Oxford: Basil Blackwell, 1952), 26–51.

ralness of human sexuality, even the sexuality of a god, as Wild notes (MA 4.1:1217). Goethe employs not only the Christian idea of incarnation, but also, repeatedly, that of the redeemability of a sinner, for example, Mary Magdalene, of whom even the Gospel of Luke says: "Ihr sind viele Sünden vergeben, denn sie hat viel geliebt."[140] "Nicht durch Reue oder Buße, sondern wegen ihrer Liebe, mit der sie sich dem Gott hingab, findet die Bajadere Erlösung."[141]

The identification of the bajadere with Mary Magdalene understates the ballad's orientalism,[142] and one of the questions it raises is the role and extent of *Goethe's* orientalism, the theme of the Goethe Society program at the 2002 MLA convention and a timely topic today. Knopf sees it as a means of alienating a scandalous topic,[143] but with his interest in Indian, Persian, Chinese, and other literatures Goethe provides ample reason why we should not underestimate his appreciation of alien cultures.

The insertion of a moral sentiment or popular maxim at the end of ballads and elsewhere (e.g. "Selige Sehnsucht") as a rhetorical strategy is in need of separate study. It is sometimes seen as ironic,[144] a view the more plausible because of the pomposity or the hyperbole in many examples of moral sententiousness in Goethe. Even the anacreontic "Unbeständigkeit" provides an example: "O Jüngling, verwein' nicht vergebens . . . !" In each instance the narrator's tone must be analyzed, with due consideration of the effect of verse as opposed to prose. As Wild observes, "Schillers Balladen stellen in einem klar geordneten, mit dramatischen Mitteln zugespitzten Durchgang durch die erzählte Handlung eine Konfliktsituation dar, in der moralisches Handeln auf der Probe steht; . . . Eine solche Einheitlichkeit in Thematik und Gestaltungsweise läßt sich in G.s Balladen, auch denen von 1797, nicht ausmachen. Sie variieren vielmehr in Form und Thematik

---

[140] Luke 7.47.

[141] Wild, MA 4,1:1217–18.

[142] Schaub, "'Gehorsam' und 'Sklavendienste,'" 40. The comparison with Mary Magdalene comes from Hegel: "Wir finden hier die christliche Geschichte der büßenden Magdalene in indische Vorstellungsweisen eingekleidet; die Bajadere zeigt dieselbe Demuth, die gleiche Stärke des Liebens und Glaubens, der Gott stellt sie auf die Probe, die sie vollständig besteht, und nur zur Erhebung und Versöhnung kommt" (G. W. F. Hegel, *Ästhetik, Jubiläumsausgabe,* 12 [Stuttgart: Fr. Frommann, 1927], 521).

[143] Knopf, "Kritiker und Konstrukteur," 378.

[144] The verse "Mit Gott im Himmel hadre nicht!" "wird als 'Schlumoral' der Ballade schon dadurch in Frage gestellt und fast zurückgenommen, daß das Gesindel vom Hochgericht, der höllische Geisterschwarm sie 'heult.' Sie erscheint auf Grund dieses Stellenwertes, der ihr den Beigeschmack einer infernalischen Ironie verleiht, wenig geeignet, ein lehrhaftes Urteil über Leonores Versündigung und gewissermaßen die Grundidee der ganzen Ballade abzugeben" (Albrecht Schöne, "Lenore," 200).

erheblich; und sie lassen auch eine unmittelbare moralische Auslegung nicht zu" (MA 4,1:1214).

The Indian setting of "Der Gott und die Bajadere" — already in its initial publication it was subtitled "eine indische Legende" — barely conceals its Christian values and its paradigmatic Christian plot, so that, in a time still struggling to accept diversity, and apparently incapable of distanced, nonpersonal toleration of "prejudice," Goethe's ballad gives double offense. Schiller, however, preferred it to "Die Braut von Korinth." And his opinion seems to be shared by some who are not put off by its theme. "Die Sprache ist gelöster," writes Staiger. "Goethe scheint sich hier freier zu bewegen und über die auch hier auf wechselvolle Gegensätze gerichtete Strophe leichter zu verfügen. Doch eben deshalb bezaubert uns hier nicht mehr das Ereignis eines Einbruchs in lang vermiedene Reiche."[145] The long-avoided realms of which Staiger speaks are no longer quite so assiduously avoided, but rarely does anyone gain any special enchantment from exoticism, except in an extreme such as vampirism.

Among the secondary themes in this ballad is the familiar one in Goethe that appearances are deceiving, but that they may also conceal a deeper truth. The professional practice and appearance of the bajadere barely disguises, through "tiefes Verderben," her "menschliches Herz" and her still unspoiled naturalness, although the hull of professionalism must be removed before the kernel of naturalness can be discovered, like the patina of accumulated smoke and grime blurring the outlines of an old painting: "Und des Mädchens frühe Künste werden nach und nach Natur." The god's deception in pretending to die barely masks his eternal vitality and brings about the final confirmation that the trafficker in love is capable of making the ultimate sacrifice in behalf of a deeper love.

"Der Gott und die Bajadere" is as pure an example of the *Liebestod* as we're likely to see, but there's more to it than approval of the girl's unconditional love. The line: "Es freut sich die Gottheit der reuigen Sünder," says something about the god's and the public's attitude toward blemished humanity. As Saint Paul Saints owner Mike Vieck once said (1996) about the baseball player Darryl Strawberry, the public loves scar tissue; we could add to Vieck's "public" God, or at least the Hindu divinity in question here, Shiva, Mahadöh, and Goethe himself. This same sympathy is one of the reasons for Lessing's claim that women with a past are more interesting than paragons of naive virtue. A book could be written about Goethe's affection for the downtrodden of the earth, which seems consonant with his manifest fondness for children. The penitent women at the end of *Faust II*, first and foremost, Gretchen, are not simply pure in their love; their imperfection and humbleness as sinners is part of their rich humanity, or else why highlight

---

[145] Staiger, *Goethe*, 2:314.

precisely penitent women? Kommerell cites Goethe's epigram: "Wundern kann es mich nicht daß uns Herr Christus mit [Huren?] / Gern und mit Sündern gelebt, gehts mir doch eben auch so."[146] Or, as Philine in *Wilhelm Meister* says to Makarie: "Ich liebe meinen Mann, meine Kinder . . . das übrige verzeihst du."[147]

---

[146] FA 1,1:465, quoted in Kommerell, *Gedanken*, 368.
[147] Quoted in Kommerell, *Gedanken*, 370.

7: *Wilhelm Meisters Lehrjahre:* Identity and Difference

WE ARE EXPLORING A NARRATIONAL FIGURE in which lovers attempt to overcome their existential opposition and blend together as one identity. There are many shades of identification, however, all of which imply, in one way or another, the submergence of duality in unity. *Wilhelm Meisters Lehrjahre* is a tour de force of identification, including multiple psychological identifications, mistaken identities, and the eventual union of sexual partners who are ideally matched but held apart by the exigencies of narrative and plot.

Among the questions the novel takes up is whether an actor can, or should, try to identify with the character he or she is playing. Challenging the view, held by many critics, that Wilhelm Meister identifies with Hamlet, Mark Bonds remarks, "Ähnlichkeit darf nicht mit Identifizierung verwechselt werden."[1] Nor identification with identity, one might add. There is a difference between absolute identity and similarity of any kind — a difference consisting in the presence of difference in any set of similars.[2] Identification too implies difference. Attired in the Count's own dressing-gown and sitting in his favorite chair, Wilhelm looks like the Count and will be mistaken for him by the pretty young Countess — or such, at least, is the Baroness's plan. As it turns out, the likeness is so great, the illusion so perfect, as to make the unexpectedly returning Count think he sees himself, just as Goethe once encountered himself riding toward himself on the road to Sesenheim (FA 1,14:545). The unequal rivals for the Countess's affection are at once double and one. Goethe makes frequent use of the idea that seeing one's double is an omen of imminent death, a sign, apparently, that a tense and fragile unity of body and soul is about to come apart and allow the separate parts to meet face to face. This is why the Count, on discovering "himself" in his own fa-

---

[1] Mark Bonds, "Die Funktion des 'Hamlet'-Motivs in 'Wilhelm Meisters Lehrjahre,'" *Goethe Jahrbuch* 96 (1979): 101–10; here, 103.

[2] Even identity may presuppose difference. See Martin Heidegger, "Der Satz der Identität," *Identität und Differenz* (Pfullingen: Günther Neske, 1957), 9–12. The possibility of division in the self is acknowledged in Wilhelm's letter to Werner: "Was [hilft es mir] ein Landgut in Ordnung zu bringen, wenn ich mit mir selber *uneins* bin?" (FA 1,9:657).

vorite chair, quietly withdraws and converts to pietistic religion.[3] Wilhelm *identifies* with the Count, however, only in the sense that, at a psychological level just below full consciousness, he would like to take his place in a more intimate and more permanent way. There is reason, too, to think that the countess would welcome Wilhelm in place of her husband, although she cannot properly admit this to herself. Wilhelm's *difference* from the Count is what makes the prospect of his "standing in" so delicious.

Wilhelm Meister's identification with Hamlet is one move in a complex game of identity and difference played out in the *Lehrjahre* (and, as it happened, in the history of its reception), as its protagonist errs along the road to self-knowledge. Hamlet, Wilhelm thinks, is like a precious vase that should have been reserved for lovely flowers but in which an oak tree has been planted instead. The roots spread and the vessel is destroyed.[4] Many critics have claimed that this description fits Wilhelm himself or Werther better than it does Hamlet.[5] Whatever the much-debated merit of this simile

---

[3] A mirror image is a double capable of capturing the soul, hence the tradition of veiling mirrors and covering vessels filled with water in a room where someone has died (see Sabine Melchior-Bonnet, *The Mirror: A History,* trans. Katharine H. Jewett [New York and London: Routledge, 2001], 102 and notes). Cf. the fisherman encountering his own reflection in the water in "Der Fischer" (the mermaid, as in Heine's "Lorelei," conventionally contemplates herself in a mirror and, via a complex metonymy, is an agent of death), and the mirror image of feminine beauty in the "Witch's Kitchen" scene of *Faust.*

[4] FA 1,9:609. In the remainder of this chapter references to the *Lehrjahre* are parenthetical and by page no. alone.

[5] Disaffection from "Goethe's" view of Hamlet as a sentimental "Zauderer" became *de rigueur* as part of the New Critical rejection of Romanticism but was expressed much earlier. For a short list of writers who reject Goethe's "conception of an unheroic, sentimental Hamlet," see Wilhelm Witte, "Deus Absconditus: Shakespeare in Eighteenth-Century Germany," *Papers: Mainly Shakespearian,* ed. G. I. Duthie, Aberdeen University Studies, no. 147 (Edinburgh: Oliver & Boyd, 1964), 83, 89 n. 19. Fischer writes, "Wie sehr gleicht der Goethe-Hamlet dem Goethe-Werther!" (Kuno Fischer, *Shakespeares Hamlet* [Heidelberg: Carl Winter, 1896], 36). Eliot reiterates this often repeated identification and claims that Goethe "made of Hamlet a Werther" (T. S. Eliot, "Hamlet and His Problems," 1919; repr. in *Selected Essays 1917–1932* [New York: Harcourt, Brace, 1932], 121). Cf. Hans Jürg Lüthi, *Das deutsche Hamletbild seit Goethe* (Bern: Paul Haupt, 1951), 23. John Dover Wilson writes angrily about "Goethe's condescending sentimentalism" toward Hamlet in *What Happens in Hamlet,* 3rd ed. (1951; repr., Cambridge UP, 1959), 43. See also 20, 50, 221, 324–25. Friendlier critics too point out that the prince is no shrinking violet. He "talks bawdry and daggers, kills Polonius like a rat, and sends Rosenkranz and Guildenstern to their death" (Wellek, *A History of Modern Criticism: 1750–1950,* 7 vols., vol. 1 [New Haven: Yale UP, 1955], 205). Cf. Henry Hatfield, *Goethe: A Critical Introduction,* Norfolk, CT: New Directions, 1963), 88.

and of Wilhelm's enactment of the role of Hamlet, which elicits Jarno's brutal judgment that Wilhelm is no actor because in playing Hamlet he was only playing himself (931), his struggle with Hamlet is an episode in the articulation of his own identity and selfhood. The very idea of personal identity, however, is employed ironically in the novel — as a useful but insufficient conceptual device.

We are told in the *Theatralische Sendung* that Wilhelm does identify with Hamlet, even to the point of becoming melancholy in his own life,[6] and there are hints, such as the name of Wilhelm's fencing partner, Laertes, that the reader is to accept this identification as well. Wilhelm's identification with Hamlet shows his aptitude for the role he is to play on the stage, just as his understanding of the master's tragedy suggests his promise, as Shakespeare's ephebe, for his theatrical mission in life. But authorial intention is always affected by the discourse in which it is realized.[7] The attribution of the passages on *Hamlet* to a fictional character affect their status and value from the very beginning, a status and value that change when the character himself is recast and resituated in the different fictional context of the later work. The transfer of the *Hamlet* criticism from the *Theatralische Sendung* into the *Lehrjahre* is its first reception — by a reader and author no longer identical to the author of the *Sendung*. A question ignored by those who take Wilhelm's views simply to be Goethe's own is why the author of the *Sendung* chose to attribute them to the hero of a work of fiction, how their

The Hamlet criticism in *Wilhelm Meister* provides the basis for another identification — that of Hamlet with the Germans. A. W. Schlegel, Adam Müller, and many others associate Hamlet with the German national character — marked by paralyzing reflectiveness and an inability to take political action — and some, such as Georg Gottfried Gervinus, do so with explicit reference to the events of 1848 (see Lüthi, *Das deutsche Hamletbild*, 63–64 n. 47, 128). "Hätte ein Deutscher den Hamlet gemacht," wrote Ludwig Börne, "würde ich mich nicht darüber wundern. Ein Deutscher brauchte nur eine schöne, leserliche Hand dazu. Er schreibt sich ab, und Hamlet ist fertig" (Lüthi, *Das deutsche Hamletbild*, 122). Heine too wrote about the Dane "welcher verrückt wurde, . . . weil er im deutschen Wittenberg vor lauter Denken das Handeln verlernt hatte." See his "Shakespeares Mädchen und Frauen," *Sämtliche Schriften*, 6 vols. (Darmstadt: Wiss. Buchgesellschaft, 1968–75), 4:241. Hamlet is, then, fully identified with Germany in Freiligrath's poem "Hamlet," which begins "Deutschland ist Hamlet!"

[6] "Die Übung der Rolle [of Hamlet] verschlang sich dergestalt in sein einsames Leben, daß endlich er und Hamlet eine Person zu werden anfingen" (FA 1,9:316). Cf. the *Lehrjahre:* "So memorierte ich, und so übte ich mich und glaubte nach und nach mit meinem Helden zu einer Person zu werden" (578–79).

[7] Cf. Roy Pascal, *The German Novel* (Toronto: U of Toronto P, 1956), 13–14; and Emil Staiger, *Goethe*, 3 vols. (Zurich und Freiburg: Atlantis, 1956–59), 2:138.

meaning is affected by this choice, and what the consequences of their later displacement into a narrative governed by irony might be.[8]

[8] Goethe scholars have long understood that the passages on Hamlet are to be considered in their novelistic context. In "Shakespeare und noch immer kein Ende," 1850, Theodor Wilhelm Danzel noticed the subjective cast of the Hamlet criticism in Goethe's novel, "wo denn doch der Hamlet im Grunde der leibhafte Wilhelm Meister selbst ist" (1850; repr. in *Zur Literatur und Philosophie der Goethezeit,* ed. Hans Mayer [Stuttgart: Metzler, 1962]), 247–85; here, 251. Alluding with his title to Goethe's own Shakespeare essay of 1813 (parts 1 and 2) and 1816 (part 3), Danzel says that Wilhelm has selected a soul-mate to enact with whom he identifies "aus innerer Verwandtschaft" (249). The larger purpose of his essay, however, is to combat the practice of exploitative reading — the abuse of literary works in behalf of the needs of the reader — and to argue for "objektive Erkenntnis" (253).

The first critic clearly to view the *Hamlet* criticism in the *Lehrjahre* as a deliberate and "romangemäße Darstellung eines Bildungserlebnisses" was Gundolf, who questions whether it represents Goethe's own view (see *Shakespeare und der deutsche Geist* [1911; repr., Munich: Helmut Küpper, 1959], 276). Cf. Ammerlahn, "Goethe und Wilhelm Meister, Shakespeare und Natalie: Die klassische Heilung des kranken Königssohns," *Jahrbuch des Freien Deutschen Hochstifts* (1978): 47–84; here, 76. William Diamond then contrasts Wilhelm's "subjective" view of Hamlet with the "objective" and correct view of A. C. Bradley. "In Wilhelm Meister's picture of Hamlet we have not an impartial critical analysis of Shakespeare's Hamlet, but a creation that resembles more strikingly Wilhelm Meister himself than Shakespeare's Prince of Denmark" (William Diamond, "Wilhelm Meister's Interpretation of Hamlet," *Modern Philology* 23 [1925–26]: 89–101; here, 91 n. 1, 92 n. 2). Diamond would like to excuse Goethe for having "foisted upon the world a brain-sick craven in place of the real Hamlet of William Shakespeare" (91) but concludes that Wilhelm's caricature of Hamlet reflects Goethe's own artistic personality and his shortcomings as a critic (101). According to Pascal, Goethe was unable to achieve the distance from his protagonists that is characteristic of Shakespeare (Roy Pascal, "Goethe und das Tragische: Die Wandlung von Goethes Shakespeare-Bild," *Goethe,* N.F. 26 [1964]: 38–53; here, 40). Jantz objects to Wellek's reading of the *Hamlet* criticism in the *Lehrjahre* "as though it were Goethe's own in reality rather than Wilhelm's in a fiction. . . . Goethe wrote these sections of *Hamlet* criticism," says Jantz, "not at all subjectively and personally, but quite objectively and calculatedly as one of a number of episodes in Wilhelm's own personal development toward maturity and insight" (Harold Jantz, "Goethe's *Wilhelm Meister:* Image, Configuration, and Meaning," in *Studien zur Goethezeit: Erich Trunz zum 75. Geburtstag,* ed. Hans-Joachim Mähl and Eberhard Mannack [Heidelberg: Carl Winter, 1981]: 103–21; here, 103–4).

Critics who see the *Hamlet* criticism in the *Lehrjahre* as an expression of Wilhelm's personal identification with Hamlet differ as to the nature, the cause, and the effects of this identification. Wilhelm is made to recognize his insufficiency for the double task of becoming both a great actor and the creator of a German national theater, says Max Hermann (*Wilhelm Meisters Theatralische Sendung: Neues Archiv für Theatergeschichte* 2, Schriften der Gesellschaft für Theatergeschichte, 41 [Berlin: Selbstverlag der Gesellschaft, 1930]: 132). Similarly, according to Pascal, "the discussions on

"Nichts weiter über Hamlets Charakter," said A. W. Schlegel, "nach dem was Wilhelm Meister gesagt: keine Ilias nach dem Homer."[9] But Schlegel himself interpreted Hamlet's character, and subsequent generations of critics have followed his example rather than his precept. They have generally concluded that Wilhelm constructs a Hamlet different from the one "objectively" encountered in the pages of Shakespeare's text — "Hamlet . . . wie er wirklich ist," in the words of Hans Reiss.[10] Students of Goethe's novel tend to view Wilhelm's preoccupation with Hamlet as an aspect of his characterization and construe whatever misprision he may suffer in reading *Hamlet* as at least a productive experience for him personally. Since Gundolf first argued the importance of context, they have either ignored or reacted sharply to quotations of Wilhelm's words out of context, as if, unmediated, they were Goethe's own. I see no reason to doubt that Goethe, in the *Theatralische Sendung,* used Wilhelm as a spokesman for his own ideas or to deny that this is of any interest.[11] And it is permissible, I suppose, to take

the play . . . circle round the issue that Goethe later called the theme of his novel — 'the great truth that man would often undertake something for which nature denied him the capacity'" (Pascal, *The German Novel,* 16). Staiger notes a more positive advantage for Wilhelm and says that in playing Hamlet: "Er schafft ans Licht, was unklar in der Tiefe seines Herzens ruht, und gewinnt damit eine innere Freiheit, die anders schwer zu finden wäre" (Staiger, *Goethe,* 2:137). But Staiger does not say what comes to light in this way. Blessin's Marxist interpretation stresses the shock to Hamlet and to Wilhelm caused by the sudden loss of inherited privilege (Stefen Blessin, *Die Romane Goethes* [Königstein/Ts: Athenäum, 1979], 21–22); while Roberts and Muenzer see the Hamlet identification as Wilhelm's means of coming to terms with his own past. He either identifies with Hamlet and enacts a psychic drama that effects a catharsis enabling him to expiate the guilt of the past (David Roberts, *The Indirections of Desire: Hamlet in Goethes "Wilhelm Meister"* [Heidelberg: Carl Winter, 1980], 103, 118–32), or he "is driven upon his own father's death to reestablish, and so personally authorize, what had seemed a preordained spiritual mission" (Clark S. Muenzer, *Figures of Identity: Goethe's Novels and the Enigmatic Self* [University Park: The Pennsylvania State UP, 1984], 58). According to Blackall, the excisions in the play proposed by Wilhelm are his way of making sure that Hamlet mirrors his own penchant for inactivity (Eric A. Blackall, *Goethe and the Novel* [Ithaca, NY: Cornell UP, 1976], 122).

[9] From Kurt Ermann, *Goethes Shakespeare-Bild* (Tübingen: Niemeyer, 1983), 317.

[10] Hans Reiss, *Goethe's Romane* (Bern: Francke, 1963), 115.

[11] See Ermann, *Goethes Shakespeare-Bild,* 198–201. "There is not the slightest doubt that Wilhelm is here expressing Goethe's own views," is James Boyd's representative pronouncement (*Goethe's Knowledge of English Literature* [1932; rep., New York: Haskell House, 1973], 32). Cf. Wellek: "Through the mouth of his hero Goethe describes the effect of Shakespeare on himself" (Wellek, *A History,* 1:204–5). K. R. Eissler adds "(Goethe)" after "Wilhelm Meister" when referring to Wilhelm's relationship to Hamlet (*Goethe: A Psychoanalytic Study 1775–1786,* 2 vols. [Detroit: Wayne State UP, 1963], 2:928). Lüthi, who hyphenates the names of the author and

umbrage at "Goethe's" view of Hamlet. We should not, however, identify the creature with the creator, and should take into account that both may change over time.

Only Bonds, to my knowledge, has *disputed* that Wilhelm identifies with Hamlet. Similarities there are, he concedes, but the introspective Wilhelm is unable to recognize them.[12] Bonds has in common with all other commentators his reliance on the subject-object dichotomy as a scaffold for describing Wilhelm's relationship to Hamlet and his wish to achieve a univocal, correct statement of what is disclosed by Wilhelm's reading of the play. The issues are widely interpreted as aspects of an *encounter* between Wilhelm as autonomous subject and Hamlet as identifiable object, unity between them being achieved, according to the usual interpretation, only at the cost of greater or lesser violence to the authoritative gauge of Wilhelm's or any reader's distortions — Shakespeare's inimitable and immutable work. That Wilhelm's views are implicitly criticized in the novel itself — that, in the pages of the *Lehrjahre,* Goethe does not commit, but, on the contrary, *exposes* the evil of adjusting a literary model to the procrustean bed of a reader's private needs — is obvious to many students of the work. Yet few consider Goethe's point elsewhere that eisegesis, rather than exegesis, is what every reader does and that it is perhaps an unavoidable evil (the work *an sich* being unavailable for independent inspection)[13] or on the likelihood that the dogmatic reliance on easy dichotomies by Wilhelm's evidently fallible critics and mentors, Jarno and the Abbé, should be read as something other than approval of such dichotomies. Rather, Goethe provides numerous hints that the face value of such common currency as "subject" and "object," self and other, and even the logical polarity of identity and difference is suspect as a representation of our ways of knowing and being.

What does it mean to say that Hamlet is an other with whom Wilhelm identifies? Goethe's works explore several kinds of otherness and ways of responding to it; some of them are articulated in plot, character, and situation, some only in metaphors and turns of phrase. Let us review several of the more or less distinct ones, conceding that finer metaphorical distinctions and the inclusion of kinds of otherness that do not concern us here would generate a longer list.

his creature (*Das deutsche Hamletbild,* 11, 29), and James W. Marchand ("A Milestone in *Hamlet* Criticism: Goethe's *Wilhelm Meister,*" in *Goethe as a Critic of Literature,* ed. Karl J. Fink and Max L. Baeumer [Lanham, MD: UP of America, 1984], 143–44) try to *demonstrate* that Wilhelm is Goethe's mouthpiece, whereas Jantz observes differences between Goethe's Shakespeare criticism and that of Wilhelm ("Goethe's *Wilhelm Meister,*" 103–4).

[12] Bonds, "Die Funktion des 'Hamlet'-Motivs," 103

[13] "Liest doch nur jeder / Aus dem Buch sich heraus, und ist er gewaltig, so liest er / In das Buch sich hinein, amalgamiert sich das Fremde" (*Episteln* 1, GA 1:212).

1. The self as identical to (or in correspondence with) the other. The "pathetic fallacy." Otherness as reflective of, or in correspondence with, the self. Goethe writes, "Es ist etwas Unbekanntes Gesetzliches im Objekt, welches dem Unbekannten Gesetzlichen im Subjekt entspricht" (FA 1,13:269). In a letter to Eckhard, he writes, "Hätte ich nicht die Welt durch Antizipation bereits in mir getragen, ich wäre mit sehenden Augen blind geblieben und alle Erforschung und Erfahrung wäre nichts gewesen als ein ganz totes vergebliches Bemühen" (E, 98). "Balde ruhest du *auch*."

2. The self viewed as both identical with and separate from the other. Self-alienation. The self objectified. Disguises and Doppelgänger, for example, Wilhelm and the Count, Goethe's disguise as a poor theology student in Sesenheim (FA 1,14:468) and his encounter with "himself" in unfamiliar clothing on the way home from Sesenheim (FA 1,14:545). The division of the self into self and other through time. In a letter to W. v. Humboldt he wrote, "Ich erscheine mir selbst immer mehr und mehr geschichtlich" (1 December 1831).

3. The admission of undistorted otherness into the self, and in such a way that the self, too, remains undistorted. In Italy Goethe "hatte die Maxime ergriffen, mich soviel als möglich zu verläugnen und das Objekt so rein als nur zu tun wäre in mich aufzunehmen" (FA 1,17:17).

4. Suppression of otherness through self-projection. It is the subject matter of the picture "der kranke Königssohn" that speaks to Wilhelm because he sees in it an image of his despair, and that of his beloved Mariane, in being denied the respective objects of their affection (FA 1,9:422–23).[14] Werther re-creates Lotte in his own image (but also, in other contexts, as his opposite and complement.)[15] In this case, the subject aspires to mastery over the object.

5. Defiance (implying acknowledgment) of the other as opposed, even hostile ("Prometheus"). The subject rejects but cannot annihilate or obliterate the other.

6. Surrender to the other or the deliquescence of the self into otherness (*Faust,* 719, 3289). The blurring of personal boundaries and effluence of the self through the letting of blood (as when Aurelie cuts Wilhelm's palm) or the injection of semen.

[14] See Christoph E. Schweitzer, "Wilhelm Meister und das Bild vom kranken Königssohn," *PMLA* 72 (1957): 419–32; here, 422. Cf. Erika Nolan, "Wilhelm Meisters Lieblingsbild: Der kranke Königssohn," *Jahrbuch des Freien Deutschen Hochstifts* (1979): 132–52. For additional variations on the theme of Antiochus and Stratonice in literature, see Donald A. Beecher and Massimo Ciavolella, *A Treatise on Lovesickness,* trans. and ed. Jacques Ferrand (Syracuse, NY: Syracuse UP, 1990), 161–62.

[15] See Blackall, *Goethe and the Novel,* 27. Cf. my "Werther's Lotte: Views of the Other in Goethe's First Novel," *JEGP* 87 (1988): 492–506; here, 494, 496–97.

7. Otherness embraced as complementary to the self according to an ideal of wholeness.[16] Wilhelm, the commoner, exchanging "bedeutende Blicke" with the beautiful Countess "über die ungeheure Kluft der Geburt und des Standes hinüber" (FA 1,9:536). Faust and Helena. Classical and Romantic. Ganymede and Zeus. Homunculus and Galatee. Tasso and Antonio. Iphigenie and Thoas. Subject and object are incomplete and mutually dependent.

8. Self and other as interactive. Polarity. The epigenesis of the eye from the action of light upon "gleichgültige tierische Hülfsorgane" (FA 1,23:24). Goethe writes, "Jeder neue Gegenstand, wohl beschaut, schließt ein neues Organ in uns auf" (FA 1,24:596) and "Wie dem Auge das Dunkle geboten wird, so fordert es das Helle; es fordert Dunkel, wenn man ihm Hell entgegenbringt, und zeigt eben dadurch seine Lebendigkeit, sein Recht das Objekt zu fassen, indem es etwas, das dem Objekt entgegengesetzt ist, aus sich selbst hervorbringt" (FA 1,23,1:41). Light and dark interacting to make the colors. Contraries marry in hierogamous or alchemical weddings.[17] In "Wiederfinden" he writes, "Allah braucht nicht mehr zu schaffen, / Wir erschaffen seine Welt."

These options are all based on the opposition of subject and object and strive to overcome otherness through the elimination of difference or the sublation of difference in a higher unity ("Geeinte Zwienatur"). As noted, this striving for identity, which may seem to be gender-neutral — symmetrical — is probably an expression of specifically masculine need and a factor in the cultural objectification of woman as the agency through which the lonely male seeks and fears to reincorporate his alienated, tormented subjectivity — as the example of Werther shows. Woman is the port the flying Dutchman seeks, the home the wanderer would return to, but she is also the *vagina dentata* that would lacerate his *Männlein* or devour him entirely. Man's *Begehren* (Hegel) or *Wunsch* (Freud) for reassimilation and his fear of engulfment have created the dominant stereotypes of women in literature — the virgin mother (Lotte) and the *femme fatale* (Adelheid von Walldorf) — in which contrary incarnations woman is both the promise of refuge and the threat of destruction (the prize and the penalty), and the goal in either case. But just as woman is objectified in literature, so do all objects tend to become functionally female, including *Hamlet* as the object of Wilhelm's probing, questing intellect. Wilhelm's struggle to penetrate and identify with

---

[16] See William Larrett, "Wilhelm Meister and the Amazons: The Quest for Wholeness," *Publications of the English Goethe Society* N. S. 39 (1968–69): 31–56.

[17] See *Faust* lines 1040–47; Ronald D. Gray, *Goethe the Alchemist* (Cambridge, UK: Cambridge UP, 1952), passim, and Evelyn J. Hinz, "Hierogamy versus Wedlock: Types of Marriage Plots and Their Relationship to Genres of Prose Fiction," *PMLA* 91:5 (1976): 900–913; here, 907.

Hamlet, like his pursuit of Mariane, Philine, the Countess, Therese, and Natalie, reflects his desire for plenitude and his will to power over the means of his fulfillment. And since this will is motivated by Wilhelm's need, his "unerläßliches Bedürfnis" (FA 1,9:659), it is also a confession of his insufficiency and his unwillingness to accept the self-identity of which insufficiency is constitutive.[18] He eventually achieves acceptance, but in the larger framework of Goethe's planned trilogy of novels, that too must be viewed as transitory.

Goethe does not analyze or explicitly critique the oppositions in his work with respect to their sexism, but he is aware of their instability. They suit his purposes, but we should not invest too much in them, as his pervasive irony reminds us. Lacoue-Labarthe and Nancy are wrong when they say that Goethe's "lack of philosophy was a little too much" for him to incarnate the Romantic ideal of fully self-conscious playfulness, that he was "not yet, not altogether, equal to the period."[19] Goethe did not use inherited *Vorstellungsarten* naively, however much he may have epitomized the naive poet to Schiller. Nor can we, if we would understand him.

Among the possible ways of describing Wilhelm's encounter with Hamlet (and *Hamlet*) — and what happens when he plays "himself" in playing Hamlet — three seem to invite special consideration. First, Wilhelm understands Hamlet correctly and discerns a true soul-mate in him, so that in enacting the part he objectifies and better understands himself (option #1 above). That is, a pre-existent self and a literary character so closely resemble each other as to constitute a genuine identity but an identity visible to the subject only as object. Hamlet is equivalent to a fortuitous objectification of Wilhelm's own self and can therefore serve as a vehicle of his growing self-knowledge. This agrees with things Goethe says elsewhere, for example, "der Mensch kennt nur sich selbst, insofern er die Welt kennt, die er nur in sich und sich nur in ihr gewahr wird" (FA 1,24:595–96).[20] Implicit in this idea is a conception of knowledge as seeing.

---

[18] Quoting Sartre, Mark Taylor argues that "from the phallocentric perspective, 'The obscenity of the feminine sex is that of everything which "gapes open." It is an *appeal to being,* as all holes are. In herself, woman appeals to a strange flesh which is to transform her into a fullness of being by penetration and dissolution'" (Mark C. Taylor, *Erring: A Postmodern A/Theology* [Chicago: U of Chicago P, 1984], 28). Conversely, to the male identity defined by his difference, woman represents plenitude and the final refuge.

[19] Philippe Lacoue-Labarthe and Jean-Luc Nancy, *The Literary Absolute: The Theory of Literature in German Romanticism,* trans. Philip Barnard and Cheryl Lester (Albany: SUNY P, 1988), 12.

[20] Cf. Goethe's corollary belief that self-knowledge is unattainable through direct introspection: "Wie kann man sich selbst kennen lernen? Durch Betrachten niemals,

The second and more often argued possibility (#4 above) is that Wilhelm subverts Hamlet's otherness by making him over in his own image — adapting the prince to his own contours, or to pre-existent material in his own consciousness. "Das Individuum [*eignet*] sich das Objekt so *an* [. . .], daß es ihm die eigentümliche Beschaffenheit benimmt, es zu seinem Mittel macht und seine Subjektivität ihm zur Substanz gibt. Diese Assimilation tritt damit in eins zusammen mit dem . . . Reproduktionsprozeß des Individuums."[21] Wilhelm, on these terms, is a consumer and exploiter of *Hamlet* — a view of him supported by statements by Jarno and the Abbé and reinforced by Goethe's evangelizing against subjectivism throughout his writings. Thus Honorio in *Novelle* shoots a perfectly tame and harmless tiger because he has just seen pictures of ferocious ones. Honorio's mental pictures are themselves objects, to be sure, but objects that have become properties of the viewing subject and that do not admit of correction by any independent other. The other appears is internalized and processed as grist for the mill of the self.

Goethe criticized this sort of subjectivism in himself and others, such as Schiller and Newton.[22] Wilhelm Meister is implicitly charged with subjectivism when he is shown to project his enthusiasm for his puppet theatre onto his mistress while she struggles to stay awake under the drone of his lengthy reminiscences and when he expresses a liking for pictorial art only to the extent that he can personally identify with its subject matter, as in the case of "der kranke Königssohn." Aurelie says he is impenetrable by anything "von außen" (621).[23] While we need not endorse the opinion of an actress who is herself prone to project herself into her roles, Wilhelm is in fact so blind to the world beyond his self that he ends up relying on the observations of his more "objective" friend Laertes and on travel books and published tables of facts for the information he needs to compose the journal he has promised his father. Acting sympathetic roles only increases his preoccupation with himself, yet he resents the message from the Tower that he should flee from the stage,[24] and says it would have been better for the ghost to have com-

wohl aber durch Handeln. Versuche deine Pflicht zu thun und du weißt gleich was an dir ist" (FA 1,13:128). See Jantz, "Goethe's *Wilhelm Meister*," 111–12.

[21] G. W. F. Hegel, *Wissenschaft der Logik II, Werke in zwanzig Bänden,* ed. Eva Moldenhauer and Karl Markus Michel (Frankfurt am Main: Suhrkamp, 1969–71), 6:483.

[22] E, 169–70; on Newton, FA 1,23,1:796.

[23] On Wilhelm's subjectivism, see Thomas P. Saine, "Wilhelm Meister's Homecoming," *JEGP* 69 (1970): 450–69; here, 451–56.

[24] An allusion to the warning "O Homo fuge!" from the *Faust* chapbook *Faust: Das Volksbuch und das Puppenspiel,* ed. Karl Simrock, 3rd ed. (Basel: Benno Schwabe, 1903), 35. Mann takes up the thread in *Der Zauberberg* when Settembrini advises Hans Castorp, on the day of his arrival, to flee from the "underworld" of the Berghof

manded: "Kehre in dich selbst zurück!" (801). It is Wilhelm who is the addressee when Jarno and the Abbé say that art and nature should be appreciated objectively rather than as clay to be modeled after the viewer's needs, opinions, and caprices (955), and there is a lesson for him in the fate of the Harfner, who spends his days narcissistically contemplating his "hohles, leeres Ich" (812–13). The primary weakness of the canoness in book 6 too derives from "zu viel Beschäftigung mit sich selbst" (897), which can "uns gewissermaßen aushöhlen und den Grund unseres Daseins untergraben" (788). Jarno's advice to Wilhelm is: "Nicht an sich denken Sie, sondern an das, was Sie umgibt" (934), for Wilhelm still has not fully realized that only through open-minded contact with the non-self is the self both revealed and enriched.

These references amount to a sufficient indictment of Wilhelm's subjectivism. Yet the work's implicitly and explicitly espoused precepts are subverted in many ways, for example in the failure of Jarno — with the Abbé, the story's chief advocate of an ideal of objectivity — to accredit Wilhelm's ability to empathize with exotic figures such as Mignon and the Harfner.[25] The Tower's understanding of Wilhelm is one-sided, incomplete, and such understanding as they have is only partially reflected in their advice to him.

An equally strong case is presented in the novel for the contrary idea that Wilhelm is a submissive (and in this sense uncommonly "objective") personality, one who surrenders himself to otherness and overcomes difference by flowing into the "real, objective" other or admitting otherness into himself in a way that expands and alters the self (#3 and #6 above). This is what is suggested when we are told that Wilhelm even takes on the burden of Hamlet's melancholy or steps more fully into Hamlet's character in his surprise at hearing the voice of his own father in the words of the ghost on stage.[26] It is a quality shared by Honorio, whose prejudice toward the tame tiger originates in a picture showing a tiger attacking a man. With characteristic irony Goethe's narrator comments, "Was denn aber auch bängliches von solchen Schreckensbildern mochte übrig geblieben sein, alles und jedes war sogleich ausgelöscht, als man, zum Tore hinausgelangt, in die heiterste Gegend eintrat" (FA 1,8:540). If the Society of the Tower

sanatorium: "Wie wäre es denn da, wenn Sie darauf verzichteten, hier älter zu werden, kurz, wenn Sie noch heute nacht wieder aufpackten und sich morgen mit den fahrplanmäßigen Schnellzügen auf- und davonmachten" ("Santana macht ehrrührige Vorschläge," Mann, *Gesammelte Werke* 3:124).

[25] See Hans Eichner, "Zur Deutung von 'Wilhelm Meisters Lehrjahren,'" *Jahrbuch des Freien Deutschen Hochstifts* (1966): 165–96; here, 183–85. Cf. Wilfried Barner, "Geheime Lenkung: Zur Turmgesellschaft in Goethes *Wilhelm Meister*," in *Goethe's Narrative Fiction: The Irvine Goethe Symposium,* ed. William J. Lillyman (Berlin: Walter de Gruyter, 1983), 85–109; here, 95–96.

[26] Saine, "Wilhelm Meister's Homecoming," 458.

ever truly regarded Wilhelm as unresponsive to things extraneous to himself, why would they have taken so strong a pedagogical interest in him in the first place? Their doing so bespeaks a belief in his educability, his malleability, for which Werner, a rigid and two-dimensional capitalist, is the chief foil. Wilhelm is the kind of protagonist that his own theory of the novel demands, "leidend, wenigstens nicht im hohen Grade wirkend"[27] — a man of passive, resilient nature, molded rather than shattered by experience and more disposed to receive the action than to drive it. Schiller commented perceptively of Wilhelm's "schöne Bestimmbarkeit" (8 July 1796), for Wilhelm is as much an open, receptive and poetic personality as he is an excessively subjective one.[28] The parenthetical characterization of him in the *Wanderjahre,* "empfänglich wie er war" (FA 1,10:499), words used verbatim to describe Eduard in the *Wahlverwandtschaften* (FA 1,8:279), fits the Wilhelm of the *Lehrjahre* just as well. Wilhelm's conjunction with Hamlet, whose story "in its tendency to subplot, to centrifugal detail, to retardation . . . is much more like a novel than a drama,"[29] cannot, then, represent a rigid personality superimposing itself upon a submissive other, but must show Wilhelm taking otherness upon himself and being transformed thereby. It is consistent with this that Natalie, whose personality Wilhelm had tried to transform in his thoughts, transforms him instead when he meets her in person. And if all this is true, then Wilhelm has always been an outward-looking young man who does not so much imprint his own identity on the world around him as gather impressions and become changed in ways unforeseen in his plans for self-development — even breaking out of his characteristic passivity.

These options suggest the futility of such questions as, What is Wilhelm in fact really like? What constitutes the indivisible core of his individuality; wherein lies the unity of his self? If he has an essential self, what is its relationship to passing states of mind such as melancholy or to wrong conclusions such as that Therese would be the right wife for him? How accurate is

---

[27] Whereas "von dem dramatischen [Helden] verlangt man Wirkung und Tat" (675). Wilhelm believes in fate rather than active self-direction.

[28] "Novalis prescribed the ideal poetic nature as follows: 'keine Anheftung an Einen Gegenstand, keine Leidenschaft im vollen Sinne — eine vielseitige Empfänglichkeit nötig." From Alice A. Kuzniar, "Reassessing Romantic Reflexivity — The Case of Novalis," *The Germanic Review* 63 (1988): 77–86; here, 81.

Rilke said in 1904: "Das tiefste Erleben des Schaffenden ist weiblich — denn es ist empfangendes und gebärendes Erleben" (Rainer Maria Rilke, *Briefe,* 2 vols. [Wiesbaden: Insel, 1950], 1:107).

[29] "The theory of the novel offered [in the *Lehrjahre*] *does* fit *Hamlet* — it deals with sentiments and events, it moves slowly, the sentiments of the main character retard the action, the hero is passive" (Jane K. Brown, "The Theatrical Mission of the *Lehrjahre,*" in *Goethe's Narrative Fiction,* 69–84; here, 75).

Wilhelm's self-image early and late as measured by the image of him trans-
mitted to the reader by the narrative through which he progresses? Which of
Wilhelm's selves is superimposed on Hamlet, if that is what is going on — a
self of his own construction or one inferable from the larger context (the
"novel") but of which Wilhelm himself is unaware or only subconsciously
aware? Is Wilhelm where he thinks, or does he think where he is not, in Lacan's famous phrase?[30]

Any representation of a moving target such as Wilhelm is bound to be
inadequate, since his identity changes over time, as the Goethean ideas of
Bildung, of "Gestaltung-Umgestaltung," and the imperative "Stirb und
werde" all suggest it must, and as Goethe's own identity had done in the in-
terval between the composition of the *Theatralische Sendung* and that of the
Lehrjahre.[31] Moreover, no representation just "represents," it replaces "ein
Sein durch ein Bild, eine Gegenwart durch eine Vergegenwärtigung."[32] Divisions of the world into a static subjective and objective, self and other both
fail to reflect the temporality of being and deny its eternal elusiveness, as
Goethe amply enables the reader to notice. Identity and continuity are fictions veiling ineluctable difference and change, fictions he used to impose a
measure of coherence on the otherwise unrepresentable complexity of a life.

"All quest-romances of the post-Enlightenment, meaning all Romanticisms whatsoever," Harold Bloom believes, "are quests to re-beget one's
own self, to become one's own Great Original,"[33] an idea that also informs
Muenzer's *Figures of Identity* and other attempts to trace Wilhelm's trajectory through the *Lehrjahre.* Romanticism is inherently teleological and cycli-
cal; it aims back to the future. However, the question of specific identity —
the difference between one individual and another in their different kinds of
insufficiency — is different from that of the difference between the individual
as self-identity (individuation occurring in time, by definition) and identity
as unity with the permanent "Grund unseres Daseins" (788). In the context
of this larger question Wilhelm Meister can be seen to waver between discomfort with his own finitude — a desire for "some mighty inhuman force"

[30] Jacques Lacan, *Ecrits: A Selection,* trans. Alan Sheridan (New York: Norton, 1977),
166.
[31] Cf. *Faust,* 182–83. Gerhart Mayer sees a "Gewinnung der Gestalt" and "Gestalt-
werdung" in the lives of subordinate characters as well as in Wilhelm's development
(*"Wilhelm Meisters Lehrjahre:* Gestaltbegriff und Werkstruktur," *Goethe Jahrbuch* 92
[1975]: 140–64;, here, 144, 147).
[32] Manfred Frank, *Was ist Neostrukturalismus?* (Frankfurt am Main: Suhrkamp,
1984), 422.
[33] Harold Bloom, *The Anxiety of Influence* (Oxford UP, 1973), 64.

to which he can yield up his identity[34] — and a contrary (and, at the novel's end, victorious) desire to embrace life as individuation and individuation as difference. In this scenario, Wilhelm, who does not inhabit a "tragic novel," goes the opposite way from Werther or from Eduard in the *Wahlver-wandtschaften,* eventually specializing as a *Wundarzt* and affirming life and himself. To be sure, the apprentice Wilhelm "must still undergo training as a journeyman before he becomes eligible for mastership."[35] And mastership will itself be but a halfway house on life's journey toward death. But to the extent that Wilhelm's progress can be mapped in terms of his occupancy of a series of trial identities underway toward the flowering of his unique, individual self,[36] the tension of identity and difference generates the novel's plot, and Wilhelm's identification with Hamlet, like the intermediate "matings" of the moth in the poem "Selige Sehnsucht," is one of several ephemeral identifications or moments of submergence along the way.[37] The quest for identity motivates his identification with *Hamlet,* but in taking leave of the stage he articulates *himself.*

Although the full *exitus-reditus* plot informing most Romantic narratives is always a spiral — from unity through individuation back to a higher unity in death — the movement in the *Lehrjahre,* as in the hymn "Prometheus," describes only the first semicircle — away from unity and toward *Ver-selbstung* (#5 above). Accordingly, Wilhelm's alliance with the group of aristocrats and *Bürger* who join in free confederation at the end of the *Lehrjahre* is based not on similarity but on complementarity.[38] This is also the significance of their interclass marriages and the difference between Wilhelm's affair with Mariane, onto whom he projects his own desires, and his love for Natalie, who in her genuine, irrepressible otherness is resistant to her lover's subjectivist leanings (516). Unlike his adopted child, Mignon, and in contrast to his literary descendant Hans Castorp, Wilhelm wins a deci-

[34] Rorty, "Nineteenth-Century Idealism and Twentieth-Century Textualism," *Monist* 64 (1981): 155–74; here, 173.

[35] Géza von Molnár, "Wilhelm Meister's Apprenticeship as an Alternative to Werther's Fate," in *Goethe Proceedings,* ed. Clifford A. Bernd et al. (Columbia, SC: Camden House, 1984), 77–91; here, 87.

[36] Cf. John O. Lyons, *The Invention of the Self* (Carbondale: Southern Illinois UP, 1978), 15: "The later Romantic hero wears disguise not to escape trouble or to deceive, but to understand himself by playing a role just to see if it fits."

[37] E.g. der kranke Königssohn and Prince Hal from *Henry IV.* See Andrew Jaszi, *Entzweiung und Vereinigung: Goethes symbolische Weltanschauung* (Heidelberg: Lothar Stiehm, 1973), passim.

[38] "Nur alle Menschen machen die Menschheit aus, nur alle Kräfte zusammengenommen die Welt" (HA 7:552 — See Muenzer, *Figures of Identity,* 64). On May 5, 1798 Goethe wrote to Schiller: "Nur sämtliche Menschen erkennen die Natur, nur sämtliche Menschen leben das Menschliche."

sive victory over the *Todessehnsucht* behind every quest for unity and finds a counterpart to his still subjective but by now more fully defined self.[39] Thus, rather than lying with Mignon in the *Saal der Vergangenheit* like an Abelard to her "nouvelle" Heloise or like Eduard with Ottilie in the renovated chapel, he separates from Natalie and goes on to new adventures in time, resisting the allure of an endless spatial permanence. "To be or not to be," that is always the question. But Wilhelm Meister goes on living and not as Hamlet but as Wilhelm. This is the point of the ending of the *Lehrjahre,* although not a crucial one for a *Bildungsroman,* as the Hans Castorp example shows. Hamlet, among other instances of otherness, speaks to Wilhelm Meister as both an exemplary contestant in the struggle between life and death and as a force that threatens prematurely to engulf a lonely subjectivity all too vulnerable to the desire for resubmergence. But, as we are led to see, Hamlet's very representation as other (an other with whom Wilhelm can identify or against whose attractive force he can articulate his own identity) is only tentatively and pragmatically presented, as a kind of narrative way station — a paradigmatic and convertible instantiation of the world vis-à-vis that does not rule out an understanding of the world as other than vis-à-vis.

Subject and object, self and other, man and model: these are only special, oppositional cases of difference — the termini of each polarity always susceptible to folding into each other and becoming identical. Such dyadic oppositions align comfortably with other, non-oppositional arrangements of identity and difference in the *Lehrjahre* and best disclose their meaning when seen within a context of other such arrangements, as when one character is superimposed on another, like different transparencies (each providing additional features of the composite portrait) or when one person is mistaken for another in a way that reveals a deeper truth about both. Wilhelm in the role of the Count is the most delightful instance, but Lothario's delighted and baffled recognition of a former sweetheart — Margarete, the Pachter's daughter — in her indifferent niece is another. Margarete herself is by now as mature as Lothario; the niece represents her as he had once known her (FA 1,9:848). The Abbé has a twin, and Natalie's handwriting is so similar to that of the "schöne Gräfin" that Wilhelm mistakes the one for the other — which has the interesting consequence that he later dreads, and tries to avoid, the meeting with Natalie, believing that he is being driven toward a reunion with the Countess, toward whom he feels so bottomlessly guilty.

[39] Wachsmuth recalls L. Oken's idea that every living being "existiere aus einem 'doppelten' Verhältnis. Es sei 'ein für sich Bestehendes und ein in das Absolute Eingetauchtes.' Daher unterliege es zwei Prozessen, einem 'individualisierenden, belebenden' und einem 'universalierenden, tötenden'" (Andreas B. Wachsmuth, "'Sich verselbsten' und 'entselbstigen' — Goethes Altersformel für die rechte Lebensführung," *Goethe* [*Jahrbuch der Goethe-Gesellschaft*] 11 [1949]: 263–92, here, 279).

When he is again in Natalie's presence, his perception of her refuses to coalesce with his recollection of the beautiful amazon whose image has guided him thither. Difference prevails. But Natalie so resembles her aunt, the canoness, that Wilhelm mistakes a portrait of the latter for Natalie herself — as though the aunt had laid aside an identity for Natalie to pick up and try on. And yet the difference between the two women is not only that the aunt is now older but that she was always too subjective — always too preoccupied with herself. In contrast, Natalie, the very epitome of objective responsiveness, might make herself available wherever a bride is lacking and would adjust to the requirements of the situation.

Wilhelm's child, Felix, is his father's second self, "und, ohne sich es zu gestehen, trug Wilhelm ihn gern vor den Spiegel und suchte dort Ähnlichkeiten zwischen sich und dem Kinde auszuspähen" (867). According to Novalis, who first liked and then rejected Goethe's novel, true self-understanding requires "leaving the self,"[40] as Wilhelm might be seen as doing when he objectifies himself in *Hamlet* and then takes his leave of that role. In reading his own *Lehrjahre,* Wilhelm "sah zum erstenmal sein Bild außer sich, zwar nicht wie im Spiegel, ein zweites Selbst,[41] sondern wie im Porträt ein anderes Selbst" (884) — which calls to mind Julie's remark, in *La nouvelle Héloïse,* that her reason for sending St. Preux the most accurate of three pictures of herself, while reserving more idealized likenesses for her mother and cousin, is that "les homages que tu rendrois à une autre figure que la mienne seroient une espece d'infidélité d'autant plus dangereuse que mon portrait seroit mieux que moi, et je ne veux point, comme que ce soit que tu prennes du goût pour des charmes que je n'ai pas" (Lettre 24).[42] The Wilhelm portrayed in the scroll *is* himself, but himself objectified and transformed. In Hamlet too Wilhelm recognizes "ein anderes Selbst," one he comes to understand as he projects it on the stage and then leaves behind, if there is ever such a thing as leaving a past self behind. Either "ein zweites Selbst" or "ein anderes Selbst" is a *contradictio in adjecto,* denying identity while asserting it.

Novalis commented on "the instability of the self in *Wilhelm Meisters Lehrjahre,*" mapping out "how the characters . . . are less persons in their

[40] Kuzniar, "Reassessing Romantic Reflexivity," 80.

[41] On 11 March 1781 Goethe wrote to Frau von Stein: "Alle meine Beobachtungen über Welt und mich, richten sich nicht, wie Marck Antonins, an mein eignes, sondern an mein zweites selbst. Durch diesen Dialog, da ich mich bey iedem dencke was Sie dazu sagen mögten, wird mir alles heller und werther" (FA 2,2:336).

[42] "The homage you would pay to a face other than mine would be a sort of infidelity, by so much the more dangerous as my portrait would be better than I. . . . I do not want you in any manner whatsoever to acquire a liking for charms I do not possess." Jean-Jacques Rousseau, *La nouvelle Héloïse,* trans. Judith H. McDowell (University Park: Pennsylvania State UP, 1968), 217.

own right than variations and transformations of other characters. Lothario is a masculine Therese; Jarno is the transition from Therese to the Abbé; Melina is a commonplace Jarno; the Count is the weak uncle; etc." If, as Kuzniar suspects, "Novalis conceived his task in writing *Heinrich von Ofterdingen* as depicting the constant mutability of the self — its ever hovering nonidentity,"[43] this was done not in opposition to Goethe but in unsuspecting imitation. When Wilhelm's dream of his future happiness as the creator of a German national theatre is described as "ein Gemälde auf Nebelgrund, dessen Gestalten freilich sehr ineinander flossen" (386–87), the fluidity of the figures is paradigmatic for the novel as a whole.

The question of identity and difference, then — the question of one or double — is a basic Goethean question, as is that of the continuity through time of personal identity. "Bin ich's noch [den du bei so viel Lichtern / An dem Spieltisch hältst]?" ("An Belinden"). The answer in the *Lehrjahre* is that Wilhelm's identity, evolving through interaction with those around him, becomes increasingly well-defined while, at the same time — through foregrounding and over-exposure — the very concept of identity is questioned and shown to be transitory — "Bin ich's *noch*? And this questioning is a factor in the diminished realism of the *Lehrjahre* or the *Wahlverwandtschaften* as compared to *Werther* or the *Theatralische Sendung,* which do not as obviously call attention to their conceptual framework.

But this framework is important; contemplation of Goethe's virtuosic use in the *Lehrjahre* of such sets of contraries as subject and object, self and other, and identity and difference suggests that we have missed something important, that our readings of this novel have been naive and constitute a reception history that takes the same dichotomies for granted (apparently without noting to what an extent they are questioned in the work itself). It is as though our preprogrammed reading were blind to the program by which it is controlled — and which Goethe lays open for our inspection and interrogation. His novel's conceptual framework is one of its themes. The reader is asked to observe not only how Wilhelm grows and becomes educated or how growth and education take place or what course Wilhelm runs or how, finally, Wilhelm wins a victory over the allure of death. Rather, we are invited as well to examine and accept only tentatively the terms in which all such events are conventionally presented and in which Goethe himself presents them. As Friedrich Schlegel recognized, Goethe, especially in the *Lehrjahre,* is a practitioner of an ironic "Poesie," one that represents "das Produzierende mit dem Produkt" and would "in jeder ihrer Darstellungen sich selbst mit darstellen, und überall zugleich Poesie und Poesie der Poesie

---

[43] Kuzniar, "Reassessing Romantic Reflexivity," 81.

sein."[44] Not that Goethe stood aloof in some non-Cartesian counter-culture and critiqued modernism from the vantage point of a non-participant. But he does, conspicuously, exhibit a reflectiveness often denied him and attributed as an original virtue to his younger contemporaries — who, for their part, were aware of their indebtedness to him. As Schlegel discerned, the fictional world of *Wilhelm Meister's Lehrjahre*, "is both sincerely presented and sincerely undermined."[45] As part of this fictional world Wilhelm's *Hamlet* criticism serves many purposes. It expresses, in all probability, Goethe's own erstwhile conviction about Shakespeare's play, while illustrating Wilhelm's tendency to amalgamate otherness to himself and diminish it in the process — a tendency that is not so much a fatal flaw as a useful error, as Wilhelm tries on foreign personae en route to an identity of his own. At the same time, this episode has a place in a larger network of identity and difference in which the very categories of self and other are denied full, "objective" validity.[46]

You can build a narrative around such dyads, and Goethe gladly exploits their diegetic potential, but he neither views them as mimetically firm nor casts his narrative as the truth pure and simple. He is no realist, if by realism is meant a belief in the identity of art and reality and a striving for an adequate representation of the world.[47] As F. Schlegel observed, "Es [konnte] nicht seine Absicht sein, hier tiefer und voller darzustellen, als für den Zweck des Ganzen nötig und gut wäre; und noch weniger konnte es seine Pflicht sein, einer bestimmten Wirklichkeit zu gleichen."[48] His looseness and seeming irresponsibility as a writer who both uses and questions his adopted discourse, while indexing a preconceptional and prepropositional reality unbridgeably beyond any story or scheme, represents a serious refusal to confuse linguistic with natural reality. His doubts about the accessibility of being through language may also explain the lack of abrupt distinctions la-

---

[44] KA 1,2:204; *Athenäums-Fragment* [238]. Bahr writes, "Goethe played a much more important role in the development of Romantic irony than scholarship in Romanticism is ready to admit. . . . [He] continued to write in the vein of Romantic irony, even after the early Romantics had abandoned it" (Ehrhard Bahr, "Goethe and Romantic Irony," in *Deutsche Romantik and English Romanticism,* ed. Theodore G. Gish and Sandra G. Frieden, Houston German Studies, vol. 5 [Munich: Wilhelm Fink, 1984], 1–5; here, 1).

[45] Neil M. Flax, *Approaches to Teaching Goethe's "Faust,"* ed. Douglas J. McMillan (New York: MLA, 1987), 40.

[46] As Goethe said, contemplation always involves theory, but theorizing should be self-conscious and ironic (FA 1,23,1:14. Cf. Eichner, "Zur Deutung von 'Wilhelm Meisters Lehrjahren,'" 192–96).

[47] Cf. Goethe on "das Dämonische" in *Dichtung und Wahrheit* (FA 1,14:839–40).

[48] Friedrich Schlegel, "Über Goethe Meister," in KA 1,2:143.

mented by Nisbet.[49] None of our categories of thinking is fundamental, he seems to say; conceptual instruments of every sort are both necessary and insufficient — always removed from identity with their ground and yet pointing rainbow-like toward terra firma beyond the pale of cognition. There is no unmediated access of this other sphere, but the longing to oc-cupy it is inextinguishable. In this skepticism and this longing lies his essential Romanticism.

The *Lehrjahre,* like *Faust,* reflects Goethe's conviction that we belong to a partial, transitory world as well as his desire for the unity behind its frag-mentary self-manifestation.[50] This desire was fed by his lifelong study of Shakespeare, of whom he said, "Wir . . . überzeugen uns abermals, daß Shakespeare, wie das Universum, das er darstellt, immer neue Seiten biete und am Ende doch unerforschlich bleibe: denn wir sämtlich, wie wir auch sind, können weder seinem Buchstaben noch seinem Geiste genügen" (GA 14:921). T. S. Eliot later said the same thing and recommended a course of action that I should like to apply to Goethe: "About anyone so great . . . it is probable that we can never be right; and if we can never be right, it is better that we should from time to time change our way of being wrong."[51]

---

[49] H. B. Nisbet, *Goethe and the Scientific Tradition* (London: Institute of Germanic Studies, 1972), 45.

[50] A belief and desire he shared with many before him, as Harold Jantz has pointed out (*Goethe's* Faust *as a Renaissance Man* [Princeton, NJ: Princeton UP, 1951], 117).

[51] T. S. Eliot, "Shakespeare and the Stoicism of Seneca" (1927), reprint in *Selected Essays 1917–1932* (New York: Harcourt, Brace, 1932), 126.

8: Poetic Ambiguity: "Selige Sehnsucht"

THE POEM "SELIGE SEHNSUCHT" from the *West-östlicher Divan* is the *locus classicus* of the love-death theme in Goethe.

SELIGE SEHNSUCHT

Sagt es niemand, nur den Weisen,
Weil die Menge gleich verhöhnet,
Das Lebend'ge will ich preisen,
Das nach Flammentod sich sehnet.

In der Liebesnächte Kühlung,   5
Die dich zeugte, wo du zeugtest,
Ueberfällt dich fremde Fühlung,
Wenn die stille Kerze leuchtet.

Nicht mehr bleibest du umfangen
In der Finsterniß Beschattung   10
Und dich reißet neu Verlangen
Auf zu höherer Begattung.

Keine Ferne macht dich schwierig,
Kommst geflogen und gebannt
Und zuletzt, des Lichts begierig,   15
Bist du, Schmetterling, verbrannt.

Und so lang du das nicht hast,
Dieses: Stirb und werde!
Bist du nur ein trüber Gast
Auf der dunklen Erde.   20

Goethe's (probably apocryphal) last words, as he went more or less gently into that good night, were, "Mehr Licht!" To have sought still greater illumination in his last moments would have been characteristic of the man who took more pride in his theory of color than in any of his belletristic achievements. Remarkably, the poem that most brilliantly exploits the light-darkness polarity is as notorious for its obscurity as his *Farbenlehre* is for its wrong-headedness. "Selige Sehnsucht" has been called "perhaps the most difficult of all of Goethe's poems,"[1] although this seems an exaggeration and must refer either to the difficulty of arriving at a definitive reading or, as Ewald Rösch believes, of fitting the poem to a procrustean preconception of what is "Goethean."[2] This short lyric is less complex in structure and syntax and employs less obscure diction than many other Goethe poems. Yet the disagreement over its meaning, the insufficiency of all attempts at translation, and the paucity of comprehensive interpretations indicate that it is in fact difficult.[3]

The relative obscurity of "Selige Sehnsucht," however, has not limited the popularity of at least part of it with the general reading public. The words of its final strophe are familiar — or perhaps we should now say *were* familiar, in view of the neglect of Goethe in school curricula since the sixties — to all passably educated speakers of German: "Und so lang du das nicht hast, / Dieses: Stirb und werde! / Bist du nur ein trüber Gast / Auf der dunklen Erde." As in the case of the equally popular words of Mephistopheles, however — "Grau, teurer Freund, ist alle Theorie, / Und grün des Lebens goldner Baum" (*Faust*, 2038–39) — even most of those who are fond of the words themselves are unacquainted with their context. In fact, the last strophe of "Selige Sehnsucht" is less uniformly understood by those who *do* know the context than by those who don't, the latter reading it as an allegory of growth and renewal and an admonition to remain able, at whatever age, to fall in love. The scholars enjoy no such consensus.

As Dorothea Hölscher-Lohmeyer has noted, the poem consists of three parts — an introduction (a "Prooemium"), a "Legende" or saint's tale, and the popular maxim.[4] In the introduction the poem's persona announces an intention to praise either (a) "das Lebendige" "the living being" that longs for a fiery death (i.e. the relative clause is restrictive) or (b) "das Lebendige" "(all) that which is alive," of which it is characteristic that it longs for a fiery death (i.e. the relative clause is only descriptive — we leave this ambiguity

[1] Konrad Burdach, "Anmerkungen," in *Goethes Sämtliche Werke, Jubiläumsausgabe* (Stuttgart: Cotta, 1904), 5:332.

[2] Ewald Rösch, "Goethe's 'Selige Sehnsucht' — eine tragische Bewegung," *Germanisch-romanische Monatsschrift*, n.s. 20 (1970): 241–56, reprint in *Interpretationen zum West-östlichen Divan Goethes,* ed. Edgar Lohner (Darmstadt: Wissenschaftliche Buchgesellschaft, 1973), 229.

[3] Emil Staiger declares the poem to be "unter den vielen geheimnisvollen seiner Umgebung [in the *West-östlicher Divan*] das geheimnisvollste" (*Goethe*, 3 vols. [Zurich and Freiburg: Atlantis, 1956–59], 3:35) but then slides over its difficulty with the explanation that its frail mystery would be crushed by scholarly analysis (36).

[4] Dorothea Hölscher-Lohmeyer, "Die Entwicklung des Goetheschen Naturdenkens im Spiegel seiner Lyrik — am Beispiel der Gedichte 'Mailied' — 'Selige Sehnsucht' — 'Eins und Alles,'" *Goethe-Jahrbuch* 99 (1982): 19–20.

unresolved for the moment) and urges the listeners to reveal this aim to none but the wise.

In the narrative part of the poem, a story of a small creature's flight into the flame of a candle, a butterfly or moth (a "Schmetterling") engaged in the natural cycle of birth and procreation is overcome by a strange feeling. "Greedy for light," the spellbound insect is driven by desire for a "higher" mating — *ripped* upward out of the darkness — and incinerated.[5] Since this plot illustrates both the blessed longing of the poem's title, which the introduction announces an intention to praise, and the death that transforms and translates a "trüber Gast / Auf der dunklen Erde," the dying and becoming of a being propelled by "Sehnsucht" is not accidental in either sense of the word. Rather, its surrender to the two primal instincts, Eros and the death instinct, is an essential self-expression, even though it results in the extinction of the self. And this death denotes a mating of a higher order than union with a sexual counterpart. Ottilie, who renounces Eduard and becomes a "bride of heaven" at the end of *Die Wahlverwandtschaften,* would be a pertinent analogy, although every true mating entails at least the abandonment of egotism and the unreserved self-submergence of the individual in a higher unity.

Love and death in Goethe, whether individually or in combination, are both a consummation and a transition, often to a new synthesis or individuation.[6] They can also be a return to the womb and matrix of being — engulfment and annulment; the pattern varies. Suicide, however, committed in the expectation of elevation, a yielding up the self with the right hand while holding onto it with the left, is hubristic, as Werther and, but for the timely intervention of the Easter chorus, Faust illustrate. The author, who in "Ganymed" glorified self-surrender, who once said, "Unser ganzes Kunststück besteht darin, daß wir unsere Existenz aufgeben, um zu existieren" (to Riemer, 24 May 1811), and who had earlier assigned the titles "Selbstopfer" and "Vollendung" to the poem now known as "Selige Sehnsucht" (see HA 2:582), speaks through the persona of the poem's nar-

---

[5] Cf. "hingerissen" = "ecstatic." Cf. also: "So, mit morgenroten Flügeln, / *Riß* es mich an deinen Mund . . ." ("Wiederfinden," lines 41–42) and the final tercet of Rilke's sonnet "Die Fensterrose": "So griffen einstmals aus dem Dunkelsein / der Kathedralen große Fensterrosen / ein Herz und *rissen* es in Gott hinein" (Rainer Maria Rilke, *Sämtliche Werke* ed. Ernst Zinn, 6 vols. [Frankfurt am Main: Insel, 1955–1966]; emphasis added).

[6] To Pandora's inquiry, "Und nach dem Tod?" Prometheus answers: "Dann lebst du auf, aufs jüngste wieder auf, / Aufs neue zu fürchten zu hoffen und zu begehren!" (FA 1,4:419).

In "Die Braut von Korinth" and "Der Gott und die Bajadere" the pairs of lovers will arise from the funeral pyre to live on another plane. In death Werther seeks eternal union with Lotte "vor dem Angesichte des Unendlichen" (FA 1,8:250–51).

rator in praise of a longing for the ecstasy of dissolution and reassimilation. But we are already deep in the text and at risk of viewing as self-evident matters that are ambiguous and problematical.

It was not possible even to read through to the poem's final strophe without noting some ambiguity underway (while passing over other instances in silence). Moving on, we acknowledge (again in passing) the ambiguity of "und" in the formula "Stirb und werde" as generative of both the "Zugleich" insisted on by Rösch[7] (that is, death and becoming are simultaneous; Rösch does not go so far as to say synonymous) and the temporal succession favored by many other critics (that is, someone or something dies *and then* becomes). In the final couplet four different meanings may be generated simply by shifting secondary accents from modifier to noun or vice versa in the phrase "ein trüber Gast auf der dunklen Erde." Is it "*trüber* Gast" or "trüber *Gast*," and "*dunkle* Erde" or "dunkle *Erde*" as opposed to a dunkel *elsewhere* (none of the four is privileged by the metric scheme)? In the first instance, an individual's guesthood on earth would not be the issue but rather one's attitude toward this status (or one's degree of illumination about it, to take only two of the many possibilities). This seems to be how Emil Staiger reads the poem: "Whoever does not know 'Stirb und werde' is . . . only a [trüber Gast] on earth. Whoever *has* experienced it will still be a guest on earth, but a guest with the utmost serenity of spirit, one no longer troubled by any care."[8] Staiger simply asserts that our (*our?*) "guesthood" is inevitable and, apparently, reads "trübe" as "betrübt" — the opposite of "heiter." The word "trübe" is crucial to any reading and demands close scrutiny. Yet Staiger might as logically have interrogated the noun "Gast" and, for starters, explored "at-homeness" or hosthood (which of the two is the "opposite" of guesthood?) as divergent possibilities for the addressee of the poem's final lines.

The word *guest* and related words (e.g. Gothic *gasts*, Latin *hostis*) fascinate because the same root generated both *hospitality* and *hostility,* but implications of strangeness and instability are always present, for instance, when Paul writes to the Hebrews that Abraham and his descendants "haben . . . bekannt, daß sie Gäste und Fremdlinge auf Erden wären."[9] Notable occurrences of "Gast" in Goethe are (a) the death-marked lovers in "Die Braut

[7] Ewald Rösch, "Goethe's *Selige Sehnsucht*," 244.

[8] Staiger, *Goethe*, 37.

[9] Hebrews, 11.13, rev. standard ed. Tanner cites Emile Benveniste (further abbreviated here): "To explain the connexion between 'guest' and 'enemy' it is usually supposed that both derived their meaning from 'stranger,' a sense which is still attested in Latin. The notion 'favourable stranger' developed to 'guest'; that of 'hostile stranger' to 'enemy'" (Tony Tanner, *Adultery in the Novel: Contract and Transgression* [Baltimore: The Johns Hopkins UP, 1979], 25).

von Korinth" — she, the revenant, as the Athenian boy's guest in her own mother's guestroom, he, the pagan, as the guest of her fanatical Christian mother (lines 17 and 27) — together they will find rest in the flames of the funeral pyre; (b) the "Gast" on the Capitol in Rom ("a second Olympus") who begs the hospitable Jupiter (Jupiter Xenius) not to expel the intruder; later he will gladly be led by Hermes into the underworld (Roman Elegy no. 7); (c) Iphigenie among the Taurians — the stranger who enjoys "eines frommen Gastes Recht" (line 282) and who rejects the king's proposal of marriage (lines 251–52), leaving him with no heir and, possibly, with a war of succession on his hands as she returns to her *home*land to bring peace and at-one-ment to the house of Atreus; (d) the parasitic ivy in "Amyntas," which as "der gefährliche Gast" because "der geliebteste,"[10] sucks the sap from the apple tree that is its host and thus destroys its own domicile.[11] All represent cases of incomplete assimilation and the tentativeness that characterizes the guest as well as all other forms of individuation. Selfhood, like guesthood, is always a matter of tenuous and temporary occupancy and is sometimes conducive of a fragile, self-assertive heroism, as in the hymn "Prometheus." Never at home in separation, the self strives always for release — *from* the mortal shell's confinement into freedom and from a lonely freedom *into* the containment of the womb. In "Amyntas" the deadly symbiosis of apple tree and ivy is cherished even by the ivy's host and victim: "Wer sich der Liebe vertraut, hält er sein Leben zu Rat?" Love takes no thought for self-preservation. Bent on love, a guest is driven by "Sehnsucht." Guesthood is in fact the issue in "Selige Sehnsucht," in Hölscher-Lohmeyer's reading, but she believes it is the mistaken "Christian-baroque" notion that we are only guests on the (planet) earth that the poem rejects.[12] It is because we are "trübe" = "unerleuchtet" (read: superstitious?) that we *think* ourselves out of place.

Faust can be made to provide an imperfect illustration of this view; imperfect because the work employs a traditional Christian cosmology as its frame of reference. A despondent Faust becomes a serene resident after temporarily and mistakenly believing himself (as a unique image of the godhead) only a guest upon the earth. In his study, a symbol of the self as a prison, he

[10] As always, the gender issue is tricky here. It is *der* Epheu but *die* Pflanze. In the poem the vine is female: "Und so saugt sie das Mark, sauget die Seele mir aus" (line 32).

[11] Wagner applies the elm-ivy topos to *Tristan und Isolde:* "Nennen wir es Tod? Oder ist es die nächtige Wunderwelt, aus der, wie die Sage uns meldet, ein Efeu und eine Rebe in inniger Umschlingung einst auf Tristans und Isoldes Grab emporwachsen?" From Hans Mayer, *Wagner,* Rowohlt Bild Monographie (Hamburg: Rowohlt, 1959), 102.

[12] Hölscher-Lohmeyer, "Die Entwicklung des Goetheschen Naturdenkens," 25, note 77.

laments that "selbst das liebe Himmelslicht / *Trüb* durch gemalte Scheiben bricht!" (lines 400–401, emphasis added) and moves toward transcending the barriers between himself and heavenly light. Death will release him from human finitude and allow him to rise to "neue Sphären reiner Tätigkeit" (line 705). On hearing the Easter music from a neighboring church, however, Faust realizes that, a man among men, he is not peculiarly out of place, and gratefully concludes his soliloquy with the insight that he is where he belongs after all: "Die Erde hat mich wieder!" (line 784). The joyous praise of an exemplary "Stirb und werde!" — Christ's mediatory death and resurrection — reminds Faust of the contingency and dependence on mediation that he shares with all creatures and restores him to the earth as his proper abode. Consistently, in the following scene he can celebrate the rebirth of spring with his fellowmen and -women — their release from "niedriger Häuser dumpfen Gemächern" (line 923) and their common resurrection from winter's darkness into the light (line 928). Thus Faust proclaims, "Hier bin ich Mensch, hier darf ich's sein" (line 940). Now viewing a recurrent dream of levitation as a passing human fancy (lines 1074–99), Faust seems cured of his self-aggrandizing Romanticism. No longer despondent, he is also no longer obfuscated, having seen the light regarding his true status and habitation. He has become the opposite of a "trüber Gast."

Not surprisingly, the obverse of this interpretation is just as demonstrable — the idea that Faust remains a "trüber Gast" and a homeless wanderer (line 3348) *throughout* his earthly life. Its exposition would rely on the same light-"trübe"-dark symbolism, beginning with the fact that Faust is described as "der . . . nicht mehr Getrübte" only after his death at the age of one hundred (lines 12073–74). It would take note of Faust's professed lack of faith (line 765) and consider the paradox that the enlightening Easter message of salvation comes from the obscurantist source of "der Kirchen ehrwürdiger Nacht" (line 927). The divergent possibilities begin to be evident.

Even if only one meaning is assigned to each of the two terms "trübe"' and "Gast" in the poem's penultimate line — let us take Staiger's for the sake of argument — three alternatives to "trüber Gast" and three potential consequences of *having* "Stirb und werde!" are generated — one might become (1) a "heiterer Gast"; (2) a "trübe" resident; or (3) a "heiter" resident. If we allow for additional definitions and divergent antonyms, while taking the phrase in question to be descriptive of an undesirable state of being, of an unhappy developmental stage, or (more "Goethean") of immutability per se — the unfortunate condition of being arrested in any stage of development, however benign or valuable in itself — we increase the readings and alternatives indefinitely. For example, we might substitute Hölscher-Lohmeyer's understanding of "trübe" as unenlightened for Staiger's "betrübt," while retaining Staiger's assumption that our guesthood on earth is inevitable, and argue that as "trübe Gäste" we are insufficiently enlightened to know that we are *not* at home on the dark earth but, ignorant of our true home, blissfully comfortable in a kind of fool's paradise (if *this* earth is the sphere designated as dark). This would mean that possession of "Stirb und Werde" (if possession is what is meant by "hast" in line 17) is prerequisite to a comprehension of human (*human* or just *someone's*?) out-of-placeness upon earth — to a realization that we do not in fact belong here. It would mean that knowledge of our own guesthood is a *consequence* of having "Stirb und werde." Guesthood, in this reading, is neither an always evident condition or status about which we may be sad or serene, as Staiger supposes, nor a misconception of the human situation, as Hölscher-Lohmeyer claims, but rather a truth only realized through a process of dying and becoming or at least of having been changed by a "fremde Fühlung" (line 7). It contains the idea of self-knowledge or at least knowledge of one's displacement and of the dark earth's essential inhospitality to beings essentially not at home, "unbehaust" refugees on earth (*Faust*, line 3348). Undergoing enlightenment, we *die* as victims of delusion and *become* enlightened guests, aware of our dislocation and distinguished by foreknowledge of the brevity and tentativeness of our stay. This may be what Staiger has in mind — someone who truly understands is a "heiter" practitioner of the intellectual love of God. We are not distressed that seven plus five equals twelve and would be as serene about our inescapable guesthood on the earth if we recognized its necessity. But the slipperiness of Goethe's poetic practice and the fecundity of language in generating oppositions make it seem unlikely that we will ever arrive at a univocal interpretation of "trüber Gast."

Let us remember, nevertheless, that in Goethe's *Farbenlehre* "die Trübe" (also "die Trübung" or "das Trübe") denotes a semi-opaque medium through whose agency the colors of the spectrum (= life) are produced.[13] In view of this we might conclude that it is not because we are unenlightened (Hölscher-Lohmeyer) or because we have become enlightened (Staiger) that we are not at home on the dark earth but because we are light-permeable or -impregnable (thus mutable) and poised to be activated or mobilized by light as Ganymede and the fisherman are ready to be mobilized by love. As "trübe Gäste," we are unactualized potential — occupants of provisional quarters, tentative and unsettled squatters ready to be

---

[13] *Zur Farbenlehre* (FA 1,23,1:74 and passim). Cf. "Sie [Morgenröte] entwickelte dem Trüben / Ein erklingend Farbenspiel" ("Wiederfinden," lines 29–30), and "Am farbigen Abglanz haben wir das Leben" (*Faust II*, line 4727).

dislodged by the first rays of light in the East.[14] The moth embraced "in der Finsternis Beschattung" (line 10) illustrates such potential. Tentatively and temporarily overshadowed and held in erotic embrace ("umfangen" — compare "umfangend umfangen" in "Ganymed"), it is already in the presence of light as the physical and semantic ground of shade (no light, no shade) and ready to be illuminated, infused with *new* desire, and drawn to the source of illumination, at the cost of life itself. (The phrase "in der Finsternis Beschattung" contains an allusion to the Song of Solomon, which Goethe had translated into German and in which overshadowing is a metaphor for sexual mounting (2.3–6; GA 15:324–29), enriching and vitalizing the references to procreation in the preceding strophe.) In this context the dark earth is antipodal to a bright elsewhere and parallel to the "coolness of love nights" (line 5) that is both the antithesis and the anticipation of the candlelight's annihilating glow.

Faust too hovers midway between antipodes and feels the pull of contrary forces. "Vom Himmel fordert er die schönsten Sterne / Und von der Erde jede höchste Lust" (lines 304–5). With two souls residing in his breast (line 1112), he is torn between his bond to the "dark earth" and the urge to escape its gravitational pull and take flight (1085–99).[15] Poised like the moth to respond to light, he is the "Erdewesen" who "dazwischen ruht im Trüben" ("Entoptische Farben," FA 1,2:505). And like the overshadowed moth, he has access not to the eternal light itself (4697) but only to its "farbiger Abglanz" (4727) and "Schein" (284).[16] Consistently with the me-

---

[14] In a paralipomenon Goethe wrote, "Empfindung der Bestimmbarkeit ohne Bestimmung ist ein unbequemer Zustand. Daher die Beängstigung, die wir im Dunkeln fühlen.

"Der höchste Moment der lebendigen Ruhe, der völligen Bestimmbarkeit bringt die Forderung der Tätigkeit hervor. Die Unmöglichkeit des Überganges von der Fähigkeit zur Tat ist die peinlichste Empfindung. Die Dichter sprechen von den Ketten der Finsterniß" (WA 2,5,2:21).

"Nachklang," another *Divan* poem, gives an ascending series of possible sources of ignition, all of them metaphors for the poet's beloved: "Laß mich nicht so der Nacht, dem Schmerze, / Du Allerliebstes, du mein Mondgesicht, / O, du mein Phosphor, meine Kerze, / Du meine Sonne, du mein Licht!" (FA 1,3,1:95).

[15] Cf. Werther's longing to fly with the cranes to the unmeasured ocean and drink from its foaming goblet just one drop of the "Seligkeit" of that Being that brings forth everything in and through itself (18 August 1771). Euphorion, Faust's son, fails to resist the urge to fly and, Icarus-like, comes crashing fatally to the earth (*Faust II*, 9900–9904).

[16] Human beings are "bestimmt, Erleuchtetes zu sehen, nicht das Licht!" (*Pandora*, line 958). The idea that contingent beings may approach, but never attain the truth, adequate ideas, pure light, is an eighteenth-century commonplace. Cf. Lessing: "Wenn Gott in seiner Rechten alle Wahrheit, und in seiner Linken den einzigen immer regen Trieb nach Wahrheit, obschon mit dem Zusatze, mich immer und ewig

dial position of "verworren" = 'con-fused' (between "dunkel" and "deut-lich") in the Leibnizian *Ideencharte,* he *serves* "verworren" (line 308).[17]

The hierarchy that situates the earthling with an urge to fly at midpoint in the great chain of being informs many other Goethean texts referring to the hybrid human as the figure suspended between the antipodes of a given polarity (analogues to the light vs. dark polarity are "Geist" vs. "Materie," above vs. below, and action vs. passion), his life consisting of movement from the negative to the positive terminal (cf. Schickaneder's Pamina and Tamino; in Goethe's sequel — *Der Zauberflöte zweiter Teil* — the Queen of the Night makes a vain attempt to reclaim at least their son for darkness). But as long as we live, we are always underway, only "strangers and pilgrims on the earth."[18] In "Selige Sehnsucht," the final phrase "dunkle Erde" re-peats "in der Finsternis Beschattung" in locating the point of origin in a darkness insufficiently shielded from the light, the goal being the candlelight that ignites longing but eventually consumes in a blaze of ecstasy the noc-turnal flyer propelled by this longing. In the poem "Wiederfinden" there is no "Sehnsucht" until morning light impregnates that which is "trübe," re-kindling the "erklingend Farbenspiel" that is life regenerate on its flight to-ward love and reassimilation.[19] But the reunion of lovers parted, after one revolution of the spiral, amounts to an annulment of separate identity and therefore to a return into the womb of night. Night (though in the latter case a bright, starlit night) explicitly resides at both ends of the polarity: ab-solute separation — not quite absolute unity (lines 3, 43).[20] But the wan-derer is neither rootless nor aimless and seeks always to return into unity and wholeness. *Exitus-reditus* is the paradigm throughout.

zu irren, verschlossen hielte, und spräche zu mir: wähle! Ich fiele ihm mit Demut in seine Linke, und sagte: Vater gieb! die reine Wahrheit ist ja doch nur für dich allein!" ("Eine Duplik," *Sämtliche Schriften,* ed. Karl Lachmann, 3rd, expanded ed. by Franz Muncker, 23 vols. [vols. 1–11, Stuttgart: Göschen; vols. 12–22, Leipzig; vol. 23, Berlin, Leipzig: de Gruyter, 1886–1924], 13:24).

[17] On Leibniz's hierarchy of ideas from "dunkel" to "verworren" to "deutlich" as a frame of reference for Herder and the Enlightenment, see Israel S. Stamm, "Herder and the *Aufklärung:* A Leibnizian Context," *Germanic Review* 38 (1963): 197–208; here, 197.

[18] Heb.11.13, King James version. Cf. *Werther,* FA 1,8:157.

[19] A clear parallel to Goethe is apparent when Freud says, "Nur das Zusammen- und Gegeneinanderwirken beider Urtriebe Eros und Todestrieb erklärt die Buntheit der Lebenserscheinungen, niemals einer von ihnen allein." "Die endliche und die unendliche Analyse" (*SA* 11:382–83). In Goethe, as in Romanticism generally, love and death are not simply opposites but opposites and an identity at the same time — a *coincidentia oppositorum.*

[20] Here "Finsternis," which separated from the light at the moment of creation (lines 17–18), is the contingent element.

Goethe does not worry about exact metaphorical equivalence in his various representations of this pilgrimage *from* love and death *to* love and death, which underscores the fact that symbolism, not allegory, is his mode of meaning. He offers *variations* on a theme, never a simple reiteration of any pattern. In the phrase "erklingend Farbenspiel," generated out of "dem Trüben" by light, the synesthesia bespeaks the sensuous vitality of the lovers' quest for reunion. Faust becomes "der . . . nicht mehr Getrübte" (lines 12073–74) — as he goes up the mountainside, blinded still by "der neue Tag" (line 12093). Like Faust, the moth of our poem's middle part is a "trüber Gast." Issuing forth from the mating of her progenitors, she mates in turn — first *in* the darkness and then *with* the light. Mating is forever in "Wiederfinden," but it leads, according to *Prometheus,* to a new selfhood and a new desiring. Alterations in the paradigm — even total reversals of valence (depending on character and circumstance, such as the contrasting valorization of individuation and self-surrender in "Prometheus" and "Ganymed" or the assignment of ontological priority to "Finsternis" and "Mutter Nacht" by Mephistopheles [lines 1350–52] and to light in "Wiederfinden") reflect Goethe's fragmentary and dialectical method. Throughout his writings, however, "trübe" as adjective or "die (das) Trübe" as noun is mediatory in function or at least medial in position. Anything so described neither reposes unborn in the womb nor is in possession of its final destiny. Whether a pilgrim itself or a temporary habitation or bridge for others (like the beautiful serpent arched across the Hermetic river in "Das Märchen"), it is always unstably in between and moving or pointing toward dissolution and rest or entropy in space. Underway toward this goal, the agitated self, propelled by "Sehnsucht," is everywhere a guest in search of love, enlightenment, and a home.

But is the escape from loneliness, obfuscation, and alienation (through transmutation) a special or a general phenomenon, the destiny of all creatures or the privilege of only a special few? I know of no commentator on "Selige Sehnsucht" who does not take the poem's esoteric rhetoric at face value, as addressed to the minority who have ears to hear.[21] Rösch goes farthest of all, claiming that it speaks not only *to,* but *about* the few "Erleuchteten" who are governed by *Geist* and whose life "eine Gesetzlichkeit des Natürlichen durchbricht," in contrast to the numerous "trübe Gäste" (philistines and dimwits all) whose secure lives on the dark earth exemplify the course of *Natur.*[22] "In unserem Gedicht aber wird nicht diese untragische Sicherung, sondern die tödliche Sehnsucht nach dem

---

[21] Corroborating reference is often sought in the first lines of another *Divan* poem, "Gingo Biloba": Dieses Baums Blatt . . . Gibt geheimen Sinn zu kosten, / Wie's den Wissenden erbaut."

[22] Rösch, "Goethe's 'Selige Sehnsucht,'" 237–38.

ungetrübten Licht selig gepriesen."[23] Creatively, Rösch translates the modifier as "getrübt" — from "trübe" in the poem — and attributes it to "Licht"
instead of to "Gast."

We cannot here review precedents in the history of prosopopeia, the
trope of apostrophe, but even a cursory consideration of this poem's rhetoric
reveals that it is not unambiguously addressed to an elite group. The very
fact of its publication by the author casts an ironic light on his command to
convey the secret to no one but the wise. The implication is that "I am going to tell all of you a secret, which, by virtue of my telling it, dies as a secret
and becomes public knowledge. I pretend to flatter you that you are the
privileged recipients of this message, but the true compliment I pay you resides in my assurance, disguised by the most transparent veil of irony, that
you are intelligent readers and will see through the flattery, appreciate my
confidence in your perceptiveness, and applaud my democratic agenda."[24]
Unlike the poems to Friederike Brion, the *West-östlicher Divan* is not essentially a private communication, and such an obvious self-reference as the
rhyme "Morgenröte — Hatem" in one of the love poems to "Suleika" invites all readers to substitute "Goethe" for "Hatem" and toast his good fortune (FA 1,3,1:87). While irony may be intrinsically elitist, discriminating
between those who see what is going on and those who don't, it is a tentative kind of elitism, fundamentally penetrable by all and in this way compa-
rable to natural revelation. There has always been a close alliance between
irony and reason. The dupe of irony is *not yet* enlightened but is not consti-
tutionally impervious to light, is not blind.

Not only is it far from self-evident that a small group of adepts are singled out and privileged by the poem's opening lines, but also the apostro-
phized moth is the addressee of the three middle strophes in only a formal,
rhetorical sense. It is already incinerated when finally named in the words,
"Bist du, Schmetterling, verbrannt" (line 16), which, seemingly, are spoken
into the void. Burned up, the moth is "nicht mehr" — "no longer embraced
in the overshadowing of darkness" (lines 9–10), no longer "getrübt" (*Faust,*
line 12074), no longer at all except as a trace in the mind of the speaker or
of his or her audience. But just as honorary citations (conventionally
couched in the second person) have another purpose than to instruct the
honoree on his or her meritorious life, it is not for the sake of the butterfly
that the story of its love and death is recounted. Rather, as the contrasting
time indicator "so lang" indicates (cf. "Es irrt der Mensch, solang' er
strebt" — *Faust,* line 317), it is but an example to the "Du" of the final

---

[23] Ibid., 249

[24] My thanks to Marshall Brown for drawing my attention to an identical irony in
Wordsworth's "Strange fits of passion have I known: / And I will dare to tell, / But
in the Lover's ear alone, / What once to me befell."

strophe, whose benighted, erring life does *not yet* exemplify "Stirb und werde" and whose persistence, so far, in an unenlightened state makes him or her the true recipient of the poem's maxim. This is also why the title names longing (the attribute of the untransmuted), not ecstasy, as the poem's subject. The pronoun is singular, arguably in contrast to the opening "Sagt" because we die, discover love, and are enlightened just one at a time.[25]

Since the poem distinguishes temporally between those who do not yet and those who already belong to light divine (Trunz, HA 2:582), thus between *before* and *after,* it provides an alternative to an elitist reading at the level of representation as well as at the level of rhetoric. The story of the moth is paradigmatic, portraying as normal a small creature's emergence out of darkness and resubmergence in darkness (in the experience of sexual conjunction), which in turn generates a "new desire" for a higher mating and a lonely flight toward a fiery death. A reading of the relative clause of lines 3 and 4 as non-restrictive and as *descriptive* of the life force as such is enabled if life is understood as the trajectory described by a living being from initial articulation through intermediate, anticipatory moments of resubmergence (in the experience of love) to ultimate reassimilation in death — the entire movement propelled by longing. Since life moves *toward,* it is always *before* the ecstasy of immolation and transmutation. The distinction, then, is not between an elite few characterized by longing and a mob lacking this driving force, but between the vital, if still unenlightened, many and the *Illuminati* (however great or small their number) who have passed through the veil, if we may here press into service the name of a second secret society devoted to enlightenment in which Goethe may have held a membership.[26] Insofar as "Stirb und werde" divides not only between sequential states of being but among a series of essences, this poem also raises the question of the continuity of personal identity.

[25] In the words of Adam Weishaupt, founder of the *Illuminatenbund,* "Der Weg, die Aufklärung allgemein zu machen ist nicht mit der ganzen Welt auf einmal anzufangen: fange erst mit dir an, dann wende dich an deinen Nächsten, und ihr beyde klärt einen Dritten und Vierten auf." (Richard van Dülmen, *Der Geheimbund der Illuminaten: Darstellung, Analyse, Dokumentation* (Stuttgart-Bad Cannstatt: Frommann-Holzboog, 1975), 184. In *Die Erziehung des Menschengeschlechts,* Lessing emphasized that Enlightenment is always individual. Moses Mendelssohn, for his part, doubted the possibility of progress toward Enlightenment for humanity as a whole (Stamm, "Herder and the *Aufklärung,*" 202).

[26] The other was the Freemasons. The member name of Abaris was reportedly assigned to Goethe in the *Illuminatenbund* (Dülmen, *Der Geheimbund,* 66 and note 130). W. Daniel Wilson, in *Geheimräte gegen Geheimbünde: Ein unbekanntes Kapitel der klassisch-romantischen Geschichte Weimars* (Stuttgart: Metzler, 1991), uses previously unpublished documents to examine Goethe's and Duke Carl August's membership. The Weimar group seems to have been singularly inactive.

The question of how radically the formula "Stirb und Werde" should be understood has generated most of the controversy over "Selige Sehnsucht." Most critics point to Goethe's fondness for the idea of metamorphosis ("Gestaltung-Umgestaltung") and images of transition such as the chrysalis and the snake repeatedly shedding its skin, and infer that he is advocating an enduring mutability in this poem.[27] Burdach finds this "moral" to be inconsistent with the "Allegorie" of the middle part, which depicts not the gentle metamorphosis of a caterpillar into a butterfly "within mortal life" but the transition from life to death. He misses any connection between the saint's tale and the "Fabula docet" "moral" of the last stanza and sees this discontinuity as evidence for Rudolf Hildebrand's conclusion that the final strophe was a later addition, although it is present in every extant manuscript of the poem.[28] Rösch applauds Burdach's strictness and argues that the "becoming" referred to in line 18 — in contrast to any merely *natural* process — is a realization of essence, a coming into being at the precise moment of death. It is thus "a tragic movement."[29] This is a common Romantic paradigm: Eibl, commenting on another soarer, writes, "Ikarus . . . ist die Sinnfigur schlechthin für eine tragische Bewegung, in der die Bahn der Selbstverwirklichung identisch ist mir der Bahn der Selbstzerstörung."[30]

---

[27] And most of them, again, take the examples of metamorphosis in nature to refer to transformations and transitions in human life, such as between childhood and youth or youth and maturity. See Johannes Klein, *Geschichte der deutschen Lyrik von Luther bis zum Ausgang des zweiten Weltkrieges,* 2nd ed. (Wiesbaden: Steiner, 1960), 353; cf. Karl Vietor, *Goethe the Poet* (Cambridge: Harvard UP, 1949), 224; and Ronald Gray: "In the end, 'Selige Sehnsucht' proves to be not a poem about entry into a higher existence in the sense of a supernatural one, but about re-entry into the natural order in a more intense ['gesteigert'] form" (*Goethe: a Critical Introduction* [Cambridge, UK: Cambridge UP, 1967], 230). Staiger says, "Die Auferstehung, die Goethe meint, [ist] diesseitig" (*Goethe,* 3:36). Kommerell observes that, "unter seinen Auslegern hat es immer zwei Riegen gegeben: solche die ängstlich gebückt waren auf Theosophisches, Astrologisches, Alchemistisches, auf das einzelne Zeugnis eines Geheimsinnes, und solche, die vergnügt mit Goethes Weltlichkeit dergleichen zur Unverbindlichkeit der dichterischen Phantasie rechneten" (Max Kommerell, *Gedanken über Gedichte,* [Frankfurt am Main: Vittorio Klostermann, 1943], 270–71).

[28] Burdach, "Anmerkungen," 334.

[29] Rösch, "Goethe's *Selige Sehnsucht*," 229–30, 237.

[30] Karl Eibl, *Das monumentale Ich: Wege zu Goethes "Faust"* (Frankfurt am Main and Leipzig: Insel Verlag, 2000), 276. Cf. Erich Trunz, "Goethes lyrische Kurzgedichte, 1771–1832" in *Goethe, Neue Folge des Jahrbuchs der Goethe-Gesellschaft,* vol. 26, 1964; repr. in *Ein Tag aus Goethes Leben: Acht Studien zu Leben und Werk* (Munich: C. H. Beck, 1991), 101–38; and Hans Pyritz, *Goethe-Studien* (Cologne: Böhlau, 1962). Hölscher-Lohmeyer harks back to Burdach and other critics who understand "Stirb und werde" to reflect Goethe's "Naturdenken" and thus to refer to natural

In the light of solid work on the sources of Goethe's worldview by Gray and Zimmermann, the burden of proof is on anyone who would deny the pertinence of the basic Hermetic paradigm of transmutation to any Goethean representation of "Stirb und werde."[31] Any becoming can be represented as a death and rebirth, as the extinction of a prior existence and the creation of a new one. There is continuity of essence, where identity resides, beneath radical discontinuity at the level of accidence. The first of the "Urworte Orphisch" proclaims: "So mußt du sein, dir kannst du nicht entfliehen, . . . Und keine Zeit und keine Macht zerstückelt / Geprägte Form, die lebend sich entwickelt." Personal identity survives accidental change — it even survives death, and may indeed be fully revealed only at the moment of death, which is the ultimate tragic meaning Rösch extracts from the poem. The verb "werden" will cover more radical change still, however — even total annihilation and obliteration, the translation of something into nothing or the absorption of a part into the whole: "Denn alles muß in Nichts zerfallen, / Wenn es im Sein beharren will" ("Im Grenzenlosen sich zu finden"). To be rescued absolutely from the prison of the self is only a more radical form of becoming than to preserve selfhood in a different guise, form, or incarnation. The blessed longing of the poem's title is for perfection ("Vollendung") in self-sacrifice ("Selbstopfer" — the two earlier titles) — for death, not for self-preservation. "Who, upon yielding to love, holds even his life in reserve?" ("Amyntas"). Such figures as the chrysalis, which implies the full sequence caterpillar — cocoon — butterfly, do illustrate Goethe's conception of metamorphosis in nature, but natural

life. She finds the poem, however, to be not about metamorphosis but about the life force as such and the ways in which it renews and "vergeistigt" itself. It is a hymn to life — to "das Lebendig-Sein" ("Die Entwicklung des Goetheschen Naturdenkens," 24) — whose dynamic force unfolds in an upward spiral of deaths and rebirths.

Benjamin Bennett views the poem as a drama of a simultaneous death and coming into being in our use of language, as an enactment of the idea "that language represents the ontological priority of communal over individual existence," while nourishing the illusion of individual autonomy. The poem is "the union or confusion of the movements of articulation and submergence [i.e., coming into being and dying] that reveals an ordinarily unremarked quality of our relation to language" (*Goethe's Theory of Poetry: "Faust" and the Regeneration of Language* [Ithaca, NY: Cornell UP, 1986], 275).

[31] *Faust* is saturated with the idea. Whether in the Easter celebration, in the concoction of a remedy for the plague by Faust's alchemist father, or in the creation of Homunculus in the alchemist's laboratory, it is a dying and becoming that is envisioned and in the latter two cases a *Liebestod* as well — the death of the Lily White and the Lion Red in the birth of the young Queen as panacea or tincture, and the death and putrefaction of human spermatazoa in the "gorde glass," according to the recipe of Paracelsus (Gray, *Goethe the Alchemist* [Cambridge, UK: Cambridge UP, 1952], 205–6).

metamorphosis may also schematize death and *ex nihilo* origination. A death precedes every beginning, every emergence is out of the void, all light the offspring of darkness, and every fulfillment a sacrifice of selfhood and reentry into nothingness. The same metaphor also adds strength to the thesis that the poem under consideration is about the flight of the soul, since the butterfly traditionally symbolizes the psyche. We recall also that Faust, after he has died, is described as "im Puppenstand" (11982). There is no need to restrict the poem's symbolic range to a particular pattern or example.

The simultaneous assertion of its continuity and discontinuity in the conditional clause, "Solang du das nicht hast," which addresses an enduring subject in possession of its own mortality and reemergent novelty — a continuity only of the cessation and re-realization of existence in an upward spiral of binary offs and ons, zeros and ones — may seem to preclude the most radical understanding of "Stirb und werde!" To *have* "Stirb und werde" (i.e. as a property of the subject) implies the endurance of the subject and thus the impossibility of "death" understood as the annihilation of the subject.[32] Neither dying nor becoming itself, the "du" of the final couplet must remain a "trüber Gast" in its failure to exemplify the mutability urged in the poem's maxim. This is paradoxical and may seem vulnerable to Occam's razor, leaving us with the interpretation of "Stirb und werde!" as a metaphor for natural metamorphosis and with a didactic reading of the poem as a lesson on life's transitions. But such an interpretation would be seriously reductive, ignoring the poem's title and obliterating the vision it affords of a love-triggered self-abandonment to a transcendent fulfillment in death. The alternative is to accept the paradox as more profound and *linguistically* natural than such *biological* naturalism — despite, or, rather, because of, its dialectical complexity and insufficiency. "Trübe Gäste" still, we do not yet understand; when enlightened, we will no longer be.

Mystification as enlightenment! Goethe's works are self-confessedly fragmentary and revel in paradox and oxymoron as reflective of life's intractableness to complete, unironic representation.[33] It is in this that his fundamental Christian-Romantic skepticism is most evident, for he does not suppose that the unequivocal truth can be told about ultimate things and thus differs fundamentally from those who would clarify his obscurity. A student of the secondary literature on "Selige Sehnsucht" can hardly fail to see

[32] Bennett stresses "the state of 'having'" as "an enduring state . . . whereas what we are supposed to 'have' in the last stanza involves the renunciation of any enduring state" (Bennett, *Goethe's Theory of Poetry*, 270).

[33] In a letter to C. L. F. Schultz, he described the epistolary record of his friendship with Schiller as "ein wahres Bild des beschatteten buntgrauen Erdenlebens" (3 July 1824, GA 21:599). In its very fragmentariness and with all its traces of conflict, suffering, and quotidian complaints, it reveals the overshadowed many-colored grayness of human life on earth.

that many of its disputes are the product of overly specific, univocal choices between mutually interactive but unreconciled alternatives in Goethe's symbolic practice. Guided, apparently, by the same operational definitions, Burdach describes Goethe's poem as an allegory (since there is no seamless metaphorical continuity between the image of a moth incinerating itself in a flame and the idea of natural metamorphosis), whereas Rösch, given his preference for symbol over allegory,[34] is obliged to find a more suitable analogy in order to valorize the poem. Thus he turns to the tragic hero, whose true essence unfolds at the moment of death.[35] Both scholars sacrifice limitless referentiality to one clear and distinct idea. But Rösch pays an additional price. Not only is Goethe required to die as Goethe and become Schiller (for it is Schiller's conception of tragedy that informs Rösch's reading), Rösch is obliged to contend that only in being consumed by the flame does the butterfly realize its essence as butterfly — to read line 16 as meaning: "only burned, butterfly, art thou (thyself)" — i.e., it is natural for butterflies to do the unnatural thing. Underlying this interpretation is a conception of "werden" as an epiphany, a revelation or unfolding of an already present quality, which Goethe's broad use of "werden" *will* tolerate.[36] But if a butterfly's essence is manifested by its flight into the flame, this must be true of the entire species, not peculiar to an exemplary few, and the image fails as a symbol of extraordinary self-sacrifice. The butterfly as either tragic hero or mystical lover is a long way from a natural association of image and idea. Rösch is aware of "antinomic structures" and of "aporetic self-conflict" in Goethe's late works,[37] yet he himself is caught in paradox by his insistence on a univocal reading of this difficult poem.

Goethe has been credited with being "the first to draw the distinction between symbol and allegory in the modern way."[38] Yet he relies not so

[34] Rösch, "Goethe's 'Selige Sehnsucht,'" 243.

[35] "Daß ihm ganze Serien solcher Flammentode zugedacht sein könnten, ist vom Sinnbild her ausgeschlossen. . . . Von einem Jenseits nach dem Flammentod wird in diesem Gedicht nichts sichtbar" (ibid., 245).

[36] This does not accord with Paul de Man's opinion; see "Intentional Structure of the Romantic Image," in *Romanticism and Consciousness,* ed. Harold Bloom (New York: Norton, 1970), 65–77; reprint in de Man, *The Rhetoric of Romanticism* (New York: Columbia UP, 1984), 1–17; here, 5. See also Wilhelm Emrich, "Symbolinterpretation und Mythenforschung," 1953, repr. in *Protest und Verheißung* (Frankfurt am Main: Athenäum, 1963): 67–94: here, 73.

[37] Rösch, "Goethe's 'Selige Sehnsucht,'" 228.

[38] René Wellek, *A History of Modern Criticism: 1750–1950,* 7 vols. (New Haven: Yale UP, 1955–1991); vol. 1: *The Later Eighteenth Century* (1955), 210.

much on the "associative analogy" between sign and referent[39] that came to characterize subsequent conceptions of symbol (and led to de Man's charging the later Romanticists with an act of ontological bad faith[40]) as on the sensuous concreteness of the image and its unlimited radiation.[41] If in symbolism the idea is infinitely effective and ineffable, the chosen imagery may be not less but more arbitrary (at least it produces an indefinitely greater sum of arbitrariness) than in allegory, which always has the circumscribed stability of convention and logical consistency. It is less likely, on the other hand, to end in aporia because of its greater tolerance of ambiguity and because it does not end at all but reverberates on into infinity.

There is difference as well as similarity in every symbol. The rainbow as a bridge to a beyond in which the "unbetrübt" eye can tolerate the light provides a natural enough association. But the arbitrariness increases when the good human being prefigures "jene geahneten Wesen," the gods ("Das Göttliche"). Thus Iphigenie is Diana, is the moon, although also mortal and contingent, in polar opposition to her immortal benefactress. With a different twist, the colors of the rainbow serve as an "Abglanz" of pure white light, a sign of its absence and proof of its presence. And in "Selige Sehnsucht," sexual union (the lower) prefigures *unio mystica* (the higher), while in "Wiederfinden," the "erklingend Farbenspiel" of lovers in search of each other, in all its present transitory multi-sensuous excitement, leads and points inexorably to the silent night of eternal rest. Difference alone is at work when the part announces the whole, the transitory reminds of the permanent, and the corrupt guarantees the pure (which baroque idea also informs the Kantian belief that God, freedom, and immortality must reside in the noumena precisely *because* of their absence from the world of the phenomena). Much of what seems allegorical in Goethe is invulnerable to displacement and resists imagistic substitution, and yet the same images convey radically different meanings in different contexts. As Emrich has established, Goethe's images are "doubly structured . . . *antinomically* formed," and interpretable only in terms of their syntagmatic inter-relationships (79).[42]

[39] Earl Wasserman, "The English Romantics: The Grounds of Knowledge," *Studies in Romanticism* 4 (1964): 17–34; here, 19.

[40] Paul de Man, "The Rhetoric of Temporality," in *Blindness and Insight: Essays in the Rhetoric of Contemporary Criticism,* 2nd, rev. ed. (Minneapolis: U of Minnesota P, 1983), 187–228; here, 211.

[41] "Die Symbolik verwandelt die Erscheinung in Idee, die Idee in ein Bild, und so daß die Idee im Bild immer unendlich wirksam und unerreichbar bleibt, und selbst in allen Sprachen ausgesprochen doch unaussprechlich bliebe" (FA 1,13:207).

[42] Emrich also shows that symbolic meaning is not automatic and "unmittelbar," but produced through reflection ("Symbolinterpretation," 88–89).

Goethe's writing is paratactic, dialectical, and self-referentially productive of a scintillating, many-colored intertextual web, articulating personal continuance through continuous metamorphosis in one context and then, without a gesture of modulation, celebrating the complete reabsorption of the individual in the next.[43] That readings at opposite ends of a number of axes may be generated by the same text Goethe was fully aware, and he took pleasure in the fact. To insist on an "obvious or univocal" reading (in Meyer Abrams's probably often regretted paraphrase of a belief attributed to him by J. Hillis Miller)[44] for "Selige Sehnsucht" or *Faust* or any other text would be to reject Goethe's precepts as well as his practice, which cannot be reduced to a single coherent statement, system, or world view. As he knew, language, like the painted panes of Faust's study, is inherently a "trübes" medium that does not simply reveal, but always refracts the truth, imprinting its own qualities on it, never affording more than a partial view (in both senses of the term); language inscribes itself on the subject. Nevertheless, he seems to have believed that our yearning is for a whole, unitary, uncorrupted truth, which is beyond language and which, though expressed in all languages, remains inexpressible and only medially available to the untransmuted self, as through a glass darkly. It is left to the guests at his symposium to pay heed and, while still "trübe Gäste" on this unilluminated sphere, to join him in looking forward to an effluence of "mehr Licht."

[43] Rösch cites the consecutively printed poems "Eins und Alles" and "Vermächtnis" as statements of the alternation of being and non-being and then of the conservation of being ("Goethe's 'Selige Sehnsucht,'" 233).

[44] Meyer H. Abrams. "Rationality and Imagination in Cultural History: A Reply to Wayne Booth," *Critical Inquiry* 2 (1976): 447–64; here, 458; J. Hillis Miller, "Tradition and Difference," *Diacritics* 2 (1972): 6–13; here, 11–12.

9: *Die Wahlverwandtschaften:* Romantic Metafiction

IN HER PRIZE-WINNING ESSAY "Hierogamy versus Wedlock," Evelyn Hinz discusses the generic classification of prose fictions in terms of the kind of marriage plot they employ.[1] Hinz refines Northrop Frye's scheme of classification, in which *Pride and Prejudice* counts as a novel but *Wuthering Heights* is a *romance,* and offers the term "mythic narrative" for lengthy prose works organized by a marriage plot and portraying the "hierogamous" union of disparate partners whose love mirrors a cosmic conjunction like "the union of earth and sky."[2] According to Hinz, marriage in a mythic narrative implicates the non-social as well as the social universe, while "novels" restrict themselves to portraying wedlock as a social contract and occasion. Hinz echoes a contemporary of Goethe's, Friedrich von Blanckenburg, in relating diverse literary genres to "einer Verschiedenheit in der Denkungsart der Menschen,"[3] as Blanckenburg puts it, and derives the difference between the mythic narrative and the novel from the difference between ancient and modern "man." As described by Mircea Eliade, "the former feels himself indissolubly connected with the Cosmos and the cosmic rhythms, whereas the latter insists that he is connected only with history."[4] Hinz agrees with Frye that *Pride and Prejudice* is an exemplary novel. *The Rainbow* and *For Whom*

---

[1] Evelyn Hinz, "Hierogamy versus Wedlock: Types of Marriage Plots and Their Relationship to Genres of Prose Fiction," *PMLA* 91:5 (1976): 900–913. Cf. Edgar Wind, *Pagan Mysteries in the Renaissance* (New Haven: Yale UP, 1958; rev. and enlarged ed. New York: Norton [The Norton Library], 1968), on the tradition of "*hieros gamos,* an ecstatic union with the god which was experienced by the neophyte as an initiation into death" (156).

[2] Hinz, "Hierogamy," 905.

[3] Friedrich von Blanckenburg, *Versuch über den Roman* (1774; facsimile repr., ed. Eberhard Lämmert (Stuttgart: Metzler, 1965), 7. The epic deals with the *Bürger* in public life, the *Roman* with the individual, private human being — e.g., Tom Jones, "mit seinem Seyn und seinen Empfindungen" (18). German criticism generally views the personal life of the characters as the distinctive province of the *Roman.* Cf. Wolfgang Kayser: "Die Erzählung von der totalen Welt (in gehobenem Tone) hieß Epos; die Erzählung von der privaten Welt in privatem Tone heißt *Roman*" (*Das Sprachliche Kunstwerk,* 1948, 6th ed. [Bern: Francke, 1960], 359).

[4] Quoted in Hinz, "Hierogamy," 905.

the Bell Tolls, by contrast, are mythic narratives. The conventions of the genre determine that the earth moves under Maria and Robert Jordan.

The question of its genre, like the bigger question of the character and literary-historical "location" of the work and its author, is never far from the center of discussions of Goethe's *Die Wahlverwandtschaften*. Stuart P. Atkins believes the work can be described as a "novel of German classicism,[5] by virtue of its "idealized naturalism" (151) rather than "naturalistic imitation" (155), its "broad human significance" (149) — it stresses the unity in human diversity — and its articulation of "Goethe's secular, strongly ethical humanism" (153).[6] It exhibits "the classical ideal of harmony of form, style, and substance" (174) and explores a threatened marriage and a spiritual "double adultery," but it also treats of "manners, ethics, landscape, music, acting, architecture, art, social pastimes, scientific and educational ideas, and socio-economic activities (social work, village betterment, estate improvement)" (173). *Die Wahlverwandtschaften* did not arise out of a mature culture and thus may lack an attribute stipulated by T. S. Eliot as essential to the classical, but, as Atkins shows, it bears most of the traits commonly associated with the classical. "Goethe responded most warmly" to Rochlitz's opinion that "'classische Gediegenheit, Rundung, Sicherheit und Harmonie' made *Die Wahlverwandtschaften* the most perfect of Goethe's narrative works" (Atkins, 180).

The German term "Roman" may refer to any long prose narrative and, in earlier discourse, to any amorous adventure as well.[7] Although it is generally held that *Die Wahlverwandtschaften* was conceived as a novella and that, in its final form, it preserves its novellistic character, Atkins doubts that the

---

[5] Stuart P. Atkins, "*Die Wahlverwandtschaften:* Novel of German Classicism," *The German Quarterly,* 53 (1980): 1–45; repr. in Atkins, *Essays on Goethe,* ed. Jane K. Brown and Thomas P. Saine (Columbia, SC: Camden House, 1995), 137–81. My frequent references to Atkins's essay will be parenthetical, usually by page no. only (page numbers refer to the reprinted version in *Essays on Goethe*). Atkins uses the terms "classical" and "classicism" to refer to *deutsche Klassik* as a program and period, but he also posits a "timeless" classical antithesis to a timeless "romantic" world view or "mode of feeling" (155). I diverge from his use of the lower case and write an "R" when referring to early nineteenth-century Romanticism as well as "C" for German Classicism, without wishing to suggest that either is a simple, uniform phenomenon.

[6] Atkins identifies the narrator as an ethical humanist with Goethe, e.g.: "for a Goethe consciously hostile to much that is romantic, *and hence for his narrator*" (155 — my emphasis). Atkins elsewhere refers to Goethe's "conciliatory humanism" (149) and to the "enlightened ethical protestantism of [the work's] narrator and its author" (167).

[7] Atkins, "Wilhelm Meisters Lehrjahre: Novel or Romance?" *Essays on European Literature in Honor of Liselotte Dieckmann,* ed. P. U. Hohendahl et al (St. Louis: Washington UP, 1972) 45–52, reprint in Atkins, *Essays on Goethe,* 130–36, esp. 130–35.

work was ever meant to be a novella. It is "the only work [that] Goethe . . . subtitled 'Ein Roman'" (25), and, more successfully than any other work of Goethe's, it conveys "the broad, even universal significance of themes treated with [the] scrupulous attention to truth of detail" that is essential to the novel — albeit "significant detail only" (1). He sees it as a *novel*, evincing "meticulous verisimilitude" of "motivation and milieu" (26)[8] — its action "largely coincides with the latter part of the War of the Third Coalition, viz., the War of Prussia and Russia against France in 1806–7" (3 and n. 6) — "normalization of diction" (26), and conscious use of the set epithet (such as *himmlisch* and *herrlich* for Ottilie — 16; nn. 43, 44). "Dramatic elements are subordinated to a deliberately epic tone in accordance with Goethe's and Schiller's essay 'Über epische und dramatische Dichtung' . . ., and an unhurried, steadily progressive mode of narration serves to minimize drama-like effects in passages of dialogue . . . or in climactic episodes" (176). It is as a grateful beneficiary of Atkins's exemplary scholarship that I here venture to make the contrary claim that Goethe's narrative is better described as a Romantic metafiction.

Remarkably, *Die Wahlverwandtschaften* has every feature of the "mythic narrative" as described by Hinz, including (at least a promise of) the conjunction of the principal characters. The union of Eduard and Ottilie, no less than the union of Tristan and Isolde in Wagner's opera, is the goal toward which the work advances, and the failure to achieve this goal is its essential tragedy. Although Hinz does not say so, it seems that the "novel" is implicitly theistic in presupposing the special status of humans, while the mythic narrative highlights the commonalities of the world, across differences of class, species, kingdoms — even across the great divide between the living and the non-living. (In which category shall we include the undead, such as the revenant in "Die Braut von Korinth"?) It shows that there is "überall nur *eine* Natur," as Goethe declared in his announcement of *Die Wahlverwandtschaften* and demonstrated to his considerable satisfaction in discovering that humans too have an intermaxillary bone. While in Hinz's scheme the novel is defined by the opposition between the natural and the human, mythic narratives display human nature in sync with the rest of the universe. Further, novels are historical, while mythic narratives, though tracing a linear trajectory toward (and beyond) the sexual conjunction of hero and heroine,[9] reflect a circular, *mythic* world view. Novels show what hap-

---

[8] Atkins notes the work's "verisimilar detail" (138), "meticulous accuracy" (139), "verisimilar exactitude" (140), "realistic historical detail" (143), and "tru[thfulness] to life" (n. 68).

[9] Objecting to the representation of love in novels as too platonic, Blanckenburg says, "der Roman endigt sich immer, und muß sich immer, bey den Voraussetzungen, daß

pened in a given situation, whereas mythic narratives show what always happens — "that which is eternally recurrent" (905). In mythic narratives the romantic coupling of the main characters, as befits its central significance, takes place at the symbolic center of the world, the *axis mundi,* a place "characterized by its extremity or ultimateness, and never is it a public building or a domestic dwelling" (909). "Wedlock" occurs in mythic narratives as well as in novels, but only to throw the more fundamental "hierogamous union into greater relief" (907). In *The French Lieutenant's Woman,* to add a strikingly pure example to those given by Hinz, John Fowles contrasts Charles Smithson's passionate secret romance with Sarah Woodruff with his proper, conventional engagement to Ernestina Freeman. "No worlds fell, no inner roar, no darkness shrouded eyes and ears, as he stood pressing his lips upon hers for several seconds. But Ernestina was very prettily dressed."[10] *Die Wahlverwandtschaften* employs the same "mythic narrative" conventions, and does so self-consciously, showing in this case too that Goethe was both appreciative of generic traditions and characteristically playful with their rules. To acknowledge this is not anachronistically to contend that the "mythic narrative" was an identified and denominated form in Goethe's time, but only to observe that its conventions were available for his use. Even the novel was not firmly defined in the restrictive, modern sense, which was no doubt a factor in Goethe's extraordinarily free experimentation with all the forms of prose (and verse) fiction. It is part of his signature as a writer, beginning with his pastoral play *Die Laune des Verliebten* and his "anacreontic" poems, that he both makes use of popular genres and exposes their conventionality. The assignment of *Die Wahlverwandtschaften* to any genre might seem to strengthen the case for its classicism, since classicism is supposed to stress the commonalities of human experience and literary genres serve to articulate commonalities — even the common experience of frustration in love (and the failure to achieve erotic or any other kind of fulfillment as characteristic of the human condition). But the work's self-conscious display and implicit interrogation of the conventions on which it relies is especially characteristic of German Romanticism.

Atkins credits Liselotte Dieckmann with having drawn attention to "the wealth of patterned or pattern-creating elements — points of view, themes, motifs, images, the use of sententious generalization, *multiple dimensions of reality,* etc. — that contribute substantive and structural density to the *Lehrjahre.*"[11] Precisely these qualities would qualify it as a mythic narrative, as Hinz uses the term. I find in *Die Wahlverwandtschaften* even greater density

wir Menschen sind, mit einer Hochzeitnacht endigen" (*Versuch über den Roman,* 480).
[10] John Fowles, *The French Lieutenant's Woman* (New York: Signet, 1969), 210.
[11] Atkins, "*Wilhelm Meisters Lehrjahre.*"

and richness of pattern than in *Wilhelm Meisters Lehrjahre,* as well as an almost geometrical abstractness. It does depict life in Germany during the Napoleonic period, but its remarkable fidelity as a picture of the age is incidental to its central project, which is to explore the longing for union of disparate and complementary lovers matched "übers Kreuz,"[12] a longing fueled by "individual passions so elemental as to justify the chemical analogy in [the work's] title."[13] Held apart in life, Eduard and Ottilie, Charlotte and the Captain, would constitute the ensuing new "compounds" after the separation of Eduard and Charlotte — who are unhappily wedded to each other — if the reaction designated by the title were allowed to proceed to its conclusion.

Ottilie and Eduard *are* symbolically and proleptically united when, in the seclusion of the forest by the mill, she gives him the medallion containing the image of her father. This symbolic union anticipates, deceptively, as it turns out, the full consummation which is desired by both and which, as Romanticism quintessentially laments, is beyond the reach of human beings — or charged particles, or the separate parts (signifier and signified) of the sign. Whether Eduard and Ottilie may be viewed as coming together in death and destined for a joint resurrection depends on what is meant by "together" as well as on how one reads or accredits the "view into eternity"[14] expressed in the narrator's last words — whether "wenn" expresses a confident "when" or a skeptical "if," and whether the reader adopts the narrator's point of view.[15] In recording the central characters' frustrated desire for a recombinant unity, it exposes the world as fragmented and its inhabitants as irrevocably disconnected, and shows the tragedy of men and women existing in a "Nacht der Ferne" ("Wiederfinden") and condemned to long for something forever beyond their reach. A Tasso may find compensation in his ability to articulate his suffering, but Ottilie's silence is the more eloquent comment on the tragedy of cosmic fragmentation. *Die Wahlverwandtschaften* is "more awesomely tragic" than *Werther, Egmont,* or the "Gretchentragödie" in *Faust,*[16] while the *Lehrjahre* is generically "comic" in (temporarily) bringing the principals together at its culmination. But the

---

[12] FA 1,8:305. In the rest of this chapter vol. 1,8 is referred to parenthetically, by page no. alone.

[13] Atkins, "*Wilhelm Meisters Lehrjahre,*" 151.

[14] *Aussichten in die Ewigkeit* is the title of Johann Caspar Lavater's popular effusions, 1768–78. See Atkins, "J. C. Lavater and Goethe: Problems of Psychology and Theology in *Die Leiden des jungen Werthers,*" *PMLA* 63 (1948): 520–76; reprint in Atkins, *Essays on Goethe,* 23–82; here, 24–31.

[15] Blackall says "this obtrusive narrator . . . is trying to describe something that is . . . beyond him" (*Goethe and the Novel* [Ithaca, NY: Cornell UP, 1976], 172).

[16] Atkins, *Essays on Goethe,* 181

implicit ideology of any work — the way it views and articulates reality, rather than the success or failure of the ambitions of its characters — is what is fundamental. Nor does it matter that the obstacles to the union of the lovers in *Die Wahlverwandtschaften* are preeminently social, for social barriers merely show that it is in society that we are most alone. Where the focus is on the manners and morals of persons and social classes rather than on the attraction/repulsion of forces in the universe, we have a novel. In the novel *someone* is alone; in the mythic narrative, and in Romanticism generally, hero and heroine are essentially alone but allied with everything else in their search for each other. We have company in our solitude, and our coupling resounds throughout the cosmos.

Since the mythic narrative celebrates the conjunction of separate selves, its natural climax is a *Liebestod*, even if the principals die one after the other, not at the same moment.[17] What is important is the lovers' victory, in dying "together," over moral, emotional and spiritual division. Persons can metonymically, but not literally, flow into each other like Charlotte's tiny globules of mercury (301), and their ashes need not actually mix, like the ashes of Faust and Gretchen on the funeral pyre at the end of Murnau's *Faust* movie. Nor must the substance of one character become incorporated into that of another, as when her Athenian bridegroom is sucked dry of blood by the vampire "bride" in "Die Braut von Korinth." Rhadames and Aida, as Hans Castorp realistically considers, do not blend together, but exist in tandem, each totally indifferent to whether he or she has company or is alone. The entombment of Eduard and Ottilie in the chapel is the more recognizable as a *Liebestod* if we see this term as an abstraction, a *coincidentia oppositorum* denoting the principals' spiritual transcendence of the individuality by which they are defined. Eduard and Ottilie are as fully united in death as are Tristan and Isolde, Romeo and Juliet, or any other pair of lovers, and Ottilie imagines and desires her death and burial with Eduard while contemplating

---

[17] Walter Benjamin (*Goethes Wahlverwandtschaften: Neue deutsche Beiträge,* ed. Hugo von Hofmannsthal [1924–25; repr., Frankfurt: Insel, 1964]), Benno von Wiese ("Nachwort und Anmerkungen" to Goethe's *Die Wahlverwandtschaften* [HA 6:672–730]), and F. J. Stopp ("'Ein wahrer Narziss': Reflections on the Eduard-Ottilie Relationship in Goethe's *Wahlverwandtschaften, PEGS* 29 [1960], 52–85), all comment on "Ding-Symbole" of love and death, e.g. the bridal chest. "Es ist ganz unverkennbar, wie das Ding-Symbol hier Träger der Liebe und des Todes ist, beides zu einer geheimnisvollen Einheit verschmelzend" (Von Wiese, as quoted by Stopp, 75–76). Stopp notes that the theme of love and death is symbolized in the hollowed-out foundation stone of the *Lustgebäude,* which, for Eduard, "is an erotic symbol which points forward to the bridal chest garnished with fine stuffs, and both are a fantasy picture of the consummation of love in the birth of a child. For him, the fantasy image turns into the counter-image of the illicitly conceived child and the coffin into which it is ultimately placed" (Stopp, "'Ein wahrer Narziss,'" 74–75).

her own image in the angels' faces painted in the chapel ceiling.[18] When she eventually does die, a wreath of asters — symbols of premature death and of "Wiedervereinigung und Erfüllung in einem andern Dasein"[19] — is placed on her head (523);[20] her bridal dress becomes her funeral dress; and, when Eduard follows her in death, they are buried together in the chapel — a place suited "nur zu einer gemeinsamen Grabstätte" (408). This is the outcome sought by the old grandmother for Kasper and Annerl in Brentano's famous story and the consummation granted to Abélard and Héloise when, twenty years after Abélard's death, his casket is opened and he reaches out to embrace Héloise for eternity.[21]

Goethe's antipathy to the excesses of some of his younger contemporaries is often cited by Germanists in support of the classicism-romanticism dichotomy. The famous quotation is, "Classisch ist das Gesunde, romantisch das Kranke," but equally harsh is, "Das Romantische ist schon in seinen Abgrund verlaufen, das Gräßlichste der neuern Productionen ist kaum noch gesunkener zu denken" (FA 1,13:239).[22] Nevertheless, German Romanticism and German Classicism[23] are not so much a polarity as a "quarrel within the family."[24] While the one may stress "Un*end*lichkeit" and the other "Vol*lend*ung" (according to Fritz Strich's still useful dichotomy), Classicists and Romantics both "strive for eternity."[25] That Goethe, the alleged Classicist, sometimes rejects what his Romantic admirers embrace does not separate the occasional adversaries as much as their common presuppositions unite them.

[18] H. G. Barnes notes Ottilie's death yearning as she contemplates her own image in the angels' faces ("Bildhafte Darstellung in den 'Wahlverwandtschaften,'" *DVjs* 30 [1956]: 41–70; here, 54).

[19] Barnes, "Bildhafte Darstellung," 58–59.

[20] Viktor Žmegač writes, "Es gibt zu denken daß die 'Wahlverwandtschaften' Richard Wagners Lieblingsroman waren. . . . Das exzeptionelle Sterben Ottilies und Eduards präludiert mit manchen seinen Zügen [*sic*] den Liebestod im romantischen Musikdrama. In beiden Werken ist die Leidenschaft absolut, verzehrend, gegen die gesellschaftlichen Konventionen gerichtet, in ihrer Einsamkeit, wenn man so will, 'asocial'" ("Zu einem Thema Goethes und Thomas Manns: Wege der Erotik in der modernen Gesellschaft," *Goethe Jahrbuch* 103 (1986): 152–67; here, 160).

[21] Fowlie, Wallace, *Love in Literature* (Bloomington: Indiana UP, 1965), 33.

[22] Atkins also quotes Goethe's description of early nineteenth-century "parochial 'romanticism'" as "wahnsinnigen, protestantisch-katholischen, poetisch-christlichen Obskurantismus" ("The Evaluation of Romanticism in Goethe's *Faust*," *JEGP* 54 [1955]: 9–38, reprint in Atkins, *Essays on Goethe,* 293).

[23] A much examined concept — see Klaus L. Berghahn, "Das Andere der Klassik: von der 'Klassik-Legende' zur jüngsten Klassik-Diskussion," *Goethe Yearbook* 6 (1992): 1–27.

[24] Hans Robert Jauss, as quoted by Berghahn, "Das Andere der Klassik," 12.

[25] Fritz Strich, *Deutsche Klassik und Romantik* (Munich: Meyer & Jessen, 1922).

Wellek long ago pointed out that every important feature of Romanticism can be found in Goethe — the mixing of genres when it suited him (which he practiced throughout his career but also sometimes deplored); a greater or lesser streak of mysticism; the view of the artist as an *alter deus* and antithesis either to thoughtless philistinism or to healthy innocence; the resulting choice of the artist or poet as a suitable subject for literary representation (preeminently in *Torquato Tasso,* but, in *Dichtung und Wahrheit,* also Goethe himself); the stronger interest in character than in event; admiration of Shakespeare and denigration of the French; a "dynamic, organic view of nature";[26] interest in the occult and the supernatural, the weird and extraordinary; fascination with dreams, the subconscious, and the dark side of human consciousness (for example, with *Doppelgänger,* as in *Dichtung und Wahrheit* and *Wilhelm Meisters Lehrjahre*); a refusal to privilege the commonsensical over idiosyncratic vision or intuition ("Erlkönig"); espousal of original genius (coupled with acknowledgment of the dependence of genius on tradition); and "a use of imagery, symbolism, and myth which is clearly distinct from that of eighteenth-century neoclassicism."[27]

Wellek believes that "Goethe perfectly fits into the European romantic movement which he, as much as any single writer, helped to create," and which regards the poet-intellectual as either uniquely equipped to see the integrity of the world or, at least, as uniquely desirous of discerning its integ-

---

[26] Wellek, "The Concept of Romanticism in Literary History," *Comparative Literature* 1 (1949): 1–23, 147–72; repr. in *Concepts of Criticism,* ed. Stephen G. Nichols, Jr. (New Haven: Yale UP, 1963), 128–98; here, 162.

[27] Wellek, "The Concept of Romanticism," 161. Atkins discusses Goethe's classicism in "*Italienische Reise* and Goethean Classicism," *Aspekte der Goethezeit,* ed. Stanley A. Corngold, Michael Curschmann and Theodore J. Ziolkowski (Göttingen: Vandenhoeck & Ruprecht, 1977), 81–96; repr. in Atkins, *Essays on Goethe,* 182–97; in "On Goethe's Classicism," *Goethe Proceedings: Essays Commemorating the Goethe Sesquicentennial at the University of California, Davis,* ed. Clifford A. Bernd et al. (Columbia, SC: Camden House, 1984), 1–21; in "Über Goethes Klassik," *Goethe Jahrbuch* 103 (1896): 278–301; and in "The Evaluation of Romanticism in Goethe's *Faust.*" Extensive discussion of German classicism continues in the *Jahrbuch der deutschen Schillergesellschaft* 32 (1988): 347–74 (essays by Wilfried Barner, Victor Lange, Hans-Georg Werner, and Terence James Reed); and 36 (1992): 409–54 (essays by Walter Müller-Seidel, John A. McCarthy, Dieter Borchmeyer, Christoph Jamme, and Anthony Stephens); also in Wolfgang Wittkowski, ed. *Verlorene Klassik: ein Symposium* (Tübingen: Niemeyer, 1986); Gert Ueding, *Klassik und Romantik: Deutsche Literatur im Zeitalter der Französischen Revolution 1789–1815* (Munich: Carl Hanser, 1987); and *Klassik im Vergleich,* DFG-Symposion 1990, ed. Wilhelm Vosskamp (Stuttgart: Metzler, 1993). Berghahn gives an overview of the debate until 1992, stressing that attempts to see the "Klassik-Legende" in its historical context are not attacks on Goethe and Schiller.

rity,[28] as in Faust's ambition to "erkenne[n], was die Welt / Im Innersten zusammenhält" (382–83). Wellek understands that Romantic striving is a limited historical phenomenon, and not a "timeless mode of feeling."[29] It also varies according to nationality and other synchronic differences. All of modernism, including Romanticism, derives from a conception of knowledge as seeing and inevitably splits the world into self and other. The *Liebestod* symbolizes the lovers' victory over separation and is symbolic of victory over every division. A complete victory is unattainable, however, and this is why the Romantics resort to irony, why in the very act of using the conventions of language and literature they put their conventionality and "falseness" on display.[30]

According to Atkins, the three most important aspects of Romanticism in *Die Wahlverwandtschaften* are "its speculative science, its art, and its religious thought" (11). He neatly disposes of these, showing that Goethe rejected or discounted Romantic theories in all three areas, but betrays a confidence in representation that Schlegel, Novalis, and, first and foremost, Goethe did not share. Specific theories aside, these three writers and many other contemporaries besides were interested in how science, art, and religion represent their truth claims, and in the intellectual implications of the fact that representation always conceals as well as reveals and that it defers whatever it demonstrates. Goethe's cognizance of the contradiction implicit in the very idea of representation and his virtuosic play with language as a representational medium suggest that his *Wahlverwandtschaften* is a Romantic metafiction that subordinates a conscientious reportorial accuracy to its own self-reflective and epistemological purposes. The work's irony highlights and throws doubt on the concepts, tropes, categories, and generic conventions that the narrative employs to depict reality and establish its claims to truth, as Romantic irony is wont to do. Granted, it is hard to encompass the various "romanticisms" in a single definition. The multiplicity of phenomena described as romantic does not let us forget Arthur O. Lovejoy's claim that "the word 'romantic' . . . has ceased to perform the function of a verbal sign,"[31] Wellek's rebuttal notwithstanding. But if a work is critical of its own conventionality and acknowledges that representation is

---

[28] Wellek, "The Concept of Romanticism," 163.

[29] Atkins, "Die Wahlverwandtschaften," 155.

[30] Even as a youth Goethe understood the need to do this: "Jede Form, auch die gefühlteste, hat etwas Unwahres, allein sie ist ein für allemal das Glas, wodurch wir die heiligen Strahlen der verbreiteten Natur an das Herz des Menschen zum Feuerblick sammeln" (*DjG*, 5 [1973], 352).

[31] A. O. Lovejoy, "On the Discrimination of Romanticisms," *PMLA* 39 (1924), 229–53; repr. in Lovejoy, *Essays in the History of Ideas* (Baltimore: Johns Hopkins UP, 1948), 228–53; here, 232.

the confirmation of a split, this reinforces the case for Romanticism. Whether self-inoculative or confidently self-inquisitorial, Goethe's tale gives ample warning not to take things at face value.

Let us return to Wellek's point that the aim of the Romanticist is to unite subject and object, self and other, art and nature, language and reality, etc. At the lexical level, alterity is denied in *Die Wahlverwandtschaften.* Goethe goes so far as to assign one name — the palindrome Otto,[32] which displays the two halves of the word as mirror images of each other and even subverts the difference between before and after — to all the principal characters: *Ott*ilie, Charl*otte,* Eduard (who has surrendered his given name Otto to his friend), and the Captain. Then there is young Otto, whose parents, at the moment of his conception, imagine themselves coupled with the lover that each, respectively, would prefer. The fruit of this "double adultery" keeps Charlotte and Eduard apart while he is alive (492), but in death he becomes a permanent barrier between Eduard and Ottilie, having drowned while in her care. The ideal lovers converge nevertheless, Ottilie early developing a hand so similar to Eduard's that both he and Charlotte mistake her writing for Eduard's own, and accompanying his erratic flute playing so effortlessly that their musical duet seems animated by one spirit. Both suffer from headaches, on opposite, complementary sides of the head. Eventually verbal communication becomes unnecessary between them. Like two magnets, they move in total unity and harmony with one another. "Nur die nächste Nähe konnte sie beruhigen, aber auch völlig beruhigen, und diese Nähe war genug." Not a glance, not a word, not a gesture or touch is needed, but only that they be close together. "Dann waren es nicht zwei Menschen, es war nur Ein Mensch im bewußtlosen vollkommnen Behagen, mit sich selbst zufrieden und mit der Welt" (516).[33]

The striving to sublate difference in an ideal higher identity and the stress on a unity of opposites that is more than mere sympathy is almost reason enough to classify a writer as a Romantic. But the highlighting of his categories is decisive. A tiny but telling example is Eduard's discovery after Ottilie's death that the glass engraved with the letters E and O is a substitute for the original: "es war dasselbe und nicht dasselbe" (527). If the entwined initials on the glass (either the original or the substitute) stand for Eduard's two names, a seeming self-identity is recast as a division. One becomes dou-

---

[32] Heinz Schlaffer, "Namen und Buchstaben in Goethes 'Wahlverwandtschaften.'" *Jahrbuch der Jean-Paul-Gesellschaft* 7 (1972): 84–102; here, 89.

[33] Cf. D. H. Lawrence's *Women in Love,* where Birkin ponders his love for Ursula: "How can I say "I love you" when I have ceased to be, and you have ceased to be: we are both caught up and transcended into a new oneness where everything is silent, because there is nothing to answer, all is perfect and at one. Speech travels between the separate parts. But in the perfect One there is perfect silence of bliss" (Cutchogue, NY: Buccaneer Books, 361–62). See Hinz, "Hierogamy," 910.

ble. If, as Edward prefers, the initials stand for Eduard and Ottilie, differ-ence, overwritten by entwinement, is represented as an identity. Two be-come one.[34]

Interlacing and entwining are secondary to metaphors of blending and correspondence as signs of unity in *Die Wahlverwandtschaften*. Both meta-phorical clusters, however, show that the polarity of unity and division is an important theme. The polarity of entwinement and unraveling — *Auflösung* — is a *leitmotif* in the narrative of *Die Wahlverwandtschaften* as well as in the inset passages from Ottilie's diary, a motif, however, whose va-lidity is called into question by frequent foregrounding and virtuosic ma-nipulation. Just into the second part of the novel the narrator compares the red thread winding through and connecting the aphorisms in the diary to that woven into the rigging ropes of the English navy. It is a thread, "den man nicht herauswinden kann, ohne alles *aufzulösen,* und woran auch die kleinsten Stücke kenntlich sind, daß sie der Krone gehören" (402).[35] This thread both denotes and denies unity. It cannot be unwound without de-stroying everything, yet it preserves separation by virtue of its difference from the uncolored threads — from one end of the rope to the other.[36]

Goethe is on record as having worked toward the "Darstellung einer durchgreifenden Idee" in the *Wahlverwandtschaften* — his only large-scale product that is so informed (643). What this idea might be is unresolved. Yet the admission by an author not proud of having ideas that his novel is in fact based on an idea, an "intentionerte Gestalt" — seen through a "durchsichtige[n] und undurchsichtige[n] Schleier," as he wrote to Karl Friedrich Zelter 26 August 1809) — is remarkable. In any case, just as the red thread denotes both linkage and separation, so the theme of unity and division is itself a red thread running through the narrative, yet separable from it, just as any theme may be contemplated apart from its context. The polarity of unity and separation is also central to the most famous aphorism in Ottilie's diary, according to which the nightingale both belongs to (is united with) and transcends (is separate from) the class of songbirds (463).

[34] Wagner employs the metaphor of entwinement in a comment on *Tristan und Isolde:* "Nennen wir es Tod? Oder ist es die nächtige Wunderwelt, aus der, wie die Sage uns meldet, ein Efeu und eine Rebe in inniger Umschlingung einst auf Tristans und Isoldes Grab emporwachsen?" From Hans Mayer, *Wagner* (Hamburg: Rowohlt, 1959), 102.

[35] Here and in the following illustrations noteworthy lexemes are italicized.

[36] Wilhelm Meister wonders whether the continental divide could erect a *Scheidewand* in his imagination between Natalie and himself. He decides that it could not: "Was könnte mich von dir *scheiden!* von dir, der ich auf ewig geeignet bin, wenngleich ein wundersames Geschick mich von dir *trennt* . . . Wie hätte ich mich losreißen können, wenn der dauerhafte *Faden* nicht gesponnen wäre, der uns für die Zeit und für die Ewigkeit *verbinden* soll" (FA 1,10:267–68).

As a metafiction, *Die Wahlverwandtschaften* both exemplifies and transcends the class of run-of-the mill, unselfconscious narratives. As an extended irony, a metafiction is a *coincidentia oppositorum*, since it makes use of generic conventions while standing free and exposing the conventionality and insufficiency of the tradition on which it feeds. The individual work, like the individual talent, is indebted but unbound.

"Dich im Unendlichen zu finden, / Mußt unter*scheiden* und dann *verbinden*," wrote Goethe in the first of three poems commemorating Luke Howard's classification of cloud forms (FA 1,2:502). He called the alternation of separating and uniting, generalizing and particularizing, transformation and specification, emergence and disappearance, solidifying and melting, hardening and flowing, expansion and contraction a "Grundeigenschaft der lebendigen Einheit." Because the oscillation of contraries occurs everywhere, a particular instance is a "Bild und Gleichniß des Allgemeinsten" (FA 1,13:48). It both exemplifies a pattern and, in its uniqueness, is the exception that confirms the pattern's generality. Goethe also said that self-manifestation and division (= individuation) are synonymous — "Erscheinung und Entzweien sind synonym." To become a phenomenon is the same as "sich *trennen, sondern, verteilen.*"[37]

An ambiguous term for the same process, "scheiden" (sweet sorrow! Compare *unter*scheiden = discriminate, in the Luke Howard poems) is woven into the fabric of *Die Wahlverwandtschaften*. *Scheiden* may, of course, mean to take one's leave from someone (it is common in this sense in Goethe) or, more philosophically, to *de*part from primal unity and arrive (through the maternal *Scheide*[38]) in being,[39] there to be driven toward reun-

---

[37] GA 17:700. The theme of separation is discussed by Heinz Politzer, "No Man is an Island: A Note on Image and Thought in Goethe's *Iphigenie*," *The Germanic Review* 37 (1962): 42–54. Klaus Müller-Salget notes the possible derivation of Werther's name from "Werth" = "die Flußinsel" ("Zur Struktur von Goethes 'Werther,'" 1981, reprint in *Goethes "Werther": Kritik und Forschung*, ed. Hans Peter Herrmann, Wege der Forschung, vol. 607 [Darmstadt: Wissenschaftliche Buchgesellschaft, 1994], 322; see also note 9).

[38] "Scheide" comes from the verb "scheiden." The meaning of its English cognate "sheath" derives from the split pieces of wood fastened together to protect a blade. The second meaning of "Scheide," from Old High German "sceida" is "Trennung, Abschied, Unter-, Entscheidung, Grenze." The use of "Scheide" for "vagina" (= sheath, first occurring with reference to the female genitalia in Plautus) is a loan translation by J. Vesling in 1678 (Friedrich Kluge, *Etymologisches Wörterbuch der deutschen Sprache*, 18th ed. [Berlin, Walter de Gruyter, 1960], 640–41).

When the gentlemen and the ladies separate after dinner in Mann's *Buddenbrooks*, the town poet laureate Jean Jacques Hoffstede permits himself a pun on "Scheide":

ion, re-creation, and wholeness through self-obliteration, as is set forth in the *Divan* poems "Wiederfinden" and "Selige Sehnsucht" as well as in "Eins und Alles." On the other hand, taking leave from a beloved person amounts to the *loss* of one's being — "*Scheiden* ist der Tod!"[40] The young actress Christiane Becker, née Neumann, who died at the age of eighteen, twice refers to herself as "*die Scheidende*" in Goethe's elegy "Euphrosyne." The dead are "Abge*schiedene.*" The day on which Anna Amalia, dowager duchess of Sachsen-Weimar, died was her "*Scheide*tag."[41] Only eternal love can divide (*scheiden*) "Geeinte Zwienatur" (*Faust,* lines 11962–65).

The issue throughout Wagner's quintessentially Romantic *Tristan und Isolde,* act 2, scene 2, in particular, is entirely one of duality vs. unity. Tristan and Isolde long for death together, a union beyond any possibility of *Scheidung* or separation and in which there is no use even for separate names: "nicht mehr Tristan, / nicht mehr Isolde; / ohne Nennen, / ohne Trennen."[42] These lovers reject even the conjunction "und," which, although a conjunction, reaffirms the separateness of the entities who long to be conjoined. What radical Romanticism longs for is total indiscrimination — a complete blending and interpenetration. All Romantics incline "zum Ungegliederten, Maßlosen, Ewigen, zum Nichts."[43] So they turn to maternal night and the immolation of the body, "daß ich luftig mit dir

> Als Sachsens Marschall einst die stolze Pompadour
> Im goldnen Phaeton — vergnügt spazierenfuhr,
> Sah Frelon dieses Paar — oh, rief er, seht sie beide!
> Des Königs Schwert — und seine Scheide!

[39] Perhaps only in German is it so easy to hypostatize "scheiden" into the opposites "die Geschiedenheit" and "die Ungeschiedenheit." Kaiser writes, "Die ungeschiedene Totaleinheit von Mutter und Kind ist mit Hilfe des Geistes zu einer Artikulation gekommen, die *durch den Reflexionsakt hindurch* in die Ungeschiedenheit zurückweist, aber auch von der Ungeschiedenheit zum Reflexionsakt" (Gerhard Kaiser, "Goethe's Naturlyrik," *Goethe Jahrbuch* 108 (1991): 61–73; here, 67.

[40] "An Werther." Cf. Hölderlin's "Der Abschied": "Trennen wollten wir uns? wähnten es gut und klug? / Da wir's taten, warum schröckte, wie Mord, die Tat?"

[41] *Vorspiel zur Eröffnung des Weimarischen Theaters am 19. September 1807 nach glücklicher Wiederversammlung der herzoglichen Familie* (WA 1,13:36).

[42] Wagner takes this directly from Gottfried von Strassburg:

> Tristan und Isot, ir und ich,
> wir zwei sîn iemêr beide
> ein dinc âne underscheide (lines 18352–54).

[43] Mann's characterization of Gustav Aschenbach's longing in *Der Tod in Venedig,* in Thomas Mann, *Gesammelte Werke in zwölf Bänden* (Oldenburg: S. Fischer, 1960), 8:475.

inniger mich mische und dann ewig die Brautnacht währt."[44] The inevitability of their failure explains their recourse to Romantic Irony, which is all that is left to anyone who longs for blending and indiscrimination but knows that division is everywhere and that the word blocks the entryway it pretends to open.

The dialectic of "Scheidung" and "Einigung" or "Einung," and "Verbindung" and "Auflösung" (= "dissolving" *and* "unraveling") in *Die Wahlverwandtschaften* begins with the discussion of the chemical analogy on which the work's title is based. "Stelle dir nur das Wasser, das Öl, das Quecksilber vor," says Eduard, "so wirst du eine *Einigkeit,* einen *Zusammenhang* ihrer Teile finden. Diese *Einung* verlassen sie nicht, außer durch Gewalt oder sonstige Bestimmung." Charlotte agreeably recalls that "schon als Kinder spielen wir erstaunt mit dem Quecksilber, indem wir es in Kügelchen *trennen* und es wieder *zusammenlaufen* lassen" (301). "Die Verwandtschaften werden erst interessant, wenn sie *Scheidungen* bewirken," opines Eduard — to which Charlotte remonstrates, "Kommt das traurige Wort . . . auch in der Naturlehre vor?" "Allerdings!" says Eduard. "Es war sogar ein bezeichnender Ehrentitel der Chemiker, daß man sie *Scheidekünstler* nannte." Charlotte answers that "das *Vereinigen* ist eine größere Kunst, ein größeres Verdienst. Ein *Einungskünstler* wäre in jedem Fache der ganzen Welt willkommen" (303), repeating a bias that Goethe had expressed to Jacobi about philosophy, on November 23, 1801: "Wenn sie sich vorzüglich aufs *Trennen* legt, so kann ich mit ihr nicht zurechte kommen . . ., wenn sie aber *vereint,* oder vielmehr wenn sie unsere ursprüngliche Empfindung, *als seien wir mit der Natur eins,* erhöht, sichert und in ein tiefes, ruhiges Anschauen verwandelt, . . . dann ist sie mir willkommen." Note also the recurrence of "willkommen" in Charlotte's rejoinder.[45]

Eduard's ardor in behalf of *Scheidekünstler* and Charlotte's preference for *Einungskünstler* not only reflects their respective attitudes toward their own marriage but also their orthodoxy in the matter of gender difference. Unity is metonymically feminine, while separation is masculine, as Chodorow shows in deriving masculine identity from a boy's difference from, and feminine identity from a girl's solidarity with, their mother. Charlotte observes that men relate to the disconnected, women to the

[44] Novalis, *Hymnen an die Nacht,* in *Schriften: Die Werke Friedrich von Hardenbergs,* ed. Paul Kluckhohn and Richard Samuel, 3rd ed., 4 vols. in 7 (Stuttgart: W. Kohlhammer, 1977–99), 1st hymn.

[45] This is common vocabulary in Goethe's old age. Thus the sculptor in the *Wanderjahre* recommends his wax fabrications as worthy surrogates for human cadavers with the words: "Sie sollen in kurzem erfahren, daß Aufbauen mehr belehrt als Einreißen, *Verbinden* mehr als *Trennen*" (FA 1,10:604). He finds the idea worth repeating: "Verbinden heißt mehr als *Trennen,* Nachbilden mehr als Ansehen" (606).

connected, "weil ihr Schicksal, das Schicksal ihrer Familien, an diesen Zusammenhang geknüpft ist, und auch gerade dieses Zusammenhängende von ihnen gefordert wird" (274–75).[46] The equation feminine = unity is implicit in the association of women with water, chaos, and death, and that of masculine = separation in the association of men with form, order (all order requires division, structure, and names) and life (= being as a separate identity). To be sure, all persons are patients, regardless of gender, since all are subject to fate and passion. As creatures we are feminine, as it were, by definition. But Eduard, "empfänglich wie er war" (279), is receptive to a degree that exceeds the givens of existential human contingency. His "passive[s] Getriebensein" and his belief in fate — for example, that his fate and Ottilie's are inseparable (390) — have been noticed, by von Wiese (HA 6:677) and others.

Love is the triumph of unity over division that Romanticism seeks and celebrates. When Ottilie agrees, in the seclusion of the mill, the "wildest place" in the landscape of *Die Wahlverwandtschaften* and the *axis mundi* generically required for the consummation of love in the mythic narrative,[47] to give Eduard the medallion containing her father's picture, it is "als wenn sich eine *Scheidewand* zwischen ihm und Ottilien niedergelegt hätte" (323). The barrier dividing the lovers and constituting them as particles is dismantled, their separation temporarily overcome, the "primordial marriage of the elements" evoked,[48] and Ottilie's father replaced by Eduard in her heart.

The idea of displacement and substitution informs the titular metaphor of *Die Wahlverwandtschaften,* as the substitution of a counterfeit glass engraved with the entwined letters E and O for the one actually caught by a

---

[46] "Western ideas of the individual are not universal . . . Particularly for boys, we value separateness: separateness from family, from community, and from the natural world . . . Even though girls are expected to retain a sense of connectedness, they are disparaged for it, while all too many boys are pushed into proving themselves by aggression and competition" (Mary Catherine Bateson, *Peripheral Visions* [New York: Harper Collins, 1994], 65). "Gender stereotypes often suggest that females emphasize continuity (this is called 'keeping the home fires burning'), while males venture forth on the new" (ibid., 86).

[47] Hinz mentions the "island in northern Quebec in *Surfacing* or the Moors in *Wuthering Heights*" as examples (Hinz, "Hierogamy," 909), while Paul de Man points to the deserted region on the northern bank of the lake in *La nouvelle Héloïse.* "Rousseau stresses that the *lieu solitaire* he describes is like a wild desert 'sauvage et désert; mais plein de ces sortes de beautés qui ne plaisent qu'aux âmes sensibles et paraissent horribles aux autres'" ("The Rhetoric of Temporality," in *Blindness and Insight,* 2nd, rev. ed. [Minneapolis: U of Minnesota P, 1983], 187–228; here, 200–201). Charles Smithson and Sarah Woodruff (*The French Lieutenant's Woman*) meet in the Edenic Undercliff (e.g., 113 and 133), "an English Garden of Eden" (59).

[48] Hinz, "Hierogamy," 909.

spectator at the cornerstone-laying on Charlotte's birthday may remind. The substitutions in the principals' minds during the "double adultery" in which Eduard and Charlotte imagine Ottilie and the Captain as their respective sexual partners are homologous with Eduard's substitution of himself for Ottilie's father and hint at the paradigmatic nature of much else in the narrative. Later, when Eduard and Ottilie first embrace, it would be impossible to "unter*scheiden*" "wer das andere zuerst ergriffen." They are seized at the same time by the same impulse (355), as though they were one person, hence subject to the same passion.

In the opposite couple, Charlotte, hoping against hope, has decided to keep to herself the Count's plan to procure employment for the Captain at a place far away, until the separation she dreads becomes certain. But when the Captain kisses her after carrying her to shore from their skiff that has run aground, she feels obliged to reveal her knowledge of the Count's plan. Separation is morally required of them after this extramarital intimacy: "Sie müssen *scheiden,* lieber Freund," she says with tragic dignity, "und Sie werden *scheiden*" (358). Charlotte intimates to Ottilie that she must renounce Eduard, but Ottilie does not take the hint, convinced by Eduard, "daß Charlotte selbst eine *Scheidung* wünsche" (364).

Eduard eventually leaves the estate, on condition that Charlotte make no attempt to remove Ottilie to another venue, but he is not ashamed of his unhappiness and refuses to behave stoically, like a gladiator dying with dignity so that the spectators "ihm beim *Verscheiden* noch applaudieren" (389). He is not obliged to make the rip in his universe pleasing to onlookers. The news that Charlotte is pregnant only drives Eduard farther away and into the dangers of military service. On returning in Part Two, having served with distinction in the wars and not having found the death he sought on the battlefield, he learns that a son has been delivered to Charlotte, which happy event, in the view of the Major, seals the union of Eduard and Charlotte forever. They must now live "*vereint*" and must "*vereint* für [the child's] Erziehung und für sein künftiges Wohl sorgen" (484). Yet to Eduard the child is divisive: "dies Kind ist aus einem doppelten Ehbruch erzeugt! es *trennt* mich von meiner Gattin und meine Gattin von mir, wie es uns hätte *verbinden* sollen" (492).

The dialectic of "Verbinden und Trennen" is repeated in the lives and the language of secondary characters as well. The Count, who wants to marry the Baroness, but is unable to win a divorce from his wife, is so preoccupied with infelicitous matches that he hits upon the idea of trial marriages. "Eine Ehe sollte nur alsdann für *unauflöslich* gehalten werden, wenn entweder beide Teile oder wenigstens der eine Teil zum drittenmal verheiratet wäre." Only by the third marriage would it become clear how a person "sich in ihren frühern *Verbindungen* betragen, ob sie Eigenheiten habe, die oft mehr zur *Trennung* Anlaß geben als üble Eigenschaften"

(342). Death ended the respective first marriages of Eduard and Charlotte, and was a more effective promoter of at least a temporary happiness than is the dogmatic Mittler (= mediator), who abhors the Count and insists that marriage must be "*unauflöslich*" in all cases. Personal misery counts for little against the general good that marriage brings (338).[49] When the death of his wife eventually leaves the Count free to marry the Baroness, Ottilie remembers every word of their earlier conversation, "was über *Ehestand* und *Scheidung,* über *Verbindung* und *Trennung,* über Hoffnung, Erwartung, Entbehren und Entsagen gesprochen ward" (425). But her hopes for a divorce between Eduard and Charlotte are destroyed forever by the death of their child — at her hand, according to her severely self-critical point of view. Her guilt sets her apart; she becomes "von allem abgesondert" (494). Even the fireworks after the collapse of the dam reflect the theme of separateness-togetherness. The show, witnessed by only two people, starts with individual bursts that are followed by others "gepaart," and goes on to great masses of explosions "alle zusammen" (371).

The thematization of union and division in Goethe's "novel" is carried out by symbol, example, and parable as well as by purely lexical or metaphorical means. Horticultural grafting, mentioned in the book's first sentence, involves unification and a manifestation of the "Grundeigenschaft der lebendigen Einheit."[50] Artificially brought together by the gardener, the separate plants *grow together* naturally. The products of art, by contrast, become separated from the artist, like the child from the parent, as Ottilie observes in her diary. Architects are denied entrance to royal rooms that they themselves have designed, and the goldsmith who made the monstrance is allowed to worship it only from afar (409). Throughout history, as Charlotte notes, times of unity alternate with times of division, epochs favoring the separation of a landowner's property by a wall or a moat giving way to others (like the time of the action), in which even the larger cities are tearing down their walls and becoming united with the surrounding countryside (454). The mason's speech on the laying of the cornerstone praises both mortar and the law as bonding materials — valuable adhesives even between stones

---

[49] This was not Goethe's view. "Was liegt daran," he sarcastically asked Chancellor von Müller, "ob einige Paare sich prügeln und das Leben verbittern, wenn nur der allgemeine Begriff der Heiligkeit der Ehe aufrecht bleibt?" (7 April 1830 — quoted by Atkins, "Die Wahlverwandtschaften," n. 31). Cf. Hatfield, "Towards the Interpretation of *Die Wahlverwandtschaften,*" *The Germanic Review* 23 [1948]: 104–14; reprint, trans. Ingo Pommerening, in *Goethes Roman "Die Wahlverwandtschaften,"* ed. Ewald Rösch (Darmstadt: Wissenschaftliche Buchgesellschaft, 1975), 175–91; here, 182.

[50] Cf. Stöcklein, "Auch hinter dem mannigfachen gärtnerischen Tun scheint eine Philosophie des Bindens und Lösens verborgen" (GA 9:696).

whose form makes them naturally fit together or between people "die einander von Natur geneigt sind" (331).

Among the references to unification in *Die Wahlverwandtschaften* are metaphors of fusion (merging, blending) as well as of resemblance, correspondence, and male/female coupling, all of which certify separateness, the precondition of their drive toward unity. Drowning is a favorite theme throughout Goethe's oeuvre, its import everywhere the same. It is the work's chief metaphor for the individual's return to a oneness before and beyond all individuation. To die in water is to reenter the undifferentiated medium from which we issued forth and in which we ourselves are dissolved. This is why Christian baptism can symbolize the death and rebirth of the self. To be immersed in the waters of baptism is, symbolically, "to die and become," to be rendered formless in the "chaotic" element — before being "reborn" as a new and better self. This is why women and water, "das schwankende Element" (356), are linked as agents of engulfment and dissolution. To enter or reenter either is to forfeit one's defining shape, but also to escape the loneliness that afflicts every denominated self. "Nicht mehr Tristan, / nicht mehr Isolde."

As noted, Wilhelm von Humboldt regarded "das häufige ins Wasser fallen und die wiederholten Rettungsversuche" as "eine Sonderbarkeit" of *Die Wahlverwandtschaften* (for example, the drowning of young Otto and the near drownings after the collapse of the dam as well as the spill into the drink of the antithetical amorous pair in the inset novella "Die wunderlichen Nachbarskinder"). This story is an inverse reflection of the primary action, inasmuch as the heroine imagines a love-death with her adversary,[51] but is eventually united with him in life, whereas Eduard and Ottilie, who long for union in life, come together (if they do come together) only in death. At the novel's end they rest beside each other in the chapel. "Und welch ein freundlicher Augenblick wird es sein, wenn sie dereinst wieder zusammen erwachen" — when — or *if* — they emerge together in their unity and difference (529).

Metaphors of fusion, merging, blending, alternate with those of separation, division, distillation, hardening throughout Goethe's oeuvre. The polarity "erstarren und fließen," "solideszieren und schmelzen," for example, is implicit in Faust's willingness "ins Nichts dahinzufließen" (line 719) if he cannot rise to "new spheres of pure activity" (line 705) and in his urge to deliquesce and, filled with love's bliss, flow back into the womb of Nature — "Bald liebewonniglich in alles überfließen" (lines 3282–89). Death, like love, dissolves fixed forms and permits their effluence into an opposed or encompassing medium or receptacle, such as water, the forest, or even "das Nichts." If Eduard divorces Charlotte, Ottilie will put an end to her sepa-

---

[51] Barnes, "Bildhafte Darstellung," 62.

rateness (put an end as well to the possibility of uniting with *him,* at least in mortal life) by drowning herself in the cold, fluid, enveloping medium into which she has let her lover's child sink and die. The blending of identities in formless unity is symbolically reiterated in the combination of three ponds to restore the original lake, a kind of *Dreieinigkeit,* analogous, as Stopp has noted, to Charlotte's "action in removing all the gravestones in the church-yard to create one indeterminate lawn," a symbol of "the elimination of in-dividual personality" in death (59). Faust's longing is for release in the moonlight or in blending together with Margarete, who means the same thing to him as moonlight,[52] and his redemption at the play's end, if we let the context bring undead metaphors up for air, involves *dis*solution as much as *ab*solution ("Den können wir er*lösen,*" 11937).[53] In no work of Goethe's, however, do the characters more transparently long for absorption in each other or do the physical events mirror more clearly the characters' quest for escape from individuation than in *Die Wahlverwandtschaften.* In organiza-tion, thought, and diction, this work relates a couple's fateful struggle to move from separateness into the unity of death. "Das Leben war ihnen ein Rätsel, dessen Auflösung sie nur miteinander fanden" (516).

Goethe also uses gardens, caves, and love grottos as places of refuge for the ego yearning to be absorbed or engulfed (as in the scene "Wald und Höhle" in *Faust*), drawing on a tradition of gardens of love that is manifest in Gottfried's *Tristan,* in the *Roman de la rose,* and in *Julie, ou La nouvelle Héloïse.*[54] A wild garden, the forest, encodes the standard Romantic longing for reassimilation, as when Werther longs to lose himself in the forest[55] or in the distant hills and valleys or, later, in the flood he surveys from above. While the intercourse between Eduard's estate and the world beyond is free and unimpeded, as Atkins shows,[56] *Die Wahlverwandtschaften* does make use of the topos of the garden as a world apart. Within the clear boundaries of the estate is the wilderness surrounding the mill (a traditional site of erotic

---

[52] Jane K. Brown, *Faust: Theater of the World* (New York: Twayne, 1992), 63.

[53] Cf. Novalis, *Hymnen an die Nacht:* "Noch einmal sah er freundlich nach der Mutter — da kam der ewigen Liebe *lösende* Hand, und er entschlief" (5th Hymn).

[54] See Claudia Brosé, "Park und Garten in Goethes *Wahlverwandtschaften,*" in *Park und Garten im 18. Jahrhundert* (Heidelberg: Carl Winter, 1978), 125–29; also de Man, "The Rhetoric of Temporality," 200–208.

[55] Cf. Eichendorff: "Lockt' dich kein Weh, kein brünstiges Verlangen / nach andrer Zeit, die lange schon vergangen, auf ewig einzugehn in grüne Scheine?'" ("Jugendandacht. 5 [8]") in Atkins, *The Age of Goethe: An Anthology of German Lit-erature 1749–1832* [Boston: Houghton Mifflin, 1969], 555).

[56] Ibid., 6–8.

conjunction[57]), where Eduard and Ottilie first become aware of their essential *Zusammengehörigkeit* (322).

Metaphors of entwinement, blending, fitting together, and linkage
through correspondence — as well as those of unraveling, separating, taking
apart, releasing and dissolving — call attention to themselves. In so subtle
and self-conscious a writer as Goethe (*pace* Schiller, who viewed Goethe as
the instinctive, "naive" poet) this cannot be inadvertent. We are intended to
notice that *resemblance,* as in the resemblance of the faces in the chapel ceiling to Ottilie (406), stops short of identity and emphasizes the tragedy of
permanent separation — as in the double resemblance between young Otto
and his respective spiritual progenitors (both of whom are absent at his conception and who are linked with his actual parents only "übers Kreuz"). The
biological improbability underscores the epistemological point that resemblance both unites and divides — for Goethe has ceased obeying the dictates
of realism and, indeed, begun to polemicize against naturalism.[58] Every mirror reverses the image and bespeaks non-identity, as he elsewhere points out
(FA 1,13:306), just as the two halves of the palindrome "Otto," each a mirror image of the other, are reversed and in opposition to each other.[59] The
similarity of subject and object, Creator and creature, only brings out the
similarity and opposition of *Gott* and *Mensch.* (417; cf. Genesis 1:26–27).
The world is opposed to, and is yet a copy of, the viewing subject, linked in
the relation of opposition to what it everywhere denies. "Wer spielt nicht
gern mit *Ähnlich*keiten?" says Charlotte, who understands that similarity implies difference and that the pairing of non-identities is a form of paradoxical
play (305). A painted portrait re-presents a person departed (399) but also
confirms his or her absence. Nevertheless, to have a picture of one's departed
lover for company (such as a picture of the absent Eduard) is reassuring,
"selbst wenn es un*ähnlich* ist," writes Ottilie in her diary. "Man fühlt auf
eine angenehme Weise, daß man zu zweien ist und doch nicht auseinander
kann" (403).

[57] See Paul Stöcklein, GA 9:694. As H. G. Barnes observes, "der Abstieg [zur Mühle
wird] zum Symbol des romantischen Liebestodes" ("Bildhafte Darstellung," 42).
See also Brosé, "Park und Garten," 126.

[58] As Friedrich Sengle observes, "Die Klassiker spielten bekanntlich mit dem
Gedanken, das Drama durch Chöre, ja sogar durch Anleihen bei der Oper dem tief
verachteten Naturalismus zu entreißen" (*Das Genie und sein Fürst* [Stuttgart:
Metzler, 1993], 182).

[59] In their youth, dancing together, Charlotte and Eduard "[bespiegelten] sich nur
ineinander." In the meantime "[hat] sich so manches verändert" (343).

Ottilie's affinity with carbon reveals her metaphorical "unity" with this feminine element (across the divide between animal and mineral),[60] just as her portrayal of the Virgin Mary in the architect's final tableau brings out her essential but unrealized maternity (439). All such linkings stress the difference hidden in every identity, as in the boundary criss-crossed forward and backward in Goethe's analogy between the personification implicit in eighteenth-century chemistry's description of a chemical event as a matter of choice and relationships and the human and personal events that are his subject in the *Wahlverwandtschaften*. Incidentally, it is a manifestation of the gender orthodoxy that we have already noticed — and yet another manifestation of the identity-difference dialectic — that Charlotte in her preference for adhesion over division extols difference, which makes complementarity possible, as providing a better basis for marital union than likeness (302–3). Her view is confirmed in "Die wunderlichen Nachbarskinder," where the similarity of the protagonists is initially a cause of quarrels: "Vielleicht waren sie einander zu ähnlich" (471). They discover their difference and their complementarity upon falling into the lake and in love. As Barnes notes, "hier ver*ein*igt das Wasser die *getrennten* Kinder" (62).

Such virtuosic play as we have been noticing could be understood as evidence of Goethe's classicism. If diverse phenomena can be understood in terms of division and reunification, then we have true unity in diversity, each separation or unification mirroring all of the others — which is what Goethe claimed when he said, "das Besonderste, das sich ereignet, [tritt] immer als Bild und Gleichnis des Allgemeinsten auf" (FA 1,13:48). This would seem to make the principle of correspondence or resemblance the fundamental principle of relation in the universe. Resemblance is the characteristic episteme of Western culture, at least until the end of the sixteenth century, as noted by E. W. M. Tillyard[61] and Michel Foucault[62] — unless the principle of attraction and repulsion is more fundamental. In any case, Goethe encountered frequent illustrations of the idea of resemblance in his study of alchemical writings during his convalescence in 1768–69, and he employs it — non-committally, as a suggestive but unbinding principle of relation, as indicative of the universal fragmentation as is the very idea of relation.

---

[60] Carbon corresponds to the female principle in Schelling's philosophy of nature, which Goethe read and approved of (Christian Rogowski, "Human Alchemy: Science and Psychology in Goethe's *Die Wahlverwandtschaften*," paper presented at MLA on 28 December 1987: 5).

[61] E. W. M. Tillyard, *The Elizabethan World Picture* (New York: Random House, n.d), ch. 6 and 7.

[62] Michel Foucault, *The Order of Things,* originally *Les Mots et les choses* (1966; trans. London: Tavistock, 1970), ch. 2.

Absolute individuation admits of no relations, hence of no comparisons; it is "etwas unvergleichbares" (463). Eduard, whose "terrible task" it becomes to imitate "das Unnachahmliche" in Ottilie's saintliness (490), remains tragically apart from his *Vorbild* (at least until death unites them). But just as there is no bridging of the difference between original and imitation or between model and imitator, neither is anything in the world of *Die Wahlverwandtschaften* absolutely discrete or other. Everything is a "Bild und Gleichnis" of everything else (FA 1,13:48). This shows that Goethe is concerned with more than verisimilitude in this work. He writes, in a "Schlußbetrachtung über Sprache und Terminologie" from his *Farbenlehre,* that "eine Sprache" is "nur symbolisch, nur bildlich" and never expresses its objects "unmittelbar." One can get at them only "gleichnisweise" (GA 16:203), and "Gleichnisse" are what his narrative mainly provides.

Die Wahlverwandtschaften is often designated a "novel of marriage" or "novel of adultery."[63] Yet according to Stöcklein, Goethe's treatment of marriage, divorce, affinity, and adultery — "Ehebruch im Ehebett" (GA 9:686) — only illustrates the more abstract issues of individuation and reunion informing this narrative and denying it the feel of realism that no degree of historical accuracy is sufficient to preserve or, probably, was intended to create. This is as true of his choice of genre and of narrational stance as it is of his choice of theme and metaphor. In *Götz von Berlichingen* and in *Werther* Goethe had demonstrated his ability to write realistically, with full psychological plausibility and well-motivated action — a style he then gave up for good when he abandoned work on *Wilhelm Meisters Theatralische Sendung,* before recasting and transforming it into something more symbolic several years later.[64] In *Werther* he had provided a dramatic formal innovation in limiting the epistolary form to the letters of the protagonist — a psychologically powerful device but an artificial one (since the "Editor" could as realistically have also provided letters from Werther's correspondents). In *Die Wahlverwandtschaften* he employs the device of Ottilie's diary, which has a function similar to that of Werther's letters in that it reveals the inner life of the taciturn Ottilie. In the works of his maturity (most of all in *Faust II*), Goethe shamelessly resorts to whatever improbabilities may suit his symbolic purpose, including the "double adultery" of a child's real parents producing a child with a double likeness to the nonparents who are, respectively, on their minds during the love act, and Ottilie's left cheek turning red while the right one turns white when she is un-

---

[63] Tanner, *Adultery in the Novel: Contract and Transgression* (Baltimore: Johns Hopkins UP, 1979), 179–232.

[64] Atkins agrees. "In the later, newly written parts [of the *Lehrjahre*] an at times transparent concern with symbolism is disturbing because of the contrast to what has gone before" (*The Age of Goethe,* 212).

pleasantly affected by an experience. Since Goethe was plainly able to obey the requisites of realism, it cannot have been his primary purpose to show the events, manners, and spirit of the times or the relation of the sexes to each other. Rather, he exposes the concepts and conventions we employ to explain the relationship of the self to otherness and interrogates the utility of such dichotomies as self and other and with them the derivative, provisional nature of all linguistic, conceptual, and cultural juxtapositions. He gave explicit voice to his resignation to representational approximation. "Man hat ein Mehr und Weniger, ein Wirken ein Widerstreben, ein Tun ein Leiden, ein Vordringendes ein Zurückhaltendes, ein Heftiges ein Mäßigendes, ein Männliches ein Weibliches überall bemerkt und genannt; und so entsteht eine Sprache, eine Symbolik, die man auf ähnliche Fälle als Gleichnis, als nahverwandten Ausdruck, als unmittelbar passendes Wort anwenden und benutzen mag" ("Vorwort" zur *Farbenlehre*, FA 1,23,1:13).[65] The effect of his virtuosic substitution is to challenge the naivete with which language is customarily used. Language approaches things "gleichnisweise," because there is no other way to approach them.

"Alles Vergängliche / Ist nur ein Gleichnis," sings the Chorus Mysticus at the end of *Faust,* and even the narcissistic Eduard realizes that the metaphor of elective affinities is only a "Gleichnisrede" (300), a word that also occurs in Goethe's advertisement of *Die Wahlverwandtschaften* (974). Analogies both mask and emphasize difference, but the ultimate *Scheidung* is between language and the world, a gap unbridged (indeed only widened) by self-critical representation and rendering mimesis an inherently futile enterprise. This is why Goethe invests so little in any particular analogy and manipulates narrational forms with unrestrained freedom, which offends some readers.[66] Anticipating the works of Joyce and other post-realist fiction, he creates in *Die Wahlverwandtschaften* an interplay of homologies that, in their resistance to closure, hint at something beyond the reach of human thought. None of the long narratives of his maturity is a novel in the usual sense. They are metafictions that make their "artefactual status thematic and self-consciously explicit."[67] And their quality as metafictions marks them as Ro-

[65] Hubert J. Meessen remarks that Goethe's procedure is similar to Vaihinger's philosophy of "Als-Ob," "wonach 'die abstrakten und allgemeinen Begriffe nur bequeme Denkmittel [sind], Werkzeuge, 'Kunstgriffe des Denkens,' zweckmäßige Fiktionen zur Beherrschung des anschaulich gegebenen Erfahrungsmaterials" ("Goethes Polaritätsidee und die *Wahlverwandtschaften*," *PMLA* 54 [1939]: 1105–23; here, 1107 n. 12).

[66] E.g. Ronald Gray, *Goethe: a Critical Introduction* (Cambridge, UK: Cambridge UP, 1967), 219–20, 224.

[67] Alastair Fowler, "The Future of Genre Theory: Functions and Constructional Types," in *The Future of Literary Theory,* ed. Ralph Cohen (New York: Routledge, 1989), 291–303; here, 293.

mantic works, of which the *sine qua non* is authorial freedom and self-consciousness.[68] Written before the constraints of realism had become obligatory, *Die Wahlverwandtschaften* exposes the artifice in every narrative. This neither invalidates nor is invalidated by the realistic *mega*fictions that were to follow. Goethe does not ask that we love fiction less because its fictionality is in view, but neither would he hide its fictionality.

These theoretical and conceptual considerations detract nothing from the importance of the social and ethical questions taken up in *Die Wahlverwandtschaften,* nor do they depreciate the value of its accurate depiction of contemporary conditions and events. However, Goethe's themes as well as his skepticism toward representation — his use of irony to highlight and mock the forms on which he has no choice but to rely — betray him as a Romantic *par excellence.* I have already quoted his comment to a fellow author, Karl Jacob Ludwig Iken, on 27 September 1827, which is almost a paraphrase of Schlegel's earlier observation: "Hat man nun einmal die Liebhaberei fürs Absolute und kann nicht davon lassen: so bleibt einem kein Ausweg, als sich selbst immer zu widersprechen, und entgegengesetzte Extreme zu verbinden."[69] It is precisely as the preeminent Romantic of world literature that Goethe is a representative author, and, the particularity of his inherited culture notwithstanding, a Classic in T. S. Eliot's sense of the word.

So is *Die Wahlverwandtschaften* a "novel of German classicism"? If the only available generic choices were "novel" or "novella," and if *Klassik* and *Romantik* were mutually exclusive concepts, Atkins would no doubt be right. But, as Wellek shows, Weimar Classicism is a Romantic epiphenomenon, its "classical" features notwithstanding. Beyond accurately depicting the historical and social realities discussed by Atkins, *Die Wahlverwandtschaften* everywhere draws attention to the medium in which these are represented and which, in turn, represents all representational media. The frustrated longing for union of Eduard and Ottilie may stand for the longing of both writer and reader for a unity of sign and referent (or of signifier and signified within the sign) — for realism, then, and reliable knowledge. But the implicit claim of *Die Wahlverwandtschaften* is that difference (dare we say dif-*férance*?) is universal and that not only signs but marriages, links, ties, bonds, compounds, analogies, and groupings of every sort are only partial, unstable, temporary, and insufficient. But if division is constitutive of being, it results in beings who long hopelessly to overcome it, which makes longing constitutive of being as well. Behind the visible and invisible veil of his de-

---

[68] "[Die romantische Dichtart] ist unendlich, wie sie allein frei ist, und das als ihr erstes Gesetz anerkennt, daß die Willkür des Dichters kein Gesetz über sich leide" (Friedrich Schlegel, KA 1,2:183, *Athenäums-Fragment,* no. 116).

[69] KA 1,2:164; Blütenstaub, no. 26.

picted world Goethe displays this longing — a kind of "intendierte Gestalt," as it were — with a sad, knowing smile.

10:   Love and Death in *Faust*

GOETHE'S *FAUST* EXPRESSES Romanticism's agony over the fact of indi-viduation and the individual's distance from its origin and destiny. Its action is propelled by a man's desire to escape from selfhood into love. *Faust* does not end in a *Liebestod,* like *Romeo and Juliet* or *Aida.* Yet what is at stake is the continuation of Faust's self-identity in time versus his dissolution, his *Entgrenzung,* in a timeless moment of bliss. The escape from selfhood into union with another, whether a lover, the world, or God, would be a *Liebestod,* and there are many echoes of the love-death theme in *Faust,* such as Margarete's longing to expire in the rapture of Faust's kisses (3406–13) and her reproach in the prison scene of the *Urfaust* (the "early version" of *Faust*): "Bist mein Heinrich und hast's Küssen verlernt! Wie sonst ein ganzer Himmel mit deiner Umarmung gewaltig über mich eindrang. Wie du küsstest als wolltest du mich in wollüstigem Todt ersticken."[1] The day of her execution was supposed to be her wedding day (4581). Gray notes that the creation of Homunculus, a stand-in for Faust, also involves a *Liebestod,* the "death" of spermatozoa in the alembic, a surrogate grave and uterus, and the birth as Homunculus.[2] This paradigm is repeated in the union of Ho-munculus with the beautiful Galatee — Homunculus as "a living flame, the 'filius ignis,'" Galatee — female and water.[3] When Homunculus breaks his glass on Galatee's scallop at the end of the *Klassische Walpurgisnacht* (8472)

---

[1] Lines 41–44 in the "frühe Fassung"; FA 1,7,1:537 — softened in the 1808 version, lines 4486–90. Hereafter, references to *Faust* are to lines in the *Frankfurter Ausgabe.*

[2] Ronald D. Gray, *Goethe the Alchemist* (Cambridge, UK: Cambridge UP, 1952), 209. Goethe knew the recipe for making artificial men in Paracelsus's *Of the Nature of Things:* "Let the Sperm of a man by it selfe be putrefied in a gourd glasse, sealed up, with the highest degree of putrefaction in Horse dung, for the space of forty days, or so long until it begin to bee alive, move, and stir, which can easily be seen. After this time it will be something like a Man, yet transparent, and without a body. Now after this, if it bee every day warily, and prudently nourished and fed with the Arcanum of Mans blood, and bee for the space of forty weeks kept in a constant, equall heat of Horse-dung, it will become a true and living infant, having all the members of an infant, which is born of a woman, but it will be far lesse. This we call Homunculus, or Artificiall. And this is afterwards to be brought up with as great care, and diligence as any other infant, until it come to riper years of understanding" (from Gray, *Goethe the Alchemist,* 205–6).

[3] Gray, *Goethe the Alchemist,* 215.

and pours "himself" into the waves: "Jetzt flammt es, nun blitzt es, *ergießet sich schon*" (8473), it is a vicarious fulfillment of Faust's desire, ridiculed by Mephistopheles, "in alles [zu] überfließen" (3289). Homunculus "marries the Ocean" (8319–21), in a *hieros gamos* that foreshadows the wedding of Faust — northern, modern, and Romantic — with Helena — southern, ancient, and classical — and foreshadows also the assumption of Faust under Margarete's guidance at the drama's end, although this is more ambiguous. The festival on the Aegean Sea ends with the sirens' words: "So herrsche denn Eros, der alles begonnen!" (8474–79). Much of the Classical Walpurgis Night traces the quest of Homunculus to "originate" (8246). The route to a new life *through nothingness* involves a dying and becoming.

Belief in an atomistic essence endowed with self-consciousness and in opposition to the world is the founding error of Romanticism. Or is it a truth, after all? On this premise, in any case, all of its struggles are based — on the belief that there *is* such a thing as a self-conscious ego torn asunder by ambivalence, by joy in its autonomy, on the one hand, and by loneliness and the longing to transcend the limits of the individual on the other. According to Goethe, "Fausts Charakter . . . stellt einen Mann dar, welcher, in den allgemeinen Erdeschranken sich ungeduldig und unbehaglich fühlend, den Besitz des höchsten Wissens, den Genuß der schönsten Güter für unzulänglich achtet, seine Sehnsucht auch nur im mindesten zu befriedigen" (1826).[4] Neither the possession of the highest knowledge nor the enjoyment of the finest goods satisfies him, for Faust's longing expresses an existential discomfort with temporality, mortality, three-dimensionality, and gravity (hence Faust's and Werther's desire to fly)[5] — in short, with individuation and separation from contiguous beings and from the source of being. Faust is driven into the arms of the devil by loneliness (6237–38). He longs to escape from his transitory selfhood in time and to become re-immersed in unity. This is why he says his life can end if he wishes time to stop and why time metaphors predominate in his projection of the outcome of his wager with Mephistopheles: "Die Uhr mag stehen, der Zeiger fallen, / Es sei die Zeit für mich vorbei!" (1705–6). Since time is constitutive of being,

---

[4] *Helena. Zwischenspiel zu Faust.* Ankündigung, FA 1,7,1:636. "Eigen ist [ihm] . . . ein außerordentliches Ausmaß an Unbefriedigtsein, ein angestrengtes Sich-nicht-abfinden-wollen mit den dem Menschen auferlegten Schranken" (Peter Michelsen, *Im Banne Fausts: Zwölf Faust-Studien* [Würzburg: Königshausen & Neumann, 2000], 54).

[5] *Faust,* lines 1074–88, cf. 287–89; cf. Werther's letter of 18 August 1771, also: "Welche Begierde fühl' ich, mich in den unendlichen Luftraum zu stürzen, über den schauerlichen Abgründen zu schweben und mich auf einen unzugänglichen Felsen niederzulassen" (*"Briefe aus der Schweiz,"* WA 1,19:199; Hans-Jürgen Schings, "Fausts Verzweiflung." *Goethe-Jahrbuch* 115 (1998): 97–123; here, 110; Michelsen, *Goethe the Alchemist,* 66).

the fatal words would be aperformative, bringing about the state they summon: the *nunc stans* of the mystics. If Faust bids the moment to stay, time will end for him and the clock stop: "Werd' ich zum Augenblicke sagen: / Verweile doch! du bist so schön! / Dann magst du mich in Fesseln schlagen, / Dann will ich gern zugrunde gehn! / Dann mag die Toten-glocke schallen, / Dann bist du deines Dienstes frei, / Die Uhr mag stehn ...!" (1699–1706). Mephistopheles will win the wager if he can create a moment of ecstasy for Faust — a paradoxical term in that "ecstasy" means standing out — outside the world, outside of time, outside of him-self.[6] Outside of time, Faust will no longer *be*. His wager amounts to a tau-tology. If he escapes the flow of time, time will be over for him. If he loves — loves ecstatically so that time stops — he will lose both the wager and his life. But he will lose nothing more, for there is nothing more to lose than his being as a separate, temporal self. The gain will be endless, unin-dividual bliss. Faust does not expect any of this to come about. Accepting the melancholy truth that he cannot have what he most wants, he resolves to live out his temporal life in the company of his fellow mortals: "Stürzen wir uns in das Rauschen der Zeit, / In's Rollen der Begebenheit!" (1750–51).

In the eschatology of Goethe's *Faust,* life here below is not the whole of human *being*. Faust's adventures are framed by two non-terrestrial scenes, the "Prologue in Heaven" and Faust's ascent through "Mountain Gorges" after his death. The Lord allows Mephistopheles to tempt Faust only "as long as he lives on earth" (315), which implies a non-terrestrial "before-" and "afterlife." But "life after death" cannot be a temporal, phenomenal, in-dividual life. Arnold's *Unparteyische Kirchen- und Ketzer-Historie,* from which Goethe gained his knowledge of Origen, the most important theolo-gian and biblical scholar of the early Greek church, refers to it as "nach der Zeit."[7] Faust declines Mephisto's offer to serve him "here" in exchange for Faust's service "drüben," where time no longer obtains.[8] The Lord has al-

---

[6] "To suffer ecstasy means to be placed outside oneself. . . . A man is said to suffer ecstasy, inasmuch as he is placed outside the connatural apprehension of his sense and reason [or] when he is overcome by violent passion or madness" (Thomas Aquinas, *Summa Theologica*, 3 vols., trans., Fathers of the English Dominican Province [New York: Benziger Brothers, 1947–48], 1:711).

[7] "daß uns nach der Zeit . . . eine wahre reinigung begegnen werde" (from Schöne, FA 1,7,2:790).

[8] The dichotomy of "hier" and "drüben" informs Faust's conception of potential spheres of action early and late ("Der Erdenkreis ist mir genug bekannt. / Nach drüben ist die Aussicht uns verrant" (11441–42) — my emphasis; cf. 940, 1663–64, 1668–70, 10181–82). Metaphorically the alternatives are often expressed as between flight and maintaining a firm footing on the earth (702–5, 1074, 1090, 9608, 9611). Euphorion attempts free flight, but, a new Icarus, he comes crashing back to the earth (stage direction 9901, 9903).

228 ♦ LOVE AND DEATH IN *FAUST*

ready declared his prior claim on Faust's service, but service can only occur in time. A body may abide forever in space, never actually performing any service, like the serving man carved in lapis lazuli in Yeats's poem and like the bold lover who will never be able to kiss his bride in "Ode on a Grecian Urn." Standing outside of time, Faust will no longer be and could never serve anyone.

It is not Faust's service, but his annihilation, that Mephistopheles seeks.[9] His goal is the destruction of being, including the *Dasein* that is Faust, the Lord's special servant (299). He is forthright about this (1338–44), and Faust accepts the challenge, for he desires, although he also fears, a "return" to a non-temporal, non-individual state of nothingness. A bargain is possible because both adversaries desire not only the mediate goal of Faust's release from his earthly hull (12088–95) but his absolute obliteration. Faust is ambivalent — willing, on the one hand, to risk flowing "into nothingness" (719), while desiring to ascend to new spheres of pure activity (705). He comes to understand that, by definition, all creatures are subject to an agency greater than themselves and that pure activity is for God alone, who has "neither body, parts, nor *passions*": "Im Anfang war," not *Leiden*, but "die *Tat*" (1237). Passion, an essential attribute of creatures, is secondary.

By the second study scene, the scene of the wager, Faust no longer expects to experience a moment of ecstasy, logically (although logic is not what causes his doubts), for an "Augenblick" of ecstasy is a contradiction, a paradox expressed in Goethe's line "Der Augenblick ist Ewigkeit" in the late poem "Vermächtnis" (FA 1,2:686). But Faust's doubt that Mephisto can usher in such a moment does not make the envisioned consummation any the less desirable. Vincent observes that "envisaging love's fulfillment as the experience of pure joy, [Faust] at the same time has a lightning awareness of the necessarily short-lived nature of that experience. Notice how he attempts to deny this awareness, however, how in his vision of imagined bliss lies an implicit demand for duration of the transitory — a demand, in other words, for the *projected* moment to stay."[10] No moment can ever stay, yet that their moment of bliss should be eternal is what Faust wants — as he later declares to Margarete. His words "kein Ende! Kein Ende! (3194) are sometimes read as meaning that Faust wishes nothing so radical (and self-contradictory) as that a moment should become an eternity, but only that love's bliss might

---

[9] Eibl sees that in "dem erfüllten Augenblick . . . sich das Telos des Daseins vollenden würde," but thinks that "Phorkyas/Mephisto" must try to prevent this outcome (Eibl, *Das monumentale Ich: Wege zu Goethes "Faust"* [Frankfurt am Main and Leipzig, 2000], 269, 271).

[10] Deirdre Vincent, *The Eternity of Being: On the Experience of Time in Goethe's* Faust (Bonn: Bouvier Verlag Herbert Grundmann, 1987), 83. In Eibl's formulation: "'Du bist so schön, dass ich mir wünsche, Du möchtest verweilen und damit Deine Eigenschaft als Augenblick aufgeben.'" (*Das monumentale Ich*, 126).

last. But to understand Goethe's text in this way would be to rationalize its paradoxes and to deny paradox in Romanticism generally, which defines love and death as synonyms, since "individuality is suspended in both, and death is the gateway to life."[11] Knowledge too, like fulfillment in love, destroys the self that "acquires" it — the self who is a spectator, looking at the world as if it were a picture.

Faust first comes into view at a moment of peak frustration. He has cruised through the faculties of the university only to discover that he is no wiser than before. Knowledge is the issue throughout the Faust tradition. What can you know? *How* can you know? In Romanticism knowing entails bridging the gap between self and other, as in a *Liebestod*. Although in possession of every academic title, Faust still does not know "was die Welt / Im Innersten zusammenhält" (382–83). Alchemy and its system of analogies fail him, since every analogy preserves a split, bespeaking the difference in every likeness or repetition. The sign of the macrocosm, too, is "Ach! ein Schauspiel nur!" (454) — an object as seen by a subject. What can be *seen* is not enough, so Faust casts this sign aside. Then he himself is rejected by the Earth Spirit, who understands Faust's words "bin deinesgleichen" (500) in terms of an epistemology of resemblance, in which "to know" something is to know what it is like and to *be* something is to comprehend something to which the self is similar: "Du gleichst dem Geist, den du begreifst, / Nicht mir!" (512–13).

Note the order of the Earth Spirit's terms. It is not that Faust "grasps" only beings like himself or that he is guilty of reducing higher things to his own size in order to comprehend them. Rather, he can only come to resemble what he is able to grasp. Knowledge is not reduction. Rather, growth depends on knowledge. Essence comes from knowing. As a separate entity, however, one can never *know* in the fullest sense. At this early moment in the drama, Faust still clings to a resemblance theory of knowledge, failing to see why he does not meet its requirements. If he was created in the image of God (Gen. 1.26–27), why does he not also resemble the Earth Spirit, a contingent *creature* like himself? But what Faust ultimately seeks is not similarity or approximation, but identity, the annihilation of difference in an eternal moment. Knowledge means becoming one with an opposite essence, the blending of subject and object.

There are many kinds of knowledge. Most of them are relational and imply "knowing" someone or something that is different from oneself. The drawing of analogies — "Gleichnisse," as in "Du gleichst dem Geist, den du begreifst" — is a visual exercise and posits a link, often a similarity, between

---

[11] "In beyden wird die Individualität aufgehoben, und der Tod ist die Pforte des Lebens" (Johann Wilhelm Ritter, *Fragmente* [1810; repr., Heidelberg: Lambert Schneider, 1969], 205).

the analogy's terms, as well as a link to the knower who "sees" their relation-ship. Even self-knowledge, as commonly understood, is relational, and im-plies a subject observing itself.[12] The very word "idea" comes from *eidomai*, to see — an unsatisfactory metaphor for knowledge, for seeing affords only a one-sided view of any object and lets us *know* only the surface of things. "That which stands-there-in-itself becomes that which re-presents itself, which presents itself in what it looks like"[13] The knower as viewer is an out-sider, a voyeur, and eavesdropper, his predicament one of opposition to what might be known in a more intimate way.

Goethe knew that his own thinking favored seeing.[14] When Schiller accused him of having preestablished ideas about the metamorphosis of plants — "Das ist keine Erfahrung, das ist eine Idee" — his retort was, "Das kann mir sehr lieb sein daß ich Ideen habe ohne es zu wissen, und sie sogar mit Augen sehe."[15] His "Anschauen" was "ein Denken," his "Denken ein Anschauen" (FA 1,24:595). But Goethe was dissatisfied with ocularcentric conceptions of knowledge, which fossilize the opposition between subject and object and, since each wants to cross over and join the other, fail to es-tablish a stable cognitive situation. Opposition begets a longing for closure, a desire for its own transcendence. "Nur *sehn* [ist] der geringste Antheil, den wir an einer Sache nehmen können," he said (*DjG* 2:271). Analysis of an object of knowledge dismembers and destroys it: "Wer will was Lebendigs erkennen und beschreiben, / Sucht erst den Geist heraus zu treiben, / Dann hat er die Teile in seiner Hand, / Fehlt leider! nur das geistige Band" (*Faust*, lines 1936–39). Goethe embraces "eine zarte Empirie, die sich mit dem Gegenstand innigst identisch macht" (FA 1,13:149) and seeks alternative metaphors to that of knowing as seeing to express this commitment.[16] In-

---

[12] As Allemann observes, "in der [indogermanischen Ausgangsform] bedeutet 'Wissen' nichts anders als 'Gesehen-Haben'" (Beda Allemann, *Zeit und Figur beim späten Rilke* [Pfullingen: Günther Neske, 1961], 289). From Scott Abbott, "'Des Dastehns großer Anfangsbuchstab': Standing and Being in Rilke's Fifth Elegy," *The German Quarterly* 60 (Summer 1987): 432–46.

[13] David Michael Levin, "Decline and Fall: Ocularcentrism in Heidegger's Reading of the History of Metaphysics," in Levin, ed., *Modernity and the Hegemony of Vision* (Berkeley: U of California P, 1993), 186–217; here, 198.

[14] "Das Auge war . . . das Organ, womit ich die Welt faßte" (FA 1,14:246).

[15] "Glückliches Ereignis," which appeared in the first number of Goethe's periodical *Zur Naturwissenschaft überhaupt, besonders zur Morphologie;* also in Cotta's *Morgen-blatt für gebildete Stände* (1817, Nr. 216–17). Reprint in FA 1,24:434–38. See commentary in FA 2,4:775.

[16] Rorty notes the ancient "inference to the 'separable,' immaterial character of voûs from a hylomorphic conception of knowledge — a conception according to which knowledge is not the possession of accurate *representations* of an object but rather the subject's becoming *identical* with the object." He goes on to say that "Aristotle had

deed, the Romantics as a group were dissatisfied with any relational conception of knowledge. Identity is traditionally understood as implying a relationship, tautologically that of A to A, or synthetically, of A to B, but Hölderlin and Novalis sought an "absolute Identität," one which implies no division and no duality.[17] The attainment of absolute identity with the object of knowledge is Goethe's desire as well, despite his sad knowledge that this goal is unattainable: "Das Wahre, mit dem Göttlichen identisch, läßt sich niemals von uns direkt erkennen, wir schauen es nur im Abglanz, im Beispiel, Symbol, in einzelnen und verwandten Erscheinungen; wir werden es gewahr als unbegreifliches Leben und können dem Wunsch nicht entsagen, es dennoch zu begreifen" (FA 1,25:274).[18]

not had to worry about an Eye of the Mind, believing knowledge to be the *identity* of the mind with the object known" (144) (Richard Rorty, *Philosophy and the Mirror of Nature* [Princeton, NJ: Princeton UP, 1979], 45, 145).

[17] "Hölderlin und Novalis . . . werden zeigen, daß, wenn einmal eine Dualität von Momenten in die Dimension des Selbstbewußtseins eingeführt ist, ihre Präreflexivität nicht mehr erklärt werden kann. Niemals könnte eine Zweiheit als Grund von strenger Identität aufgeboten werden. Diese Kritik setzt eine Radikalisierung der Bedeutung des Terms 'Identität' voraus, denn Identität ist in der Tradition durchaus als Relation bestimmt worden" (Manfred Frank, *Selbstbewußtseinstheorien von Fichte bis Sartre*, ed. Manfred Frank [Frankfurt am Main: Suhrkamp, 1991], 450).

[18] Heidegger recommends a conception of knowing as hearing (Levin, "Decline and Fall," 186–217, esp. 212), whereas Derrida objects to metaphors of knowledge as hearing because of the "proximity, appropriation and property (*Eigentlichkeit*) implied" in them (Jürgen Trabant, "Language and the Ear: From Derrida to Herder," *Herder Yearbook* 1(1992): 1–22; here, 1.

Sound from the radio or an orchestra envelops a listener. One is always *inside* hearing, never across from it. The ear "is responsible for the intra-uterine well-being [that the self experiences in hearing] — 'la plus familiale demeure' . . . for the 'obedience' of thought" in the sense of "*ob-audientia*" or, in German, "*Hörigkeit*" = "sexual bondage" (Trabant, "Language and the Ear," 1). To be sure, sounds come from different directions. And echoes may deceive us as to their source, just as a reflection may make us think something is here when in reality it is over there. The ventriloquist Proteus deceives Homunculus and his companions as to his location. He seems now close, now far away — "bauchrednerisch, bald nah, bald fern. Hier! und hier!" (8227).

"To listen to (*hören auf*) the other," says Heidegger, "is to be in bondage (*hörig*) to the other, and so to belong (*zugehören*) to her (366/266)" (Theodore Kisiel, *The Genesis of Heidegger's Being and Time* [Berkeley: U of California P, 1993], 379). Hearing envelops the listener, who is inside the world or the womb, like the prey of a large reptile that swallows its dinner whole. Alternatively, hearing may imply a devouring self which takes sound into its ears and digests it in its mind. Levin believes that seeing generates an active will to power, a will "to grasp and fixate, to reify and totalize . . . to dominate, secure and control," whereas hearing is passive and receptive (212). But while *hearing* may be passive, *listening* is active.

As an interaction between the self and the non-self, knowledge is relational, whether conceived as the observation of an object by a subject or even in terms of such more intimate metaphors as penetration or incorporation. In the "biblical" meaning of to know sexually, knowledge implies uniting with another and in this way transgressing the boundaries of the self.[19] Mary Ann Doane speaks of "the imbrication of knowledge and sexuality."[20] Adam and Eve's transgression is traditionally construed as sexual. Mephistopheles autographs the student's album with Satan's words to them: "Eritis sicut Deus, scientes bonum et malum." A correct answer to a question, says Goethe, is like "ein lieblicher Kuß" (FA 1,13:288),[21] but a kiss is fleeting, and knowledge, like love, wants permanence.

Terrestrial love is an unstable, tension-filled form of cognition, its temporary unions always followed by another division and the return of the autonomous self. Matussek finds that "das Wesen der Erkenntnis ist das Festhalten, [aber] das der Erotik [ist] die Flüchtigkeit."[22] If Eros und *Erkenntnis* fail to come together in *Faust*, however, it is not because they have contrary aims. It is the incompleteness and transitoriness of creaturely love that makes it unsatisfactory and arouses desire for "a higher mating" ("Selige Sehnsucht") and a final, absolute surrender of the self. The *Liebestod* is irreversible — "nicht mehr Tristan, nicht mehr Isolde." The desire for knowledge, too, is a desire for a permanent erasure of the boundary between the knower and the known, a longing for the demolition of representational

---

[19] This applies to either sex. "Adam knew Eve his wife; and she conceived, and bare Cain" (Gen. 4:1), while Mary replies to the Gabriel's announcement that she will conceive the Christ child with the words, "How shall this be, seeing *I know* not a man?" (Luke 1:34). "*Adam vero cognovit Evam uxorem suam;* vgl. auch Wiener Genesis, hg. von Kathryn Smits, Berlin 1972, Verse 1051–53: *Adam sin wip erchande / so noch site ist in demo lande. / er hete mit ir minne*" (Rüdiger Schnell, *Suche nach Wahrheit: Gottfrieds "Tristan und Isold" als erkenntniskritischer Roman* [Tübingen: Max Niemeyer, 1992], 228 n. 83).

The narrator of *Der Zauberberg* says of the departed Claudia Chauchat's abiding presence to Hans Castorp: "Aber war sie unsichtbar-abwesend, so war sie doch zugleich auch unsichtbar-anwesend für Hans Castorps Sinn, — der Genius des Ortes, den er in schlimmer, in ausschreitungsvoll süßer Stunde . . . *erkannt und besessen* hatte" (Thomas Mann, *Der Zauberberg*, "Veränderungen," 485–86).

[20] Mary Ann Doane, *Femmes Fatales: Feminism, Film Theory, Psychoanalysis* (New York and London: Routledge, 1991), 1, 3.

[21] "Diese Analogie ist einem alten Menschheitsgefühl gemäß, das sich etwa in den Sprachen zeigt, die dasselbe Wort für 'erkennen' und 'begatten' brauchen" (Hermann Schmitz, *Goethes Altersdenken im problemgeschichtlichen Zusammenhang* [Bonn: H. Bouvier, 1959], 173; ref. to Franz von Baader, Über die Analogie des Erkenntniss- und des Zeugungs-Triebes, *Sämmtliche Werke*, ed. Franz Hoffmann et al. [Leipzig: Herrmann Bethmann, 1851], 41–48).

[22] Peter Matussek, "Faust I," *Goethe-Handbuch* 2 (1997): 352–90; here, 387.

structures in "an outright merger."[23] Love is fundamental to an epistemological tradition that is older than the Renaissance epistemology of resemblance. In "the Neo-Platonic, mystical literature of the Middle Ages," writes Ernst Cassirer, "the act of knowledge and the act of love have one and the same goal, for both strive to overcome the separation in the elements of being and return to the point of their original unity. . . . To know an object means to negate the distance between it and consciousness; it means, in a certain sense to become *one* with the object: *cognitio nihil est aliud, quam Coitio quaedam cum suo cognobili.*"[24] Goethe's answer to F. H. Jacobi's *Von den göttlichen Dingen und ihrer Offenbarung* (1811) was that if he were to publish a similar encomium to Artemis, the words on the back of the title page would be: "Man lernt nichts kennen, als was man liebt, und je tiefer und vollständiger die Kenntnis werden soll, desto stärker, kräftiger und lebendiger muß Liebe, ja Leidenschaft sein" (10 May 1812; FA 2,7:59). The "Gelehrtentragödie" and the "Gretchentragödie" of *Faust* are parallel manifestations of a single impulse — Faust's desire for a complete blending with the object.

There is an "etymological (and Biblical) connection of knowledge with eating as well as with sex (in Latin, *sapere*)."[25] Kilgour points out that "in French, to consume and to consummate are the same word" — *consommer.*[26] *Carnal* knowledge is *carnivorous* knowledge. When Milton describes Eve eating the forbidden fruit: "Greedily she ingorg'd without restraint, / And

---

[23] "Knowledge, thinks Graeme Nicholson, is always representation of an object and can never be more than that, never outright merger with the object" (*Illustrations of Being: Drawing Upon Heidegger and Upon Metaphysics* [New Jersey: Humanities Press, 1992], 184).

[24] Ernst Cassirer, *The Individual and the Cosmos in Renaissance Philosophy*, trans. Mario Domandi (New York: Barnes & Noble, 1963), 134. He writes, "Knowledge is nothing but a specific stage on this road back. It is a form of striving, for the 'intention' towards its object is essential to all knowledge" (*intensio cognoscentis in cognoscibile* — loc cit). Cassirer documents his quotation as from Francesco Patrizzi, *Panarchia* XV: "De intellectu" (*Nova de universis philosophia;* Ferrara, 1591), fol. 31.

Schnell writes, "Für Augustin, Anselm von Canterbury wie für Thomas von Aquin ist Lieben mit einem Erkenntnisvorgang gekoppelt: *Nullus potest amare aliquid incognitum* ('Niemand liebt ihm völlig Unbekanntes.' *Amare* und *cognoscere* sind untrennbar verbunden. 'Was man ganz und gar nicht kennt, kann man in keiner Weise Lieben,' schreibt Augustin (De trinitate X 1). Für Gregor den Großen ist 'die Liebe selbst Erkenntnis' (*Amor ipse cognitio est*)" (Schnell, *Suche nach Wahrheit,* 226–27).

[25] Jocelyne Kolb, *The Ambiguity of Taste: Freedom and Food in European Romanticism* (Ann Abor: U of Michigan P, 1995), 20.

[26] Maggie Kilgour, *From Communion to Cannibalism: An Anatomy of Metaphors of Incorporation* (Princeton, NJ: Princeton UP, 1990), 7.

knew not eating Death" (*Paradise Lost*, 9:791–92), he may be doubly understood as saying that Eve did not know either that with the apple she was eating death or that Death would soon devour her.[27] Both Adam and Eve partake of the fruit, and the twin results of their eating were knowledge and mortality. In love they also partake of each other. "A lover can well say to his sweetheart that he would like to eat her up," notes Theodor Reik, "and thus express his tender desire for incorporation." Maggie Kilgour, from whose book I take this quote, adds, "Like eating, intercourse makes two bodies one"[28] and disrupts the binarism of me and you, just as knowing transgresses the boundary between subject and object and collapses both into one. Yeats's sonnet "Leda and the Swan" asks, "Did she put on his knowledge with his power / Before the indifferent beak could let her drop?"[29] — "indifferent," not only because of a male's ennui after sex, but because the difference between giver and receiver has been erased. In Goethe's "Amyntas" the ancient marriage topos of elm and ivy — in this case, *apple tree* and ivy — host and parasite turn out to be so intimately intertwined that removing the latter would also destroy the former, although they are goners either way. "Schone den Armen," he pleads to the gardner, "Der sich in liebender Lust, willig gezwungen, verzehrt!" (lines 43–44). The poem ends with the rhetorical question, "Wer sich der Liebe

---

[27] The *New Princeton Encyclopedia of Poetry and Poetics*, 1993, Article: "Pun," 1005.

There have been many paintings of "Death and the Woman" since the Renaissance, e.g. by Hans Baldung, a.k.a. Hans Baldung Grien, 1484/85–1545 — see Willibald Sauerländer, "German Art: The Return of the Repressed," *The New York Review of Books* 43, no. 5 (March 21, 1996): 33–36. In *The Three Ages and Death* (Vienna) a girl contemplating herself in a mirror is approached by death from behind (reproduced in Sabine Melchior-Bonnet, *The Mirror: A History*, trans. Katharine H. Jewett [New York and London: Routledge, 2001], 211). Aries mentions the Baldung paintings "Rider with Death and a Maiden" in the Louvre and "Death and the Woman" in Basel (Philippe Aries, *Western Attitudes toward Death: From the Middle Ages to the Present*, trans. Patricia M. Ranum [Baltimore: The Johns Hopkins UP, 1974], 56). An Egon Schiele painting entitled "Tod und Mädchen" is in the Oberes Belvedere, Vienna. Klara, in Hebbel's *Maria Magdalena*, asks Death to take her instead of her old father, who will otherwise be killed by the news of her pregnancy: "Nimm mich für ihn! Ich will nicht schaudern, wenn du mir deine kalte Hand reichst, ich will sie mutig fassen und dir freudiger folgen, als dir noch je ein Menschenkind gefolgt ist" (2.2).

[28] Kilgour, *From Communion to Cannibalism*, 7. See also her notes 14, 15, and 16, pp. 250–51.

[29] The male redback spider injects into the female and is consumed by her (James Meek, "Sex is best when you lose your head," *London Review of Books*, 16 November 2000; a review of *Promiscuity: An Evolutionary History of Sperm Competition and Sexual Conflict* by Tim Birkhead [Cambridge, MA: Harvard UP, 2000], 9).

vertraut, hält er sein Leben zu Rat?" (FA 1,2:195). If to eat is to love and to love is to know, then to eat is to know.

Isomorphically speaking, ingesting food is a female activity, while to feed or stab or infuse poison into someone is male, despite the common association of both feeding and poisoning with women in literature. Both knowledge and love may take either a male or a female form — as penetration (donational) or incorporation (receptive). A teacher may infuse knowledge into a student's mind, who may receive and incorporate what he or she has been "given," but a good student extracts more from a book or a lecture than the author or teacher put into it.[30] Hearing is passive and receptive, but listening is active reception — extraction.

Am I the cannibal or the missionary; Jonah or the whale? A given metaphor may assign a locus of consciousness to predator or to prey or confer priority on the one or the other.[31] Either knowing as penetration or knowing as devouring allows for two possible identities and centers of consciousness, however. The rapist's misogynist fantasies either deny the consciousness of his victim or imagine it in a way that the victim would not recognize. The myth of the *vagina dentata,* too, may seem to assign consciousness to the terrified phallus. Yet the action is in the vagina. It is easy to imagine consciousness and even primary value located there as well. Is it penetration or incorporation when a guest enters a house or a convert is immersed in the waters of baptism? In either case, personal identity seems to remain intact, identifiable and contained in its boundaries, yet, symbolically, it is absorbed and obliterated. Is it penetration or incorporation when I descend into myself, like a miner going down into the shaft,[32] at the risk of discovering there my incompleteness and need for a complement?[33] Alluding to Aristophanes'

---

[30] Robert Tobin writes of "the slipperiness of the distinction between pedagogy and pederasty in the Greek tradition" (*Warm Brothers: Queer Theory and the Age of Goethe* [Philadelphia: U of Pennsylvania P, 2000], 136).

[31] Hegel "unabashedly [makes] clear that . . . perception or conception ends up in incorporation and in the following digestion of the conceived, as in real life. What the metaphysical hand seizes is eaten up" (Trabant, "Language and the Ear," 14). In at least in two passages of the *Phenomenology,* Hegel "makes it very clear that the Spirit is the Big Incorporator and Digester" (Jürgen Trabant's letter to me, 2 December 1993).

[32] Mines are seen as orifices in the body of Mother Earth throughout Romanticism. See Ziolkowski, *German Romanticism and its Institutions* (Princeton, NJ: Princeton UP, 1990), 18–63. Kleist's Penthesilea compares her own bosom to a shaft in which she will find the ore for the poisoned dagger with which she will pierce her breast (lines 3025–34). There is probably a reflection of the death of Juliet in this passage, despite the metaphorical expansion of sheath [= Scheide] into shaft in *Penthesilea.*

[33] But "Natur hat weder Kern / Noch Schale, / Alles ist sie mit einem Male" (FA 1,2:507).

tale of divided humans in Plato's *Symposium* and also to the parable of the cave, Goethe observes that "Wer in sich recht ernstlich hinabsteigt wird sich immer Nur als Hälfte finden, er fasse nach her ein Mädchen oder eine Welt um sich zum Ganzen zu constituiren das ist einerlei" (FA 1,13:391). To know fully, the self must disintegrate and blend with the non-self, there perhaps to find itself again. Metaphors of deliquescence and influence imply either penetration of the other or ingestion of the other into oneself, as when Stella "drinks" Fernando's soul with trembling lips (FA 1,4:544) or Werther wants to "drink" Lotte. Mann's Adrian Leverkühn receives "seltsame Eingiessungen" from the Devil (*Doktor Faustus*, 665), but Leverkühn has actively courted the Hetaera Esmeralda, and deliberately contracted syphilis from her, so there is a strong element of reciprocity in the transaction. Both penetration and incorporation occur when the river flows into the ocean in "Mahomets Gesang" *In*fluence begets *con*fluence, *in*fusion *con*fusion: "Und wiederkehrt / uralte Verwirrung" (Hölderlin, "Der Rhein"). Subject and object oscillate back and forth and are symbiotic, just as sadism and masochism imply each other. The masochist's enjoyment of pain may come from his vicarious experience of the sadist's pleasure in inflicting pain. It is hard to tell where this sort of mirroring and substitution stops.[34]

Human, as opposed to *divine,* subjectivity is essentially receptive, for "to *be* a subject," unless one is God, "is already to live in a world"[35] and to accept "gifts," conditions, conceptual habits, and categories of mind that do not originate with oneself. "Ja, das ist das rechte Gleis, / Daß man nicht weiß, / Was man denkt, / Wenn man denkt; / Alles ist wie geschenkt," says Goethe in one of his *Zahme Xenien* (FA 1,2:631). But interaction with the world is the only path to true knowledge, and mortal creatures may be either benefactors or beneficiaries, or both at once: "Der Mensch kennt nur sich selbst, insofern er die Welt kennt, die er nur in sich und sich nur in ihr gewahr wird" (FA 1,24:595–96), hence Goethe's word about "eine zarte Empirie, die sich mit dem Gegenstand innigst identisch macht." Denied access to the object of their most passionate desire, those twin sons of Tanta-

---

[34] As Zagermann observes, "die orale Phantasie der Inkorporation, Introjektion des Objekts" does not contradict imagined containment in the object. "Denn die Inkorporation stellt nach unserer Ansicht . . . paradoxerweise gerade einen Versuch der Herstellung dieses Zustands der Enthaltenheit dar, insofern die, sozusagen, Verdauung und Metabolisierung des inkorporierten Objekts dem Ich die fusionäre Einheit mit diesem Objekt und damit eben wieder die Enthaltenheit im Schutz- und Gewährungsraum des Objekts gewinnen soll" (Peter Zagermann, *Eros und Thanatos* [Darmstadt: Wissenschaftliche Buchgesellschaft, 1988], 246).

[35] John Mepham, "The Structuralist Sciences and Philosophy," in *Structuralism: An Introduction,* ed. David Robey (Oxford: Clarendon Press, 1973), 126.

lus, Faust and Werther,[36] try to transcend the walls of separation. Werther destroys himself in pursuit of an eternal union with Lotte before the benign countenance of God. Faust, likewise "a hungerer after the unreachable" (8204–5), is interrupted on the verge of the same desperate solution, but made to see that transcendence, like knowledge, is a gift and cannot be demanded (672–75). Christ is not a Hermes leading mortals into the beyond but a bridge and mediator between them and the Father. Unlike Werther, who wished to emulate the death and resurrection of Christ, Faust is reminded by the Easter pageant that we are contingent beings, patients. There can be no such thing as self-translation or even self-sufficiency. And there is no life outside of time — no literal *ecstasis,* except in death. The self-imagined "Übermensch" (490) and *Himmelsstürmer* had been at the point of hubris, but, reminded of our dependence on (in this case, *divine*) mediation, he puts down the cup of poison, delivers himself up to a temporal life "here,"[37] and will immerse himself in "was der ganzen Menschheit zugeteilt ist" . . . Und so mein eigen Selbst zu ihrem Selbst erweitern (1770–74). He is given, in the nick of time, a vision of the redemptive act of *the* necessary being and accepts the contingency he shares with all humankind. It is we mortals, not the gods, who suffer passion and to whom, as patients, life's limits and accidents are given, and Faust will become *one* with his fellows and suffer directly what *they* experience on the sojourn through life. He is mistaken in thinking that he is "vom Wissensdrang geheilt" (1768), for he still wants to know, but now experientially.

Let us not squeeze any of Goethe's paradigms harder than Goethe does himself. To restrict him to any exclusive theory, doctrine, or model is to mistake the freedom and the irony in his use of inherited materials. Much of traditional *Faust* scholarship has amounted to reductive elaborations of one theme or element to the exclusion of others and attempts to resolve the paradoxes that Romanticism cannot avoid. *Faust* contains Christian as well as non-Christian ideas, and both are expressed in both orthodox and heterodox forms. An ambiguous balancing of grace and "good works," broadly understood as including striving or daring, is a legacy from the Renaissance that is memorably on display in Marlowe. Proceeding from work by Burdach, Hen-

---

[36] "Und seiner Unersättlichkeit / Soll Speis' und Trank vor gier'gen Lippen schweben; / Er wird Erquickung sich umsonst erflehn" (*Faust,* lines 1863–65). Cf. Werther: "Weiß der große Gott, wie einem das tut, so viel Liebenswürdigkeit vor einem herumkreuzen zu sehen und nicht zugreifen zu dürfen" (30 Octbr. 1772).

[37] The dialectic of temporal-eternal is reflected in that of terrestrial-celestial, and dark and light. Mephisto had credited Faust with an appetite for more than *earthly* food — "Nichtirdisch ist des Toren Trank noch Speise" (301). "Vom Himmel fordert er die schönsten Sterne / Und von der Erde jede höchste Lust" (304–5). The moth in "Selige Sehnsucht" escapes from "der Finsternis Beschattung" and, greedy for light, flies into the candle's flame.

kel, and Breuer, Schöne reads Faust's death and resurrection at the play's end in terms of Origen's theory of apocatastasis,[38] according to which everyone, even Lucifer, will be gathered up in the arms of a conciliatory God, an influence that is likely, if not undisputed.[39] Goethe portrays Being in terms of the ancient paradigm of *exitus-reditus*, as a series of divisions and reunions, articulations and reabsorptions, life in time characterized by becoming, "life" beyond time by being as nothingness. But Goethe agrees with Kant that direct presentation of any absolute is impossible. "Es ist nichts trauriger anzusehn als das unvermittelte Streben ins Unbedingte in dieser durchaus bedingten Welt," he once said (FA 1,13:83 — cf. *Faust,* line 341), in the light of which remark much of *Faust* reads like an allegory of its author's beliefs about the need for mediation of many kinds — above all, the mediation of language and play.[40]

Among the paradigms employed in *Faust* is the "die-and-become!" model of alchemy,[41] the "science" with which Goethe experimented during his convalescence after returning home ill from his studies in Leipzig and which he exploited in "Selige Sehnsucht." The idea of transmutation is schematically equivalent to the coincidence of opposites in a higher synthesis and, as a model, informs every dialectic, including irony. Consistently, therefore, Novalis and Friedrich Schlegel call irony the "*menstruum universale*" and the "universal solvent," for it dissolves "established boundaries, real and imaginary, linguistic and mental."[42] Irony too, like the tincture or the philosophers' stone, or like Jesus Christ (who is both God and mortal), sublates opposites in a transcendent unity. Every paradigm, every metaphor, and every image is only provocative or deictic, never truly mimetic. And this ap-

[38] Schöne, FA 1,7,2:788–92.

[39] Disputed by Hans-Rudolph Vaget, "'Mäßig boshaft': Fausts Gefährte: Goethes Mephistopheles im Lichte der Aufklärung," *Goethe-Jahrbuch* 118 (2001): 234–46; here, 244, who cites Zimmermann, Eibl, and Jochen Schmidt and finds a more satisfactory influence in Spaldings *Die Bestimmung des Menschen* (1748).

[40] Jane K. Brown, *Goethe's* Faust: *The German Tragedy* (Ithaca: Cornell UP, 1986), 101.

[41] Implicit in Faust's rejuvenation in the witch's kitchen and in his regenerating sleeps, first in the alpine meadow (4613–78) and again in Wagner's laboratory, from which sleep "to life he'll waken" (7054) when he is set down in Greece. It is further restated in the "birth" of Homunculus (6848–79) — which presupposes the "death" and putrefaction of human spermatozoa in a laboratory retort — and in his (projected) rebirth, when, in the pageant on the Aegean Sea and shore, his wish to (die and) become is granted (8466–73). Faust takes pleasure in the "resurrection" (922) of the townspeople whom he and Wagner join outside the town wall. Finally, there is Faust's death and rebirth to a higher existence at the end of the play.

[42] Jochen Schulte-Sasse, "Romanticism's Paradoxical Articulation of Desire," in *Theory as Practice* (Minneapolis: U of Minnesota P, 1997), 30.

plies as much to Goethe's employment of fashionable psychologies and ephemeral scientific theories as to his use of theologies. He did not need to believe in the atonement to use it as a symbol of mediation, any more than he needed to believe in devils to create in Mephistopheles a witty, urbane Enlightener of a devil and then let this devil admit his own consignment to the rubble heap of history: "Den Bösen sind sie los, die Bösen sind geblieben" (2509). By allowing them to stand, Goethe even authorized "inconsistencies" resulting from the long genesis of his *Faust*.[43] To one attempt to rationalize his work, he replied, "Das wäre ja Aufklärung. Faust endet als Greis, und im Greisenalter werden wir Mystiker."[44]

The "die-and-become" model is prominent in the scene "Vor dem Tor" on Easter Sunday. Walking with his famulus Wagner, Faust remarks that, just as Christ was reborn, the colorful throng of picnickers has been resurrected from the dank chambers in which they have spent the winter. It is a warm and cheerful scene of vivacious flirting and joyful singing and dancing. When the revelers toast Faust for his struggle against the plague in his days as a young doctor, he guiltily recalls that the cure administered by him and his "obscure" alchemist father was worse than the disease (1034–36).

In the alchemists' work "the lion red, a wooer daring" (sulfur, probably) was wed "in tepid bath" to the lily (possibly mercury), resulting in a "marriage" of "das Widrige."[45] This is a hierogamous "marriage" and another of the many *coincidentiae oppositorum* in the Goethean opus.[46] The alchemists knew that the chemical mixing of contraries could yield a deadly poison, and drew the paradoxical inference that out of poison may come healing, just as life comes out of death. The philter drunk by Tristan and Isolde is both a medicine and a poison. It heals what afflicts them and makes them whole while annihilating them as separate individuals. Potions and poisons, such as the poison administered by the cook in "Es war eine Ratt' im Kellernest" and the witch's potion that rejuvenates Faust and kindles his craving for a

---

[43] As Schöne points out, the ruptures in continuity are constructive: "Indem die personale Charakterkonstanz sich verliert, gewinnt das Prinzip der Verwandlung selber Konstanz" (*Die deutsche Lyrik,* 52).

[44] As reported by Friedrich Förster, in *Goethes Gespräche,* auf Grund der Ausgabe und des Nachlasses von Flodoard Freiherrrn von Biedermann, ed. Wolfgang Herwig, 5 vols. in 6 (Zürich and Stuttgart: Artemis, 1972), 3.2:295, no. 6187. Undated, between 1825–28.

[45] Mircea Eliade, *The Forge and The Crucible,* trans. Stephen Corrin (New York: Harper Torchbook, 1971), 151.

[46] Faust teaches Helena to rhyme and let one word "caress" the other (9371). Rhyme, like irony, involves mediation — and yields a wedding and coincidence of opposites. Oneness destroys twoness through the erasure of boundaries between selves, words, or meanings.

woman, are favorite props in tales of love-death.[47] Poison is the great suture
and healer — not least of the individual's eruption into finitude, hence
Faust's near recourse to poison on Easter morning.

In *Faust* the activity generated by the coincidence and interplay of opposites, what Goethe called "Polarität," generates the dynamic striving that is
Faust's outstanding quality, for the positive and negative poles constantly
attract or repel each other and prevent the state of rest that their eventual
sublation in a higher synthesis would yield. As the Lord had proclaimed, opposed forces are in conflict in Faust's breast (304–5), one of his two souls
holding fast to the world below "in crude desire for love" while the other
soars to the haunts of great ancestors (1112–17). Torn between his bond to
the "dark earth" and the drive to escape its gravitational pull and take flight
(1085–99), Faust is poised like the moth to respond to light, the "earth-
being" who "rests in the medial gloom between" ("Entoptische Farben,"
FA 1,2:505). Opposition is in force on the horizontal scale as well, Faust as
"das irrend Strebende, Tätige und Gewaltsame"[48] in need of redemption at
the hands of the eternal-feminine — first and last Margarete and, on different symbolic levels, by Helena and the Mater Gloriosa. In arranging a love
affair for him, Mephistopheles aims to generate a moment of ecstasy that will
sate and annihilate Faust.

Brander's song "Es war eine Ratt' im Kellernest" is another illustration
of Goethe's virtuosic employment of substitutions. This song is a parody of
Faust's inability to satisfy the hunger in his own "deeply-moved breast"
(307). Since "Unersättlichkeit" defines Faust (1863), absolute [*unbedingte*]
rest would (and *will*) be the death of him — inevitable in any case, but not
soon (341). This is why Mephistopheles, as tempter and provocateur
(342–43), is given a free hand with Faust "solang' er auf der Erde lebt"
(315). The rat's racing about and slurping from every puddle (Bohm notes
the pun on Pfütze and Fotze) "mirrors" the knowledge-thirsty Faust's own
frenzied chase — through the curricula of the university, through experiments in magic, to the erstwhile attempt to escape from the confines of this
world, which both Faust and the lovesick rat experience as stifling (2131),
and then to his self-dedication to a life of tumult and pain — not really cured
of "Wissensdrang" (1768), but only of the desire for academic, non-
experiential knowledge. Life is a sign in *Faust,* its frantic deeds and frenetic
events an illustration of being's erring toward entropy, drawn on by the
promise of timeless love. The wicked joke here is that rat poison is an aphro-

---

[47] Augustin, in the *Lehrjahre,* acquires a means of suicide in a vial of laudanum, but
because he has the ability to take his life, he is able to live: "Er führt nun in einem
festen geschliffenen Glasfläschen dieses Gift als das sonderbarste Gegengift bei sich"
(FA 1,9:979).

[48] Schöne, *Die deutsche Lyrik,* 786.

disiac, like the potion that rejuvenates Faust in the Witch's kitchen: "Du siehst, mit diesem Trank im Leibe / Bald Helenen in jedem Weibe" (2603–4). The repetition of the words "im Leibe" from the song about the rat reaffirms Faust's identity with the fellow sufferer in love. He sets out on a quest for a woman in the flesh.

When Faust and Margarete eventually meet and converse, Margarete's endearing tale of caring for her baby sister during her sick mother's convalescence inflames Faust's passion, just as Lotte's surrogate motherhood to her young siblings attracts Werther, and Ottilie's "scheinbar" motherhood ignites the adoration of the architect in *Die Wahlverwandtschaften* (FA 1,8:438–39). The "Mothers" from whose realm Faust will retrieve the shade of Helena and the divine mother as *mater dolorosa* and as *mater gloriosa* define the *arché* and the *telos* of *Faust.*[49] As a foil to Faust's and Margarete's blossoming love we are given, in alternating revolutions around the stage, Mephistopheles's evasive dance with the eager harridan Frau Marthe Schwerdtlein, the contrasting pairs both showing Goethe's early mastery of dramatic conventions and his reliance on polarities. Margarete, who feels a strong antipathy toward his uncanny Cicerone (3470–75), longs for him, when he is away, with unashamed desire: "Mein Schoos! Gott! Drängt / Sich nach ihm hin!" (FA 1,7,1:519),[50] while Faust is ashamed of what he is doing to her, like his unfaithful counterparts Clavigo and Fernando. Fearing Faust's conscience, Mephistopheles arrives to entice him back to the pleasures of which Margarete's own longing is plainly promising. What Faust wants, says Mephisto in provocative metaphors, is to lie on the mountains in the night and the dew, embrace [*umfassen*] heaven and earth, swell up into a divine state, "bore through" [*durchwühlen*] the marrow of the earth with a prescient thrust [*Ahnungsdrang*], and then flow over into everything (3283–89). Faust's "Liebeswut" (3307) was like a mountain stream overflowing its banks with the rush of melted snow. But now the brook is shallow and must be fed. From the *Song of Songs* Mephisto takes the image of twin roe deer grazing among the roses to remind Faust of Margarete's succulent breasts (3337), themselves an image of the breasts of Nature (455–59), and declares with a *double-entendre,* "Ihr sollt in eures Liebchens Kammer / Nicht etwa in den Tod" (3343–44).

It had not been Faust's purpose on Easter morning to destroy himself. Rather, frustrated in his earthly efforts, he sought translation to a distant shore: "In's hohe Meer werd' ich hinausgewiesen, / Die Spiegelflut erglänzt zu meinen Füßen, / Zu neuen Ufern lockt ein neuer Tag" (699–701). The risk he is willing to take is that he might just "flow" into nothingness (719),

[49] Terms from Clark S. Muenzer, *Figures of Identity: Goethe's Novels and the Enigmatic Self* (University Park: The Pennsylvania State UP, 1984), passim.

[50] "Schoos" is toned down to "Busen" in the 1808 version (line 3406).

that he might deliquesce and disappear into the open womb of "Nature." It might then be said of him as of the fisherman of the ballad: "Halb zog sie ihn, halb sank er hin, / Und ward nicht mehr gesehn" (FA 1,1:303). Faust conceives of nothingness as a female *something*, if we take the metonymy seriously, and identifies himself with seminal fluid. Faust's rhetoric at this crucial moment marks the close association between love and the kind of knowledge he seeks. Flowing into his sexual opposite, he would cease to be, which, as Michelsen notes, is also the goal of Gretchen's longing, "denn nicht nur — das spürt man — auf die petite mort der Liebeserfüllung ist dieses Verlangen gerichtet, sondern, weiter und tiefer, auf ein Sich-Verlieren, Hinuntersinken, Untergehen."[51] Accepting the risk, Faust returns and impregnates her, but is rudely expelled from their moment of bliss by the threat of prosecution for the murder of Valentin, a prefiguration of Kurwenal's "Rette dich, Tristan!" in the Wagner opera, and by Margarete's disgrace; indeed, one of Goethe's early purposes in writing *Faust* had been to satirize the cruel treatment of unwed mothers in a supposedly modern, supposedly Christian society. Distraught and guilty of drowning her baby, Gretchen, for her part, is hunted down, imprisoned, and executed — on what was supposed to have been her wedding day (4581).

Faust's journey to "the Mothers" to retrieve Helen of Troy in Part Two of the drama reflects the Romantic character of *Faust* in four ways: (1) Faust will be propelled by loneliness (6226–27), just as his pact with the devil and his pursuit of Margarete were motivated by loneliness (6236–38). (2) His quest is paradoxical. In the boundless "Nichts" into which Mephisto is sending him (6246, 6248) he hopes to find "das All" (719; 3289). (3) The Mothers reside outside of time and space, and Faust can get to them either by sinking or by climbing. Finally (4), beyond time and space, the mothers defy representation and are a "Nichts" in this sense too. Goethe steadfastly refused to explain the Mothers, but — source and sanctuary — they yield up Helena's shade, prompting an ardent, still impatient Faust to carry his quest for the "real," unmediated, Helena back through time and space to ancient Greece and the shores of the Aegean Sea.

The context indicates what the Mothers "stand for." Eliade notes the alchemists' belief that "'he who would enter the Kingdom of God must first enter with his body into his mother and there die.'"[52] Indeed, the whole world must "'enter into its mother,' which is the *prima materia*, the *massa confusa*, the *abyssus*, in order to achieve eternity."[53] "It is obvious that the 'mother' symbolizes, in these different contexts, nature in her primordial state, the *prima materia* of the alchemists, and that the 'return to the

[51] Michelsen, *Im Banne Fausts*, 86.
[52] Paracelsus, as quoted by Eliade, *The Forge and the Crucible*, 154.
[53] Eliade, ibid., 154–55.

mother' translates a spiritual experience corresponding to any other 'projection' *outside Time* — in other words, to the reintegration of a primal situation."[54] Hatfield denies that the Mothers are "symbols of some romantically conceived *Ur*-womb,"[55] but the value and voltage assigned to mothers and motherhood throughout Goethe's oeuvre cannot be ignored. He could have named them something else, after all. Compare the Earth Spirit's words "Geburt und Grab / Ein ewiges Meer" (504–5). The Mothers' abode is more formless even than the unfathomable ocean, where Faust might at least see waves and an occasional dolphin (6239–44).

As a representation, Helena links presence and absence. Her very "literariness" bespeaks the Romantic character of Goethe's *Faust,* which exposes its own fictionality while pointing to an inner sanctum beyond its reach, like Phorkyas before the palace of Menelaus. Helena is herself a fiction. "She arrives parodying classical Greek trimeters, identifies herself as the subject of ancient legend and fable, and faints when others remind her of less flattering versions of her myth. She then seals her union with Faust by learning how to imitate medieval poetry — that is, by rhyming her speech — and she bears a son who is a reincarnation of Byron."[56] As a reproduction, she is, if not false, then, at least in disguise, and has her dissemblance in common with Mephistopheles, who appears as a poodle, an itinerant student, a professor and freshmen adviser, a court jester, and eventually as Phorkyas, Helena's ugly servant. Like signs, veils, shades and masks of every sort, disguises both conceal and reveal. They are signs of signs, signifiers of signification, but also obstructors of presence, and proof of the split in the knowing process and in allegory. They expose difference and lack and, like the distance between lovers, they both tantalize and frustrate.

The authors of one *Faust* commentary note that "three festivals of love form the culminating points of three almost equal parts of the FAUST poem. The Northern Walpurgis Night (3835–4222), symbolizing deepest confusion in Faust's mind, is carnal debauchery. The Classic Walpurgis Night (7005–8487), fantastic and weird in its beginnings, ends in a celebration of creative Eros. The conclusion of the FAUST poem is a *Magnificat* to Divine Love. At each of these points a higher and clearer state of existence is foreshadowed."[57] Faust's redemption and release from terrestrial bonds is hardly a conventional "salvation," rewarding the "goodness" of a man who has left

---

[54] Eliade, ibid., 155, emphasis added.

[55] Henry Hatfield, *Goethe: A Critical Introduction* (Norfolk, Connecticut: New Directions, 1963), 184, footnote.

[56] Neil M. Flax, "The Presence of the Sign in Goethe's Faust," *PMLA* 98:2 (1983): 183–203; here, 195.

[57] R.-M. S. Heffner, Helmut Rehder, and W. F. Twaddell, *Goethe's Faust,* 2 vols. (Boston: Heath, 1955), 1:94.

Margarete to her fate, caused the death of her mother, murdered her brother; and, near the end of the drama, violently dispossessed an aging couple, who die of shock at seeing their front door battered down. Faust's crimes, which he too late regrets, hardly reflect moral merit or even moral growth. Yet the angels say, "Den können wir erlösen" (11937). How can this be possible? What does it mean?

Schöne outlines the soteriological debate, and, noting the pervasive theme of *Tätigkeit* in *Faust,* joins Burdach, Henkel, and Breuer in citing Goethe's knowledge of Origen's theology (788–92). Schöne and others contrast Faust's restlessness with quiescence, reclining on a "Faulbett," rather than with the fulfillment toward which it strives. We can make the necessary adjustments if we note that Faust stipulates multiple conditions that must be satisfied if he is to lose the wager. These conditions are augmentative and mutually reinforcing.

The reference to a "Faulbett" occurs seven lines before the phrase "Werd' ich zum Augenblicke sagen." In between, Faust mentions two other conditions — (a) that Mephistopheles so delude him that he will be self-satisfied and (b) that he deceive him with "Genuß" (1694–96). These terms are precisely not a series of ever more intense synonyms, a progressive raising of the stakes, as it were. Yet to be pleased with oneself *is* more than mere laziness or even than the languor after sex that is implied by the baroque associations of "Faulbett." "Genuß" means positive pleasure, and the requirement that Mephistopheles provide a moment of such intense beauty that Faust will not want it to cease is of a higher order still, a superlative like Tristan and Isolde's "höchste Liebes-Lust." The common denominator of the three conditions, culminating in the proposal of the "ewiger Augenblick,"[58] is the cessation of activity, ultimately in a moment of supreme, timeless joy. The joy that Mephistopheles contracts to deliver is not, then, merely a "state of complacent inertia,"[59] but a pleasure so intense that Faust will long for nothing more. And the contrastive term to *Tätigkeit* is not comfort or complacence, but *Leiden* — passivity, "die unbedingte Ruh" that humans prematurely seek (341),[60] as in the *Leiden* of young Werther. Gretchen's meeting with Faust generates in her a longing for a fulfillment[61] for which she heretofore had no conscious desire and whose beckoning now deprives her of her "Ruhe": "Meine Ruh' ist hin." Goethe's *Faust* is not a homily against sloth.

---

[58] See Andreas Anglet, *Der "ewige" Augenblick: Studien zur Struktur und Funktion eines Denkbildes bei Goethe* (Weimar: Böhlau, 1991), passim.

[59] Vincent, *The Eternity of Being,* 64.

[60] It is as an aide in keeping "des Menschen Tätigkeit" alive and hopping, in not letting it prematurely expire, that the Lord welcomes the diabolical "Schalk" Mephistopheles to a tête à tête (or, as Eibl proposes, a levee) at the drama's beginning.

[61] Michelsen, *Im Banne Fausts,* 85.

It is a probing of the contingency and incompleteness of humankind, of our need for a "höhere Begattung." The threat and promise to Faust, like the threat and promise to the moth in "Selige Sehnsucht," is that he will be drawn — "hingerissen," *ripped* — into an ecstasy that will suspend time and make the moment eternal. Temporal travail contrasts with eternal rapture and, intermediately, with the buffeting about that is the human lot, however frenetically Faust may strive and kick against the pricks. Vulnerability to passion — patient-hood, receptiveness to God's action — this is what it means to be a creature.

The term by which the angels mark Faust's destiny denotes release as much as redemption: "Wer immer strebend sich bemüht, / Den können wir er*lösen*" (11936–37). It is reasonable, and this idea should startle only those readers who take for granted that Faust's striving is a merit and justification of his salvation, to read "erlösen" as meaning that the angels can release a man from a life of frenzied activity, from the rat race toward death — "*Wer auch immer strebend sich bemüht.*" "Whoever it is who is striving and exerting himself," him we can release.[62] We once again face the respective democratic and aristocratic alternatives encountered in our discussion of "Selige Sehnsucht." It is in the nature of all human creatures to strive and to err, but the promise of release is extended to them all.

Faust's *Erlösung* involves not only release and absolution but also *dis*solution, the *Auflösung* of "geeinte Zwienatur" (11962–65), the end of hybridity and hypostasis,[63] and the conclusion of life as an individual. It is important to heed the semantic links between "lösen," "er*lösen*,"

---

[62] Schöne cites this plausible formulation from Wilhelm Böhm, *Goethes Faust in neuer Deutung* (Cologne: E. A. Seemann, 1949), 297 (Schöne, FA 1,7,2:801).

[63] Cf. Novalis, *Hymnen an die Nacht:* "Noch einmal sah er freundlich nach der Mutter — da kam der ewigen Liebe *lösende* Hand, und er entschlief" (5th Hymn). "Der Vater, der in der Urszene dem fusionären Sog des primären Objekts gegenübertritt, ohne ihm zu erliegen, ohne ihn zu fürchten, schafft dadurch erst die Mutter als ungefährliches und verläßliches, eindeutiges und sozusagen 'objektales' Objekt im Sinne des Eros, denn unter dem Aspekt des Todestriebs ist der objektale Charakter der Mutter sehr zweifelhaft-zweideutig: Sie ist ja hier, unter der thanatalen Definition, kein Objekt im üblichen, abgegrenzt-objektalen Sinne, sondern interessant, begehrenswert, dämonisch als Durchgangsstation, als Tor zum Nicht-Sein, zur Aufhebung des Ich wie des psychischen Objekts. Die fusionäre Mutter ist . . . eigentlich ein Medium, ein Mittel: die objektale Verdichtung des Todestriebs, die Manifestation des Nichts im Sein. Sie ist so dasjenige Objekt, das das Objektale selbst aufhebt. Die Angst vor ihr, die eine Produktion des opponierenden Lebenstriebes ist, die Angst vor der verschlingenden Imago ist in Wahrheit der horor vacui" (Zagermann, *Eros und Thanatos,* 109).

"Ablösung"[64] and *"auf*lösen."[65] The etymology of "erlösen" and the metaphor of dissolution, for example, by means of love, the ultimate *Menstruum universale* in *Faust*, has been neglected in interpretations of the angels' words, although it is prominent in Romantic discourse, erasing the boundary between image and referent, deception and truth, and self and non-self, and folding opposites into each other.

Longing for dissolution informs the lyric, "*Lösest* endlich auch einmal / Meine Seele ganz" ("An den Mond"), and motivates the descent of the fisherman into the mermaid's "tiefe[n] Himmel" (FA 1,1:303).[66] Faust is propelled by love and longing for restoration, thus by the lack of and the need for a complement. It is *from* activity that he is saved — *from* the frenzy of a life of loneliness and longing, *confusedly* underway toward joy. Joy cannot be found close at hand or at once, which is why the Lord greets Mephistopheles as provocateur at the play's beginning. But rest, ecstasis, release is the goal — love and death. "Das Ziel alles Lebens ist der Tod."[67]

Faust imagines, but does not experience, the ecstatic moment to which he *could* say "Verweile doch! du bist so schön!" Although granted a premonition of such high happiness, he remains unsatisfied to the end, falling victim to time while being delivered from its sway: "Die Zeit wird Herr, der Greis hier liegt im Sand" (11592). "Wer immer strebend sich bemüht," *can* (not *must*) be redeemed. Faust's redemption is due not to his own good works or even to the restless activity resulting from his lack and dissatisfaction, but to Divine Love. Purification, as in the smelting of metal in the fire of love, must be gratefully received (12099). Love divides and reunites. And it is love, which began everything (8479), that "forms all things and all protects" (11873), and that will dissolve the boundaries and usher in the void. As Schöne notes, love is the crucial word in this final scene, recurring fourteen times.[68] But love is a gift and cannot be earned, whether through striving or in any other way. In *Faust* love is a *female* donation, embodied in the

[64] "Gewiss ist die 'Erlösung' eine 'Ablösung' vom 'Erdenrest,' und damit eine 'Auflösung' der Person. . . . Dem entspricht auch, dass die seligen Knaben die 'Flocken' der im 'Puppenstand' befindlichen Seele, also den Kokon 'lösen' (11985)" (Eibl, *Das monumentale Ich*, 337).

[65] Weighing the testamentary disposition of his property, Goethe remarked in a letter to Zelter: "Übrigens begreifst du, daß ich ein testamentarisches und kodizillarisches Leben führe, damit der Körper des Besitztums, der mich umgibt, nicht allzuschnell in die niederträchtigsten Elemente, nach Art des Individuums selbst, *sich eiligst auflöse*" (23 November 1831; my emphasis). FA 2,11:487.

[66] In *Die Wahlverwandtschaften* Eduard and Ottilie long for absorption in each other. "Das Leben war ihnen ein Rätsel, dessen Auflösung sie nur miteinander fanden" (FA 1,8:516).

[67] Sigmund Freud, "Jenseits des Lustprinzips," *SA* 3:248.

[68] Schöne, *Die deutsche Lyrik*, 786.

transfigured Margarete, who intercedes on Faust's behalf. Goethe's *Faust* does not lead to the lovers' burial together in the chapel. No rose arches over from Faust's grave and takes root in the grave of the executed Margarete. But one of the penitents in the play's last scene, "otherwise known as Gretchen" (stage direction 12069, 12084), invokes the image of rejuvenation through the shedding of a hull or a skin: "aus ätherischem Gewande / . . . tritt erste Jugendkraft [hervor]" (12090–91). His opposite and complement, she will lead him upward and on.

Eventually Faust is ripe for removal to a new sphere. Even "drüben," on "neuen Ufern," as the description of Faust as "a chrysalid entity" implies (11982), he may metamorphose into something higher and finer. He is (*again*, as in "Anmutige Gegend") blinded by the new day (11982, 12093). Development as metamorphosis, decay and renewal, death and rebirth is interwoven in *Faust* with the dichotomies of time and eternity, terrestrial and celestial, dark and light. Faust dies and is transported — carried heavenward (he levitates, as he had imagined doing in the scene "Vor dem Tor" [1074–99]) and relocated beyond time, passing such anchorites as St. Philipp Neri, the probable model for the Pater Ecstaticus of lines 11854–65, as he rises upward through mountain gorges.[69] Reborn and borne into the clarity promised in the "Prolog im Himmel" (309), he becomes "der . . . nicht mehr Getrübte" (12074), now delivered from the domain of "Mutter Nacht" (1351, 8812).

In "Selige Sehnsucht" a continuous subject is exhorted to "have" its own dying and becoming, to possess its own oscillation between being and non-being, between self-assertion and surrender to love and death. This paradox is the paradigm for Goethe's conception of knowledge, in which the subject seeks identity with the object, through self-immersion, penetration, infusion, or incorporation. Incorporation or infusion may be either seminal or sanguinal and entails self-sacrifice, even the suspension of cognition. It may be that the kind of knowledge sought by Goethe and the Romantics is not appropriately termed knowledge at all. If an individual "identifies so completely with the 'other' that this other can be neither represented nor remembered . . . If I am you or he is she, then you, she, 'the other' cannot be recalled"[70] or "known." The knowledge most worth having obliterates the separations on which relational knowledge depends. Indeed, it annihilates the agents of knowledge, the knowers.

---

[69] Goethe wrote of Philipp Neri, "the humorous saint," reeling and stumbling before the altar, levitating, and biting into the communion cup as though he were slurping the blood of Christ (Zweiter Röm. Aufenthalt, FA 1,15,1:495–508).

[70] Mikkel Borch-Jacobsen, "Little Brother, Little Sister," a review of *Mad Men and Medusas: Reclaiming Hysteria and the Effects of Sibling Relationships on the Human Condition*, by Juliet Mitchell, *London Review of Books* 23 (24 May 2001): 16.

Goethe hovers, tenuously, in between — a "geeinte Zwienatur" attracted both to identity as self-articulation and to the contrary attraction of a seamless identification with the object: "Fühlst du nicht an meine Liedern, / Daß ich eins und doppelt bin?" This is as good a paradigm of Romantic Irony as could be found, for irony is always double, both entrance and withdrawal. It is a guest and parasite, never inescapably lodged in any dwelling and always ready to withdraw. Coitus interruptus. "Folgt man der Analogie zu sehr, so fällt alles identisch zusammen; meidet man sie, so zerstreut sich alles in's Unendliche. In beiden Fällen stagnirt die Betrachtung, einmal als überlebendig, das andere Mal als getödtet" (FA 1,13:46). In both seeking and shunning more intimate knowledge than mere inspection can provide, Goethe is the quintessential ironic poet.

Five days before his death Goethe wrote to Wilhelm von Humboldt about *Faust* — "these very serious jests." He had considered publishing the completed work and was curious to see how the public might respond: "Der Tag aber ist wirklich so absurd und konfus, daß ich mich überzeuge, meine redlichen, lange verfolgten Bemühungen um dieses seltsame Gebäu würden schlecht belohnt und an den Strand getrieben wie ein Wrack in Trümmern daliegen und von dem Dünenschutt der Stunden zunächst überschüttet werden. Verwirrende Lehre zu verwirrtem Handel waltet über die Welt, und ich habe nichts angelegentlicher zu tun, als dasjenige, was an mir ist und geblieben ist, womöglich zu steigern und meine Eigentümlichkeiten zu kohobieren, wie Sie es, würdiger Freund, auf Ihrer Burg Ja auch bewerkstelligen" (17 März 1832).

To "cohobate" is to purify through repeated distillation and reconstitution. It is indicative of the importance in *Faust* of alchemy and its paradigms of dividing and reuniting, dissolving and blending, articulation and resubmergence, that an alchemical image should inform Goethe's last recorded thoughts of it. As he contemplated his own translation to a new sphere of activity, *Faust* was on his mind. "Der frühe Geliebte, / Nicht mehr Getrübte,[71] / Er kommt zurück," says Gretchen (12073–75) — coming back, and stripping off earth's bonds as he goes (12088–89).

What beckons in Faust's reunion with Margarete is what he had challenged Mephistopheles to deliver — the ecstasy of "a shared nonbeing." Thus the ending of *Faust* mirrors both the paradoxes informing the play and

---

[71] The word here "Getrübte," from "Trübe" ("obfuscation"/"cloudiness") and derivative forms ("betrübt": "obfuscated," "troubled") designates in Goethe's theory of optics ("Die Farbenlehre") a semiopaque medium imparting color either to pure white light (from yellow to ruby red, as the opacity of the medium increases), or, if luminous, to pure dark (from violet to light blue). A familiar non-technical use may be found in Schubart's "Die Forelle" (musical setting by Schubert): "[Der Fischer] macht das Bächlein tückisch trübe, . . ." Only after troubling the waters does the poem's fisherman catch the trout.

the contradictions in Faust the man, still himself and still separate from the beloved who has him in tow. The idea of separation necessarily inhabits that of conjunction. And what this final paradox repeats and reinscribes are the conceptual categories and divisions that are posited and ironized in a great work that is aptly described as "Romantic."

11: Truth. Paradox. Irony.

Truth

WIEDERHOLTE SPIEGELUNGEN! The paradox of the love-death tradition is mirrored in Goethe's conception of truth and in the Romantic irony with which he shows that any representation of reality that is free from irony only masks it further. His passion for the truth, however, is an enduring flame, as is evident in the energy he expended on scientific experimentation and in his polemics against Newton.

Goethe's position on the truth, on the accessibility of ultimate things to human cognition, and on the faculties with which we access and communicate "truth" rewards careful study. Johann Christian Kestner wrote of the twenty-three-year-old Goethe: "Er strebt nach Wahrheit; hält jedoch mehr vom Gefühl derselben, als von ihrer Demonstration" (FA 2,1:262). Serlo, in the *Lehrjahre,* speaks of "erlogene Wahrheit" as the quality to be striven for in the theater (FA 1,9:677). And the poet in the "Vorspiel auf dem Theater" says: "Ich hatte nichts und doch genug: / Den Drang nach Wahrheit und die Lust am Trug" (192–93). Truth is a prize never finally or inalienably secured. Only as refracted in the mist of a waterfall, the painted panes of Faust's study, or the conventional categories of a culture is truth available to "Erkennende." "Jede Form," wrote Goethe at a young age, "auch die gefühlteste, hat etwas Unwahres, allein sie ist ein für allemal das Glas, wodurch wir die heiligen Strahlen der verbreiteten Natur an das Herz der Menschen zum Feuerblick sammeln" (*DjG* 5:352). Conceptual categories are not transparent lenses, but refractory and opaque with native significance. We cannot simply reach out and grasp *nuda veritas.* We cannot even approach her unless we are aware of the terms in which we couch our quest and of those in which truth reveals itself. "Das Wahre ist gottähnlich; es erscheint nicht unmittelbar, wir müssen es aus seinen Manifestationen erraten" (FA 1,13:53). Goethe's irony illuminates and dismantles these "Manifestationen."

Abstractly considered, Goethe's theory of truth is the Realist one that "the . . . fact expressed by the sentence must obtain in a world independent of mind."[1] He does not suppose that behind the phenomena there is nothing, and he is consistently critical of any theory that seemed to "crop" or adjust meta-realities to one's own purpose, just as he disliked writers who recreated the world in their own image. "Solange [der Dichter] bloß seine wenigen subjektiven Empfindungen ausspricht, ist er noch keiner zu nennen; aber sobald er die Welt sich anzueignen und auszusprechen weiß, ist er ein Poet" (E, 169–70). "Ich kenne freilich ihrer genug," says Jarno in the *Lehrjahre,* "die sich bei den größten Werken der Kunst und der Natur sogleich ihres armseligsten Bedürfnisses erinnern, ihr Gewissen und ihre Moral mit in die Oper nehmen, ihre Liebe und Haß vor einem Säulengange nicht ablegen, und das Beste und Größte, was ihnen von außen gebracht werden kann, in ihrer Vorstellungsart erst möglichst verkleinern müssen, um es mit ihrem kümmerlichen Wesen nur einigermaßen verbinden zu können" (FA 1,9:955). On the other hand, he insists on the truth of phenomena as they present themselves.[2] Newton's way, he says, leads away from the "sinnlich wahrnehmbaren Natur als konkrete Umwelt des lebenden Menschen" into "die Abstraktion von zerlegten, apparativ zu bearbeitenden Naturobjekten, die nicht mehr in ihrem ursprünglichen Zusammenhang geschaut werden können" (FA 1,23,1:1080–81).

Goethe does not claim that there is no God but only simulacra of God or that signifiers had taken on a life of their own and were no longer subservient to the signifieds they pretend to represent,[3] as did Baudrillard much later. In agreement with German idealism generally, however, he regards ultimate, unmediated reality as inaccessible to the finite human mind, as unknowable. "Das Unendliche . . . oder die vollständige Existenz kann von uns nicht gedacht werden. Wir können nur Dinge denken die entweder beschränkt sind, oder die sich unsre Seele beschränkt. Wir haben also in so fern einen Begriff vom Unendlichen, als wir uns denken können, daß es eine vollständige Existenz gebe welche außer der Fassungskraft eines beschränkten Geistes ist."[4] Goethe neither denies that there is anything be-

---

[1] Richard L. Kirkham, *Theories of Truth: A Critical Introduction* (Cambridge, MA: MIT Press, 1992), 118.

[2] "In Schellings Ideen habe ich wieder etwas gelesen, und es ist immer merkwürdig sich mit ihm zu unterhalten; doch . . . was habe ich denn an einer Idee, die mich nötigt, meinen Vorrat von Phänomen zu verkümmern" (To Schiller, 21 February 1798; GA 20:539).

[3] Jean Baudrillard, "Simulacra and Simulations," *Selected Writings,* ed. Mark Poster. (Stanford CA: Stanford UP, 1988), 167–69.

[4] "Studie nach Spinoza" (FA 1,25:14). Baudrillard outlines "the successive phases of the image: 1. It is the reflection of a basic reality. 2. It masks and perverts a basic reality. 3. It masks the *absence* of a basic reality. 4. It bears no relation to any reality whatever; it is its own pure simulacrum. Against this framework, Goethe appears to be at phase two, but the entire framework is based on ocularcentric imagery which

hind the simulacra nor reduces what we can know to a mere index of this reality. Respect for the autonomy of phenomena informs his definition of symbolism and his distinction between symbolism and allegory. Percepts are more than signifiers of the abstractions to which they refer. An *Abglanz* (*Faust*, line 4727), not only (mis)represents a higher, infinite, and infinitely displaced, reality, it supplants it to a greater or lesser degree, while referring to it analogically or as an incorporated opposite. It is because we can recognize limitation that we can imagine something unlimited. The nobility of "der edle Mensch" is like that of the gods ("Das Göttliche"), while their "Unendlichkeit" is confirmed by contrast with his or her finitude and temporality. Similarly, the transitory is a "Gleichnis" of the eternal, the rainbow refracts pure white sunlight, of which each color of the spectrum is a both a vicar and a distortion. "Alles Drängen, alles Ringen" is "ewige Ruh in Gott dem Herrn" ("Wenn im Unendlichen dasselbe"). It is fun at Goethe's expense when Nietzsche pans the *Hinterweltler's* denigration of this world as only an "Abglanz" of a greater one beyond the clouds, "Alles *Un*vergängliche — das ist nur ein Gleichnis! Und die Dichter lügen zuviel" (*Werke*, 2:345), but he knew that Goethe shared his love for the fleeting forms and colors of human life. Goethe said to Eckermann:

> Es hätte auch in der Tat ein schönes Ding werden müssen, wenn ich ein so reiches, buntes und so höchst mannigfaltiges Leben, wie ich es im Faust zur Anschauung gebracht, auf die magere Schnur einer einzigen durchgehenden Idee hätte reihen wollen! Es war im Ganzen [. . .] nicht meine Art, als Poet nach Verkörperung von etwas *Abstraktem* zu streben. Ich empfing in meinem Innern *Eindrücke*, und zwar Eindrücke sinnlicher, lebensvoller, lieblicher, bunter, hundertfältiger Art, wie eine rege Einbildungskraft es mir darbot; und ich hatte als Poet weiter nichts zu tun, als solche Anschauungen und Eindrücke in mir künstlerisch zu runden und auszubilden und durch eine lebendige Darstellung so zum Vorschein zu bringen, daß Andere dieselbigen Eindrücke erhielten, wenn sie mein Dargestelltes hörten oder lasen." (E, 616)

There are at least four kinds of relationship between cognition and reality: (a) Thought mirrors reality; (b) Thought represents reality, but in terms of its own categories (Kant); (c) Thought generates reality; (d) Thought is generated by reality, but not in an iconological or mimetic way, not as an imitation. The last possibility may be subdivided into a variety of forms, including the materialist one of the neuroscientists that brain and mind are identical and the contextualist one that thought results from the confluence of a variety of physical and social/intellectual currents, much as life, mysteri-

Goethe ultimately sees a need to overcome (Baudrillard, "Simulacra and Simulations").

ously, originated from the confluence of materials and structures that were themselves not alive. Marx is not the materialist that the term "dialectical materialism" may make him seem. He does not conceive of the convergence of economic, social, and material reality that yields the superstructure of mores, values, and ideals as a simple, transitive consequence of the underlying material foundation. The platonist option (a) is derivational and implies that the result is less than the cause. Options (c) and (d) imply that the result is greater than the cause. If thought imposes its own categories on reality (b), this involves a reduction, but an inevitable one. Goethe especially disliked (c). All four scenarios are fundamentally temporal. Every reproduction involves a "before" and an "after."

Goethe's orientation *is* broadly platonist: "Wir leben innerhalb der abgeleiteten Erscheinungen und wissen keineswegs, wie wir zur Urfrage gelangen sollen" (FA 1,13:76). The derivative nature of experience does not diminish its worth, however. The "erklingend Farbenspiel" of life is valuable in itself and not only as a manifestation of its origin (the genetic fallacy) or as a sign of some higher signified. The downward vector of the prefix "ab" in "Abglanz," notwithstanding, I see no reason to privilege Goethe's neoplatonism over his evolutionism or to ignore his affirmation of the transitory event, the "Gunst des Augenblickes": "Stund' um Stunde / Wird uns das Leben freundlich dargeboten, / Das Gestrige ließ uns geringe Kunde, / Das Morgende, zu wissen ist's verboten" ("Elegie").

When Goethe juxtaposes "gegenüber gestellte und sich gleichsam ineinander *ab*spiegelnde Gebilde,"[5] it is a compliment to the reader, whom he may tease but with whom he is united in lacking access to the ultimate, absolute truth. Far from affecting a superior aloofness, his fictions are allegories of our common becloudedness. Language, the "schlechter Stoff" in which he chose to carry out his artistic/intellectual mission (*Venezianische Epigramme* # 29, FA 1,1:449), is inherently a "trübes" medium, like the prism, the atmosphere, or a veil ("der Dichtung Schleier aus der Hand der Wahrheit"), or like a fan which both conceals and reveals, affording only a partial and partisan view of the pair of pretty eyes peeking through its ribs (in the *Divan* poem "Wink"). Since the limitations of the thinking and viewing subject must be taken into account, we require a hermeneutic "Bewußtsein" and "Selbstkenntnis" — insight into our blindness. Among the means of self-criticism available to the ironic mind is linguistic "alienation" or "conceptual distance," which separates a statement from its "normal" meaning and either subverts its claim to truth or exposes the scaffolding on which it rests. Respect for truth requires displaying our means of representing it, including the writer's own subjectivity. "Als literarische Strategie," observes Karl Eibl, "dient [Goethe's] Ironie nicht der Entwertung der Sachen, von

---

[5] To Carl Jacob Ludwig Iken, 27 September 1827. My emphasis.

denen geredet wird, sondern der Relativierung der Formulierungsmittel gerade um der Sachen willen."[6] When Nietzsche said, "gerade Tatsachen gibt es nicht, nur Interpretationen" (*Werke* 3:903), he was echoing Goethe, who exposes the hopeless quest for transparent representation, for instance, in the realistic novel or confessional autobiography. Goethe puts intertextuality on display and alerts us to the power of convention and self-referentiality. We must therefore be wary of such declarations as that the disloyal lovers in his early plays reflect his own guilty conscience or that confession is "das poetologische Prinzip" of his work.[7] The act of confessing one's transgressions ironically alienates them. Adam Müller characterized Goethe's method and imitated his love of oxymorons when he wrote: "An gegensätzlicher Kunst . . . an fester Beweglichkeit, an wahrer Ironie, an Weltreichtum wissen wir ihm keinen Meister an die Seite zu setzen."[8]

In observing phenomena we are unavoidably theoretical: "Und so kann man sagen, daß wir schon bei jedem *aufmerksamen* Blick in die Welt theoretisieren" (FA 1,23,1:14 — my emphasis). In the letter to Iken, Goethe expresses his intention to reveal truth to "dem Aufmerkenden," for it is one of his aims to keep the reader alert. This is a reason for his use of paradox, even self-contradiction, suggesting that any truth will be partial, tenuous, and ephemeral, that it must be neither non-assertion nor counter-assertion, but a self-conscious and medium-conscious assertion, displaying "das Produzierende mit dem Product," as Friedrich Schlegel put it, the painter as well as the painting. It would "in jeder ihrer Darstellungen sich selbst mit darstellen, und überall zugleich Poesie und Poesie der Poesie seyn." Goethe's love of paradox is evidence not only of his pleasure in the trickiness of language. It is akin to Brecht's "Verfremdungseffekt," a way of keeping us alert, inquisitive, and aware of our limitations, and of avoiding the deceptions of illusionist writing. This is why books 7 and 8 of the *Lehrjahre* depart so conspicuously in tone and narrational style from the parts taken over from the more realistic *Theatralische Sendung* and why they appear carelessly to ignore the techniques of realism. Goethe not only provides "a picture of eighteenth-century society,"[9] the "Weltreichtum" of which Müller speaks, but "frames" the picture in its own concrete materiality.

[6] Karl Eibl, *Das monumentale Ich: Wege zu Goethes "Faust"* (Frankfurt am Main & Leipzig: Insel Taschenbuch, 2000), 76.

[7] Klaus-Detlef Müller in FA 1,14:1147.

[8] Adam Müller, "Die Lehre vom Gegensatze," in *Kritische, Ästhetische und philosophische Schriften,* ed. Walter Schröder und Werner Sieberl, 2 vols. (Neuwied: Luchterhand, 1967), 2:237.

[9] W. H. Bruford, "Goethe's *Wilhelm Meister* as a Picture and Criticism of Society," *PEGS,* NS 9 (1933): 20–45.

What does Goethe mean, however, in saying that the true is *identical* with the divine? As we have seen, visual knowledge is not enough. "Nur *sehn* [ist] der geringste Antheil, den wir an einer Sache nehmen können" (*DjG* 2:271), said the self-declared "Augenmensch." He expressed his faith in "eine zarte Empirie, die sich mit dem Gegenstand innigst identisch macht"[10] and said that a correct answer to a question is "wie ein lieblicher Kuß" (FA 1,13:288). Faust's love for Margarete contains as much epistemological as sexual lust. Like Hölderlin and Novalis, Goethe is dissatisfied with every relational conception of knowledge. In both love and knowledge he sought an "absolute identity," with no division and no duality. The truth most worth having erases the separations on which truth, in the usual sense, depends.[11] Truth as identical to the divine only comes to a seeker who is reunited with the divine and no longer *is* as an opposed, alienated individual. Knowledge annihilates the knower. For the self still locked in the prison of individuality, truth can only be an ambition or a desire, a blue flower beckoning from afar. What we seek is "Erlösung," release from desire and the escape from self-hood into death. The remedy for "Lieb im Leibe" is self-submergence — "in die ganze Menschheit," in the body and soul of a lover, or in an ontological "Ganzes" — as when the igneous Homunculus unites with Galatee and is extinguished in the water of the Aegean Sea. Whether as the sadistic cook in the kitchen, as Gretchen, as the other penitent women in "Felsbuchten," or as the Mater Gloriosa, das Ewig-Weibliche is an agent of dissolution, an infinity in which selfhood slithers away.

Every fulfillment is only transitory and insufficient, yet a "Gleichnis" of something eternal, both a bridge and a barrier between us and divine truth: "Und deines Geistes höchster Feuerflug / Hat schon am Gleichnis, hat am Bild genug" ("Prooemion"). Bahr speaks of Goethe's "mystische Ironie" and calls Goethe a "mystischer Ironiker."[12] "Ironischer Mystiker" would be

[10] FA 1,13:149. Cf. Bultmann: The "religionsgeschichtliche Schule" "recognized . . . the importance of enthusiastic and cultic piety and of cultic assemblies; they understood in a new way the conception of knowledge (γνῶσις) which as a rule does not mean theoretical, rational knowledge, but mystical intuition or vision, a mystical union with Christ" (Rudolf Bultmann, *Jesus Christ and Mythology* [New York: Scribners, 1958], 48).

[11] "Love and knowledge have one and the same goal," writes Ernst Cassirer, "for both strive to overcome the separation in the elements of being and return to the point of their original unity. . . . To know an object means to negate the distance between it and consciousness; it means, in a certain sense to become one with the object: *cognitio nihil est aliud, quam Coitio quaedam cum suo cognobili* (*The Individual and the Cosmos in Renaissance Philosophy*, trans. Mario Domandi [New York: Barnes & Noble, 1963], 134).

[12] Ehrhard Bahr, *Die Ironie im Spätwerk Goethes* (Berlin: Erich Schmidt Verlag, 1972), 169.

better, as Bahr concedes when he says "Goethes Mystik ist eine ironische Mystik, und die Einheit mit Gott wird höchstens als dichterisches Gleichnis 'des Wünschenswertesten' ins Auge gefaßt."[13] Like the traveler bounced over "Stock Wurzeln Steine" in "An Schwager Kronos," or like the love-driven rat of Brander's song, we rush toward primal confusion — Hölderlin's "uralte Verwirrung." On arrival we may not care whether "Drunten von ihren Sitzen / Sich die Gewaltigen lüften."

Paradox

"Alle höchsten Wahrheiten jeder Art sind durchaus trivial," writes Friedrich Schlegel, "und eben darum ist nichts notwendiger, als sie immer neu, und wo möglich immer paradoxer auszudrücken, damit es nicht vergessen wird, daß sie noch da sind, und daß sie nie eigentlich ganz ausgesprochen werden können."[14] The same principle informs the title "Dichtung und Wahrheit." Goethe's love of paradox reflects a double legacy, that of alchemy and that of Christianity. The philosophers' stone, like Goethe's *Urphänomen*, is "zugleich überall und nirgends, unauffindbar und allbekannt, billig und unerschwinglich, verborgenes Geheimnis und greifbares Präparat."[15] In Christian theology the creator becomes a creature, the fall is fortunate, and the believer's ability to acquiesce in God's power to save is accounted as strength. "The last shall be first."

Paradox pervades the love-death tradition and, like it, is dyadic in structure. "The paradox of a love [for Marianne von Willemer] which is requited but not fulfillable accounts for much of the dual, 'single and double' tone of the *Divan*," writes Hatfield.[16] Like the *pharmakon* that is at once a poison, a panacea, and a love potion, or Jesus Christ, who is both bigger than the heavens and small enough to fit in Mary's womb,[17] "lovers" blending to-

---

[13] Bahr, *Die Ironie im Spätwerk Goethes,* 165. Bahr hedges when he says, "Der Begriff Mystik wird vermieden, da keine ekstatische Vereinigung erfolgt, sondern nur ein Verknüpfen der 'entferntesten Dinge,' ein Zusammen-Schauen 'des Verschiedenen als identisch,' aber keine eigentliche Identität" (64). Later he says, "Durch das Gegengewicht und den Ausgleich der Ironie lassen sich die Bedenken gegenüber einer reinen Mystik bei Goethe beseitigen" (169).

[14] "Über die Unverständlichkeit," KA 1,2:366.

[15] From *Pseudodemokritica,* ed. Pizzimenti 1573, cited in Hermann Schmitz, *Goethes Altersdenken im problemgeschichtlichen Zusammenhang* (Bonn: H. Bouvier, 1959), 207, who, in turn, cites Edmund Oskar von Lippmann, *Entstehung u. Ausbreitung der Alchemie* (Berlin: J. Springer, 1919), 346.

[16] Henry Hatfield, *Goethe: A Critical Introduction* (Norfolk, Connecticut: New Directions, 1963), 115.

[17] "Den aller Himmel Himmel nicht umschloß, der liegt nun in Mariä Schoß." A church hymn quoted by Hegel. From *Hegels theologische Jugendschriften,* ed.

gether in the *Liebestod* are at once opposites and identical. Love and death are themselves opposites, linked in paradoxical coincidence. Like Christ as both God and man, like a straight line and a circle with an infinite radius, like freedom and fatality,[18] or like absence and presence coinciding in the sign, they are both one and double. Perfect being is the death of being.[19]

The signs and servants of truth — language or the forms of the imagination — inscribe themselves both on the subject and on what the subject receives from her surroundings or from the past. No individual can encompass unity or the absolute, only embrace a "nicht-Wissen, das sich als solches weiß, . . . eine *docta ignorantia*" (Frank 474). Such formulations as "Dauer im Wechsel"[20] and "Offenbar Geheimnis,"[21] "im Gegenwärtigen Vergangnes" are common in Goethe. "Freywillige Abhängigkeit ist der schönste Zustand und wie wäre der möglich ohne Liebe?" (FA 1,13:440). "Voluntary dependence," is an oxymoron, but love resolves the contradiion, makes the irreconcilables compatible. "Der bejahrte Jüngling" in "Der Mann von funfzig Jahren" practices his "Verjüngungskunst" on his clients and recommends cosmetics to his friend, the Major (FA 1,10:438–39). The *Divan* says: "Daß du nicht enden kannst das macht dich groß / Und daß du nie beginnst das ist dein Loos" (*Divan*, "Unbegrenzt"). "Im Grenzenlosen sich zu finden, / Wird gern der Einzelne verschwinden, . . . Denn alles muß in Nichts

Hermann Nohl (Tübingen, 1907), 349. The astrologer at the emperor's court in *Faust II* says, "Unmöglich ist's, drum eben glaubenswert." This is a translation of Tertullian's: "Crucifixus est dei filius . . . et sepultus resurrexit; certum est, quia impossible est" (Schmitz, *Goethes Altersdenken*, 47–48).

[18] Schiller's Lord Burleigh says to Queen Elisabeth: "Raube Dir nicht die Freiheit, das Notwendige zu tun." See Cassirer, "Giovanni Pico Della Mirandola," *Journal of the History of Ideas* (1942), 323.

[19] Cf. Coleridge, who "cries out silently [to Wordsworth] in his notebook, 'O that my Spirit purged by Death of its Weaknesses, which are alas! my *identity*, might flow into *thine*, and live and act in thee, and be Thou" (Maggie Kilgour, *From Communion to Cannibalism: An Anatomy of Metaphors of Incorporation* [Princeton, NJ: Princeton UP, 1990], 189).

[20] Related to "der stehende Augenblick" the "nunc stans" of the mystics (see Peter Matussek, "Faust I," *Goethe-Handbuch* 2 (1997): 352–90; here, 384). If Faust asks the moment to stand, if he wants to escape from temporality in a moment of ecstasy, he will lose the wager.

[21] See Marlis Helene Mehra, *Die Bedeutung der Formel "Offenbares Geheimnis" in Goethes Spätwerk* (Stuttgart: Hans-Dieter Heinz Akademischer Verlag, 1982. Cf. "Offenbar Geheimnis" (FA 1,3,1:32–33). See Jakob Hermann Obereit (1725–98), "Das offene Geheimnis aller Geheimnisse," repr. in Zimmermann, *Das Weltbild des jungen Goethe: Studien zur hermetischen Tradition des deutschen 18. Jahrhunderts*, vol. 2 (Munich: Wilhelm Fink, 1979), 406–12. Goethe saw Gotter's play *Das öffentliche Geheimnis* (he calls it "das Offenbaare Geheimniss") in Leipzig in 1781 (GA 18:616).

zerfallen, Wenn es im Sein beharren will."[22] "Was kann der Mensch im Leben mehr gewinnen," asks Hamlet-Goethe, contemplating Schiller's skull, "Als daß sich Gott — Natur ihm offenbare, / Wie sie das Feste läßt zu Geist zerrinnen, / Wie sie das Geisterzeugte fest bewahre." In tiny Weimar, a microcosm of the geopolitical world, Goethe says, "Ich bin Weltbewohner, / Bin Weimaraner" (FA 1,2:661).[23] "Epirrhema" expresses the unity of inside and outside, the one and the many, secrecy and openness, truth and illusion, earnestness and play:

Nichts ist drinnen, nichts ist draußen;
Denn was innen das ist außen.
So ergreifet ohne Säumnis
Heilig öffentlich Geheimnis.

Freuet euch des wahren Scheins,
Euch des ernsten Spieles:
Kein Lebendiges ist ein Eins,
Immer ist's ein Vieles. (FA 1,2:498)

Goethe referred to *Faust II* as "diese sehr ernsten Scherze" in the last letter he wrote, to Wilhelm von Humboldt on 17 March 1832. Paradox is pervasive in *Faust*. Mephistopheles is "ein Teil von jener Kraft, / Die stets das Böse will und stets das Gute schafft" (line 1336). Gretchen's tragic fate is caused by her desire for one of life's highest goods: "Doch — alles, was

[22] "Eins und alles," FA 1,2:494–95. Anglet eliminates the paradox (Andreas Anglet, *Der "ewige" Augenblick: Studien zur Struktur und Funktion eines Denkbildes bei Goethe*, Kölner Germanistische Studien, vol. 33 [Weimar: Böhlau, 1991],57–62). Cf. Boyle, "Kantian and Other Elements in Goethe's 'Vermächtniß,'" *Modern Language Review* 73 (1978): 532–49. Goethe writes, "Unser ganzes Kunststück besteht darin, daß wir unsere Existenz aufgeben, um zu existieren" (FA 1,13:32).

[23] Weimar, with its 6,000 inhabitants, was the smallest and the least significant of principalities, which enabled Goethe to resist, whenever he could, Karl August's adventurism in world politics. Further examples of paradox are: "Natur hat weder Kern / Noch Schale, / Alles ist sie mit einemmale; / Dich prüfe du nur allermeist, / Ob du Kern oder Schale seist" (FA 1,2:507–8); "Jemehr du fühlst ein Mensch zu sein, / Desto ähnlicher bist du den Göttern" (ibid., 660); "In der Beschränkung zeigt sich erst der Meister / Und das Gesetz nur kann uns Freiheit geben" (839); and "der Augenblick ist Ewigkeit" (686). "Dem Taumel weih ich mich," says Faust, before following Mephistopheles into the world of human trials, "dem schmerzlichsten Genuß, / Verliebtem Haß, erquickendem Verdruß" (lines 1766–67). Familiar oxymorons are: "willig gezwungen" ("Amyntas," FA 1,1:633), "grenzenlose Zeit" (*Faust,* line 10173), "häßlich-wunderbar," "dunkel-hell," "zart--kräftig," "ernst-freundlich," "geeinte Zwienatur," "tätige Weile," "kluge Torheit," "Schweres Leichtgewicht," "Rachesagen," "Wechseldauer" (The last ten quoted from Bahr, "Goethe and Romantic Irony," 30).

TRUTH. PARADOX. IRONY.   ◆   259

dazu mich trieb, / Gott! War so gut! Ach war so lieb!" (3585–86). The day of her execution was to have been her wedding day — "Mein Hochzeitstag sollt' es sein." If Faust says to a moment of ecstasy: "Verweile doch, du bist so schön!" he will lose the wager, but gain release from the prison of his self and enter eternal bliss. Ordered to retrieve the shade of Helen of Troy from the realm of the Mothers, outside of both space and time (6214), Faust says to Mephisto, "In deinem Nichts hoff' ich das All zu finden" (6256). "Versinke denn!" commands Mephisto. "Ich könnt' auch sagen: steige!" (6275). The drama *Faust* resolves in the paradoxes of the *Chorus mysticus:* "Alles Vergängliche / Ist nur ein Gleichnis; / Das Unzulängliche, / Hier wird's Ereignis; / Das Unbeschreibliche, / Hier ist's getan; / Das Ewig-Weibliche / Zieht uns hinan" (12104–111).

Paradox has its "doubleness" in common with disguises and with irony.[24] There is unity in duality — a "geeinte Zwienatur" — in every paradox. One does not contradict oneself in saying that a proposition denied is preserved by its denial, as Fichte points out.[25] The truth beneath Wilhelm's disguise in the Count's housecoat and chair is that the pretty young Countess is in love with Wilhelm and wishes *he* were her husband, instead of the older, unromantic Count to whom she is wedded. Truth and illusion also coincide in the Count's belief that he sees himself in the imposter Wilhelm, out of body, as it were.

Hurt by Herder's "spirit of contradiction" (FA 1,14:439–40), Goethe used his own "Waffen der Paradoxie" against Basedow (FA 1,14:671). He admired the paradoxical spirit of Arnolds *Unparteyische Kirchen- und Ketzer-historie.* "Der Geist des Widerspruchs und die Lust zum Paradoxen steckt in uns allen" (FA 1,14:382). About his "Urworte Orphisch," he wrote to Riemer, "Ich werde selbst fast des Glaubens, daß es der Dichtkunst vielleicht allein gelingen könnte, solche Geheimnisse gewissermaßen auszudrücken, die in Prosa gewöhnlich absurd erscheinen, weil sie sich nur in Widersprüchen ausdrücken lassen, welche dem Menschenverstand nicht einwollen" (28 October 1821).

Goethe's fondness for paradox separates him from Lessing, who in *Wie die Alten den Tod gebildet* rejects Bellori's claim that the cherub-like figure on ancient sarcaphogi — standing with crossed legs and holding his torch

---

[24] Before he met Friederike Brion in Sesenheim, Goethe's lips were kissed and cursed by a prior flame, Lucinde (FA 1,14:432). "Jede Weihe enthält ja beides" (both a blessing and a curse) (ibid., 496). Goethe then came in disguise to the Pfarrhaus in Sesenheim (468–81).

[25] Frederick Copleston, S. J., *A History of Philosophy,* rev. ed., 7 vols. (New York: Image Books, 1962–1994), 7,1:67.

upside down — is Amor.[26] Lessing's reply is, "Keine allegorische Figur muß mit sich selbst im Widerspruche stehen. In diesem aber würde ein Amor stehen, dessen Werk es wäre, die Affekten in der Brust des Menschen zu verlöschen. Ein solcher Amor ist eben darum kein Amor."[27] To Renaissance humanists, however, "Thanatos and the funerary Eros were one"[28] — a *coincidentia oppositorum.* Goethe prefers an oblique hint of ambiguous truth to a futile attempt at collapsing paradoxical contradictoriness into a comprehensible inanity.

Goethe may not have worried excessively about how a given paradox is to be resolved. Schmitz speaks of his "geringes Bedürfnis, sich mitzuteilen und bestätigt zu werden" (56).[29] Some unwillingness to make many concessions to the reader is evident already in his youth. To Jacobi he wrote on 21 August 1774: "Sieh lieber, was doch alles schreibens Anfang und Ende ist die reproducktion der Welt um mich, durch die innre Welt die alles packt, verbindet, neuschafft, knetet und in eigner Form, Manier, wieder hinstellt, das bleibt ewig Geheimniss Gott sey Danck, das ich auch nicht offenbaaren will den Gaffern u. Schwäzzern" (*DjG* 4:243–44). To Zelter he wrote that the "Hexeneinmaleins" and the "Weissagungen des Bakis" were not accessible to "dem schlichten Menschenverstande" (4 December 1827). Nevertheless, he took pains to cultivate his readership, a primary motive in his writing of *Dichtung und Wahrheit.*

The power of paradox to penetrate the veil covering truth derives from its ability to combine contradictory concepts in a brief formulation and to inspire a search for their reconciliation. It partakes of the succinctness of the *leitmotiv,* with which Wagner and Mann keep previously narrated themes and events before the reader's mind. Rhyme, quotation, repetition, and imitation (including the *mimesis* of realistic art), serve a related function. Syn-

[26] "Diese Figur, sagt Bellori, sei Amor, welcher die Fackel, das ist: die Affekten, auf der Brust des verstorbenen Menschen auslösche. Und ich sage: Diese Figur ist der Tod!" (Gotthold Ephraim Lessing, "Wie die Alten den Tod gebildet," in *Sämtliche Schriften,* ed. Karl Lachmann. Third, expanded, ed. by Franz Muncker. 23 vols. [vols. 1–11, Stuttgart: Göschen; vols. 12–22, Leipzig: Göschen; vol. 23, Berlin, Leipzig: de Gruyter, 1886–1924], 11:10).

[27] Ibid., 11:11.

[28] Edgar Wind, *Pagan Mysteries in the Renaissance* (New Haven: Yale UP, 1958; rev. and enlarged ed. New York: Norton [The Norton Library], 1968), 158.

[29] Schmitz, *Goethes Altersdenken,* 56. Goethe said, "Was ich recht weiß, weiß ich nur mir selbst; ein ausgesprochenes Wort fördert selten, es erregt meistens Widerspruch, Stocken und Stillstehen" (FA 1,13:54). Zimmermann comments, "Goethe bekümmert sich immer weniger um die Mitteilbarkeit, also um die objektive Rechenschaft über seine Art und seine Gedanken. Er lebt seine Individualität, und ob andere diese Individualität begreifen, ist nicht seine Sorge" (Zimmermann, *Das Weltbild des jungen Goethe,* 1:82).

thetic, synchronous and non-discursive, paradox also has in common with counterpoint the ability to assert more than one meaning at the same time — two mutually exclusive meanings, seemingly: "In dieser Armut, welche Fülle! / In diesem Kerker, welche Seligkeit!" (2693–94). Paradox, however, only *seems* to rank as equivalent the contradictory meanings it asserts. More often it points to a contrary higher truth behind a foregrounded particular. All symbolism is paradoxical and richer than allegory, which is why it was preferred by the Romantics. Goethe said his occasional poems were "alle durch mehr oder minder bedeutende Gelegenheit aufgeregt, im unmittelbaren Anschauen irgendeines Gegenstandes verfaßt worden, . . . darin jedoch [kommen sie] überein . . ., daß bei besondern äußern, oft gewöhnlichen Umständen ein Allgemeines, Inneres, Höheres dem Dichter vorschwebte" (FA 1,1:729).

"Die *Paradoxie* ist für die Ironie die conditio sine qua non, die Seele, Quell[e] und Princip," according to Schlegel,[30] "hence the very incarnation of irony: 'Ironie ist die Form des Paradoxen.'"[31] Irony instantiates the paradoxical, just as a symbol is both itself and a reference to something higher and more abstract. The extensiveness and subtlety of Goethe's irony, combined with a love of paradox that is sometimes just playful, recommends their separate treatment.

Irony

In the "foreword" to the most ambitious of his scientific works, the *Farbenlehre,* and of all his writings the one of which he was proudest, Goethe acknowledges the necessity of theory as opposed to mere observation. "Denn das bloße Anblicken einer Sache kann uns nicht fördern. Jedes Ansehen geht über in ein Betrachten, jedes Betrachten in ein Sinnen, jedes Sinnen in ein Verknüpfen, und so kann man sagen, daß Wir schon bei jedem aufmerksamen Blick in die Welt theoretisieren." But if this process is to be scientifically productive, it must be carried out "mit Bewußtsein," "Freiheit," and "Selbstkenntnis" or, in other words, "*mit Ironie*" (FA 1,23,1:14).

Romantic irony is present in Goethe's earliest writings. In "Die Mitschuldigen," Söller, eavesdropping on the lovers Sophie and Alcest, employs what has become known as a "stage separator,"[32] whispering to the people in the parterre: "Es ist mein großes Glück daß ihr da unten seid; /

<hr />

[30] *Schriften aus dem Nachlaß,* KA 2,16:174; "Fragmente zur Litteratur und Poesie," no. 1078.

[31] KA 1,2:153; *Lyceums-Fragment,* no. 48.

[32] John Haiman, "Sarcasm as Theatre," *Cognitive Linquistics* 1–2 (1990):181–205; here, 182.

Da schämen sie sich noch" (FA 1,4:694). In the *Wanderjahre* Wilhelm Meister meets a painter who has done portraits of Mignon in her native setting, and we realize not only that he can have known her only from reading the *Lehrjahre,* but that the painter's reading is part of the story. When the narrator in "Die neue Melusine" rebuffs his beloved's admonition not to drink too much wine with the words "Wasser ist für die Nixen," he unwittingly takes a bow to the cultural literacy of the reader, who knows that the literary ancestress of this "new" Melusine is a water maiden, although the present token of the type has no marine connection whatsoever. In the *Wanderjahre* narrational illusion is abandoned altogether, just as illusionist theater is rejected in favor of world theater in *Faust.*[33] The *Verfremdungseffekte* of Tieck, Jean Paul, Brentano, Büchner, and Brecht have many precedents in Goethe. They not only expose *as fiction* the fiction in which they are embedded but also erect a fictional construction upon it. Irony is the servant of truth. But Goethe goes further and asks the reader to supplement ["supplieren"] what is given. An example is the word "Stau" embedded in "staunt zurück" in the poem "Mächtiges Überraschen," where Oreas blocks the onrushing mountain torrent, splashes it back into itself and creates "ein neues Leben." This association is not simply "there," *in the poem,* as it were. It elicits the cooperation of the reader, and has the additional merit of saying what actually happens.

As Schlegel's remark about the importance of displaying "das Produzierende mit dem Produkt" shows, Goethe was not alone in understanding the materiality of language and other media of representation — their tendency to distort in order to focus and foreground. Since all lexical and grammatical forms are quotations, they are unoriginal, untrue and "unverbindlich." As Flax says, "the parousia can occur only as a quotation, but to the extent that it is a quotation, it cannot be a parousia.[34]" Thomas Mann notes that even the ejaculations of religious ecstatics are conventional. And conventional, too, are the mores of amour. This is why in his *Römische Elegien* Goethe adopted the themes and verse forms of the ancients, whose amorous adventures he enjoyed reliving or, at least, relating in poems. The more "realistic" the imitation, the greater the deception. And the more honestly its fictionality is exposed, the stronger is its truth value. Bahr points out that "Goethe played a much more important role in the development of Romantic irony

[33] Thanks to Stuart Atkins (passim) and Jane K. Brown (*The German Tragedy*, 18–19), we now understand Goethe's use of the generic traditions of "world theater" and no longer mistake him for a practitioner of neo-Aristotelean tragic theory, striving with incomplete success to make the reader or viewer identify and suffer with his characters.

[34] Neil M. Flax, "The Presence of the Sign in Goethe's Faust," *PMLA* 98:2 (1983): 183–203; here, 194.

than scholarship in Romanticism is ready to admit, and . . . continued to write in the vein of Romantic irony, even after the early Romantics had abandoned it."[35] We are often left to wonder where his bottomless irony stops; an irony which, like Schlegel's, "will not let us relax in joyful laughter."[36]

In saying that theory must be done "mit Ironie," Goethe declares the importance of self-knowledge. But truth about oneself is hard to get.[37] A narcissistic self-centeredness is harmful precisely because it involves self-deception — Sartre's *mauvais foi*. Wilhelm, the "schöne Seele" of Book Six, and the Harfenspieler are all mistaken in thinking that the self with which they are obsessed is their own real self instead of the effigy and surrogate that it must be. Irony is isomorphic with the paradox of love and death in that both irony and the *Liebestod* constitute a *coincidentia oppositorum*. Love and death coincide yet deny each other. In Romantic Irony, too, affirmation and denial coincide. I both affirm and question what I assert. "Romantische Ironie vermag . . . Heterogenitäten nicht etwa im Kompromiß auszugleichen, sondern eher im Hegelschen Sinne 'aufzuheben' oder die Cusanische *coincidentia oppositorum* herbeizuführen."[38] It has this unity in duality in common with metaphor and with the symbol, which both is and is not what it represents. Both linkings would have it both ways, and both mark the point where incompatibles meet and dissolve into one another.[39]

In "Romantic irony"[40] a speaker or an author implicitly critiques his or her own discourse. Ironizing the very idea that irony could be classified and

---

[35] Bahr, "Goethe and Romantic Irony," in *Deutsche Romantik and English Romanticism*, ed. Theodore G. Gish and Sandra G. Frieden, Houston German Studies, vol. 5 (Munich: Wilhelm Fink, 1984), 1.

[36] Paul de Man, "The Concept of Irony," Columbus, Ohio, 4 April 1977, in *Aesthetic Ideology*, ed. Andrzei Warminski, *Theory and History of Literature*, vol. 65 (Minneapolis: U of Minnesota P, 1996), 163–84; here, 167.

[37] Goethe confesses in "Bedeutende Fördernis durch ein einziges geistreiches Wort" that the ancient admonition: "erkenne dich selbst" is suspect to him as a likely trick of secret, conspiratorial priests with the aim of confusing humankind by demanding the impossible and leading us "zu einer innern falschen Beschaulichkeit" (FA 1,24:595).

[38] Helmut Prang, *Die Romantische Ironie* (Darmstadt: Wissenschaftliche Buchgesellschaft, 1972), 13.

[39] "Pursued to the end, an ironic temper can dissolve everything, in an infinite chain of solvents" (Wayne Booth, quoted by Paul de Man, "The Concept of Irony," 166).

[40] Schlegel never actually spoke of "romantic irony." This term originates with Hermann Hettner, in *Die Romantische Schule in ihrem Zusammenhang mit Göthe und Schiller* (quoted in Lilian Furst, *Fictions of Romantic Irony* [Cambridge, MA: Harvard UP, 1984], 30).

made into a system,[41] F. Schlegel playfully lists the following varieties: "die grobe Ironie," "die feine oder die delikate Ironie," "die extrafeine Ironie," "die redliche Ironie," "die dramatische Ironie," "die doppelte Ironie," and, finally, "die Ironie der Ironie."[42] In "Über Goethes Meister," Schlegel notes that the novel's narrator seldom mentions the protagonist without irony and appears "auf sein Meisterwerk selbst von der Höhe seines Geistes herabzulächeln" (KA 1,2:133). Goethe himself speaks of his "realistischer Tic": "Ich komme mir vor wie einer, der, nachdem er viele und große Zahlen über einander gestellt, endlich mutwillig selbst Additionsfehler machte um die letzte Summe, aus Gott weiß, was für einer Grille, zu verringern" (to Schiller, 9 July 1796).

Romantic irony relativizes the means by which the human speaker seeks to reveal the self-concealing God or "the truth." It exposes the perverseness of language and of generic and conceptual systems of all sorts. It thus reveals, and enjoys revealing, the inherent fictionality and ambiguity of art, as when the poetic hero of Brentano's novel *Godwi* writes about his author and creator, Maria, who in turn is the fictional creation of the "real," but here *fictional,* author, Brentano. As in *Wilhelm Meisters Lehrjahre* and *Die Wahlverwandtschaften,* the conceptual framework of Goethe's fiction is also one of its themes — "es stellt sich auch selbst dar" (KA 1,2:134). Goethe's irony shows the futility of transparent representation, the necessity of mediation, our reliance on symbols as bridges to the truth. His narrators are critiqued as interlocutors, yet the criticism does not discredit what is communicated. The play of irony "consists in the mobility that results from [a system's] various logical and conceptual shortcomings. . . . And this play cannot be separated from the seriousness, the playful seriousness that lies in the system's self-reflexivity, in the way it calls attention to itself *as* system and undermines itself, that is, in the implied statement about systems as such."[43]

Irony is more complex than paradox, covering a greater range of shadings in a greater number of directions and dimensions. In paradox a seeming contradiction is easily seen through and resolved, whatever the frequency or the duration of the oscillation between its antipodes or between the surface contradiction and the underlying coherence. Irony also differs from paradox in the greater variety of its forms (which are not always antithetical and may be unstable) and from virtuosity in its zeal to point the way to some honest seeker, often at the expense of the obtuse or the dishonest. Irony does refer

[41] "Es ist gleich tödlich für den Geist, ein System zu haben, und keins zu haben. Er wird sich also wohl entschließen müssen, beide zu verbinden" (KA 1,2:173; Athenäums-Fragment no. 53).

[42] "Über die Unverständlichkeit," KA 1,2:369.

[43] Peter Burgard, *Idioms of Uncertainty: Goethe and the Essay* (University Park: Pennsylvania State UP, 1992), 31.

to reality, especially linguistic reality, but not directly. Irony disguises. Since truth is not directly approachable or communicable, irony self-consciously illuminates the angle, means, and method of the pursuit of truth. Irony pricks and deflates the presumption of those who fail to see that God hides, while confessing the misprision of its own map. Irony pretends to be humble. It does not promise more than it can deliver, but even its modesty is a striptease, feigning superior wisdom and hinting at distant satisfactions.

Goethe agrees with Kant that the phenomena cannot embody essence, or, if essence, only the essence of the phenomena themselves. His intention is not so much to penetrate the phenomena as to mark their illusoriness and unreliability, even if, as Weinhandl supposes, they are the only manifestations of reality. Irony reflects on the human knower, showing that the conceptual apparatus brought to bear on a reality affects how thoroughly and how accurately that reality can be discerned and revealed. "Alles, was wir gewahr werden und wovon wir sprechen können, sind nur Manifestationen der Idee" (FA 1,13:124).

Goethe took alienation into the bargain when he translated prose versions of *Faust* and *Iphigenie auf Tauris* into verse. Any thought cast in verse, especially in rhyming verse, is alienated. Setting verses to music further alienates them, as anybody knows who has sung words he or she would have been uncomfortable pronouncing in naked confessional prose. But even confessional prose is inevitably alienated by virtue of its reliance on the conventions of language: something has always been done to it before it comes to you. Goethe would not have considered writing his *Farbenlehre* in verse, although he easily could have, as his verses in "Die Metamorphose der Pflanzen" or those on cloud formations show. As Kayser observes in his *Kleine deutsche Versschule*, "Zu Versen gehört nun einmal die Bindung," and this "Bindung," the anchoring of a thought or sentiment in a metric scheme, removes it by a step from the representational pose of prose (the *mauvais foi* of prose) and makes it a less *im*mediate statement. A thought or narrative thus "bound" is, paradoxically, set free — allowed to float like a kite or an untethered balloon. Verses free a text from any pretense of communicating "direct" mimetic truth. Their artificiality is itself a mask, and the claim of truth the stronger for all its seeming falseness. Goethe neither views any *Vorstellungsart* as mimetically grounded nor casts his narrative as the truth pure and simple. He does not provide false consolation. His freedom is responsibility, an admission that all representation is *mis*representation and all truth based on convention.

To what extent Goethe's irony is not only a rhetorical technique or a means of argumentation but also an expression of a world view — to what extent it is metaphysical irony, is hard to decide. We have his own testimony as to its rhetorical purpose: "'Aber mit dem Positiven muß man es nicht so ernsthaft nehmen, sondern sich durch Ironie darüber erheben und ihm dadurch die Eigenschaft des Problems erhalten"[44] As we have seen, even (or especially) in scientific writing, irony is indispensable.[45]

"Die meisten Menschen," says Wilhelm in the *Wanderjahre*, "erreichen nicht jene herrliche Epoche, in der uns das Faßliche gemein und albern vorkommt." "Es ist ein Mittelzustand zwischen Verzweiflung und Vergötterung," replies Jarno (FA 1,10:47). Does this mean that Goethe doubted the intelligibility of the universe? I doubt it. What is certain is that he both uses and questions his adopted discourse while indexing a precon-ceptional and prepropositional reality beyond the reach of any story or scheme, and that he does not confuse linguistic with "natural" reality. Con-ceptual instruments of every sort are both necessary and insufficient, always removed from identity with their ground yet arching rainbow-like toward *terra firma* on the far side of cognition. There is no unmediated access to this distant terminal, but the longing to occupy it is inextinguishable. In his skepticism and his longing — what Kilgour calls "nostalgia for total inside-ness"[46] — lies Goethe's Romanticism.

Goethe did not rank it as a matter of great importance that his words should reach the widest possible audience or even that they should be under-stood. "Das Närrischste ist," he wrote, "daß jeder glaubt überliefern zu müssen, was man gewußt zu haben glaubt" (FA 1,10:579). His confidence in the communicability of his insights might have been greater if he had been part of a cohesive national culture instead of writing for the readers of "world literature," the "Gemeinschaft der Heiligen."[47] Had he been born in England, he told Eckermann, he would have become a duke or, better still, a bishop with 30,000 pounds a year and would have lied through his teeth to preserve ignorance all about (E, 715–16). We have considered whether Goethe deserved to be called a Classic in T. S. Eliot's sense of the term, as arising out of a mature culture. This is one side of the matter.

On the other side is Goethe's far-flung allusiveness and the confidence in his readership that this reflects. He expects the motto "Gedenke zu leben"

[44] Letter to Caspar Maria Graf v. Sternberg, 19 September 1826, WA 4,41:169.

[45] "Die Äkuivokation kann ein bloßes Versehen sein und ist dann ein Fehler, der die Untersuchung stört; sie kann aber auch der Absicht entspringen, ein in sich vielgesichtiges, vielleicht paradoxes Phänomen angemessen zu beschreiben" (Schmitz, *Goethes Altersdenken*, 33).

[46] Kilgour, *From Communion to Cannibalism*, 10.

[47] Letter to C. F. Zelter, 18 June 1831 (WA 4,48:241). Boyle writes, "Goethe in his maturity . . . was not writing for the settled, self-confident, imperialist bourgeoisie of nineteenth-century France and England, and what he wrote should not be compared with the works of the great realistic novelists whom those societies produced" (Nicholas Boyle, "Introduction: Goethe and England; England and Goethe," *Goethe and the English-Speaking World*, ed. Nicholas Boyle and John Guthrie [Rochester, NY: Camden House, 2002], 1–20; here, 15).

of the *Saal der Vergangenheit* in the *Lehrjahre* to be recognized as the obverse of the motto of the medieval cloister Cluny: "memento mori."[48] And when Wilhelm, about to sign on as an actor, finds on the stage a veil inscribed with the words, "Flieh, Jüngling, flieh!" the reader, and perhaps Wilhelm too, is expected to recognize this as a translation of "o homo fuge," the warning to Faust before he signs the pact in virtually every version of the legend, including the 1587 chapbook. Goethe relied on a united European literary culture.[49] A privileged financial and social status, his good private education, frequent visits to the Frankfurt French theater and regular intercourse with representatives of French culture, and his absorbing and retentive mind gave Goethe a familiarity with world literature enjoyed by few other Europeans of his own time or since. Goethe *spoke* Latin.

Asked about the bridging of time and space in the juxtaposition of the medieval North and the ancient "South" of Helena and Menelaus in *Faust II*, act 3, Goethe is supposed to have answered: "Ja, ja, ihr guten Kinder, wenn ihr nur nicht so dumm wäret."[50] He was a wistful Enlightener, had weaker pedagogical leanings than Schiller, not to mention Lessing, and resolutely refused to interpret his works. When asked by Eckermann what the Mothers in *Faust* signified, he is said to have answered only by repeating line 6217: "Die Mütter! Mütter! — s'klingt so wunderlich!" (E, 374) He doubted whether reliable representation, therefore accurate communication, was possible. He *wanted*, always, to penetrate to the core and achieve a unity so intimate as to dissolve the boundaries of selfhood and the barriers separating self from object, thus his fondness for metaphors of engulfing and penetration, and for the idea of flowing. Facing the chasm between self and other, he developed the doctrine of *Entsagung*. Like Lessing, Goethe would preserve a respectful humility toward the inscrutability of ultimates, "denn es möchte doch immer gleich schädlich sein, sich von dem Unerforschlichen ganz abzusondern oder mit demselben eine allzuenge Verbindung sich

---

[48] Schiller, for one, did notice. "Die Inschrift 'gedenke zu leben' ist trefflich und wird es noch viel mehr, da sie an das verwünschte Memento mori erinnert und schön darüber triumphiert" (to Goethe, 3 July 1796; GA 20:191). "Vgl. Spinoza 'Ethica' IV, 67: 'Homo liber de nulla re minus, quam de morte cogitat, & ejus sapientia non mortis, sed vitae meditatioest' . . . Vgl. die Losung, die Lenardo dem Auswandererbund der *Wanderjahre* (III, I, B. 17) mitgibt: 'Haben doch lebensmüde, bejahrte Männer den Ihrigen zugerufen: 'Gedenke zu sterben!' so dürfen wir lebenslustige jüngere wohl uns immerfort ermuntern und ermahnen mit den heitern Worten: 'Gedenke zu wandern!'" (MA 5:836). FA 1,9:1490 too refers to Spinozas *Ethik* (Lehrsatz 67). Both editions credit Oskar Walzel with discovering this correlation (Oskar Walzel, *Kommentar zur Festausgabe*, 11:605).

[49] Ernst Robert Curtius, *Europäische Literatur und lateinisches Mittelalter*. 1948. 3rd ed. Bern: Francke, 1961

[50] Eibl, *Das monumentale Ich*, 252.

anzumaßen."[51] The limitations of language and rhetoric are always there, happily when considered from this angle. Complete in ourselves, we may be free of longing, while "unvollständige Menschen," "deren Sehnsucht und Streben mit ihrem Tun und Leisten nicht proportioniert ist" are consumed by their insufficiency. "Derjenige, der sich mit Einsicht für beschränkt erklärt ist der Vollkommenheit am Nächsten," says Goethe (FA 1,13:79). The limitations of language free the poet or thinker from any need for the precise *mot juste* and encourage uninhibited experimentation.

"*Je inkommensurabeler und für den Verstand unfaßlicher eine poetische Produktion, desto besser.*"[52] This, however, can also be an excuse. Goethe once spoke of das "angenehme Gefühl . . ., uns zwischen zwei entgegengesetzten Meinungen hin und her zu wiegen und vielleicht bei keiner zu verharren."[53] But a refusal to commit oneself has consequences for a writer's reputation with a posterity that has been taught to expect greater mimetic strictness than did Goethe's immediate public. Hans-Egon Hass speaks of Goethe's "Verantwortungslosigkeit,"[54] a word that gives strikes a chord in any reader of Goethe's longer prose works. The equally large question, then, is whether Goethe "faltered as an artist."[55] Does his irony represent a cavalier rejection of accountability or an amused condescension toward his reader? An eighteenth-century French or a nineteenth-century English writer might have felt obliged better to harmonize books 7 and 8 of the *Lehrjahre,* for example, with books 1–5, or to tie up the loose ends in the plot and thought of *Iphigenie auf Tauris.* Goethe tosses his bread upon the waters, mixes apples and oranges. He sets novellas such as the "Pilgernde Törin" and the song she sings into the *Wanderjahre,* and does so, one feels, more for fun than for the light they shed on the encompassing frame: "Da kamen Brüder, / Da stand ein Vetter und ein Ohm!" However, no categorization of Goethe as a mystifier explains his purposes or provides a reliable judgment on the legitimacy of such liberties. We know something about Goethe's skepticism and we can see the freedom he allows himself as a writer. The thought suggests itself that the two may be connected.

[51] "Der deutsche Gil Blas, Fromme Betrachtung," FA 1,21:63.
[52] E, FA 2,12:616. Trunz comments, "Je älter Goethe wird, desto genauer wird er" (Erich Trunz, "Goethes lyrische Kurzgedichte 1771–1832," *Goethe: Neue Folge des Jahrbuchs der Goethe-Gesellschaft,* vol. 26, 1964; repr. in Trunz, *Ein Tag aus Goethes Leben: Acht Studien zu Leben und Werk* [Munich: C. H. Beck, 1991], 101–38; here, 121).
[53] "Wunderbares Ereignis," GA 17:557.
[54] Hans-Egon Hass, "Über die Ironie bei Goethe," in *Ironie und Dichtung,* ed. Albert Schaefer (Munich: C. H. Beck, 1970), 59–83; here, 61–62.
[55] Furst's word; see *Fictions of Romantic Irony,* 14.

12: Virtuosity

"SEID IHR WOHL GAR EIN VIRTUOS?" is the question put to Mephistopheles by Frosch in Auerbach's Keller (2201), in an effort to embarrass the uncanny intruder. "O nein! says Mephistopheles with a quick rhyme on Frosch's word, "die Kraft ist schwach, allein die Lust ist groß" (2195–2204). Goethe's (and Mephisto's) power over language is anything but "schwach." Linguistic dexterity may seem to presuppose no ideology or epistemology. Fun is fun. Still irony, paradox, and virtuosity are all dyadic (not triadic, for instance), and suggest a reliance on binary choices, even if God transcends all opposition between contraries. Irony and paradox subvert, contradict, or modulate more or less specific terms of reference, while virtuosity depends on a renunciation of reference to things beyond the prison house of language in favor of play within the system. Many, different maneuvers are employed in virtuosic performance, as in any other kind of game. Irony and paradox may themselves be among the tools and tricks of a virtuoso, as my colleague Gitta Hammarberg has pointed out to me. Any game, however, is self-contained and governed by local rules. It may make gestures toward a world beyond its artificial universe, but it is ultimately modest, foregoing metaphysical statements, or making them only with a twinkle in its eye. The same is true of virtuosity in language. Skeptical of the iconicity of language, Goethe was the freer to exploit its possibilities. Here we let a sample of his virtuosity pass in revue in order to suggest that his linguistic adventurism has something to do with his doubts about the power of language to represent any non-linguistic reality. Like love and death, or Tristan and Isolde, words and the world remain forever apart, however much we may long for them to come together.

In a letter to Herder of 10 July 1772 Goethe seems to *equate* virtuosity with mastery: "Wenn du kühn im Wagen stehst, und vier neue Pferde wild unordentlich sich an deinen Zügeln bäumen, du ihre Krafft lenckst, den austretenden herbey, den aufbäumenden hinabpeitschest, und iagst und lenckst und wendest, peitschest, hältst, und wieder ausjagst biss alle sechzehn Füsse in einem Tackt ans ziel tragen. Das ist Meisterschafft, επικρατειυ, Virtuosität (*DjG* 2:256). In nineteenth-century discourse the word becomes a dismissible frivolity. Wagner and the French late Romantics were "lauter Fanatiker des *Ausdrucks*," "Virtuosen durch und durch" says Nietzsche (*Werke* 2:1091). They were sick, so without obligation, exhibiting an "Unheilbarkeit im Wesen," like Herr Albin in *Der Zauberberg*, who enjoys

shocking the ladies with his careless handling of knives and pistols. No need
for a man who is going to die anyway to take precautions. *Doktor Faustus*
satirizes the German nationalists' censure of virtuosity. The program of the
farewell concert by Rudi Schwerdtfeger with the Munich Zapfenstößer, Berlioz, and Wagner on the program, was a mixture of "welschem Virtuosen-
und deutschem Meistertum," therefore a "Geschmacklosigkeit," according
to Professor Gilgen Holzschuher, a Dürer expert. The conductor, a Dr. Edschmidt, was known to be a republican, thus "national unzuverlässig."[1] Both
Robert and Clara Schumann distinguished between "wahre Musik" and
"Virtuosenthum."[2] Virtuosity is performance without responsibility. A good
virtuoso can be a bad musician,[3] indifferent to the beautiful and the durable.
He or she dazzles and disappears in a veil of mist, like Helena.

It is tempting to charge Goethe, if not with a "virtuos antikünstlerischen
Gesinnung, der Lästerung, des nihilistischen Frevels,"[4] then at least with
decadence, a swank insouciance that, despairing of the truth, indulges its
own cleverness. More justly, one might say that his art, freed from the obligation to be epistemology, can be itself. This would be another distortion,
ignoring both the sorrow implicit in any *Entsagung* and the mystical hope
for higher knowledge in another world.

There are at least three reasons why language affords only a partial and
partisan view. First, the forms of language cast unformed thoughts, feelings,
"ideas" into a preestablished mode. Forms are an instrument of refraction,
like the magnifying glass. Thus are the disorganized impressions and feelings
of a newborn baby compressed into a language and set of structures current
before the baby's birth and received as he or she learns to communicate and
speak. Second, all linguistic forms are quotations. They have been used before so that every subsequent use involves imitation, "the repetitive stutter of
tautology."[5] Since every utterance is an imitation, there is an implicit denial
of responsibility in every claim of truth, an implied indirect discourse. Fi-

---

[1] Thomas Mann, *Dr. Faustus, Gesammelte Werke* 6:593.

[2] Barbara Meier, *Robert Schumann* (Hamburg: Rowohlt Taschenbuch Verlag, 1995),
81:

[3] "Aller Passagenkram ändert sich mit der Zeit; nur, wo die Fertigkeit höheren
Zwecken dient, hat sie Werth" (Robert Schumann, "Musikalische Haus- und
Lebensregeln" [Textanhang zu Robert Schumman's Album für die Jugend], *Neue
Zeitschrift für Musik*, Supplement to vol. 32, no. 36 [1850], 2; no. 20).

[4] Gilgen Holzschuher's criticism of Leverkühn's one-movement symphony about
the universe: "Das Wunder des Alls" (Th. Mann's *Doktor Faustus, Gesammelte Werke*
6:366).

[5] De Man, "The Epistemology of Metaphor," *Critical Inquiry* 5, 1 (autumn 1978):
13–30. Reprint in *Aesthetic Ideology*, ed. Andrzei Warminski, Theory and History of
Literature, vol. 65 (Minneapolis: U of Minnesota P, 1996), 38.

nally, every proposition is only a dim, distorted reflection of non-linguistic reality. There is an inverse relation between any pretense of realism and the amount of actual truth conveyed but a positive correlation between the deliberateness with which an author exploits the artifice of traditional forms and the truthfulness of his or her narrative. The more self-conscious the imitation, the more authentic the representation. This is, at least, good Romantic doctrine. And the more modest claim of truth yields a greater truth than rhetorical imperiousness, as Eibl implies in saying that Goethe's early anacreontic poems in the collection *Annette* are "durchaus konventionell, ein Durchprobieren gängiger Formen, die recht virtuos und routiniert gehandhabt werden" (FA 1,1:783). Greater "originality," however, may only betray greater innocence, which may be why Goethe reverted to the distichs of the *Römische Elegien*. In the *West-östlicher Divan* he affirms his brotherhood with earlier poets: "Und der Wandrer wird kommen, / Der Liebende. Betritt er / Diese Stelle, ihm zuckt's / Durch alle Glieder. / Hier! vor mir liebte der Liebende! / . . . Er liebte! Ich liebe wie er, / Ich ahnd' ihn!" (FA 1,3,1:603). We recall that Goethe's nickname was "der Wandrer."

At its best, Goethe's poetry exhibits the most unostentatious simplicity. Wilkinson overstates the case when she says that in "Über allen Gipfeln" there is "not a simile, not a metaphor, not a symbol."[6] What, if not a symbol of the unity of subject and the object, self and the creation, is the ontological progression from mineral to vegetable to animal to human, and the direction of the reader's eye, by the poet's baton, from far to close, to closer still, and finally into oneself? The elaborate verse forms of his 1797 ballads aside, Goethe is not a creator of intricate structures. Easy felicity, rather than spectacular ingenuity, characterizes his writing. Goethe's poetry is often deceptively simple, in any case, his inventiveness seldom on display, just as in *Dichtung und Wahrheit* the focus is on the world of Goethe's youth, rather than on himself.

But that only conceals his cleverness. Eibl notes Goethe's use of the ancient palindrome "Roma-Amor" ("Roma tibi subito motibus motibus ibit Amor") in the apostrophe to "Ewige Roma" in *Roman Elegy # 1* (FA 1,1:1099–1100). And listen for the onomatopoeia and alliteration in "Die Winde schwangen leise Flügel, / umsausten schauerlich mein Ohr" ("Willkommen und Abschied") or "Noch andres Zeug zischt zwischen drein" (*Faust*, line 7225).[7] Hatfield finds the onomatopoeia of the "Walpur-

---

[6] Elizabeth M. Wilkinson, "Goethe's Poetry," 316–29; here, 317.

[7] Cf. "Da pfeift es und geigt es und klinget und klirrt, / Da ringelt's und schleift es und rauschet und wirrt, / Da pispert's und knistert's und flüstert's und schwirrt; / Das Gräflein, es blicket hinüber, / Es dünkt ihn, als läg' er im Fieber" ("Hochzeitlied").

gisnacht" in *Faust* iconically justified: "Besides actual music, we hear the storm above, the crashing of trees and moaning of boughs, the shouts of witches overhead, and above all the onomatopoeic force of the German language . . ., as in Mephisto's description of the witches: 'Das drängt und stößt, das ruscht und klappert! / Das zischt und quirlt, das zieht und plappert! / Das leuchtet, sprüht und stinkt und brennt! / Ein wahres Hexenelement!'" (4016–19).[8] As he swims toward Leda, the swan's "Gefieder bläht sich schwellend, / Welle selbst, auf Wogen wellend" (7305). There is no art of language that Goethe does not employ with a flair. Eibl notes a displaced verb, synecdoche, zeugma and litotes all in the four lines 10267–70 of act 4 of *Faust.*[9]

As much a "serious" German as Bach or Beethoven, Goethe exhibits an infectious love of lightness. His insouciance suggests indifference to formal perfection and pedantry, what Zagari describes as the "für viele Dichter der Moderne wesentlich gewordenen Unverbindlichkeit und Willkürlichkeit des eigenen Verhältnisses zur Umwelt, zur Tradition, zur eigenen Identität," *in contrast to Goethe.*[10] I would frame the contrast differently. Knowing the limits of representation, Goethe both exploits the richness of language and shows his reader that any "truth" must be tenuous and ephemeral. On the other hand, he regrets the impossibility of unambiguous representation, and wishes he could succeed in a more obviously representational and more lasting medium than the German language. But part of his mastery of this "poorest medium" (FA 1,1:449, no. 29) depends on the ephemerality of the word, its ability to kiss and run away.

Goethe's is a relaxed virtuosity, reflecting the agility and spontaneity of his talent. Gleim gives an illustration from a poetry-reading in 1777 to the small circle of Anna Amalie's *Musenhof.* Gleim himself had read aloud, from the newly published *Göttinger Musenalmanach,* when a stranger volunteered to relieve him. For a while the newcomer dutifully read from the new publication but then began to experiment with a variety of verse and strophic forms not found in his text. Impressed with the guest's "vexatorische Begabung" and his skill at versifying, Gleim shouts out, "That's either Goethe or the Devil!" To which Wieland replied, "Beide!"[11]

---

[8] Henry Hatfield, *Goethe: A Critical Introduction* (Norfolk, CT: New Directions, 1963), 171.

[9] Karl Eibl, *Das monumentale Ich: Wege zu Goethes "Faust"* (Frankfurt am Main and Leipzig: Insel Verlag, 2000), 160.

[10] Luciano Zagari, "Der Lyriker Goethe: Der erste der Modernen, der letzte der Vormodernen," *Goethe-Jahrbuch* 108 (1991): 125.

[11] Related by Helmut Brandt in "Goethes Sesenheimer Gedichte als lyrischer Neubeginn," *Goethe Jahrbuch* 108 (1991): 31–46; here, 34.

The virtuosity visible in those fragments of his juvenalia that happened to escape the "auto-da-fé" of 1766 was a gift in which the young Goethe took pleasure — more pleasure than pride.[12] The two poems written to his grandparents on New Year's Day 1757, when he was eight years old, contain three abba strophes each, a becoming self-irony, and a lot of playful hyperbole. His "Poetische Gedancken über die Höllenfahrt Jesu Christi" (1764 or 1765), possibly written at the behest of Susanna von Klettenberg, employs chiasmus, enjambement,[13] and intensification through an imitation of Caesar's asyndetonic *veni, vedi, vici* — "Ich litt, Ich bat, Ich starb für sie."[14] As a sixteen-year-old he wrote "deliberately strained" hexameters, comically imitating Klopstock and having fun at the expense of Professor Gottsched. He "read to [his sister Cornelia] from Homer . . ., translating extemporaneously from a Latin version into metrical German."[15]

Poems and *Briefgedichte* written in the anacreontic mode during Goethe's year and a half in Leipzig as a student and on into the eighties — Eibl titles the writings of this period "Leipziger Witzkultur" (FA 1,1:25–99) — have a wittiness of diction and phrasing matching the wittiness of their content. The poem "Hochzeitlied, An meinen Freund" (FA 1,1:87–88) exploits the various meanings of the prefix *ver-* in the lines "Wie glühst du nach dem schönen Munde, / Der bald verstummt und nichts versagt." "Verstummen" is an inchoative, meaning "stumm werden" — 'to become mute.' Silence can be eloquent, as the *Schenke* notes in the *West-östlicher Divan* poem "Nennen dich den großen Dichter." The boy will hear when the poet sings, but he will listen when the poet is silent. Talk is cheap, but "der Kuß, der bleibt im Innern." "Singe du den andern Leuten," he concludes. "Und verstumme mit dem Schenken'" (FA 1,3,1:110). The *Divan* poem "Höheres und Höchstes" contains two verbs with different meanings of the prefix *ver-* in a single line: "Ungehemmt mit heissem Triebe / Lässt sich da kein Ende finden, / Bis im Anschaun ewiger Liebe / Wir verschweben, wir verschwinden" (FA 1,3,1:445). "Verschweben," is a cessative, meaning to 'hover away' (i.e. to dissipate), whereas the root verb "schweben" means to continue to hover, to remain aloft and present. "Verschwinden" and "schwinden," on the other hand, are almost synony-

---

[12] Eibl estimates that Goethe must have shown his father some 1500 to 2000 quarto magiore pages of poetry before leaving to begin his university studies in Leipzig (FA 1,1:750).

[13] "Er schwingt Sich aus den dunklen Orten / In seine Herrlichkeit zurück."

[14] Cf. "Ich sah, ich liebte, schwur dich zu genießen" ("Das Tagebuch," line 80, FA 1,2:845).

[15] Meredith Lee, *Displacing Authority: Goethe's Poetic Reception of Klopstock* (Heidelberg: Winter, 1999), 20, 23. The words "deliberately strained" from p. 25.

1

mous, except that it is "schwinden" rather than "verschwinden," which has the stronger inchoative character.

The wit in the line "der bald verstummt und nichts versagt" derives from the contrast between "stummen" (cf. "schweigen") and "sagen," opposed meanings both being expressed by verbs with the prefix *ver-*, one of them intransitive, the other transitive, but with some overlap since "versagen" imposes a reticence or muteness *on someone*. Soon these pretty lips will forbid no expression of love whatsoever. "Versagt" ought to be a synonym of "verspricht," where the prefix *ver-* converts "speaking" to "promising." And they are in fact synonyms in their participial forms, such as when Lotte Buff was "versagt," that is, "versprochen," to her fiancé Johann Christian Kestner and therefore shielded from excessive overtures by a too ardent Goethe, as Goethe wistfully points out in *Dichtung und Wahrheit* (FA 1,14:591, 594). Since Lotte was "versagt" to Kestner, a prize that Goethe passionately desired, or at least claimed to desire, was "versagt," in the opposite sense, to him.[16]

In another anacreontic poem, on the occasion of Goethe's friend Behrisch's departure from Leipzig into service with the Prince of Anhalt in Dessau, a prematurely wise, eighteen-year-old Goethe urges stoicism on his friend. "Lehne dich nie an des Mädchens / Sorgenverwiegende Brust," he says with an twinkle in his eye.[17] What red-blooded young man amidst the trials of a new job is going to deny himself the cushion of a lovely girl's "sorgenverwiegende Brust"? — a better cure for Care than denying its existence, as the aged Faust is eventually blinded for trying to do. Goethe adopts a similar pretense of wisdom in "Unbeständigkeit": "O Jüngling, sei weise, / verwein' nicht vergebens / Die fröhlichsten Stunden des traurigen Lebens, / Wenn flatterhaft je dich ein Mädchen vergißt." Take them as they are. "Es küßt sich so süße der Busen der zweiten / Als kaum sich der Busen der ersten geküßt."

Why will the bride of "Hochzeitlied" fall silent? Because she is struck dumb with love? Because she can't talk while being smothered with kisses?[18] Or because she has neither any reason nor inclination to deny her young husband anything? The futurity implied by "bald," by "beim Schlag der

---

[16] In "Die Braut von Korinth" there is the ambiguous line: "Doch kein Gott erhört, / Wenn die Mutter schwört, / Zu versagen ihrer Tochter Hand" (lines 169–75). As a votive offering to her Christian God, the newly converted mother has *committed* her daughter to a convent and *denied* her hand in marriage to the youth to whom she was betrothed when they were children. Cf., from "Der Gott und die Bajadere," the lines: "Ach, und die gelenken Glieder, / Sie versagen allen Dienst."

[17] *Dritte Ode an meinen Freund*, HA 1:23.

[18] Thanks to John Haiman for this insight and for an explanation of cessatives and inchoatives.

Stunde," and by the parallel with "verstummt" (= "will soon *become* silent") is important. She will *soon no longer* deny him anything. The deceptive parallelism between the transitive "versagt" and the intransitive "verstummt" = her silent surrender in the growing darkness of the wedding night is accompanied by the dying down of the little watchman's flame, which ensures their privacy (MA 1,1:796).

In the later of two versions of this poem the verb "glühst" replaces "blickst" of the first version: "Wie *glühst* du nach dem schönen Munde." Goethe loves the verb "glühen." Pygmalion, in an early experiment on that theme, "glühte schon eh er sie [Galatee] sah, Jetzt glüht er zweimal mehr" (FA 1,1:68–69). Comparing himself with the rat that has eaten poison, Goethe says "ihr innerstes glüht von unauslöschlich verderblichem Feuer" (To Auguste Stolberg, 14–19 September 1775). Prometheus, in the eponymous hymn, asks his own heart; "Hast du's nicht alles selbst vollendet / Heilig glühend Herz?" He adds, full of scorn and indignation, "Und glühtest jung und gut, / Betrogen, Rettungsdank / Dem Schlafenden dadroben." In "Wandrers Sturmlied," the rain-drenched wanderer prudently advises himself: "Glüh entgegen / Phöb Apollen," lest the god refuse to bestow a reciprocal warmth. The compound "Siegdurchglühter Jünglinge" — cf. "Knabenmorgenblüthetraume" from "Prometheus" or "des Mädchens Sorgenverwiegende Brust" — depicts the crackling whips of chariot-driving while Pindar's soul "glühte . . . Mut" [at] "Gefahren." The meanings multiply if we add the parallel noun "Glut" in "Pygmalion" (line 32) and "Wandrers Sturmlied": "Nur so viel Glut / Dort meine Hütte, Dort hin zu waten!" The Princess von Este admonishes Torquato Tasso: "Wenn ich dich, Tasso, länger hören soll, / So mäßige die Glut die mich erschreckt" (lines 3265–66). Tasso's "Glut" must "verglühen," or the sympathetic ear of the princess will be "versagt" to him.

Politzer, who writes appreciatively of Goethe's "Sprachzauber,"[19] admires the lines: "Nun am östlichen Bereiche / Ahn' ich Mondenglanz und -glut, Schlanker Weiden Haargezweige / Scherzen auf der nächsten Flut" (52–56). "Schlanker Weiden Haargezweige / Scherzen" is a miracle of linguistic grace, as is "Mondenglanz und -glut." Compare "Füllest wieder Busch und Tal / Still mit Nebelglanz. / Lösest endlich auch einmal meine Seele ganz." Goethe, notes Hatfield,[20] was proud of the lines: "Wie traurig steigt die unvollkommne Scheibe / Des roten Monds mit später Glut heran" (*Faust,* 3851–52), a reference to his own belated passion, humorously allegorized in "Locken, haltet mich gefangen," with its image of a volcano raging beneath a cap of snow. Finding only a pile of ashes, his beloved will

[19] Heinz Politzer, "Goethe's Sprachzauber," *Versuche zu Goethe* (Heidelberg: Lothar Stiehm, 1976), 52–56.

[20] Hatfield, *Goethe: A Critical Introduction,* 171.

shrug her shoulders and say: "Der verbrannte mir." But let us not overlook the sadness in this Heine-like self-irony, sadness at his own imperfection and a too-late glow.

Poems in a great variety of forms were written for the eyes of one young woman, Friedericke Brion — others, later, for Charlotte von Stein. Only three of the nine Sesenheim poems were ever published by Goethe himself, and these not in their original form. "Kleine Blumen, Kleine Blätter," its exquisite lightness infused with unexcelled poignancy in the last line, both fulfills and transcends the anacreontic mode, coming as close as any poem in any language to the wit and grace of a Watteau painting or a Mozart opera, while investing it with a chaste and "un-French" reverence. In the sonnet "Natur und Kunst, sie scheinen sich zu fliehen," Goethe is effortlessly profound. Trunz speaks of "der leichte geistige Witz" and of Goethe's "sublime Heiterkeit" in the *West-östlicher Divan*. "Über die hohen Dinge des Lebens wird fast immer ganz leicht gesprochen. Das ist Übermacht, Geist, Lächeln der Weisheit, Virtuosität, Altersstil. Vollendete Ironie und keine Spur von Zynismus. Welche Gesundheit gehört dazu, dies zu erreichen!" (HA 2:562). I am reminded of Hesse's portraits of the serene Goethe and Mozart in *Der Steppenwolf,* not unlike those of the aged Chinese men in Yeats's "Lapis Lazuli": "Their ancient glittering eyes are gay." But Goethe's wisdom reflects not so much stoical acceptance of whatever is as a sovereign amusement at the self-importance of young and old alike, a self-ridiculing pose he assumed when he himself was young, as in the feigned pompousness of "Unbeständigkeit" and the hyperbole of "Willkommen und Abschied."

Goethe wrote easy alexandrines in *Die Laune des Verliebten* and *Die Mitschuldigen,* Klopstockian free verse with a "harte Fügung" in his *Sturm und Drang* hymns, and iambic pentameter and trimeter in his classical plays. Wilkinson has pointed out Goethe's use of the figure of *enumeratio* in Faust's so-called "credo."[21] He replicates medieval church liturgy in the liquid lines of the Easter chorus in the scene "Nacht" from *Faust,* which Vischer almost as smoothly parodied in his *Faust III,*[22] and employs such a variety of verse forms throughout that it would take excessive space just to list them. How shall we span the distance between the rough *Knittelverse* of *Faust I* and the iambic pentameters of *Torquato Tasso* or the classical trimeter in act 3 of *Faust II,* or even recognize them as the work of the same poet?

[21] Elizabeth M. Wilkinson, "Theologischer Stoff und dichterischer Gehalt in Fausts sogenanntem Credo," in *Goethe und die Tradition,* ed. Hans Reiss (Frankfurt am Main: Athenäum, 1972), 242–58.
[22] Friedrich Theodor Vischer, *Faust: Der Tragödie Dritter Theil,* gedichtet von Deutobold Symbolizetti Allegoriowitsch Mystifizinsky (Tübingen: Verlag der Laupp'schen Buchhandlung, 1918).

The ballads "Der Schatzmeister" and "Der Zauberlehrling" exhibit *"eine zur Virtuosität gesteigerte Meisterschaft."*[23] Goethe's sonnets of 1807–8, preceded by only two poems in sonnet form in 1800, may have been motivated in part by a desire to master the sonnet form and go one better than the Romantics. Goethe adopted the madrigal, distichs, ottava rima ("Zueignung," "Epilog zu Schillers 'Glocke'"), the terza rima of "Im ernsten Beinhaus" and the beginning of *Faust II* (lines 4679–4727) and invented many new verse and strophic forms, including those of "Die Braut von Korinth," on which Staiger confers the highest prize.[24] A poem with a higher claim, but the same deft lightness is:

> Wenn im Unendlichen dasselbe
> Sich wiederholend ewig fließt,
> Das tausendfältige Gewölbe
> Sich kräftig ineinander schließt,
> Strömt Lebenslust aus allen Dingen,
> Dem kleinsten wie dem größten Stern,
> Und alles Drängen, alles Ringen
> Ist ewige Ruh in Gott dem Herrn.

Here in simple, unforgettable language Goethe portrays the movement and agitation of beings as eternal quietness at the source of all being — "Kern und Schale," center and periphery at the same time.[25] This is a different "Dauer im Wechsel" from that in the poem of that title, which ends with the words, "Danke, daß die Gunst der Musen / Unvergängliches verheißt, / Den Gehalt in deinem Busen / Und die Form in deinem Geist" (FA 1,1:78–79, 493–94).

Goethe is neither shy about trafficking in contradictions nor quick to resolve them. His "Märchen," at the end of *Unterhaltungen deutscher Ausgewanderten,* shows his "carelessness," as does the "curse" scene of *Faust* (second study scene). Images and ideas collide, emit a flash of light, and

---

[23] Emil Staiger, *Goethe,* 3 vols. (Zurich and Freiburg: Atlantis, 1956–59), 2:307 — emphasis added. In Staiger's usage, *Virtuosität* is a degree above *Meisterschaft;* Edschmidt — the Th. Mann character — uses it as the antithesis of *Meisterschaft.*

[24] Staiger, *Goethe,* 2:311. Staiger and Elizabeth Wright like the line in "Die Braut von Korinth": "Golden reicht sie ihm die Kette dar," "for by means of the transferred epithet something of the beauty and preciousness of the metal goes over to her" (Elizabeth Wright, "Ambiguity and Ambivalence: Structure in Goethe's 'Die Braut von Korinth' and 'Der Gott und die Bejadere,'" *PEGS* 51 (1980–81): 114–32; here, 118); also the phrase "'Brautigams und Braut,' wo der Artikel und also bei 'Braut' die Genitivbezeichnung fehlt"; and "'So zur Tür hinein,' was uns als unvollständiger Satz in diesem Stil ein wenig überrascht" Staiger, *Goethe,* 2:311).

[25] Cf. "Sobald der Pol den Pol berührt" (FA 1,2:381).

ricochet apart without becoming reconciled in a single triumphant perspective.[26] Many contradictions are only apparent. Faust's imperious, "Vergangenheit sei hinter uns getan!" (9563) *seems* pleonastic, but acknowledges something still present and troublesome that, impossibly, must be banished to the past. "Wir alle leben vom Vergangenen und gehen am Vergangenen zugrunde" (FA 1,13:20). "Der Wandrer" in the eponymous poem observes that the inscriptions on the stones of the path leading to the temple are "verloschen" — "weggewandelt," in a Klopstockian transitive locution for *vergangen*. Trodden away by tired feet, they remain present in their pastness for whoever can see what is no longer there. The concision of "Ein Hügel hemmet uns zum Teiche" and the composite "Schlangewandelnd" in "Mahomets-Gesang" among other reflections of the power of Klopstock's example, have been widely admired.

Every poetic form was new and fascinating to Goethe as his powers matured. In *Die Laune des Verliebten* he exploited the conventions of the pastoral play and, in *Die Mitschuldigen*, those of the classical farce. In these and other quickly dashed-off works (*Clavigo* in a single week) he eclipsed more than a hundred contemporary practitioners of either genre in Germany alone. Many of his works, like the sonnets of 1808, were *études, vocalises,* experiments in whatever form, theme, or idea caught his attention. No poet ever rhymed more effortlessly — not Byron, not Heine, not even Rilke.[27] Note the triple rhyme repeated in every strophe of "Lebendiges Andenken."[28] Yet few poets have used trite rhymes more shamelessly —

---

[26] "Goethe liebt . . . grammatische Mehrdeutigkeiten, so im Schlußvers der 'Novelle'" (Hermann Schmitz, *Goethes Altersdenken im problemgeschichtlichen Zusammenhang* [Bonn: H. Bouvier, 1959], 60.

[27] See Katharina Mommsen, "Spiel mit dem Klang: Zur Reimkunst im 'Westöstlichen Divan,'" in: *"Sei mir, Dichter, willkommen!" Studien zur deutschen Literatur von Lessing bis Jünger,* ed. Klaus Garber and Teruaki Takahashi, Europäische Kulturstudien 4 (Cologne, Weimar, Vienna: Böhlau Verlag, 1995), 29–46.

In *Don Juan,* Byron irreverently rhymes "phthisical" with "metaphysical" and with "this I call," "burlesque" with "desk," and "laureate" with "Tory at." Heine creates the rich rhyme "ästhetisch" and "Teetisch"; and rhymes "Rettich" with "wett ich!" (in "Disputation," from *Romanzero*) and "melancholisch" with "katholisch" (in "Miserere"). Clever rhymes from Rilke are "Fragonard: war; Grüne: Phryne; Volière: Imaginäre" (W. Kayser, *Kleine deutsche Versschule* [Bern and Munich: Francke, 1946], 94) and "Verschwender" with "Sechzehn-Ender" (Rilke, *Sonette an Orpheus,* 2nd part sonnet 3, *Sämtliche Werke,* ed. Ernst Zinn, 6 vols. [Frankfurt am Main: Insel, 1955], 1:508).

[28] H. A. Korff, *Goethe im Bildwandel seiner Lyrik,* 2 vols. (Hanau am Main: Werner Dausien, 1958), 1:40.

"lieben" with "Trieben,"[29] "fließen" with "genießen," and "Kätchen" with "Mädchen." Quirkier are "Religion" and "Indigestion,"[30] "stechen" and "radebrechen" ("An Lotten"), "Rohr" and "Perlentor" ("Mit einer Zeichnung"), "Gegacker" and "Gequacker"; "Geschnatter" and "Geflatter," "Boulingreen" and "hin" ("Lilis Park"), and the rich rhyme "Pantoffel" and "Kartoffel" ("An Merck mit einer Zeichenmappe"). Faust's "Erdenrest" is as indivisible as "Asbest" (11954–56). All in all, Goethe did not craft many strange rhymes. "Seele" and "Pamele" (= Pamela, "An die Unschuld"), "Exempel" and "Tempel" ("Hans Adam war ein Erdenkloß"), "ich weiß nicht wie" and "Hypochondrie" ("Freuden des jungen Werthers"), "Sarkasmen" and "Pleonasmen,"[31] "Wie das Wort so wichtig dort war, / Weil es ein gesprochen Wort war," "Papiere" and "Skapuliere," "Namen" and "Amen," "entmantelt" and "handelt," "beschieden" and "Sassaniden," the last five from the *West-östlicher Divan*,[32] the very last from a poem *about* rhyme, are about as outlandish as he gets — except, perhaps, for the rhymes in Proteus and Thales' blow-by-blow reportage of Homunculus's quest for Galatee. Thales: "Bis jetzt gibt ihm das Glas allein *Gewicht*, / Doch wär' er gern zunächst *verkörperlicht*. Proteus: Du bist ein wahrer *Jungfern-Sohn*, / Eh du sein solltest bist du *schon*! Thales *leise*: Auch scheint es mir von andrer Seite *kritisch*, / Er ist, mich dünkt, *hermaphroditisch*" (8245–56).

One scholar is ridiculed by another for observing that conjunction via rhyme is like sexual conjunction and that in Faust's union with Helena it leads to sex,[33] but rhyme does become a symbol of unity in duality, and is so interpreted by Helena (9369–71).[34] Like other conjunctions, such as the "süß[es] Wörtlein 'und'" in *Tristan und Isolde* (*Liebestod* music; 2.2), rhyme is paradoxical, holding apart in spatial, consonantal, and semantic difference what it binds together in the identity of the final stressed vowel and subsequent syllables.[35] Goethe sometimes lets his readers furnish the signaled but

[29] Motto Verse zur zweiten Ausgabe der *Leiden des jungen Werthers*, 2nd ed., 1775.

[30] In *Satyros*, FA 1,4:400, lines 7–8.

[31] To Johann Jakob Riese, 8 November 1765.

[32] FA 1,3,1:12, 14, 15, 42, 92.

[33] Eibl, *Das monumentale Ich*, 267. See also 390 n. 11. "The erotic image is important" (Hatfield, *Goethe: A Critical Introduction*, 204).

[34] See Erich Trunz, *Ein Tag aus Goethes Leben: Acht Studien zu Leben und Werk* (Munich: C. H. Beck, 1991), 681.

[35] The Faust-Helena dialogue employs both end rhymes and internal rhymes. "Helena: Ich fühle mich so *fern* und doch so *nah*, / Und sage nur zu *gern*: da bin ich! *da*! Faust: Ich atme *kaum*, mir zittert, stockt das *Wort*, / Es ist ein *Traum*, verschwunden Tag und *Ort*. Helena: Ich scheine mir *verlebt* und doch so *neu*, / In dich *verwebt*, dem Unbekannten *treu*. Faust: Durch grüble *nicht* das einzigste *Geschick*. / Dasein ist *Pflicht* und wärs ein *Augenblick*" (9411–18).

unstated rhyme word, as in the naughty "Annonce": "Ein Hündchen wird gesucht, / Das weder murrt noch beißt, / zerbrochene Gläser frißt, / Und Diamanten. . . ." His "rhyme": "Morgenröte" — "Hatem" in the *Divan* poem, "Locken, haltet mich gefangen!" (FA 1,3,1:87), employs a "Reim-Aposiopese,"[36] the same trick as the song "Sweet Violets" or the "rhymed" quatrain on the glories of canned milk: "No tits to pull, no hay to pitch, just punch a hole in the son-of-a-gun." Mommsen calls attention to the implied reference to the "Buch der Bücher" behind the spoken "Tuch der Tücher" in the *Divan* poem "Beiname," a reference to the handkerchief of Saint Veronika. It would have been tactless toward his Muslim mentor Hafis for the poet of Goethe's narrative to have singled out the Bible as the "book of books."[37]

Students sometimes fail to notice that "Über allen Gipfeln ist Ruh" rhymes, just as they overlook that *Iphigenie auf Tauris* is in verse. Goethe rhymed easily, unobtrusively. As a television comic acknowledged:

> Goethe war gut.
> Mann, der konnte reimen!
> Wenn ich es versuch,
> schwitz ich Wasser und Blut,
> und ich merk jedesmal:
> Goethe war gut.[38]

Translators despair at rendering lexical neologisms such as "umsausten," "Hexenheit" (*Faust*, line 4015 — "witches' race"),[39] the transitive "anglühen" ("Ganymed") or the compounds "sorgenverwiegend," "Knabenmorgenblütenträume" ("Prometheus"), "Kraftbegeistet" (rhymes with "geleistet," *Faust*, 10216–17). Goethe's lexical inventiveness actually increases in his old age, as Trunz observes: "'Silenus' öhrig Tier (10033); Unglücksbotschaft häßlicht ihn (9437); Ringsum von Wellen angehüpft, Nichtinsel (9511); eigensinnig zackt sich Ast an Ast (9543); zweighaft Baum

[36] Ehrhard Bahr, *Die Ironie im Spätwerk Goethes: Studien zum "West-östlichen Divan," zu den "Wanderjahren" und zu "Faust II"* (Berlin: Erich Schmidt Verlag, 1972), 77.

[37] Mommsen, "Spiel mit dem Klang," 33–34.

[38] Dagmar Matten-Gohdes, *Goethe ist gut* (Weinheim and Basel: Beltz, 1982), 5.

[39] Cf. "was der ganzen Menschheit zugeteilt ist" (line 1770): "Der Begriff 'Menschheit' ist da an einer begriffsgeschichtlichen Wasserscheide angesiedelt. Einerseits bezeichnet er noch im älteren Sinne das 'Wesen' des Menschen, die Menschennatur (wie in Goethes Gedicht *Grenzen der Menschheit*). Da Herder aber meint, dass alle Anlagen der Menschheit bei keinem einzelnen Menschen zur Gänze anwesend seien, sondern nur auf alle Menschen verteilt . . ., kann Menschheit schon hier auch die Gesamtheit aller Menschen bedeuten" (Eibl, *Das monumentale Ich*, 67–68).

gedrängt an Baum' (9541); ähnlich ist es in der späten Lyrik: 'auf Gipfelfels' hochwaldiger Schlünde (HA 1:344); . . . So nährt es doch, das Schaf bewollt sich dran, / Die Wiese grünt, gehörnte Herde braunt . . . (HA 1:352); Ros 'und Lilie morgentaulich . . .'"[40] Goethe is equally bold in shaping German syntax to his rhetorical purpose, especially in the free rhythmic hymns of his Sturm und Drang period.[41] "Die Sonne bebt. Es bebt die Welt" (FA 1,1:17) is a case of chiasmus, as are "Die Kunst ist lang, und kurz ist unser Leben" (*Faust*, line 558); and "Bewundert viel und viel gescholten, Helena" (line 8488).

As "Annonce," the "Rattenlied," and the scatological "Erst zur Flasche, dann zur [Fotze]," show, Goethe was no prude. Hatfield points out that in the Witches' Sabbath "deliberate ugliness reminds us of the horror of the nightmare world: "Das Kind erstickt, die Mutter platzt" (line 3977). The contrast between the Walpurgis Night of *Faust I* and the Classical Walpurgis Night of *Faust II*, culminating in a pageant of "magnificent imagery" and "brilliant spectacle" in the scene "Rocky Coves of the Aegean Sea" — "one of the splendors of the entire poem"[42] — could hardly be greater. In Margarete's prayer to the *mater dolorosa* and the variation on it in *Bergesschluchten* seven lines contain three rhymes; linking Margarete and Mary, and promising the deceased Faust new clarity of vision.

A broader dimension of Goethe's virtuosity is in the variety of his fictional characters and in the range of experience and emotion to which they are subject — from Gretchen's innocent trust in Faust to her tragic incomprehension that she could have murdered her own baby, from Werther's ecstatic self-immersion in the wonders of Nature to his discovery that she is a self-destructive monster, from Wilhelm Meister's awkward delight in Philine's coquettish naughtiness to Faust's and Prometheus's titanic struggle against the creation itself. Or in ideas — incorporating a heritage ranging from the conceptual framework of alchemy, neoplatonism, and Renaissance nature philosophy to a scientific paradigm beyond mechanistic physics,[43] demanding that the scientist remain self-aware while scrutinizing the wonders of the natural world. Goethe pondered the effects of an inchoate industrial revolution and not only envisioned great land reclamation projects and new political systems but also studied the revolutions and counter-revolutions that had taken place. He foresaw others still to come.

The limits of language present a challenge to so fecund a thinker and so facile and inventive a writer. Acceptance of how little can be said affords the freedom to attempt the impossible, the license to sparkle within the limits.

[40] Trunz, "Goethe's Altersstil," 1953, *Ein Tag aus Goethes Leben*, 142.

[41] See Trunz, "Goethe's Altersstil," *Ein Tag aus Goethes Leben*, 143.

[42] Hatfield, *Goethe: A Critical Introduction*, 195.

[43] "Was wär ein Gott, der nur von außen stieße!" — FA 1,2:379.

"In der Beschränkung zeigt sich erst der Meister (FA 1,2:389). But mastery can be overrated. "Auf alles was ich als Poet geleistet habe, bilde ich mir gar nichts ein."[44] "Über allen Gipfeln" — perhaps the most famous poem in the German language — was left out of the first three editions of his poems.[45]

Goethe was too wise to think that if it is clever it must also be true. The suggestion here, presented, I hope, with no more than due emphasis, is that his virtuosity is to some degree indebted to his epistemology or, perhaps more precisely, his mysticism, and that there is a relationship between his mysticism and his fondness for the love-death topos. The relationship in question is between a signifier and a signified, the paradox in the signifier amounting to an acknowledgment of a mystery that no linguistic formulation could presume to represent. "Alles Vergängliche ist nur ein Gleichnis"! The coincidence of love and death in the figure of the *Liebestod* informs Goethe's conception of meaning, truth, goodness, reconciliation, and reality. It illustrates his conception of the sign, of symbolism, of knowledge, and of whatever means human beings employ in trying to access such things as the mystery of signification. Virtually everything Goethe thinks and writes about the human and the divine, Nature and human nature, subject and object, self and other, fate and freedom, time and eternity, spirit and word requires that a presupposed duality be sublated in a higher unity, as in the *Liebestod*. The yearning of subject for object or of subject for opposed subject is always for absolute identity, but approximation of this ideal is all that contingent, derivative, time-bound beings can have. Let us grasp, and glory in, the gifts that are ours — the ability to move toward, if never in life to gain, the true, the timeless, the beautiful and the boundless. Perfection is death, says Goethe. "Gedenke zu leben!"

---

[44] Goethe continues: "Daß ich aber in meinem Jahrhundert in der schwierigen Wissenschaft der Farbenlehre der einzige bin, der das Rechte weiß, darauf tue ich mir etwas zu gute, und ich habe daher ein Bewußtsein der Superiorität über Viele" (E, 19 February 1829; 320).

[45] Those of 1789, 1800, and 1806. "Erst 1815, als Fünfundsechzigjähriger, gab er es zum Druck" (Erich Trunz, "Goethes lyrische Kurzgedichte 1771–1832," *Goethe: Neue Folge des Jahrbuchs der Goethe-Gesellschaft* 26 (1964), repr. in *Ein Tag aus Goethes Leben*, 101–38; here, 110).

Works Cited

Goethe's Works, Diaries, Letters, and Conversations

Goethe, Johann Wolfgang von. *Gedenkausgabe der Werke, Briefe und Gespräche,* Ed. Ernst Beutler. 24 vols. Zürich: Artemis, 1948–1954. Cited as GA.

———. *Goethes Sämtliche Werke.* Jubiläumsausgabe. 40 vols. Ed. Eduard von der Hellen. Stuttgart: Cotta, 1902–1907.

———. *Sämtliche Werke. Briefe, Tagebücher und Gespräche.* 40 vols. Eds. Hendrik Birus, Dieter Borchmeyer, Karl Eibl, Wilhelm Voßkamp, et al. Frankfurt am Main: Deutscher Klassiker Verlag, 1985–2003. = Frankfurter Ausgabe. Cited as FA.

———. *Sämtliche Werke nach Epochen seines Schaffens.* Ed. Karl Richter with Herbert G. Göpfert, Norbert Miller, and Gerhard Sauder. 21 vols. in 31. Munich: Carl Hanser, 1985–98. = Münchener Ausgabe. Cited as MA.

———. *Werke.* Ed. Erich Trunz. 14 vols. Hamburg: Christian Wegner, 1948–60. Munich: Beck, 1981. = Hamburger Ausgabe. Cited as HA.

———. *Werke. Weimarer Ausgabe.* Eds. Gustav von Loeper, Erich Schmidt, et al., im Auftrage der Großherzogin Sophie von Sachsen. Four parts, 133 vols. in 143. Weimar: Hermann Böhlau, 1887–1919. Cited as WA.

Goethes Briefe an Charlotte von Stein. 2 vols. in 4. Ed. Julius Petersen. Leipiz: Insel, 1923.

Goethes Briefe an Frau von Stein. 2 vols. Ed. Adolf Schöll. Second enlarged ed. Prepared by Wilhelm Fielitz. Frankfurt am Main: Rütten and Loening, 1883–85.

Goethes Gespräche. Auf Grund der Ausgabe und des Nachlasses von Flodoard Freiherrrn von Biedermann. Ed. Wolfgang Herwig. 5 vols. (in 6). Zürich and Stuttgart: Artemis, 1965–1987.

Gräf. Hans Gerhard. *Goethe über seine Dichtungen: Versuch einer Sammlung aller Äußerungen Goethes über seine poetischen Werke.* Three parts in 9 vols. Frankfurt am Main: Ruetten & Loening, 1901–1914.

Der junge Goethe. Ed. Hanna Fischer-Lamberg. 6 vols. Berlin: Walter de Gruyter, 1963–74. Cited as *DjG.*

Primary Sources, Other Authors

Adorno, Theodor W. *Minima Moralia: Reflexionen aus dem beschädigten Leben.* 1951. Reprint Frankfurt am Main: Suhrkamp, 1980. Vol. 4 of *Gesammelte Schriften.* 22 vols. Frankfurt am Main: Suhrkamp, 1971–1980.

Aquinas, Thomas. *Summa Theologica.* 3 vols. Trans. Fathers of the English Dominican Province. New York: Benziger Brothers, 1947–48.

Atwood, Margaret Eleanor. *Alias Grace.* New York: Nan A. Talese, 1996.

Barrett, William. *Irrational Man: A Study in Existential Philosophy.* Garden City, New York: Doubleday Anchor Book, 1962, c.1958.

Baudelaire, *L'Art Romantique, Oeuvres complètes de Charles Baudelaire.* Ed. Félix François Gautier. 14 vols. Éditions de la Nouvelle Revue Française, 1918–1931.

Bellini, Vincenzo. *I Capuleti e I Montecchi.* Libretto by Felice Romani. EMI Classics, 1975.

Boehme, Jacob. *Sämtliche Schriften.* Ed. Wilhelm Erich Peuckert. 11 vols. Stuttgart: Frommann, 1955–61.

Brontë, Emily. *Wuthering Heights.* 1847. New York, Norton, 2003.

Byatt, A. S. *Possession.* New York: Random House, 1990.

———. *The Virgin in the Garden.* London: Chatto and Windus, 1978. New York: Vintage 1992.

Dante Alighieri. *The Divine Comedy.* Trans. with a commentary by Charles S. Singleton. 2 vols. Princeton, NJ: Princeton UP, 1970.

Dickens, Charles. *Nicholas Nickleby.* 1839. Ed. Paul Schlicke. Oxford, New York: Oxford UP, 1990.

Dürrenmatt, Friedrich. "Der Theaterdirektor." In *Die Stadt.* Zürich: "Die Arche," 1952. 57–71.

Eliot, George. "Leaves from a Note-Book." In *Essays of George Eliot.* Ed. Thomas Pinney. New York: Columbia UP, 1963. 437–51.

Eliot, T. S. "Hamlet and His Problems," 1919. Reprint in *Selected Essays 1917–1932.* New York: Harcourt, Brace, 1932. 121–26.

———. "Shakespeare and the Stoicism of Seneca." 1927. Reprinted in *Selected Essays 1917–1932.* 107–20.

Ferrand, Jacques. *A Treatise on Lovesickness.* Ed. and trans. Donald A. Beecher and Massimo Ciavolella. Syracuse, NY: Syracuse UP, 1990.

Ficino, Marsilio. *Commentary on Plato's Symposium on Love.* Trans. Sears Reynolds Jayne. Dallas, Texas: Spring Publications, Inc. 1985.

Fleming, Paul. *Deutsche Gedichte.* Ed. J. M. Lappenberg. 2 vols. Stuttgart: Litterarischer Verein, 1865. Reprint, Darmstadt: Wissenschaftliche Buchgesellschaft, 1965.

Fowles, John. *The French Lieutenant's Woman.* New York: Signet, 1969.

Freud, Sigmund. *Gesammelte Werke: Chronologisch Geordnet.* 18 vols. London: Imago, 1940–1968. Cited as GW.

———. "Letter to Wilhelm Fliess." *The Origins of Psychoanalysis: Letters to Wilhelm Fliess, Drafts and Notes.* Trans. Eric Mosbacher and James Strachey. New York: Basic Books, 1977.

———. *Studienausgabe.* Eds. Alexander Mitscherlich, Angela Richards, and James Strachey. 11 vols. Frankfurt am Main: S. Fischer, 1969–75. Cited as SA.

Gargam, Georges. *L'Amour et la Mort.* Paris: Editions du Seuil, 1959.

Grimmelshausen, Hans Jakob Christoph von. *Der abenteuerliche Simplicissimus.* 1668–69. Ed. Alfred Kelletat. Munich: Winkler, 1956. Reprint, Darmstadt: Wissenschaftliche Buchgesellschaft, 1967.

Hazleton, Lesley. *The Right to Feel Bad: Coming to Terms with Normal Depression.* Garden City, New York: Doubleday, 1984.

Hegel, Georg Wilhelm Friedrich. *Hegels Theologischen Jugendschriften.* Ed. Hermann Nohl, Tübingen: Niemeyer, 1907.

———. *Werke in zwanzig Bänden.* Eva Moldenhauer and Karl Markus Michel, eds. Frankfurt am Main: Suhrkamp, 1969–1971.

Heidegger, Martin. *Gesamtausgabe.* 87 vols. Frankfurt am Main: Vittorio Klostermann, 1975–(2004).

———. "Der Satz der Identität." In *Identität und Differenz.* Pfullingen: Günther Neske, 1957.

———. *Sein und Zeit.* 16th ed. Tübingen: Niemeyer, 1986.

Heine, Heinrich. *Geständnisse.* Vol. 6 of *Sämtliche Schriften.* Munich: Carl Hanser Verlag, 1968–75. 443–514.

———. "Shakespeares Mädchen und Frauen." Vol. 4 of *Sämtliche Schriften.* Darmstadt: Wiss. Buchgesellschaft, 1968–75. 171–293.

Hemingway, Ernest. *For Whom the Bell Tolls.* New York: Scribner's, 1940.

Heraclitus. *Fragments: The Collected Wisdom of Heraclitus.* Trans. Brooks Haxton. New York: Viking Penguin, 2001.

Herder, Johann Gottfried. *Briefe in einem Band.* Berlin: Aufbau, 1970.

———. *Sämtliche Werke.* Ed. Bernhard Suphan. 33 vols. Berlin: 1877–1913; reprint, Hildesheim: Georg Olms, 1967. Abbreviated Suphan.

Hölderlin, Friedrich. *Sämtliche Werke und Briefe.* 3 vols. Frankfurt am Main: Deutscher Klassiker Verlag, 1992. Vol 2: *Hyperion.*

Hugo, Victor. *Le Rhin: Lettres a un Ami.* In *Oeuvres Complètes,* vol. 28. Paris: La Librarie Ollendorff, 1906.

Humboldt, Wilhelm von. *Briefwechsel zwischen Schiller und Wilhelm von Humboldt.* 3rd expanded ed. Ed. Albert Leitzmann. Stuttgart: Cotta, 1900.

James, P. D. *The Skull Beneath the Skin.* New York: Scribner, 1982.

Jung, C. G. *Gesammelte Werke.* 20 vols. Stuttgart: Rascher, 1958–1994. Reprint, Olten and Freiburg im Breisgau: Walter-Verlag, 1966–1994.

Kaplan, Alice. *French Lessons.* Chicago: U of Chicago P, 1993.

Lawrence, D. H. *Women in Love.* Cutchogue, NY: Buccaneer Books, 1976.

Lessing, Gotthold Ephraim. *Sämtliche Schriften.* Ed. Karl Lachmann. Third, expanded ed. by Franz Muncker. 23 vols. Vols. 1–11, Stuttgart: Göschen; vols. 12–22, Leipzig: Göschen; vol. 23, Berlin, Leipzig: de Gruyter, 1886–1924.

Mann, Thomas. *Gesammelte Werke in zwölf Bänden.* Oldenburg: S. Fischer, 1960.

Marvell, Andrew. *The Complete English Poems.* Ed. Elizabeth Story Donno. New York: St. Martin's P, 1972.

Nietzsche, Friedrich. *Werke in drei Bänden.* Ed. Karl Schlechta. Munich: Carl Hanser, 1966. Cited as *Werke.*

Novalis. *Schriften. Die Werke Friedrich von Hardenbergs.* Eds. Paul Kluckhohn and Richard Samuel. 3rd ed. 4 vols. in 7. Stuttgart: W. Kohlhammer, 1977–99.

O'Hehir, Diana. *I Wish This War Were Over.* New York: Washington Square Press, 1984.

Praetorius, Johannes. *Anthropodemus Plutonicus.* Magdeburg 1666.

Rilke, Rainer Maria. *Briefe.* 2 vols. Wiesbaden: Insel, 1950.

———. *Sämtliche Werke.* Ed. Ernst Zinn. 6 vols. Frankfurt am Main: Insel, 1955–1966.

Ritter, Johann Wilhelm. *Fragmente.* Heidelberg: Mohr & Zimmer, 1810. Facsimile reprint, Heidelberg: Lambert Schneider, 1969.

Rousseau, Jean-Jacques. *The Confessions.* Trans. J. M. Cohen. Harmondsworth, England: Penguin, 1954.

———. *La nouvelle Héloïse.* Trans. Judith H. McDowell. University Park: Pennsylvania State UP, 1968.

———. *Oeuvres complètes.* 5 vols. Paris: Gallimard, 1959 [1995].

Runge, Philipp Otto. *Briefe und Schriften.* Ed. Peter Betthausen. 1981. Munich: C. H. Beck, 1982.

Schelling, Friedrich Wilhelm Joseph von. *Historisch-Kritische Ausgabe.* Ed. Hans Michael Baumgartner, et al. Stuttgart: Frommann-Holzboog, 1976–2001.

―――. *Sämmtliche Werke*. Ed. K. F. A. Schelling. Stuttgart: Cotta, 1856–61.

Schiller, Friedrich. *Sämtliche Werke*. 5 vols. Munich: Carl Hanser, 1960–65.

Schillers Briefe: Kritische Gesamtausgabe. Ed. Fritz Jonas. 7 vols. Stuttgart, Leipzig, Berlin, Vienna: Deutsche Verlags-Anstalt, 1892.

Schlegel, Friedrich. *Kritische Friedrich-Schlegel-Ausgabe*. Ed. Ernst Behler, et al. 35 vols. Munich, Paderborn, Vienna: Ferdinand Schöningh, 1958–2002. Abbreviated as KA.

―――. *Kritische Schriften*. Munich: Carl Hanser, 1964.

―――. *Literary Notebooks 1797–1801*. Ed. Hans Eichner. Toronto and London: Toronto UP, 1957.

Schopenhauer, Arthur. *Werke in zwei Bänden*. Ed. Werner Brede. Munich: Carl Hanser, 1977.

Schumann, Robert. "Musikalische Haus- und Lebensregeln." Appendix to Robert Schumman's *Album für die Jugend*. *Neue Zeitschrift für Musik*, Supplement to vol. 32, no. 36 (1850). 1–4.

Shakespeare, William. *The Complete Works*. Ed. George Lyman Kittredge. Boston: Ginn & Co., 1936.

Strassburg, Gottfried von. *Tristan*. Trans. with an introduction by A. T. Hatto. Rev. ed. Harmondsworth: Penguin Books, 1967, c1960.

―――. *Tristan und Isolde*. In Auswahl herausgegeben von Friedrich Maurer. 5th ed. Berlin: Walter de Gruyter, 1986.

Updike, John. *Brazil*. New York: Knopf, 1994.

Verdi, Giuseppe. *Otello*. Libretto by Arrigo Boito, trans. Walter Ducloux. New York: Schirmer, 1962.

Verlaine, Paul. *Selected Poems*. Trans. C. F. MacIntyre. Berkeley: U of California P, 1970.

Vischer, Friedrich Theodor. *Faust. Der Tragödie Dritter Theil*. Gedichtet von Deutobold Symbolizetti Allegoriowitsch Mystifizinsky. Tübingen: Verlag der Laupp'schen Buchhandlung, 1918.

Wilde, Oscar. *The Collected Works*. Ed. Robert Ross. 15 vols. London: Routledge, 1993.

Secondary Sources

Abbott, Scott. "'Des Dastehns großer Anfangsbuchstab': Standing and Being in Rilke's Fifth Elegy." *The German Quarterly* 60 (Summer 1987): 432–46.

Abraham, Claudes. "Theme and Variations: Liebestod in Tristan." *Papers on French Seventeenth Century Literature* 12 (1979–1980): 39–51.

Abrams, Meyer H. *Natural Supernaturalism: Tradition and Revolt in Romantic Literature.* New York: W. W. Norton, 1971.

———. "Rationality and Imagination in Cultural History: A Reply to Wayne Booth." *Critical Inquiry* 2 (1976): 447–64.

Adamzik, Sylvelie. *Subversion und Substruktion: Zu einer Phänomenologie des Todes im Werk Goethes.* Berlin: de Gruyter, 1985.

Allemann, Beda. *Ironie und Dichtung.* 1956. 2nd ed. Pfüllingen: Neske, 1969.

———. *Zeit und Figur beim späten Rilke.* Pfullingen: Günther Neske, 1961.

Allen, Virginia M. *The Femme Fatale: Erotic Icon.* Troy, NY: Whitston, 1983.

Ammerlahn, Hellmut. "Goethe und Wilhelm Meister, Shakespeare und Natalie: Die klassische Heilung des kranken Königssohns." *Jahrbuch des Freien Deutschen Hochstifts* (1978): 47–84.

Andrews, Mildred Tanner. "The Water Symbol in German Romanticism Culminating in Fouqué's Undine." Diss., University of Washington, 1969.

Anglet, Andreas. *Der "ewige" Augenblick: Studien zur Struktur und Funktion eines Denkbildes bei Goethe.* Kölner Germanistische Studien, vol. 33. Weimar: Böhlau, 1991.

Aries, Philippe. *Western Attitudes Toward Death: From the Middle Ages to the Present.* Trans. Patricia M. Ranum. Baltimore: The Johns Hopkins UP, 1974.

Arrizabalaga, Jon, John Henderson, and Roger French. *The Great Pox: The French Disease in Renaissance Europe.* New Haven, CT: Yale UP, 1997.

Atkins, Stuart. *The Age of Goethe: An Anthology of German Literature 1749–1832.* Boston: Houghton Mifflin, 1969.

———. *Essays on Goethe.* Eds. Jane K. Brown and Thomas P. Saine. Columbia, SC: Camden House, 1995.

———. "The Evaluation of Romanticism in Goethe's *Faust.*" *JEGP* 54 (1955): 9–38. Reprint in Atkins, *Essays on Goethe,* 293–321.

———. *Goethe's Faust: A Literary Analysis.* Cambridge, MA: Harvard UP, 1958.

———. "*Italienische Reise* and Goethean Classicism." In *Aspekte der Goethezeit.* Eds. Stanley A. Corngold, et. al. Göttingen: Vandenhoeck & Ruprecht, 1977. 81–96. Reprint in Atkins, *Essays on Goethe,* 182–97.

———. "J. C. Lavater and Goethe: Problems of Psychology and Theology in *Die Leiden des jungen Werthers.*" *PMLA* 63 (1948): 520–76. Reprint in Atkins, *Essays on Goethe,* 23–82.

———. "On Goethe's Classicism." In *Goethe Proceedings: Essays Commemorating the Goethe Sesquicentennial at the University of California, Davis.* Ed. Clifford A. Bernd et al. Columbia, SC: Camden House, 1984] 1–21.

———. "Über Goethes Klassik." *Goethe Jahrbuch* 103 (1986): 278–301.

————. "Die Wahlverwandtschaften: Novel of German Classicism." *The German Quarterly* 53 (1980): 1–45. Reprint in Atkins, *Essays on Goethe,* 137–81.

————. "*Wilhelm Meisters Lehrjahre:* Novel or Romance?" In *Essays on European Literature in Honor of Liselotte Dieckmann.* Eds. Peter Uwe Hohendahl, et al. St. Louis: Washington UP, 1972. 45–52. Reprint in Atkins, *Essays on Goethe,* 130–36.

Auerbach, Nina. *Woman and the Demon: The Life of a Victorian Myth.* Cambridge: Harvard UP, 1982.

Baader, Franz von. "Über die Analogie des Erkenntnis- und Zeugungs-Triebes." *Sämmtliche Werke.* Sec. 1, vol. 1. Leipzig: Herrmann Bethmann, 1851. 39–48. 16 vols. in 9. 1850–60.

Bade, Patrick. *Femme Fatale: Images of Evil and Fascinating Women.* New York: Mayflower, 1979.

Bahr, Ehrhard. "Goethe and Romantic Irony." In *Deutsche Romantik and English Romanticism.* Ed. Theodore G. Gish and Sandra G. Frieden. Houston German Studies, vol. 5. Munich: Wilhelm Fink, 1984. 1–5.

————. *Die Ironie im Spätwerk Goethes: Studien zum "West-östlichen Divan," zu den "Wanderjahren" und zu "Faust II."* Berlin: Erich Schmidt Verlag, 1972.

Baker, R. J. "Laus in Amore Mori: Love and Death in Propertius." *Latomus* 29 (1970): 670–98.

Bakhtin, Mikhail. *Rabelais and His World.* Trans. Hélène Iswolsky. Cambridge, MA: MIT Press, 1968.

Barner, Wilfried. "Geheime Lenkung: Zur Turmgesellschaft in Goethes *Wilhelm Meister.*" In *Goethe's Narrative Fiction: The Irvine Goethe Symposium.* Ed. William J. Lillyman. Berlin: Walter de Gruyter, 1983. 85–109.

Barnes, H. G. "Bildhafte Darstellung in den 'Wahlverwandtschaften.'" *DVjs* 30 (1956): 41–70.

Barrett, William. *Irrational Man: A Study in Existential Philosophy.* Westport, CT: Greenwood Press, 1977.

Bataille, Georges. *Death and Sensuality: A Study of Eroticism and the Taboo.* New York: Walker, 1962.

Bateson, Mary Catherine. *Peripheral Visions.* New York: Harper Collins, 1994.

Baudrillard, Jean. "Simulacra and Simulations." In *Selected Writings.* Ed. Mark Poster. Stanford, CA: Stanford UP, 1988. 167–69.

Baus, Lothar. *Johann Wolfgang Goethe — Ein "genialer" Syphilitiker: Das Ende einer langen Kontroverse.* Homburg/Saar: Asclepios, 2001.

Beck, Jonathan. "Formalism and Virtuosity: Franco-Burgundian Poetry, Music, and Visual Art, 1470–1520." *Critical Inquiry* 10 (1984): 644–67.

Behler, Ernst. *Klassische Ironie — Romantische Ironie — Tragische Ironie.* Darmstadt: Wissenschaftliche Buchgesellschaft, 1972.

Benjamin, Walter. *Goethes Wahlverwandtschaften: Neue deutsche Beiträge.* Ed. Hugo von Hofmannsthal. 1924–25; reprint, Frankfurt: Insel, 1964.

Bennett, Benjamin. *Goethe's Theory of Poetry: "Faust" and the Regeneration of Language.* Ithaca, NY: Cornell UP, 1986.

———. "Goethe's *Werther:* Double Perspective and the Game of Life." *The German Quarterly* 53 (1980): 64–81. Reprint in Bennett, *Goethe as Woman.* Detroit, MI: Wayne State UP, 2001. 43–62.

———. "Prometheus and Saturn: The Three versions of *Götz von Berlichingen.*" *The German Quarterly* 58 (1985): 335–47. Reprint in Bennett, *Goethe as Woman,* 83–103.

Bentley, Greg. "Melancholy, Madness, and Syphilis in *Hamlet.*" *Hamlet Studies* 6 (1984): 75–80.

Bentley, Greg W. *Shakespeare and the New Disease: The Dramatic Function of Syphilis in Troilus and Cressida, Measure for Measure, and Timon of Athens.* New York: Peter Lang, 1989.

Benwell, Gwen, and Arthur Waugh. *Sea Enchantress: The Tale of the Mermaid and Her Kin.* 1961; reprint, New York: Citadel: 1965.

Berghahn, Klaus L. "Das Andere der Klassik: von der 'Klassik-Legende' zur jüngsten Klassik-Diskussion." *Goethe Yearbook* 6 (1992): 1–27.

Bettelheim, Anton. *Beaumarchais: Eine Biographie.* Frankfurt, Rütten & Loening, 1886.

Beutler, Ernst. "'Der König in Thule' und die Dichtungen von der 'Lorelay.'" In Beutler, *Essays um Goethe.* Wiesbaden: Dieterich, 1947. 307–69. Reprint, Frankfurt am Main: Insel, 1995. 333–88.

Bijvoet, Maya C. *Liebestod: The Function and Meaning of the Double Love-Death.* New York and London: Garland, 1988.

Blackall, Eric A. *The Emergence of German as a Literary Language 1700–1775.* Cambridge, UK: Cambridge UP, 1959.

———. *Goethe and the Novel.* Ithaca, NY: Cornell UP, 1976.

Blanckenburg, Friedrich von. *Versuch über den Roman.* Leipzig und Liegnitz: David Siegerts Wittwe, 1774. Reprint, ed. Eberhard Lämmert. Stuttgart: Metzler, 1965.

Blessin, Stefan. *Die Romane Goethes.* Königstein/Ts: Athenäum, 1979.

Bloch, R. Howard. *Medieval Misogyny and the Invention of Western Romantic Love.* Chicago: U of Chicago P, 1991.

Bloom, Harold. *The Anxiety of Influence.* Oxford UP, 1973.

Blumenthal, Hermann. *Zeitgenössische Rezensionen und Urteile über Goethes "Götz" und "Werther."* Berlin: Junker und Dünnhaupt, 1935.

Bode, Wilhelm. *Goethe in vertraulichen Briefen seiner Zeitgenossen.* 3 vols. 1917; new ed. Berlin: Aufbau, 1979.

Bohm, Arnd. "The Tell-Tale Chalice: 'Es war ein König in Thule' and *Orlando Furioso.*" *Monatshefte* 92,1 (2000): 20–34.

———. "Typology and History in the 'Rattenlied' (*Faust I*)." *Goethe Yearbook* 10 (2001): 65–83.

Böhm, Wilhelm. *Goethes Faust in neuer Deutung.* Cologne: E. A. Seemann, 1949.

Bohning, Elizabeth E. "The Meaning of Death: A Topical Approach to German Literature." *Eighteenth Century Life* 5.iii (1979): 21–27.

Bonds, Mark. "Die Funktion des 'Hamlet'-Motivs in 'Wilhelm Meisters Lehrjahre.'" *Goethe Jahrbuch* 96 (1979): 101–10.

Boney, Elaine E. "Love's Door to Death in Rilke's Cornet and Other Works." *Modern Austrian Literature* 10 (1977): 18–30.

Booth, Wayne C. *A Rhetoric of Irony.* Chicago and London: U of Chicago P, 1974.

Borch-Jacobsen, Mikkel. "Little Brother, Little Sister," a review of *Mad Men and Medusas: Reclaiming Hysteria and the Effects of Sibling Relationships on the Human Condition* by Juliet Mitchell. *London Review of Books* 23 (24 May 2001).

Bordo, Susan. "The Cartesian Masculinization of Thought." *Signs* 11 (1986): 439–56. Rev. as "The Cartesian Masculinization of Thought and the Seventeenth-Century Flight from the Feminine." In *The Flight to Objectivity: Essays on Cartesianism and Culture.* Albany: SUNY Press, 1987. 97–118.

Bormann, Alexander von. "Erlkönig." In *Goethe-Handbuch.* Vol. 1. Stuttgart, Weimar: Metzler, 1996. 212–17.

Boyd, James. *Goethe's Knowledge of English Literature.* 1932; reprint, New York: Haskell House, 1973.

———. *Notes to Goethe's Poems.* 2 vols. Oxford: Basil Blackwell, 1944 & 1949.

Boyle, Nicholas. *Goethe: The Poet and the Age.* Vol. 1: *The Poetry of Desire (1749–1790).* Vol. 2: *Revolution and Renunciation (1790–1803).* Oxford: Clarendon Press, 1991, 2000.

Boyle, Nicholas, and John Guthrie, eds. "Introduction: Goethe and England; England and Goethe." In *Goethe and the English-Speaking World: Essays from the Cambridge Symposium for His 250th Anniversary.* Rochester, NY: Camden House, 2002. 1–20.

Brady, Patrick. "Manifestations of Eros and Thanatos in L'etranger." *Twentieth Century Literature* 20 (1974): 183–88.

Brandt, Helmut. "Goethes Sesenheimer Gedichte als lyrischer Neubeginn." *Goethe Jahrbuch* 108 (1991): 31–46.

Breuer, Dieter. "Goethes christliche Mythologie. Zur Schlußszene des 'Faust.'" *Jahrbuch des Wiener Goethe-Vereins* 84/85 (1980/81). 7–24.

Bronfen, Elisabeth. *Over Her Dead Body*. New York: Routledge, 1992.

Brosé, Claudia. "Park und Garten in Goethes *Wahlverwandtschaften*." In Wolfgang Baumgarten, ed., *Park und Garten im 18. Jahrhundert*. Heidelberg: Carl Winter, 1978. 125–29.

Brown, Jane K. *Faust: Theater of the World*. New York: Twayne, 1992.

———. *Goethe's "Faust": The German Tragedy*. Ithaca: Cornell UP, 1986.

———. "The Theatrical Mission of the *Lehrjahre*." *Goethe's Narrative Fiction*. 69–84.

Brown, Norman O. *Love's Body*. New York: Random House, 1966.

Browning, Robert M. *German Poetry: A Critical Anthology* (New York: Appleton-Century-Crofts, 1962.

Bruford, W. H. "Goethe's *Wilhelm Meister* as a Picture and Criticism of Society." *PEGS* N.S. 9 (1933): 20–45.

Buck, Theo. "Goethes 'Ginkgo [sic] biloba.'" *Études Germaniques*. Année 53. Paris 1998. No. 2: 277–90.

Bultmann, Rudolf. *Jesus Christ and Mythology*. New York: Scribners, 1958.

Burdach, Konrad. "Anmerkungen." *Goethes Sämtliche Werke. Jubiläumsausgabe*. Vol. 5. Stuttgart: Cotta, c. 1904.

Burgard, Peter J. *Idioms of Uncertainty: Goethe and the Essay*. University Park: Pennsylvania State UP, 1992.

Burschell, Friedrich. *Friedrich Schiller: Mit Selbstzeugnissen und Bildokumenten*. Hamburg: Rowohlt, 1958.

Butler, E. M. "Pandits and Pariahs." In *German Studies Presented to L. A. Willoughby*. Oxford: Basil Blackwell, 1952. 26–51.

Cassirer, Ernst. *The Individual and the Cosmos in Renaissance Philosophy*. Trans. Mario Domandi. New York: Barnes & Noble, 1963.

Castle, Eduard. "*Stella:* Ein Schauspiel für Liebende." 1924. Reprint in *Jahrbuch des Wiener Goethe-Vereins* 73 (1969): 125–46.

Chasseguet-Smirgel, Janine. "Vorwort" to Peter Zagermann, *Eros und Thanatos*. Darmstadt: Wissenschaftliche Buchgesellschaft, 1988, IX–XIX.

Chodorow, Nancy. *The Reproduction of Mothering: Psychoanalysis and the Sociology of Gender*. Berkeley: U of California P, 1978.

Churchland, Paul M. and Patricia S. Churchland. *On the Contrary: Critical Essays, 1987–1997.* Cambridge, MA: Bradford/MIT Press, 1998.

Cirlot, J. E. *A Dictionary of Symbols.* Trans. Jack Sage. New York: Philosophical Library, 1962.

Clark, Robert T., Jr. "The Psychological Framework of Goethe's Werther." *The Journal of English and Germanic Philology* 46 (1947): 273–78.

Conrad, Peter. *A Song of Love and Death: The Meaning of Opera.* New York: Poseidon, 1987.

Conway, J. F. "Syphilis and Bronzino's London Allegory." *Journal of the Warburg and Courtauld Institutes* 49 (1986): 250–55.

Copleston, Frederick. *A History of Philosophy.* Vol. 7,1. New York: Image Books, 1962–1994.

Curtius, Ernst Robert. *Europäische Literatur und lateinisches Mittelalter.* 1948. 3rd ed. Bern: Francke, 1961.

Danzel, Theodor Wilhelm. "Shakespeare und noch immer kein Ende." 1850. Reprint in *Zur Literatur und Philosophie der Goethezeit.* Ed. Hans Mayer. Stuttgart: Metzler, 1962. 247–85.

de Man, Paul. "The Concept of Irony." Paper presented at Columbus, Ohio, 4 April 1977. Published in *Aesthetic Ideology.* Ed. Andrzej Warminski. Theory and History of Literature, vol. 65. Minneapolis: U of Minnesota P, 1996. 163–84.

———. "The Epistemology of Metaphor." *Critical Inquiry* 5, 1 (autumn 1978): 13–30. Reprint in *Aesthetic Ideology.* 34–50.

———. "Intentional Structure of the Romantic Image." In *Romanticism and Consciousness.* Ed. Harold Bloom. New York: Norton, 1970. 65–77. Reprint in Paul de Man, *The Rhetoric of Romanticism.* New York: Columbia UP, 1984. 1–17.

———. "The Rhetoric of Temporality." In *Blindness and Insight: Essays in the Rhetoric of Contemporary Criticism.* 2nd, rev. ed. Minneapolis: U of Minnesota P, 1983. 187–228.

Demetz, Peter. "The Elm and the Vine: Notes Toward the History of a Marriage Topos." *PMLA* 73 (1958): 521–32.

Derrida, Jacques. *Dissemination.* Trans. Barbara Johnson. Chicago: U of Chicago P, 1981.

———. *Of Grammatology.* Trans. Gayatri Chakravorty Spivak. Baltimore: The Johns Hopkins UP, 1974.

———. *Specters of Marx: The State of the Debt, The Work of Mourning, and the New International.* New York and London: Routledge, 1994.

Die deutsche Lyrik: Form und Geschichte. Ed. Benno von Wiese. Düsseldorf: August Bagel Verlag, 1964.

Diamond, William. "Wilhelm Meisters' Interpretation of Hamlet." *Modern Philology* 23 (1925–26): 89–101.

Diez, Max. "The Principle of the Dominant Metaphor in Goethe's *Werther.*" *PMLA* 51 (1936): 821–41; 985–1006.

Dijkstra, Bram. *Evil Sisters: The Threat of Female Sexuality in Twentieth-Century Culture.* New York: Henry Holt, 1996.

Dinnerstein, Dorothy. *The Mermaid and the Minotaur: Sexual Arrangements and Human Malaise.* New York: Harper, 1976. Harper Colophon, 1977.

Diski, Jenny. "Oh, Andrea Dworkin." *London Review of Books* 23, 7 (6 September 2001): 11–12.

Doane, Mary Ann. *Femmes Fatales: Feminism, Film Theory, Psychoanalysis.* New York and London: Routledge, 1991.

Dobbek, Wilhelm. "Die coincidentia oppositorum als Prinzip der Weltdeutung bei J. G. Herder wie in seiner Zeit." *Herder Studien.* Ed. Walter Wiora with Hans Dietrich Irmscher. Würzburg: Holzner. Vol. 10 (1960): 16–47.

Donovan, Josephine. "Toward a Women's Poetics." *Tulsa Studies in Women's Literature* 3 (1984): 99–110.

Drux, Rudolf. "Ganymed," *Goethe-Handbuch.* Vol. 1. 115–18.

———. "'Wie reimt sich Lieb und Tod zusammen?': Gestalten und Wandlungen einer Motivkombination in der barocken Lyrik." *Der Deutschunterricht* 37.5 (1985): 25–37.

Dülmen, Richard van. *Der Geheimbund der Illuminaten: Darstellung, Analyse, Dokumentation.* Stuttgart-Bad Cannstatt: Frommann-Holzboog, 1975.

Dye, Robert Ellis. "The Easter Cantata and the Idea of Mediation in Goethe's Faust." *PMLA* 92 (1977): 963–76.

———."Man and God in Goethe's Werther." *Symposium* 29 (1975): 314–27.

———. "Werther's Lotte: Views of the Other in Goethe's First Novel." *JEGP* 87 (1988): 492–506.

Eagleton, Terry. *The Idea of Culture.* Oxford: Blackwell, 2000.

———. *Literary Theory: An Introduction.* 2nd ed. Minneapolis: U of Minnesota P, 1996.

Eibl, Karl. "Consensus: Eine Denkfigur des 18. Jahrhunderts als Kompositionsprinzip Goethescher Gedichtsammlungen." In *Insel-Almanach auf das Jahr 1999: Johann Wolfgang Goethe. Zum 250. Geburtstag.* Frankfurt am Main and Leipzig: Insel, 1998. 93–112.

———. *Das monumentale Ich: Wege zu Goethes "Faust."* Frankfurt am Main & Leipzig: Insel Taschenbuch, 2000.

Eichner, Hans. "Zur Deutung von 'Wilhelm Meisters Lehrjahren.'" *Jahrbuch des Freien Deutschen Hochstifts* (1966): 165–96.

Eissler, K. R. *Goethe: A Psychoanalytic Study 1775–1786*. 2 vols. Detroit: Wayne State UP, 1963.

Eliade, Mircea. *The Forge and The Crucible*. Trans. Stephen Corrin. 1962; reprint, New York: Harper Torchbook: 1971.

Eliot, T. S. *Selected Essays 1917–1932*. New York: Harcourt, Brace and Co., 1932.

———. "Shakespeare and the Stoicism of Seneca." 1927. Reprint in *Selected Essays*. 3rd, rev. enlarged ed. London: Faber, 1951. 126–40.

Emrich, Wilhelm. "Symbolinterpretation und Mythenforschung." 1953; reprint in *Protest und Verheißung*. Frankfurt am Main: Athenäum, 1963. 67–94.

Ennemoser, Maria. *Goethes magische Balladen*. U of Münster P, 1940.

Ermann, Kurt. *Goethes Shakespeare-Bild*. Tübingen: Niemeyer, 1983.

Eschenburg, Barbara. *Der Kampf der Geschlechter: Der neue Mythos in der Kunst 1850–1930*. Ed. Helmut Friedel. Munich: Lenbachhaus; Cologne: DuMont Buchverlag, 1995.

Faber, M. D. "The Suicide of Young Werther." *Psychoanalytic Review* 60 (1973): 239–76.

Fairley, Barker. "Nietzsche and Goethe." *Bulletin of the John Rylands University Library*. Manchester, UK: The Library, vol. 18 (1934). 298–314.

Feise, Ernst. "Die Gestaltung von Goethes 'Braut von Korinth.'" *Modern Language Notes* 76,2 (1961): 150–54.

———. "Goethe's Werther als nervöser Charakter." *The Germanic Review* 1 (1926): 185–253.

———. "Gotthilf Heinrich Schubert und Goethes 'Selige Sehnsucht.'" *Modern Language Notes* 59 (1944): 369–74.

Fetzer, John Francis. "Schatten ohne Frau: Marginalia on a *Werther* Motif." *The Germanic Review* 46 (1971): 87–94.

Ficino, Marsilio. *Commentary on Plato's 'Symposium' on Love*. Trans. Sears Jayne. Dallas, TX: Spring Publications, 1985.

Fiedler, Leslie. *Love and Death in the American Novel*. 1960; revised edition, New York: Stein and Day, 1966.

Fischer, Kuno. *Shakespeares Hamlet*. Heidelberg: Carl Winter, 1896.

Flax, Neil M. *Approaches to Teaching Goethe's "Faust."* Ed. Douglas J. McMillan New York: MLA, 1987.

———. "The Presence of the Sign in Goethe's Faust." *PMLA* 98:2 (1983): 183–203.

Focke, Alfred. *Liebe und Tod: Versuch einer Deutung und Auseinandersetzung mit Rainer Maria Rilke.* 1885; reprint, Vienna: Herder, 1948.

Foucault, Michel. *The Order of Things.* (English translation of *Les Mots et les choses,* 1966.) London: Tavistock, 1970.

Fougères, Michel. *La liebestod dans le roman francois, anglais et allemand au XVIIIe Siecle.* Ottowa, Canada: Naaman, 1974.

Fowler, Alastair. "The Future of Genre Theory: Functions and Constructional Types." In *The Future of Literary Theory.* Ed. Ralph Cohen. New York: Routledge, 1989. 291–303.

Fowlie, Wallace. *Love in Literature.* Bloomington: Indiana UP, 1960.

Frank, Manfred. *Selbstbewußtsein und Selbsterkenntnis.* Stuttgart: Reclam, 1991.

———. *Selbstbewußtseinstheorien von Fichte bis Sartre.* Ed. Manfred Frank. Frankfurt am Main: Suhrkamp, 1991.

———. *Die Unhintergehbarkeit von Individualität.* Frankfurt am Main: Suhrkamp, 1986.

———. *Was ist Neostrukturalismus?* Frankfurt am Main: Suhrkamp, 1984.

———. *What is Neostructuralism?* Trans. Sabine Wilke & Richard Gray. Minneapolis: U of Minnesota P, 1989.

Friedenthal, Richard. *Goethe: Sein Leben und Seine Zeit.* Munich: R. Piper, 1963.

Friess, Ursula. *Buhlerin und Zauberin: Eine Untersuchung zur deutschen Literatur des 18. Jahrhunderts.* Munich: Wilhelm Fink, 1970.

Fritz, Horst. "Die Dämonisierung des Erotischen in der Literatur des Fin de Siècle." *Fin de siècle: Zu Literatur und Kunst der Jahrhundertwende.* Ed. Roger Bauer et al. Frankfurt am Main: Klostermann, 1977. 442–64.

Fromm, Erich. *The Art of Loving.* New York: Harper and Row, 1956.

Furst, Lilian. *Fictions of Romantic Irony.* Cambridge, MA: Harvard UP, 1984.

Gargam, Georges. *L'Amour et la Mort.* Paris: Editions du Seuil, 1959.

Gilman, Sander L. "Black Bodies, White Bodies: Toward an Iconography of Female Sexuality in Late Nineteenth-Century Art, Medicine, and Literature." *Critical Inquiry* 12,1 (1985): 204–42.

———. *Disease and Representation: Images of Illness from Madness to AIDS.* Ithaca: Cornell UP, 1988.

Gilmore, David. *Misogyny: The Male Malady,* U of Pennsylvania P, 2001.

Goethe und die Tradition. Ed. Hans Reiss. Frankfurt am Main: Athenäum, 1972.

Goethes Roman 'Die Wahlverwandtschaften.' Ed. Ewald Rösch. Darmstadt: Wissenschaftliche Buchgesellschaft, 1975.

Gordon, Rosemary. "The Death Instinct and its Relation to the Self." *The Journal of Analytic Psychology,* no. 2 (1961): 131–32.

Gottfried von Strassburg. Ed. Alois Wolf. Darmstadt: Wissenschaftliche. Buchgesellschaft, 1973.

Gräf, H. G. *Goethe über seine Dichtungen.* 3 parts in 9 vols. Frankfurt am Main: Ruetten & Loening, 1901.

Graham, Ilse. *"Die Leiden des jungen Werther:* A Requiem for Inwardness." *Goethe and Lessing: The Wellsprings of Creation.* London: Paul Elek, 1973. 115–36.

———. "Die Theologie tanzt. Goethes Balladen 'Die Braut von Korinth' und 'Der Gott und die Bajadere.'" In Ilse Graham, *Goethe: Schauen und Glauben.* Berlin: Walter de Gruyter, 1988. 253–84.

———. "Wintermärchen. Goethes Roman Die Wahlverwandtschaften." In Ilse Graham, *Goethe: Schauen und Glauben.* 167–208.

Granville-Barker, Harley. *Prefaces to Shakespeare.* 2 vols. Princeton, NJ: Princeton UP, 1947.

Gray, Ronald D. *Goethe: A Critical Introduction.* Cambridge, UK: Cambridge UP, 1967.

———. *Goethe the Alchemist.* Cambridge, UK: Cambridge UP, 1952.

Green, Mandy. "'The Vine and her Elm': Milton's Eve and the Transformation of an Ovidian Motif." *The Modern Language Review* 91, Part 2 (April 1996): 301–16.

Greenberger, Ellen. "'Flirting' with Death: Fantasies of a Critically Ill Woman." *Journal of Projective Techniques and Personality Assessment,* 30, 2 (1966). 197–204.

Gulzow, Monte, and Carol Mitchell. "'Vagina Dentata' and 'Incurable Venereal Disease': Legends from the Viet Nam War." *Western Folklore* 39 (1980): 306–16.

Gundolf, Friedrich. *Goethe.* 1930; reprint, Darmstadt: Wissenschaftliche Buchgesellschaft, 1963.

———. *Shakespeare und der deutsche Geist.* 1911; reprint, Munich: Helmut Küpper, 1959.

Härtl, Heinz, ed. *"Die Wahlverwandtschaften": Eine Dokumentation der Wirkung von Goethes Roman 1808–1832.* Berlin: Akademie Verlag, 1983.

Hafner, Katie. *The Well: A Story of Love, Death, & Real Life in the Seminal Online Community.* New York: Carroll & Graf, 2001.

Haiman, John. "Sarcasm as Theatre." *Cognitive Linguistics* 1–2 (1990): 181–205.

Harrison, A. H. "Eros and Thanatos in Swinburne's Poetry: An Introduction," *Journal of Pre-Raphaelite Studies* 2.1 (November 1981): 22–35.

Hart, Gail. "Voyeuristic Star-Gazing: Authority, Instinct and the Women's World of Goethe's Stella." *Monatshefte* 82 (1990): 408–20.

Hart, Lynda. *Fatal Women: Lesbian Sexuality and the Mark of Aggression.* Princeton, NJ: Princeton UP, 1994.

Hass, Hans-Egon. "Über die Ironie Bei Goethe." In *Ironie und Dichtung.* Ed. Albert Schaefer. Munich: C. H. Beck, 1970. 59–83.

Hatfield, Henry. *Goethe: A Critical Introduction.* Norfolk, Connecticut: New Directions, 1963.

———. "Towards the Interpretation of 'Die Wahlverwandtschaften.'" *The Germanic Review* 23 (1948): 104–14. Reprint (trans. Ingo Pommerening) in Rösch. 175–91.

Heffner, R.-M. S., Helmut Rehder, and W. F. Twaddell. *Goethe's Faust.* 2 vols. Boston: Heath, 1955.

Heller, Erich. *Thomas Mann: The Ironic German.* Cleveland, OH: World Publishing Co., 1961.

Henkel, Arthur. "Das Ärgernis Faust." 1976. Reprint in *Goethe-Erfahrungen: Studien und Vorträge.* Stuttgart: Metzler, 1982. 163–79.

Hermann, Max. *Wilhelm Meisters Theatralische Sendung: Neues Archiv für Theatergeschichte* 2, Schriften der Gesellschaft für Theatergeschichte 41 Berlin: Selbstverlag der Gesellschaft, 1930.

Herrmann, Hans Peter, ed. *Goethes 'Werther': Kritik und Forschung.* Wege der Forschung, vol. 607. Darmstadt: Wissenschaftliche Buchgesellschaft, 1994.

Hess, Günther H. "*Stella* und *Die Wahlverwandtschaften.*" *Seminar* 6 (1970): 216–24.

Hinz, Evelyn J. "Hierogamy versus Wedlock: Types of Marriage Plots and Their Relationship to Genres of Prose Fiction." *PMLA* 91:5 (1976): 900–913.

Hirschenauer, Rupert. "Johann Wolfgang Goethe: Erlkönig." In *Wege zum Gedicht,* vol. 2 *Interpretation von Balladen.* Eds. Rupert Hirschenauer and Albrecht Weber. Munich: Schnell und Steiner, 1963. Reprint, 1964. 159–68.

Hölscher-Lohmeyer, Dorothea. "Die Entwicklung des Goetheschen Naturdenkens im Spiegel seiner Lyrik — am Beispiel der Gedichte 'Mailied' — 'Selige Sehnsucht' — 'Eins und Alles.'" *Goethe-Jahrbuch* 99 (1982): 11–31.

Hoelzel, Alfred. *The Paradoxical Quest: A Study of Faustian Vicissitudes.* New York: Peter Lang, 1988.

Hoffmeister, Gerhart. "Dirnen-Barock: "Evil Women" in 17th-Century German Prose and its Roots in Reality." In *Studies in German and Scandinavian Literature after 1500: A Festschrift for George C. Schoolfield.* Ed. James A. Parente, Jr. and Richard Erich Schade. Columbia, SC: Camden House, 1993. 67–80.

Irion, Ulrich. *Eros und Thanatos in der Moderne: Nietzsche und Freud als Vollender eines Anti-Christlichen Grundzugs im Europäischen Denken*. Würzburg: Königshausen & Neumann, 1992.

Irving, John S. "The Quest/Goal Pattern and its Thematic Transformation in Goethes Works Through 1786: An Experiment in Morphological Criticism." Diss., UCLA, 1964.

Jantz, Harold. *Goethe's Faust as a Renaissance Man*. Princeton, NJ: Princeton UP, 1951.

———. "Goethe's *Wilhelm Meister:* Image, Configuration, and Meaning." In *Studien zur Goethezeit: Erich Trunz zum 75. Geburtstag*. Eds. Hans-Joachim Mähl and Eberhard Mannack. Heidelberg: Carl Winter, 1981. 103–20.

Jantz, Rolf-Peter. "'Sie ist die Schande ihres Geschlechts.' Die femme fatale bei Lessing." *Jahrbuch der Deutschen Schiller-Gesellschaft* 23 (1979): 207–21.

Jaszi, Andrew. *Entzweiung und Vereinigung: Goethes symbolische Weltanschauung*. Heidelberg: Lothar Stiehm, 1973.

Jeßing, Benedikt. *Johann Wolfgang Goethe*. Stuttgart and Weimar: Metzler, 1995.

John, David G. "Ein neuer Schluß für Goethes *Stella*." *Goethe Jahrbuch* 111 (1994): 91–101.

Jones, Hugh Lloyd. *Blood for Ghosts: Classical Influences in the Nineteenth and Twentieth Centuries*. Baltimore: Johns Hopkins, 1982.

Kämpchen, Paul Ludwig. *Die numinose Ballade*. Mnemosyne 4. Bonn: Ludwig Röhrscheid, 1930.

Kaempfer, Wolfgang. "Das Ich und der Tod in Goethes 'Werther.'" In *Goethes "Werther": Kritik und Forschung*. Ed. Hans Peter Herrmann. Darmstadt Wissenschaftliche Buchgesellschaft, 1994. 266–95.

Käsemann, Ernst. "The Pauline Doctrine of the Lord's Supper." In Käsemann, *Essays on New Testament Themes*. London: SCM Press, 1964.

Kaiser, Gerhard. "Goethes Naturlyrik." *Goethe-Jahrbuch* 108 (1991): 61–73.

———. "Zum Syndrom modischer Germanistik." *Euphorion* 65 (1971): 194–99.

Kaufmann, Walter. *From Shakespeare to Existentialism*. Garden City, New York: Doubleday, Anchor, 1960.

Kayser, Wolfgang. *Geschichte der deutschen Ballade*. Berlin: Junker und Dünnhaupt, 1936.

———. *Kleine deutsche Verschule*. Bern & Munich: Francke, 1946.

———. *Das sprachliche Kunstwerk*. 1948. 6th ed. Bern: Francke, 1960.

Kemper, Dirk. "Goethes Individualitätsbegriff als Receptionshindernis im Nationalsozialismus." *Goethe-Jahrbuch* 116 (1999): 129–43.

Kerényi, Karl. "Das Ägäische Fest: Die Meergötterszene in Goethes 'Faust II.'" 1949. Reprint, *Aufsätze zu Goethes "Faust II."* Ed. Werner Keller. Darmstadt: Wissenschaftliche Buchgesellschaft, 1992. 160–89.

Kilgour, Maggie. *From Communion to Cannibalism: An Anatomy of Metaphors of Incorporation.* Princeton, NJ: Princeton UP, 1990.

Kirkham, Richard L. *Theories of Truth: A Critical Introduction.* Cambridge, MA: MIT Press, 1992.

Kisiel, Theodore. *The Genesis of Heidegger's Being and Time.* Berkeley: U of California P, 1993.

Klein, Johannes. *Geschichte der deutschen Lyrik von Luther bis zum Ausgang des zweiten Weltkrieges.* 2nd ed. Wiesbaden: Steiner, 1960.

Kluckhohn, Paul. *Die Auffassung der Liebe in der Literatur des 18. Jahrhunderts und in der deutschen Romantik.* 1922; Tübingen: Max Niemeyer, 1966.

Knopf, Jan. "Kritiker und Konstrukteur der erlesenen Kunstgebilde: Zur Goethe-Rezeption im Werk Bertolt Brechts am Beispiel von 'Der Gott und die Bajadere.'" In *Spuren, Signaturen, Spiegelungen: Zur Goethe-Rezeption in Europa.* Eds. Bernhard Beutler, Anke Bosse. Cologne, Weimar, Vienna: Böhlau, 2000. 367–79.

Kolb, Jocelyne. *The Ambiguity of Taste: Freedom and Food in European Romanticism.* Ann Abor: U of Michigan P, 1995.

Kommerell, Max. *Gedanken über Gedichte.* Frankfurt am Main: Vittorio Klostermann, 1943.

———. "Goethes indische Balladen." In *Goethe-Kalender auf das Jahr 1937.* Ed. Frankfurter Goethe-Museum. Leipzig: Dieterich, 1937. 158–85.

———. "Johann Wolfgang Goethe: Der Gott und die Bajadere." In *Wege zum Gedicht,* 2. 186–89.

Kontje, Todd. "Goethe's Multicultural Masquerades." Paper presented at MLA 2000, Washington, DC, December 2000.

Korff, H. A. *Goethe im Bildwandel seiner Lyrik.* 2 vols. Hanau am Main: Werner Dausien, 1958.

Kramer, Lawrence. *After the Lovedeath: Sexual Violence and the Making of Culture.* Berkeley: U of California P, 1997.

Kurth-Voigt, Lieselotte E. "La Belle Dame sans Merci: The Revenant as Femme Fatale in Romantic Poetry." In *European Romanticism: Literary Cross-Currents, Modes, and Models.* Ed. Gerhart Hoffmeister. Detroit: Wayne State UP, 1990. 247–67.

Kurzke, Hermann. *Thomas Mann: Das Leben als Kunstwerk.* Munich: C. H. Beck, 1999.

Kuzniar, Alice A. "Reassessing Romantic Reflexivity — The Case of Novalis," *The Germanic Review* 63 (1988): 77–86.

Lacan, Jacques. *Ecrits: A Selection.* Trans. Alan Sheridan. New York: Norton, 1977.

Lacoue-Labarthe, Philippe, and Jean-Luc Nancy. *The Literary Absolute: The Theory of Literature in German Romanticism.* 1978. Trans. Philip Barnard and Cheryl Lester. Albany, NY: SUNY Press, 1988.

Lakoff, George. *Women, Fire, and Dangerous Things: What Categories Reveal about the Mind.* Chicago and London: U of Chicago P, 1987.

Larrett, William. "Wilhelm Meister and the Amazons: The Quest for Wholeness." *Publications of the English Goethe Society,* N.S. 39 (1969): 31–56.

Layton, Lynne. "Current Issues in Theories of the Self." Paper given at the MLA Convention, December 29, 1991. 15 pp.

Lederer, Wolfgang. *The Fear of Women.* New York: Grune & Stratton, 1968.

Lee, Laurie. *My Many-coated Man.* New York: Coward-McCann: 1957.

Lee, Meredith. *Displacing Authority: Goethe's Poetic Reception of Klopstock.* Heidelberg: C. Winter, 1999.

Leitzmann, Albert. *Die Quellen von Schillers und Goethes Balladen.* Bonn: A. Marcus and E. Weber, 1911.

Lemaitre, Georges. *Beaumarchais.* New York: Alfred A. Knopf, 1949.

Lermontov, Mikhail. *A Hero of Our Time.* Trans. Vladimir Nabokov and Dimitri Nabokov. New York: Doubleday, 1958.

Levin, David Michael. "Decline and Fall: Ocularcentrism in Heidegger's Reading of the History of Metaphysics." In *Modernity and the Hegemony of Vision.* Berkeley: U of California P, 1993. 186–217.

Lewes, George Henry. *The Life and Works of Goethe.* 2nd ed. 1864; reprint with an introduction by Victor Lange, New York: F. Ungar, 1965.

Lichtenstern, Christa. "Jupiter — Dionysos — Eros/Thanatos: Goethes symbolische Bildprogramme im Haus am Frauenplan." *Goethe-Jahrbuch* 112 (1995): 343–60.

Lloyd-Jones, Hugh. *Blood for the Ghosts: Classical Influences in the Nineteenth and Twentieth Centuries.* Baltimore: Johns Hopkins UP, 1982.

Lohner, Edgard, ed. *Interpretationen zum West-östlichen Divan Goethes.* Darmstatt Wissenschaftliche Buchgesellschaft, 1973.

———. *Studien zum West-östlichen Divan Goethes.* Darmstadt: Wissenschaftliche Buchgesellschaft, 1971.

Lovejoy, Arthur O. "On the Discrimination of Romanticisms." *PMLA* 39 (1924): 229–53. Reprint in Lovejoy, *Essays in the History of Ideas.* Baltimore: Johns Hopkins UP, 1948. 228–53.

Lüthi, Hans Jürg. *Das deutsche Hamletbild seit Goethe*. Bern: Paul Haupt, 1951.

Luhmann, Niklas. *Liebe als Passion: Zur Codierung von* Intimität. Frankfurt am Main: Suhrkamp, 1982.

Lukács, Georg. "Die Leiden des jungen Werther." 1936. Reprint in *Goethe und seine Zeit*. Bern: A. Francke, 1947. 17–30.

Lyons, John O. *The Invention of the Self*. Carbondale: Southern Illinois UP, 1978.

MacKinnon, Catherine. "Pornography, Civil Rights and Speech." Reprint in *Pornography: Women, Violence and Civil Liberties, A Radical View*. Ed. Catherine Itzin. Oxford UP, 1992.

Madland, Helga Stipa. "Poetic Transformations and Nineteenth-Century Scholarship: The 'Friederikenliteratur.'" *Goethe Yearbook* 8 (1996): 28–44.

Marchand, James W. "A Milestone in *Hamlet* Criticism: Goethe's *Wilhelm Meister*." In *Goethe as a Critic of Literature*. Eds. Karl J. Fink and Max L. Baeumer. Lanham, MD: UP of America, 1984.

Martin, Laura. "Who's the Fool Now? A Study of Goethe's Novella 'Die pilgernde Törin' from his Novel *Wilhelm Meisters Wanderjahre*." *The German Quarterly* 66.4 (1993): 431–50.

Mason, E. C. 'Wir sehen uns wieder!' Zu einem Leitmotiv des Dichtens und Denkens im 18. Jahrhundert." *Literaturwissenschaftliches Jahrbuch der Görres-Ges*. NF 5, 1964.

Matten-Gohdes, Dagmar. *Goethe ist gut*. Weinheim and Basel: Beltz, 1982.

Mattenklott, Gert. "Faust II." In *Goethe-Handbuch*. Vol. 2. Stuttgart: Metzler, 1997. 391–477.

Matussek, Peter. "Faust I." In *Goethe-Handbuch*. Vol. 2 (1997): 352–90.

Matzen, Raymond. *Goethe: Friederike und Sesenheim*. Kehl: Morstadt Verlag, 1989.

Mayer, Gerhart. "*Wilhelm Meisters Lehrjahre:* Gestaltbegriff und Werkstruktur." *Goethe Jahrbuch* 92 (1975): 140–64.

Mayer, Hans. *Wagner*. Rowohlt Bild Monographie. Hamburg: Rowohlt, 1959.

———. "Das zweite Geschlecht und seine Aussenseiter." In *Aussenseiter*. Frankfurt am Main: Suhrkamp, 1975. 33–167.

Mayer, Mathias. "Goethes Vampirische Poetik: Zwei Thesen zur *Braut von Corinth*." *Jahrbuch der deutschen Schillergesellschaft* 43 (1999): 148–58.

Mayer, Paola. *Jena Romanticism and Its Appropriation of Jakob Böhme: Theosophy — Hagiography — Literature*. Montreal & Kingston: McGill-Queen's UP, 1999.

McFarland, Thomas. *Romanticism and the Forms of Ruin: Wordsworth, Coleridge and the Modalities of Fragmentation*. Princeton, NJ: Princeton UP, 1981.

Meagher, Robert Emmet. *Helen: Myth, Legend, and the Culture of Misogyny.* New York: Continuum: 1995.

Mecklenburg, Norbert. "Poetisches Spiel mit kultureller Alterität: Goethes 'indische Legende' *Der Gott und die Bajadere.*" *Literatur in Wissenschaft und Unterricht* 33 (2000): 107–16.

Meessen, Hubert J. "Goethes Polaritätsidee und die *Wahlverwandtschaften.*" *PMLA* 54 (1939): 1105–23.

Mehra, Marlis. *Die Bedeutung der Formel "offenbares Geheimnis" in Goethe's Spätwerk.* Stuttgart: Hans-Dieter Heinz Akademischer Verlag, 1982.

Meier, Barbara. *Robert Schumann.* Hamburg: Rowohlt Taschenbuch Verlag, 1995.

Melchior-Bonnet, Sabine. *The Mirror: A History.* Trans. Katharine H. Jewett. New York and London: Routledge, 2001.

Mepham, John. "The Structuralist Sciences and Philosophy." In *Structuralism: An Introduction.* Ed. David Robey. Oxford: Clarendon Press, 1973.

Michelsen, Peter. *Im Banne Fausts: Zwölf Faust-Studien.* Würzburg: Königshausen & Neumann, 2000.

Miller, J. Hillis. "The Critic as Host." In *Deconstruction and Criticism.* Ed. Harold Bloom. New York: Seabury Press, 1979. 217–54.

———. "Tradition and Difference." *Diacritics* 2 (1972): 6–13.

Molnár, Géza von. "Confinement or Containment: Goethe's *Werther* and the Concept of Limitation." *German Life and Letters* 23 (1970): 226–34.

———. "Wilhelm Meister's Apprenticeship as an Alternative to Werther's Fate." *Goethe Proceedings.* Eds. Clifford A. Bernd et al. Columbia, SC: Camden House, 1984. 77–91.

Mommsen, Katharina. "Spiel mit dem Klang: Zur Reimkunst im 'West-östlichen Divan.'" In "*Sei mir Dichter, willkommen!*": *Studien zur deutschen Literatur von Lessing bis Jünger; Kenzo Miyashita gewidmet.* Eds. Klaus Garber and Teruaki Takahashi. Europäische Kulturstudien 4. Cologne: Böhlau Verlag, 1995. 29–46.

Moog-Grünewald, Maria. "Die Frau als Bild des Schicksals: Zur Ikonologie der Femme Fatale." *Arcadia* 18,3 (1983): 239–57.

Müller, Adam Heinrich. "Die Lehre vom Gegensatze." In *Kritische, ästhetische und philosophische Schriften.* 2 vols. Eds. Walter Schröder and Werner Sieberl. Neuwied: Luchterhand, 1967.

Müller-Seidel, Walter. "Goethe: Die Braut von Korinth." In *Geschichte im Gedicht.* Ed. Walter Hinck. Frankfurt am Main: Suhrkamp, 1979. 79–86.

Muenzer, Clark S. *Figures of Identity: Goethe's Novels and the Enigmatic Self.* University Park: The Pennsylvania State UP, 1984.

Munzer, H. W. "Das Liebesproblem und Todesproblem bei Johann Christian Günther." Diss. U of Pennsylvania, 1951.

Naumann, Walter. "'Staub entbrannt in Liebe': Das Thema von Tod und Liebe bei Properz, Quevedo und Goethe." *Arcadia* 3 (1968): 157–72.

Nethercot, Arthur Hobart. *Road to Tryermaine.* Chicago: U of Chicago P, 1939.

New Princeton Encyclopedia of Poetry and Poetics. Eds. Alex Preminger & T. V. F. Brogan. Princeton, NJ: Princeton UP, 1993.

Nicholson, Graeme. *Illustrations of Being: Drawing Upon Heidegger and Upon Metaphysics.* New Jersey: Humanities Press, 1992. Paperback, 1997.

Nisbet, H. B. *Goethe and the Scientific Tradition.* London: Institute of Germanic Studies, 1972.

———. "Goethe und die naturwissenschaftliche Tradition." *Goethe und die Tradition.* Ed. Hans Reiss. Frankfurt am Main: Athenäum, 1972. 212–41.

Nolan, Erika. "Wilhelm Meisters Lieblingsbild: Der kranke Königssohn," *Jahrbuch des Freien Deutschen Hochstifts* (1979). 132–52.

Øhrgaard, Per. "Der König in Thule." *Goethe-Handbuch.* Vol. 1. 132–34.

Papanghelis, Theodore D. *Propertius: A Hellenistic Poet on Love and Death.* Cambridge, Engl.: Cambridge UP, 1987.

Papineau, David. *Thinking About Consciousness* by David Papineau. Oxford, Engl.: Oxford UP, 2002.

Pascal, Roy. *The German Novel.* Toronto: U of Toronto P, 1956.

———. *The German Sturm und Drang.* New York: Philosophical Library, 1953.

———. "Goethe und das Tragische: Die Wandlung von Goethes Shakespeare-Bild." *Goethe,* N.F. 26 (1964): 38–53.

Pater, Walter. *The Renaissance: Studies in Art and Poetry.* London: Macmillan. 2nd rev. ed., 1877.

Paulin, Roger. "'Wir werden uns Wieder Sehn!': On a Theme in Werther." *Publications of the English Goethe Society.* N.S. 50 (1980): 55–78.

Pepper, Stephen C. *World Hypotheses: A Study in Evidence.* Berkeley: U of California P, 1957.

Pikulik, Lothar. "Stella. Ein Schauspiel für Liebende." *Goethes Dramen: Neue Interpretationen.* Ed. Walter Hinderer. Stuttgart: Reclam, 1980. 89–103.

Politzer, Heinz. "Goethes Sprachzauber." *Versuche zu Goethe: Festschrift für Erich Heller.* Heidelberg: Lothar Stiehm, 1976. 38–56.

———. "No Man is an Island: A Note on Image and Thought in Goethe's *Iphigenie.*" *The Germanic Review* 37 (1962): 42–54.

————. "Das Schweigen der Sirenen." *Deutsche Vierteljahrsschrift für Literaturwissenschaft und Geistesgeschichte* 41 (1967): 444–67.

Pool, Daniel. *What Jane Austen Ate and Charles Dickens Knew: From Fox Hunting to Whist — The Facts of Daily Life in Nineteenth-Century England.* New York: Simon & Schuster, 1993.

Powers, Elizabeth. "The Artist's Escape from the Idyll: The Relation of Werther to Sesenheim." *Goethe Yearbook* 9 (1999): 47–76.

Prang, Helmut. *Die Romantische Ironie.* Darmstadt: Wissenschaftliche Buchgesellschaft, 1972.

Pruys, Karl Hugo. *Die Liebkosungen des Tigers: Eine erotische Goethe Biographie.* Berlin: Edition q, 1997.

Pyritz, Hans. *Goethe-Studien.* Cologne: Böhlau, 1962.

Rabuzzi, Kathryn. *The Sacred and the Feminine: Toward a Theology of Housework.* New York: Seabury, 1982.

Rehm, Walter. *Der Todesgedanke in der deutschen Dichtung vom Mittelalter bis zur Romantik.* Halle/Saale, 1928. Second ed. Tübingen: Max Niemeyer Verlag, 1967.

Reiss, Hans. *Goethe und die Tradition.* Frankfurt am Main: Athenäum, 1972.

————. *Goethes Romane.* Bern: Francke, 1963.

————. "Die Leiden des jungen Werthers: A Reconsideration." *Modern Language Quarterly* 20 (1959): 81–96.

Ricoeur, Paul. *Soi-meme come un autre.* Trans. by Kathleen Blamey as *Oneself as Another.* Chicago: U of Chicago P, 1992.

Ritter, Johann Wilhelm. *Fragmente.* Heidelberg: Mohr & Zimmer, 1810. Facsimile reprint Heidelberg: Lambert Schneider, 1969.

Ritter-Santini, Lea. *Ganymed: Ein Mythos des Aufstiegs in der deutschen Moderne.* Trans. Birgit Schneider. Munich: Carl Hanser, 2002.

Roberts, David. *The Indirections of Desire: Hamlet in Goethes "Wilhelm Meister."* Heidelberg: Carl Winter, 1980.

Robinson, Henry Crabb. *Diary.* Ed. T. Sadler. 1869. 3rd ed. New York: AMS Press, 1967.

Robinson, Paul. *Opera and Ideas.* Ithaca, NY: Cornell UP, 1985.

Rölleke, Heinz. "Und ward nicht mehr gesehen: zur Geschichte eines Goethe-Zitats." *Germanisch-romanische Monatschrift* 58, N.F. 27,4 (1977): 433–45.

Rösch, Ewald. "Goethe's 'Selige Sehnsucht' — eine tragische Bewegung. *Germanisch-romanische Monatsschrift* N.S. 20 (1970): 241–56. Reprint in *Interpretationen zum West-östlichen Divan Goethes.* Ed. Edgar Lohner. Darmstadt: Wissenschaftliche Buchgesellschaft, 1973. 228–49.

Roetzel, Calvin J. *The Letters of Paul: Conversations in Context.* 2nd ed. Atlanta: John Knox Press, 1982.

Rogowski, Christian. "Human Alchemy: Science and Psychology in Goethe's *Die Wahlverwandtschaften.*" Paper presented at MLA, 28 December 1987.

Rolland, Romain, 1866–1944. *The Game of Love and Death.* New York: H. Holt and company, 1926.

Rorty, Richard. "Nineteenth-Century Idealism and Twentieth-Century Textualism." *Monist* 64 (1981): 155–74.

———. *Philosophy and the Mirror of Nature.* Princeton, NJ: Princeton UP, 1979.

Ross, Werner. "Johann Wolfgang Goethe: Es war ein König in Thule." In *Wege zum Gedicht* 2. *Interpretationen von Balladen.* Ed. Rupert Hirschenauer and Albrecht Weber. Munich and Zürich: Schnell and Steiner, 1963. 147–53.

Rougemont, Denis de. *Love in the Western World.* Trans. Montgomery Belgion. New York: Fawcett, 1940. Rev. ed. New York: Pantheon, 1956.

Rudolph, Enno. "Individualität." *Goethe-Handbuch.* Vol. 4/1. Stuttgart: Metzler, 1998. 524–31.

Runge, Philipp Otto. *Briefe und Schriften.* Ed. Peter Betthausen. Munich: C. H. Beck, 1982.

Saine, Thomas P. "The Portrayal of Lotte in the Two Versions of Goethe's *Werther.*" *Journal of English and Germanic Philology* 80 (1981): 54–77.

———. "Wilhelm Meister's Homecoming." *JEGP* 69 (1970): 450–69.

Saint-Armand, Pierre. "Terrorizing Marie Antoinette." Trans. Jennifer Curtiss Gage. *Critical Inquiry* 20,3 (spring 1994): 379–401.

Sauder, Gerhard. "Heidenröslein." In *Goethe-Handbuch.* Vol. 1. Stuttgart: Metzler, 1996. 127–32.

Schade, Richard. "Thesen zur literarischen Darstellung der Frau am Beispiel der Courasche." In *Literatur und Volk im 17. Jahrhundert,* part 1. Ed. W. Brückner et al. Wiesbaden: Harrasowitz, 1985.

Schaub, Ute Liebmann. "'Gehorsam' und 'Sklavendienste': Komplementarität der Geschlechtrollen in Goethes Ballade 'Der Gott und die Bajadere.'" *Monatshefte* 76.1 (1984): 31–44.

Scherpe, Klaus. *Werther und Wertherwirkung.* Bad Homburg: Gehlen, 1970.

Schings, Hans-Jürgen. "Fausts Verzweiflung." *Goethe-Jahrbuch* 115 (1998): 97–123.

Schlaffer, Heinz. "Namen und Buchstaben in Goethes 'Wahlverwandtschaften.'" *Jahrbuch der Jean-Paul-Gesellschaft* 7 (1972): 84–102.

Schmitz, Hermann. *Goethes Altersdenken im problemgeschichtlichen Zusammenhang.* Bonn: H. Bouvier, 1959.

Schneider, Wilhelm. "Goethe: 'Selige Sehnsucht.'" *Liebe zum deutschen Gedicht.* Freiburg im Breisgau: Herder, 1954. 298–309. Reprint in Lohner, *Interpretationen.* 72–83.

Schnell, Rüdiger. *Suche nach Wahrheit: Gottfrieds "Tristan und Isold" als erkenntniskritischer Roman.* Tübingen: Max Niemeyer, 1992.

Schöne, Albrecht. *Goethes Farbentheologie.* Munich: C. H. Beck, 1987.

———. "Lenore." In *Die deutsche Lyrik.* Ed. Benno von Wiese. 2 vols. Düsseldorf: August Bagel, 1964. 190–210.

Scholes, Robert. "Is There a Fish in this Text?" In *On Signs.* Ed. Marshall Blonsky. Baltimore, Maryland: The Johns Hopkins UP, 1985. 308–20.

Schulte-Sasse, Jochen. "Romanticism's Paradoxical Articulation of Desire." In *Theory as Practice: A Critical Anthology of Early German Romantic Writings.* Minneapolis: U of Minnesota P, 1997.

Schumann, Detlev W. "Some Notes on Werther." *JEGP* 55 (1956): 533–49.

Schweikert, Patrocinio P. "Toward a Feminist Theory of Reading." In *Gender and Reading: Essays on Readers, Texts, and Contexts,* eds. Elizabeth A. Flynn and Patrocinio P. Schweikert. Baltimore: Johns Hopkins UP, 1986. 54–55.

Schweitzer, Christoph E. "Wilhelm Meister und das Bild vom kranken Königssohn." *PMLA* 72 (1957): 419–32.

Searle, John R. *Mind, Language, and Society: Philosophy in the Real World.* New York: Basic Books, 1998.

Sengle, Friedrich. "Die didaktischen und kulturkritischen Elemente im 'West-östlichen Divan.'" *Neues zu Goethe: Essays und Vorträge.* Stuttgart: Metzler, 1989.

———. *Das Genie und sein Fürst.* Stuttgart: Metzler, 1993.

Seyhan, Azade. *Representation and its Discontents: The Critical Legacy of German Romanticism.* Berkeley: U of California P, 1992.

Simpson, James. "Freud and the Erl King." *Oxford German Studies* 27 (1998): 30–63.

Simrock, Karl, ed. *Faust: Das Volksbuch und das Puppenspiel.* 3rd ed. Basel: Benno Schwabe, 1903.

Singer, Dorothea Waley. *Giordano Bruno: His Life and Thought.* New York: Henry Schuman, 1950.

Snyder, Alice D. *The Critical Principle of the Reconciliation of Opposites as Employed by Coleridge.* Ann Arbor, MI: Ann Arbor Press, 1918.

Staiger, Emil. *Goethe.* 3 vols. Zurich and Freiburg: Atlantis, 1956–59.

Stamm, Israel S. "Herder and the *Aufklärung:* A Leibnizian Context." *Germanic Review* 38 (1963): 197–208.

Stammler, Wolfgang. *Frau Welt: Eine mittelalterliche Allegorie.* Freiburger Universitatsreden, N.F. Nr. 23. Freiburg: Universitätsverlag Freiburg in der Schweiz, 1959.

Steinhauer, Harry. Trans. & afterword. *Goethe: The Sufferings of Young Werther.* New York: Norton, 1970. 97–125.

Stephens, Walter. *Demon Lovers: Witchcraft, Sex, and the Crisis of Belief.* U of Chicago P, 2002.

Stewart, Susan. *Crimes of Writing: Problems in the Containment of Representation.* New York: Oxford UP, 1991.

Stilling, Roger. *Love and Death in Renaissance Tragedy.* Baton Rouge: Louisiana State UP, 1976.

Stopp, F. J. "'Ein wahrer Narziss' Reflections on the Eduard-Ottilie Relationship in Goethe's Wahlverwandtschaften." *PEGS* 29 (1960): 52–85.

Strawson, Peter F. *Individuals: An Essay in Descriptive Metaphysics.* London: Methuen, 1959.

Strich, Fritz. *Deutsche Klassik und Romantik.* Munich: Meyer & Jessen, 1922.

Strieber, Whitley. *Confirmation: The Hard Evidence of Aliens Among Us.* New York: St. Martin's Press, 1998.

Strohschneider-Kohrs, Ingrid. *Die romantische Ironie in Theorie und Gestaltung.* 1960. rev. ed. Tübingen: Niemeyer, 1977.

Sword, Helen. "Leda and the Modernists." *PMLA* 107 (1992): 305–18.

Tanner, Tony. *Adultery in the Novel: Contract and Transgression.* Baltimore: The Johns Hopkins UP, 1979.

Tatar, Maria M. *Lustmord: Sexual Murder in Weimar Germany.* Princeton, NJ: Princeton UP, 1995.

Taylor, Charles. *Sources of the Self: The Making of the Modern Identity.* Cambridge, MA: Harvard UP, 1989.

Taylor, Mark C. *Erring: A Postmodern A/Theology.* Chicago: U of Chicago P, 1984.

Tellenbach, H[ubertus]. "The Suicide of the 'Young Werther' and the Consequences for the Circumstances of Suicide of Endogenic Melancholics." *Israel Annals of Psychiatry and Related Disciplines* 15 (1977): 16–21.

Thalheim, Hans-Günther. "Goethes Ballade 'Die Braut von Korinth.'" *Goethe* 20 (1958): 28–44.

Theweleit, Klaus. *Männerphantasien.* Frankfurt am Main: Verlag Roter Stern, 1977.

———. *Male Fantasies.* Trans. Stephan Conway, with Erica Carter and Chris Turner. Foreword by Barbara Ehrenreich. Minneapolis, MN: U of Minnesota P, 1987.

Thornton, R. K. R. *Poetry of the Nineties.* Harmondsworth, Middlesex, England: Penguin Books, Ltd., 1970.

Tillyard, E. W. M. *The Elizabethan World Picture.* London: Chatto & Windus, 1943. Reprint, New York: Random House, [1959].

Tobin, Robert. *Warm Brothers: Queer Theory and the Age of Goethe.* Philadelphia, PA: U of Pennsylvania P, 2000.

Trabant. Jürgen. *Apeliotes oder der Sinn der Sprache: Wilhelm von Humboldts Sprach-Bild.* Munich: Wilhelm Fink Verlag, 1986.

———. "Language and the Ear: From Derrida to Herder." *Herder Yearbook* 1(1992): 1–22.

Trevelyan, Humphry. *Goethe and the Greeks.* Cambridge, UK: Cambridge UP, 1941.

Trunz, Erich. "Goethe's Altersstil." *Wirkendes Wort* 5 (1954–55), 134–39. Reprint in Trunz, *Ein Tag aus Goethes Leben: Acht Studien zu Leben und Werk.* Munich: C. H. Beck, 1991. 139–46.

———. "Goethes lyrische Kurzgedichte. 1771–1832." In *Goethe. Neue Folge des Jahrbuchs der Goethe-Gesellschaft.* Vol. 26, 1964. Reprint in *Ein Tag aus Goethes Leben.* 101–38.

Tunner, Erika. "The Lore Lay — a Fairy Tale from Ancient Times?" In *European Romanticism: Literary Cross-Currents, Modes, and Models.* Ed. Gerhart Hoffmeister. Detroit: Wayne State UP, 1990. 269–86.

Unseld, Melanie. *"Man Töte Dieses Weib!": Weiblichkeit und Tod in der Musik der Jahrhundertwende.* Stuttgart and Weimar: Metzler, 2001.

Unser Goethe: Ein Lesebuch. Eds. Eckhard Henscheid & F. W. Bernstein. Zürich: Diogenes, 1982.

Vaget, Hans Rudolph. "'Mäßig boshaft': Fausts Gefährte: Goethes Mephistopheles im Lichte der Aufklärung." *Goethe-Jahrbuch* 118 (2001): 234–46.

Vietor, Karl. *Goethe the Poet.* Cambridge: Harvard UP, 1949.

Vincent, Deirdre. *The Eternity of Being: On the Experience of Time in Goethe's Faust.* Bonn: Bouvier Verlag Herbert Grundmann, 1987.

———. "Text as Image and Self-Image: The Contextualization of Goethe's *Dichtung und Wahrheit* (1810–1813)," *Goethe Yearbook* 10 (2001): 125–53. Abbreviated "Text."

———. *Werther's Goethe and the Game of Literary Creativity.* Toronto: U of Toronto P, 1992.

Wachsmuth, Andreas B. "'Sich verselbsten' und 'entselbstigen' — Goethes Altersformel für die rechte Lebensführung." *Goethe (Jahrbuch der Goethe-Gesellschaft)* 11 (1949): 263–92.

Waidson, H. M. "Death by Water: or the Childhood of Wilhelm Meister." *Modern Language Review* 56, No. 1 (January 1961): 44–53.

Warner, Maria. "Peroxide Mug-Shot." *London Review of Books.* Vol. 20, No. 1 (1 January 1998): 10–11.

Wasserman, Earl. "The English Romantics: The Grounds of Knowledge." *Studies in Romanticism* 4 (1964): 17–34.

Wege zum Gedicht 2: *Interpretationen von Balladen.* Eds. Rupert Hirschenauer and Albrecht Weber. Munich and Zürich: Schnell und Steiner, 1963. Reprinted 1964.

Weinhandl, Ferdinand. *Die Metaphysik Goethes.* Berlin: Junker und Dünnhaupt, 1932. Reprint, Darmstadt: Wissenschaftliche Buchgesellschaft, 1965.

Wellbery, David E. "Morphisms of the Phantasmatic Body: Goethe's 'The Sorrows of Young Werther.'" In *Body & Text in the Eighteenth Century.* Eds. Veronica Kelly and Dorothea von Mücke. Stanford, CA: Stanford UP, 1994. 181–208.

———. *The Specular Moment: Goethe's Early Lyric and the Beginnings of Romanticism.* Stanford, CA: Stanford UP, 1996.

Wellek, René. "The Concept of Romanticism in Literary History." *Comparative Literature* 1 (1949): 1–23, 147–72. Reprint in *Concepts of Criticism,* ed. Stephen G. Nichols, Jr. New Haven: Yale UP, 1963. 128–98.

———. *A History of Modern Criticism: 1750–1950.* 7 vols. New Haven: Yale UP, 1955–1991. Vol. 1: *The Later Eighteenth Century.* 1955.

———. "Romanticism Re-examined." *Concepts of Criticism.* 199–221.

Wiese, Benno von. "Nachwort & Anmerkungen" to Goethe's *Die Wahlverwandtschaften.* HA 6:672–730.

Wilkinson, Elizabeth M. "Goethe's Poetry." *German Life and Letters* 2 (1948–49): 316–29.

———. "Theologischer Stoff und dichterischer Gehalt in Fausts sogenanntem Credo." In *Goethe und die Tradition.* Ed. Hans Reiss. Frankfurt am Main: Athenäum, 1972. 242–58.

Willems, Marianne. *Das Problem der Individualität als Herausforderung an die Semantik im Sturm und Drang: Studien zu Goethes "Brief des Pastors zu *** an den neuen Pastor zu ***," "Götz von Berlichingen" u. "Clavigo."* Studien u. Texte zur Sozialgeschichte der Literatur, 52. Tübingen: Niemeyer, 1995.

Wilson, John Dover. *What Happens in Hamlet.* 3rd ed. 1951; Reprint, Cambridge UP, 1959.

Wilson, W. Daniel. *Geheimräte gegen Geheimbünde: Ein unbekanntes Kapitel der klassisch-romantischen Geschichte Weimars.* Stuttgart: Metzler, 1991.

Wind, Edgar. *Pagan Mysteries in the Renaissance.* New Haven: Yale UP, 1958. Revised and enlarged edition, New York: Norton (The Norton Library), 1968.

Witte, Wilhelm. "Deus Absconditus: Shakespeare in Eighteenth-Century Germany." In *Papers: Mainly Shakespearian.* Ed. G. I. Duthie. Aberdeen University Studies no. 147. Edinburgh: Oliver & Boyd, 1964.

Wittkowski, Wolfgang. "Homo homini lupus. Homo homini Deus: 'Götz von Berlichingen mit der eisernen Hand.'" In *Andeuten und Verschleiern in Dichtungen von Plautus bis Hemingway und von der Goethezeit bis Sarah Kirsch.* Frankfurt am Main: Peter Lang, 1993. 31–56.

Wolff, Cynthia G. "Thanatos and Eros: Kate Chopin's 'The Awakening.'" *American Quarterly* 25 (1973): 449–71.

Wright, Elizabeth. "Ambiguity and Ambivalence: Structure in Goethe's 'Die Braut von Korinth' and 'Der Gott und die Bajadere.'" *PEGS* 51 (1980–81). 114–32.

Zagari, Luciano. "Der Lyriker Goethe: Der erste der Modernen, der letzte der Vormodernen." *Goethe-Jahrbuch* 108 (1991): 117–27.

Zagermann, Peter. *Eros und Thanatos.* Darmstadt: Wissenschaftliche Buchgesellschaft, 1988.

Zimmermann, Rolf Christian. "Goethes Polaritätsdenken im geistigen Kontext des 18. Jahrhunderts." *Jahrbuch der Deutschen Schillergesellschaft* 18 (1975): 304–47.

———. *Das Weltbild des jungen Goethe: Studien zur hermetischen Tradition des deutschen 18. Jahrhunderts.* 2 vols. Vol. 1. Munich: Wilhelm Fink, 1969. Vol. 2: Munich: Wilhelm Fink, 1979.

Zimmermann, Werner. "Johann Wolfgang Goethe: Der Fischer." In *Wege zum Gedicht* 2. 154–58.

Ziolkowski, Theodore. *German Romanticism and its Institutions.* Princeton, NJ: Princeton UP, 1990.

———. "The Telltale Teeth: Psychodontia to Sociodontia." *PMLA* 91 (1976): 9–22. Reprint in *Varieties of Literary Thematics.* Princeton, NJ: Princeton UP, 1983. 3–33.

Žmegač, Viktor. "Zu einem Thema Goethes und Thomas Manns: Wege der Erotik in der modernen Gesellschaft." *Goethe Jahrbuch* 103 (1986): 152–67.

Index: Persons and Subjects

"la petite mort," 7, 24, 33, 69, 242

Lacan, Jacques, 35, 81, 111, 139, 175

Lacoue-Labarthe, Philippe and Jean-Luc Nancy, 171

Laocoon, 140

Lameir (Isolde's lament), 121

Laßberg, Christine (Christel) von, 123

Lavater, Johann Caspar, 42 n. 3, 83, 94, 103 n. 15, 105, 137

Lawrence, D. H., works by: *The Rainbow*, 200; *Women in Love*, 209 n. 33

Leda, 49 (Rilke's poem), 56, 59, 234 (Yeats's poem), 272

Lederer, Wolfgang, 36 n. 80, 64 n. 11, 68, 118–19 n. 15

Lee, Laurie, works by: "Song by the Sea," 120

Lee, Meredith, 273 n. 15

Leibniz, Gottfried Wilhelm, 190

Leiden, 32, 47, 48, 174, 228, 244. *See also Tätigkeit*

Leidenschaft, 32

leitmotif, 92, 210, 260

Leitzmann, Albert, 44, 144 n. 96

Lengefeld sisters (Caroline and Charlotte von): Schillers love for, 45

Lessing, Gotthold Ephraim, 81, 260

Lessing, Gotthold Ephraim, works by: "Eine Duplik," 190 n. 16; *Hamburgische Dramaturgie*, 138; *Laokoon*, 77, 126; *Miß Sara Sampson* (Marwood, 39, 62 n. 2, 71, 126); *Wie die Alten den Tod gebildet*, 259

levitation: Faust's desire to levitate, 57, 89 n. 33, 187, 189, 247. *See also* flight

Liebestod: meaning of, 17, 19, 21, 25, 29, 35, 282. *See also* love-death

light, 136, 170, 184, 187, 188, 189, 190, 191, 196, 198, 240, 247, 248 n. 71. *See also* color, Goethe's theory of; optics, science of

Lewes, George Henry, 134

lightness, Goethe's love of, 64, 272, 276, 277

Lillo, George, works by: *The London Merchant* (Lady Millwood), 39, 71, 126, 147

Lola, Lola Lola, Lorelei Lee (Marilyn Monroe as), Lulu, 73, 75, 118

longing: blessed longing, 182–99 *passim;* constitutive of being, 223; for death, 3; for dissolution ("Entgrenzung"), 88, 246; for fulfillment, 244; informs subjectivity, 20; for love, 24, 204; for love and death (Werther's), 82 (Margarete's), 22; mystical longing, 94; for reassimilation, 218; for release, 19, 218; to return to the womb, 29, 90; for self-submergence (self-surrender), 24, 29; for union, 223

Lorelei (Lore Lay), 12, 34, 65, 76, 118, 119, 120, 126, 164 n. 3

love and knowledge, 232, 233

love-death: anti-individualistic, 33; a male construct, 36–40; misunderstandings of, 31–32; neglect of, 8; and subject-object dichotomy, 35

love potion, 121 n. 27, 256. *See also pharmakon;* poison(s); potion(s)

Lovejoy, Arthur O., 208

loyalty in love, theme of, 51, 71, 156, 157

Theweleit, Klaus, 36
Tieck, Ludwig, 262
Tillyard, E. W. M., 220
time (temporality, temporal flux),
21, 25, 28, 31, 39, 78, 124,
175, 179, 192, 224, 226–27,
228, 237, 238, 243, 244, 245,
247, 282; Faust's timeless
moment, 31, 40; the
Marschallin's reflections on, 58.
See also Augenblick
Tobin, Robert, 235 n. 30
Todessehnsucht, 37, 177
Trabant, Jürgen, 231 n. 18
transfusion, 155
transmutation, 33, 120, 153, 154,
158, 195, 199
*trennen und verbinden
(vereinigen)*, 22, 113, 211,
213, 215
Tristan und Isolde (Iseult), 1, 2,
7, 9, 14, 15, 17, 20, 27, 93,
212, 217, 232, 244 ("höchste
Liebes-Lust"), 269, 279
trübe, das (die) Trübe, 10, 188,
191, 199, 248 n. 71, 253; "dem
Trüben" ("Wiederfinden"),
188 n. 13, 190, 191, 248 n. 71;
"im Trüben," 189
("Entoptische Farben"); "der
nicht mehr Getrübte," 187,
191, 247, 248; "trüber Gast,"
130, 152, 182–85, 186, 187
Trunz, Erich, 82, 87, 88, 125,
193, 276, 280
truth, Goethe's conception of,
250–56 *passim*
Tunner, Erika, 73 n. 51, 120
twins (*Zwillinge*), 15
two souls, Faust's, 189, 240

Übermensch, 237
"und": ambiguity of the
conjunction, 185 (in "Stirb *und*

werde"), 212, 279 (in Tristan
und Isolde)
Undine, 12, 34, 118 n. 14, 119,
121
unfaithful lovers, 108, 126, 241
unio mystica, 131, 149 (in
Novalis), 198. *See also*
mysticism, Goethe's
unity: and division, 210, 216; in
duality, 14, 259; vs. duality,
212; as feminine, 213–14
unterscheiden und verbinden
Updike, John: works by: *Brazil*, 7
Urfrage, 10, 253; *Urphänomen*,
256; Ur-womb, 243

Vaget, Hans Rudolph, 115 n. 4,
238 n. 39
vagina dentata, 12, 19, 68–69,
90, 170, 235
vampire(s), 34, 141–55 *passim*;
lamia as vampires, 67
vampirism, 89 (*vampirisme
fusionnel*), 145, 146, 158
veil(s) (*Schleier*), 13, 101 (of St.
Veronica), 110, 112
("Zueignung"), 243, 253, 260,
267 ("Flieh, Jüngling, flieh!")
venereal disease, 12, 48, 62, 69,
71. *See also* syphilis
Venus, 64, 65, 90; Mary and, 29,
66
Venus and Adonis, 29
veracious imagination, 85
verbinden und trennen, 213, 215.
See also trennen
Verdi, Giuseppe, works by: *Aida*,
2, 7, 205, 225; *Don Carlo*, 59;
Otello, 4; *Rigoletto*, 140
Verfremdungseffekt, der, 254, 262
Verlaine, Paul, 4
Vincent, Deirdre, 83, 98, 100,
112, 228
virgin and whore, woman as, 62
virtuosity, 269–82 *passim*